BY PRESCRIPTION ONLY

Econ 690B

BY PRESCRIPTION ONLY

A REPORT ON THE ROLES OF THE UNITED STATES
FOOD AND DRUG ADMINISTRATION, THE AMERICAN
MEDICAL ASSOCIATION, PHARMACEUTICAL MANUFAC-
TURERS, AND OTHERS IN CONNECTION WITH THE
IRRATIONAL AND MASSIVE USE OF PRESCRIPTION DRUGS
THAT MAY BE WORTHLESS,
INJURIOUS, OR EVEN LETHAL

BY MORTON MINTZ

REVISED EDITION

ORIGINALLY PUBLISHED AS
THE THERAPEUTIC NIGHTMARE

BEACON PRESS : BOSTON

FOR ANITA

℞

Severe criticism was visited on physicians by some lay journals in the earlier days of the reform movement for being willing to use means of treatment without having any real knowledge of their composition or action, when their responsibilities are so great. It was indeed an evil state of things, but the fault lay less with the individual than with the conditions under which he did his work. Circumstances practically forced him to use many of these substances, and he could not learn anything but what the manufacturer told him. The reproach fell on the profession as a body, rather than on the individual practitioner, for putting its head into the noose and not seeing the trap until it was in it. The spectacle astonishes one now that it can be viewed from the perspective of growing distance: a learned scientific profession doing about one half of what is its chief work — treating the sick — on the strength solely of information received from advertisements and detail men.

DAVID L. EDSALL, M.D.
in The Journal of the American
Medical Association, *November 12, 1910*

℞

ACKNOWLEDGMENTS

IF ANY should care to throw stones after having read this book, let them come out of their glass houses and throw them at mine. If any should care to strew flowers, let them stop at many doors.

I had a great deal of help. Without it, some gravely flawed and lesser effort might have been possible, but not this book. Although some feeling of friendship may have motivated those who gave so generously of their knowledge, their time, and their wisdom, the predominant consideration was to serve the public interest.

Most of all, I refer to Dr. Barbara Moulton, a physician, her husband, Dr. E. Wayles Browne, Jr., an economist, and other persons — two in particular — who, to my deep regret, must remain anonymous. All are public servants whose sacrifices of their private time and effort were unstinting.

My debt extends to many others. The Washington *Post* granted me a leave of absence to accept a fellowship awarded by the Nieman Foundation at Harvard University. The Nieman Fellowship, for which I shall be forever grateful, not only let me partake of the intellectual joys of Harvard, but also afforded me the opportunity to undertake a book. That *this* book came about is attributable to the action of the *Atlantic* in commissioning me to write a long article focused principally on the performance of the Food and Drug Administration in the field of

Acknowledgments

prescription drugs. To the disappointment of all concerned, this project died — but not before giving birth to this book.

From several members of the Harvard faculty who were kind enough to read an early, rudimentary manuscript I received wise counsel and encouragement. They included Professor-emeritus Arthur M. Schlesinger, Sr., Professors John Kenneth Galbraith, Theodore Morrison, and James Q. Wilson, and Charles L. Trozzo, then a teaching fellow in economics. I am grateful to all of them. To Professor Schlesinger I owe the greatest debt. His advice was invaluable. His expression of confidence in me sustained, over a period of months, my sometimes flagging determination to see this effort through.

My gratitude goes also to Dr. John M. Blair, chief economist of the Senate Subcommittee on Antitrust and Monopoly, and to C. Michael Curtis, of the *Atlantic*. To my editor at Houghton Mifflin, Anne Barrett, to Helen Phillips, and to the editor-in-chief, Paul Brooks, I offer an unsolicited testimonial. They were wonderful to work with, unfailingly.

MORTON MINTZ

Cambridge, Massachusetts,
and Washington, D.C.
1964

℞

HOWEVER naïve it may seem to us today, the myth that science has no drawbacks was extremely tenacious. In 1896 Elihu Thomson, then of General Electric, found that X-rays were injurious to body tissues. Radiologists have learned this to their sorrow: even today, despite vastly improved shielding and other precautions, their lifespan is shortened.

In 1923, a year after an estimated one hundred radiologists had died in the practice of their profession, there sprang up a business employing beauticians to remove unwanted hair with a series of X-ray treatments. This enterprise in folly, surely dependent on a blind faith that such a symbol of science as X-rays could cause no harm, spread across the United States and Canada and flourished for six years. The consequences were horrifying — thousands of cases of X-ray burns, cancer, and even death.

In 1927 Hermann J. Muller, the geneticist whose work was ultimately honored with a Nobel Prize, reported that X-rays cause mutations of the genes. Clearly, it was at this point that the threat from promiscuous use of X-rays should have been recognized. But recognition was very slow in coming. Hair removal by X-ray remained a prosperous business into 1929 before it at last came under public condemnation. The attack was from the American Medical Association. Professor Donald

Fleming of Harvard, a historian of science in America, has found that not once during the six-year life of the enterprise was action taken against it by government — federal, state, or local. And not until after Hiroshima did Muller win a serious hearing for his case that physicians and dentists were so casually using X-rays as to give far more radiation than necessary.

We went through a similar cycle with pesticides. The reception accorded DDT, which was introduced during World War II, was overwhelmingly favorable. The late Rachel Carson taught us that while we need DDT we must also fear it.

The problem I dealt with in *Silent Spring* is not an isolated one [Miss Carson wrote in the *New York Times Book Review* for December 2, 1962]. The excessive and ill-advised use of chemical pesticides is merely one part of a sorry whole — the reckless pollution of our living world with harmful and dangerous substances. Until very recently, the average citizen assumed that "Someone" was looking after these matters and that some little understood but confidently relied upon safeguards stood like shields between his person and any harm. Now he has experienced, from several different directions, a rather rude shattering of these beliefs.

Almost simultaneously with the publication of *Silent Spring*, the problem of drug safety and drug control, which had been simmering in the press for many months, reached its shocking culmination in the thalidomide tragedy.

The tragedy of a sedative that caused birth deformities taught us that although we need drugs, which like pesticides also are chemicals, we must be aware of their hazards.

The pages that follow demonstrate, I believe, that we have engaged to a frightening extent in sometimes senseless pollution of our bodies with harmful and dangerous drugs, of which thalidomide was but one. The "Someone" we have trusted to look after us is the United States Food and Drug Administration. We take the drugs physicians, osteopaths, and others prescribe; yet they, too, have trusted blindly.

Dr. Louis S. Goodman, professor of pharmacology at the University of Utah College of Medicine, and co-author of *The Pharmacological Basis of Therapeutics*, touched on this at a hearing conducted by the late Senator Estes Kefauver. "From a considerable contact with physicians, both former students of mine and many others," Dr. Goodman said, "I have formed the impression that most medical doctors do, in fact, believe that the drugs which they now prescribe have been appropriately scrutinized by some Governmental agency for proof of efficacy. They may not know the name of the agency, but they take for granted that there has been some sort of expert and official review preceding the release of the drug for distribution and sale."

They — and we — have taken for granted entirely too long the existence of expert and official review of drugs to assure not only that they are efficacious, or do what is claimed for them, but also that they are safe. This book documents case after case in which our shields against harm have been as imaginary as the emperor's clothes, with death and injury to the innocent being the consequences.

✓ ✓ ✓

However grievous the Food and Drug Administration's failures in drug regulation may be, the fault is not confined to the agency alone. Although it deals literally in matters of life and death, a pervasive apathy has afflicted many who might have been expected to monitor its performance. FDA has been neglected by schools of medicine, university departments of governmental affairs, students of regulatory agencies, the lay press, the White House, and Congress. Agencies that deal with financial matters do not usually suffer such an extensive want of attention (nor should they). A great lack of interest has been shown by the American Medical Association, but one should be aware that the AMA has been receiving about half of its revenues from the pharmaceutical industry. If others have been apathetic, uninterested, or ignorant, the industry has not. Its lobbying — in the Executive Branch, on Capitol Hill, in numerous congressional districts, in the lay and medical press — has made that of other major industries seem somewhat pathetic by comparison. Meanwhile, the industry's technological inventiveness has outpaced FDA's capacities. All of this has helped to erode FDA's zeal to protect the public interest. So has that erratic, nebulous, and, on occasion, nonexistent Something called the Corporate Conscience.

In recent years, the Corporate Conscience, whatever it is, has been disturbing a good many people, not least in the big corporations themselves. Most of the discussion, however, has focused on price-fixing, on conspiracy to violate the antitrust laws, on executive stock-option plans, on oil-depletion allowances and other tax gimmicks so admirably described by Philip M. Stern in *The Great Treasury Raid*, on usurious interest rates, on exorbitant profits on defense contracts, on scandals in quiz shows, vegetable-oil tanks and liquid-fertilizer tanks, on subsidies, on sharp practices in the selling of securities, and on what Jessica Mitford called *The American Way of Death*.

This book is about the American Way of Drugging and, therefore, more about injury and death to the innocent than about money. Here we shall see that there have been instances when our excessive trust in certain Corporate Consciences has been rewarded with inadequately and even fraudulently tested drugs, with useless drugs and inferior versions of good drugs, with protraction of illness, and with waste of our money. In order that sales may begin and continue, regardless of whether we are healed and spared pain, evidence of serious and even lethal effects has been withheld from the responsible government agency and concealed from the medical profession and the public.

ʽ ʽ ʽ

After you have read this book you may agree that it would not be fanciful to portray a John Doe of a few years back who went through a nightmare that began when a manufacturer who had tested his new drug on six mice, four rats, and two dogs for eight days, and on no humans, and had brought pressure on FDA to release it to the market, planted a story in one of the media proclaiming it a certain cure for John Doe's chronic disease. Seeking relief from his suffering, John Doe asked his physician for a prescription for the drug; the doctor prescribed it because he had been brainwashed into believing that it was effective; John Doe had the prescription filled at prices so high he had to give up eating meat; he was made sicker by the drug than he would have been had he let nature take its course; he entered a hospital for therapy; the drugs given him there made him sicker still; he was treated with the special drugs created to overcome the ill effects of other drugs; and he became impoverished by the cost of all of this.

John Doe was more fortunate than some — he did not die. He never learned that the exorbitant ˌprices he had paid for the drugs he didn't need had contributed to the wildly excessive pharmaceutical advertising, receipts from which helped the American Medical Association in financing its war against the Medicare he needed but was denied.

In *U.S.A.: The Permanent Revolution* the editors of *Fortune* assure us that "Big business, if only because it is subject to the most pressure, exercises its power with a strong and growing sense of responsibility." Maybe. But the evidence here points to the more persuasive conclusion of Bernard D. Nossiter in *The Mythmakers* that "there is nothing in the logic or practice of concentrated corporate industries that guides or compels socially responsible decision making."

The truth of this is attested by Warren Kiefer, a former public relations man for Pfizer International, Inc., and a witness before the Senate Subcommittee on Antitrust and Monopoly. In a letter appearing in the *Saturday Review* for September 3, 1960, Kiefer said: "It was my experience in the drug industry that most executives were honest most of the time. But they were businessmen, who, in the old American tradition, placed company interest first. *Public* interest was F&DA's lookout . . . Drug executives are responsible to stockholders who pay their salaries. If in the course of their duties they also serve the public interest, as they frequently do, it is to their special and individual credit. But regulatory officials are responsible to the people . . ."

I do not undertake to deal, except peripherally, with the question of how FDA met its responsibilities to the people in regard to nonprescription drugs, foods, cosmetics, pesticides, and other products within its purview, for to do so would be beyond my scope. I would not suggest that FDA's performance is other than enterprising in regard to its police functions. But I do suggest that its persistence and success in, say, fighting medical quackery, while assuredly winning headlines and public trust, have served to obscure its quite unpublicized failures in coping with the dangers posed by powerful and worthless drugs marketed not by smalltime quacks, who generally menace relatively few, but by giant corporations, any one of whose products may be taken by millions.

It cannot be too strongly emphasized that whatever FDA's abilities and dedication may be, it is severely and discouragingly handicapped by a lack of consistent, effective, and intelligent public support. Unlike the fickle public, the lobbyists for the multibillion-dollar drug industry are as constant and available as aspirin in an all-night drugstore. The arguments of the industry are heard, a medical educator has said, "loudly and incessantly . . . the other side only sporadically and feebly . . . The consumers . . . have no paid advocates." Indeed, Vice President Hubert H. Humphrey has said, they are "almost never represented, except by FDA itself, when FDA sits down with industry to negotiate new drug regulations. Virtually all of the organized pressure brought to bear on FDA is *against* firm regulation for the public health." The Minnesota Democrat provided this illustration:

In February, 1964, FDA proposed immensely significant regulations, which would require records and reports on the safety and effectiveness of all drugs on the market. Not a single physician or medical group in the Nation wrote in to express *support* of these proposed regulations, in whole or in part.

Virtually, every specific and substantive comment which FDA received on individual provisions in the regulations was in *opposition*. Indeed, only a single individual doctor in the Nation wrote in on specifics of the regulations; he *opposed* a principal provision.

All *other* comments came from: —

(a) individual drug companies, drug organizations or companies in related fields,

(b) 5 individual citizens — none of whom commented on any *specific* details of the regulation.

Criticism of the pharmaceutical industry, or of leaders of FDA whose performance satisfied the industry, usually brings anguished complaints of injury and unfairness from industry spokesmen and their sometimes obsequious advocates in the trade press. It is doubtful that the anguish has run very deep. The apathy of the public and the medical profession about how FDA meets its responsibilities has remained undisturbed. Each year the number of prescriptions written has increased substantially. Year after year drug-industry profits have reached fantastic levels.

On June 11, 1962, after Senator Estes Kefauver's drug-reform bill had been gutted in a secret meeting, and before the thalidomide episode rescued it, he took the Senate floor to make an extraordinary protest. "I was surprised and put out that I, as chief sponsor of the bill, had neither been invited to the meeting nor knew anything about it," he said. He went on to say that the weakened bill "as it stands is admittedly agreeable to the Senator from Illinois [Everett M. Dirksen] and the Senator from Nebraska [Roman L. Hruska]. They have generally, and I think admittedly, taken the position on these issues set forth by the pharmaceutical manufacturing industry."

Senator Kefauver and Senator John A. Carroll, a Colorado Democrat, also had some uncomplimentary things to say about the ambiguous and disturbing role played in this strange episode by the Kennedy Administration.[1] Then Carroll returned to the action of members of the Senate Committee on the Judiciary in reducing the reform measure to a shadow. "We must not blame it all on the Republicans," he said. "Most of the Democrats voted that way, too . . . We are hitting into one of the biggest industries of the nation . . ."

Those who fight for the public interest rather than the vested interest often do so against hopeless odds, overwhelming discouragement, and wounding ridicule. There could be no better example than Estes Kefauver. I speak no praise his foes did not freely concede. "I like his relentlessness," Senator Dirksen, the Minority Leader, told the Senate after Kefauver had termed him a voice of the pharmaceutical industry. "He is as single-purposed as an Apache Indian. He is as gracious as a Victorian lady . . . His patience is certainly equal to that of Job. I think he makes Job look a little like an amateur."

In 1962, somewhat more than a year before Kefauver died, an enormously productive and far-reaching inquiry into FDA's mis-

---

[1] For a superb and thorough account of the background and history of the drug reforms of 1962 the reader is referred to Richard Harris's *The Real Voice* (New York: Macmillan, 1964), which appeared in condensed form in *The New Yorker* for March 14, 21, and 28, 1964.

handling of drugs was begun by Senator Humphrey, who is a licensed pharmacist and co-author of the Durham-Humphrey Act of 1951, which established separate legal categories for prescription and nonprescription drugs. Senator Humphrey carried on the inquiry for two years, despite the enormous burdens imposed on him by his post as Assistant Majority Leader of the Senate, by his leadership of the successful fight for enactment of the Civil Rights Act of 1964, and by his active concern for other causes ranging from public education in the District of Columbia to disarmament. It cannot be said that he was as single-purposed as Dirksen's Apache Indian, but this only served to make his dedication and accomplishment the more impressive.

On several occasions, on the floor of the Senate and elsewhere, Senator Kefauver had expressed appreciation for the indispensable contributions made to drug reforms by the staff of his Senate Subcommittee on Antitrust and Monopoly, including Paul Rand Dixon, formerly counsel and staff director, John M. Blair, the chief economist, and another economist, E. Wayles Browne, Jr. Mr. Humphrey too has praised the professional staff of his Senate Subcommittee on Reorganization and International Organizations. And well he might have — incredibly, it consisted of but one man, Julius N. Cahn, a brilliant and selfless public servant. The publications of the two subcommittees are the primary sources of this book.[2] The Kefauver subcommittee's testimony, exhibits, and memoranda fill 13,260 pages, and the Humphrey subcommittee's about 4000. There is significant reliance also on hearings held by the House Intergovernmental Relations Subcommittee.[3] The terminal date for

[2] Of which these are of special importance: U.S. Senate, Subcommittee on Antitrust and Monopoly of the Committee on the Judiciary, *Study of Administered Prices in the Drug Industry*, 87th Cong., 1st Sess., 1961, Report No. 448; and U.S. Senate, Subcommittee on Reorganization and International Organizations, *Hearings* on "Agency Coordination Study," 87th Cong., 2nd Sess., 1962, and 88th Cong., 1st Sess., 1963.

[3] Of the Committee on Government Operations. U.S. House of Representatives, *Hearings*, 88th Cong., 2nd Sess., March 24, 25, April 8, and June 3, 1964.

the material covered in the text of this book is the end of 1964.

No drug is perfectly safe. A drug powerful enough to do good is powerful enough to do harm. For that reason, to demand observance of a standard of absolute safety is not only to demand the impossible, but also to demand that good and necessary drugs no longer be made available. What we have a right to demand, I suggest, is that the ratio of benefits to risks be calculated intelligently, in full knowledge of the facts.

In this book I shall deal with how and why it came about that drugs went on sale which had not been thoroughly tested, had not been demonstrated to be safe, were worthless, and were irrationally prescribed. I write as one who hopes that the Food and Drug Administration will be helped and strengthened. I do not write as an antidrug faddist. My wife uses medicines, our children use them, and I use them, and they have spared us a good deal of suffering. I do write as a reporter who believes there has been insufficient reporting in an area of the most profound importance to all of us.

MM

By Prescription Only is not merely *The Therapeutic Nightmare* in a new dress, but is a significantly more useful book. Except for certain footnotes permitted by a kind if not indeed indulgent publisher, the Houghton Mifflin Company, the cutoff date for material used in *Nightmare* was December 31, 1964. At that time it was expected — prophetically, as it turned out — that within a year Commissioner George P. Larrick would retire from the Food and Drug Administration into earned obscurity. What was quite uncertain was whether a disastrous era of regulation — or nonregulation — of prescription drugs would be perpetuated. That possibility was foreclosed in August 1965 when President Johnson named John W. Gardner Secretary of the Department of Health, Education, and Welfare, of which the FDA is a constituent agency. Gardner had an earned reputation for a dedication to excellence; he had no intention of losing it by fumbling the challenge posed by FDA.

The man chosen to succeed Larrick was Dr. James L. Goddard, about whom I shall have something to say later on. For the moment, I want to say only that he led a bureaucratic renaissance which produced a large flow of news. I had the privilege of reporting it for the Washington *Post*. This assignment enabled me to bring to *By Prescription* not simply an abundance of new material, but a perspective on the Larrick era from a fresh vantage point. In addition, enough time has elapsed to permit at least a preliminary assessment of the Goddard regime. And so this is a different book worthy of a different title; and I am indebted to Donald Cutler, my editor at Beacon Press, for coming up with a fine one.

To retain the old while blending the new into *By Prescription Only* I have incorporated the Acknowledgments, the Preface, and all eighteen chapters of *The Therapeutic Nightmare*. The discovered errors — and I am most relieved to report that I know of very few — were minor and have been corrected. The original text has additionally been amended where it seemed necessary, primarily to delete references to the Appendixes which had been included in *The Therapeutic Nightmare* but which were dropped from this edition in order to make room for a wealth of new material of much greater timeliness and relevance.

The Glossary has been supplemented to accommodate material newly presented in this edition. Such new material is now to be found in this Preface, in an Afterword to each of the first seventeen chapters, and in an Epilogue. I have retained the contents of Appendix V, but its "Additional Notes" have been distributed to the appropriate sections of the Afterwords.

I have tried to confine my additions to matters that have lasting significance and instructiveness and to matters that have an important effect upon public health.

I think the reader will be struck by the enduring validity of basic themes set out in *Nightmare*. One is the simply incalculable importance of Congressional oversight, or monitoring, of Executive agencies charged with major responsibilities. A mistake with but one drug can have frightful consequences. FDA is responsible for thousands of drugs, and for food additives and pesticides as well. Yet since late 1964 no subcommittee of the Senate has given informed, serious, and sustained attention to the agency's performance. The burden has rested entirely on the

House Intergovernmental Relations Subcommittee. W. Donald Gray, the senior investigator, spends almost all of his time — including countless nights and weekends — on FDA matters. Delphis C. Goldberg, the professional staff member, is concerned with the agency, too — but also with oversight of the National Institutes of Health and, indeed, of the entire Department of Health, Education, and Welfare. Even with this minute staff the Subcommittee, which is headed by Representative L. H. Fountain, a North Carolina Democrat, has done a first-rate job — careful, fair, thorough, and very, very tough-minded. Lives have been saved and drug injuries have been prevented because of the work of this dedicated but underfinanced and understaffed Subcommittee — how many lives and injuries there is no way of knowing, but surely the number is substantial.

A related theme is the great need for informed reporting and auditing in the lay press, which is obligated to provide, Walter Lippmann has said, "an adequate supply of what the public will in the longer run need to know." There was a story told in World War II — I do not know if the story is true — that General Douglas MacArthur's public relations officers were allowed to report his dramatic arrivals, or wade-ins, at the Pacific beachheads but not his departures. Similarly, there is a tendency — discussed in *Nightmare* and persisting still — to report the arrivals of drugs but not their departures, to conjure up a sky which has silver linings but no clouds. This threatens what the philosopher Hannah Arendt has called "the sense by which we take our bearings in the real world." Survival requires, she said in a memorable speech last year at the annual convention of the American Political Science Association, "men willing to do what Herodotus was the first to undertake consciously, namely, *legein ta eonta*, to say what is." In *Minority Report*, H. L. Mencken said, "The only way that democracy can be made bearable is by developing and cherishing a class of men sufficiently honest and disinterested to challenge the prevailing quacks. No such class has ever appeared in the United States. Thus, the business of harassing the quacks devolves upon the newspapers. When they fail in their duty, which is usually, we are at the quacks' mercy." The press often fails today because of an inability to recognize that quackery is practiced not only by barkers at carnivals, but also by men with doctoral degrees who are members and officers of prestigious medical-scientific organizations and who are shielded from detection and criticism by such organizations, by public officials, and by governmental, corporate, and organizational secrecy and public relations. It is, I think, a disturbing and revealing commentary, that in the entire Washington press corps there is but one lay reporter whose assignment has included sustained reporting about FDA's regulation of prescription drugs and about related matters. "The American Government," John Kenneth Galbraith reminded us in *The Liberal Hour*, "works far better — perhaps it only works — when the Federal Executive and influential business and the respectable press are in some degree at odds. Only then can we be sure that abuse or neglect, either public or private, will be given the notoriety that is needed. In the time of Coolidge and Hoover, the Federal Executive, business and the press were united. These are the times in our democracy when all looks peaceful and much goes wrong."

A third theme, which is related to the preceding ones, is the continuing and largely unmet need for attention to FDA in the universities. In the fall of 1966, when I covered the American Political Science Association convention on an assignment for the Washington *Post*, I made my way through a blizzard of papers. Most seemed to me to be a lot of Simple-Simon propositions, leaf-raking or material otherwise peripheral to things that really matter. Informally, I inquired whether anyone knew of a single paper of quality that had been presented to the Association, in any year within memory, on FDA, an agency with a grip on the health and lives of all of us. No such paper could be recalled. Doubtless the same situation prevailed as to other agencies. Thus, for example, nothing was to be heard about the unusual meshing of the Federal Aviation Agency and business interests that is intended to produce with a supposedly temporary billion-dollar subsidy a project as dubious as the Supersonic Transport. I was not alone in my dismay. In a brilliant paper on the Office of Education, Stephen K. Bailey of Syracuse University termed it "passing strange" that really close examination of a Government department or agency — which he called "microanalysis" but which sounded to me like depth reporting — is a rarity. What political scientists prefer, Bailey said, are the "incomparably greater dividends" of "macroanalysis" — spatial comparisons between, say, the Office of Education and the Bureau of Reclamation or the FBI.

A fourth theme is that massive efforts continue to be made to deceive and mislead physicians about prescription drugs, that all too frequently these efforts succeed, and that when they do it is the patients whose pocketbooks are exploited and who may be injured or killed. Not infrequently the threat is to a fetus, which is surely in a poor position to invoke the doctrine of *caveat emptor*. In *By Prescription* the reader will find evidence that in at least one case the American Medical Association was involved in noncompliance with the law. That evidence, published here in the Afterword to Chapter 4, has been previously disclosed in the Washington *Post* and in *The Progressive* magazine and has not been challenged. The case concerned a drug called Pree MT, a product of Wallace Laboratories (now Wallace Pharmaceuticals).

A fifth theme is that we owe a continuing debt of great magnitude to those described by former Senator Paul H. Douglas as "lonely soldiers of the common good." I include among them those anonymous public servants who have imperiled their careers in order to bring to light nonfeasance and misfeasance that would unless exposed cause needless injury and loss of life.

To my knowledge, no such risks have been run by anyone in those pharmaceutical companies and medical advertising agencies where drug testing has been falsified and misrepresented and where knowledge of drug-caused death and injury has been suppressed. Such rigidly conformist loyalty to the corporation as this indicates, and which is to be found in numerous other industries besides the pharmaceutical, is heedless of ethical and human values. It is a phenomenon worthy of examination by those who care about the nature of our society.

✓ ✓ ✓

I turn now to January 17, 1966, when within a few hours, in different cities, two events occurred that had interlocking and far-reaching consequences. In Trenton, New Jersey, the Wallace firm, a division of Carter-Wallace, Inc., switched its plea from innocent to no-contest and was sentenced in the Pree MT episode, the first case brought under the false-advertising provisions of the Kefauver-Harris Amendments to the Food, Drug, and Cosmetic Act. In Washington, D.C., Dr. James Goddard, who was destined to make a crackdown on false prescription-drug ads a proud chapter in his career in the Food and Drug Administration, was sworn in as Commissioner of the agency.

"We searched long and hard to find the best man," Secretary John Gardner said at the ceremony, "and we found him. I am sure that you will find his leadership stimulating and strengthening." Gardner went on to say that in November 1965 he had appointed a Committee to study the major problems facing the agency. "The Committee, in reporting to me, spoke of the intense pressures surrounding the operations of the Food and Drug Administration," the Secretary continued. " 'Because of these pressures,' it asserted, 'the agency *must* maintain a high standard of excellence, *must* be skillfully managed, *must* be clear as to policies, *must* function with spotless integrity.' " There were some polite bows to the past, but Gardner said, "Putting the matter bluntly, they [members of the Committee] asserted that the FDA must be far better managed in the future. . . . Given the life or death character of so many of FDA's decisions, 'laxity in management cannot be tolerated,' to quote the Committee."

Few of the several hundred FDA and HEW officials and employees who were at the ceremony had seen Dr. Goddard before. He was coming to the agency from Atlanta, where for three years he had headed the Communicable Disease Center of the Public Health Service. Earlier he had been chosen by General Elwood R. Quesada to be the first Civil Air Surgeon of the Federal Aviation Agency. He was young (42), tough, vigorous, and articulate. "[W]e must never forget that our reason for existence, as a government agency, is to serve the *public* interest," he said. "And the public has very little voice unless it is ours. My professional commitment as a physician and my career commitment to public health combine to fix my ultimate standard for judgment — the safety and well-being of the individual citizen." He promised to build and strengthen the agency's staff, to seek to base decisions "upon the best scientific capability that exists, wherever it exists," to give a top priority to "a systematic program of career development," and to administer the law, "both in its language and intent, for the fullest protection of the American people." He concluded:

> Mr. Secretary, I am proud to accept the challenge that you and the President have put before me. I am not unaware of the fact that this is one of the hottest of the governmental hot-spots. But I am also aware that few if any governmental agencies have a more delicate or critical part to play in assuring that the American people advance into the future with safety and confidence. I'm going to give it everything I've got.

With that, the crewcut physician took command of an agency with about 5,000 employees scattered among 27 district offices, with mixed regulatory and public health functions and with varying authority over industries whose products take 25 cents out of each dollar spent by consumers. Soon after he took over the new Commissioner ordered a teletype system set up to connect Washington with the district offices. Messages went out from headquarters. There were no responses. After several days the first came in. It said, "What hath Goddard wrought?"

He wrought change. Some called him "Go-Go Goddard." He had power and did not hesitate to use it. He had the authority earned as a physician with special training in public health, and he used that authority as, alas, a poor Larrick never could. He had a finely honed sense of public relations. This was aided by enormous energy and by an extremely quick mind. Some said he looked a bit like a graying astronaut, but he had only to let his spectacles descend the bridge of his nose to soften his appearance with a touch of bedside manner. In his first 100 working days he drew attention from news media rivaling that, according to *Medical World News*, "given to the President himself." The New York *Times*, which had not before his appointment used his picture, used one for the tenth time on September 19, 1966; in addition, there was a picture spread in the *Times Magazine* for May 15. He seemed to be making speeches at a faster rate than they could be produced by anything less than a platoon of literate speech-writers. *Life* magazine photographed him wearing a sanitary hat in a drug plant, sniffing animal feed and leaping from a boxcar at a Ralston-Purina facility. "My nature is such that I can't be in a factory or store or hotel ten minutes before I see all sorts of things wrong and start trying to reorganize the whole place," *Life's* issue for August 23, 1966, quoted him as saying, "Even my relaxation can be tense."

I think the intelligent reader should be as tense about the kind of adulatory tone that pervaded the *Life* article as he should be about the sarcasm implied by a phrase like "Go-Go." Neither adulation nor sarcasm is going to help us. Dr. Goddard has delivered an inordinate number of speeches — but a Commissioner of the FDA who is going to make a politician, corporation, or organization think twice about trying to apply improper pressures *must* build a popular base of support. Dr. Goddard's disposition "to reorganize the whole place" was entirely appropriate to FDA — but that is not to say the old skeletons swept out of the closet will not someday be replaced by new ones. Dr. Goddard is an almost infinite improvement over his predecessor; he is a public servant of a quality far higher than we often get in the Federal bureaucracy, and a brave, intelligent, and winning man, to boot. But like all of us he can slip, his performance requires fair and informed auditing, and he responds to heat. To express reservations of this sort is to be neither carping nor unfair, and I venture that Dr. Goddard himself would be among the first to say so. I am suggesting merely that a clearcut distinction is to be made in one's attitude toward God and Man, whether at Yale or at the Food and Drug Administration.

The Committee upon which Secretary Gardner relied provided the basis for an example illustrating the point I am making. "The Commissioner, Deputy Commissioner, and Associate Commissioner for Science," the Committee said, "should be viewed as a team to achieve maximum strength in both management and scientific competence. This whole top team must be sufficiently outstanding to win the immediate confidence of the public, industry, Congress and the scientific-professional community." The departure of George Larrick from FDA was accompanied by several other departures from FDA's top echelons, including that of Deputy Commissioner John L. Harvey. One who remained was Assistant Commissioner Winton B. Rankin. He was no more likely "to win the immediate confidence" of Congress than Larrick, because there had been innumerable occasions when the two former inspectors seemed to be interchangeable if not indistinguishable. Nonetheless Dr. Goddard made Rankin Deputy Commissioner after finding their working relationship "compatible and fruitful." I do not argue that Dr. Goddard was wrong in making this selection, but rather that his choice was one that the Committee had seemingly carefully precluded, that no compelling reason for ignoring the Committee has been advanced, and the situation induced a certain wariness.

The third member of the "top team" has of this writing not been chosen. At one point there were rumors — denied by agency spokesmen — that the Associate Commissioner for Science would be Dr. Arthur E. Wentz, who since August 1966 has been in charge of FDA's extramural research. Again, he had the confidence of Dr. Goddard; but whether he had the confidence of Congress may be questioned, on the basis of a scalding report issued in September 1966 by the House Government Operations Committee following an investigation by its Research and Technical Programs Subcommittee and the General Accounting Office.

In 1960, the year after Dr. Goddard became Civil Air Surgeon of the Federal Aviation Agency, the FAA set a mandatory retirement age of 60 for airline pilots. An outcry followed from the pilots, although I daresay that few passengers would question that their safety was advanced by an action that was unavoidably arbitrary. The pilots complained that no meaningful correlation had been demonstrated between a man's chronological age and his physiological age or capabilities. In what was widely regarded as an attempt to take off the heat, applied by a powerful and well-financed group, General Quesada and Dr. Goddard argued before a House Appropriations subcommittee that the FAA should make a pilot aging study of its own — with new and limited facilities — even though the aging process was being researched at the National Institutes of Health, at medical schools, and by the armed forces and the Veterans Administration.

The Government Operations Committee reported that a short time later the FAA awarded a $26,785 contract to the Lovelace Foundation for Medical Education and Research in Albuquerque to devise a plan for a long-term study of pilot aging. But seven months before this effort was completed the Agency began the very long-term study that had not yet been devised. "Thus, the planning study funds were wasted," the Subcommittee said. The long-term study was undertaken by Dr. Wentz at the Georgetown University Clinical Research Institute. It was to last twenty-five years but was abandoned in April 1966 after an FAA advisory group found a mountain of test data for which no satisfactory statistical analysis had been designed, which had not been analyzed, and which had been accumulated at a 5-year cost to the taxpayers of more than one million dollars. In a criticism implicitly including Drs. Goddard and Wentz among its targets, the Committee said it "can only conclude that FAA's failure to take earlier action evidences poor management and an inadequate sense of responsibility for public funds." In the *Life* article, Dr. Goddard was quoted as saying that the post of FDA Commissioner "should never again be filled by a non-scientist." But the episode revealed by the House Committee was the product of a kind of political science.

Dr. Goddard took command of the FDA with a public promise from Secretary Gardner of "the strongest support that the Office of the Secretary can provide." Without such support the Commissioner could not have gone to Boca Raton, Florida, eleven weeks after taking office to deliver the toughest speech ever given to the Pharmaceutical Manufacturers Association by an official of the FDA. The PMA, which is made up of 140 firms that produce more than 90 per cent of the nation's prescription drugs, had enjoyed a cozy relationship with George Larrick and once had given him an award for "devoted service to the public welfare" and for his "understanding of mutual problems." No such award is likely to be conferred by the PMA on Dr. Goddard. He told the industry's decision-makers that in his brief time in office he had "seen evidence that too many drug manufacturers may well have obscured the prime mission of their industry: to help people get well." He said he was "alarmed" by what he had found and told why:

Let me begin with Investigational New Drugs. I can say that I have been shocked at the quality of many submissions to our IND staff. The hand of the amateur is evident too often for my comfort.

✦ ✦ ✦

In addition to the problem of quality, there is the problem of dishonesty in the Investigational New Drug Stage. . . . And I will admit that there are gray areas in the IND situation.

But the conscious withholding of unfavorable animal or clinical data is not a gray-area matter.

The deliberate choice of clinical investigators known to be more concerned about industry friendships than in developing good data is not a gray-area matter.

The planting in journals of articles that begin to commercialize what is still an Investigational New Drug is not a gray-area matter.

✦ ✦ ✦

Let us move on to New Drug Applications. This is the takeoff stage, as you know, for a new product of this industry. . . . But once again, I have been shocked at the materials that come in to us. I have been shocked at the clear attempts to slip something by us. I am deeply disturbed at the constant, direct, personal pressure some industry representatives have placed upon our people.

Dr. Goddard documented his charges with several specific examples. In these he saw "symptoms of a disease that drugs cannot cure. . . . That disease is irresponsibility. You cannot afford to have it in your midst any longer," he said. Even before that the bold Commissioner had begun to increase the price of "irresponsibility." That story is told in the Afterwords to several chapters of this book.

May 1967   MM

℞

CONTENTS

℞

FOLLOWING is a glossary of prescription drugs mentioned in *The Therapeutic Nightmare*. The list is not all-inclusive: it excludes most of the foreign trade names and, in addition, the drugs mentioned solely in the appendixes. Generic names are italicized. An asterisk denotes that the product has been removed from the market.

The reader may find useful the following definitions of some of the descriptive terms used in the glossary. An amphetamine is a potent stimulant. An antibacterial agent kills bacteria or inhibits their growth. An antibiotic is an antibacterial agent of biologic origin, although some antibiotics can be produced synthetically. An antidepressant acts against mental depression. An antidiabetic acts against diabetes. An antidiarrheal agent prevents or overcomes diarrhea. An antimalarial agent prevents or suppresses malaria. An antispasmodic tends to relieve spasm.

A barbiturate is a derivative of barbituric acid and is used as a potent sedative or hypnotic (sleeping pill). A diuretic increases the flow of urine. A hormone is produced in an organ of the body and has a highly specific effect on some other, distant organ; some hormones can be produced synthetically.

A tranquilizer has a sedative or calming effect without inducing sleep. *However, most so-called tranquilizers and most so-called sedatives can either calm or induce sleep, depending upon the dosage.* Except in the case of potent tranquilizers, the difference between so-called tranquilizers and so-called sedatives is commonly more apparent than real.

Achrocidin, a combination product used in respiratory infections which contains the antibiotic *tetracycline hydrochloride* and other substances, including a pain-killer

Achromycin (*tetracycline*), an antibiotic

Altafur* (*furaltadone*), an antibacterial agent

Antivenin (*Crotalidae polyvalent*), an anti-snakebite serum

Atabrine (*quinacrine*), an antimalarial agent

Atarax (*hydroxyzine hydrochloride*), a mild tranquilizer

Aureomycin (*chlortetracycline*), an antibiotic

Bacitracin, an antibiotic

Capla (*mebutamate*), used against hypertension

Catron* (*pheniprazine*), an antidepressant

Ceporin, an antibiotic derived from the cephalosporium mold

Chlorcyclizine hydrochloride, an antihistamine

Chloromycetin (*chloramphenicol*), an antibiotic

Compazine (*prochlorperazine*), a potent tranquilizer

Cortisone, an anti-inflammatory hormone much used against arthritis

Cuprimine (*penicillamine*), used in an uncommon affliction known as Wilson's disease

Deaner (*deanol*), an antidepressant

Decadron (*dexamethasone*), an anti-inflammatory hormone

Demerol (*meperidine*), a synthetic narcotic used as a pain-killer

Deprol (*meprobamate* plus *benactyzine*), a mild tranquilizer combination

Dexedrine (*dextroamphetamine*), a potent stimulant

Diabinese (*chlorpropamide*), an oral antidiabetic

Dihydrostreptomycin, an antibiotic

Diuril (*chlorothiazide*), a diuretic

Doriden (*glutethimide*), a sedative

Dornwal * (*amphenidone*), a mild tranquilizer

Efocaine,* a long-acting anesthetic

Elavil (*amitriptyline*), an antidepressant

Enovid (*norethynodrel* plus *mestranol*), a combination of hormones used as an oral contraceptive

Entoquel * (*thihexinol methylbromide*), an antidiarrheal agent

Equanil (*meprobamate*), a mild tranquilizer

Eutonyl (*pargyline hydrochloride*), an antidepressant

Flexin* (*zoxazolamine*), a muscle relaxant and anti-gout agent

Gramicidin, an antibiotic

Insulin, an antidiabetic hormone

Keflin, an antibiotic derived from the cephalosporium mold

Kevadon (*thalidomide*), a sedative; although never officially approved for marketing in the United States, 2.5 million pills were distributed

Librium (*chlordiazepoxide hydrochloride*), a mild tranquilizer

Mandelamine (*methenamine mandelate*), a urinary-tract antiseptic

Marplan (*isocarboxazid*), an antidepressant

Marsilid * (*iproniazid*), an antituberculosis drug later used as an antidepressant

Meclizine hydrochloride, an antihistamine

Medrol (*methylprednisolone*), an anti-inflammatory hormone

Meprospan (*meprobamate*), a mild tranquilizer in sustained-release capsules

MER/29 * (*triparanol*), a cholesterol-blocking agent

Meticorten (*prednisone*), an anti-inflammatory hormone

Miltown (*meprobamate*), a mild tranquilizer

Monase* (*etryptamine acetate*), an antidepressant

Naquival (*trichlormethiazide* plus *reserpine*), a diuretic

Nardil (*phenelzine sulfate*), an antidepressant

Neomycin, an antibiotic

Niamid (*nialamide*), an antidepressant

Noludar (*methyprylon*), a sedative

Norinyl (*norethindrone* plus *mestranol*), a combination of hormones used as an oral contraceptive

Norlestrin (*norethindrone* plus *ethinyl estradiol*), a combination of hormones used as an oral contraceptive

Norlutin (*norethindrone*), a hormone used in gynecologic disorders

Orabilex* (*bunamiodyl sodium*), a radio-opaque dye used as a diagnostic aid

Orinase (*tolbutamide*), an oral antidiabetic

Ortho-Novum (*norethindrone* plus *mestranol*), a combination of hormones used as an oral contraceptive

Parnate (*tranylcypromine*), an antidepressant

Penicillin, an antibiotic

Peritrate (*pentaerythritol tetranitrate*), used against angina pectoris

Placidyl (*ethchlorvynol*), a sedative

Polymyxin, an antibiotic

Pree MT*(*meprobamate* plus *hydrochlorothiazide*), a combination of a mild tranquilizer and a diuretic used in premenstrual tension

Probenecid, an anti-gout agent

Provest (*medroxyprogesterone acetate* plus *ethinyl estradiol*), a combination of hormones used as an oral contraceptive

Seconal (*secobarbital*), a sedative

Serpasil (*reserpine*), a tranquilizer

Sigmamycin (*oleandomycin* plus *tetracycline*), a combination of antibiotics; succeeded by Signemycin

Signemycin (*tetracycline* with *oleandomycin* as *triacetyloleandomycin*), another combination of antibiotics

Soma (*carisoprodol*), a muscle relaxant

Sparine (*promazine hydrochloride*), a potent tranquilizer

Streptomycin, an antibiotic

Terramycin (*oxytetracycline*), an antibiotic

Thalidomide, a sedative; although never officially approved for marketing in the United States, 2.5 million pills were distributed

Thorazine (*chlorpromazine hydrochloride*), a potent tranquilizer

Tigan (*trimethobenzamide hydrochloride*), an anti-nausea product

Tofranil (*imipramine hydrochloride*), an antidepressant

Tyrothricin, an antibiotic

Valmid (*ethinamate*), a mild tranquilizer

V-Cillin (Penicillin V or *phenoxymethyl penicillin*), an antibiotic

℞

GLOSSARY 1967

Amplus (*dextroamphetamine sulfate* plus *hydroxyzine hydrochloride* plus various *minerals* and *vitamins*), an antihistamine-containing combination product

Anhydron K (*cyclothiazide* plus *potassium chloride*), a thiazide-potassium diuretic

Anhydron KR (*cyclothiazide* plus *potassium chloride* plus *reserpine*), a thiazide-potassium diuretic plus an antihypertensive agent

Antivert (*meclizine hydrochloride* plus *nicotinic acid*), an antihistamine-containing combination product

Apascil (*meprobamate*), a mild tranquilizer

Ataraxoid (*prednisolone* plus *hydroxyzine*), an anti-inflammatory hormone plus an antihistamine

Atraxin (*meprobamate*), a mild tranquilizer

Atromid-S (*clofibrate*), a cholesterol reducing agent

Aventyl HCL (*nortriptyline hydrochloride*), a drug used in anxiety and depression

Biobamat (*meprobamate*), a mild tranquilizer

Bonadettes (*meclizine hydrochloride*), an antihistamine

Bonadoxin (*meclizine hydrochloride* plus *pyridoxine hydrochloride*), an antihistamine-containing combination product

Bonamine (*meclizine hydrochloride*), an antihistamine succeeded by Bonine

Bonine (*meclizine hydrochloride*), an antihistamine

Bucladin, a combination product containing the antihistamine *buclizine hydrochloride*

Calmiren (meprobamate), a mild tranquilizer

Cartax (pentaerythritol tetranitrate plus hydroxyzine hydrochloride), an antihistamine-containing combination product

Chloral (chloral hydrate), a sedative/tranquilizer

Cirpon (meprobamate), a mild tranquilizer

Clomid (clomiphene citrate), an antisterility drug

C-Quens (mestranol and mestranol plus chlormadinone acetate), a combination of hormones used as a sequential oral contraceptive

Cyrpon (meprobamate), a mild tranquilizer

d, dl-Desoxyephedrine, stimulants

d-, dl-Methamphetamine, stimulants

Deltasone (prednisone), an anti-inflammatory hormone

Deltra (prednisone), an anti-inflammatory hormone

DMSO (dimethyl sulfoxide), an experimental drug

Dyazide (triamterene plus hydrochlorothiazide), a diuretic

Ecuanil (meprobamate), a mild tranquilizer

Elipten* (amino-glutethimide), an anticonvulsant

Enarax (oxyphencyclimine hydrochloride plus hydroxyzine hydrochloride), an antihistamine-containing combination product

Enduron (methyclothiazide), a diuretic-antihypertensive agent

Enduronyl (methyclothiazide plus deserpidine), a diuretic-antihypertensive agent

Esidrix (hydrochlorothiazide), a diuretic

Esidrix-K (hydrochlorothiazide plus potassium chloride), a thiazide-potassium diuretic

Hydrodiuril-Ka (hydrochlorothiazide), a thiazide-potassium diuretic

Hydropres-Ka (hydrochlorothiazide plus reserpine), a diuretic and hypertensive agent

Harmonin (meprobamate), a mild tranquilizer

Indocin (indomethacin), a drug used in rheumatoid arthritis

Indoklon (flurothyl), a convulsant agent for psychiatric use

Kynex (sulfamethoxypyridazine), a long-acting sulfonamide

Lasix (furosemide), a diuretic

Lincocin (lincomycin hydrochloride monohydrate), an antibiotic

Madribon (sulfadimethoxine), a long-acting sulfonamide

Madricidin* (sulfadimethoxine), a long-acting sulfonamide

Marax (*hydroxyzine hydrochloride* plus *ephedrine sulfate* plus *theophylline*), an antihistamine-containing combination product

Marezine (*cyclizine*), an antihistamine

Measurin, a delayed-absorption aspirin

Meclizine, an antihistamine

Mepantin (*meprobamate*), a mild tranquilizer

Mepavlon (*meprobamate*), a mild tranquilizer

Meproleaf (*meprobamate*), a mild tranquilizer

Meprosin (*meprobamate*), a mild tranquilizer

Meprotabs (*meprobamate*), a mild tranquilizer

Midicel (*sulfamethoxypyridazine*), a long-acting sulfonamide

Miluretic* (*meprobamate* plus *hydrochlorothiazide*), a combination of a mild tranquilizer and a diuretic used in premenstrual tension

MK-665 compound, a combination of hormones once used as an experimental oral contraceptive

Naturetin č K (*bendroflumethiazide* plus *potassium chloride*), a thiazide-potassium diuretic

Nervonus (*meprobamate*), a mild tranquilizer

Neuramate (*meprobamate*), a mild tranquilizer

Norgesic, an analgesic and muscle relaxant

Oasil (*meprobamate*), a mild tranquilizer

Oracon (*ethinyl estradiol and dimethisterone* plus *ethinyl estradiol*), a combination of hormones used as a sequential oral contraceptive

Ortho-Novum SQ (*mestranol and mestranol* plus *norethindrone*), a combination of hormones used as a sequential oral contraceptive

Pamaco (*meprobamate*), a mild tranquilizer

Panediol (*meprobamate*), a mild tranquilizer

Paraldehyde, a mild tranquilizer

Pediamycin (*erythromycin ethyl succinate*), an antibiotic

Perazil (*chlorcyclizine hydrochloride*), an antihistamine

Pertranquil (*meprobamate*), a mild tranquilizer

Perequil (*meprobamate*), a mild tranquilizer

Pertranquil (*meprobamate*), a mild tranquilizer

Placidon (*meprobamate*), a mild tranquilizer

Pre-Sate (*chlorphentermine rydrochloride*), an appetite inhibitor

Probamyl (*meprobamate*), a mild tranquilizer

Quanil (meprobamate), a mild tranquilizer

Quilate (meprobamate), a mild tranquilizer

Rautrax-N (rauwolfia serpentina whole root plus bendroflumethiazide plus potassium chloride), a thiazide-potassium diuretic plus an antihypertensive agent

Rautrax-N Modified (rauwolfia serpentina whole root plus bendroflumethiazide plus potassium chloride), a thiazide-potassium diuretic plus an antihypertensive agent

Relay, a delayed-absorption aspirin

Renese (polythiazide), a diuretic

Renese-R (polythiazide plus reserpine), a diuretic plus an antihypertensive agent

Rondomycin (methacycline hydrochloride), an antibiotic

Sedabamate (meprobamate), a mild tranquilizer

Sedasil (meprobamate), a mild tranquilizer

Serax (oxazepam), a mild tranquilizer

Serc (betahistine chloride), used against certain symptoms of Menière's Syndrome

Softran (buclizine hydrochloride), an antihistamine

Stendin, a delayed-absorption aspirin

Tegopen (sodium cloxacillin monohydrate), an antibiotic

Tigacol (trimethobenzamide plus nicotinyl alcohol), used against certain symptoms of Menière's Syndrome

Urbil (meprobamate), a mild tranquilizer

Valium (diazepam), a mild tranquilizer

Viobamate (meprobamate), a mild tranquilizer

Vistaril (hydroxyzine), an antihistamine

℞

LIST OF COMMITTEES
AND SUBCOMMITTEES

IN THIS BOOK there are references to several committees and subcommittees of the Congress. For the sake of clarity and completeness these are listed below. First mention in each chapter gives the formal title, succeeding mention adopts the informal reference; asterisks indicate the two exceptions where informal title only is given.

UNITED STATES SENATE

Subcommittee on Reorganization and International Organizations
of the Committee on Government Operations
Subcommittee on Antitrust and Monopoly
of the Committee on the Judiciary
Hill subcommittee*
of the Committee on Appropriations
Subcommittee on Health
of the Committee on Labor and Public Welfare

HOUSE OF REPRESENTATIVES

Intergovernmental Relations Subcommittee
of the Committee on Government Operations
Subcommittee on Legal and Monetary Affairs
of the Committee on Government Operations

Antitrust subcommittee*
   of the Committee on the Judiciary
Committee on Interstate and Foreign Commerce
Subcommittee on Departments of Labor and Health, Education, and
   Welfare, and Related Agencies Appropriations
Intergovernmental Relations Subcommittee of the Committee
   on Government Operations, *Hearings* on "Drug Safety,"
   88th Cong., 2nd Sess., 1964, Part I, March 24 and 25, and
   June 3; Part II, April 22, 23, 28, and 29, May 6, and June 17
   and 18; 89th Cong., 1965, 1st Sess., Part III, March 23 and
   24, May 4, and June 8, 9, 10, 24, and 25; Part IV, July 20,
   22, and 27, August 3 and 10, and September 24; 2nd Sess.,
   1966, Part V, March 9 and 10, May 25 and 26, and June 7,
   8, and 9.

BY PRESCRIPTION ONLY

1

THE GREAT THERAPEUTIC MISADVENTURE

In his Consumers' Protection Message of March 15, 1962, the late President Kennedy told Congress that new drugs marketed since 1938, when the Federal Food, Drug, and Cosmetic Act was enacted, have "saved countless lives and relieved millions of victims of acute and chronic illnesses." Having acknowledged this, he went on to say:

> . . . new drugs are being placed on the market with no requirement that there be either advance proof that they will be effective in treating the diseases and conditions for which they are recommended or the prompt reporting of adverse reactions. These new drugs present greater hazards as well as greater potential benefits than ever before — for they are widely used, they are often very potent, and they are promoted by aggressive sales campaigns that may tend to overstate their merits and fail to indicate the risks involved in their use. For example, over 20 percent of the new drugs listed since 1956 in the publication *New and Nonofficial Drugs* were found, upon being tested, to be incapable of sustaining one or more of their sponsor's claims regarding their therapeutic effect. There is no way of measuring the needless suffering, the money innocently squandered, and the protraction of illnesses resulting from the use of such ineffective drugs.

One clue to the extent of the needless suffering is provided by the United States Public Health Service, which says that we have each year 1,368,000 nonfatal, so-called therapeutic misadventures. All of these are iatrogenic, that is, doctor-caused; most of them are induced by drugs, including vaccines; a significant but undetermined proportion are induced by useless drugs, and many of these so induced are more damaging than the original disease. Indeed, by 1960 at least 40 new diseases or syndromes had been attributed to drugs used in therapy.

The Public Health Service figure includes merely those injuries severe enough to cause the victim to seek medical care or to restrict his activities for at least one day. Large though a toll of 1,368,000 misadventures a year may appear, the PHS terms it "probably an underestimate." This chapter deals with six basic reasons why it is almost certainly an underestimate, and why a figure on *fatal* therapeutic mishaps cannot even be conjectured.

1. *Some drug mishaps are not recognized as such.* Consider the testimony given in 1962 before Representative Emanuel Celler's House Antitrust subcommittee by Dr. M. Harold Book, director of laboratories at the Norristown State Hospital in Pennsylvania and assistant professor of neuropathology at the University of Pennsylvania: "In the last eight or nine years," he said, "I, and many other pathologists, have noticed a distinct increase in the number of serious adverse effects, even deaths, resulting from the widespread use of the newer, so-called wonder drugs."

Dr. Book said the approximately 2000 autopsies he had performed left him "firmly convinced that the ill effects of some of these drugs go unrecognized. Sometimes it is apparent that the treatment has shortened the life of the patient. This might be considered a sort of involuntary euthanasia . . . Many of these unusual effects of drugs and mistakes in diagnosis are only uncovered at autopsy. Unfortunately, postmortems are done in only a small percentage of deaths in this country . . ." To put it another way, the evil is oft interred with their bones.

While Dr. Book was speaking primarily of elderly persons, Dr. Sydney H. Kane, of the Foundation for Medical Research, Perinatal Study, Philadelphia, dealt with the understatement of adverse drug effects in the newborn, especially the premature. In a letter to then Senator Hubert H. Humphrey, Dr. Kane said:

> . . . there have been no adequate procedures for evaluating pharmacologic effect on newborns comparable to those methods used in adults . . . data obtained from animal experimentation . . . cannot be readily transferred to newborn humans. Thus, many therapies administered to the mother have an indirect or continuing effect on the newborn infant. Even more disturbing is the specter of the long-range effects of drug therapy given to newborns.
>
> Innumerable examples can be cited in the experience of the last few years concerning the difficulties and risks involved when transferring information obtained from older human beings to the newborn infant and especially to the premature child. Many of the untoward results reported were completely unpredictable on the basis of previously acquired scientific information. In fact, some of these reactions have been heretofore totally unreported in medical practice, especially as they relate to premature infants. In this general category of drug reactions noted in the last few years have been liver failure, jaundice, and the unusual production of pigmented substances within the body of the premature infant. As to the long-term effect of some of these difficulties, one can only speculate.
>
> Many of these undesirable responses to drug therapy go undetected or unrecorded because of their infrequency of occurrence in a given hospital or a given physician's experience. It is only when the problem becomes widespread in nature that reporting of such hazards and undesirable reactions begins to appear in the medical literature.

A problem of a quite different kind is posed by the patient who has taken several drugs, or has taken drugs in combination with other substances, including alcohol and even certain foods. In such cases it is frequently difficult to establish just what caused harm.[1] Uncertainty of this sort attended the death in February 1964 of Alan Ladd, the actor, whose body was found in his home at Palm Springs, California. The coroner said the case would be signed out as an accidental death. Three drugs were involved: Seconal, a barbiturate sleep-inducer; Sparine, a potent tranquilizer; and Librium, which has been advertised as a successor to mild tranquilizers. "The combination of alcohol [with the three drugs] produced together the total effect the depressants had on the central nervous system with the high level of alcohol being the major factor," the coroner, Dr. James S. Bird, Jr., said, according to an Associated Press report. The *National Observer* reported that Dr. Bird had termed such deaths from alcohol and drug mixtures "far from uncommon" in his Riverside County jurisdiction.

Additional reasons for the nonrecognition of drug-induced mishaps are cited in a report to Senator Humphrey's Subcommittee on Reorganization and International Organizations by Forrest E. Linder, director of the National Center for Health Statistics. He said that the families involved in the nationwide survey on which the 1,368,000 mishap figure is based "can pass on to the interviewer only such information as has been given them by the physician who treated the case.

"To the extent that the physician does not know that the illness was the result of the preventive measure of treatment . . . or, knowing of it, the physician does not pass on this information to the patient (or parent, in the case of a child) — to this extent, the cases will not be reported in the interview."

---

[1] "Heredity does influence and may determine the response of a person to drugs," Dr. Werner Kalow of the Department of Pharmacology at the University of Toronto, said in a paper presented on December 30, 1964, at the annual convention of the American Association for the Advancement of Science. "One dares no longer to predict with certainty the action of a drug in one person even if it has been examined in another one, and a drug found to be safe in one racial group is not necessarily safe in another."

2. *Even if recognized, certain therapeutic misadventures are not officially acknowledged to be such.* One illustration is provided by tranquilizers, which have been advertised with such claims as "Does not impair . . . normal behavior" and "Restores drive and interests." But it is not uncommon for tranquilizers to induce temporary impotence in men. Even if a victim should suspect a connection between his use of the tranquilizer and the impairment of his normal sexual behavior he may be quite unwilling to discuss it with anyone, his physician included; and if he should mention it impotence would not be listed as a therapeutic misadventure.

3. *Systems for reporting even recognized and acknowledged therapeutic misadventures often are unreliable or nonexistent.* "The number of deaths listed usually includes only the number of deaths mentioned in published literature," Senator Humphrey said. "The number of deaths not published, but known and validated, may be much higher, perhaps several times higher."

Reporting of adverse reactions consumes precious time, carries a reward that is nebulous at best, and is not required by law. This may help to explain why some observers, as two pharmacologists wrote in the Canadian Medical Association *Journal* for April 1, 1959, "are disinclined to publish reports of additional cases of a well-known toxic reaction." In August 1964, Arnold Elkind of New York City, head of the products liability exchange of the American Trial Lawyers Association, estimated that "90 to 95 per cent of therapeutic misadventures never see the light of day."

Most hospitals do not have a system to encourage staff members to recognize, record, and report drug reactions. In an article about this in the July 14, 1962, issue of the *Journal* of the American Medical Association, Dr. Dale G. Friend expressed his belief "that only a small percentage of all drug reactions is ever recorded." Dr. Friend, who is senior associate in medicine at the

Peter Bent Brigham Hospital in Boston and assistant professor of medicine at the Harvard Medical School, could have cited a spot check made by the Food and Drug Administration in 1952–1953 of 95 hospitals in 11 cities.

FDA found 84 unreported cases of penicillin shock, of which 25 were fatal. A decade later, in Baltimore, the Committee on Pharmacy and Therapeutics of the Johns Hopkins Hospital, where there *is* a reporting system, said in its July 1962 *Drug Letter:* "The reporting of drug reactions during the past 12 months has been variable and it is estimated that no more than 10 per cent, at the most, of all drug reactions have, in fact, been reported . . . In addition to failure to report, there is little doubt that occasionally the fact that one is dealing with a drug reaction may be entirely missed . . ."

In the December 10, 1955, *Journal* of the AMA, Dr. David P. Barr wrote about a careful survey made in the medical service of a large New York hospital which disclosed that 1 patient in 20 had been admitted as the result of "sanctioned and well-intentioned" use of drugs.

One who was shocked by this was Dr. Walter Modell, whose qualifications included being editor of *Drugs of Choice,* a biennial physician's manual, editor-in-chief of *Clinical Pharmacology and Therapeutics,* a journal with the central purpose of publishing information about the effects of drugs in man, head of an FDA new-drug advisory committee, and associate professor of pharmacology at the Cornell University Medical College. "One needs," he said, "only to read Moser's *Diseases of Medical Progress* (what an ironic title!) to realize the dimensions of this danger."

The dimensions were further indicated by two later surveys. One was made over an eight-month period in 1960–1961 at Grace–New Haven Community Hospital in New Haven, Connecticut. Among 1014 patients, 103 — or 1 in 10 — suffered a total of 119 reactions to drug therapy given in the hospital. Although 61 episodes were judged minor and 44 moderate, Dr. Elihu M. Schimmel of the Yale University Medical School has reported in the *Annals of Internal Medicine* for January 1964 that 10 were of major severity and 4 were fatal. In November 1964, physicians at the Johns Hopkins Hospital reported an intensive, two-year study that there, too, patients had been admitted because of adverse reactions to medicines — 1 patient in 20. Excluding patients brought in with drug reactions, 3 out of every 20 patients under drug therapy developed side effects — a rate 50 per cent greater than that found by Dr. Schimmel. Of the 3, 1 was serious enough to prolong the patient's stay in the Baltimore hospital by two or more days. In addition, the number of adverse reactions was said by Dr. Leighton Cluff, who directed the study project, to have increased in proportion to the number of drugs administered.

4. *Physicians are sometimes loath to indict themselves: for example, to record as the cause of death a disease induced by drugs they had prescribed — needlessly.* Consider the antibiotic Chloromycetin. In September 1960, eleven and one-half years after it had been marketed, Harry J. Loynd, president of Parke, Davis & Co. of Detroit, the sole American manufacturer, testified before the Senate Subcommittee on Antitrust and Monopoly that its use had resulted in 25 damage suits. Most of them were settled out of court, on undisclosed terms. In 1962, for the first time, a Chloromycetin case went to a jury. The Law Department of the American Medical Association reported:

A record judgment of $334,000 was awarded to a California woman [Mrs. Carney Love, of Palo Alto] . . . A jury held the doctor who prescribed the drug and the company which manufactured it liable for damages. A pharmacist was exonerated.

It was claimed that the drug caused the patient to contract aplastic anemia [a blood disease which has a fatality rate of at

least 50 per cent]. Testimony at the trial showed the following:
The doctor prescribed the antibiotic for a sore gum after a
tooth extraction and again for a bronchial condition. A prescription was refilled six times, upon authorization from the
doctor's office — usually from his nurse. The patient under-
went 60 blood transfusions and massive dosages of male hormone to combat the [aplastic] anemia. Thereafter a beard
grew on her face, her complexion became red, and her face was
disfigured by acne.[2]

This case helps to explain why the Public Health Service considers it "understandable" that physicians are reluctant to record
adverse drug reactions when to do so sets up a potential basis for
litigation.[3]

Chloromycetin, which has the chemical name chloramphenicol, was marketed in 1949, was aggressively promoted, and won
wide acceptance, in part because it was freer of certain side effects

[2] On the ground that Mrs. Love's trial counsel had engaged in "[m]isconduct
. . . egregious beyond any in our experience," the verdict and judgment against
the physician and Parke, Davis were reversed by an appellate court. A new jury
trial then was held in Superior Court in Redding, California. This time, Mrs.
Love was awarded a $180,000 judgment against Parke, Davis alone. According
to *Drug News Weekly* for March 1, 1965, Mrs. Love has taken an appeal, contending that she was entitled to a larger sum and that there was error in the
failure to assess damages against the doctor.

[3] Walter V. Schaefer, a justice of the Supreme Court of Illinois, has said about
drugs that may be dispensed only upon prescription: ". . . recent cases indicate
that the duty to warn of potential danger runs primarily to the physician, so that
if a physician is properly warned of the dangerous propensities of a drug, the
drug manufacturer will be effectively insulated from liability. Misuse by a physician is not regarded as a foreseeable risk that the manufacturer must guard against.
He must, however, properly warn the physician, and if a patient is injured as a
result of a physician's adherence to inadequate instructions or warnings, the
manufacturer will be liable to the patient."

The quotation, from which Justice Schaefer's citations have been deleted,
is taken from *Drugs in Our Society*, edited by Paul Talalay (Baltimore: Johns
Hopkins Press, 1964). This book stems from a four-day conference on the problems involved in making safe and effective drugs available to the public. The
conference, sponsored by the Johns Hopkins University, was held late in 1963 in
Baltimore. The participants were a small group of specialists in various relevant
fields. Justice Schaefer was one of them.

than other antibiotics. In the first eleven years after its introduction it was prescribed to 40 million persons, according to testimony given by Parke, Davis president Loynd before Estes Kefauver's Senate Antitrust subcommittee. In 1949, the first year in
which Chloromycetin was sold, sales amounted to $9 million. In
1951 they reached $52 million. A year later, when reports of
aplastic anemia in association with Chloromycetin were in the
news, they fell off to $47 million. Although there were further
setbacks, the confidence of physicians in chloramphenicol was so
effectively rebuilt that in 1960 sales reached a record $86 million.
In part because of the unfavorable impact of the Kefauver hearings, sales then declined. In 1963 they totaled $59 million, a
substantial 31 per cent of all Parke, Davis sales.

The sales figures are of interest in the light of a report made in
November 1962 by the California State Department of Public
Health, which had undertaken a study of Chloromycetin under
a resolution adopted twenty-two months earlier by a committee
of the state senate. "Positive and statistically significant correla-
tions," the Department said, "were found between rates of chloramphenicol sales by the drug manufacturer and rates of aplastic
anemia deaths, in both California and the United States, when
the death rates were compared to sales rates 1 and 2 years previously — allowing time for the drug to reach the patient and time
for a fatal effect to occur."

The Department concluded that among those for whom Chloromycetin was prescribed the incidence of fatal aplastic anemia
is "conservatively" 1 in 60,000. In 1960, in his testimony before
the Kefauver subcommittee, Loynd had acknowledged a rate one
fourth as large, 1 in 225,000 (eight years earlier the company's
estimate had been 1 in 400,000). Using Loynd's estimate of
40 million users, it would appear that 666 or 177 users of Chloromycetin died, depending upon which incidence — 1 in 60,000 or
1 in 225,000 — is accepted. Neither computation, of course,
takes into account fatalities among the several million persons

who have been given chloramphenicol in each year since 1960.

Even the figure of 666 for the initial eleven years may be low. The California authorities say the "actual risk is probably higher," one reason being that they worked from official records in which the cause of death was forthrightly listed as aplastic anemia and from hospital records that, unlike others, actually showed Chloromycetin to have been prescribed. In any event, the fundamental question is the same. Did any suffer or die needlessly? Clearly, the answer of the California State Department of Public Health is yes.

The California Public Health department said that among the fatal cases it investigated chloramphenicol "had been prescribed frequently for viral infections against which antibiotics are not effective." In many other cases "there was no evidence . . . that another less toxic drug would not have been as effective . . ." Here are some specific cases cited by Barbara Yuncker on September 12, 1962, in the New York *Post*:[4]

Parke, Davis says, quite correctly, that the percentage of risk is much higher in anesthesia and blood transfusion. But that hardly explains a case like this, which has turned a California publisher into an angry avenger.

Brenda Lynn Elfstrom, 19, came home from college on a September week-end in 1959 with a sore throat. She was given Chloromycetin.

In January she was given Chloromycetin again for a minor urinary infection — and again in April for another sore throat (which happens to be a first sign of drug-induced blood disease). In May a slight bump turned into a huge bruise (another blood disease clue), but still no tests were made. A week later she could no longer swallow, and aplastic anemia was finally diagnosed. She died on June 8.

[4] Excerpts quoted here and on page 231 are from a series of articles by Miss Yuncker entitled "Pills and You." Copyright 1962, New York Post Corporation.

Her grieving father, Edgar F. Elfstrom, publisher of the Fullerton (Calif.) News Tribune, is determined that at the very least a doctor should be required to warn his patients before giving the drug.[5]

Brenda Lynn's case is unfortunately not unique. The New York Post's random file includes such cases as a 20-year-old college sophomore treated for acne who died in 1960; another pretty coed whose death from aplastic anemia followed Chloromycetin therapy for an infected mosquito bite on her cheek; a 30-year-old wife and mother who was given the drug for pneumonia and whose year-long losing fight against thrombocytopenic purpura (another blood disease caused by Chloromycetin) was a horror story of severe reactions from repeated blood transfusions and agonizing efforts to obey her doctor and stay on her feet; a baby girl who got Chloromycetin 5 times for a cold, a sty, and an infected finger and who died at 2.

Many Chloromycetin deaths may not be so identified. A California father has testified [before a California state senate committee] that the doctor who used the drug on his 5-year-old daughter not long before she died from aplastic anemia said the death probably resulted from some toxic household product. The father found the prescription [for Chloromycetin] in the drugstore file.

Dr. Albe M. Watkins, a La Canada, California, physician prescribed Chloromycetin to his own son, and in 1952 the boy died. In November 1961 the physician went before a California senate committee. "I do not know of one single victim who wouldn't be alive today had he only been permitted to get well by him-

---

[5] A suit filed by Elfstrom was settled in July 1964. His lawyer, David M. Harney of Los Angeles, said that Parke, Davis had agreed to pay $12,600, two physicians $21,000, and a third doctor $1400. "Insofar as I can ascertain," Harney said, the $35,000 settlement "is the largest . . . ever made in the United States concerning the death of a child of Brenda's age." Elfstrom said that his proceeds, after attorney's fees, would be donated to St. Jude Hospital in Fullerton for a project of its choice for the benefit of children.

self, by nature, without the use of this antibiotic," he said. "And for those doctors who claim such curative power of this drug, I would ask them if they tried any other less potent antibiotic before taking such a 'calculated' risk or playing 'Russian roulette' with some innocent unsuspecting patient.

"We have waited 10 years for my profession to police itself, which obviously it has failed to do," Dr. Watkins continued. "Although I am a doctor of medicine I must, naturally, include other members of the healing arts [such] as osteopaths and dentists."

At the same hearing another California physician, Dr. Franklin Farman, a Whittier urologist, told the state senate committee that in June 1952 "we lost our daughter — 5 years old — through the administration of Chloromycetin . . . Her death was one of many similar cases of blood dyscrasias [which] have not been recognized." Later in his statement he said: "I know of no more torturous death, especially in children . . ."

During his presentation Dr. Farman cited Parke, Davis advertising in 1952–1953 that contained this statement: ". . . it is particularly significant that Chloromycetin therapy is notably free of untoward reactions. In those few instances where reactions do occur, they are generally limited to mild nausea or diarrhea and rarely has severity of the reaction required discontinuance of treatment with the drug. No cumulative effects have been reported, and it can be said with justification that Chloromycetin is well tolerated by adults and children alike."

The first reports associating Chloromycetin with aplastic anemia were published early in 1950, at least two years before the statement cited by Dr. Farman. During 1952 FDA became so alarmed that it took the drug off the market pending a study by the National Research Council. After considering 410 cases of serious blood disorders, of which 177 were definitely associated with Chloromycetin, the Council issued recommendations that FDA implemented in August 1952.

Deciding that chloramphenicol should be available "for careful use by the medical profession in those serious and sometimes fatal diseases in which its use is necessary," FDA directed that the circular, or brochure, in the package, warn that "Chloromycetin should not be used indiscriminately or for minor infections." (In November 1960, FDA asked the National Research Council to appoint a committee of physicians to advise whether Chloromycetin should be banished, whether its use should be restricted to persons in hospitals, or whether it should remain available for general use. Two months later, the committee recommended that general availability continue and made certain suggestions about labeling that FDA followed.)

In a letter to Senator Humphrey in March 1963, Commissioner George P. Larrick said that FDA's Division of Antibiotics considered Chloromycetin the "drug of choice" in typhoid fever. Like many others, they were saying that chloramphenicol is *the* drug to use in that disease. Larrick further wrote that the National Health Survey Division of the National Center for Health Statistics "reports approximately 1,100 cases of typhoid a year, but cautions that the sampling error is so great that the actual number of cases may be 50 or 60 times greater than reported." In other words, the Commissioner indicated the possibility that there were actually 55,000 to 60,000 cases of typhoid a year — a major epidemic unknown to the public and the medical profession. The more cases, the greater the need for Chloromycetin.

However, Forrest Linder, the director of the Center for Health Statistics, told Mr. Humphrey in September 1964 that "the actual number of cases may be 50 to 60 *percent* greater (or less) than reported." (My italic.) This meant not 55,000 or 60,000 cases but between, roughly, 500 and 1700 and indicated a much smaller need for Chloromycetin. FDA's error seems even odder when one considers that Linder told Humphrey that the most reliable source of communicable disease information is the Communicable Disease Center of the Public Health Service, which annually publishes the number of cases of typhoid in *Morbidity and Mortality*. This publication reported 814 cases in 1961, 608 in 1962, and 566 in 1963. In each of the five years 1958–1962 there were fewer than 30 deaths.

In his letter to the Senator, Commissioner Larrick also said that Chloromycetin is an "alternative drug" — not to be used in minor infections, in newborns, or where less hazardous agents are effective — in various intestinal infections attributed to Gram negative bacteria, such as salmonella; in rickettsia diseases, such as Rocky Mountain spotted fever; and in diseases due to large viruses, such as psittacosis (parrot fever). The Commissioner said the Public Health Service estimate is that there are 135,600 cases of these diseases a year, but that again there are large sampling errors.

Let us look now at what we have here. Chloromycetin is the drug of choice in typhoid fever — of which there are a few hundred cases a year. It is an alternative drug in a couple hundred thousand cases of other diseases. But in one year alone, Chloromycetin was prescribed for 4 *million* Americans. Perhaps 3.7 million of them, perhaps 3.8 million, perhaps more need not have received it. Perhaps some of them, maybe 60, maybe 16, needlessly died.

Since 1952, the AMA and its *Journal* have carried one warning after another against promiscuous use of Chloromycetin. In the *Journal* of October 31, 1959, for example, Dr. Sidney P. Kent and Dr. Gilder L. Wideman reported on a study at University Hospital in Birmingham, Alabama, of infants born after premature rupture of the fetal membranes. In 1954, when there was no program of prophylaxis with antibiotics, the death rate among the infants was 29 per 1000. In 1958, when there was such a program, the rate was 144 per 1000, or five times as great.

Between January and May of 1958, 160 newborn babies received antibiotic prophylactic treatment. Twenty-five — almost one sixth — died. All 25 had received Chloromycetin. "When the use of chloramphenicol in the nursery was discontinued on June 13, 1958," Dr. Kent and Dr. Wideman wrote, "the neonatal death rate dropped back to and remained at about the level present before the use of chloramphenicol."

In the *Journal* for December 3, 1960, a Boston blood specialist, Dr. William Dameshek, said: "By some means, whether by regulation or by self-discipline, promiscuous use of the drug should be avoided and its use restricted to impelling circumstances, i.e., for conditions in which no other antibiotic is currently effective." Among 30 cases of aplastic anemia seen within the previous three years, he said, 8 had received Chloromycetin, "almost invariably for minor infections. Of the most recent 10 cases . . . 5 had followed therapy with chloramphenicol. The tragic thing about all these seriously ill cases, most of whom died, is that the drug need never have been given."

If a physician needlessly prescribes chloramphenicol to a patient, and the patient dies, what is he to do? That some respond by concealing the true cause, deplorable though this may be, was suggested by Dr. Watkins, who for ten years after his son's death traced Chloromycetin reactions and fatalities around the country. The obstacles he encountered included denial of access to hospital records of pharmacy prescriptions, families who feel " 'it is God's will' and wish to be left alone," prescribing physicians from whom "it is next to impossible to obtain an interview," and, most relevant, what he described as "wrong diagnoses either through ignorance or by willful intent." He said he found victims of aplastic anemia listed under such headings as brain hemorrhage, which is something like attributing the death of a man whose throat has been slit to loss of blood. "I never knew so many babies and children could die of brain hemorrhage," Dr. Watkins said.

But the physician who needlessly prescribes chloramphenicol and then honestly records aplastic anemia on the death certificate may find himself a defendant in a law suit. He could hardly blame his misprescribing on the *Journal* or the AMA. He might have to admit that he relied for his education in the uses of Chloromycetin on Parke, Davis salesmen, or detailmen, as they are called in the trade. They, in turn, had been educated in an appalling campaign launched by the company immediately following FDA's 1952 warning that Chloromycetin "should not be used indiscriminately for minor infections."

In a letter to its detailmen the company construed this as a government clearance "with *no restriction* on the number or range of diseases for which Chloromycetin may be administered." [6] (Italics in original.)

There was an entire series of such miracles in translation, and sales of Chloromycetin, which had been depressed, regained their old zip.[7] The Senate Antitrust subcommittee majority discusses this whole episode in detail in that portion of its report entitled "See 'Advertising and Promotion of Drugs' which constitutes Part IV of the *Study of Administered Prices in the Drug Industry* by the Senate Subcommittee on Antitrust and Monopoly (1961)."

[6] Richard Harris wrote in *The Real Voice*, "It was only by accident that Kefauver found out about Parke, Davis's instruction to its detail men; the F.D.A. had decided to return the directions without making copies of them, or taking any further action, but Mrs. Goodwin [Dorothy D. Goodwin, a subcommittee attorney] had come across them, and had had photostatic copies made before they were sent back to the company."

[7] Chloromycetin, it should be realized, is sold not only in the United States but over the world. In the *British Medical Journal* for March 16, 1963, a committee of the Association of Clinical Pathologists of the United Kingdom reported that a random sampling had unearthed 40 cases of aplastic anemia among users of chloramphenicol in the years 1953–1962. Thirty-one of the patients died, and in 27 of them "death was attributed directly to chloramphenicol therapy." Notably, 35 of the 40 cases were "hitherto unpublished."

A few months after the report in the British journal, an author of several books on medical subjects, Brian Inglis, wrote in the *Nation* for August 24, 1963: "Nor, in Britain at least, are there many cases of Rocky Mountain fever, or of psittacosis, the only other disorders for which it is seriously claimed that chloramphenicol is invaluable. Yet Chloromycetin has continued to be sold here as a 'broad spectrum,' general-purpose antibiotic; the manufacturers, Parke, Davis, have continued to advertise it for that purpose; and medical journals — though their articles have been warning that Chloromycetin should never be prescribed except for typhoid — have continued to accept those advertisements."

5. *Certain manufacturers have failed to pass on to FDA and the medical profession reports that have come to them of injurious and lethal side effects.* While this information has dwelled in its corporate limbo, physicians unaware of the true extent of the risks involved have prescribed the drugs in question to more and more people, among whom there have been still more mishaps.

In a memorandum to members of his subcommittee in June 1964, Senator Humphrey put some of the blame for this situation on FDA. After a new-drug application had been approved, the Senator said, many companies felt they "had complete leeway not to report if *absolute* cause-and-effect proof of a drug's guilt was not available. Rarely is such absolute proof available," he added. "The result was that companies could suppress great numbers of suspected, but 'unproven' incidents. FDA never bothered, prior to the enactment of the new [1962] law, to tell the companies it wanted *all* cases of suspicious effects reported, not just cases when proof of etiology was available."

A remarkable instance of secretiveness about side effects was brought out by the Kefauver subcommittee. The drug involved was Diabinese, an oral antidiabetic. It was put on sale in 1958 by Chas. Pfizer & Co., Inc., of Brooklyn, in competition with Upjohn's Orinase. The clinical testing on Diabinese was conducted by Dr. Dominic G. Iezzoni. In a memorandum addressed to Pfizer president John E. McKeen, the physician ominously reported several instances of adverse effects that had not been known to occur in patients treated with the rival product. Five weeks later, Dr. Iezzoni submitted to his chiefs a summary showing that among 1922 persons treated with Diabinese a staggering 27 per cent, or 513, had suffered one or more side effects — not only minor irritations but also severe injuries to the central nervous system and the liver.

If business pressures are great enough, "the medical director will be overruled," Dr. A. Dale Console, himself a former medical director for a large manufacturer, once told the Kefauver subcommittee. "He has one vote."

Despite the report of Dr. Iezzoni, Pfizer waited only a week to file its new-drug application for Diabinese. FDA waited only two months to clear it, providing its version of in-by-nine, out-by-five service. In October 1958 Diabinese was on the market. In the advertising campaign that followed, Pfizer withheld the facts from physicians, claiming for Diabinese an "almost complete absence of unfavorable side effects." The original package insert began, "Side effects are generally of a transient and nonserious character." Not until two years had elapsed was the labeling changed to warn the physician of the danger of jaundice, at the rate of 4 cases per 1000.

For a hearing on Diabinese Senator Kefauver naturally sought the appearance of Dr. Iezzoni. He didn't show up. McKeen provided not explanations but statements avoiding the issue: "Mr. Chairman, may I make a brief statement at this time?" "With regard to Dr. Iezzoni, Dr. Warner is now in charge . . ." Later, Kefauver said Dr. Iezzoni was not brought to the hearing because "his studies showed many side effects."

The facts cited here were obtained by the Antitrust subcommittee with great difficulty. The report Dr. Iezzoni made in 1958 showing 27 per cent side effects was withheld from the subcommittee until the very morning of the hearing. For a fuller account of this fantastic episode the reader is referred to Part IV of *Study of Administered Prices in the Drug Industry* by the Senate Antitrust and Monopoly Subcommittee (1961).

For a period of years, crucial information about a widely used drug called Flexin was withheld from FDA by the manufacturer, McNeil Laboratories, Inc., of Fort Washington, Pennsylvania, which on January 15, 1959, became a subsidiary of Johnson & Johnson. Even before passage of the 1962 Kefauver-Harris amendments, FDA regarded the sustained failure of a manufacturer to submit reports of adverse effects as "a serious violation" of the purpose of the new-drug clearance procedures. Yet, in the

Flexin case FDA attempted to withhold information sought by a committee of Congress seeking to find out if the agency had met its responsibilities.

Flexin (zoxazolamine) was intended originally for use in the relief of muscle spasm in musculo-skeletal disorders and neurological diseases, and was later recommended for use in gout. The handling of the drug by FDA was such as to persuade Representative L. H. Fountain, a North Carolina Democrat, that an inquiry was needed by his House Intergovernmental Relations Subcommittee. The inquiry culminated in two days of hearings in April 1964, at which FDA Commissioner George Larrick was the principal witness. The chronology that follows was derived from the testimony and exhibits in the hearings record. A few references come from materials published by Senator Humphrey.

1955

November 14. McNeil submitted its new-drug application for Flexin, asserting it to be "an entirely new drug" against muscle spasm, and explaining that consequently there were in the medical literature no safety data on Flexin. FDA also was told in the application that jaundice "has not been reported in any patient receiving Flexin."

December 2. McNeil received from Dr. Bernard Alpers, of Jefferson Medical College in Philadelphia, who had been testing Flexin in a series of patients, a report that one, a woman, had died. She had received Flexin three or four times a day for several months. She died of hepatitis, a liver disease of which jaundice is a symptom. Although the company's new-drug application was pending before FDA, it did not report the case. Indeed, it waited five and a half years to do so, until mid-1961.

1956

January 5. Dr. William E. Delaney, who had conducted a postmortem examination on the woman, and was a resident in pathology at Jefferson Medical College, wrote to Dr. James M.

Shaffer, director of McNeil's Division of Clinical Investigation. "The conclusion that the hepatic changes may be due to drug therapy and in addition cannot be differentiated from fulminating viral [infection-caused] hepatitis is concurred in by my chief, Dr. Peter A. Herbut," Dr. Delaney said.

January 13. FDA released Flexin to the market, which ultimately swelled to an estimated 3 million users.

August 14. McNeil submitted to FDA a supplemental application so that it could sell Flexin in a new dosage form. Accompanying the application were five copies of a proposed brochure for physicians. Two copies contained the original claim that jaundice "has not been reported in any patient." In the remaining three copies this claim was deleted. The deletion was not detected by FDA.

Not until long afterward, Commissioner Larrick told Representative Fountain, did the agency know that as of this date — August 14, 1956 — physicians had informed McNeil "of six cases of liver damage . . . including one death." During the following twenty-two months Flexin continued to be sold, Larrick said, "with still no reports . . . from either the firm or the medical community . . . [of] increasing numbers of severe and fatal cases of liver damage."

October 18. Dr. Shaffer discussed with a vice president of the firm, R. L. McNeil, Jr., the possibility of including a positive warning statement in the labeling for Flexin. At this time, FDA had approved a draft version (in connection with the supplemental application) without a warning to physicians that Flexin might cause hepatitis. The question was whether to include a warning in the final printed version.

"As indicated in our telephone conversation today," Dr. Shaffer said in a memorandum to the company president, "a new problem must be considered in relation to this index card [a form of labeling] revision.

"On page 3, the last paragraph is the statement concerning

liver damage as suggested by Doctor Dripps. [Dr. Robert D. Dripps, Jr., of Philadelphia, a consultant to the firm. His suggestion was that the labeling say: "Liver damage, with or without jaundice had been suggested (reported?) in approximately 15 patients. Data are inconclusive on a cause-effect relationship. The incidence of hepatic involvement appears low, i.e., 12 cases from a patient population of approximately 500,000. Nevertheless this possibility must be kept in mind by the physician prescribing Flexin."] On page 3a is an alternate statement pertaining to the same subject."

The alternate statement said: "Liver damage, possibly related to administration of Flexin, has been reported in approximately 15 patients during nine months of general clinical use of this new drug. In most of these patients a definite cause and effect relationship is difficult to establish. The incidence of hepatic involvement appears to be low (probably less than .05 or one per cent). Nevertheless, this possibility should be kept in mind by the physician prescribing Flexin."

During the hearings, W. Donald Gray, of the Fountain subcommittee staff, brought out the fact that although the proposed warnings got to R. L. McNeil they never got to FDA. "For some reason," Gray remarked at the hearings, "neither form of this statement was included in the final printed version of the labeling."

December 14. Dr. Shaffer wrote and filed a memorandum on a telephone conversation with one of three physicians who had thought it worthwhile to write a sixteen-page paper on liver damage in four users of Flexin. "No instance of liver damage had been published, to our knowledge, as of Oct. 1, 1956," the authors said. The paper reported that in each of the four patients manifestations of liver damage developed after Flexin had been administered for a few weeks — but disappeared promptly when the drug was withheld. In the memorandum, the McNeil physician said he had been informed that the paper "will not be submitted for publication," and that it had been reviewed by three other physicians, each of whom said that the evidence "was inconclusive and that the material would probably not be accepted by the editor of any journal."

I confess that I find this assertion surprising. The authors had impressive credentials, being from the Departments of Medicine and Neurology at the Columbia University College of Physicians and Surgeons and on the staff of the Presbyterian Hospital and Neurological Institute in New York. Their paper, which I have read, struck me as objective and sound research — and far more careful than much of what many journals have published, particularly when a drug is being praised. What the authors reported was in accord with the information the company had been receiving independently but not passing along to FDA. In any event, it is a pity that no editor was given a chance to make a judgment. The paper was written by Dr. Albert Damon, Dr. William Amols, and Dr. Donald Holub. In his memorandum Dr. Shaffer said he had talked with Dr. Amols.

1958

June 11. McNeil submitted a supplemental new-drug application for use of Flexin in gout, which afflicts an estimated 300,000 Americans. The company claimed, "The reports received on patients with gout treated with Flexin indicate that there have been no adverse effects or undesirable side reactions caused by the drug."

In an accompanying brochure, however, the firm allowed a slight shadow to be cast. Since 1955, it said, there have been "occasional reports" of jaundice. Although the possibility exists that Flexin, "in rare cases, may produce hepatitis and jaundice," the company said, "careful inquiry" cannot exclude a virus rather than the drug as a possible cause.

"The facts are," Commissioner Larrick testified, "that at that time the firm had received reports of seven deaths from hepatitis

. . . The total number of cases known to the firm of patients who had developed liver damage while taking Flexin was 29. The firm had not conducted a 'careful inquiry' into many of the cases."

1959

February 18. The then Surgeon General of the Public Health Service, Dr. Leroy E. Burney, announced the discovery of a powerful new drug for the treatment of gout "which is now undergoing clinical trial by scientists at the National Institute of Arthritis and Metabolic Diseases." The drug being tested at the Institute for use in gout was zoxazolamine, or Flexin, which FDA had approved for general, nonexperimental use against gout two and one-half months earlier. At the Intergovernmental Relations Subcommittee hearings, Representative Fountain termed it "rather curious" that the Surgeon General "announced this discovery by a press release" *after* FDA had cleared Flexin for the new use. Although Flexin had been developed by McNeil, its use in gout was the result of research by scientists at the National Institutes of Health and others working under a grant from the Institutes.

About three weeks later, the president of the company, Henry S. McNeil, sent a letter to doctors assuring them that the firm had nothing to do with the press release, but happily quoting from it.

September 29. In a supplemental application for Flexilon, a drug containing Flexin, McNeil acknowledged that during the past three and one-half years of use of Flexin it had received "a total of 32 reports . . . suggesting that the administration of the drug may have been associated with the development of hepatitis with jaundice." But, the company said soothingly, "Flexin has produced no irreversible toxic reactions when administered to patients daily for periods of over six months."

In refutation, Commissioner Larrick testified: "The submission did not show that instead of 32 cases of reversible liver damage, with two deaths probably unrelated to use of the drug, the firm then knew of 39 cases of hepatitis in patients taking Flexin, including 11 fatalities, and that 20 of the cases, including 6 deaths, had been ascribed directly to Flexin by the reporting physicians." Reports such as these continued to be received by the firm, but were not passed along to FDA.

1961

February 3. The *Medical Letter,* an authoritative, nonprofit drug-evaluating service for physicians, warned of possible liver damage from use of Flexin, and said that until experience is much greater there is no compelling reason to substitute it for the anti-gout agent of first choice, probenecid.

July 13. At a meeting requested by the company — very soon after medical journals with large circulation had published reports of liver damage in two Flexin users — McNeil Laboratories disclosed to FDA that it had received a total of 54 reports of hepatitis in Flexin users. Fifteen of the cases were fatal. Of the remainder, 26 had survived. Whether the other 13 had lived or died was not ascertained. The company suggested that the situation could be handled with a stronger warning to physicians. As phrased by the firm, Larrick testified, the warning "minimized, qualified, and cast doubt upon the validity of the reactions attributed to Flexin and did not inform about the high incidence of fatality . . ."

October 6. At FDA's suggestion, McNeil agreed to withdraw Flexin from the market and requested that the new-drug application be suspended.

October 13. FDA formally suspended the new-drug application.

1962

May 2. In a letter to Commissioner Larrick, Representative Fountain asked that arrangements be made for W. Donald

Gray, of the subcommittee staff, to examine FDA files on Flexin and on MER/29, another drug withdrawn from the market and the subject here of Chapter 11.

May 10. "We have uniformly declined to make the files on new drugs available to anyone except employees of the Food and Drug Administration," Larrick wrote in a letter of reply to the Congressman. However, he promised to supply as promptly as possible summaries containing "all pertinent information" about the two drugs.

June 20. Representative Fountain appeared before the House Committee on Interstate and Foreign Commerce, headed by Representative Oren Harris, the Arkansas Democrat whose name was later to be joined to Senator Kefauver's as a co-author of the drug amendments, to testify against an FDA-sponsored proposal that would have made it virtually impossible to get from the agency any information it acquired under the Federal Food, Drug, and Cosmetic Act. In speaking against this proposal, which was later defeated, Representative Fountain referred to Commissioner Larrick's assertion that FDA had permitted no one but its own employees to see new-drug files. "The fact is that our subcommittee staff has examined such files in the past, and FDA had not previously in our experience claimed confidentiality for these records," Fountain testified.

The Congressman went on to say that when informed of this Assistant FDA Commissioner Winton B. Rankin had promised reconsideration of the matter by the agency, but that in the ensuing weeks, despite numerous telephone calls by the subcommittee staff, no action had been taken, nor had the promised summaries been received. Fountain told Harris: "To me it is unthinkable that information, other than trade secrets, which is available to officers and employees of the Department of Health, Education, and Welfare [of which FDA is a part], as big as it is, as well as to the courts, should not also be available to the Congress, which passes the legislation and appropriates the funds necessary for the Department's operations." Eventually, the summaries Larrick had promised were supplied, but they contained serious information gaps. However, the Commissioner reconsidered and agreed to give the subcommittee access to anything in his agency's files having a bearing on its administration of the law.

1963

August 12. In response to an inquiry, Commissioner Larrick said that since October 1961, when FDA had taken Flexin off the market, it had received reports of 30 additional reactions in patients who had taken Flexin or products containing it. These included 12 cases of liver damage, for a total of 66, and 2 cases of blood disease.

1964

April 28. During the Fountain hearings, Larrick was asked whether McNeil had submitted "a fraudulent application." He replied that the "entire file" had been turned over to the general counsel of the Department of Health, Education, and Welfare "a long time ago."

April 29. Questioning by Representative Fountain developed that "a long time ago" was not 1961, when FDA had learned of the company's withholding of information, but December 1963. Not until then, an FDA staff officer, R. C. Brandenburg, insisted, did the agency have "complete evidence." Fountain asked William W. Goodrich, the Department's assistant general counsel for FDA, when the matter had been referred to the Department of Justice. The answer was, about ten days earlier — ten days before the hearings opened. In trying to find out why FDA and HEW had been so slow — the justifications given were not very persuasive — Fountain drew from Goodrich this acknowledgment: "The statute [of limitations] expired in five years . . . What occurred prior to April of 1959 is of course barred . . . How the case will be worked up in the Department of Justice, how many counts or what they will do with it is something that is beyond me."

◢ ◢ ◢

What the Department of Justice did in the case of withholding of information about a tranquilizer called Dornwal was to present the case to a grand jury in Washington. In August 1964 an eight-count indictment was returned against the manufacturer, Wallace & Tiernan, Inc., of Belleville, New Jersey. Its former medical director, Dr. Charles E. Hough, and its former director of clinical research, Robert T. Conner, were named in five counts each. They reportedly had resigned for reasons unrelated to their handling of the Dornwal matter.

After the indictment was returned, the company said that an "estimated 160,000 prescriptions [had been] written" for Dornwal before the drug was removed from the market in November 1961. Months before sales were halted, however, when one might expect that the figure would have been smaller, the manufacturer was suggesting a larger one. In a proposed brochure submitted to FDA, Wallace & Tiernan said that "hundreds of thousands" of adults and children had received Dornwal.

Dornwal (amphenidone) had been released by FDA, in April 1960, with a label warning that its administration be limited to three months. On October 31, 1960, the company requested FDA's permission to delete the warning. It said in a supplemental new-drug application that one patient on Dornwal had developed a marked leukopenia, in which there is a decrease in the ability of the blood's white cells to combat infection, but assured FDA that Dornwal was not likely to be held responsible. The reason given was that at least one other medication known to depress the bone marrow, where blood components are formed, had been prescribed for the patient.

The indictment charged that in order to influence FDA delete the warning against more than three months of use,

Wallace & Tiernan and Dr. Hough "knowingly and willfully concealed" from FDA information about a second patient, an elderly woman who had been a patient of Dr. Walter J. Sperling at Mountainside Hospital, Montclair, New Jersey. She had, the indictment charged, developed bone-marrow depression under circumstances suggesting that it had occurred "as a direct effect of Dornwal itself." The accused were said to have known this in early January 1961.

The agency medical officer handling the Dornwal matter was Dr. Frances Oldham Kelsey, who in 1962 was to be awarded the gold medal for Distinguished Federal Civilian Service for preventing the marketing of thalidomide, the baby-deforming sedative. A supplemental new-drug application that the company submitted in the spring of 1961 went to her. In it the firm claimed to have supplied FDA with all the reports and data in its possession on the safety of Dornwal.

In fact, the indictment alleged, Wallace & Tiernan and Dr. Hough had concealed from Dr. Kelsey information in their possession on three patients who had died and on at least six others, including the New Jersey woman, who had incurred the bone-marrow disease, all while on Dornwal.

Among the other charges of concealment in the indictment is one dealing with what is said to have happened on September 22, 1961, which was after the company had received reports on the three deaths and six or more injuries. The firm at that time sent to FDA a brochure that "falsely and fraudulently . . . represented that":

Dornwal has proved remarkably safe in clinical evaluations over a two-year period. Its extremely low toxicity and relative freedom from side effects make it an ideal tranquilizer . . . Total side effects . . . have been dramatically low . . . All were minor and transitory in nature.

Five days later, on September 27, 1961, Dr. Hough, of Morris Plains, New Jersey, and Conner, who later moved to Los Angeles, conferred in Washington with Dr. Kelsey. She asked, the indictment said, if "there was any evidence of hematological or blood troubles in the use of Dornwal," but her visitors from Wallace & Tiernan failed to mention the nine cases about which they were said to have known.

About three weeks afterward, Dr. Kelsey attended a meeting at the National Institutes of Health in the Washington suburb of Bethesda, Maryland. Also present was Dr. Douglas Goldman of Longview State Hospital in Cincinnati. According to the indictment, he had reported to Wallace & Tiernan on a female patient who had died two months before "under circumstances showing an association of [bone-marrow disease] with the administration of Dornwal tablets for a period of several months."

In a memorandum written a few days later, and published by the Senate Reorganization subcommittee, Dr. Kelsey said Dr. Goldman mentioned that he had told the company of the death "about 1 month ago," and that "he assumed the company had apprised us of this case." Dr. Kelsey went on to say that Dr. Hough and Conner had not mentioned the case on September 27 when they visited her, nor had Conner said anything about it in a subsequent telephone conversation. As a result, she had allowed Wallace & Tiernan to use the brochure quoted from above.

The day after the meeting in Bethesda, Dr. Kelsey telephoned Conner. In the memorandum published by the Humphrey subcommittee, she said that

he readily admitted they had the information on this case at the time their supplemental application was under consideration, and that there was no question that Dornwal was the offending agent. He further stated they had received five other reports . . . in patients on Dornwal but in these cases, other drugs resulting in bone morrow depression had been used. Only one of these cases was drawn to our attention. In this case the patient was apparently also taking chloramphenicol.

On the day the indictment was returned a statement was issued by the public relations firm of Hill & Knowlton, Inc., in which the president of Wallace & Tiernan, Robert T. Browning, said:

> The question raised by this indictment is whether a practice generally followed by the drug industry in 1960 and 1961, and known to the Food and Drug Administration, constituted a criminal act. We are convinced that it did not, and we look forward to a vindication of our position.
>
> As a matter of principle, we intend to fight this charge, even though the drug involved has been off the market for more than two and one-half years, and is not a factor in our sales and earnings.
>
> . . . the company suppressed nothing. Instead, it had exerted every effort to obtain all available data on the reports and then had retained independent consultants for the express purpose of studying this material in depth and evaluating it so that the company could then make a meaningful report to FDA.
>
> The only legal question raised . . . is whether the company was required to turn over raw, unevaluated information to FDA under the law then existing. No charge of inconsistency has been made relating to the scientific data submitted to FDA.
>
> .   .   .   .
>
> . . . Reports of the type received are nearly meaningless either to the company or to the FDA until they have been supplemented by hospital records and other detailed medical data . . . to determine what part, if any, the drug played . . .

It was therefore the general practice in the drug industry to make a scientific evaluation of each report before forwarding it to the FDA. In the case of Dornwal, we engaged two specialists in hematology for such a study and evaluation, with the understanding that their findings and recommendations would be turned over to the FDA.

Just as this study was completed as fully as possible and was to be forwarded to Washington, the FDA learned independently about one of the cases and inquired of the company about it . . .

. . . .

[Until enactment of the 1962 Kefauver-Harris amendments] the practice of the pharmaceutical industry was to follow the course we took in the Dornwal matter . . .

A searching review convinces us that the company and the former employees named in the indictment . . . are innocent of these charges. Moreover, we believe the facts that may be elicited at a trial will prove that we conscientiously sought information about possible harmful drug effects and acted to protect the public.

This was not to be understood, apparently, as meaning that the company wanted to hasten the advent of its day in court. On November 2, 1964, the company won dismissal of the indictment through the invocation of an obscure provision in the District of Columbia Code. The provision said that a special grand jury had to be convened by order of the Chief District Judge or the Presiding District Judge, whereas the special grand jury that indicted Wallace & Tiernan had, the firm pointed out, been convened by order of the judge presiding in the assignment court of the criminal division. However, the Department of Justice said it would seek either to reinstate the indictment through the appellate process or would seek a new indictment.[8]

[8] In February 1965 the Justice Department filed an appeal intended to reinstate the indictment.

Nonreporting of side effects, a form of reticence that has depressed Dr. Kelsey even if it has not depressed sales curves, has involved numerous other drugs. Those that will be discussed in subsequent chapters, on the basis of reports by congressional committees, include: Orabilex, E. Fougera & Company's diagnostic aid; Marsilid, a psychic energizer that was made by Roche Laboratories, a division of Hoffmann-La Roche, Inc., of Nutley, New Jersey; and MER/29, the William S. Merrell Company's anticholesterol product. According to an FDA chronology published by the Humphrey subcommittee, Hoffmann-La Roche received initial reports of liver damage in September 1957, but did not tell FDA until a half-year had passed. The toll later known to FDA was 53 deaths and 193 injuries.

Finally, it should be mentioned that the Merrell Company, which had been pressing Dr. Kelsey to release thalidomide, had, she has said, learned but "not forthrightly disclosed" to her that peripheral neuritis had been discovered among a few users. Quite by accident she came across a letter reporting this effect in the *British Medical Journal* for February 1961. This discovery was a crucial factor in firming her resolve not to let the sedative go on sale. It has been estimated that, had she released the drug in February 1961, 10,000 American babies would have been born without arms and legs before marketing could have been halted.

6. *Figures on therapeutic mishaps do not take into account patients who are undertreated because their physicians are fearful of drugs they do not understand.* Dr. Walter Modell, the editor of *Drugs of Choice*, says that such patients "may suffer . . . may even die because they received inadequate treatment with an adequate drug." In a memorable editorial in the January–February 1961 issue of *Clinical Pharmacology and Therapeutics*[9] the Cornell pharmacologist gave some particularly force-

[9] Published by the C. V. Mosby Company.

ful reasons why physicians do not always understand and can be fearful:

> Too often new drugs are not introduced for the only proper reasons: because there is a real or presumed need for them, because they are genuinely superior to those in current use. Too often they are turned loose on the public to horn in on a market which has been created by someone else's discovery, to compete with drugs which have recently been established as good and useful. Too often they are hurried into use to get in on a market before it vanishes. I know of a pharmaceutical company in possession of a series of congeners [molecular modifications] which kept what it deemed to be the best for its own use and licensed the inferior ones to other distributors, to be sold by them to the medical profession for use on patients. Thus, drugs are being marketed and promoted and advertised by precisely the same techniques used for soaps and detergents.

A large proportion of claims for superiority for new drugs are patently invalid. But in addition, it is impossible that of the huge number of new drugs available, each one is the "best" for a separate medical indication. Thus for the approximately forty-five different tranquilizers, the thirty different sedatives, the eighteen different psychic energizers, the twenty-five different antihistamines, the thirty-two different antispasmodics, the thirty different diuretics on the market at this writing (and this census accounts only for different chemical entities and not different brands), each manufacturer claims his to be the best. Is each . . . the "best"? The best for what? The best for whom? There is a manufacturer who sells one drug entity in this country and a congener in another country, making precisely the same claims in each case: namely that each is the best for the same purpose. We are accustomed to this in soap advertisements, but drugs are not soaps. Since

more than one drug cannot be the best for the same indication, we simply don't have enough diseases to go around. At
the moment the most helpful contribution is the new drug to
counteract the untoward effects of other new drugs; we now
have several of these.

It is too bad that the American Medical Association gave
up the publication of that small and masterful book, *Useful
Drugs*. It provided a good, unbiased formulary for everyone.
This, or its equivalent, is one way of ensuring both safe and
effective use of drugs as well as limiting their number through
authoritative suggestion. Is it the only way? Perhaps not, but
how else clarify the confusion created by excessive numbers of
unproved new drugs promiscuously and prematurely introduced into the drug market? Of course there would be no
confusion if the pharmaceutical industry saw the immorality
in claiming a drug to be the best when a better drug was in
fact available, if the sole criterion for the introduction of a
drug was the good of the patient.

A memorable illustration of the dangers of confusion about
drugs has been provided by a famed pediatric cardiologist at the
Johns Hopkins Hospital who holds the Presidential Medal of
Freedom. She is Dr. Helen B. Taussig, the co-discoverer of the
blue-baby operation and a firsthand investigator of the thalidomide tragedy in Europe. In the *New England Journal of Medicine* for July 11, 1963, Dr. Taussig said that a year earlier a
writer for the Brazilian magazine *Ocruziero* had been assured by
health authorities in Brazil that thalidomide was not being sold
there. But in an inquiry precipitated by the birth of an armless
and legless baby, he found 50 other cases of phocomelia. Then
he discovered that thalidomide was indeed being sold — under
such unrevealing names as Sedin, Sedalis, Slip, and Verdil. (In
other countries it was sold under a total of 50 to 100 names.) In
a surprise ten-day search of São Paulo suppliers and pharmacies,

authorities unearthed a stock of 2.5 million thalidomide pills (or boxes of pills), 46,000 flasks containing the sedative, and 103.5 *tons* of the pure substance.

The first warning about thalidomide in an American publication of general circulation was carried in *Time* on February 23, 1962. "I'm very proud of it," the magazine's medicine editor, Gilbert Cant, said later. He went on, however, to relate "how utterly and miserably ashamed [he was] of [himself] for having been two months late with it." The story of the delay involved, once again, confusion over names. Cant told it in October 1963 at a symposium on communications and medical research at the University of Pennsylvania. Immediately after the thalidomide disaster in West Germany became known at the end of November 1961, *Time* correspondents cabled Cant, "describing the drug as Contergan and then giving the generic name thalidomide."

At this time I checked, and found that it was not marketed in the United States, and I put it aside. It did not seem to me then of general interest for an American audience. (Our magazine, though it has an international circulation, is primarily an American magazine.)

During December a man called me who was the father-in-law of a German Occupation bride who had borne a thalidomide baby. He wanted me to do a story. (He was an American.) I told him I was sorry, but I didn't think this was yet a matter for the American market.

Not until February did somebody put a piece of paper in front of my face which just happened to say "Kevadon — Thalidomide." Only then did I realize that Kevadon was the same drug for which I had attended a promotion in Canada. I knew that it was being widely sold in Canada and that there was a new drug application pending for it in the United States.

I have confessed my error, but may I plead this in extenuation. The business of communication in this whole field would be greatly expedited if we used generic names, and if we had started earlier using generic names . . . we would have communicated much better — and I could have communicated the dangers of thalidomide two months earlier than I actually did.

✓ ✓ ✓

At the outset of this chapter, it will be recalled, President Kennedy was quoted on the impossibility of measuring the suffering, protraction of illness, and waste of money resulting from the use of ineffective drugs. It is the crucial issue of worthless drugs that will be explored in the next chapter.

A MAIN POINT in Chapter 1 concerned the failure of certain manufacturers "to pass on to FDA and the medical profession reports that have come to them of injurious and lethal side effects." Following submission of the manuscript for *The Therapeutic Nightmare* more examples of this failure became known. Those presented here struck me as of especial importance because each illuminates relevant problem areas in addition to non-reporting of adverse effects. The examples concern the anticonvulsant known as Elipten, the solvent called DMSO that came to be — and still is — regarded by many as a "miracle drug," the experimental oral contraceptive designated as MK-665 compound, and a group of thiazide-potassium preparations. Following these accounts there is a summary of the outcome of the Dornwal case.

ELIPTEN

Elipten (amino-glutethimide) was an anticonvulsant drug prescribed for the control of epilepsy. When it was removed from the market the Food and Drug Administration disclosed that it masculinized some young girls and caused sexual precocity and other "untoward effects" in certain children. In September 1964 a report summarizing materials in FDA's files on the drug was submitted to then Medical Director Joseph F. Sadusk, Jr., and other agency officials by Dr. John O. Nestor, a courageous medical officer some of whose other services to the public health are set out later in this book. Predictably the report was consigned to oblivion, which was where some in FDA would have liked to send Dr. Nestor for having made it. It recalled that in 1959, while an application by the CIBA Pharmaceutical Company to market Elipten was pending, FDA pharmacologists urged that the firm be required to make a one-year study in rats. Although such a study was done, the agency did not demand — and did not receive — results before releasing Elipten for sale in 1960. Indeed, it was not until 1964 — five years later — that CIBA got around to submitting even partial results. These were ominous. They made clear a need for FDA action. They established beyond doubt, the Nestor report said, that Elipten had an effect on the thyroid gland. Also in 1964, Dr. Nestor discovered, FDA knew of ten cases of hypothyroidism and/or goiter — eight of which had been reported by CIBA — in children on the drug. FDA did nothing. This was not surprising. The agency had let Elipten go on sale in the first place on the basis of what Dr. Nestor termed "very inadequate and uncontrolled studies." The labeling approved by the agency was so loose that it failed to inform physicians that 90 per cent of the children in one test group developed skin rashes which were "sometimes very serious."

Nor did FDA do anything in the last six months of the Larrick regime with the "secret information" its inspectors found at the CIBA plant in Summit, New Jersey, when they at last were sent there in July 1965 — ten months after Dr. Nestor's report was turned in. The rat study, the inspectors discovered, showed not only serious toxic effects on the thyroid, but also on the adrenal glands and on ovaries and uteri.

Meanwhile, a key phase of the story was developing at Sinai and Children's Hospitals in Detroit. A 3-year-old boy was admitted to Sinai. He was very ill, his thyroid gland was prominent, and his skin color was deep bronze. Dr. Ralph Cash, a pediatrician, had laboratory studies done which showed the boy's adrenal glands were not working properly. His thyroid activity was also altered. Elipten became suspect when it was discovered that five months before entering the hospital the boy had started taking the drug to control his epileptic seizures. To test the suspicion Elipten was given to some rats. Marked changes were produced in the experimental animals' adrenals and thyroid. Unbeknownst to Dr. Cash and his associates, of course, similar results had been obtained in the rat study that CIBA had undertaken in 1959 but had been slow in reporting. In the Detroit *News* of February 20, 1966, Charles S. Marwick reported what Dr. Cash said happened then (the boy was, for convenience, called Tommy):

> In the midst of this work, with Drs. Alvro Comacho and Joseph Brough . . . in Children's Hospital, I studied two other children. We found that their adrenals — like Tommy's — had been affected in the same manner.
>
> And they, like Tommy, were also receiving Elipten.
>
> All this work took about a year and a half. By that time we had it nailed down.

In October 1965 CIBA was informed of the findings; Dr. Cash also reported them in the same month at the annual meeting of the Midwest Society for Pediatric Research. No action was taken by CIBA. On January 25, 1966 — eight days after Dr. James Goddard became Commissioner of the FDA — the findings were reported directly to the agency by Dr. Piero P. Foa, director of research at Sinai, and Dr. Herbert Ravin, chief of medicine at the hospital. Sinai is a participating hospital in the FDA's Adverse Drug Reaction Reporting Program.

On February 15, 1966, Dr. Goddard announced that at FDA's request Elipten was being withdrawn from sale. He said he had been advised by agency scientists that had the results of the 1959 rat studies been in hand before marketing was approved in May

1960 they would not have recommended it. In an implicit reference to the Sinai episode, he said that "some of the clinical experience reported to CIBA by physicians using the drug was not in turn reported by CIBA to the FDA as required by law." He went on to make the chilling disclosure about the potential of Elipten to cause sexual precocity and to masculinize little girls. He struck at assumptions that such risks were worth taking when he said, "There is a question as to the effectiveness" of the drug in the treatment of convulsions — and he, as had Dr. Nestor before him, pointed out that more than a dozen other anticonvulsant drugs were available.

CIBA issued a statement in which it said that "5000 persons have been successfully treated annually" with Elipten. No prosecution for withholding data was instituted.

DMSO

DMSO (dimethyl sulfoxide) is an industrial solvent that for a century has been a byproduct of papermaking. Starting in the early 1960s it received massive and frequently hysterical publicity as a "wonder drug" useful in most any medical problem from arthritis to headaches. After learning of numerous reports of eye damage in human users, the Food and Drug Administration on November 10, 1965, suspended clinical trials. On March 9, 1966, a hearing was held by Representative L. H. Fountain's House Intergovernmental Relations Subcommittee.

Wyeth Laboratories, a division of American Home Products Corporation, sponsored certain studies in which DMSO was used in rabbits. Adverse eye effects occurred. Wyeth was notified of this in a typewritten report in December 1964, but did not pass along the information to FDA until the day eleven months later when the agency decided to discontinue all investigations with DMSO. The Congressman asked whether Wyeth had not been "required to submit this information to FDA *immediately* after it came to their attention?" (My italic.) "They were," replied Dr. Joseph F. Sadusk, Jr., whose title of Medical Director of FDA was born when he came to the agency but which was abolished on his departure.

Adverse effects on the eyes of dogs treated with DMSO were reported to Merck Sharp & Dohme, a division of Merck & Co., Inc., which waited eight months to tell FDA about them — until filing an application on May 28, 1965, to market DMSO. In a report to the Subcommittee after the hearing, FDA said it had found in Merck files five other DMSO studies recording damage in dogs, rabbits, and rats that had not been reported at all to the agency. But the Fountain hearing disabused observers of any confidence they might have had that a prompt report by Merck would have brought a prompt reaction from FDA. The significance of the eye changes in dogs that were reported in May by Merck, Dr. Sadusk testified, "was not immediately noted." That was understatement; six months went by before the significance was effectively noted and acted upon.

In a second paper filed with the Subcommittee after the hearing, FDA provided a list of firms that were found during field investigations to have failed to report reactions to DMSO in humans and to report DMSO animal studies. These firms were Syntex Laboratories, Inc., the E. R. Squibb & Sons division of Olin Mathieson Chemical Corp., and Schering Corporation. Merck Sharp & Dohme and Crown-Zellerbach Corp. were listed for having failed to report clinical reactions, and Wyeth and Ayerst Laboratories, which is also a division of American Home Products, for failure to report animal studies.

The same FDA table listed the following firms in connection with various other "discrepancies" found in the field investigations of the experimental handling of DMSO:

"Shipment to unlisted clinical investigator" — White Laboratories, Inc., its parent Schering Corporation, Syntex, Squibb, Merck Sharp & Dohme, Crown-Zellerbach, and Ayerst.

"Use of animal grade DMSO" — White, Schering, Geigy Chemical Corporation, and Ayerst.

"Use in treating conditions not in protocol," that is, in the approved experimental plan — Syntex, Squibb, Schering, and Crown-Zellerbach.

"Everything that could go wrong went wrong in this situation," Commissioner James L. Goddard testified. Much had gone wrong in the pre-Goddard FDA. Animal data sufficient to justify trials in humans — as many as 50,000 may have been getting DMSO from authorized and unauthorized investigators — had not been submitted when these trials began; the trials began simply because FDA had allowed the situation to drift. Ordinary clinical trials often involve only about 100 patients. Three companies — Merck, Squibb, and Syntex — alone gave a go-ahead to 1,206 investigators. FDA recommended limits on numbers of patients, on duration of testing, and on testing of DMSO in combination with other drugs — and then failed to enforce them. Merck drew up a plan to try a combination of DMSO and Indocin, a then new anti-arthritic, in humans, although an FDA medical officer testified that there was "really a paucity of animal data." W. Donald Gray, the Subcommittee's senior investigator, brought out that Merck also notified FDA of plans to try DMSO on human mucous membranes in the ear, mouth, and nose. "Did they submit separate animal studies to justify those new [and unapproved] routes of administration?" Gray asked. "No," the FDA's Dr. Harold Anderson answered.

The DMSO hearing, and other developments that followed, were a blow to Dr. Frances O. Kelsey, heroine of the thalidomide episode. In recognition of her achievement in blocking marketing of the baby-deforming drug she had been promoted from medical officer to head of the Investigational Drug Branch. It was in that Branch that many of the slipups occurred — concerning not only DMSO but also other experimental drugs. There is no question but that Dr. Kelsey was seriously handicapped by insufficient personnel and other factors. But there is also little doubt that administration was not her forte. This came out with a special poignancy in the Fountain hearing when she acknowledged uncertainty about whether all of the thirteen firms authorized to test DMSO in humans had been told not to try it in women of child-bearing age — although her branch had received reports of birth defects in animals treated with the drug.

MK-665 COMPOUND

MK-665 compound was an experimental Merck Sharp & Dohme oral contraceptive that combined the estrogen called mestranol, which was used in some marketed birth control pills, with a progestogen, ethynerone, which was not used in pills then being sold. On January 21, 1966, the manufacturer told the Food and Drug Administration that breast cancer had been found in four of six beagles which had been sacrificed after receiving large doses of the product for twelve months. The company said it had halted testing in 340 women that was being conducted by authorized investigators, and in 127 others who were receiving MK-665 from two other Merck investigators who had not been cleared by the firm to do this testing but who also had not been intercepted. No trace of cancer was found in the patients, who will remain under observation.

The discovery of cancer in the dogs was an "alarming finding," William W. Goodrich, FDA's counsel, testified at an inquiry held by the House Intergovernmental Relations Subcommittee on March 10, 1966. As such, it was required under FDA regulations to be reported "immediately" without awaiting evaluation. But the regulations were violated, Goodrich said under questioning by W. Donald Gray of the Subcommittee staff.

The dogs were sacrificed on July 30, 1965. Tissue sections were not examined under the microscope until four months later. The explanation for the delay was that the findings had been negative in a group of dogs sacrificed in February after a six-month toxicity trial, and the July findings were made inconveniently in a vacation period. If reasons of this kind can provide immunity from the law's reporting requirements, Gray told Goodrich, "a company could do animal studies and not make final tissue examinations and reports for years." So far as Gray was concerned, the four-month delay was clearly a violation. In November 1965 Merck applied to FDA to begin large-scale clinical testing. The application cited the negative results from the test dogs sacrificed in February after six months of testing but of course ignored, because they had not yet been examined, the tissues taken from the dogs in the more meaningful year-long testing. On December 9, 1965, cancer in the beagles' breast tissue was found. Merck "should have reported the results of the tissue examination immediately," Goodrich testified, but was instead "getting in touch with their consultants." FDA was not notified until 43 days later. ". . . that was a violation," Goodrich told the Subcommittee. Late in the day of the hearing, Merck issued a statement saying it had "acted responsibly and as promptly as warranted."

Although I deal thoroughly with questions about the safety of oral contraceptives in Chapter 13 and its Afterword, a troubling consequence of the MK-665 matter may appropriately be discussed here. It is relatively easy to accomplish the withdrawal of an experimental birth control pill that is being tried in but a few hundred women and in which the financial and other stakes are quite limited. But one is awed to contemplate what the consequences would be to public officials who would attempt to take off the market oral contraceptives which — according to an FDA estimate of April 1967 — were being taken by eleven million women around the world. The question was what relation, if any, existed between MK-665 and the marketed pills. As noted, the experimental compound contained one hormone, mestranol, found in some pills that have been sold for years. The second hormone, ethynerone, is chemically similar to progestogens widely used in other contraceptives. That similarity led some to suggest that the biological impacts of ethynerone and other progestogens might differ only in degree. In August 1966, the FDA's Advisory Committee on Obstetrics and Gynecology concluded that to call a halt to testing of MK-665 was warranted but that to halt use of marketed oral contraceptives was not. Although the Committee report was unanimous it included a report that took a different view of the MK-665 matter. The report was written by Dr. Roy Hertz, a member of the Committee, former scientific director of the National Institute for Child Health and Human Development and former chief of the Endocrinology Branch of the National Cancer Institute. After discussing the chemical resemblance between ethynerone and accepted progestogens he said that "either the marketed products are also to be condemned on the basis of certain expectable animal findings or ethynerone should not have been condemned." It is essential to understand what Dr. Hertz was saying and what he was not saying. He was saying that he saw no sound scientific basis for distinguishing between the possible carcinogenic potential of ethynerone and hormones in the same chemical family; he was saying that he saw no sound scientific basis for either accepting or questioning the safety of one of these substances but not the others. But he was *not* saying the occurrence of cancer in the breasts of beagles treated with MK-665 was a sufficient basis for a conclusion that ethynerone will, or will not, cause cancer in the breasts of women; he was *not* saying that the MK-665 experience provided a basis for concluding that *any* birth control pill will, or will not, cause breast cancer. The reason for Dr. Hertz's position — and it was a *scientific* position — was primarily that testing of the pills had been wholly inadequate as to many diseases and certainly as to those types of cancer that are not reliably detectable during latency periods of ten years or so. The lack of proper testing — a major thrust of Chapter 13 and its Afterword — compelled the kind of caution evidenced by Dr. Hertz. Doubtless it was unsatisfying; how pleasant it is to be assured, in contrast, that the pill one wants to believe is safe, is safe. Dr. Hertz looked up at a sky that is dark and unrevealing and said, I cannot be certain but there may be a cloud; Commissioner Goddard looked up at the same sky and said, lo, I see a silver lining. The parallel drawn by Dr. Hertz between MK-665 and the other birth control pills, Dr. Goddard told me in October 1966 in response to a question, "does not exist. . . . No component of the marketed oral contraceptives has produced breast cancer in dogs." But the eyesight of Dr. Goddard in perceiving this silver lining was demonstrably blurred. He had failed to notice the finding of the Advisory Committee to his own agency that insufficient testing of the pills in dogs had been undertaken and its recommendation that there be more.

THIAZIDE-POTASSIUM DIURETICS

In the condition known as edema the tissues swell with water. The condition occurs in association with congestive heart failure, and occasionally with high blood pressure and pregnancy, among other things. Diuretics, of which the thiazides comprise one group, treat edema by increasing the flow of urine. Unavoidably the body's potassium supply is simultaneously reduced. Almost always a deficiency in potassium can be made up by diet supplementation, i.e., by consuming more potassium-rich foods such as bananas and oranges and orange juice, or by taking potassium itself in, say, liquid solution. In this situation the physician retains individual control of the dose, which leading medical scientists consider sound practice.

Late in 1959 applications were submitted to the Food and Drug Administration for the marketing of pills combining a thiazide diuretic with potassium chloride. Each tablet had a so-called enteric coating designed to prevent dissolution in the stomach. In behalf of Hydrodiuril-KA Merck Sharp & Dohme submitted clinical reports from 15 investigators on about 135 patients. The submission included no animal studies, and none was asked for by the agency on the theory that they had been made redundant by wide experience with the ingredients as separate entities. In behalf of Esidrix-K the CIBA Pharmaceutical Company submitted a similar application except that the number of patients was 235. Within a few months both products had a go-ahead from FDA. So popular were the combinations that in the period November 1961 to September 1964 an estimated seven million persons began to use them — an average rate of 206,000 per month.

On July 22, 1964, CIBA informed FDA of a case of a stenotic lesion of the small bowel, or ulcer of the small intestine, "allegedly associated with the ingestion of Esidrix-K." In the four months that followed the agency learned, mostly from the manufacturers, of 120 such cases associated with ingestion of the enteric-coated tablets. In consultation with FDA, CIBA and Merck sent telegrams to a total of 420 hospitals in the United States and abroad requesting reports on their experience with the pills. All told, the agency had learned of 15 fatal and 218 nonfatal cases by the first week in January 1965; they had occurred in cardiovascular patients whose average age was 60.

Against this backdrop, the House Intergovernmental Relations Subcommittee developed a picture of bumbling and sharp practice (or worse) that taxes credulity. This picture would not have emerged had FDA had the sense and the courage to have compelled the withdrawal from sale of Esidrix-K, Hydrodiuril-KA, and similar preparations marketed then or later, including Hydropres-KA (Merck); Naturetin $\bar{c}$ K, Rautrax, Rautrax-N Modified, and Rautrax-N (E. R. Squibb & Sons), and Anhydron K and Anhydron KR (Eli Lilly & Co.). At a hearing on June 10, 1965, Delphis C. Goldberg and W. Donald Gray of the Subcommittee staff developed a line of questioning intended to show that withdrawal would have been the safer course. Their case was highly persuasive. The danger, it appeared, was created by the enteric coating which caused potassium chloride to be retained too long in the lower bowel; potassium could be ingested safely in other ways, and, therefore, combination tablets entailed needless risk. The rebuttal arguments, made by Dr. Joseph F. Sadusk, Jr., FDA's Medical Director, were transparently weak. But he was in the position of defending not only a *fait accompli*, and of trying to save face, but also of fending off a challenge to his regulatory philosophy. That philosophy was that by and large the practicing physician could and should be the judge of the efficacy of drugs. Even if that philosophy were not gravely flawed — it is, as demonstrated in subsequent chapters — it did not measure up to the law.

On January 6, 1965, FDA met with representatives of CIBA and Merck — and in their presence decided on, or formalized, a course of action. The propriety of this kind of consensus decision-making was questioned by L. H. Fountain, the Subcommittee chairman. At first Dr. Sadusk said the meeting served merely to ratify a decision that had been reached by him and his staff; but then he conceded to Donald Gray that before that he had made a "purely verbal" agreement with the companies. The gist of the agreement was that a warning drafted by CIBA and Merck would be mailed by them to physicians and incorporated in a revised labeling for the drugs, and that Dr. Sadusk would make special arrangements for prompt publication of the warning and for editorial mention in the *Journal* of the American Medical Association. These things were done. The warnings were mailed in March 1965.

Although FDA did not know of it at once, the letters were sent third-class, bulk-rate "junk" mail. The return address on the envelope was, "120 Brighton Road/Clifton, New Jersey 07012." This, it turned out, was the address of a mailing company; the names of CIBA and Merck nowhere appeared on the envelope. In the lower left-hand corner were the words "IMPORTANT

INFORMATION." This kind of mail is commonly pitched unopened into doctors' wastebaskets, Representative Fountain pointed out. There was nothing on the envelope to alert physicians that an important drug warning was enclosed. Asked if the method used here "was adequate to call this matter forcibly" to the attention of physicians, Dr. Sadusk said, "I think it was . . ." It is arresting that Dr. Sadusk persisted in this defense until the end of the hearing, by which time Assistant Commissioner J. Kenneth Kirk had promised that thereafter first-class mail with a drug-warning legend on the envelope should and would be used in such situations.

The "junk" mailing, which Fountain at one point called "a mighty insignificant . . . and a rather careless way to warn a doctor about a drug," had also caused deep concern within FDA or, more precisely, to Dr. Robert S. McCleery, head of the Medical Advertising Branch. Dr. McCleery, who is as brave, dedicated, informed, and wise a public servant as I know of, sent a memo soon after the mailing to Dr. Howard I. Weinstein, director of the Division of Medical Review, saying that the features of the envelopes "create the very great probability that only a small percentage of those that survived the bulk handling and eventually reached physicians' offices will be opened and read by them." Such envelopes, Dr. McCleery said, are familiar to physicians who are the objects of promotions for "insurance, radios, ties . . ." He ventured that companies presumed by Dr. Sadusk to be "responsible" had taken "unfair advantage" of him (subsequently, a Merck spokesman insisted to me that the "junk" mailing was undertaken by company personnel who, had they consulted with top executives, would have been directed to do no such thing). Finally, Dr. McCleery proposed that a professional survey be commissioned to ascertain reliably how many physicians had in fact received "a message of vital importance concerning a new danger." Dr. Weinstein thought so little of the memo that he failed even to forward it to Dr. Sadusk. He had not known, he testified, that the warning was going third-class bulk mail, "[b]ut that would have been all right." He held to this incredible position until questioning by the Congressman and Donald Gray made it apparent even to him that it was untenable.

When a pharmaceutical manufacturer's "self-interest impels it to get a message through the 'nurse curtain' to the physician," the McCleery memo said, there is a "great difference" between its tactics and those used in this case by Merck and CIBA. He made his point with the behavior of E. R. Squibb & Sons, a division of Olin Mathieson Chemical Corporation, in exploiting a momentary advantage. On March 18, which was a brief time after issuance of the Merck and CIBA warning, Squibb representatives met with the FDA about their brand of thiazide and potassium chloride combination, Naturetin c̄ K. The company was told, the agency's Dr. Weinstein testified, "that their product is no different from the others and should contain the exact same warning as the Merck and CIBA product." He also said that the warning these firms had distributed, which mentioned no brand names, was intended to apply to *all* thiazide potassium diuretics. Finally, the official recalled to Donald Gray, the Squibb representatives had given no indication that they were planning to send a so-called warning letter of their own.

Yet such a letter, which was dated the next day, March 19, was sent. Signed by Dr. Thomas J. Ormsby, Squibb's Senior Associate Medical Director, it turned out to be a piece of promotion — even though to pierce the "nurse curtain" it bore the legend "IMPORTANT DRUG INFORMATION ENCLOSED" and the firm's name on the envelope and was mailed first-class. Dr. Ormsby called attention to publicity given small bowel lesions associated with thiazide-potassium diuretics. Although more than 300 million tablets of the Squibb brand purportedly had been marketed since January 1960, his letter boasted, "To date we are aware of no clinical reports of small bowel ulceration with Naturetin with K." As soon as FDA became aware of this — the name of the game was shell — it called Squibb in to force a retraction. On April 15 this enterprising firm sent out a second "Dear Doctor" letter saying that the agency "had on file reports of small bowel lesions associated with the administration of Naturetin with K, which cases had not previously come to our attention." Enclosed was a prescribing brochure revised to incorporate the same warning that CIBA and Merck had adopted. The mailing was first-class. On the lower left-hand corner of the envelope were the words "IMPORTANT DRUG WARNING." "Did the first letter not actually mislabel the product within the meaning of the law?" Gray asked. "In our judgment," replied Kirk, the Assistant Commissioner, "this is true." Preparations were made in the agency to cite Squibb to a hearing at which the firm would be allowed to show cause why it should not be prosecuted, but Dr. Sadusk generously recommended to then Commissioner George P. Larrick that in view of Squibb's prompt — and forced — agreement to the second letter "any pending regulatory action against Squibb be withheld."

The unanswered question was how effective the various warnings had been, that is, how many patients were being injured or killed because their physicians hadn't gotten the word. The FDA could ignore Dr. McCleery's suggestion for a professional survey; it could not ignore the oversight mechanisms of the House Intergovernmental Relations Subcommittee. Thus it was learned that in the 16 months starting in March 1965, when the "junk" mailing went out, 63 new cases were reported to FDA; 14 of the reports were made by Squibb. And, it should be noted, Commissioner James L. Goddard has himself emphasized that adverse reactions to drugs of all kinds are grossly underreported. Of the 63 cases 51 required surgery and 8 were fatal. In December 1966 Dr. Goddard told Representative Fountain that the prescribing instructions for thiazide-potassium products would have to be further restricted to emphasize the "recognized risk." The agency then drafted a letter intended to be sent out by the manufacturers. One or more refused to send it on the ground that such a letter was unnecessary. Yet the draft was weak, Fountain has pointed out. For one thing, it substituted the weak phrase "potential danger" for the "recognized risk" acknowledged by Dr. Goddard, it minimized even the "potential danger," and it made a highly questionable assertion about a reduction in the toll of death and injury. Finally, in March 1967, FDA sent a "Dear Doctor" letter of its own to almost 300,000 civilian and military physicians, osteopaths, and hospital pharmacies. Although stronger than the draft the companies had rejected, even this document was deficient. The letter, which was signed by Dr. Herbert L. Ley, Jr., who succeeded Dr. Sadusk as director of the Bureau of Medicine, told physicians that the combination products may be used in edema responsive to thiazides "only where development of even a mild degree of hypokalemia [abnormally low potassium content in the blood] might have serious consequences," and for those few who could not tolerate liquid potassium. For reasons stated in the foregoing, the letter might more wisely have said that the indications for using the combinations have been restricted to *very serious* thiazide-responsive types of edema, such as those associated with heart and liver decompensation, in which even a mild degree of hypokalemia might have serious consequences; that indications for use in less serious types of edema, *such as in pregnancy*, have been eliminated, and that the previous warning allowing use *only when adequate dietary supplementation is not practical* remains in force. The letter announced a new labeling but — if your strained credulity can bear to hear this — failed to state its purpose. In addition, Representative Fountain said in a statement, the FDA letter failed to tell physicians how the new labeling "differs from or is more restrictive than the old labeling."

DORNWAL

On November 8, 1965, Wallace & Tiernan, which had looked forward to "vindication" in the case of the tranquilizer called Dornwal, pleaded no contest in District Court in Washington and was fined $10,000 — the maximum allowed — on each of four felony counts. Dr. Charles E. Hough, the former medical director, pleaded *nolo contendere* to a felony count charging willful failure to inform the Food and Drug Administration of deaths and injuries in users of Dornwal. He was put on probation for a year. Four other counts were dismissed by Chief Judge Matthew F. McGuire. Robert T. Conner, the former director of clinical research, pleaded guilty to two misdemeanor counts, which were in an information substituted by the Justice Department for the original indictment. The Judge put Conner on probation for six months.

2

DANGERS OF
WORTHLESS DRUGS

INEFFECTIVE DRUGS can be dangerous drugs. There is no fact more crucial to an understanding of why we have wasted our money and our health. Dr. Louis S. Goodman, of the University of Utah College of Medicine, testifying as "a teacher of pharmacology to medical students and postgraduate physicians, as a research worker, and as a textbook author," told the Kefauver Senate Subcommittee on Antitrust and Monopoly in 1961: ". . . I find it difficult, if not impossible, to separate the problem of drug safety from considerations of therapeutic use and efficacy." He used as a "homely example" water, table salt, and sugar: "These three simple and usually safe articles of our diet are really potent drugs and can, under certain not uncommon circumstances, cause serious physiological derangements and markedly aggravate existing diseases or disorders."

Dr. Goodman explained, "A daily intake of water which would make most of us quite ill or decidedly uncomfortable is absolutely essential to maintain the health of a patient with diabetes insipidus. An amount of table salt which most of us find necessary to make our food palatable would cause serious illness or death in a patient with dropsy caused by congestive heart failure. Even a modest excess above an allowable sugar intake may precipitate a metabolic crisis in a patient with diabetes mellitus."

The late Dr. Lawson Wilkins, in his May 10, 1962, presidential address before the American Pediatric Society, warned that "many of the new remedies have more subtle and obscure side effects producing bizarre iatrogenic [doctor-caused] disturbances which may be misdiagnosed and lead to further and perhaps dangerous mistreatment of the patient."

"Extreme remedies are appropriate for extreme diseases," Hippocrates said. What was true twenty-four centuries ago is true today. Dr. Barbara Moulton, a former FDA medical officer now with the Federal Trade Commission, summed it up before the Kefauver subcommittee: "No physician, no one who has ever been responsible for the welfare of individual patients, will accept the idea that safety can be judged in the absence of a decision about efficacy. No drug is 'safe' if it fails to cure a serious disease for which a cure is available. No drug is too dangerous to use if it will cure a fatal disease for which no other cure is available. To attempt to separate the two concepts is completely irrational . . ."

If a bad experiment allows an inefficacious drug to become accepted in therapy, Dr. Walter Modell, the Cornell University Medical College pharmacologist, told the American Association for the Advancement of Science in 1962, the result is

. . . a more insidious menace than the introduction of a toxic drug, because toxic effects attract more attention than failure to produce effects, and are usually promptly noted. It is much more difficult to identify the ineffective drug once it is in actual clinical use, because it is usually combined with a number of other therapeutic measures, and because it is very difficult to make a careful, thorough experimental examination of a drug once it has been accepted. Thus archaic drugs like strychnine continue to be used 50 years after it has been established that they have no use in medicine. The adverse effects of the useless drug are more subtle than that of the toxic drug. The useless drug is harmful because it engenders a false sense of security which may lead to a lessening of attention and failure to look for and observe critical features of the progress of the disease.[1]

The established use of so many ineffective drugs in therapy is attributable in varying degrees to bad experiments, bad science, and wishful thinking. This is hardly a new discovery. In 1861, for example, D. W. Cheever wrote in the Boston *Medical and Surgical Journal:* "Effects are ascribed to drugs which really flow from natural causes, and are but the usual succession of the morbid phenomena; sequences are taken for consequences, and all just conclusions confused. From the want of this knowledge [of the natural history of disease]; from defective observation, rash generalizations, and hasty conclusions a priori, have arisen the thousand conflicting theories which have degraded Medicine from its true position as a science, and interfered with its advancement as a practical art."

Dr. William B. Bean, professor of internal medicine at the Medical College of the University of Iowa, described to the Senate Antitrust subcommittee his experience with seriously ill victims of pellagra in the South in the 1930's:

> If a person at a certain stage of acute pellagra is put to bed and given a pellagra-producing diet, he will improve. This improvement is short lived, but it may last for several days, or even a week. Any treatment, any procedure used at such a time is followed by this nonspecific improvement. Thus, everything that was ever used by physicians, and this included almost every drug available in the pharmacopoeia, was praised as a specific cure.

[1] This address was published in the *Hearings* of the Humphrey Subcommittee on Reorganization and International Organizations, and also in *Science* under the title "Hazards of New Drugs." The quotations here and on pages 57, 76, 152, 170, 215, 246, and 307 are from *Science,* Vol. 139, No. 3560 (22 March 1963), pages 1180–1185; copyright 1963 by the American Association for the Advancement of Science.

Only when recognition of this nonspecific phase of improvement had been gained by clinical investigation was a proper evaluation of therapy possible . . .

Physicians are desperately anxious to relieve, to succor, and to restore to health the patients who come to them in their difficulty. It is only natural that as physicians we are pleased to ascribe to our own efforts such good changes as occur and blame on the nature of the disease, the patient's refractoriness, orneriness, or something else, failures we encounter. The observer parallax or body English, our intense hopes, make it extraordinarily difficult for anyone to observe his clinical results dispassionately.

Yet another example was given by Dr. Michael Shimkin, chief of cancer biology at the Fels Research Institute in Philadelphia, in a lecture before that city's College of Physicians in December 1963. Dr. Shimkin, who is also a professor of medicine at Temple University School of Medicine, told this story:

In important medical journals there appears a full-page advertisement of a respected pharmaceutical company, of a progestational compound for the treatment of threatened abortion [miscarriage]. A lovely girl, heavy with child, looks mistily into a blossoming tree. The trade name of the compound, in large red letters, is followed by the claim that 80 per cent of threatened abortions are salvageable. There is a reference to an article documenting the claim. But there are two studies, one in Australia . . . and one in Texas in which the progestational agent was used along with a parallel group of controls that received a placebo. In both investigations 80 per cent of the threatened pregnancies were saved. This was also exactly the result in both placebo-treated groups.

Bad experiments and bad science can account for but a part

of the persistence of ineffective drugs into the present.[2] Another part of the explanation must be sought in our political and social history.

✓ ✓ ✓

Not until the 1880's was the first bona fide federal pure food and drug legislation introduced (by Senator A. A. Paddock of Nebraska). It and other efforts like it were defeated by a durable alliance of quacks, ruthless crooks, pious frauds, scoundrels, high-priced lawyer-lobbyists, vested interests, liars, corrupt members of Congress, venal publishers, cowards in high office, the stupid, the apathetic, and the duped.

It took a twenty-five-year fight to win enactment of the Pure Food and Drugs Act of 1906. The leader of that fight was Dr. Harvey W. Wiley, who said that "the most wretched and disgraceful evil" was that of patent medicines foisted on humanity by what he called "this group of ghouls." He wrote in his autobiography, published in 1930, the year in which he died:[3]

One quack nostrum I studied carefully may be cited as an example of the whole sorry lot. The concoction was a weak solution of sulphuric and sulphurous acids, with an occasional trace of hydrochloric and hydrobromic acids, and the bulk of it was water. Here is what its blatant announcers guaranteed it would "cure": asthma, abscess, anemia, bronchitis, blood poison, bowel troubles, coughs, colds, consumption, contagious diseases, cancer, catarrh, dysentery, diarrhea, dyspepsia, dandruff, eczema, erysipelas, fevers, gall-stones, goiter, gout, hay

[2] In *The Decline of Capitalistic Civilization* Beatrice and Sidney Webb suggest that "a man will buy only two or three boxes of pills which can and do really cure him of an ailment, but he will continue to buy for years those remedies which never do him any good."

[3] This and the quotations on pages 44 and 132 are from *Harvey W. Wiley: An Autobiography,* copyright 1930 by The Bobbs-Merrill Company, Inc., R. 1957 by Mrs. Harvey W. Wiley, reprinted by permission of the publishers.

fever, influenza, la grippe, leucorrhea, malaria, neuralgia, piles, quinsy, rheumatism, scrofula, skin diseases, tuberculosis, tumors, throat troubles, and ulcers—all arranged nicely in the advertisements in alphabetical form so that your particular ill could easily be located — and, so the announcements continued, "all diseases that begin with fever, all inflammations, all catarrh, all contagious diseases, and all the results of impure or poisoned blood; in nervous diseases our remedy acts as a vitalizer, accomplishing what no drugs can do."

Of course most of the quack medicines which afflicted that generation were positively harmful in their effects. The "headache powders" were quite uniformly drugs, and vicious habit-forming drugs at that. Women and girls became addicted to their use in tragic numbers. The pain-killers and pain-relievers usually depressed the heart of the victim who used them, and the reaction made the pain far worse. Poisonous "women's remedies" were sold in amazing quantities, and the sum total of their harmful effects will never be known. Poor mothers doped their babies into insensibility at night with soothing syrups containing opium or morphine. Catarrh cures, depending on cocaine and opium for their efficacy, had a rushing sale.

The most vicious of the whole circus of medical frauds was the group which preyed on incurables. Cancer "cures" flooded the market. Quacks did not stop at duping actual sufferers . . . Patients with tuberculosis were usually willing to spend the last cent obtainable to recover their health, and the fiends who preyed upon them many times got their last cent in exchange for a mixture of cod-liver oil and poisonous drugs.

. . . The patent-medicine manufacturers furnished a great bulk of the average newspaper's advertising, and therefore its income. Advertising contracts were held as clubs over the heads of the editors and publishers, and many newspapers were definitely under the influence of the quacks. The average publisher, grateful for the steady stream of money that poured in from medical advertisers, supinely accepted "editorial and news" matter written by the advertiser himself, telling of the wondrous cures the nostrum had effected and how all humanity was about to be blessed by this amazing discovery and boon to mankind . . . The amount of blood money coming in from patent-medicine advertisements in newspapers and periodicals in this country at the beginning of the century I estimate to have been about a hundred million dollars annually.[4]

Yet, as Dr. Wiley himself had emphasized, indispensable support in bringing about passage of the 1906 law came from the muckraking press, particularly Samuel Hopkins Adams and Norman Hapgood in *Collier's* weekly and Mark Sullivan and Edward Bok in the *Ladies' Home Journal*, with notable assists from others including William Allen White, editor of the Emporia *Gazette* in Kansas. In later battles, Dr. Wiley had almost universal press support, although not from trade papers such as those "devoted to the interests of adulteration."

The 1906 law prohibited false *or* misleading labels on drugs. This quickly proved to be not much of a restraint. In *Food and Drug Regulation*, Stephen Wilson tells how a huge loophole was opened in 1911: "The Supreme Court . . . in the first drug case to come before it, ruled that such statements related only to the identity of the product and not to its curative properties. The Sherley Amendment was then passed [in 1912] to offset the

---

[4] In *Freedom of the Press* George Seldes, citing a November 1905 exposé in *Collier's* entitled "The Patent Medicine Conspiracy against the Freedom of the Press," tells of an address made to the Proprietary Association of America by its president, Frank J. Cheney, who manufactured a catarrh "cure." Cheney told the Association, which was spending about $40 million a year on newspaper advertising, how to influence the press: ". . . I, inside of the last two years, have made contracts with between fifteen and sixteen thousand newspapers [presumably including a great many weeklies] . . . This is what I have in every contract I make: 'It is hereby agreed that should your State, or the United States Government, pass any law that would interfere with or restrict the sale of proprietary medicines, this contract shall become void' . . . I have carried this through and know it is a success. I know the papers will accept it . . . It throws the responsibility on the newspapers . . ."

Supreme Court's decision, and forbade false and fraudulent therapeutic claims on the label. This simple change in phraseology practically legalized false therapeutic statements because, to be illegal, they had to be both false and fraudulent, a fact very difficult to prove [because fraud involves intent to deceive]." Wilson wrote that "the phraseology was advocated at the hearings on the amendment by Charles M. Woodruff of Parke, Davis and Co."

Nor did the 1906 law provide any control over *advertising* of drugs, as distinguished from labeling. Thus, after spending ten years to get fraudulent tuberculosis claims off the label of a horse liniment called "B & M Remedy," Wilson said, the government could do nothing about the same claims being made for it on the radio, in newspapers, and in other media. Nostrum advertising boomed. The damage to health, the waste of life, the squandering of money for worthless medications — all of these kept pace.

In 1913, two years after the Supreme Court ruled that the law did not bar false therapeutic claims for nostrums used by men, women, and children, Congress passed a law prohibiting the marketing of worthless serums and other drugs for the treatment of hogs, sheep, and cattle. Efforts to do as much for people failed. After adoption of the Eighteenth Amendment to the Constitution, to be sure, a few dozen efficacious patent medicines were promoted. These claimed, accurately, to be effective against the effects of Prohibition.

✦   ✦   ✦

"The trouble now," Dr. Wiley wrote in 1930 in his autobiography, "is that no one takes much interest in the Food and Drugs Act — that is to say, no one in Congress. It is regarded as established and in perfect operation. This is a great mistake." Among the public at large, too, the Act was mistakenly thought to be providing adequate protection, for reasons that will be made clear in a moment.

After Franklin D. Roosevelt took office in 1933, Rexford G. Tugwell, then Assistant Secretary of Agriculture, who was aware of the many deficiencies of the 1906 law, appointed a committee to draft new legislation. On June 12, 1933, the bill that resulted was introduced by a physician-member of the Senate, Royal S. Copeland, of New York.

In *Food and Drug Regulation*, which was published in 1942 by the American Council on Public Affairs in Washington, Stephen Wilson tells of a "17 plans" attack quickly launched by the United [patent] Medicine Manufacturers of America, and disclosed at Senate hearings by Alice L. Edwards, executive secretary of the American Home Economics Association. The "plans" commended to the patent-medicine makers included these:

2. Secure cooperation of newspapers in spreading favorable publicity, particularly papers now carrying advertising for members of the association.

3. Enlist all manufacturers and wholesalers, including those allied to the trade, and induce them to place the facts before their customers through salesmen, and in all other possible ways to secure their cooperative aid.

4. Secure the pledge of manufacturers, wholesalers, advertising agencies, and all other interested affiliates to address letters to Senators to gain their promise to vote against the measure.

5. Line up with other organizations, such as Drug Institute, Proprietary Association, National Association of Retail Druggists, and others, to make a mass attack on bill . . .

9. Convey by every means available — radio, newspaper, mail, and personal contact — the alarming fact that if the bill is adopted, the public will be deprived of *the right of self-*

diagnosis and self-medication, and would be compelled to secure a physician's prescription for many simple needs . . .
[My italics.]

11. Enlist the help of carton, tube, bottle and box manufacturers.

12. Defeat the use of ridicule by the American Medical
Association — who favored the measure — by replying with
ridicule.

The bill contained provisions, which although probably requiring changes in wording, were intended to assure effectiveness
of drugs, patent *or* prescription. One provision said that a drug
shall be deemed misbranded "if its labeling bears any representation, directly or by ambiguity or inference, concerning the effect
of such drug which is contrary to the general agreement of medical opinion." A second clause, bitterly opposed by publishing
interests, read, in part: "An advertisement of a food, drug, or
cosmetic shall be deemed to be false if in any particular it is untrue, or by ambiguity or inference creates a misleading impression regarding such food, drug, or cosmetic."

President Roosevelt not only authorized the proposed revision
of the 1906 law but sent a message to Congress about it, and
several times asked leaders of Congress to help get it passed. In
addition, there were numerous hearings in the Senate and
House, hearings frequently rich in newsworthy material. Yet
for five years the initial bill and subsequent versions were met by
what Wilson called a "conspiracy of silence," during which the
legislation was watered down while being blocked. At a Senate
hearing it was brought out that a patent-medicine maker had
written to newspapers warning, "If this bill should become law,
we will be forced to cancel immediately every line of advertising."

David F. Cavers, now of the Harvard Law School, who was a
member of the committee that drafted the original bill and was
adviser to the Department of Agriculture on food and drug legis-

lation, wrote in the Winter 1939 issue of *Law and Contemporary Problems*:

> Perhaps the most striking characteristic of the history of the Food, Drug, and Cosmetic Act [which became law in June 1938] is the fact that this measure, which was of consequence to the health and pocketbook of every citizen of the country and which importantly affected industries whose annual product totals roughly ten billion dollars, never became the object of widespread public attention, much less of informed public interest. The affected industries were kept posted by their associations and journals; some national women's organizations sought to apprise their membership of major developments; but the public at large, including persons ordinarily well-informed on national affairs, knew little or nothing of what was transpiring in Congress. I suspect that today only a small fraction of the public knows that a new law has been enacted.
>
> For the existence of this situation, the nation's press must stand primarily accountable. In the long history of the bill, the *New York Times* seems to have seen fit to give it front-page mention on but a single occasion and then only to report a disturbance in the Senate galleries. The *Times'* policy was not exceptional.

In a footnote, Professor Cavers said that the only newspapers of consequence to give consistent support to the measure were the St. Louis *Post-Dispatch*, the *Christian Science Monitor*, and William Allen White's Emporia *Gazette*.

Three decades earlier large-circulation magazines had been militant in behalf of food and drug legislation. But during the 1930's, Cavers said, they "were silent or unfriendly . . . That this policy was due in no small measure to advertising revenues seems inescapable."

There *were* breakthroughs in the news boycott nonetheless. One was achieved by the Food and Drug Administration's "Chamber of Horrors" exhibition, which received particularly widespread attention when it was visited by Eleanor Roosevelt. This exhibition deserved a book in itself, and indeed one was published about it in 1936 — Ruth deForest Lamb's *American Chamber of Horrors.*

Among other things, the exhibition showed that existing law could not prevent lethal and useless nostrums from flourishing. "Radithor," to cite one, was truthfully labeled "Certified Radio-Active Water, Contains Radium and Mesothorium in Triple-Distilled Water." It was advertised as a source of pep and vitality, and as a cure for venereal diseases. Because it was neither adulterated nor misbranded, FDA could take no action against it.

Nor did the 1906 legislation prevent use of an eyelash cosmetic that caused blindness, or of thallium, which is now recognized as too hazardous even for consumer use as rat poison, as a depilatory.

The critical breakthrough came in 1937, when the S. E. Massengill Company, of Bristol, Tennessee, marketed an "Elixir of Sulfanilamide" to meet a market demand for sulfanilamide in liquid form. The solvent was diethylene glycol, a chemical relative of permanent radiator antifreeze. FDA Commissioner George P. Larrick, who has several times testified before congressional committees about this episode, told the Senate Antitrust subcommittee in 1960, "Animal testing would have exposed the danger from this poisonous Elixir. But the manufacturer did not test his liquid." Instead, the company checked it for appearance, flavor, and fragrance. Of the 240 gallons manufactured, 11¾ were dispensed across drug counters and by prescription.

In October 1937, FDA received the first reports of deaths. Seizures were begun at once. All but the 11¾ gallons were confiscated. The seizures were possible only because the drug was misbranded — it was called an "Elixir," which wrongly implied that it contained alcohol. Had the stuff been called a "solution" instead, FDA could not have sustained its case through the courts.

When it was all over, 108 persons were dead, including the pharmaceutical chemist who had developed the product. Unlike the others, his death was a suicide. It took a catastrophe and thirty-two years to bring about the first major overhaul of the 1906 law.

✝ ✝ ✝

As a direct result of the Elixir tragedy the Federal Food, Drug, and Cosmetic Act of 1938 contained, among many other important advances, a section under which a manufacturer had to test any new drug for safety and report the results to the Food and Drug Administration. Unless FDA acted within 60 to 180 days to prevent marketing, the drug automatically could be placed on sale. FDA was empowered through hearing procedures to delay release even longer if, for example, it found that the manufacturer's tests did not show the drug to be safe under the recommended conditions. The agency also was authorized to remove from the market a drug it could prove to be unsafe.

Note that these provisions, which were to be applied solely to *new* drugs to be sold in interstate commerce, did not require a producer to show that his product was *effective* as well as safe for its intended use. In killing the efficacy requirement proposed in the original 1933 bill, Congress was, some contend, recognizing the economic, lobbying, and political — not the medical — facts of life.

The 1938 law went far to curb the excesses in the patent-medicines business. The huge "false and fraudulent" loophole created in 1912 by the Sherley amendment was closed. A drug could be deemed misbranded if its labeling was false or misleading. Separate legislation gave the Federal Trade Commission

clear powers to regulate patent-medicine advertising, but made
its control over prescription-drug advertising restricted and ambiguous. In 1958 a House Subcommittee on Legal and Monetary
Affairs charged that the FTC had "completely ignored" its responsibilities in regulating advertising of prescription drugs. The
pharmaceutical lobby had not wanted authority vested in FDA,
where, of course, it properly belonged.

During the entire era discussed above the chief problem concerned nonprescription products. These had been the greatest
menace. Generally, the properties of prescription products were
well understood by physicians, and in an average year a mere
handful of new ones were marketed. Furthermore, a high standard was observed by such firms as Eli Lilly, Merck, and Squibb.
The end of World War II brought the "drug revolution." New
prescription medicines, some of hitherto unimagined chemical
formations and with utterly unknown effects, came to be marketed at the rate of 300 to 400 a year. For the first time —
and this is the key point — the problem of efficacy in drugs, of
assuring that they were not worthless for the purposes for which
they were promoted, shifted heavily to the so-called ethical
products.

✶   ✶   ✶

"How in the world," Dr. Lawson Wilkins asked his fellow
pediatricians, "can any physician be expected to keep up with
the new pharmacy?" The answer of Dr. Dale G. Friend, of the
Harvard Medical School and Peter Bent Brigham Hospital, is
that he cannot. Writing in *Clinical Pharmacology and Therapeutics* for January–February 1963, Dr. Friend said that it is
"utterly impossible for the practicing physician to have enough
information to select the drugs he uses in the treatment of his
patients wisely." Dr. Friend, who advocated a national prescription formulary, continued: "It is obvious that among the
nearly 8,000 preparations now available, there are many agents

that are unwanted, useless, undesirable, of limited value, or actually harmful. This huge number of preparations has served to increase the cost of medical care and the cost of drugs and has placed a severe burden on the physician and the pharmacist." About 90 per cent of the drugs in current use have been marketed since 1950. They include powerful new chemical agents that have a potential to do more good and — if improperly used — more harm than earlier preparations.

Between 1938 and 1960 an average of 375 new drug products a year cleared FDA. Only a handful in each year have been really new drugs — the unique agents, the chemical entities, that are reviewed by the Council on Drugs of the American Medical Association.

The reader will recall President Kennedy's statement in 1962 that more than 20 per cent of the new entities listed since 1956 in the Council's *New and Nonofficial Drugs* had been found "incapable of sustaining one or more of their sponsor's claims." In other words, at least one out of five was not shown by substantial evidence to be effective in treating the diseases and conditions for which it was recommended. It could hardly be said that the late Chief Executive's message brought a speedy improvement in this regard. The 1963 edition of *New and Nonofficial Drugs* listed 26 new chemical entities. The acting secretary of the Council, John Lewis, wrote in the AMA *Journal*, that 22 — all but 4 — necessitated inclusion of "some statement to the effect that the Council [on Drugs] considered the data inadequate or insufficient in one way or another."

Between 1938 and 1962 pharmaceutical manufacturers filed 13,623 new-drug applications, of which FDA's Bureau of Medicine cleared 9097. One should not be misled by that large figure. It includes multiple brands of identical products. It also includes various dosage forms. Most important, it includes a large but undetermined proportion of products containing one or more of the agents that the Council had challenged — in those drug combinations that are nothing more than "shotgun therapy," and in those delayed- or sustained-action products that have been shown to be unreliable. Although the Council has decried the trend toward drug combinations as "irrational," most of the drugs physicians prescribe are combinations.

These things help to explain why Dr. Friend declared that physicians cannot keep abreast of the proliferation of drug products. But they also must contend with the presence of additional prescription products for which FDA chose not to require new-drug applications, and with hundreds of additional products consisting of or containing certifiable antibiotics. The certifiable antibiotic preparations, for which the law required evidence of potency, which logically cannot be divorced from efficacy, were handled separately, by FDA's Division of Antibiotics.

It is possible to talk in stark terms about the magnitude of the efficacy problem. In 1963 about 800 million prescriptions were written, for which the consumers paid an estimated $2.2 billion. A substantial proportion was for products containing one or more of the agents that the AMA's Council on Drugs found did not live up to at least one of the sponsor's claims.

AFTERWORD TO CHAPTER 2

In October 1965 the Food and Drug Administration approved for sale a prescription product and an accompanying prescribing brochure that included three pages on why and how the drug should be used and nine on why it should not. "The average physician would find it difficult to administer this product with any degree of assurance," Professor Anthony T. Buatti of St. John's University College of Pharmacy said two months later at the annual Food and Drug Administration-Food Law Institute Conference in Washington. "Unless some important overlying health objective is to be served," Buatti went on to say, pharmaceutical products requiring so much data on cautions, precautions, side effects, and warnings "perhaps ought not to be marketed." This gets to the point made in Chapter 2 by Dr. Dale G. Friend of Harvard Medical School, that it is "utterly impossible for the practicing physician to have enough information to select the drugs he uses in the treatment of his patients wisely." Yet in the reign of Commissioner James L. Goddard, as in that of his predecessor, FDA has approved drugs — some of doubtful value at best — with prescribing instructions of great length and complexity, and studded with ifs, ands, buts, and other qualifiers until — as the late A. J. Liebling might have said — backward reels the mind. If such labeling — sometimes in very small type — was actually *read* and, to the extent possible, *understood* and *remembered*, the products for which it was written might be so seldom prescribed as to make marketing of them uneconomic. But because such products are profitably produced and commonly prescribed one can conclude only that the labeling is widely unread or insufficiently heeded by practitioners. There are many reasons for this. Over the broad range they doubtless include overwork and laziness, ignorance and arrogance; surely they include in the average practitioner, whose training is twenty years old, a scientific background that has been said by Dr. Joseph R. DiPalma, of Hahnemann Medical College and Hospital, to be "completely inadequate" for coping with a torrent of new chemical therapeutic agents. With all of this, however, there remains the omnipresent detailman, the drug-company salesman whose person-to-person contact with physicians so often overcomes such prescribing inhibitions as may be present. He may give the physician advice which flatly contradicts the printed labeling; he is more likely to fudge it. In any event the detailman poses a most difficult regulatory problem; he enjoys, as do we all, the right of free speech. It is with these thoughts in mind that the following specific cases are offered. They involve Clomid, the first antisterility drug to win marketing approval; the long-acting sulfonamide products, and Serc, whose effectiveness against vertigo may approximate that of a placebo.

CLOMID

On the night of February 1, 1967, Mrs. Lionel A. Harris, a 31-year-old Brooklyn, New York, woman, gave birth to quintuplets. She had been unable to bear a child but conceived the quints five months after starting to take Clomid (clomiphene citrate), an antisterility drug which had been in experimental status but which by coincidence won marketing approval from the Food and Drug Administration on the day her children were born. One of the quintuplets was stillborn and a second died when 5½ days old; but the survivors were reported at the time to be in good condition. Ten days after the birth of the Harris infants, quintuplets were born three months prematurely to Mrs. Allen Bradley, of Big Piney, Wyoming, who also had taken an experimental antisterility drug — which one, her doctors refused to say. Three of the quints lived a matter of seconds and one for four hours. The fifth, a 1½-pound girl, died 29 hours after birth. These two cases of drug-induced multiple birth were among those that were on the mind of Representative L. H. Fountain, chairman of the House Intergovernmental Relations Subcommittee, when on February 14, 1967, he wrote FDA Commissioner James L. Goddard to express concern about whether the benefits of antisterility drugs outweighed the risks. He also raised a question that was more relevant in the context of this Afterword — whether the officially approved labeling or prescribing instructions for Clomid made the benefit/risk ratio — whatever that ratio was assumed to be — clear to physicians. This can be seen to have a special importance because of the understandable inclination of married couples who want but have been unable to have children to come to their doctors with a feeling of despair that sometimes is accompanied by a predisposition to gamble.

The labeling for Clomid tells the doctor that it "has been demonstrated to be a useful new therapy." Clinical trials were conducted with 2616 women. At an early point in the labeling there is a statement that "successful therapy characterized by pregnancy" occurred in 548 cases; subsequently, a figure of 672 is cited and relied upon thereafter. It may be that such an apparent discrepancy is readily explainable, but the point I am making is precisely that a lack of clarity of which this is symptomatic breeds confusion and danger.

Of the 672 completed pregnancies, 457 had "a favorable outcome," meaning that an infant survived. This disclosure is on page 4 of a small, 24-page booklet; 14 pages later there is a related disclosure, that 12 of the infants resulting from the 672 pregnancies had birth defects. How many of the 12 survived is not revealed. (It may be argued that physicians are provided with 18 references to articles in the medical literature, but to assume that the articles will routinely be looked up and studied is to assume too much.) What the prognosis seemed to come down to was that a sterile woman who takes Clomid has a 21 per cent chance of becoming pregnant; if she does become pregnant she has a 68 per cent chance of having a living child, and a 1.8 per cent chance of having a defective child. As noted, the physician is not told in the labeling how many of the 12 defective infants survived. It is, however, made explicit that the defects are serious. Two of the 12 infants had deformed hearts, two had undescended testes, two had abnormally small heads, and one had an abnormal channeling of blood between an artery and a vein. In addition, the labeling reported additional birth defects in the 12 children including blindness, heart disease, excess fingers or toes, harelip, cleft palate, and sunken chest. Three of the 12 infants were conceived four to ten months after the mothers had stopped taking the drug. The brochure says that "no causative evidence of a deleterious effect . . . on the human fetus has been seen." Whether this statement is optimistic remains to be revealed by longer and wider experience with the drug and may possibly depend upon how "causative evidence" is defined. In any case, one might expect a juxtaposition of the statement and the listing of birth defects — but they were eight pages apart. The statement was followed instead by a disclosure that causative evidence of a deleterious effect on the fetus of the rat and rabbit "has been presented." Because of this, Clomid "should not be administered in pregnancy."

Precautions are advised to prevent inadvertent ingestion of the drug by a pregnant woman. In her home the patient must take her so-called basal body temperature, which can indicate whether she has ovulated. How she would be protected against the risk of inadvertent use in the event of conception on the first day of ovulation, is not made clear. In addition, the basal body temperature must be taken by the patient throughout all the cycles of her treatment — every day, at the same time of day, and before arising, drinking, eating, or smoking. Then she must record it on a graphic chart. The sufficiency of this temperature-taking safeguard is implicitly questioned in the labeling itself. There it is reported that of the 672 women who completed their pregnancies 42 — 6 per cent — "inadvertently received [clomiphene citrate] during early pregnancy." Among the 12 deformed infants was one whose mother had inadvertently received Clomid in early pregnancy.

The incidence of multiple pregnancy, including triplets and quadruplets, is increased by Clomid, the labeling says, "up to tenfold." Patients and their husbands are to be advised of this and of its potential hazards "if conception occurs during a cycle in which Clomid is given." Is the doctor to understand from this muddy instruction that he is to advise about the risks before starting to give Clomid, or after the patient is pregnant? "From 50 multiple pregnancies, 72 infants survived, including 1 set of triplets," the labeling says. But it does *not* say how many infants were born in the multiple pregnancies, or how many died.

The first page of text in the brochure points out that Clomid is chemically related to MER/29 (triparanol), a cholesterol inhibitor to which Chapter 11 is devoted. This drug, which was removed from the market in 1962, raised the levels in the blood of another steroid, desmosterol, and was associated with a so-called classical triad of injuries — cataracts, hair loss, and severe skin reactions. The manufacturer of Clomid and MER/29, the William S. Merrell Company, a division of Richardson-Merrell, Inc., says in the labeling for the antisterility compound that patients "should be advised that blurring or other visual symptoms may occasionally occur," although their significance "is not yet understood." The symptoms are said to be temporary but "may render such activities as driving a car . . . more hazardous than usual . . ." After being severely diminished the eyesight of one patient "returned to normal on the third day after treatment was stopped." In a few patients "moderate, reversible hair loss has been reported." Turning to animal studies, the labeling says that in 53-week trials 4 of 29 rats developed cataracts. They had been given large doses of Clomid; cataracts did not develop in rats given smaller amounts. A "dot-like opacity" occurred in the eye of a dog on Clomid. Rabbits in other 53-week trials experienced thinning of fur, "with incidence related to dose and duration of therapy." Malformed offspring were in one of five litters born to rats heavily dosed with Clomid. In rabbits, deformed fetuses were seen following ingestion of large amounts of the drug by the mother.

I do not pretend to know precisely how much weight should be given to such findings. I contend simply, as I did at the conclusion of the Preface to *The Therapeutic Nightmare*, that "we have a right to demand . . . that the ratio of benefits to risks be calculated intelligently, in full knowledge of the facts." This objective was not diligently pursued in the labeling approved for Clomid by the FDA.

LONG-ACTING SULFONAMIDES

Sulfonamide drugs, which arrest or hinder the growth of bacteria, are among those preferred for the treatment of acute infections of the urinary tract. In most other infections the drug of choice is one or another of the antimicrobial agents that kill bacteria, such as the penicillins. The original sulfonamides were short-acting, that is, required multiple doses — sometimes as few as two, however — each day. Especially in the case of children, administration of the drugs was often inconvenient, especially when a child resisted swallowing them. In 1957 there came one of those solutions that, in retrospect, recall an admonition of the ancient Hippocrates in *On Wounds of the Head, 1:* "For they praise what seems outlandish before they know whether it is good, rather than the customary which they already know to be good; the bizarre rather than the obvious." The solution was, or seemed to be, the long-acting sulfonamides. Within about eight years an estimated 605 million doses had been administered in the United States alone. The long-actings had the advantage of convenience — a once-a-day dose. Ultimately, the view came to be held in the scientific community that convenience was the *only* advantage, because of a preponderance of evidence that there were no medical conditions in which the long-actings were any more or any less effective than the short-actings.

Although the short-actings are metabolized and excreted with reasonable speed, the long-actings linger for from five to seven days before bodily processes get fully rid of them. That this characteristic of the long-actings should harbor a potential for trouble may not surprise those who are wary of the proposition that one can get something for nothing. After a time it became apparent that users of the long-acting sulfonamides were being stricken far more frequently than users of the short-actings with Stevens-Johnson Syndrome. This is characterized by fever, by large blisters of the skin and mucous membranes (including ulceration), and by damage to internal organs. The Syndrome lowers a patient's resistance, permitting sometimes fatal infections to gain a foothold.

In Poland the long-actings were taken off the market. In Britain they were omitted from the National Formulary, an official drug guide for doctors. In the United States their use was abandoned in numerous hospitals and by many physicians. There was also concern, although neither the medical nor the lay public knew anything about it, in the Food and Drug Administration. In December 1964 Lederle Laboratories, a division of American Cyanamid Company, and the principal producer of long-acting sulfonamides, submitted a proposed new prescribing brochure containing a boxed warning on Stevens-Johnson Syndrome. Clearly this was done to head off harsher action — removal of Kynex from the market; such removal would have had consequences for Hoffmann-La Roche's Madribon and Parke, Davis' Midicel. At the time, there was also pending in the agency a removal from the market of its Kynex and similar or identical products (Hoffmann-La Roche's Madribon and Parke, Davis' Midicel). At the time, there was also pending in the agency a proposed Kynex brochure which had been submitted earlier by Lederle and which lacked the boxed warning about the Syndrome. Even the producer, obviously, had given up on this one — but that was the one that the agency approved in January 1965. Another of those bizarre, ghoulish foul-ups that seemed to proliferate in George Larrick's FDA (but on which it certainly had no monopoly among government agencies).

While the companies were profiting from a reprieve that must have seemed all but inexplicable even to them, FDA's drug surveillance unit in the Bureau of Medicine undertook a survey of the world's medical literature. Reports were found on 27 fatal and 63 nonfatal cases of Stevens-Johnson Syndrome associated with the use of long-acting sulfonamides. The actual incidence, of course, was much higher, not only because of the customary gross under-reporting of drug reactions, but because cases inevitably had occurred in countries where adverse reaction reporting is nonexistent. Five months later, in August 1965, the survey was updated. The reported deaths included 16 in the United States and 13 elsewhere; serious injuries numbered 65 in this country and 22 elsewhere. The American figures — 16 deaths, 65 injuries — occurred, it will be recalled, with an estimated 605 million doses. FDA learned of no deaths and of only four cases of Stevens-Johnson Syndrome associated with 683 million doses of the short-acting drugs. Of the 29 deaths of users of the long-actings that were reported world-wide 16 were in children, who are highly susceptible to the Syndrome. The convenience of the long-actings, FDA was told by Dr. Harry C. Shirkey, chairman of the Committee on Drug Dosage of the American Academy of Pediatrics, "does not outweigh the morbidity or mortality that is found in a small percentage of children . . ." In the Bureau of Medicine there were physicians who could see no medical or scientific justification for permitting continued sale of the long-acting products, especially for use in children. They expected that any effort to end marketing would arouse the wrath of influential and powerful manufacturers. The discouraging thing, however, was that the Medical Director of the FDA, Dr. Joseph F. Sadusk, Jr., had shown a persistent disposition to avert actions that could seriously offend companies in the industry. And so the battle came to be waged not over a hopeless cause — ending sale — but over whether a strong or a weak warning would go out to physicians. Even the battle for a strong warning might have been a hopeless cause had it not been reported by the Washington *Post.*

The strategy elected by a group of FDA medical officers was to agree to reinstate the boxed warning that in December 1964 had been proposed by Lederle itself — only to be lost in the agency's paper-shuffling. But they also wanted to incorporate a supplemental statement that long-acting sulfonamides are indicated for use only when the short-actings are ineffective.

On August 30, 1965, Dr. Sadusk acknowledged in writing that "the long-acting sulfonamides are *identical* to the shorter-acting sulfonamides in their effectiveness," that their "*only advantage*" is the "convenience of less frequent administration," and that their "significant disadvantage" is a greater tendency to cause serious and often fatal effects. (My italics.) Assistant (and acting) Commissioner Winton B. Rankin then asked Dr. Sadusk to inquire of FDA's Medical Advisory Board, a group of outside consultants whose chairman was Dr. Sadusk, "whether there are urgent medical reasons for having the long-acting sulfonamides available to practicing physicians . . ." Neither from FDA nor from members of the Board was I able to learn what such "urgent medical reasons" might be. On September 7, in one of those actions that raise troubling questions about the utility of such bodies in government, the Board struck out the supplemental language recommended by FDA staff members. The Board, in other words, conceived its obligation to the public to be approving a warning that a party at interest, Lederle, had itself proposed nine months earlier. Winton Rankin, however, agreed with the staff that the public deserved something more. On October 25, 1965, he proposed adding this sentence: "Since the short-acting sulfonamides are effective for the same conditions, their use should be ruled out before the long-acting sulfonamides are employed." This, of course, was consistent with what Dr. Sadusk had said on August 30 were the facts; it was inconsistent only with the final policy decision later rendered by the Agency and with the "medical reasons" that were at once "urgent" and invisible.

Visible but underestimated was a trump card in the hands of Lederle. This was an obscure claim that had been added to the Kynex brochure which had won FDA's accidental approval in January. The claim was that Kynex was effective in leprosy and trachoma. In the United States these diseases are so rare that in 1964, according to the Public Health Service, only 1836 persons were newly afflicted by them. This claim, which was based on some research done somewhere in Asia, was an awfully weak reed, but in the hands of the manufacturers it seemed to be a big stick. On December 21 Winton Rankin, who would later become Deputy Commissioner under Dr. James L. Goddard, backed away from the tough language he had proposed two months earlier. In a letter to Parke, Davis, Hoffmann-La Roche, and Lederle, he proposed a warning which would say the short-actings were effective not in the "same conditions" as the long-actings, but in "most of the same conditions." The exceptions were not specified; they were, of course, leprosy and trachoma —

diseases that most American physicians would not see in a century of practice. In October Rankin had said the short-actings "should be ruled out" before resort to the long-actings; now he substituted the weak word "considered." Formally, the responsibility for these dilutions fall on Rankin; realistically it might well be shared by Dr. Sadusk, who unlike Rankin was a physician, and by the Medical Advisory Board of which he was Chairman.

Adoption of the vague, watered-down warning was announced by FDA on January 11, 1966. In addition to its intrinsic faults the warning may well have been illegal. The law says that marketing of a drug shall be halted by the Secretary of Health, Education, and Welfare if he finds a "lack of substantial evidence that the drug will have the effect it purports . . . to have under the conditions of use . . . suggested in the labeling . . ." No evidence — not even from somewhere in Asia — had been submitted to show that Madribon or Midicel was effective in leprosy or trachoma. The defense that the three products were chemically identical was unavailable. Kynex is sulfamethoxypyridazine, which is not the same thing as sulfadimethoxine (Madribon). Kynex and Midicel are chemically identical, but again there was no defense — under the law as FDA had regularly interpreted it a claim that a product is effective in a hitherto unlisted condition must be backed by substantial evidence, even if the same claim has been approved for a different brand of the same formulation. The effect of the substitution of the phrase "most of the same conditions" for "the same conditions" of use was to synthesize a claim that there is a difference between Madribon (and Midicel) and the short-acting sulfonamides in the treatment of leprosy and trachoma. No legally qualified evidence was submitted to back up that claim.

Such was the mess that Dr. Goddard inherited when he took office six days after the warning went out. He acted with dispatch to straighten it out. On March 2, 1966, the new Commissioner announced that the three manufacturers had been told to change their prescribing instructions to say that "since the short-acting sulfonamides are effective for the *same* conditions, their use should be *ruled out* before the long-acting sulfonamides are employed." (My italics.) Lederle was allowed an exception only for trachoma. Finally, Dr. Goddard directed Hoffmann-La Roche to stop selling Madricidin, a combination product containing Madribon and claimed by its maker to offer "palliative treatment of the common cold." There is "a lack of substantial evidence that Madricidin is effective for the conditions for which it is recommended," the Commissioner said; nor has it been "shown to be safe . . ."

Not long after this Dr. Sadusk resigned from the agency. He was no longer *the* physician in the house. He went on to Baltimore, where he became an associate dean and professor of medicine at the Johns Hopkins School of Medicine. Less than a year later, in March 1967, he was named vice president for medical affairs of Parke, Davis.

SERC

Serc (betahistine chloride) is a histamine-like product that was written up as far back as 1948 in medical literature. It aroused little interest. Eighteen years later it reached the market. The labeling approved by the Food and Drug Administration made one wonder why a physician who read it would want to prescribe the product. The explanation may lie in, among other places, the medical section of *Time* magazine, which, unlike FDA and the authoritative *Medical Letter*, indicated that Serc was just great.

There is a cluster of symptoms known as Menière's Syndrome. A principal one is vertigo — severe dizziness. Another is tinnitus — a ringing in the ear. Others are nausea, vomiting, and headache. In the *Journal* of the American Medical Association for April 11, 1966, Dr. Joseph P. Elia of the Washoe Medical Center, St. Mary's Hospital, Reno, Nevada, said that Serc controlled these symptoms and made surgery unnecessary. He based this claim on a study that, he said, had been "double-blind," that is, one in which neither doctor nor patient knew which was the drug and which was the fake pill or placebo until a code was broken at the end of the experiment.

This report led some bells to be rung in the ear of FDA, which had long had before it a marketing application for Serc. The manufacturer, Unimed, Inc., of Morristown, New Jersey, was understandably anxious to put the drug on sale. In the year ended September 30, 1966, Unimed grossed only about $180,000. The approval of Serc, which the agency granted late in 1966, changed the outlook drastically. Unimed forecast revenues in calendar 1967 of four million dollars, but forecast also that the annual sales rate would exceed seven million dollars by the end of 1967. Within a few weeks after Serc was approved for sale, Unimed stock on the over-the-counter market went up from about 15 to about 37 — and even the higher figure was more than doubled by May 1967. Doubtless some credit for this success story is owed to *Time*, which on December 16, 1966 — shortly after Serc had won FDA clearance — said in its best authoritative-promotional style that the drug already had been administered to "14,000 patients under the care of almost 300 physicians." And, *Time* said, "excellent results" had been reported by Dr. Elia in a "careful double-blind study."

The name of the Reno physician got into *Time* but not into the FDA-approved prescribing brochure — an omission that if deliberate is so unusual as to induce vertigo. Nor did the brochure proclaim "excellent results." It did say — with emphasis in the original:

There is some evidence suggesting that SERC may reduce the frequency of episodes of vertigo associated with Menière's syndrome in some patients. Clinical studies designed to evaluate the efficacy of SERC have been concerned only with a small portion of the clinical spectrum of Menière's syndrome. Such a subgroup of patients have been characterized by a high frequency of vertiginous episodes ranging from once a day to once per two weeks. An inference of efficacy with respect to the larger population of Menière's syndrome which is characterized by *occasional episodes of vertigo* cannot be made.

No inference can be made . . . that SERC has any role in the prophylaxis and/or treatment of tinnitus . . . it has not been demonstrated that . . . SERC influences the future course of a given patient with respect to the subsequent need for surgical procedures directed at ameliorating incapacitating vertigo.

On April 21, 1967, the *Medical Letter* pointed out that the law requires a manufacturer to demonstrate the efficacy of a drug with "substantial evidence" — "adequate and well-controlled investigations" performed by specialists qualified in their particular fields. But, said the nonprofit publication, which evaluates drugs for more than 30,000 physician-subscribers, in the case of Serc there had been "no well-controlled trials which will permit the conclusion" that the drug is effective in preventing or treating "any" of the symptoms in the Syndrome. The suggestion, in short, was that the release of the drug violated the law. The study characterized by Dr. Elia and *Time* as "double-blind," the *Medical Letter* continued, used controls that "were seriously inadequate"; in addition, "similar code designations were used for all drug samples, with different code designations for all placebo samples." Dr. Elia had used "almost identical procedures" — of which the *Medical Letter* thought poorly — in finding another drug "to be highly effective against the symptoms of Menière's Syndrome." The publication identified the drug as Tigacol, a Hoffmann-La Roche, Inc., product combining trimethobenzamide with nicotinyl alcohol. Dr. Elia's boost for Tigacol was published in 1965 by *Medical Times*. His published clinical evidence on the effectiveness of Serc consisted of the article in the AMA *Journal*, another, in 1965, in *Angiology*, and what *Medical Letter* dismissed as "uncontrolled observations." Even before the *Medical Letter* article appeared a preliminary investigation into FDA's handling of the Serc matter had been begun by the House Intergovernmental Relations Subcommittee.

3

DRUG SUCCESS = NEWS;
DRUG FAILURE = NON-NEWS

PERHAPS IT WAS inevitable that the Food and Drug Administration remained police-minded and inspector-dominated. Only after long struggle had it got some of the tools it needed to cope with the inexhaustible supply of fly-by-nights, adulterators, charlatans, frauds, and quacks. Food plants had to be inspected. Contaminated products had to be seized. Standards of purity had to be maintained. The prescription-drug revolution radically changed the situation, creating a whole new set of problems while the old ones persisted.

What FDA had to do now was to make sure that the powerful new drugs with which it was being deluged were safe and efficacious. This called for a vastly expanded and more important role for science and scientists, and an end to the dominance of inspectors. FDA was required, in short, to meet the demands of a radically new era of pharmaceutical science with equally radical shifts in conceiving its responsibilities to the public welfare, in the allocation of its resources, in its organization, and in its very psychology. How grossly FDA failed to meet this challenge will be brought out as we proceed. For the moment it is sufficient to say that instead of becoming, as it should have, a scientific agency of high caliber — such as the National Institutes of Health — FDA became a scientific backwater, a prisoner, in a sense, of a glorious past that had become somewhat irrelevant.

On the record, to be sure, FDA recognized that, however unclear the foundation was in law, considerations of safety and efficacy could not be separated in its evaluation of drugs for life-threatening diseases. "It is clear that the use of an ineffective drug for the treatment of a serious disease is not a safe practice," Deputy Commissioner John L. Harvey has said. "Many infectious diseases are progressive and life-threatening. To hold off treatment by the use of an ineffective remedy is clearly unsafe. The usefulness and effectiveness of a drug under such conditions is clearly relevant and material to the safety of its use."

In 1960 a forceful statement of FDA's position was made by Julius Hauser, assistant to the medical director. He said FDA would not concede the safety of a drug intended for use in a life-threatening condition

> until its efficacy has been demonstrated; this is particularly true when other reliable treatments are known . . .
>
> Secondly, there are very few drugs which are not capable of producing some harmful effects. In such cases, FDA will not conclude that the drug is safe until there is adequate evidence to show that its usefulness outweighs its hazards. When the evidence establishes that the potential hazards of the drug are extremely small in comparison to the number of lives saved or prolonged in serious diseases, the drug is regarded as safe.

In actual practice this standard was all too infrequently observed by FDA; and to the extent that it was respected, much of the credit was owed to scrupulous manufacturers and plain luck. Nevertheless, there were lapses. A case in point involves Altafur (furaltadone), which was offered for use against infection in adults, children, and infants. Dr. Louis Lasagna, of the Departments of Medicine, Pharmacology, and Experimental Therapeutics of the School of Medicine at the Johns Hopkins University, has seen in furaltadone a clear example of the danger of an ineffective drug. If first used in patients with severe staphylococcal infections it "might well lead to mortality, whereas if such patients received more effective treatment first, they might be saved," he told the Kefauver Senate Subcommittee on Antitrust and Monopoly.

The new-drug application was filed by Eaton Laboratories, a division of the Norwich Pharmacal Company. FDA released Altafur for sale in July 1959. Only seventeen months later, in December 1960, FDA found it unsafe and tried to halt marketing; but marketing continued while the action was appealed. Reportedly, the manufacturer filed the appeal to test FDA's contention that it could invoke efficacy as relevant to Altafur's safety. The appeal brought a protracted, secret, and unprecedented hearing conducted by an independent hearing examiner, Edward E. Turkel, of the Social Security Administration. In November 1961 he ordered Altafur off the market.

Turkel's decision was remarkable in several respects. Perhaps most importantly, he held that, the ambiguity of the law notwithstanding, therapeutic efficacy is "material and relevant" in ascertaining safety. More, he found that a drug "must be sufficiently reliable in curing or treating patients"; to have cured or helped "some" patients "is not enough." Altafur, Turkel found, had an awesome apparent incidence of side effects — about 33 per cent. This rate was much higher than that occurring with other antibacterial drugs available for the purposes for which Altafur was offered. The examiner continued: ". . . tests show that Altafur is not sufficiently efficacious in the treatment of infections to justify the risk of the serious toxic effects . . ." These effects, "generally not irreversible," included "paralysis of the nerves affecting vision, swallowing and speech," double vision, "serious blood disturbances," skin reactions ("one with possibly life-threatening severity"), and "particularly serious" sensitivity reactions. In one study, among 50 postoperative patients menaced by infection and treated with Altafur, 5 developed staphylococcol infections *while under treatment* with the drug. Yet, Turkel pointed out, Altafur had been represented as "especially effective against staphylococci."

Turkel had harsh words for FDA's handling of the new-drug application (NDA) in the first place. Although the agency had repeatedly insisted that it recognized efficacy as inseparable from safety, he said: "Most of the reports in the NDA fail to show adequate clinical research data to evaluate the efficacy and safety of use of Altafur, particularly in the light of additional investigations to determine such matters after the NDA became effective."

Again, there had not been sufficient evidence even of *safety*. Despite this finding, the examiner's report apparently had little effect on FDA's bureaucratic inertia. In March 1963 an FDA medical officer testified about the Altafur case before the Humphrey Senate Subcommittee on Reorganization and International Organizations. Turkel's findings, Dr. John O. Nestor disclosed, had not succeeded in bringing about "an internal appraisal to determine how this drug was allowed to clear the FDA new-drug procedure."

↑ ↑ ↑

The advent of the wonder drugs, some of which truly were fantastically effective against a broad range of human afflictions, radically changed the role of the lay press in the scheme of things. In an earlier era it was a common thing for a newspaper to be corrupted and silenced by what Harvey Wiley had called the "blood money coming in from patent medicine advertisements." The 1938 Federal Food, Drug, and Cosmetic Act imposed strong new controls on the nostrum business. This, and the maturing and general improvement of newspapers as well, reduced the old evils of nostrum advertising to relatively minor proportions.

Now came the rush of wonder drugs. These were ethical preparations — drugs that physicians prescribe, not products for self-medication. They were not — could not be — advertised to laymen in newspapers, magazines, television, and such media. Instead, they were advertised in the journals and other publications intended for physicians. In this radically changed situation, the public hungered for news of wonder drugs that promised to save lives, curb disease, and ease pain; and the press tried to provide such news in fulfillment of its responsibilities. This is not to suggest that all news reports on the wonder drugs were written in a spirit of wide-eyed innocence, but rather to say that a conscientious effort to inform the public prevailed in responsible publications.

In the new atmosphere certain elements of the drug industry saw something quite different: an opportunity to get — free — precious publicity that could not be bought, news space devoid of the stigma of doubt drug advertising might carry. For some in the industry the temptation to exploit this opportunity, sometimes viciously, by withholding from reporters literally vital facts, by distorting, and even by lying, was irresistible.

"The desire to take medicine is perhaps the greatest feature that distinguishes man from animals," Sir William Osler once said. This was hyperbole, of course; but the irresponsible planting of drug stories converted the desire to take medicine in the sick, the suffering, and others in the lay public into something like a positive lust. The patient aroused by a drug news story he had read or heard on radio or television could not get the new medicine merely by asking for it at the corner drugstore. He had to have a physician's prescription. And so physicians found themselves under enormous pressure from medically ignorant patients — not that this was a surprise to drug manufacturers and their advertising and publicity agencies.

The planting of "what appear to be news items" was termed "insidious" by Dr. Walter Modell at the 1962 convention of the American Association for the Advancement of Science. He condemned the "salted items" that ". . . lead the patient to bring the existence of the new drug to the attention of the physician before very much is known about it, and to press him to use it instead of other therapy he may have been contemplating . . . the physician is urged to abandon the therapy he knows well and to use therapy he has had little or no experience with."

There have been instances of market-building publicity even *before* FDA has acted on the new-drug application. One such case involved Norlestrin, a Parke, Davis oral contraceptive. Stories appeared in the New York *Herald Tribune* and papers in Detroit, the firm's headquarters city, on August 8 and 9, 1963, which was well before FDA approval was granted. "Parke, Davis has denied that it was the source of this report," Commissioner Larrick wrote to Senator Humphrey. Another case involved Merck's drug for rheumatoid arthritis, Decadron. (Other aspects of the Decadron case are discussed in the Afterword to Chapter 7.

Patients have been known to desert physicians who have refused to prescribe new drugs they demand, to go to other doctors who prescribed what they asked, and to die as the consequence. The Kefauver Senate Antitrust subcommittee was told, for example, of a woman with an acute common cold and also chronic asthma. Dr. Perrin Long, of the State University of New York College of Medicine, recalled what happened: "She imperiously demanded that she be given penicillin, which my friend refused to give her, because it is not a good idea to give asthmatics penicillin. The patient got very angry, dismissed the doctor, saying 'I'll get a doctor who will do what I say.' She did. He gave her an injection of penicillin, and in less than five minutes she died from an anaphylactoid reaction produced by the penicillin."

The desire for wonder drugs has often been inspired by stories in what Dr. Haskell J. Weinstein, a former acting medical director of J. B. Roerig & Company, a division of Chas. Pfizer & Co., Inc., called "the eminent medical journals such as *Reader's Digest, Time,* and the *Wall Street Journal.* Some of this is legitimate good reporting," the physician told the Senate Antitrust subcommittee. "However, much of what appears has in essence been placed by the public relations staffs of the pharmaceutical firms." The witness was among those who wondered aloud what effects announcements of new drugs in the *Wall Street Journal* and in the financial pages of other publications "may have on stock market quotations." The question answers itself.

The exploitation of the lay press by certain pharmaceutical houses — an exploitation of the public, really — was laid bare with quite shocking documentation by the Kefauver subcommittee. All of the media had been caught up — the great wire services, the daily newspapers, country weeklies, magazines, health columns, television, radio. What Senator Kefauver uncovered about this abuse of the press was in itself an important story; it was one of the most under-reported stories of 1962. Further developments are discussed in the afterwords of several chapters of this volume.

In 1952 the publisher of a drug industry weekly, *F-D-C Reports,* usually referred to as the Pink Sheet, was able to say that the industry had been enjoying a "sensationally favorable" press. A decade later such a claim would have been absurd, at least in regard to a few important newspapers such as the New York *Herald Tribune,* the New York *Post,* the Washington *Post,* and the Washington *Evening Star.* "It is encouraging to be able to record the interest now expressed in drug marketing problems by such conservative newspapers as the *Wall Street Journal,*" John Lear wrote in the *Saturday Review* for September 5, 1964. "But it may be asked where were the potent organs of the daily press when the drugmakers were pulling political and economic strings to try to prevent the facts from being exposed? When SR began reporting the worst abuses in drug marketing in 1959, only two newspapers were willing to assume responsibility for wider dissemination of *SR*'s independently obtained information. One of those two was the St. Louis *Post-Dispatch*; the other was *Advertising Age*."

"My concern is that the record would show that 90 per cent of the stories we have written about new drugs have gone down the drain as failures," Arthur J. Snider, science editor of the Chicago *Daily News*, said in October 1963 at a national symposium on communications and medical research at the University of Pennsylvania. "We have either been deliberately led down the primrose path or have allowed ourselves through lack of sufficient information to be led down the primrose path. The remaining 10 per cent of the drug stories we've written have had to be subjected to re-evaluation."

As if this were not serious enough, there was also the statement of Alton L. Blakeslee, science writer of the Associated Press. Earlier in the same symposium, which was financed by Merck Sharp & Dohme, Smith Kline & French Laboratories, and Wyeth Laboratories, and sponsored by the university's School of Medicine and Annenberg School of Communications, Blakeslee said he hoped that someone would, one day, come up with "an ethics pill." He explained:

It is not exactly not needed. Recently, I was approached by a man who said he had an opportunity for me to place an article in a magazine on a free-lance basis. He described very frankly his own rather curious organization. He and his associates were representing a company which had developed a new product to treat a very common ailment. They guaranteed to find the medical researchers who would test it, and had done so. Further, they had a method of getting it published more quickly in a medical journal than might otherwise be done, so that it became "legitimate" news.

At this point he went to a magazine and suggested a story

on the general topic, and told the magazine editor that the company would place a large amount of advertising with them if the story were used. He also volunteered to find a science writer who would write the story, and this is what he was talking to me about. He said I would make my deal with the magazine editor, and perhaps be paid $1,500 or $2,000 for the article, and all I had to do was to mention this new product by trade name twice, and never mention any other product. The company, he said, knew that writers were never paid what they were worth, so the company would give me $5,000 on the side. Then if the article were picked up and reprinted by a certain outlet, I would get that reprint fee, and the company would be so delighted with the advertising achieved that way they would pay me $10,000 more.

This added up to $17,000 — as I mentally kept track of the arithmetic — but apparently something else showed because when he finished this explanation, he said, "Why are you looking at me like I just crawled out from under a rock?" And when I tried to explain to him, as gently and as easily as I could, why I didn't want to have any part in such a planted story I simply said that I'd like to be able to sleep at night. He had a curious answer. He said, "I wish I could."

It is herewith duly noted that in May 1958 the Pharmaceutical Manufacturers Association, the trade organization for the 140 companies that produced 90 per cent of the nation's prescription drugs, and most of which also produced nonprescription preparations, adopted this "Principle of Ethical Promotion":

The release to the lay public of information on the clinical [human] use of a new drug or on a new use of an established drug prior to adequate clinical acceptance and presentation to the medical profession is not in the best interests of the medical profession or the laymen.

On March 12, 1956, the Pink Sheet had said: "In recent years, virtually all important drugs have gone through a similar cycle — lavish praise by the medical profession on introduction, then after widespread use the publication of papers reporting side effects. *When the latter are not reported in the lay press* they don't usually have too much effect on the market position of a drug — unless the side effects are very serious." (My italics.)

The press has exhibited a tendency to regard drug successes, or *claimed* drug successes, as news, and drug failures as non-news. This has been a highly significant factor in the lack of public awareness that some of the highly touted prescription drugs laymen demand, and get, are ineffective and therefore dangerous.

The classic illustration of this kind of editorial myopia, which, fortunately, is on the decline, was provided by thalidomide. In November 1961, Australia became the first country to take this sedative off the market. It acted on the findings of a gynecologist, Dr. W. G. McBride, who had raised the first suspicions that thalidomide was linked to an outbreak of birth deformities in Australia. Later in the same month, the much larger outbreak of phocomelia in West Germany was linked to the drug by Dr. Widukind Lenz, a Hamburg pediatrician. The German manufacturer immediately withdrew the sedative, and the German Ministry of Health issued a warning to women of child-bearing age. "Immediately the issue became top news in European newspapers, magazines, radio and television," Arthur E. Rowse of the Washington *Post* wrote in *Nieman Reports* for December 1962. "But for some reason, American mass media did not pick it up." On February 22, 1962, the Canadian Department of Health and Welfare had reported the situation publicly. "This set off widespread reaction in the Canadian press," Rowse wrote.

But still no news of the international sensation reached the readers, viewers and listeners of American mass media except in *Time* magazine. The issue of February 23 carried an article entitled "Sleeping Pill Nightmare."

On March 30, the magazine made another reference to thalidomide and mentioned "a sharp-eyed woman doctor on the FDA staff" whom it did not name. Even *Time*, however, did not follow up its own lead on Dr. Kelsey's epic struggle.

It was crucially important to alert physicians with utmost authority and speed to the dangers of thalidomide. Every day counted, because the deforming effect occurred only within a very few days in early pregnancy. Dr. Helen B. Taussig, of the Johns Hopkins Hospital, undertook a one-woman crusade to do this after she had personally investigated the thalidomide disaster in Europe. Incredibly, she encountered serious resistance from the leading medical journal. This was indicated in a memorandum, prepared on June 14, 1962, by the FDA's Dr. Frances Kelsey. The memorandum, recounting a conference she had had that day with Dr. Taussig and an FDA colleague, Dr. John O. Nestor, has been published by the Senate Reorganization sub committee. It contains this paragraph:

> Dr. Taussig mentioned that since she wished authentic information concerning the hazard of this drug to reach the practicing physician as rapidly as possible, she submitted a letter to the AMA for publication shortly after her return from Europe in the late winter. She was told that *inasmuch as* Time Magazine *had already run an item on the drug, they would not be interested in publishing such a letter* [my italics]. They are however publishing an article but this inevitably entails a considerable delay. [The article was published in the *Journal* of the American Medical Association the following summer, on June 30, 1962.]

And so it went until July 15, 1962, when the Washington *Post* broke the story about how Dr. Kelsey's devotion to duty had kept thalidomide off the American market. In some organs of the lay press the impediment certainly had not been fear of or subservience to a major industry. In *Time,* as the medical editor, Gilbert Cant, said, the delay was occasioned by confusion caused by brand names and by news judgment. Other news organizations also have believable explanations. But one is struck by the frequency with which news that might adversely affect powerful business interests encounters indifference and lethargy. The doings of Elizabeth Taylor are routinely reported from London or Rome. The findings of Dr. Widukind Lenz were not routinely reported from Bonn. In Washington there is an army of reporters, and they cover obvious events in regiments and platoons. The reporter concerned with how a regulatory agency is meeting its responsibilities to consumers or concerned with the real issues in the Communications Satellite legislation need not be overly worried about competition. In writing about the problems of pesticides Rachel Carson, I venture, had no fear that she would be scooped.

The conclusion of the California State Department of Public Health that among those prescribed Chloromycetin, the antibiotic taken by 40 million persons in 11 years, the incidence of fatal aplastic anemia was at least 1 in 60,000, four times the rate previously acknowledged, was largely ignored outside California. Was this not news? Was not chloramphenicol prescribed in every other state and around the world?

In October 1962, on the floor of the Senate, Hubert Humphrey disclosed a hitherto confidential chronology on MER/29, the anticholesterol drug. The chronology contained a charge by FDA that in connection with the drug the manufacturer had submitted *fraudulent* test data. The disclosure was little noted.

In March 1964 the manufacturer, the William S. Merrell Company of Cincinnati and Richardson-Merrell, Inc., with which it had been merged, entered pleas of no contest to a total of 8 of 12 counts in a federal indictment. This unprecedented development drew minor attention in many newspapers. The New York *Times* carried an item buried on an inside page. *Time* carried a brief article that soft-pedaled the serious implications and neglected altogether the careless and inept role FDA had played in permitting sale of MER/29. Yet, even *Time*'s gentle coverage was so outstanding — comparatively — that it could draw a letter like this from a New York physician: "May I applaud, congratulate, and simultaneously breathe a sigh of relief. Of all the public media, including newspapers and TV as well as professional journals, your publication was the only one to date to carry a competent account of the atrocity story of our day . . ." The writer of the letter inadvertently may have exaggerated — *Time*'s account wasn't all that competent, and some newspapers, including those in Washington, did carry adequate accounts. But the fundamental point, that a major and significant story had been given inadequate attention, was correct.

✓ ✓ ✓

Surely, a layman might say, the medical journals have been keeping the medical profession fully and promptly informed: of the safety and efficacy of the drugs it prescribes; of the facts about how the Food and Drug Administration evaluates the drugs submitted to it; of the recall by FDA of more than two dozen drugs it had released as safe; of many other drugs implicated in fatalities and serious injuries; and of the grounds on which the federal agency so trusted by physicians decides whether to take a dangerous and ineffective drug off the market promptly or whether to let it linger with a warning letter, rather like a condemned but still-occupied slum. How rash such a sweeping presumption would be was strikingly indicated when the Humphrey subcommittee asked the National Library of Medicine, which subscribes to 2000 medical journals, to search its files for any detailed, thorough postmortem analysis of a drug disaster.

The Library found *none*. The autopsies have been left to a few reporters for a few lay publications.

Only four times in its memory, perhaps in a quarter-century, FDA informed Senator Humphrey in February 1964, has any medical organization — or any informal group of two or more doctors — bothered to ask FDA to re-evaluate the safety of a specific drug. The national health organizations also have shown a notable apathy in this area. For example, the American Heart Association was invited by the Humphrey subcommittee to comment on the MER/29 episode, which was one certainly in the purview of its interest because before the drug was taken off the market it had been prescribed for more than 400,000 persons with heart and related diseases. The Association's response was simply unresponsive.

A few years ago, an American physician, concealing his name to avoid embarrassment to his colleagues, wrote a highly critical article on our pharmaceutical industry in the *Lancet*. Why in an English journal?

Dr. William B. Bean, of the University of Iowa College of Medicine, told the Kefauver subcommittee that some American journals had "refused to publish articles criticizing particular drugs and methods of therapy, lest advertising suffer."

Although the *New England Journal of Medicine* was cited as a notable exception, physicians have told the Humphrey subcommittee of pressures on medical journals so great as to cost the jobs of editors who have incurred the wrath of the drug industry.

In 1958 Walter L. Griffith, director of product advertising and promotion for Parke, Davis & Co. in a speech to the American College of Apothecaries which was put into the record of the Kefauver hearings, estimated that the prescription-drug industry had turned out "3,790,908,000 pages of paid journal advertising."

Dr. Haskell Weinstein, who had been on the medical staff of Pfizer and of its Roerig division, told the Antitrust subcommittee that "a substantial number of the so-called medical scientific papers that are published on behalf of . . . drugs are written within the confines of the pharmaceutical houses concerned."

In an address of 1962 before a Connecticut State Congress on Medical Quackery, Irving Ladimer, of the National Better Business Bureau, denounced a number of medical journals that "regrettably become inadvertent co-promoters of quackery, when they permit their pages to be filled with questionable or spurious reports." The address, published in the *Food, Drug, Cosmetic Law Journal* for August 1963, also held that

> these journals, either because of interest in advertising, reprint sales or perhaps sheer incompetence or lack of time on the part of editors, allow such things as a paper comparing an alleged new over-the-counter item with a prescription drug, although no prescription drug was used in the tests; a paper signed by doctors who turned out to have no medical degree; a paper based on a test presumably prepared by the author but in fact done by another; a paper with references to a product claimed to be the same as that under study but in fact different; and numerous papers without identification of samples, method of selecting subjects and, of course, conclusions based on statistics not given or improperly computed.
>
> I must conclude here that although not all journals are lax in screening, there are enough cases to warrant much closer scrutiny.

That the journals receive close scrutiny in the executive suites of industry is apparent. In March 1959 *Northwest Medicine*, the official organ of the medical societies of Washington, Oregon, Idaho, and Alaska, attacked John Lear of the *Saturday Review* for questioning the propriety of Henry Welch's editing two antibiotics journals sustained by revenue from antibiotics manufacturers. Welch was FDA's antibiotics chief. *Northwest Medicine* said: "Lear seems to think there is something evil . . . Logically extended this argument would condemn most of the medical journals published in this country since their major if not their entire source of income is from advertising."

Four months later, Harry J. Loynd, president of Parke, Davis, wrote the then Secretary of Health, Education, and Welfare, Arthur S. Flemming: "Lear seems to think there is something wrong . . . Logically extended, this argument would condemn most of the medical journals published in this country today since their major, if not entire, source of income is from advertising."

Loynd acknowledged before the Kefauver subcommittee that his company had contributed $100,000 to Welch's enterprise to start a British edition of one of his journals. The venture collapsed but bequeathed Welch an unexpended balance of $18,973.

✓   ✓   ✓

Another phenomenon in medical publishing should be noted. It is the rise of publications that although enormously expensive to produce are distributed free of charge to physicians. They are technically superb. *Medical World News,* for example, is printed on glossy paper, makes lavish use of costly color photography and printing, and is, in a Sunday-supplement kind of way, "interesting." The technical articles are breezily written and presented in an attractive typographical setting. There is a swarm of features. And there is also reporting about, say, the activities of congressional committees, the Food and Drug Administration, the drug industry, and the American Medical Association. It is not the kind of reporting likely to offend seriously the advertisers who make this huge giveaway possible. Almost all of them are pharmaceutical manufacturers.

Counting the covers, the May 22, 1964, issue of *Medical World News* has 212 pages. The front cover has a striking color photograph of Dr. Komei Nakayama, "Japan's Master Surgeon." The front cover also proclaims that inside the physician-reader will find an "Illustrated Guide to San Francisco AMA MEET-ING," which consists of 15 pages, some in beautiful color, that tell doctors "where to eat and what to see." Sylvia Porter has a crisp column on the "Economics of Health Quackery." Dr. Morris Fishbein, former editor of the AMA *Journal,* offers a full-page editorial on "The Psychiatrist's Image." There is a page for "Product News" and more than a page for "Names in the News." A report on the hearings held by Representative L. H. Fountain on Flexin is cursory. There are sufficient feature-type scientific articles ("Lasers Fire on Human Cancer," "Triple Play with Hydrogen Peroxide Infusion") to allow a physician who cares to do so to cultivate the notion that he is keeping up.

This collage is dropped in amid advertisements, most of which, according to the index of advertisers, are placed by about 40 pharmaceutical manufacturers for about 75 products. The advertisements occupy well over half of the 212 pages. One alone, for Warner-Chilcott's Mandelamine, a urinary tract antiseptic, takes 13 solid pages.

It's a free country, isn't it, and the physician is free to read what he wants to read, including advertiser-sponsored entertainment and trivia that arrive biweekly in an eye-catching glossy package. Obviously, though, while the physician keeps up with the world, courtesy of the drugmakers, he is simultaneously reading neither the *Medical Letter,* which has no advertising and provides objective evaluations of drugs, nor difficult, somber professional articles.

✓ ✓ ✓

Most immune from criticism, for reasons that by now should be apparent, are the drug companies. In an interview in 1962 published by the Center for the Study of Democratic Institutions at Santa Barbara, California, Dr. Herbert Ratner, of the Stritch School of Medicine of Loyola University, told what happened in the 1940's:

I showed a former dean of our medical school a talk I had prepared for a Religious Emphasis Week at a State medical school. When he came to the lines, "Modern man ends up a vitamin-taking, antacid-consuming, barbiturate-sedated, aspirin-alleviated, benzedrine-stimulated, psychosomatically diseased, surgically despoiled animal; nature's highest product turns out to be a fatigued, peptic-ulcerated, tense, headachy, overstimulated, neurotic, tonsilless creature," the dean said: "Gee, Herb, I wish you'd not use that line. It will antagonize the drug houses, and we are trying to build up research funds." [1]

[1] The Pharmaceutical Manufacturers Association has estimated that in one year (1958) the industry donated $20 million to medical education and research. This statement was critically examined in September 1959 in the *Journal of Medical Education*. Dr. Solomon Garb, of Albany Medical College, Albany, New York, made the following points:

The figure was indicated by Dr. Garb's contacts with other medical educators to be "far too high." Whether the sum actually given was $20 million or less, the credit belonged more to certain firms than to the industry as a whole. Rather than being unrestricted grants, a portion of the contributions was based on contracts for specified research.

Dr. Garb contended that in reality the medical schools were subsidizing the industry, rather than vice versa. He estimated that it would cost the companies between $100 and $200 million a year to buy on the market "the services they now get so cheaply from medical schools." Even when his college has a government training grant, Dr. Garb wrote, "we subsidize each Ph.D. to the extent of about $3000 per year, or $12,000 per degree."

The $20 million amounted to less than $100 per practicing physician. About $3500 per physician per year was being spent on drug advertising and promotion.

THE EXPLOITATION of purported successes of new drugs has continued unabated in certain news media. Some make a specialty of it. One such is *Pageant*. During the winter of 1966–67, in a statement granting an injunction requested by the federal government, District Judge James C. Connell of Cleveland, Ohio, said, "a pilgrimage [was] made to Cleveland by many who were ill, many who literally had one foot in eternity; and they have all come because this magic magazine has told the world, 'Here, at last, is the cure.' " The disease was cancer — terminal cancer. The "cure" was a vaccine whose ingredients included substances contaminated by bacteria; a possible residue of benzidine, which can *produce* cancer, and a substance carefully labeled not for humans, but "for chemical and investigational use only" and for "laboratory research on animals." The "only effect" on 12 cancerous mice that received the vaccine, the Judge recalled from expert testimony, was "to hurry the end of the existence of the creatures . . ." In summing up a case in which the whole episode was developed, United States Attorney Merle M. McCurdy said that if the laboratory in which the vaccine had been produced had "been a butcher shop, it would have been closed up by the health authorities." The vaccine was packaged in unlabeled vials and, said Judge Connell, illegally carried from Cleveland into interstate — and even foreign — commerce by, among others, Dr. J. Ernest Ayre, medical and scientific director of the National Cancer Cytology Center, Inc. But it is time to pause and say that although the *Pageant* episode induces a special horror, other involving more prestigious publications cannot be passed over. In addition to the vaccine case, then, I will summarize instances of publicity hazardous to health and life concerning DMSO, the "wonder drug" discussed in the Afterword to Chapter 2, and oral contraceptives.

THE VACCINE

The cover of the December 1966 *Pageant* was a classic example of one way to build circulation: "AT LAST! SCIENTISTS REPORT / ANTI-CANCER VACCINE / Claim 12 dying patients saved in / first experiments! 75 doctors in 35 Ohio hospitals now attacking / all kinds of cancers / in hundreds / of cases / FIRST & EXCLUSIVE DOCUMENTATION." The impact of that cover and of the article inside, and of a *second* cover story and article in the January 1967 issue — publisher Gerald A. Bartell knew a good thing when he had it — was staggering. The Food and Drug Administration knew of hundreds of cancer victims who came to Cleveland, but does not pretend to know of all who came. Many traveled great distances, in pain and with financial sacrifice. They had been given hope that their cancer was not terminal, and because the Government attacked that hope at its source the Government came to be hated.

In November, soon after the "AT LAST" cover appeared on the newsstands, R. C. Brandenburg, who for practical purposes is FDA's chief investigator, saw one on a stand in Falls Church, Virginia. He ordered an investigation made. It culminated in a petition by the Government for an injunction against further manufacture of the vaccine.

In a proceeding before District Judge James C. Connell in Cleveland the petition was contested by the Rand Development Corporation and its president, H. James Rand, who in 1949 was acclaimed Cleveland's Outstanding Young Man and who more recently was named by the Cleveland Press Club as the City's Outstanding Man in the Field of Science. The transcript of the proceeding, which ended on March 2, 1967, when the Judge granted the restraining order, is the primary source of this account. I was aided also because in December 1966 Howard Simon;, an assistant managing editor of the Washington *Post*, had seen *Pageant* and asked me to see what it was all about. The upshot was a story published on December 27 which blew a whistle on a piece of ghoulish magazine pageantry. "The Government," the *Post* article began, "has refused to allow interstate shipment of an experimental anticancer vaccine that was given cover-story treatment in the December and January issues of Pageant magazine . . ."

The refusal was based on the repeated and sustained failure of James Rand to comply with the requirement of the law that certain reports routinely required of drug makers be filed, to enable the Government to assure that proper and safe human testing procedures would be observed. "The mystery [of noncompliance] is explainable when we see," Judge Connell said in his opinion, "how cleverly stock market operations went on . . . how the stock went up every time the scientist involved [Rand] had an interview with anybody who had anything to do with publications."

To be understood, that is, the affair has to be viewed as an elaborate plan to drive up the price of Rand Development stock and to unload large blocks of shares before the bubble would burst. Within a few months in 1966 the price per share went from $2 to $3 to $54; and large blocks were unloaded. The stock would have been retained in expectation of even higher prices, the Court and the Government reasoned, if James Rand and certain associates had, or really believed they had, a cure for "all kinds" of cancer. This was a venture that promised and yielded very large profits. It was intricate; it had to be built on a foundation of carefully timed and controlled publicity. Rand was well situated to obtain publicity, not only because of his elite status in the community, but also because cancer victims within the boundaries of Ohio could be given the vaccine without restriction, so long as it was provided through physicians. Rand thus brought into being a constellation of circumstances in which he could, and did, make claims of miraculous promise and even results; but he had to find, and he did, reporters such as *Pageant's* who would not check out the claims. In addition, there had to be a "cover" to argue his good faith and serious intent. And so an application to be allowed to test the vaccine in states other than Ohio was duly filed with the Division of Biologics Standards of the National Institutes of Health. While demonstrating good faith, the application also served as an incentive to a New York brokerage firm to agree to try to raise one million dollars in capital that would be needed, supposedly, to gear up for large-scale production. Finally and perhaps most importantly, the application provided *Pageant* with a superficially authentic news peg (the Division and the FDA, as a matter of policy, do not publicize applications of the kind filed by Rand — and for a very good reason; the law and implementing regulations were drawn precisely to prevent publicity's being given to uses of a drug for which it has been inadequately tested). Rand, of course — not the Government — publicized the application. Biologics Standards found the application unsatisfactory and asked for more information. Rand stalled. In fact, he never did supply the required data. The reason, the Government suggested in court, was that he could not — and had not intended to.

The first batch of vaccine was manufactured on May 7, 1966. Before the month was out, McCurdy, the United States Attorney, told the Court, "it was being injected into the bodies of human beings" — although it had not yet been injected into a mouse or a rabbit or a dog to find out if an animal would survive. "Then there commenced to be some news leaks," McCurdy said. Rand tried to interest Edwin L. Seitz, then the medical writer for the Cleveland *Press*. Although in the second *Pageant* article Rand would claim encouraging results on a thousand patients, "he wouldn't tell the Government the name of one, and he wouldn't tell Ed Seitz the name of one," Judge Connell said. "He constantly annoyed Mr. Seitz trying to steam him up to write something that would help him, and Seitz was too ethical a writer to put anything in the newspaper which wasn't first in some fashion reported through proper medical or scientific circles, as a result of which Seitz lost the story."

In mid-August Rand made his last effort. He warned Seitz that he might be scooped. So be it, Seitz said. On August 19 the Cleveland *Plain Dealer* carried a 7-column headline saying, "Stock Jumps on Cancer Cure Rumor." It had indeed jumped — from about $16 on the eve of publication to $54 on the day of publication. The story, signed by John E. Bryan, the financial editor, said the stock had been driven up from a recent price of about $10 by investors who "bet on a new miracle" and by rumors spread by "cured" patients and their physicians. "A cure for cancer," Bryan said, "may be imminent."

Rand testified that he "would never go to *Pageant*" for publicity "because it is only one step above the *Police Gazette*. . . . I think it's worse than that." But there was admitted into evidence an overtly made tape recording in which Rand said to a *Pageant* reporter, "I'm talking to you because the chairman of the board of my company, Mr. J. Elroy McCaw, has an agreement with your publisher, and that's why I'm talking to you."

The reporter was a free-lance named Lester David, of Woodmere, New York, who had been assigned to the story by Jim Hoffman, editor of *Pageant*. David interviewed Rand on September 6, 1966, in Darien, Connecticut. Rand testified that he granted the interview because David was "a top-flight medical writer." This estimate, the United States Attorney established, was *not* based on "Boys and Girls Together?", an article David wrote for *This Week,* but was based instead on a body of David's works specifically including the "World's First Clam Farm" in *Popular Science,* "Suicide Is Dangerous" and "How Old Is Your Spouse?" in *Coronet,* and "The Shocking Price of Parental Anger" in *Good Housekeeping.* "He never exaggerated," Rand testified about David. "He was accurate." David *was* accurate when he testified that he got his material from Rand. He asked the executive, "What types of cancer have responded, or are responding, to this vaccine, Mr. Rand?" Rand replied, "As far as we know, all types."

The January 1967 article in *Pageant* was done by William Barry Furlong, a Lake Forest, Illinois, free-lance who testified that the publications for which he has written include the *Saturday Evening Post, Reader's Digest, Harper's,* the New York *Times Magazine, Sports Illustrated, Sport,* and *Pageant.* On September 27, 1966, he flew to Cleveland, met a *Pageant* photographer at the airport, and, over a period of a few days, interviewed Rand. He proved to be, the testimony brought out, a generous host; commingled with the conversation was a goodly amount of eating and drinking. Unfortunately, Furlong testified, he ran "into pretty much of a dead end on specific persons who had been tested with the vaccine," other than those who under Rand's selection processes had already been publicized. Rand "could not give me the names, he could not tell me on whom it had been tested," Furlong told the Court. Yet Furlong's *Pageant* article proclaimed, the Judge pointed out, encouraging early results in "a thousand or more patients." The presentation, Connell noted, had "the desired effect on the vast army of the desperately ill . . . the pilgrimage began to Cleveland in full."

The Judge devoted much attention to Dr. J. Ernest Ayre, medical consultant to the Rand firm and medical director of the National Cancer Cytology Center, Inc., which has facilities in New York City and Miami, Florida. The vaccine was promoted for use in *terminal* cancer patients; Dr. Ayre had himself administered it to women with cervical tissue diagnosed as pre-cancerous. The vaccine was untested. Some of it was contami-nated; some may have contained benzidine, a carcinogen. Dr. Ayre took 150 to 200 vials to physicians in various states and even to the Dominican Republic. Under the law the vials could not be taken out of Ohio; nor could they be tested elsewhere. Dr. Ayre knew, Judge Connell said, that every vial he gave was "a violation of law. . . . He said he administered vaccine to pa-tients for psychological purposes . . . to make them feel good."

In June 1966 news media received, and many derived stories from, a Cytology Center release headlined, " 'THE PILL' FOUND SAFE/FOR USE BY PATIENTS WITH/EARLY CERVICAL CANCER." The suggested subheadline was, "Re-search by Cytology Center Will Ease/Fears of Millions Who Take/Oral Contraceptives." This highly questionable release was based on "a daring three-year study" on the "influence of the pioneer birth control pill on women predisposed to cancer of the cervix." The study was backed by G. D. Searle & Co., Inc., manufacturer of Enovid, and published in the July 1966 issue of *Obstetrics and Gynecology*, official journal of the American College of Obstetricians and Gynecologists. Doubtless the study was "daring"; so is Dr. Ayre. He had also been involved with DMSO. In March 1966, at a symposium sponsored by the New York Academy of Science shortly *after* abuses surrounding the drug had been exposed by the House Intergovernmental Rela-tions Subcommittee, Dr. Ayre appeared to claim that DMSO had a significant potential in human cancer therapy.

Dr. Ayre had a significant potential for remaining credible. This was demonstrated on May 10, 1967, when the Associated Press sent over the news wires an interview in which Dr. Ayre made the claim that tests with Enovid showed it will not cause, and may inhibit, uterine cancer. The next day in New York City, Dr. Ayre delivered a paper to that effect. But the fact is that all known human carcinogens have a latency period of about a decade — far longer than the period involved in the "daring" studies made by Dr. Ayre. Therefore, the Advisory Committee on Obstetrics and Gynecology of the Food and Drug Administration has said, "any valid conclusion must await accurate data on a much larger group of women" than has been reliably studied. On the same day that Dr. Ayre delivered his paper before a Pan-American medical group of which he was founding president, the FDA confirmed to me that it was investigating Dr. Ayre in connection with his transportation of the Rand vaccine across state lines. In Chicago, a spokesman for the Searle firm said it was evaluating Dr. Ayre's work to determine whether to renew a grant for research by the Cytology Center on Enovid. The grant, for an undisclosed amount, was made originally in 1963 and had been renewed each year since. The spokesman said the relation with Dr. Ayre began when he approached Searle with potentially promising but preliminary test data indicating that Enovid had no effect on cancer of the cervix.

DMSO (AGAIN)

Dr. Joseph F. Sadusk, Jr., who was the Food and Drug Administration's top physician during much of the DMSO mess described in the Afterword to Chapter 2, made an entirely warranted compaint about the role played by news media in bringing about use of a highly experimental drug by perhaps 50,000 persons. At a time in early 1964 when the agency was calling for meaningful _animal_ studies, and when it had agreed only to very cautious and highly limited human studies involving application of the industrial solvent to the skin, "very extensive publicity appeared in the popular press," Dr. Sadusk testified before the House Intergovernmental Relations Subcommittee. This publicity, he said, represents DMSO "to be a wonder drug for the treatment of a variety of diseases."

As of the day of his testimony — March 9, 1966 — there was "a probable relationship" between use of DMSO and eye injuries. At least one of several known deaths in DMSO users appeared to be related to the drug. Applications associated with topical application were severe enough to cause discontinuation of DMSO therapy in about 7 per cent of 900 users in one study, or about 63, Dr. Sadusk testified; 54 per cent experienced burning, 43 per cent a skin affliction called erythema, and lesser percentages tenderness, scaling, and other problems. There is, Dr. Sadusk told the Subcommittee, "no substantive pharmacological data" to support the belief of many physicians "that DMSO is a relatively safe drug." He dealt with the efficacy of DMSO in his discussion of the press:

> Despite enthusiastic reports concerning alleged benefits derived from DMSO treatment, published in some medical journals as well as the lay press, it is the view of the medical staff of FDA that at the present time there is a lack of substantial evidence of the effectiveness of DMSO. This, of course, does not rule out the possibility that careful scientific investigations may yet establish a place for DMSO in the therapeutic armamentarium of the physician.
>
> As a result of excessive publicity about the value and safety of DMSO and of unwarranted enthusiasm among some physicians about this drug, what was approved as a limited study involving the cutaneous application of DMSO to a few patients, rapidly grew to a widespread use of DMSO alone and in combination with a variety of other drugs for the treatment of several diseases.

The drug companies involved in all of this were named, and they should have been; but an even-handed standard, it seems to me, imposed on Dr. Sadusk an obligation to name those publications which he believed had behaved irresponsibly. If one believes, as do I, that the Congress must oversee the Executive, and that the press must exercise oversight of both, then one must also believe that immunity from oversight is not owed the press and in fact is a disservice to it and the public. In the DMSO case, however, the specific roles of *Life*, *Newsweek*, and the *Saturday Evening Post* were set out in an article entitled "Razz-ma-Tazz in the Drug Industry" and published in the *Nation* for April 11, 1966. The writer, Robert G. Sherrill, Washington correspondent of the *Nation*, said that at the point when FDA considered even the animal testing inadequate:

> . . . what the promoters needed was publicity. They got it. *Newsweek* was soon quoting one researcher to the effect that DMSO was "the most exciting thing I know of in medicine. It's unbelievable." It was reportedly good, said *Newsweek*, for the common cold, swellings, pain and even as a method of "injecting" insulin. Just rub it on! Why, "it could even make the hypodermic needle obsolete."

✓ ✓ ✓

Life, bringing its medical wisdom to the public on July 10, 1964, admitted that it was "hard to talk about" this "fantastic" drug "without sounding like a carnival salesman." Nevertheless, *Life* was willing to take that risk by touting DMSO as a cure-all for "arthritis, sinusitis, headaches, earaches, sprains, burns" . . . and it "reduces swelling, kills pain, fights germs, tranquilizes, enhances other drugs. . . ."

The *Saturday Evening Post* was soon reciting even more wonderful results. First, of course, there was the usual disclaimer: "The strange powers of this newly explored drug make it sound like Indian snake oil. Yet it may create a breakthrough in medicine comparable to the discoveries of insulin and penicillin. . . . Nearly 2,000 research centers over the world have asked for it." No wonder. Dr. Jacob [Dr. Stanley W. Jacob, who discovered first the skin-penetrating abilities of DMSO and then his own abilities to penetrate the presumed normal skepticism of medical reporters] was quoted as saying that "if it continues to show no serious toxicity . . . it will be useful to every known malady." Even lame race horses in Florida, after a good rubdown with DMSO, were up and running again, said the *Saturday Evening Post*.

At that point, any control the FDA might have had over the experimental program became impossible. All across the country . . . *Life* and *Post* and *Newsweek* readers with aches and pains trooped to their family doctors and demanded to be swabbed down with DMSO. For that matter, the doctors themselves were excited by the stories. So, goaded by their patients and by their own curiosity, they went to work with a passion.

ORAL CONTRACEPTIVES

In January 1966 a book by Dr. Robert A. Wilson, a Brooklyn, New York, gynecologist, was published under the title *Feminine Forever*, and by August it had sold 100,000 copies. Dr. Wilson could lay claim to literary license, although not on the basis of his prose, but he had no scientific license to say that anything that lives is *forever*. Questions like this did not deter *Look*, which published excerpts in its issue of January 11, 1966; *Vogue*, which did the same in its issue of June 1966; King Features Syndicate, which syndicated the book in various newspapers, and those news and women's magazines that gave the book a ride. One claim in the excerpts published by *Look* was "that no woman who uses the birth control pills containing the proper amount of a suitable estrogen and an estrogenic progestogen (i.e., norethynodrel) will ever experience menopause." Although there are many formulations of oral contraceptives, only one, Enovid, contains the particular progestogen called norethynodrel. Enovid is a product of G. D. Searle & Co. That firm's Searle Foundation, James Ridgeway and Nancy Sommers disclosed in the *New Republic* of March 19, 1966, had given $17,000 in 1964 to the Wilson Research Foundation, Inc., of which Dr. Robert A. Wilson was president. In the same year the

Wilson Foundation received $8,700 from the Ayerst Laboratories division of American Home Products Corporation. In an interview, George Lardner, Jr., of the Washington *Post* reported on August 15, 1966, Dr. Wilson said he personally does not prescribe birth control pills in treating patients, but dispenses instead "conjugated estrogens." These are an Ayerst specialty. The Wilson Foundation received $5,600 from the Upjohn Company. Lardner wrote, "In a magazine article he [Dr. Wilson] said the progestin he prescribed [to supplement the "conjugated estrogens"] is 'medroxy-progesterone acetate.' . . . Upjohn makes medroxy-progesterone acetate."

If the foregoing suggests a certain symmetry one should beware reading much if anything into it. There is little doubt that Dr. Wilson is a true believer. "He has recommended the therapy," Lardner wrote, "for women young and old, from nuns in a convent to a 72-year-old Englishwoman he says he put on a 'crash program' to ready her for her wedding night." The lady was well within the boundaries laid down by Dr. Wilson when he said that oral contraceptives can make sex more enjoyable "regardless of age." In *Feminine Forever*, the gynecologist said the pills "provide probable protection against breast and genital cancers thanks to keeping the woman estrogen-rich." There is no question but that estrogens have a place in therapy, especially in postmenopausal women; but to hold out the pills as cancer preventives is to make a claim that is unwarranted by the evidence. Generally, the data are so inadequate that no one really knows, for instance, whether the pills may either promote or retard breast cancer. In November 1966 Commissioner James L. Goddard of the Food and Drug Administration wrote the Searle company about a claim that Dr. Wilson had made in, among other places, the *Look* article. He "has publicized the use of Enovid in lay publications, stating that it is effective in preventing the symptoms of the menopause," Dr. Goddard said. "Our investigational drug regulations provide that neither the sponsor nor anyone on its behalf may disseminate promotional material claiming that the drug has been shown to be effective for the conditions for which it is being investigated. Dr. Wilson has disseminated such information. He is therefore unacceptable as an investigator for 'Enovid in the Menopause.' " The performance of *Look, Vogue,* and other publications in this and similar cases also was unacceptable. That, too, ought to be said.

4

THE ASTONISHING POSTURES OF
THE AMERICAN MEDICAL ASSOCIATION

THE KEFAUVER HEARINGS, which spanned two and one-half years, established beyond doubt that useless drugs were being wantonly marketed and prescribed, with resultant extensive death and injury. The Senator from Tennessee made the logical proposal that the law be amended to give the Food and Drug Administration specific legal authority to require substantial evidence that a prescription drug for which marketing permission was sought lived up to the maker's claims of therapeutic effectiveness.

The point should be made very clear. If a maker claimed to FDA that his new drug was effective (and safe) against, say, pneumonia, and there was substantial evidence that this was so, FDA would, under the Kefauver amendment, release the drug for that use. If the maker then claimed the same drug to be effective against, say, cancer, but could not substantiate the claim, FDA would not allow the claim to be made in labeling or promotional literature.

Even the Pharmaceutical Manufacturers Association, the industry's own trade organization, was willing to go along with the efficacy requirement Senator Kefauver proposed. But *not* the American Medical Association. Its position seemed to be that it is bad for you to buy a worthless medicine for self-medication but acceptable for you to get a worthless medicine prescribed by a physician: it is right for the AMA to cooperate with FDA in fighting quacks who peddle worthless medicines sold without a prescription, but wrong for the AMA to support a government effort to curb the peddling of worthless prescription medicines (which are, of course, advertised in the AMA's journals).

To put it another way, and very simply: the AMA had become Sganarelle in this dialogue from Molière's *The Physician in Spite of Himself:*

> GERONTE: Yes, I have but one daughter; and I would never get over it if she were to die.
>
> SGANARELLE: Do not let her do anything of the kind. She must not die without a prescription of the physician.

Needless to say, the AMA did not state its position in quite this way. In July 1961, when its spokesmen appeared before the Senate Subcommittee on Antitrust and Monopoly, its position against the efficacy proposal somehow was made to sound pro-logic, pro-science, pro-America. Fortunately, however, the AMA position was examined by some first-rate diagnosticians. The "official position of the American Medical Association" was presented to the Kefauver subcommittee by Dr. Hugh H. Hussey, Jr., chairman of the AMA's board of trustees. It quickly developed that the trustees had, in arriving at the "official position," bypassed the AMA's own Council on Drugs — a group of leading specialists set up to advise them on drug matters. "Our opinions were not asked," one Council member, Dr. Louis S. Goodman of the University of Utah, testified. The witness, co-author of *The Pharmacological Basis of Therapeutics*, went on to say, "And several of us resented it . . . and we were told, 'Well, you are only an advisory body' . . ."

The core of the AMA's position as stated by Dr. Hussey, who was then dean of the Georgetown University School of Medicine in Washington, was in a passage which has here been divided into three numbered sections:

1. "A physician is trained during his many years in medical school, internship, and residency, and continuously learns after he enters into the practice of medicine, to use his professional judgment in determining what particular drug is best for a particular patient suffering from a particular disease or condition."

Yet, a physician as eminent as the late Dr. Lawson Wilkins found it necessary to include this admonishment in his 1962 presidential address to his fellow pediatricians of the American Pediatric Society:

> . . . one of the great shortcomings of our medical teachers of the present generation is a failure to inculcate into students and interns a cold, scrutinizing, skeptical state of mind which would make them leery of accepting any therapeutic claim without proof. If the young physician were less credulous and gullible he would be less enthusiastic about trying every new sample of the 400 new drugs handed to him annually, and he might do less damage to his patients.

Dr. Goodman termed Dr. Hussey's argument "specious." He said: "The average practicing physician — and I have helped to train hundreds of them — just does not have the time, the facilities, the skill, nor the training to be an expert in the determination of drug efficacy. He is not capable of, or interested in, carrying out the elaborate and extensive controlled clinical and laboratory tests to determine drug efficacy. He rightly depends (or should depend) on the published opinions of . . . experts in this field."

2. "We believe [Dr. Hussey continued] that only the physician has the knowledge, ability, and the responsibility to make that decision [as to what particular drug is best] in regard to that particular patient and that he should not be deprived of the use of drugs he believes are medically indicated for his patient by a governmental ruling or decision."

Dr. Walter Modell, the editor of *Drugs of Choice,* a member of the Council on Drugs, testified in rebuttal:

> By sheer superiority of numbers alone the problem of handling new drugs literally threatens to overwhelm the practicing physician.
>
> And, as if that were not serious enough, promotional pressures and near-truths in and outside professional literature as well as high-pressure peddling by detail men and confusing mumbo-jumbo in advertising, have led the practicing physician to use new drugs promptly on their introduction into the market and before he has been able to acquire the substantial information he needs in order to deal safely and effectively with new drugs he uses. Unfortunately substantial information arrives late while the insubstantial promotional information, like the poor, is always with us.

Another member of the Council on Drugs, Dr. Maxwell Finland, professor of medicine at the Harvard Medical School, saw in Dr. Hussey's view

> . . . an invitation to all manufacturers to dump into the hands of busy practitioners any and all types of good and bad, useful or useless, drugs and devices and let them learn, at the expense and perils of their patients, whether they may be of help in each instance . . . With over 200,000 physicians and their patients as potential prey, the result would be untold harm [that] might take long to appreciate and evaluate. The manufacturer would have little difficulty in obtaining and publicizing testimonials as to the value of his products from those who may have gained favorable impressions or from those who were fortunate enough not to see harmful effects or who could not recognize them, while those whose results were

indeterminate or unfavorable would hesitate to report them or would not be heard.

Wisely, perhaps, Dr. Hussey had not sought the counsel of the distinguished Dr. Harry F. Dowling, who later became chairman of the Council on Drugs. Four years earlier Dr. Dowling had said at an American Medical Association section meeting in New York City: "Most practicing physicians do not see a sufficient number of patients with any one disease to make a critical trial of a new drug themselves . . . But today the 'commercials' are so loud, so incessant, and brash that they jam the channels of communication. The bewildered physician prescribes by suggestion and not from information."

Edward Turkel, the examiner who held months of hearings on Altafur, the antibacterial drug which FDA released with inadequate evidence of safety and efficacy, had to conclude that even medical specialists are "not necessarily competent to conduct clinical investigations . . . in their specialty" [because] adequate evaluation of safety and effectiveness requires research "not done in the private practice of medicine."

3. "Medical history and experience [Dr. Hussey said in his peroration] clearly demonstrate that the only possible final determination as to the efficacy and ultimate use of a drug is the extensive clinical use of that drug by large numbers of the medical profession over a long period of time."

During Dr. Hussey's appearance he was accompanied by C. Joseph Stetler, general counsel of the AMA and director of its Socioeconomic Division. Later, however, Stetler became executive vice president of the Pharmaceutical Manufacturers Association. Speaking in 1963 for the PMA but taking a stand as inseparable from Dr. Hussey's as safety is from efficacy, he acclaimed drugs "amply proven to be safe and effective as a result of the best of all possible tests — widespread use in actual medical practice over an extended period of time." It is, I think, a logical progression to designate this the Hussey-Stetler Test of Time.

The Hussey-Stetler Test of Time has frequently proved as enlightening as permanently monochromatic litmus paper. There is a long list of drugs upon which physicians relied for decades and even centuries (chaulmoogra oil for leprosy, calomel for syphilis, strychnine for heart disease, buccal enzymes for phlebitis) that were shown to be valueless by a few well-designed experiments. For hundreds of years the Hussey-Stetler Test of Time was passed with flying color — red — by the leech.

About 1930 a new pain-killer, meperidine, sold as Demerol, was introduced as a substitute for morphine with the unhedged, categoric claim that it was not addictive. "The work on which the claim was based was shoddy," Dr. Modell recalled in his speech before the American Association for the Advancement of Science in 1962, "yet use of the drug was vigorously promoted. Experience soon proved that meperidine was highly addictive, and that in this respect it certainly had no advantage over morphine."

This didn't stop meperidine from passing the Hussey-Stetler Test. "Even now, 30 years later," Dr. Modell said in the speech, which has been published by the Humphrey Subcommittee on Reorganization and International Organizations,

few physicians seem to accept the fact that meperidine is highly addictive. Many seem to assume that the original contention must have had some validity, and they continue to use meperidine as though it were less hazardous than morphine. The medical profession uses morphine with great respect and, as a result, a very small number of patients become addicted to it as an accident of therapy. But this is not the case with meperidine. As a result, many more victims are admitted to the hospital for addicts at Lexington, Kentucky, as a result of meperidine therapy than are admitted because of morphine therapy.

What the Hussey-Stetler Test exalts is a collection of impressions in the mind of the physician. A collection of impressions simply cannot be relied upon to furnish the truth.

"If he is honest," Harvard's Dr. Finland told the Antitrust subcommittee,

> the individual physician will admit that he can only gather impressions concerning the effect of the remedy he uses in an individual patient, but he cannot even in that case determine the likelihood that the response was a matter of chance or was due to any of the different methods of treatment that he employed, nor can he say what might have been the result were some other drug used.
>
> Only when adequate numbers of properly studied cases are gathered and the responses analyzed and compared with similar data from other well demonstrated experiences can one gain some approximation of the effectiveness of any remedy.

Dr. Dowling provided the subcommittee with a simple statistical illustration. Among 100 patients with pneumococci pneumonia about 30 will die. The rest will recover without the use of any specific remedies. "If a doctor," Dr. Dowling said, "were to use a drug that had no effect on the recovery rate — let us say aspirin — and his patient recovered, this would mean nothing with regard to the aspirin because 7 times in 10 the patient would have recovered anyway." But aspirin would have passed the Hussey-Stetler Test in a disease against which it is ineffective.

Yet another weakness of the Hussey-Stetler Test was brought out by Dr. Charles D. May, a member of the Council on Drugs and professor of pediatrics at New York University. "How," he asked, "can the individual physician be expected to evaluate drugs sensibly when often the only evidence made available to him in promotional material is limited to: 'unpublished reports,' 'cases in the company's files,' 'exhibits in meetings' long since dismantled, and citations of selected papers from relatively inaccessible or inferior journals often quoted out of context?"

✶ ✶ ✶

One of the most devastating characterizations of the position of the American Medical Association was offered to the Kefauver subcommittee by Dr. William Bean, of the University of Iowa. He said:

> Because of its very real and serious apprehensions of the centralization of Federal authority, the American Medical Association in its fear has euchred itself into the astonishing posture of supporting the position that it is better to have non-efficacious drugs or those whose efficacy is as yet unestablished released freely to the American physician and the American public, rather than have those made available only when their usefulness in therapy has been determined or its probability is of so high an order that no one could object.

Less kind was Dr. Allan M. Butler, professor of pediatrics emeritus, Harvard Medical School, and director of clinical services at the Metropolitan Hospital of Detroit. If the AMA's posture was "astonishing" to Dr. Bean, it was "untenable" to Dr. Butler. Citing the sources of AMA revenues, he said that "it is difficult to disregard the existence of a 'conflict of interest' . . . It is there and should be recognized . . . And, as is well known, the AMA and the drug companies have cooperated in opposing legislation concerning the financing and distribution of medical care."

✶ ✶ ✶

The American Medical Association was, once upon a time, a courageous and progressive force in American life. "Into the darkest recesses of the [nostrum] industry the Association probed, never hesitating to reveal the most sordid aspects of the business," James G. Burrow wrote in *AMA: Voice of American Medicine*. "No other organization in the nation after 1906 remotely rivaled the AMA in exposing the graft and ravages of the nostrum vendors."

Alongside Harvey Wiley and the muckrakers, and again in the 1930's, the AMA fought for progressive food and drug legislation and for safe and effective medicines. In order to provide its members with reliable information on the safety and effectiveness of drugs, the AMA set up in 1905 what is now its Council on Drugs.

During the 1940's the government began to require that insulin and then antibiotics be certified for efficacy as well as safety. This was *not* opposed by the AMA. But the prescription-drug revolution was just beginning to make its impact felt on the AMA's revenue structure.

In 1950 the AMA derived $5 million from dues and subscriptions. Only slightly more than half as much, $2.6 million, came from advertising in its journals. In the seven-year period ending in 1953, however, the advertising revenues of some medical journals increased about half, while those of the AMA's periodicals rose by only 3 per cent. This contrast was shown by a survey that the AMA had commissioned, and to which Kefauver called attention at his subcommittee hearings. There followed major changes in the AMA's policies, some of which are described below. And in 1957 advertising revenue exceeded dues and subscription income for the first time. In 1960 advertising revenue was top-heavy — $8 million — compared to income from dues and subscriptions of $6 million. Other activities — for example, making mailing lists available to drug manufacturers for a fee — added $2 million. The total income was $16 million. Half came from advertising, and more than half of that, or $4.5 million, was provided by a mere 22 ethical-drug firms.

In 1963, according to an analysis published by the Chicago

Sun-Times, the AMA's total income was $22.5 million. Almost half, or $10.1 million, came from advertisements in its 12 journals and in its laymen's monthly, *Today's Health.* During that year the AMA *Journal* carried 5262 pages of advertisements — more than in any other national weekly except the *New Yorker* and the *Oil and Gas Journal.* As a nonprofit organization, the AMA has not had to pay income taxes on its publishing activities, which compete with publications that do pay taxes. The *Sun-Times* story, which appeared in August 1964, reported that the Internal Revenue Service was going to propose new regulations to subject advertising revenues such as the AMA's to income taxes, in the conviction that the sale of advertisements in periodicals like the AMA's is not related to the nonprofit purposes for which it was chartered. No such regulations had been proposed by the end of the year.

While advertising from the drug houses was becoming a primary source of revenues, other significant changes were occurring simultaneously. To illustrate: it was brought out at a Kefauver subcommittee hearing that the Council on Drugs, which had acquired a deservedly lustrous reputation for its evaluations of the risks and benefits of prescription drugs, had — in the era of the deluge, the drug revolution — been experiencing budget cuts. In 1955 the Council was allocated $152,000. In 1958 it was getting less than half that sum, $75,000. The $75,000, incidentally, amounted to $\frac{1}{10,000}$ of the annual spending by the industry on advertising and promotion.

The AMA's public relations department was doing rather better. In 1955 it received $425,000. In 1958 it got $69,000 more, or $494,000. In 1964, according to the *Sun-Times* story cited earlier, the number of full-time AMA lobbyists in Washington was four.

Perhaps chastened by the disclosures being made at the Kefauver hearings, the AMA more than tripled the budget of the Council on Drugs, from $75,000 in 1960 to $262,000 in 1961. To the credit of the AMA, the allocation for the Council has been increased in each year since, reaching $619,000 for 1964.

The AMA had published a small book widely regarded as valuable, *Useful Drugs*. After thirty-nine years of publication it was abandoned in 1952. Eight years later, in a proposal filed with the Department of Health, Education, and Welfare, the AMA proposed to publish "an annual 'Handbook of Drugs' based on information previously presented in the monthly 'Authorized Brochures on Drugs' including the summaries of the Council on Drugs." With some pride the proposal went on to say, "This volume would be similar to desk reference books and drug encyclopedias now available but would present more complete information about action, uses, side effects, and dangers of drugs than similar existing volumes." Speaking for the AMA's board of trustees, Dr. F. J. L. Blasingame added: "Assuming that the program [which included several other items] is approved in February [1961] by our Board of Trustees, as we anticipate it will be, and, if it is acceptable to the Food and Drug Administration and the other organizations and individuals involved, we believe that it can be made effective within 6 months of date of approval [which indicated that the program would be in operation by July 1961]."

During 1961, in the course of assuring the Kefauver subcommittee that drug reforms were not needed, the AMA said the handbook was on its way. In March 1963, when there was still no sign of it, Senator Humphrey wrote to the AMA to ask what had happened to it. As of November 1964, the handbook still was not out. Indeed, Mr. Humphrey had not even received an answer to his letter.

In its journals the AMA had permitted advertising of only those drugs that had won the affirmative approval of the Council on Drugs. In 1955 the Council's role was cut back — if its members and consultants were invited to do so, they could give advice on specific advertisements. Also in 1955 the AMA abandoned its famed seal-of-acceptance program.

The Council was stripped of effective power to require manufacturers to submit data for evaluation before advertising would be accepted. In some instances, the AMA *Journal* published claims in advertisements even before the advertiser had responded to the Council's request for data with which to evaluate the claims.

Changes like these, and Dr. Hussey's explanations of them, distressed the distinguished *New England Journal of Medicine,* which is edited by Dr. Joseph Garland. In an editorial of November 2, 1961, the publication said:

> Whatever their motives, it was the administrative officials of the Association who made the decisions . . . It is doubtful . . . whether many leading medical educators were consulted and approved these moves. However, there are some among them who believe that these decisions had much to do with encouraging the introduction of relatively inferior drugs and minor medications and undesirable combinations of drugs . . . These changes have done little to help but may have done much to confuse the physician in his efforts to practice good medicine.

The AMA is not a monolith. There are contending forces within it that account for many of the confusing zigs and zags in its record. The AMA's journals require observance of higher advertising standards than most (which is not a great compliment), and they print some blistering reports on drugs. For a dozen years the AMA has maintained an invaluable registry of drugs associated with serious and fatal blood diseases, and this central registry is now being vastly expanded. The record, in short, resists sweeping generalization.

And yet it is difficult to escape the conclusion that too often the AMA leadership has been blind, doctrinaire, and something more than an embarrassment to countless decent, humane, sensitive, and sensible physicians who are too busy doing their jobs to pay attention to the politics of their professional organization. That this characterization is not an overstatement can, I believe, be readily demonstrated.

At the request of Senator Kefauver, the Library of Congress surveyed drug advertising in six leading medical journals published in the nine-month period ending in March 1959. The survey covered 34 important trade-name products whose advertising was found in a total of 2033 pages. In 89 per cent of the advertisements, the Antitrust subcommittee said, there was "no reference to side effects at all or only a short dismissal phrase which was typically less a warning than a reason for prescribing." The drugs about which the advertisements were so discreet included Diabinese, the oral antidiabetic that Pfizer marketed despite a report by a member of its medical staff of an incidence of 27 per cent side effects, and Norlutin (norethindrone), a Parke, Davis product for gynecologic disorders.

On March 5, 1960, the *Journal* of the American Medical Association — one of the publications in the Library of Congress survey — published a report that physicians had encountered 35 baby girls with male sexual characteristics born to mothers who had been given Norlutin during pregnancy. In the same issue there was a Norlutin advertisement that did not mention this chilling side effect. This advertisement for Norlutin continued to appear regularly in the AMA *Journal* during the ensuing three months, although the article had warned, "During the past year or two, Norlutin has caused fetal masculinization with sufficient frequency to preclude its use or advertisement as a safe hormone to be taken during pregnancy."

Dr. Martin Cherkasky, director of Montefiore Hospital in New York, who testified before the Senate and House Antitrust subcommittees in behalf of himself and of the Greater New York Hospital Association, said to the Senate group: "I would like for you to think a moment about the human values involved for [female] children . . . born with masculinization so that you have difficulty in determining whether it is a male or a female.

"All drugs have dangers and you cannot point up a bad result of one sort or another as a reason for not using drugs when they have values, *but should not the doctors know when they use a drug just what kind of risks they run?*" (My italics.)

There was this exchange between Senator Kefauver and Julian Farren, executive vice president of L. W. Frohlich & Co., Inc., of New York, the advertising agency that had the Norlutin account:

> SENATOR KEFAUVER. After the March article, did J.A.M.A. [the *Journal* of the AMA] ask you to put any warning in?
>
> MR. FARREN. No, they did not, to my knowledge. As a matter of fact, Senator, I would like to add to my last statement that if they had requested us to put the warning statement in, we undoubtedly would have done so.

In September 1960 and again in October — more than six months after the article appeared — advertisements for Norlutin in the *Journal* carried a citation to an article in the *American Journal of Obstetrics and Gynecology*. However, this publication, it was pointed out to the Kefauver subcommittee by its chief economist, John M. Blair, "would be read by specialists to a greater degree than by the general practitioner [on whom many women with gynecologic disorders rely]."

No warning of possible masculinization of female babies was included in these advertisements; nor, indeed, was one included until about a year after the article had been published. Parke, Davis did include a reference to the AMA *Journal* article in the package insert, the folder sent to the pharmacist but usually not seen by the physician.

The incidence of masculinization may be small, and some authorities consider Norlutin a valuable drug. Three, for example, have said that when norethindrone is properly used it can be "remarkably efficacious in relief of many disturbances of menstruation and reproduction." A most dubious view, however, has been repeatedly expressed by the AMA's own Council on Drugs.

In *New and Nonofficial Drugs* for 1960 — the year in which the advertisements in question were running in the AMA *Journal* — the Council said:

> Norethindrone, as well as other progestogens, has been tried in a more or less empirical manner for the treatment of threatened or habitual abortion [miscarriage]. At present, there is a dearth of convincing evidence that any agent of this type can reduce the incidence of fetal loss. There is likewise insufficient evidence at hand to establish the proposed use of norethindrone for the treatment of premenstrual tension of dysmenorrhea [difficult or painful menstruation].

The Council was saying that it was not convinced that a woman who ran the risk of having a hermaphrodite by taking norethindrone had any more assurance that she would avoid a miscarriage than if she took no drug at all, or took a different type. The 1961 edition of *New and Nonofficial Drugs* repeated the paragraph quoted above. The Council's skepticism was set out again in the 1962 edition. The 1963 and 1964 editions contained this paragraph:

> *Maintenance of Pregnancy:* The use of norethindrone for threatened and recurrent abortion *is not justified* since its value has not been proved by controlled studies and its administration during pregnancy has been associated with varying degrees of masculinization of the human female fetus. [My italics.]

All of this serves to underscore the importance of the question raised by Dr. Cherkasky: Should not the physician, who is always informed of a drug's benefits, actual and claimed, also be told of its risks?

On one fundamental point probably everyone — the AMA, the manufacturers, FDA, the subcommittees and their witnesses — professed agreement: physicians *should* make their decisions on whether to prescribe a drug on the basis of published studies, so as to be fully informed on the ratio of benefits to risks. The question was the extent to which they *do* make such decisions on the basis of medical literature, rather than on the basis of advertising and promotion.

In December 1960 one answer came from the Pharmaceutical Manufacturers Association, which with United Marketing Services had sponsored a survey of the attitudes of 1552 physicians and surgeons, "a sample of medical profession leaders in the United States." In a report the PMA said: "The preferred source of information about new drugs, in all geographical regions of the United States, is literature detailed by manufacturers' technical representatives [detailmen]."

The former medical director for E. R. Squibb & Sons, Dr. A. Dale Console, said at one point in his testimony before the Kefauver subcommittee: "There is a simple maxim, I learned from detail men . . . 'If you can't convince them, confuse them.' "

"*Physicians' Desk Reference* [the PMA continued] and 'journal articles or papers' closely vied for second place of preference." But in the *Physicians' Desk Reference*, an annual with quarterly supplements, all material about every drug listed is prepared, edited, approved, and paid for by the manufacturer. Although *PDR*, as it is usually called, indicates this quite clearly, and although it is distributed free to physicians, "very few users realize that it is paid advertising," according to a report made to the Public Health Service.

One need not limit the search for evidence of the massive reliance placed by physicians on manufacturer-controlled sources of drug information to the PMA. Under auspices of the AMA itself, a marketing-analysis firm undertook an earlier study in a representative Midwestern community, Fond du Lac, Wisconsin. Among 55 physicians 28, or half, rated promotional sources, including advertising and company detailmen, "most important" in their education about new drugs.

✓ ✓ ✓

The leaders of the American Medical Association refused to be convinced even by its own survey, even by the Norlutin episode, that drug advertising should be required to carry warnings of side effects and list conditions for which use was not indicated.

Instead, the AMA opposed the Kefauver proposal, which was backed by President Kennedy and the Food and Drug Administration, to require such disclosure. In doing so the AMA's spokesmen invoked such specious arguments as that physicians look on the advertisements merely as "reminders" about drugs, and that to summarize the side effects in them would be to discourage doctors from turning to the full literature.

In speaking such sophistries, in rejecting the plea of Dr. Cherkasky to consider the human values involved, the AMA was assuming another astonishing posture. This one was separated from the PMA's by no more than a hyphen. The AMA-PMA position must have been prepared by men who had become accustomed to each other's face. It might just as well have been prepared by one man.[1]

---

[1] For reasons that probably are obvious by now, the drug industry through its advocates in Congress, particularly Senator Roman L. Hruska of Nebraska and Representative J. Arthur Younger of California, fought bitterly against a disclosure provision. That they lost this battle, with a consequent avoidance of incalculable injury and death among the population, was due in large measure to the brilliant, last-minute battle on the floor of the House of Representatives led by Representatives John D. Dingell of Michigan and John A. Blatnik of

In June 1960 several hyphens had seemed to separate the American Medical Association from the Pharmaceutical Manufacturers Association. Feeling the heat of the Kefauver inquiry, the AMA's House of Delegates at that time adopted a resolution to "establish a special commission which shall make a comprehensive study of the pharmaceutical industry in the United States, with special reference to the research, development, control and marketing of the medicaments essential to the modern practice of medicine." The bold separation of powers having been proclaimed, the AMA thereupon began to narrow the gap between it and the PMA. Soon they were once again a hyphenated name. Just enough space was left between them to let the "comprehensive study" slide through and drop to oblivion.

On November 28, 1960, the AMA's board of trustees pushed the resolution to the brink of the memory hole. "After investigating the scope of such a study," the board said, it was decided that the AMA "does not have either the resources or the authority to conduct such a study. It is the intention of the Board to maintain an active interest in the legislative proposals which may stem from the current congressional investigations of the pharmaceutical industry and to present the position of the American Medical Association on any proposals which affect the private practice of medicine."

Two days later, on the recommendation of its Reference Committee on Public Health and Occupational Problems, the House of Delegates deleted the sentence saying that the AMA lacked the resources and authority for the study and approved the rest. With that the special commission to make a comprehensive

---

Minnesota, and to the steadfastness in a Senate-House conference committee of Representative Kenneth A. Roberts of Alabama and Senator Kefauver.

Congressman Dingell, for instance, cited a finding of the Senate Antitrust subcommittee about an advertisement for Upjohn's Medrol, a cortical steroid. What appeared to be before-and-after X-rays adorned the advertisement, and suggested that Medrol was highly effective against ulcerative colitis. Making his case with a display of enlarged photostats of the X-rays, Dingell said that each of the two X-rays was of a different person. Neither person had taken Medrol.

study of the pharmaceutical industry disappeared down the memory hole.

↗ ↗ ↗

In yet another important area the hyphenated distance between the American Medical Association and the Pharmaceutical Manufacturers Association had appeared to be wide. The issue was legislation that Senator Thomas J. Dodd had introduced to fight the illegal traffic in amphetamines ("pep pills") and barbiturates (sedatives colloquially called "goof balls"). The Connecticut Democrat, who is chairman of the Senate Subcommittee to Investigate Juvenile Delinquency, summed up the situation on August 3, 1964, before a Senate Subcommittee on Health of the Committee on Labor and Public Welfare:

> . . . I refer to the staggering amounts of psychotoxic drugs that are diverted every year into illegal channels, millions of which end up in the hands of our Nation's youths.
>
> I reported to the Senate on August 24, 1961, that in the year 1960, drug companies in this country produced 5¾ billion [*billion*] capsules of barbiturates and 4 billion tablets of amphetamine drugs. This is in addition to millions of bootleg drugs that find their way into the black market.
>
> . . . .
>
> . . . during the last five years, the illegal use of the billions of these pills . . . has reached epidemic proportions. The results of this traffic which have come to our attention, revealed the following picture:
>
> The illegal use of these drugs is increasing at a fantastic rate among juveniles and young adults.
>
> The use of these drugs has a direct causal relationship to increased crimes of violence.
>
> The use of these drugs is replacing, in many cases, the use of the "hard" narcotics, such as opium, heroin, and cocaine.
>
> The use of these drugs is more and more prevalent among

the so-called white-collar youths who have never had prior delinquency or criminal records.

The use of these drugs is increasingly identified as causes of sexual crimes.

Mr. Chairman, I feel this bill has had as much study, analysis, and consideration at this point as any piece of legislation I have ever been associated with.

Since May 23, 1961, when I first introduced this bill, it has been subjected to the scrutiny of the President's Commission on Narcotic and Drug Abuse; the Department of Health, Education, and Welfare; Treasury; Justice; and State; the law enforcement agencies in New York City and the State of California, where this problem is greatest; the Association of Juvenile Court Judges; the International Juvenile Police Officers Association; the Pharmaceutical Manufacturers Association; and the distinguished representatives of a number of religious faiths. All of these groups, without exception, have approved of or endorsed this bill over the last 3½ years. Thousands of parents have written to me urging passage of the bill. Even the president of the largest producer of stimulant drugs in the United States personally wrote to me and endorsed this legislation.

This is a bill which tightens acknowledged inadequacies which are permitting a wave of narcotic addiction to go unchecked in this country. It was publicly and repeatedly supported by the late President Kennedy. It has the support of every group that knows anything about this problem. It has been backed by every witness who testified before the Juvenile Delinquency Subcommittee, including three drug company presidents.

Mr. Chairman, I do not know anyone who is against it.

A few minutes later, Dodd learned that there *was* someone against his bill. The news came from Senator Ralph W. Yarborough, the Texas Democrat who was presiding at the hearing. "We have a letter against it, but it just came in today," Yarborough said. "The first letter, I am advised. It is from the American Medical Association, dated July 31, 1964, and it is opposed to the bill. I will order it printed in the record, but I will read a few sentences to illustrate their point: 'The American Medical Association is well aware of the addicting and habituating properties of barbiturates, amphetamines and certain other psychotoxic agents. It considers, however, that education and appropriate local and State laws, rather than the Federal regulation envisioned in S. 2628, is the appropriate answer.' "

The AMA's position was in the old lobbyists' pattern. When the existence of an evil cannot be denied, stall by calling for "education." But who educates the AMA? To say we should not do any more than educate, Dodd told the hearing, "is to say nothing, in my opinion, and I cannot really find words strong enough to express my disapproval of that course of conduct. The house is on fire, and we do not need a lesson in how to prevent the starting of fires. What we need now is to put the fire out and go on with our fire prevention work." Despite yet another astonishing posture of the AMA the Senate was willing to try "to put the fire out" and passed the Dodd bill without dissent.

The Senator having publicly credited the PMA with being among the groups that had "approved or endorsed the bill over the last 3½ years," there seemed to be a large gap between it and the AMA. To his dismay Dodd was to find out that the PMA had been rendering lip-service. Later in the day during which he testified the PMA submitted a letter in which it so qualified its support as to make it almost meaningless. Dated August 3, 1964, the day of the hearing, the letter was signed by the president of the PMA, Dr. Austin Smith. That the AMA, which at least had been frank, and the industry were in reality again a mere hyphen apart subsequently became clear. "Some drug interests are known to be trying to kill the bill," *Drug Trade News* reported on August 18, 1964. On September 1 the same publication said, "Retail and manufacturing sections of the pharmaceutical industry are pressing hard this week to delay House action on the controversial psychotoxic drug bill . . ." [2] The account said that the bill was unacceptable to the PMA.

[2] The House allowed Dodd's bill to die, but in the new session of Congress, on March 10, 1965, passed a similar measure 402 to 0 and sent it to the Senate. This remarkable development followed a series of events that began on September 2, 1964, when CBS Evening News presented the first of three reports on a fine piece of journalistic enterprise by a CBS news producer, Jay McMullen.

In a rented office in New York, McMullen had set up McMullen Services, an "import-export" firm. Simply by using its letterheads he obtained from nine suppliers — none a member of the Pharmaceutical Manufacturers Association — the equivalent of 1,075,000 barbiturate and amphetamine pills worth more than $50,000 at retail and between $250,000 and $500,000 on the black market. His cost was $600.28. Ten other manufacturers demanded proof that McMullen Services was licensed or was registered with the Food and Drug Administration.

Public opinion also was aroused by one story after another in the press on the victimization of young people. FDA Commissioner Larrick reported that organized criminal rings were heavily involved in the illegal traffic. And President Johnson called on Congress to act. Seeing the handwriting on the wall, the AMA and the PMA tried to create the impression that apart from minor caveats they supported reform legislation. Actually, they sought crippling amendments. Thus on January 28, 1965, the AMA urged the House Committee on Interstate and Foreign Commerce, without success, to exclude from control psychotoxic drugs other than amphetamines and barbiturates, such as mild tranquilizers. These are heavily advertised in AMA publications.

SINCE *The Therapeutic Nightmare* was published in November 1965 the American Medical Association has been repeatedly exposed as a leading purveyor of false or misleading drug advertisements to its approximately 215,000 physician-members. They have shown no significant disposition to do anything about it. That is regrettable; but one cannot let it go at that, because an ad that misinforms a physician can be, as Dr. James L. Goddard, Commissioner of the Food and Drug Administration, has said, "a clear and present danger to the patient."

The AMA has called itself the "largest publisher of prescription drug advertisements in the world." Most of these ads are carried in the weekly AMA *Journal*; others are distributed among the Association's ten medical specialty journals. In 1966 the AMA's revenues from advertising (including some from the laymen's publication *Today's Health*) totaled $13,290,714, or 47.9 per cent of all income. Clearly the members of this professional organization are of lesser financial importance than the advertisers; members' dues provided only 27 per cent, or 20.9 percentage points less, of gross income. The ad income has been tax-exempt on the ground that it was substantially related to the AMA's professed purpose of promoting the "art and science of medicine and the betterment of public health." Every issue of the *Journal* says that the advertisements therein "have been reviewed to comply with the principles governing advertising in AMA scientific publications." In some advertisements for itself in the *Journal* the AMA has said that "every statement" in the ads it accepts "must be backed by substantiated facts . . . or we won't run it!" The purity theme also has been emphasized by Glenn R. Knotts, Director of Advertising Evaluation. On April 9, 1965, he told a meeting of the Parenteral Drug Association that since the *Journal* was established in 1883 the AMA "has maintained screening boards to enforce high standards of advertising" and to limit advertising claims "for useful products to those which can be documented *by scientific fact.*" (My italics.) Knotts said his office is staffed by "scientifically trained individuals"; they use "comprehensive" procedures; they correspond with "approximately four hundred consultants"; they maintain "liaison with centers of research in medical schools, hospitals, industry, agencies of the government, and branches of the military services."

On January 17, 1966, in District Court in Trenton, New Jersey, a plea of *nolo contendere* was entered in the first criminal prosecution brought under the advertising provisions of the Kefauver-Harris Amendments to the Food, Drug, and Cosmetic Act. The plea was entered by the Wallace Laboratories division of Carter-Wallace, Inc., of Cranbury, New Jersey. The drug involved was Pree MT (previously Miluretic), which was commonly prescribed for premenstrual tension, congestive heart failure, and high blood pressure, and which combined meprobamate (the sedative/tranquilizer most widely known as Miltown and Equanil) with the diuretic hydrochlorothiazide (which removes excess water from the tissues). The advertising was characterized in the criminal information as "false and misleading." The medium was the AMA *Journal*. The ad on which the two counts in the information were based was an elaborate 2-page affair that was published in four successive issues starting on June 1, 1964. The Government said the ad violated the law because it misled physicians by suppressing data on adverse effects and by

falsely claiming, "Contraindications: None known." (A contraindication is a medical condition in which a drug should not be
used.) For Pree MT the omitted side effects and contraindications included a warning that patients be carefully watched for
signs of a blood disease that is serious and sometimes fatal.

Since October 1960 contraindications had been listed *millions*
of times by Wallace Laboratories in the FDA-approved prescribing brochure in every package and in the *Physicians' Desk Reference*, the prescribing guide of which about a half-million copies
are distributed annually. Is it credible that these millions of
listings could have escaped detection by the massive screening
resources of the AMA's Office of Advertising Evaluation?
Contraindications were also listed by the AMA itself in *New
and Nonofficial Drugs*, which was published by the Council on
Drugs. Are we to believe that even this simply slipped by? Is
it unreasonable to expect that one of the "approximately 400
consultants" might have noticed that *Modern Medicine* was
carrying an ad listing contraindications for Merck Sharp &
Dohme's Cyclex — a product of exactly the same formulation as
Pree MT?

The issue of the AMA *Journal* for June 29, 1964, was the
first subsequent to those listed in the criminal information. It
carried a Pree MT ad identical to the earlier one except for one
thing: The false claim "Contraindications: None known" had
been chiseled off the *Journal*'s printing plate. The FDA was told
by Wallace that this was "a correction" — one that was, however, not made until after someone in the agency may have
leaked word of impending legal action to the company. But no
euphemisms about "a correction" can explain the behavior of the
AMA — even if one is credulous enough to believe it was unaware of contraindications listed millions of times. After running an ad saying contraindications did not exist, the AMA
was suddenly asked to remove the claim. What reason could
there have been for the request but that the invalidity of the

claim had been recognized? What conclusion other than that there were contraindications possibly could have been drawn by the AMA? So long as the claim appeared the law was being violated by a lie; when the claim was deleted a new ad legally was created — and then the law was being violated by noncompliance. The AMA was a party to noncompliance. But the Kefauver-Harris Amendments do not provide for prosecution of medical journals.

Wallace Laboratories was arraigned on December 6, 1965, before Judge Arthur S. Lane. Its plea was innocent. As part of my coverage of the story for the Washington *Post* I telephoned the AMA in Chicago to put the obvious questions: What was the explanation of the deletion of the claim of no contraindications? How had such a claim slipped through the screening apparatus? Hours later, a spokesman replied. He said the AMA "exercises caution in acceptance of advertisements" but does "not attempt to operate a censorship program." Wallace Laboratories, which was a leading *Journal* advertiser, was praised as "a highly reputable pharmaceutical firm." No serious effort was made to reconcile the disclaimer of a censorship program with the claim that every statement in every ad "must be backed by substantiated facts." Nor was it explained how a "highly reputable" manufacturer could acknowledge millions of times that there were contraindications to the use of its drug and then claim in the *Journal* that there were none. In District Court six weeks later the company said the *Journal* ad had resulted from "a mistake" of a sort that would not be allowed to recur (which was not to say that "mistakes" would not occur in ads in the *Journal* for other Wallace products; the reader is referred to the material on Deprol and Miltown in the Afterword to Chapter 14). The original plea of innocent was switched to *nolo contendere*, which averted the publicity that would have attended a trial. Judge Lane imposed the maximum penalty allowed for a misdemeanor violation — a fine of $1,000 on each of two counts. In 1964, the year of the offense, the net income after taxes of Carter-Wallace, Inc., of which Wallace Laboratories is a division, was $11.3 million, or 5,650 times more than the fine.

The Pree MT case was but the beginning. Within six weeks after Dr. James L. Goddard became Commissioner of FDA the agency initiated a series of crackdowns on advertising. Some were criminal actions. Some were seizures of interstate shipments — a civil procedure that can be undertaken with greater speed. Both methods — along with such others as admonitory private correspondence and citations of a company to closed hearings — are gravely flawed. The principal reason is that however well they perform a regulatory function they fail to perform a vital *public health* function — informing the physician. He may never learn that he has been deceived, especially because the professional press, dependent as it is upon advertising from a single source, the drug industry, is apathetic about reporting such matters. When comparable apathy is shown by general news media, as it usually is, the patient hasn't a chance of avoiding exploitation, or worse. Realization of this within the FDA, along with prodding by the House Intergovernmental Relations Subcommittee, finally produced, early in 1967, the corrective letter. This is a device of wondrous simplicity and virtue. It is an individual communication in which a manufacturer says, in effect, "Dear Doctor: In that advertisement we ran we deceived you. We're sorry. Now, here are the facts." When a corporation has to send a letter of that kind to each of more than 200,000 prescribing physicians, it behaves as though it were a *person* not merely in law, but also in fact. If a corporation had a soul this would be good for it. Naturally, pharmaceutical manufacturers have not rushed into FDA's Medical Advertising Branch to confess to Dr. Robert S. McCleery, its chief, and ask to do penance; he must catch them out and then they must be told that the consequences of not sending a corrective letter will be very unpleasant. Nonetheless the letter is *remedial*; it is to be valued because it can save the patient the evil consequences of an ad that has misinformed his doctor — and do it with a certainty and speed denied by punitive procedures.

None of the techniques — criminal and civil proceedings and corrective letters — is available to the FDA for use against the American Medical Association, which has preserved its *Sacred Trust*, as Richard Harris called it, by accepting with apparent equanimity the use of its *Journal* as an instrument for the criminal deception of its members. On April 13, 1967, the Internal Revenue Service formally proposed regulations to tax magazine advertising revenues of nonprofit groups, provided those revenues are unrelated to the public purposes for which the groups had been given tax exemptions. In an interview with Harvey H. Segal of the Washington *Post*, Bernard D. Hirsh, head of the AMA's legal department, said that the Association would fight the proposed new rules. Advertising in the *Journal*, he told Segal, has "educational value"; this, of course, is a corollary of what Hirsh called the AMA's "rigid standards of acceptability for publication."[1]

A few days later, Abbott Laboratories wrote a "Dear Doctor" corrective letter at FDA's request and sent it to all prescribing physicians. The letter said that the agency considered "misleading" an ad for Enduron and Enduronyl, which are related drugs used in patients with high blood pressure or congestive heart failure. The ad had run in the AMA *Journal*. If the AMA had a soul it would be morally refreshed by sending a letter acknowledging to its members that the main promotional theme of the questioned ad was contradicted by the 1965 through 1967

[1] But when the AMA's purpose was to block adoption of advertising regulations by FDA the Association avoided a claim of "educational value"; instead, it said in a brief filed with the agency on August 30, 1963, the value of the ads it carries is in "reminding" doctors of a product's availability and usefulness in certain conditions. The AMA and the Pharmaceutical Manufacturers Association were as one in insisting that physicians should of course be educated about drugs by medical and scientific literature and sources. The trouble is, they all too often are not.

editions of *New Drugs* — the annual guidebook issued by the AMA's own Council on Drugs. Needless to say, no such letter was sent. The theme of the ad, which was headlined "Thiazide-potassium/problems, doctor?", was that the loss of potassium with the Abbott brands is less than with similar products. The ad omitted several warnings — including one about the possibility of serious blood diseases — that are carried in *New Drugs*. The letter sent by Abbott Laboratories said in part:

> The ad suggests that any physician taking a patient off a thiazide-potassium combination may wish to consider Enduron as alternative therapy. It states that the product will "do an outstanding job for you *without* routine potassium supplementation," and that it has "potassium-sparing characteristics."
>
> The FDA believes that these claims could lead to the erroneous conclusion that . . . potassium supplementation is less often necessary with Enduron than with other thiazides.
>
> In point of fact, the need to consider potassium supplementation, dietary or otherwise, is no less with Enduron or Enduronyl than with any other thiazide drug.

The "rigid standards" about which AMA lawyer Hirsh spoke did not include taking the AMA's *New Drugs* off the shelf, just as in the Pree MT case the same standards did not involve a look at the AMA's *New and Nonofficial Drugs*, the predecessor volume. Here, in chronological order, are other advertising cases in which the *Journal*, sometimes along with medical publications that at least do not claim to have standards, was the medium for a false or misleading message:

PERITRATE SA

On February 27, 1967, the Food and Drug Administration seized shipments of Peritrate SA, which is sold by the Warner-Chilcott Laboratories division of the Warner-Lambert Pharmaceutical Company. The drug is pentaerythritol tetranitrate. Discovered in Sweden, it has been prescribed since 1952 to millions of coronary artery disease patients. It has been widely used to relieve the massive chest pain of the heart condition known as angina pectoris. But the five- and even ten-page ads that ran in six issues of the *Journal* of the American Medical Association — the issues dated December 6, 1965, each of the four weeks thereafter, and the issue of February 7, 1966 — went far beyond the approved claim for usefulness in angina pectoris to suggest that Peritrate kept more patients alive while they were in the hospital, and diminished the likelihood of attacks after they had been released. · An estimated one million dollars was spent on such promotion of Peritrate — a sum that in the same time period was exceeded for only two other prescription products. The claims, which FDA deemed false and misleading, were laid down in a bed of lavish color pictures — waves quivering on the surface of the sea, seagulls in the air, a hand reaching out toward a rising sun. The headline, one which did not bother the AMA but which Dr. James Goddard, Commissioner of FDA, said would "make any responsible physician cringe — although it might make advertising copywriters puff with pride," was, "Is Peritrate Life-Sustaining?"

The claims to which FDA objected were based primarily on a single study sponsored by the manufacturer and executed by Dr. Alexander Oscharoff, a New York City cardiologist. The advertisements were "distasteful," he told me when I interviewed him for the Washington *Post.* He had had "nothing to do" with them; and after he saw them, he said, he had objected to the company. Although FDA referred in court papers to his "purportedly well-controlled clinical investigation," it said his study had been falsely presented in the advertising.

Of the initial hundred patients, about half received Peritrate and half a fake pill. According to the ads, the survival rate after two years was 22 per cent higher among the Peritrate patients than among the controls who were given a placebo. But Peritrate had not been established by the study to be responsible for the higher survival rate. Similarly, the ads indicated that in the period of hospitalization immediately following cardiac attacks only two patients on Peritrate died — nine fewer than those who were given the placebo. Dr. Oscharoff has acknowledged, however, that the ads failed to report the results of his clinical trials when they were repeated. Again, a hundred patients were involved; in all major respects they were similar to the initial group. Yet among them the number of deaths of patients on the drug was 10 — and the number of fatalities among the placebo patients was identical.

Physicians whose curiosity was not numbed by the waves and the seagulls may have seen a footnote citing a research study supposedly supporting a claim that Peritrate stimulates collateral circulation. There was such a study. It had been done, the FDA said, "in a manner which in no way approximates the human disease situations." The footnote, that is, failed to disclose that the study had been done in piglets. Questioned about all of this, an AMA spokesman said the ads "met our standards."

SERAX

Serax (oxazepam), a tranquilizer/sedative produced by the Wyeth Laboratories division of the American Home Products Corporation, was introduced in mid-1965 with an initial, 6-month advertising budget of $350,000 for medical journals; another $250,000 was budgeted for direct mail promotion. This advertising and promotion, Commissioner James Goddard of the Food and Drug Administration has said, "has been consistently characterized by misleading statements and excessive claims." On May 23, 1966, FDA seized a quantity of Serax. The agency charged that it had been falsely and misleadingly advertised in the *Journal* of the American Medical Association for April 25, 1966 (and in certain issues of the *American Journal of Psychiatry* and *Medical Economics*). The advertising referred to a study made with Serax involving "148 elderly patients." Although some of these patients were in fact as old as 97, there were among them women as young as 33 and men as young as 35. The ad also promoted a "dangerous use for the elderly," FDA said, "by quoting from the study a dosage of up to 40 milligrams per day while the FDA-approved labeling for Serax limits the initial dosage in 'older patients' to 30 . . ." In addition, the agency said, the ad "promotes the drug's effectiveness by the claim 'controls . . . anxiety-linked depression' which is not permitted in the approved labeling. This may be dangerous because psychotic patients may be depressed and Serax should not be used for treating psychotics." Finally, FDA said, the requirement of fair balance was not met by the ad, because it cited one study that emphasizes the "favorable aspects of Serax treatment in relation to a competitive product" — but "fails to mention other studies which present different views." (In March 1967 the Roche Laboratories division of Hofmann-La Roche, Inc., sent a corrective letter to physicians concerning Librium, a tranquilizer/sedative in the same clinical family as Serax; the letter is discussed in the Afterword to Chapter 9. This is among the advertising episodes which did not involve the AMA *Journal*. The episodes other than the Librium episode are dealt with in a broader discussion of prescription-drug advertising in the Afterword to Chapter 8.)

ESIDRIX AND ESIDRIX-K

On September 22, 1966, in District Court in Newark, New Jersey, the Justice Department filed a 4-count criminal information against the CIBA Pharmaceutical Company, manufacturer of the diuretic drugs Esidrix and its potassium-containing chemical brother, Esidrix-K. The misdemeanor action was based in part on advertisements in the *Journal* of the American Medical Association for September 21, 1964, and April 5, 1965 (and on circulars mailed in February 1964), that, in the view of the Food and Drug Administration, tended to exaggerate the usefulness of Esidrix and Esidrix-K while downplaying problems associated with their use. By the time the second ad appeared, it may be recalled from the Afterword to Chapter 1, CIBA had sent out a warning letter about Esidrix-K in a bulk-rate "junk" mailing. The action was further based on entries in the *Physicians' Desk Reference,* the hardcover annual that, although advertising matter, is the medical profession's most generally relied upon guide to prescribing. The PDR entry supplied for Esidrix failed to alert physicians to the need to be cautious and gradual in administering other drugs for high blood pressure to patients on the CIBA product; the entry for Esidrix-K failed to warn that some patients may require — from dietary or other supplementation — more potassium than the combination drug provided. In a statement, CIBA said the charges were "of the most technical nature," unrelated to any injury known to the company and free of a claim of "intentional error." A plea of innocent was entered. As of late May 1967 the case was awaiting trial.

LINCOCIN

On October 27, 1966, the Food and Drug Administration went into District Court in Cincinnati to file papers to seize several cases of Lincocin, an antibiotic introduced in January 1965 by the Upjohn Company. The agency charged that the product was misrepresented in the *Journal* of the American Medical Association for October 3, 1966. The objections made by FDA included these: The ad contained claims that Lincocin caused no serious kidney or nervous disorders — but failed to give prominence to a "frequency of severe diarrhea" that is "a unique feature" of therapy with the antibiotic and to information that a sometimes fatal blood disease may occur during its use. The ad omitted precautionary advise to physicians that before relying exclusively on Lincocin for antibiotic therapy they should perform bacterial studies to see if it is apt to help the patient; in addition, there was a specification neither of the serious nature of the reactions that may occur in persons who may be hypersensitive to Lincocin, nor of the drugs that should be at hand for emergency treatment if such reactions should occur. In the FDA-approved prescribing instructions was a statement that certain adverse reactions were "observed in a small proportion of patients"; but in the ad, the agency said, this has been "misleadingly changed" to, "Side effects of small proportion." Finally, Lincocin's efficacy in the conditions for which it was approved was said not to be fairly shown.

Lincocin was one of eight drugs which within the year of their introduction (1965) became very popular — popular enough to join the list of the 200 medicines most prescribed. Seven days before the FDA action against Lincocin, these "big eight" drugs were discussed by William W. Goodrich, FDA's counsel, in a speech before the Pharmaceutical Advertising Club in New York City. "If the advertising copy for the 'big eight' is typical of what is going on. Madison Avenue's new disease of 'Behavioral Drift' is out of hand," Goodrich said.[2] The ad for Lincocin "obscures," he said, "the most important information that the physician needs in using this drug — that hematologic toxicity can occur, and that the frequency of severe diarrhea is a unique feature of Lincocin therapy." (The other seven products are discussed in the Afterword to Chapter 8.)

---

[2] "Behavioral Drift" was a phrase coined by Madison Avenue, picked up by the able and tough Goodrich, and used by him to describe the process by which drug ads are laid out and written so as to distort and go beyond the claims of safety and usefulness authorized by FDA. "As tempted as you may be by a new piece of investigative work that may be whispered to you to mount a new campaign to capture an entire market," Goodrich told an overflow audience of ad agency executives and copywriters, "you must remember that the approved claims are the limits beyond which promotion cannot go . . . you have an obligation in developing ad copy to tell the whole truth — good and bad . . . the entire advertising message must be designed around these basic ideas." Sensibly doubtful that the creativity of his listeners could be held within the boundaries of social usefulness by "the placebo of talk," Goodrich said, "more likely some stronger medicine will be necessary."

The Upjohn Company was being treated in a style to which it was unaccustomed. In Kalamazoo, Michigan, R. T. Parfet, Jr., the president, defended the ad, criticized FDA, and said his firm "has never intended either to mislead or misinform." Then in what was regarded by the FDA as an effort to incite powerful pressures to be brought by diverse sources against the agency, Upjohn said it was canceling its December 1966 advertising in some three dozen medical publications, including the *Journal* of the AMA. A "constant threat of court action" — not "Behavioral Drift" between Madison Avenue and Kalamazoo — was of course blamed. On November 14, 1966, *Barron's National Business and Financial Weekly*, published by Dow Jones & Company, stepped up the pressure on FDA with one of the most startling journalistic performances of 1966 (or maybe most any year). Neatly centered at the top of page one was the headline "Angels of Death." The subhead was, "FDA Has Become a Threat to U.S. Health and Welfare." The Lincocin case was given prominence as a justification for saying, among other things, that the agency, "in the doctrinaire hands of its new Commissioner, Dr. James L. Goodard, has become a clear and present danger to the nation's health and welfare." In the hands of whoever it was who wrote this baronial bilge, Dr. Goddard had demonstrated what a threat he was by acting against Elipten, the anticonvulsant whose adverse effects, it may be recalled from the Afterword to Chapter 1, CIBA Pharmaceutical Company had long failed to report, and by urging doctors to prescribe the short-acting sulfonamide drugs, whose superior safety over the long-acting versions was documented in the Afterword to Chapter 2. In the same baronial hands, the Pharmaceutical Manufacturers Association became a noble force "[f]ortified by the support of the scientific community" for resisting "pharmaceutical dictatorship." The concluding paragraph said, "What the nation already owes the drug makers can never be repaid." There came a recital of how the death rate has declined — with an implication that credit was due wholly to firms such as CIBA, Hoffmann-La Roche, and Upjohn. "Viewed in this light, the medicine men of FDA, all unwittingly perhaps, are angels of death," *Barron's* said in the peroration. "The 90th Congress should clip their wings." In the light of the record, it would be appropriate to wonder what Robert M. Bleiberg, the editor of *Barron's*, would feel he owes the FDA if, say, it had prevented an epileptic daughter from being masculinized by Elipten, or had protected a son from serious or fatal Stevens-Johnson Syndrome by denying him Madricidin to treat a cold. Possibly the view from the editorial offices of *Barron's* at 30 Broad Street in Manhattan would be different had Bleiberg himself suffered blood destruction or dangerously severe diarrhea because his doctor had been misled by an ad for Lincocin in the *Journal* of the AMA.

LASIX

On November 22, 1966, the Food and Drug Administration filed papers in District Court in Philadelphia for a seizure of Lasix, a diuretic newly marketed by Hoechst Pharmaceuticals, Inc. (formerly Lloyd Brothers, Inc.), of Cincinnati. The agency acted on the basis of advertisements that it said lacked fair balance and suggested uses that had not been authorized. The ads were in the *Journal* of the American Medical Association for October 10, 1966 (and, at about the same time in *Medical World News*, *Medical Economics*, and *MD Medical News Magazine*). There was a mention of the usefulness of Lasix in edematous patients, who have acute swelling, usually about the face; in support of this a study was cited. What the ads did not reveal was, FDA said, "that the study was not conducted on edematous patients." Lasix was featured as a "nonthiazide diuretic." This was condemned as misleading — Lasix shares many adverse effects, contraindications, and warnings with the thiazide diuretics, FDA said.

RONDOMYCIN

On May 22, 1967, the Pfizer Laboratories division of Chas. Pfizer & Co., Inc., mailed a corrective "Dear Doctor" letter to physicians concerning an advertisement for Rondomycin, a broad-spectrum antibiotic. The ad, which had appeared in the *Journal* of the American Medical Association for May 1, and in earlier issues, was regarded by the Food and Drug Administration as "potentially misleading." Dr. John L. Watters, the Laboratories' medical director, said. He went on to acknowledge that the ad failed to identify Rondomycin as a member of the tetracycline family that did not kill bacteria but instead arrested their growth. For that reason, Dr. Watters said, physicians should know that administration of the product for ten days "is especially important" in treating certain streptococcal infections. Finally, the company said, the warning information in the ad "is considered inadequate."

5

WHO KNOCKS AT FDA'S DOOR?

UNTIL 1938 drugs did not have to be shown to be either safe or effective. Starting in 1938 the Food and Drug Administration was authorized to prevent marketing of a drug product unless it could be shown to be safe. Drug products now must be shown to be safe *and* effective. The requirements for efficacy affect different groups of preparations in different ways:

1. Drugs marketed before 1938 were exempted by the legislation of that year; no showing of safety or efficacy is or can be required.

2. Under the Kefauver-Harris reforms of 1962, all applications for FDA marketing approval of new drugs, and for new uses of drugs legally considered to be "new," must be supported by substantial evidence of the makers' claims for therapeutic effectiveness, as well as safety. This requirement has been in effect since June 20, 1963.

3. There remains the largest group of drug products — the thousands marketed with FDA consent in the quarter-century between enactment of the Food, Drug, and Cosmetic Act of 1938 and June 20, 1963. Congress authorized FDA to demand for these drugs the same evidence of efficacy as for the wholly new products. The effective date set by law was October 10, 1964, the second anniversary of the signing of the bill by President Kennedy.

For many reasons it was the last group that posed the biggest problems for FDA. There were also many reasons for forebodings about how FDA would meet the challenge.

✓   ✓   ✓

As early as November 1963, with the public's memory of thalidomide fading, the Pharmaceutical Manufacturers Association was prepared to assume that the Food and Drug Administration would be "reasonable." The PMA proceeded to propose itself as a "sort of clearinghouse of information" on those drugs whose effectiveness might be brought into question. To be sure, the PMA was not conceding that the problem of ineffective drugs could amount to much. In the ears of cynics the PMA proposal might have sounded like a preposterous example of a goat volunteering to guard the cabbage patch. Probably the idea did not sit too well, either, with those who are aware that inadequate knowledge on the part of a physician about a drug's efficacy can injure a patient as surely as a drug's toxic action.

Not unexpectedly, the PMA's executive vice president and council, C. Joseph Stetler, trotted out that deathless dinosaur, the Hussey-Stetler Test of Time, "the best of all possible tests — widespread use in actual medical practice over an extended period of time." A month later there was heard the loud, incessant, and even more dismaying voice of the American Medical Association. In December 1963 the House of Delegates of the AMA — from whose Socioeconomic Division Stetler had migrated, and which had remained frozen in the ludicrous posture into which it had euchred itself — demanded outright repeal by Congress of the efficacy provisions[1] of the 1962 Kefauver-Harris

[1] Before this radical surgery was proposed, the AMA had applied a tight tourniquet to FDA. In January 1962 the AMA stopped sending FDA copies of the confidential *Bulletin* of the Council on Drugs. This publication, Commissioner George Larrick told Senator Humphrey, "was helpful to our reviewing medical officers in the Bureau of Medicine." Why the AMA thought it desirable to cut off the flow of valuable data to those who must make delicate decisions affecting our health and lives has not been persuasively explained.

amendments, which, it may be noted, were adopted without a single audible dissent in either the House or the Senate. The voice of the people was, typically, also inaudible, except as it was being expressed by one man, Senator Humphrey.

Unexpectedly, while FDA was considering what to do, the voice of President Lyndon B. Johnson was heard. Only eleven days after the assassination of John F. Kennedy he summoned the heads of the independent regulatory agencies to the White House. "I know the pressures that you feel and the duties you must discharge," he said. "When those pressures are honorable, respect them; when they are not, reject them. Accord to the honorable citizen . . . the full respect and honor that he is due, but let the venal and the self-seeking and the tawdry and the tainted fear to enter your building and fear even more to knock on your door." Perhaps some in Washington could translate this Johnsonian prose into clear guidelines for the guards at the building entrances and the receptionists outside the office doors, but the President's message may have seemed inscrutable at FDA. For one thing, FDA is not an independent regulatory agency, such as the Securities and Exchange Commission, but part of the sprawling domain of the Department of Health, Education, and Welfare. For another, it was not invited to the White House meeting.

Perhaps FDA's overriding problem was a tendency to impute the knocks on its doors to a concern for the general good rather than to self-interest. The regime of Commissioner George P. Larrick, Stephens Rippey wrote in *Drug Trade News* on June 29, 1959, "can be characterized as one of sweetness and light, togetherness, of loving one's neighbor [which the columnist defined as industry and Congress] as one's self . . . The changes in FDA in recent years have resulted in speculation that law enforcement has been sacrificed on the altar of good fellowship." [2] A year earlier, the PMA had honored the Commissioner

---

[2] Certainly this kind of togetherness was not unique to FDA. In *Conflict of Interest and Federal Service* (Cambridge: Harvard University Press, 1960), a book

with an award for "devoted service to the public welfare" and for his "understanding of mutual problems."

To one seeking a tough, vigorous approach by the Food and Drug Administration to the efficacy problem these were not the only discouraging factors. Another was that the skeletons in the drug industry's closet included some that FDA had helped to put there; and this could tend to inhibit the agency. Let us open the closet door for a moment.

About 1950, some four years before Commissioner Larrick's regime, there came into use a substitute for streptomycin, a lifesaving drug in tuberculosis. The chief drawback of streptomycin is that it can cause loss of the sense of equilibrium by damaging the vestibular branch of the eighth cranial nerve. A close chemical relative, dihydrostreptomycin, was introduced as a replacement. Because of the close chemical relationship between the two antibiotics, one would think that FDA would have been meticulously careful to get clear answers to questions that might occur even to a moderately curious layman. Can dihydrostreptomycin also affect the eighth cranial nerve? If it does not affect the vestibular branch of the nerve, where the sense of balance is controlled, might it affect the auditory (cochlear) branch and thereby cause deafness?

Adequate studies were not required. FDA certified dihydrostreptomycin as safe by itself and in combination with other products. Some of the combinations were promoted for use in trivial illnesses.

---

in which FDA is not even mentioned, the authors, a Special Committee on the Federal Conflict of Interest Laws of the Association of the Bar of the City of New York, say: "An agency — especially a promotional or regulatory agency [the Departments of Commerce and Labor being instances of the former] — is apt to develop close working relations with the particular industries and firms to which its program relates, and to find itself negotiating continuously with this interest group constituency. On occasion, the voice of this constituency becomes very strong, and opposition voices begin to refer to the agency as a 'captive agency' — a crypto-representative within government of an interest outside it. In a sense, the whole agency and its executive can become caught up in one big conflict of interest."

By 1951 it was a published fact that dihydrostreptomycin in sustained use caused permanent deafness. Not long afterward it became evident that this could result even when the dose was small and the duration of treatment brief. Perhaps the most graphic in a series of warnings was published in the August 1, 1959, issue of the *Journal* of the American Medical Association. Eight specialists, who practiced medicine in four widely separated cities, reported that since 1955 they had collectively encountered 32 cases of permanent deafness in patients who had been given dihydrostreptomycin. The authors said that the "prescribing physician usually had not the remotest idea of the eventual disastrous results."

It could be said that, so far as the prescribing physicians were concerned, dihydrostreptomycin had survived the Hussey- Stetler Test of Time. They had not known that there was a "latent period of from several weeks to as long as six months between the administration and the onset of the hearing loss." Even if they had known of the risk, they might not have been aware they were taking it because, again quoting the *Journal* article, "drug companies market multiple combinations of antibiotics combining penicillin, dihydrostreptomycin, and streptomycin under names that do not clearly indicate the presence of dihydrostreptomycin."

FDA's former antibiotics chief, Henry Welch, who had approved fixed combinations of antibiotics, "apparently first became concerned about this problem" in 1959, the Kefauver Subcommittee on Antitrust and Monopoly was told by Dr. Barbara Moulton. This, she noted, was "roughly 10 years after the drug was first certified as safe." Action "to remove some of the combination products from the market" was taken during her tenure as an FDA medical officer. Finally, on September 22, 1960, a proposal was published to require strong warning statements. That was about seven months after her father, Dr. Harold G. Moulton, former president of the Brookings Institution, had been prescribed an antibiotic combination that contained dihydrostreptomycin, which his condition did not require. "My father is now noticeably hard of hearing," the physician testified shortly before the requirement of strong warning statements became effective.

Among the 32 victims mentioned in the 1959 *Journal* article were several who had received dihydrostreptomycin not as a life-saving measure but pointlessly — for infections against which it was ineffective, including a cold, flu in three cases, upper respiratory infection, and mononucleosis, and "prophylactically" in uninfected surgical patients. One victim of this kind of prophylactic precaution became considerably depressed over her disabling loss of hearing. She was a thirty-nine-year-old telephone operator.[3]

✦ ✦ ✦

The magnitude of the drug-efficacy problem had been compounded by long overlooked failures of the Food and Drug Administration. Here are some of them.

FDA allowed drugs to go on the market on the basis of what some of its own medical officers, including Dr. Frances Kelsey and Dr. John Nestor, have disdainfully called mere testimonials; Commissioner Larrick acknowledged to Representative L. H. Fountain's House Intergovernmental Relations Subcommittee that even as he spoke — in 1964 — there were drugs on the market that had not been tested in animals before being tested in humans; Senator Humphrey has spoken of his "understanding that a number of drugs which are still labeled for 'infant use' were never even tested in infants — or in a substantial number

[3] On April 13, 1964, the *Journal* of the AMA reported a talk given by Dr. Merlin K. Du Val on the common use of antibiotics to prevent infection after operations. He had told a sectional meeting of the American College of Surgeons that among 1000 surgical patients studied more wounds became infected when various antibiotics were given than when they were withheld. He said the side effects included allergic reactions, deafness, aplastic anemia, liver damage, and near-fatal inflammation of the small intestine. A more comprehensive report on the unrestrained use of antibiotics in hospitals will be found in the afterword to this chapter.

of infants — before the labeling was proposed and approved."
FDA assured Congress and the public that it had demanded a
showing of efficacy in drugs it had released for use in life-threatening situations, but the agency had not consistently imposed
such demands — as was demonstrated by Altafur and by other
drugs.

And FDA had not kept adequate records of which drugs were
on the market, of which drugs no longer were being sold, of
which drugs had been cleared but had not yet been placed on
sale. When a manufacturer took a drug off the market and FDA
did not know of it, two dangers were posed. One was that the
company could change its mind and put the product on sale
once again. Another was that, with no report in its file on
toxicity, FDA would have no reason not to clear for sale a new-
drug application for the same product submitted by a different
manufacturer. Finally, FDA had lost track of whether promotional claims conformed with the new-drug application and the
labeling. All of these situations and possibilities have been
brought out by congressional inquiries.

Senator Humphrey's Subcommittee on Reorganization and
International Organizations, for example, developed the case of
Efocaine, a long-acting anesthetic introduced commercially in
January 1952 by E. Fougera & Company, Inc. According to a
bibliography prepared for the subcommittee by the National
Library of Medicine, the first death attributed to the use of
Efocaine was reported in the October 10, 1953, issue of the
Journal of the American Medical Association. Numerous inju-
ries, including paralysis, also were reported. In an editorial of
May 15, 1954, the *Journal* said that "in the best interests of
patients continued use of the present formula does not seem
justified." Four months later, the *American Surgeon* editorial-
ized:

. . . it now appears obvious that Efocaine can be extremely
damaging to the tissues and to the nerves themselves. We

therefore make a strong plea that Efocaine be abandoned, especially for use in the paravertebral [alongside the spinal column] region . . .

Our experience, we believe, has been another example of the use of drug therapy in human beings producing disastrous results before adequate . . . studies have been completed in the experimental animal.

How inadequate the studies were was indicated in 1955, when, in connection with a civil suit brought against Fougera in the Federal Court in New York City, a deposition was taken from Clifford H. Bradney, executive vice president of the company. In response to questions by the attorney for the plaintiff, Bradney said that up until the time the new-drug application was submitted to FDA — in August 1951 — the number of researchers who had done animal studies on Efocaine was "just one." The researcher was Dr. Tobias Weinberg, a pathologist at Sinai Hospital in Baltimore. Bradney also said that Dr. Weinberg's studies were begun in March or April of 1951, that the final results were reported the following July, and that up to August 1952 no further animal studies of the effects of Efocaine were undertaken.

In another Efocaine suit in the Supreme Court of Bronx County, New York, Bradney was again subjected to pretrial examination. He was asked by Arnold Elkind, who had also represented the plaintiff in the Federal Court case, if he had been "aware of the fact that Dr. Weinberg's animal studies did disclose, on autopsies of animals, that there had been atypical reactions in the brachial plexus [a nerve center] of these animals following injection of Efocaine?" Bradney conceded, "I had knowledge of it." Later, these exchanges took place:

Q. Was any attempt made by . . . E. Fougera & Co., Inc., to warn the medical profession of any of the claims of atypical results which had come to the attention of E. Fougera & Co., prior to November 19, 1952 [when the *Sinai Hospital Journal* published a report on Efocaine by Dr. Weinberg]?

A. Not to the best of my knowledge there was not.

. . . .

Q. What knowledge did the defendant . . . have prior to November 19, 1952, of the technique involved in performing a paravertebral nerve block?

A. The knowledge that was available to us is the knowledge available to anyone who had studied the text book on technique of paravertebral or intercostal [between the ribs] nerve block.

Q. And how was this knowledge made available to E. Fougera & Co., Inc.? Do they have such text books?

A. Yes, we have such text books.

Q. And these are texts describing the techniques and procedure to be used in paravertebral and intercostal nerve block? Is that correct?

A. That is correct.

Such was the foundation of the new-drug application — textbooks, and animals studied by one researcher who found and reported atypical reactions. And such was the foundation of the clearance given Efocaine by FDA two months after the application was filed. When Senator Humphrey obtained FDA's official chronology he found that there was a complete blank for the nine years between September 14, 1954, and June 20, 1963. In a letter to Mr. Humphrey, lawyer Elkind wrote: ". . . I simply cannot understand why the FDA file should be a vacuum [for nine years], and I also find it hard to understand, in the light of the medical literature [the National Library of Medicine bibliography listed 28 reports of adverse reactions, some of them multiple, to Efocaine], why the FDA file only mentions one complaint of adverse reactions from Efocaine and that this was basically a complaint of local soreness."

"What does the astonishing account indicate?" the Senator asked in a memorandum published by his subcommittee. "For one thing, the Efocaine history illustrates that nobody knows how many unsafe drugs were withdrawn from the market without FDA being notified and without FDA caring very much, prior to the 1964 regulation."

✦ ✦ ✦

The Food and Drug Administration announced its draft regulations on efficacy for the 1938–1963 drug products on February 28, 1964. The industry reaction was mild. Manufacturers are "reacting favorably," *Chemical Week* reported. "A spokesman for the Pharmaceutical Manufacturers Association says drug companies are not worried. 'A few drugs may be affected, but we do not anticipate any real difficulty.' " *Business Week* reported predictions by trade observers that the proposed efficacy regulations "may mean considerable relabeling of established drugs but won't remove many from the market . . . 'In contrast with the violence of the Kefauver hearings . . . FDA's current proposals are a welcome relief,' one drug executive says."

"Industry had feared," said the *PMA Newsletter*, "that the government might insist on extensive and unnecessary controlled clinical tests for all drugs involved, even though they might have been well regarded and successfully used for years.

"Instead the regulations adhere in principle [to] informal plans FDA had discussed with representatives of the [PMA]. The important point is that . . . clinical experience may be recognized as substantial evidence of effectiveness."

In order to gain some perspective on all of this, the distinction must be drawn between clinical *experience* and the "adequate, well-controlled clinical *investigations*" (my italic) that FDA was authorized to demand by the Kefauver-Harris amendments of 1962.

In a first-rate clinical investigation possible bias is eliminated. "Clinical investigation cannot be strong while bias persists," Dr. Henry K. Beecher of Boston said in a guest editorial in the *Journal* of the American Medical Association for January 3, 1953. "It cannot be strong while unsound clinical impression has authority."

Examples of his point abound. For the moment two will suffice. One was reported in April 1964 in the *Archives of Dermatology*. It involved a study of anti-itching pills. Four groups of tablets were used. Each group was of a different color, and each group was placed in an envelope. Twelve itchy patients were instructed to take tablets from envelope *A* four times daily for two weeks. Then they were told to do the same with the tablets from envelope *B*, then from envelope *C*, and finally from envelope *D*, until all four types of tablets had been consumed. All four types of tablets were lactose placebos, the article disclosed, but in about 66 per cent of the cases the patients reported a beneficial effect from one or more of the four groups. They believed the pills would help, and so they did. The second example, reported in May 1964 in *Worldwide Abstracts of Medicine*, published by Warner-Chilcott Laboratories, was based on an article printed in 1963 in the *Scandinavian Journal of Psychology*. When what was actually a placebo was introduced as a "depressant" it produced a statistically significant fall in pulse rate, blood pressure, and subjective reaction speed. When the placebo was presented as a "stimulant" it produced significant changes of the opposite kind.

The double-blind system eliminates bias. The investigator does not know which pill contains the drug with which he is working, which contains a placebo, or which may contain another drug. The patient is similarly uninformed. The pills are identified by a code number. Not until the investigation has been completed and the results tabulated is the code broken.

Clinical experience is almost self-defining. It is the experience of practicing physicians in treating sick patients with a drug.

The worth of this experience can vary extremely. It can consist of a high order of observation, or of nothing more than a collection of impressions — all of them wrong. A large number of drugs went on the market with claims of efficacy supported not by controlled studies but by clinical experience — even mere testimonials, as Dr. Kelsey and others have found. The unhappy fact was that, as a practical matter, FDA could not demand clinical investigation of all the drugs marketed in a quarter-century and still being sold. There are, by estimate of Commissioner Larrick, 6000 of these — prescription and nonprescription.

Many reasons are to be found for this. One of the most compelling is that there is a severe and critical shortage of fully trained clinical pharmacologists (a shortage that neither the industry nor the federal government has made any major effort to overcome). It would be highly unrealistic and probably impossible to add to the workload of this elite group the retesting of thousands of products that have been on the market for years, particularly since they understandably prefer to work on the frontiers testing new drugs. Further, the industry is undoubtedly correct in saying that many old drugs have established their safety and worth through prolonged and carefully observed clinical experience.

It is, I think, clear that although FDA must demand clinical investigations to support claims for *new* drug products, and although it should demand them for some of the old, it could not now demand them for 6000. The Commissioner gave Senator Humphrey written assurance that ". . . [FDA] will not accept collections of medical testimonials as proof of effectiveness."

✓ ✓ ✓

The regulations that the Food and Drug Administration proposed — discussed in some detail below — were far-reaching and strong. For thirty days the record was held open for filing of comments. Once again FDA was thrown heavily on the defensive. "Not a single physician or medical group in the nation," Senator Humphrey said, "wrote in to express *support* of these proposed regulations, in whole or in part." But there *was* substantial pressure to hold firm, apart from the spirit and the letter of the law itself. It came principally from Senator Humphrey, who repeatedly made it clear that he was going to keep FDA under continuing scrutiny.

The industry — numerous trade associations and individual firms — was upset most about FDA's insistence that its proposed regulations covered old drugs that had been cleared by the agency for sale and were no longer legally classified as "new" drugs. The industry contended that marketing and promotion of these products should continue without evidence of efficacy being submitted. An estimated 1500 preparations were involved. The agency stood fast, insisting that the law required it to make sure that these drugs are effective for the purposes claimed. In July 1964 the PMA, joined by 41 manufacturers, sought a declaratory judgment in the Federal Court in Wilmington, Delaware. This kind of bitter-end resistance would be serious enough if only money were involved. Much more than that — suffering, protraction of illness — may be at stake with at least some of the 1500 preparations. And what of the Hussey-Stetler Test of Time? If it really is, as claimed, the best of all possible tests, why have a court test? Why not merely submit the evidence that the 1500 preparations can meet the claims made for them?

The final regulations were announced on May 28, 1964, about two months before the suit was filed at Wilmington. They differed little from those that had been proposed. In a lengthy press release FDA listed areas in which it had *not* yielded to industry views. These included:

1. A requirement that a responsible officer of the firm sign a

statement attesting to the accuracy of current promotional material in the light of clinical and other experience available to the company. FDA refused to delegate responsibility for review of an individual firm's detailed data to the industry.

2. The argument that advertising of over-the-counter products was outside FDA's jurisdiction. The agency rejected this view. It ruled that it had a right to call for a review of advertising of nonprescription preparations, and to halt sale of those that are promoted for uses it has not approved.

3. The suggestion that a manufacturer should not be required to explain why sale of a drug had been discontinued, or why marketing had not commenced. FDA, in rebuffing this, said that the reasons why a firm stops marketing or fails to begin it "may have an important bearing on safety of the same drug marketed by others either now or in the future."

4. Protests that discontinuance of a new drug or failure to market it was not a ground for suspension of the new-drug application, such suspension ending the possibility of marketing. FDA went part way on this. It changed the regulation to state that failure to market, or discontinuance, "may" be the basis for a notice to withdraw approval, and to show that the withdrawal of approval will be undertaken on one of the statutory grounds.

This is what the regulations announced by the Food and Drug Administration on May 28 required:

1. Manufacturers marketing drugs and antibiotics approved since 1938 must examine their promotional materials and their clinical records to be sure that all claims — *for efficacy and safety* — are justified by experience, and that the promotional materials include all necessary warnings, contraindicated uses, and side effects and untoward reactions that may have appeared after the drugs had been put on the market.[4]

---

[4] The 1962 drug amendments transferred jurisdiction over advertising of prescription drugs from the Federal Trade Commission to FDA. The FTC had had ill-defined and seldom-used powers over advertising of ethical drugs that was not legally considered labeling.

2. Manufacturers were directed to report to FDA by September 25, 1964, whether the labeling and promotional claims then current offered the drug only for conditions covered in the original new-drug application. Manufacturers were directed to disclose simultaneously if there had been brought to their attention any claims, side effects, untoward reactions or contraindications that were not adequately covered by the labeling and advertising.

3. Also by the September 25, 1964, deadline, manufacturers were directed to tell FDA what they planned to do about discontinuing or obtaining the agency's acceptance of unsubstantiated claims.

4. By July 27, 1964, manufacturers were directed to report to FDA which approved drugs had never been marketed, which had been taken off the market, and which remained on the market.

5. Manufacturers were directed to prepare to submit annually — on the anniversary date of approval of the new-drug application — reports on each approved drug, including any changes or additions to information previously filed.

Commissioner Larrick said the task of considering the information would be "monumental." How much time will be needed? how many drugs will be withdrawn from the market voluntarily or by compulsion? how many labels will be changed? how many claims will be abandoned? — to such questions there were no clear answers.

The Commissioner told Senator Humphrey that "special attention" would be given to drugs said by the Council of Drugs of the American Medical Association to lack scientific proof of efficacy. He also said that the following groups of drugs would be given "priority attention": psychotherapeutic drugs, including "most tranquilizers"; topical, ophthalmic antibiotic-steroid combinations; other topical antibiotic combination products; pediatric dosages; progestational (hormonal) agents; drugs used in pregnancy; topical antihistamines; topical pain-killers; oral and injectable proteolytic enzymes; bioflavonoids; nonprescription iron preparations; hormone creams; a number of sustained-release drugs.

✓ ✓ ✓

Let there be no mistake about it. The regulations and the law behind them have an enormous potential to reduce the unnecessary suffering, protraction of illness, and waste of money that the late President Kennedy attributed to ineffective drugs. Commissioner Larrick correctly said, when the final regulations were announced, that Congress had given the Food and Drug Administration a "unique opportunity to review past medical decisions permitting several thousand new drugs to go on the market. This review will include not only a new look at the safety of these drugs, but a first-time comparison of the actual promotional claims with the medical evidence on which they were based."

No matter what the potential of the law and the regulations, however, what counts in the final analysis is their implementation — *how* FDA enforces them. It would be unfair and unwise to presume that FDA will fail to implement the efficacy regulations vigorously and in the public interest. It has little excuse for such a failure. It has an enlarged staff, a new medical director, more money, and other tools that will be discussed in Chapter 18. Yet it would be folly to forget or minimize FDA's past record, which includes serious instances of nonimplementation or poor implementation of the 1938 law — a record further developed here in succeeding chapters.

In a letter that Senator Humphrey wrote in February 1964, he asked, in the matter of drug efficacy who represents the consumer? His answer was ". . . thus far, apparently no one except FDA itself. And its record is not very consistent as regards standing up for the consumer — the public — in some contro-

versies regarding prescription drugs." After years of looking into
FDA's operations, and learning more about them than probably
any other member of Congress, the Senator felt compelled to
caution, "The past record of laxity of the Food and Drug Administration leaves considerable doubt that it will administer
this key [efficacy] provision of the law in a strong, effective manner."

Senator Kefauver and President Kennedy, both of whom were
concerned with this problem, are dead. Although Senator
Humphrey told Commissioner Larrick that he intends to maintain his interest in FDA, his subcommittee's inquiry came to an
end on the day the regulations were announced, and he has
been elevated to the vice presidency.

Over the long run, then, the quality of FDA's implementation of the efficacy regulations, and of its responsibilities for
drugs generally, will depend heavily upon the interest shown by
the public and the medical profession. This is not very encouraging. "There is strong organized pressure on FDA against firm
implementation," Senator Humphrey had warned. "There appears to be no organized effort to encourage FDA *toward* firm
implementation."

The situation might have had a familiar ring to a public
servant as wise in the ways of government as Senator Paul H.
Douglas of Illinois. In his *Ethics in Government,* a book em-
bodying the substance of the Godkin Lectures he gave at Harvard in 1952, Douglas wrote:

. . . on any concrete issue the stake of each member of the
general public as taxpayer and consumer will be small, while
that of the special interest group will be large. The concentrated private interest will, therefore, usually triumph over the
diffused general interest. A form of social control which began
in ardent good faith as an attempt to help the weak and the

poor may therefore wind up as an instrument to enrich the greedy and the powerful. Something of this sort has been happening in our national life during these last few years.

THE "MORE COMPREHENSIVE REPORT on the unrestrained use of antibiotics in hospitals" referred to in footnote 3 of Chapter 5 is reprinted here from the Appendixes of *The Therapeutic Nightmare*, and is followed at once by a brief discussion of the status of the drug-efficacy situation.

✓ ✓ ✓

In March 1963 the president, director, and statistician of the Commission on Professional and Hospital Activities, whose sponsors include the American College of Physicians, the American College of Surgeons, and the American Hospital Association, reported: "There are now comforting and concrete indications that the medical profession is fully aware of the hazards of the unbridled use of antibiotics and is exercising restraint in the prescription of these dangerous and frequently ineffective drugs." Dr. Du Val's report of a year later, raises the question whether the Commission was not being optimistic.

In the *Bulletin* of the American College of Surgeons for March–April 1963, the Commission officials — Dr. Robert S. Myers, Dr. Vergil N. Slee, and statistician Richard P. Ament — told with dismay about what was revealed by a study of 85,734 discharges in 1961 from a random sample consisting of 20 hospitals to determine the therapeutic use of antibiotics.

Almost half of the antibiotic use, 46 per cent, was determined to be prophylactic. "The patients in this group," the experts reported, "were given antibiotics to prevent infections which did not exist, should not occur, and in all probability never would happen. Such prophylactic use has been denounced for years as a dangerous, unnecessary, and expensive practice." The report continued:

For instance, one study has shown that 38 per cent of patients undergoing surgical repair of simple inguinal hernias [in the region of the groin] received antibiotics, and of these, at least 74 per cent were given these drugs needlessly, that is, for prophylaxis. Since [this] is one operation in which infection should not occur if proper selection and preparation of patients are observed, and if adequate surgical aseptic technique is followed, then this unnecessary prophylactic use is illogical, unscientific, and contrary to the welfare of the patient.

Our experience . . . has also revealed excessive and ill-advised use of antibiotics in other fields . . . For example, there was the large teaching hospital in which . . . almost every patient admitted for tonsillectomy received a prophylactic injection of antibiotics upon entrance to the hospital . . . This is bad surgical practice, for in the years before the discovery of antibiotics, very few patients developed postoperative infections of any consequence after tonsillectomy. Moreover, such widespread use of the antibiotics exposes the patients to the dangers of serious and even fatal complications, to say nothing of wasting the patients' money and the nurses' time.

There is also the case of the large medical center in which a substantial number of internists routinely gave prophylactic antibiotics to all patients admitted with coronary thrombosis, on the theory that pulmonary edema [excessive accumulation of fluids in the lungs] and pneumonitis [pneumonia] might develop later. Obviously, there is no way of determining in advance the proper antibiotics for such cases and insufficient concern was shown for the probability that the needless use of these drugs exposed the patients to more danger than would occur from the occasional pulmonary infection.

The reader will find a fuller discussion of the needless use of antibiotics in Chapter 10.

✓ ✓ ✓

With the appointment of Dr. James L. Goddard as Commissioner of the Food and Drug Administration there came into being a reasonable basis for hoping that the question of the efficacy of the drugs marketed between 1938 and 1962 would be handled with more concern for the interests of the public and less for those of the pharmaceutical industry. One development of crucial importance was the resignation of Dr. Joseph F. Sadusk, Jr., as Medical Director of FDA. In view of President Kennedy's eloquent discussion of the importance of assuring that drugs are useful, in his Consumers' Protection Message of March 15, 1962, it is little short of incredible that the man chosen, a few months after the assassination of Mr. Kennedy, to implement those views, by then embodied in the law, could have been Dr. Sadusk. He did not believe in the provisions of the law that put on FDA responsibility for requiring evidence that a drug was not worthless in the medical conditions for which it was being offered; he wanted physicians to be allowed to do pretty much as they pleased. Inevitably he brought no vigor to the task of dealing with the 1938–62 drugs (Dr. Goddard has estimated the total at as many as 4000) that had been marketed under a law requiring only that safety be shown. After hearings in which FDA's performance under the efficacy provisions of the Kefauver-Harris Amendments were reviewed, Chairman L. H. Fountain of the House Intergovernmental Relations Subcommittee said on June 25, 1964, "Serious questions have been raised . . . as to compliance with those portions of the . . . Amendments which specify that a drug must be shown effective as well as safe in order to continue to be marketed." The Congressman had particular reference to Dr. Sadusk's role in connection with Parnate, an antidepressant (discussed in Chapter 9 and its Afterword), and with certain antihistamines with a suspected capacity to cause birth defects (see Chapter 12 and its Afterword).

Dr. Sadusk left FDA on March 22, 1966, accompanied by Dr. Joseph M. Pisani, his deputy. A few weeks later it was announced that the efficacy review would be undertaken by the National Academy of Sciences-National Research Council. Understandably, because of such factors as FDA's limited resources, Commissioner Goddard was "grateful." Frederick Seitz, president of the NAS-NRC, who joined Dr. Goddard in making the announcement, said the review is of "extraordinary importance to the medical profession and the Nation. It is essential that the study have the strongest possible professional base; we shall, therefore, depend on the cooperation, not only of many individual scientists, but also of the major professional societies interested in therapeutic drugs."

A tendency to greet all of this with vast relief would be quite natural, but it may be premature and unwise to let one's guard down to the point of indulging in uncritical admiration. The structure of the Academy, Ralph E. Lapp, the nuclear scientist, has pointed out, is one that has permitted its policies on the space program to be shaped by space advisors who happen to work for space contractors. Therefore, until the drug-efficacy study is submitted, at some still-indefinite date, one cannot exclude the possibility that the views of the drug industry, closely meshed as it is with various educational and research institutions and professional societies, will not to some degree be reflected at the expense of the public health. I am talking about a possibility; I am not making a presumption. The FDA surely must give great weight to the NAS-NRC study. Surely also, if in any respect that study is inconsistent with the public interest, the agency must act in a manner consistent with its primary obligations. "But we must never forget that our reason for existence, as a government agency, is to serve the *public* interest," Dr. Goddard said when he was sworn in as Commissioner. "And the public has very little voice unless it is ours."

6

FDA: THE EROSION OF ZEAL

NOT LONG BEFORE Senator Humphrey had expressed pessimism about the capacity and will of the Food and Drug Administration to administer vigorously the efficacy provisions that were to take effect in October 1964, he had seen FDA update its "past record of laxity" into the present. This happened in an episode involving Orabilex, a contrast medium. It makes the gallbladder of a patient who takes it more visible for examination on X-ray plates.

The Senator knew enough about the Orabilex story to be distressed and angered. However, after his involvement had ended several extremely revealing chapters were written by Representative L. H. Fountain's House Intergovernmental Relations Subcommittee. In two days of hearings during June 1964, the subcommittee developed information showing that the situation had been even worse than Senator Humphrey realized. The account that follows was taken from the records of both the Fountain and Humphrey subcommittees.

By FDA's admittedly rough estimate, Orabilex (bunamiodyl sodium) was administered to 2.7 million persons in its first three and one-half years on the market. FDA's records indicate that 25 deaths were associated with its use, although in perhaps 7 of these cases the agency regarded the association as tenuous. There is, however, some controversy about the toll. Dr. John E.

Wennberg, a Johns Hopkins Hospital research fellow who was in large measure responsible for the removal of the drug from the market, has cited reports of 17 fatalities in the Baltimore-Washington area alone, and he has extrapolated from this a national total of at least 100 deaths. Even this figure is considered by some to be conservative. Dr. Francis J. Borges, director of the Division of Hypertension-Renal Diseases at the University of Maryland School of Medicine, wrote to Senator Humphrey in April 1964 that the medical literature he had seen showed 27 fatal and nonfatal cases of acute renal (kidney) damage in persons given Orabilex. "However," he added, "it is reasonable to assume that the recorded data is a small representation of the total experience."

On the other hand, several physicians argued vehemently that Orabilex was safe. For example, two California doctors certified by the American Board of Radiology, Dr. M. L. Weinstein and Dr. N. E. Roberti, wired the Department of Health, Education, and Welfare after a warning letter had been issued that they had used the drug "thousands of times" without harm to their patients.

The value of Orabilex as a diagnostic aid is also in dispute. Dr. Weinstein and Dr. Roberti said in their telegram that other dyes lacked the "consistency and reliability" of Orabilex, and that if it were to become unavailable the consequence would be "much needless surgery" with "resultant increased surgical mortality rate." A view irreconciliable with this one was expressed in March 1964 in a letter to Senator Humphrey from Dr. Martin W. Donner, an associate professor in the Department of Radiology at the Johns Hopkins Hospital. The "one unqualified prerequisite of a diagnostic medium is its safety," he said and, that being so, Orabilex could not be considered "an indispensable drug, unique in its field." At the Fountain hearings, FDA's principal witness, Assistant Commissioner for Planning Winton B. Rankin, was asked by D. C. Goldberg, of the subcommittee staff, if Orabilex was "superior to other contrast media." "No," Rankin answered.

Orabilex was a product of E. Fougera & Company, Inc., the Hicksville, Long Island, firm that had also marketed Efocaine, the long-acting anesthetic taken up in Chapter 5. FDA received the new-drug application on July 7, 1958, and cleared it, after requesting more data, on October 24, 1958. The initial labeling authorized by the agency claimed that the drug had "spectacularly low" toxicity and "notable absence of side effects." In a disillusioned look back on FDA's clearance of the drug for sale, the AMA *Journal* said in an editorial of November 2, 1963, that the agency had acted on the basis of "a false assumption" that similar chemicals had proved safe, and on the basis of an opinion derived from animal studies that "appear inadequate."

Later, a similar dismay was expressed by Dr. Clarke Davison, a George Washington University pharmacologist whom the Fountain subcommittee had engaged as a consultant. He said, "[I have] examined this [new-drug] application in its entirety and feel that the information Fougera submitted was completely inadequate to demonstrate the safety of the drug. I also feel FDA was quite remiss in approving the application with so little pharmacological [animal test] and clinical data."

Bunamiodyl sodium had been tried on only 10 dogs. There was suggestive but inconclusive evidence that the kidneys of all of them had been affected — including, oddly enough, the one dog, the control, that had not been given Orabilex. In those dog data W. Donald Gray, of the subcommittee staff, found some perplexing material. For one thing, the internal organs of the dog *not* given Orabilex were described in lavish detail, whereas those of the 9 experimental animals were described, tersely, as normal. The report had been prepared for the manufacturer by Leberco Laboratories of Roselle Park, New Jersey. In a part that dealt with gross, or naked-eye, examination of the organs of the autopsied dogs it said, "Dog No. 10 was dead on the 9th day of the experiment and an autopsy could not be performed because rigor mortis had completely set in." But the same report described the results of a microscopic examination of the kidney, spleen, liver, and other organs as "normal." As Gray pointed out, the organs "could not have been examined and found normal if the dog was not autopsied." Dr. Bert J. Vos, director of FDA's Division of Toxicological Evaluation, conceded that the report was "impossible." The impossibility had not, however, been discovered by FDA.

The supplemental dog data submitted to FDA before it released the drug contained additional evidence, albeit inconclusive, that Orabilex could impair kidney function. The hearings brought out that years later this had been recognized even by a consultant whom the manufacturer had engaged. The FDA pharmacologist who had reviewed the data had said, however, "The added submission on kidney function tests indicates this drug is safe."

"On what basis did he arrive at that conclusion?" Representative Fountain inquired. It developed that no one in the FDA delegation before him really knew. In keeping with the casual ways that were followed in the agency, a conclusion like this could be reached with no requirement that the person reaching it summarize his reasons in writing. In 1960, a committee of the National Academy of Sciences and the National Research Council had found it necessary to make the elementary recommendation that such summaries be prepared.

"It is inconceivable to me," the North Carolina Democrat told Rankin sharply, "that it would take a group or committee of the National Academy of Sciences to impress upon someone in the Food and Drug Administration the importance of such a procedure, and I am surprised that it was not required a long time ago. That you would permit this drug or any drug to be approved, without a summary of the basis upon which the pharmacologist or medical officer made the decision, is inconceivable to me."

The subcommittee's medical consultant found that the examination of rats to which Orabilex had been given was inadequate. According to the report, only four types of tissue, Dr. Davison said, had been examined grossly for evidence of drug effects. None of the body tissues had been examined under a microscope. Representative Fountain asked Dr. Vos if he would agree that this was insufficient. "Yes," the FDA toxicologist replied, "I would agree . . ."

In Rankin's prepared statement the Assistant Commissioner said, "The clinical work conducted by 19 physicians on 757 patients showed no serious adverse side effects." The subcommittee was not persuaded that the physicians had been encouraged to look for serious adverse effects. It turned out that they had used a report form, supplied by the manufacturer, which listed a number of side reactions — all of them relatively minor — that might be encountered. Representative Fountain asked Dr. Ralph G. Smith, director of FDA's Division of New Drugs, ". . . the extent to which the clinical investigators performed diagnostic tests, such as kidney and liver function tests, or blood counts, which would be likely to reveal serious adverse effects?" "Tests of that nature were not performed," Dr. Smith admitted. "Do you have any information or evidence indicating whether or not the company ever suggested the advisability of such tests?" Mr. Fountain asked. "No, I have no information as to that," Dr. Smith said.

The original physicians' brochure for Orabilex said it was not to be used for a patient with impaired kidney function. Despite this, it was brought out by Gray of the subcommittee staff, FDA had not felt it necessary to require that simple tests be done on humans to see if the drug had particular effects on the kidney. Representative Fountain asked Dr. Smith for his opinion at that moment as to whether the kidney-function test should have been made in 1958. By this time, Dr. Smith was finding the atmosphere chillingly unlike that of ten weeks before, when, in the auditorium of the Department of Health, Education, and

Welfare, he had received the Distinguished Service Award, the Department's highest honor. He had this colloquy with the Congressman:

DR. SMITH. Well, I would be a lot happier now if they [the tests] had been done in 1958, and if we had required them.

MR. FOUNTAIN. I didn't ask you what would make you happy. I asked you what ought to have been done.

DR. SMITH. Well, if I had to go back to 1958, and had to do it over again, I would have required them.

During an exchange with Gray, Dr. Smith conceded that, in the absence of kidney function and other key diagnostic tests, the total of 757 patients was insufficient to turn up a side effect that might occur in 1 patient among, say, 2500.

The E. Fougera firm had claimed in the original brochure, "No derangement of any organ attributable to Orabilex has been reported." The company submitted a supplemental application on October 14, 1960. The claim was not in the application, Representative Fountain noted, but FDA approved it only twenty-five days later. This disclosure, as did others, seemed to catch Rankin and Dr. Smith off guard. It appears from what they said that the deletion had not been detected, or, if it had been detected, nothing had been done to find out what lay behind it. There was this inquiry:

MR. FOUNTAIN. Had you followed up on the deletion . . . wouldn't you have discovered in 1960, rather than in 1962, that cases of kidney damage had occurred in association with the administration of Orabilex?

DR. SMITH. We might have.

MR. FOUNTAIN. Well, if you followed through properly

you certainly would have unless the company misrepresented the facts or refused to give you the information.

DR. SMITH. That is true . . .

In his prepared statement, Assistant Commissioner Rankin said that for three and one-half years FDA had received "no reports from the firm or the medical community that its [Orabilex's] use was associated with cases of acute renal failure." The first report, he testified, came on April 23, 1962, from a University of Pennsylvania radiologist who passed along information on three cases that had come to his attention. At that time, Rankin said, the number of users totaled an estimated 2.7 million. There must have been a good many more, because the drug remained available long afterwards.

The manufacturer had not told FDA of several cases of acute kidney failure that had been reported to it. In November and December of 1958, a matter of weeks after Orabilex had been released, physicians at the University of Maryland Hospital in Baltimore had reported two cases, both of which ended in death. In March 1960, one fatal and two nonfatal cases had been reported to the company by a radiologist in Grand Rapids, Michigan. In the same month, the Fougera firm was told of a nonfatal case at the Columbia-Presbyterian Medical Center in New York. In April a fatality was reported by a surgeon from the Harvard Medical School. In 1960-1961 two fatalities were reported from the George Washington University Hospital.

By the summer of 1961, Dr. John Wennberg, the Johns Hopkins research fellow, said in a letter of June 1964 to Senator Humphrey, "at least seven university faculty members and at least one private radiologist had independently contacted the manufacturer to report cases. Each was apparently led to believe that his cases were unique."

The manufacturer was adamant in denying a cause-and-effect relationship. A drug that is innocent until proved guilty can remain on the market even though "proof" in these matters is extraordinarily difficult, if not impossible, to come by. In September 1962 the firm's medical director, Dr. F. J. Sanen, said in a memorandum to physicians that the "extensive" animal studies and "vast clinical experience" with Orabilex ruled out a priori the possibility of an inherent kidney-poisoning property. He said it "would certainly appear" that other factors than the use of Orabilex caused kidney failure.

Dr. Wennberg's letter to Senator Humphrey reported that by 1961 "at least four university hospitals had discontinued use of the drug because it was considered too dangerous. Although the cases reported by these groups contained at least nine fatalities, the manufacturer reported none of this experience to FDA. This silence served to isolate the experiences of each of these individuals; and they, therefore, had little influence on the habit of usage of this drug."

One denial, for instance, was made by Clifford H. Bradney, vice president of E. Fougera, on March 30, 1960, in a letter to Dr. Francis Borges of the University of Maryland School of Medicine. "We find," Bradney wrote, "no evidence that employment of Orabilex was more than coincidental" in the deaths of the two patients who had died in 1958 at the University Hospital although neither had any previous history of renal disease.

Despite all this, FDA was shown to have had very little excuse for such unawareness of what was going on. Dr. Wennberg pointed out that the *Journal* of the AMA, for March 11, 1961, which one might reasonably expect officials of the FDA to read, published the report of Dr. James A. Gunn on the three cases of renal failure which had occurred in Grand Rapids. Dr. Gunn, director of radiology at Blodgett Memorial Hospital, was, like Dr. Borges, told by the manufacturer that Orabilex was innocent and, like Dr. Borges, disagreed. In addition, a report on a nonfatal case in November 1960 at the University of North Carolina Hospital was written by Dr. William B.

Blythe and Dr. James W. Woods and published in the May 18, 1961, issue of the *New England Journal of Medicine*, another indispensable professional publication.

Perhaps it was too much to expect FDA to know what was being published. The Fountain hearings established that the agency's spokesmen had come to the hearings without knowing even of reports that the subcommittee had found in FDA's own files. Two reports of acute kidney disease in Orabilex patients, the hearings brought out, had been made on May 31 and June 5, 1961 — eight and one-half months before receipt of the report Assistant Commissioner Rankin had described as the first that FDA knew about. In addition, Representative Fountain produced a memorandum about the two reports from the Division of Research to the Division of New Drugs. It was dated January 10, 1962, which would have been four and one-half months before the first case was said to have been reported to FDA. Rankin — who had testified earlier, "we investigate every report of significant injury or death from every drug" — confessed, "I am frankly quite surprised that this has developed."

Ten weeks after the Fountain hearings on Orabilex, Rankin wrote the subcommittee, which by this time could hardly be surprised by anything that developed insofar as FDA was concerned, that the reports of May 31 and June 5 referred to the same case but had been assigned different serial numbers by FDA. The Assistant Commissioner also said that the memorandum of January 10, 1962, should have been dated January 10, 1963, an error in dating having occurred. Note that these errors were not discovered by the agency until *after* the Fountain hearings.

In a post-hearings letter dated August 27, 1964, Rankin additionally advised Representative Fountain that "no further action was considered necessary on the basis of the reports of this case due to the obvious overdose (13½ grams) of Orabilex administered, and the reporting physician's description of the reaction as an idiosyncrasy of the drug." The validity of the description and FDA's acceptance of it aside, a check by the subcommittee staff showed that the dose had been not a single one of 13.5 grams, but three separate doses of 4.5 grams administered on successive days.

At the hearings the subcommittee's reservoir of unhappy disclosures had not yet been drained. Representative Fountain revealed that the subcommittee staff and its consultant, Dr. Davison, had found in an examination of FDA files "that fully half of the summary letters from the original clinical investigators containing their conclusions with respect to the safety and the effectiveness of Orabilex, were virtually identical, except for the number of cases reported." The Congressman asked Dr. Ralph Smith if there was "anything indicating that this fact was noted?" "No, sir," the FDA executive replied.

In closing the hearings, Representative Fountain commented "on a matter which [he found] very disturbing":

> In examining the files of the manufacturer of Orabilex, it was found that several of the articles which appeared in the medical literature purportedly providing an objective clinical evaluation of Orabilex were in fact written in whole or in part by the manufacturer or by an outside agency retained by the manufacturer for this purpose.
>
> These articles were also included in the bibliography which constituted part of the later versions of the brochure approved by FDA as part of the new-drug application, and which thereby became the major source of information for the medical profession concerning this product.

Mr. Fountain then put into the record correspondence between the E. Fougera company and the authors of the articles. He deleted the names of the doctors involved "in order to spare them personal embarrassment." Resuming, he said:

While this practice may not violate any law or regulation, it appears to me it surely raises questions of medical ethics and strikes at the very roots of scientific integrity. Unfortunately we do not know how widespread this practice [which is discussed in Chapters 3, 5, and 16, and elsewhere in this book] may be. I feel that the subcommittee will want to bring this matter to the attention of the appropriate scientific bodies.

The articles appeared during 1960, in the *Journal* of the AMA, in *Radiology* (which is published by the Radiological Society of North America, Inc.), and in the *Journal* of the Southern Medical Association. One of the physicians wrote to Clifford Bradney, the E. Fougera executive, "If you could prepare a preliminary draft . . . it would probably stir me from my lethargy. Please follow the general style as used in the AMA Journal . . ." Bradney routed the request to a "Bob Chase." In the case of a physician and his associates who had prepared a draft for the Southern Medical Association *Journal* and had sent it for initial clearance to the manufacturer, Bradney told Chase that it "leaves much to be desired. Will you be good enough to assign this paper to the agency [retained by the company]."

In August 1962 a Philadelphia physician told FDA of a patient who had been seized by convulsions after taking a double dose of the drug. By this time FDA knew of 9 nonfatal cases, in 7 of which the dose of Orabilex had been larger than recommended. "The physician's report," Assistant Commissioner Rankin testified, caused FDA to make an inspection of the Fougera firm's files in October. Inspectors found 6 fatalities that had not been reported to FDA. Dr. Wennberg told Senator Humphrey that this file did not include all the cases which had been reported to the firm.

In November 1962 a Washington kidney specialist, Dr.

George E. Schreiner of the Georgetown University Hospital, reported 4 more fatalities to FDA. The agency then retained him and three other consultants. "Their consensus was," Rankin testified before Fountain, "that the Orabilex labeling should bear a warning against use of double or repeat doses and against use in patients with chronic renal disease." Later, Dr. Schreiner was to make it clear that he believed FDA would have been justified in stopping sale of the drug.

In the following month, there was a meeting of kidney specialists from the Baltimore-Washington area at the Walter Reed Army Hospital in the capital. Dr. Wennberg conducted an informal poll which revealed more than 40 local cases of acute kidney failure associated with Orabilex. Also in December 1962, FDA notified the manufacturer that a warning letter to physicians would be required. The firm resisted. Only after the agency proposed an order to take the drug off the market did the firm consent to issue a warning letter. It was sent, on March 29, 1963, to 136,266 physicians, and it was said by Rankin to have reduced use of the drug by five sixths. The letter advised that complications had followed when a dose exceeding 4.5 grams was given.

More than a month earlier, however, the firm's medical director, Dr. Sanen, had gone to Baltimore, where Dr. Borges of the University of Maryland told him of two cases of acute kidney failure, one of them fatal, in patients who had received a single dose of 4.5 grams. Dr. Wennberg and others told Dr. Sanen that they believed the 4.5-gram dose to be toxic and that it would bring further cases of renal failure.

In April 1963 University of Maryland and Johns Hopkins physicians, including Dr. Wennberg and Dr. Borges, held a conference at which Dr. Arthur A. Ruskin, then acting head of FDA's Division of New Drugs, was told of a total of 16 cases, half of them fatal. He disagreed with Dr. Wennberg's opinion that Orabilex should be removed from the market. In June Dr.

Wennberg wrote to FDA. He summarized the problem, cited the proliferation of unfavorable reports in the medical literature, and appealed for a halt to sales of Orabilex. FDA did not reply. In the same month, the *Medical Letter* advised, "In view of the hazards of Orabilex, [the *Letter's*] consultants do not recommend its use."

More reports of injuries and deaths — some on single, 4.5-gram doses — were published. By August the *Medical Letter* was saying, "Even if the company's claim that single doses . . . have caused no deaths is true, it is also true that any contrast medium which cannot be given in double the recommended dose without fear of fatality is best avoided." The November 2 issue of the *Journal* of the AMA, which had published reports of injuries and deaths, said in a blunt editorial that the hazards of Orabilex had been established "by relatively simple methods," and that these "provide an alternative to the sometimes dangerous method of establishing drug safety by means of mass exposure." FDA allowed mass exposure to continue.

Meanwhile, Dr. Wennberg learned of additional cases of kidney failure following single 4.5-gram doses. In December he wrote to Senator Humphrey for the first time. He took this step, he told the Baltimore *Sun* afterward, because, although he had been "embarrassed that [such a step] was necessary," he had been forced to turn to Congress by the frustration he had met "in using the usual means of communication." In his letter to the Senator, Dr. Wennberg said that 25 cases of acute kidney failure associated with Orabilex had been reported, that 17 of them had occurred in but two hospitals, that 11 of them were fatal, and that the nationwide death toll presumably exceeded 100.

Senator Humphrey forwarded Dr. Wennberg's letter to FDA. Although in August 1963 a nonfatal case in Frederick, Maryland, had been reported to the manufacturer, FDA apparently did not know of it, assumed that no new cases had occurred since its warning letter in March, and declined to take further action. On December 6 Mr. Humphrey informed the Senate about the problem, telling it of the letter in which Dr. Wennberg had recounted the history of the drug and FDA's handling of it. Finally, the Senator turned to the White House. The President's Office of Science and Technology then looked into the matter.

In January 1964, Dr. Wennberg learned of a fatal case of renal failure which had occurred in July 1963 in the Baltimore area. He informed the agency of this and a nonfatal case on January 14, 1964. Just before a scheduled conference between President Johnson's representatives and FDA the agency asked the manufacturer to withdraw Orabilex from sale. Recall letters and telegrams were sent by E. Fougera during the next few weeks. Even in April 1964, however, FDA inspectors still found so much of the drug available that the agency had to require the firm to issue an "additional, stronger" recall.

For Senator Humphrey, Orabilex came close to being a last straw. In a letter to the President he appealed for help in making FDA "a scientific regulatory agency of the highest caliber." As it is, he wrote, the agency appears to be run "by a group of ex-inspectors, basically, as a police-type operation." [1]

✓ ✓ ✓

Almost a half-century old now, FDA originated as the Bureau of Chemistry in the Department of Agriculture. It remained

---

[1] In February 1964, television reporter Martin Agronsky discussed the Orabilex case on NBC's "Today" show with Mrs. Esther Peterson, President Johnson's newly appointed Special Assistant for Consumer Affairs. "It's a terrible tragedy," she said. After the program, she received a call from Anthony J. Celebrezze, Secretary of Health, Education, and Welfare, "who, in so many words, advised her to stay out of matters she does not understand," according to *Advertising Age*. Later, after a conversation with FDA Commissioner George Larrick, she said in a statement, "I am convinced that [FDA] acted responsibly in handling the 'Orabilex' case . . . These matters are never black and white." In a speech in March 1964, reported by *Drug Trade News*, S. L. Mayham, executive vice president of the Toilet Goods Association, said that Mrs. Peterson's appointment "is not likely to accelerate the pace of the consumer protection movement too sharply."

in the Department — becoming the Food, Drug, and Pesticide Administration in 1927 and the Food and Drug Administration in 1931 — until 1940, when it was transferred to the Federal Security Agency. When the Security Agency attained Cabinet status as the Department of Health, Education, and Welfare in 1953, FDA became part of it.

A quarter-century ago FDA was getting along on $2 million or so a year. In 1952 the figure was $5.6 million, five years later $6.8 million. In 1962 a spacecraft launched toward Venus failed, the reported cause being the omission of a hyphen in some mathematical data fed into a computer. The estimated cost to the taxpayer was $18.5 million, a mere $10 million less than the 1962 appropriation of $28.5 million for FDA. For the 1965 fiscal year the FDA's operating budget is $39.2 million. This amounts to a mere 19 cents per capita, although about 30 cents of every dollar the consumer spends is for articles within the jurisdiction of FDA. With its appropriation FDA must enforce laws against adulterated and misbranded foods, drugs, cosmetics, therapeutic devices, and household products containing hazardous substances; and must also carry out its responsibilities under the Kefauver-Harris amendments.

FDA has about 4000 employees at its headquarters and in 18 district offices. Annually they inspect about one third of the 100,000 establishments in the agency's jurisdiction and make 106,000 laboratory analyses.

One of the first to characterize FDA as a police-type operation in a new age of pharmaceutical science was Robert P. Fischelis. In 1953, while secretary of the American Pharmaceutical Association, a national professional society of pharmacists, he protested to congressional committees about:

> . . . the trend of administrative supervision within the FDA . . . neither the Commissioner, nor any of the personnel . . . at the policy-making level, include a pharmaceutically trained executive. So much of the administrative activity

of the FDA deals with drugs that it is difficult to understand the deliberate omission of pharmaceutically-trained personnel in this agency at the policy-making level.

While it is true that the agency has a medical department, it has not been able to retain top-ranking medical personnel in this section. The reason which has been assigned for this failure to retain highly qualified physicians is the relatively low salary schedule. We do not believe that this is a major consideration. On the contrary, we wish to point out that when this agency was headed by professional men like Dr. Harvey Wiley, Dr. Carl Alsberg and Mr. Walter Campbell . . . they were able to attract scientific and professional personnel of a very high order and to keep them there continuously . . .

In recent years the line of succession in the administration of the FDA has been on the basis of its policing activity and those who have headed it have been in a position to dominate and overrule the professional personnel within the administration. In our judgment, this is the real cause for failure of professional personnel to look upon this activity as a career.

People of the stripe of Dr. Harvey Wiley — able scientists, idealists filled with zeal to protect the public interest — often have found the atmosphere uncongenial. Civil Service forced them to start at the bottom, where they were ruled and overruled by men who had risen to power by seniority and by winning the backing of powerful elements among the regulated.

✓ ✓ ✓

George P. Larrick, who became Commissioner of the Food and Drug Administration in 1954, was born on November 19, 1901, in Springfield, Ohio. He attended Wittenberg College (now University), in his home town, and Ohio State University.

He was graduated from neither, but holds honorary degrees from Wittenberg, the Drexel Institute of Technology, and the Philadelphia College of Science and Pharmacy. The Commissioner, who is married and has three sons and a daughter, joined FDA in 1923 as an inspector in Memphis, a humble beginning emulated by now Deputy Commissioner John L. Harvey two years later. Both rose through the ranks. Larrick became a supervising inspector, and was chief inspector from 1930 to 1945. Later he became an Associate Commissioner and then Deputy Commissioner, the post from which he was promoted to the top job.

In addition to the Pharmaceutical Manufacturers Association award conferred on him in 1958, Larrick received the National Civil Service League's career service award, its highest honor, "for outstanding contribution to the national welfare" in 1959. Four years later, the American Pharmaceutical Association bestowed an honorary membership on Larrick. He is, the Association said, a "public servant, administrator [and] humanitarian, whose 40 years of Government stewardship in the public health field has fulfilled the finest tradition of service above self and whose constancy and judicious application of authority has earned the respect of pharmacists everywhere . . ."

The genial Larrick once remarked at a Kefauver hearing, "I regard myself as a political eunuch." There are compensations. FDA's district office in Detroit has been designated the George P. Larrick Building. The district office in Los Angeles has been named the John L. Harvey Building. Other district offices have been named for various FDA underlings. These honors to living men have been conferred quietly and without ceremony. This reticence, if that is what it is, has precluded attention being drawn to the fact that none of the district offices has been designated the Harvey W. Wiley Building in honor of the physician and chemist who was the father of the agency, and who is dead.

It was symbolic of the ascendancy of the drug industry that

Larrick, a former inspector not trained as a scientist, was chosen to be its chief regulator, an episode that received negligible attention in the lay press at that time.

The Pink Sheet, the drug-industry trade paper with a $150 annual subscription price, reported on December 22, 1958, how Commissioner Larrick had "recalled that in 1953, when it was rumored that former HEW Secretary Oveta Culp Hobby might name a political appointee to replace the late Charles W. Crawford as FDA Commissioner, industry flooded Mrs. Hobby with telephone calls and telegrams. Larrick said he was well satisfied with the results." Also well satisfied was James Bradshaw Mintener, a former counsel for Pillsbury Mills in Minneapolis, who in 1952 had spearheaded the so-called Minnesota Miracle of write-in primary votes that won the state's Republican presidential nomination for General Eisenhower.

In 1954 Commissioner Crawford had been withholding announcement of his impending retirement. When the news broke, the Pink Sheet for December 15, 1958, nostalgically recalled, "the regulated industries [again] rallied in support of a 'nonpolitical' FDA by making their views known via letters, telegrams, telephone calls, and personal visits." One fateful personal visit was made by Bradshaw Mintener. As the Pink Sheet recounted it, "it took heroic efforts on the part of industry to maintain the career tradition for the top spot. Brad Mintener, a long-time friend of President Eisenhower, went to the White House on the matter, and subsequently agreed to resign his post in industry to become Assistant HEW Secretary, thus insuring Larrick's appointment as FDA Commissioner." His responsibilities were to include "policy supervision of FDA," said *Chemical Week* on September 11, 1954. The magazine predicted he would be "especially valuable in supplementing the work of FDA's career officials" by, for example, giving industry "a supra-FDA office" to which it could bring its complaints.

After but two years at HEW, Mintener entered into a private

food and drug law practice in Washington. Among those he represented were E. Fougera & Company, Inc., in the Orabilex case and Richardson-Merrell, Inc.

ʄ   ʄ   ʄ

In late 1961 and early 1962 Richardson-Merrell was fighting fiercely to block or soften actions by the Food and Drug Administration against MER/29, the anticholesterol drug for which, FDA said later, fraudulent test data had been submitted to the agency. Deputy FDA Commissioner John Harvey has confirmed the fact that during this period representatives of the company appeared in his office with Mintener.

While representing Richardson-Merrell, Mintener also was chairman of the drugs subcommittee of an FDA Citizens Advisory Committee to which he had been nominated — by FDA or, to be realistic, Larrick. In October 1962 this committee issued a report that drew the following "not acceptable" rating from the publication of the Consumers Union, *Consumer Reports* for March 1963:

Few documents in history purporting to review matters of serious public concern can have been so inauspiciously timed or so poorly conceived. The report failed to mention at all the big problem in drug testing — whether it is wise to allow manufacturers to control the clinical testing of their own products. Aside from this, the report gave *as its first and most urgent recommendation that the FDA take a more lenient attitude toward industry to the end that "mandated self-inspection and self-regulation" should eventually supersede control by regulatory investigation and legal enforcement.* As one drug trade commentator put it, the pro-industry bias of the Committee's report was so plain that even Congressmen out to pin something on the FDA or its Commissioner, George P. Larrick, could not use it for that purpose.

No more than one of the 16 members of the . . . Committee, Miss Anne Draper of the AFL-CIO, is on record as opposing the Committee's pro-industry philosophy. Nor, with the exception of Miss Draper, has anyone spoken out about the remarkable shortcomings of the report. Privately, a good many Washington officials have characterized it as a report to end all such reports. But publicly Senators, Congressmen, and the officers of the FDA and the Department of Health, Education, and Welfare have allowed the report to stand without opposition. In January the Pharmaceutical Manufacturers Association gave the report a strong endorsement.

It seems to CU that . . . the Congress might well [investigate] how a citizens committee happened to come out with so uncitizenlike a philosophy.

Control of industry by itself — by "mandated self-inspection and self-regulation" — was a daring vision of a startling synthesis, of a PMA-fda-PMA molecule. Hopefully, this bold molecular manipulation will be crystallized in time to provide the wisdom that the president of the Warner-Lambert Research Institute, Dr. L. Earle Arnow, tells us we shall need to cope with the drugs of the future. Some of these, he has predicted, will "put the 'pep pills' to shame . . . will increase the ability to concentrate . . . speed up thinking . . . remove grief, allay sadness, and induce good humor."

Before you lose your capacity to grieve, before you trade the tear in your eye for a pill on your tongue, hark to Miss Draper, of the AFL-CIO, the Citizens Advisory Committee's lone protester. She said the committee, which was for practical purposes Larrick's creation, took no account "of the extremely important issues in pesticide problems which formed the subject of Rachel Carson's book, *Silent Spring*." She did not find this surprising, because "consumers and consumer groups . . . had very little representation."

✓ ✓ ✓

It is time to say that the invocation of the career tradition, as defined and vigorously praised by Mintener, the Pharmaceutical Manufacturers Association, and the Pink Sheet, falls harshly on the ears of many employees who try to carry on in the career tradition not of George Larrick but of Dr. Harvey Wiley. The contrasts between Larrick and Dr. Wiley and their approach to their responsibilities are stark. It is indeed hard to believe they were members of the same branch of the federal service or were separated by such a short space in time.

In a biography of Wiley, *The Health of a Nation*, published in 1958, Oscar E. Anderson, Jr., wrote that the 1906 food and drug legislation was "one of the great achievements of the progressive era in American politics . . . the work not only of political leaders and muckrakers but also of chemists and food officials. Wiley was the most important of these . . . mostly because of the righteous indignation he brought to the cause and the imagination with which he fought for it." In the last six years of his stay in government Wiley "contended against his superior, the Secretary of Agriculture, frequently forcing the fight to the White House itself. In 1912, finally convinced that the Republican party, to which he had given unswerving loyalty, had become the shield of the cheat and the adulterator, he resigned his post and campaigned for Woodrow Wilson. For eighteen more years he fought on as a private citizen, directing a constant barrage of criticism against what he considered the lax administration of the law."

In Wiley's autobiography there is a passage that seems to be little remembered in the executive offices of the FDA, that never won PMA acclaim for understanding of mutual problems, that may not always be sufficiently kept in mind by the leaders of the American Medical Association, that probably was not quoted by Bradshaw Mintener to Dwight Eisenhower, and that must have been ignored by the Citizens Advisory Committee which proposed a PMA-fda-PMA molecule. This is what Wiley wrote in 1930:

There is a distinct tendency to put regulations and rules for the enforcement of the law into the hands of the industries engaged in food and drug activities. I consider this one of the most pernicious threats to pure food and drugs. Business is making rapid strides in the control of all of our affairs. When we permit business in general to regulate the quality and character of our food and drug supplies, we are treading upon very dangerous ground. It is always advisable to consult business men and take such advice as they give that is unbiased, because of the intimate knowledge they have of the processes involved. It is never advisable to surrender entirely food and drug control to business interests.

The industry's praise of the career tradition mocks the spirit Harvey Wiley brought to the federal service. It makes a good cover story but would be instantly discarded if the career tradition were to bring to the top tomorrow a man like Harvey Wiley — a possibility on which not a moment's thought need be wasted. How wonderful it must be to appear a noble defender of the career tradition while being regulated by an amiable Larrick.

At a hearing in 1963 Senator Ernest Gruening of Alaska asked witnesses, "Have you ever heard the comment made that the FDA, instead of regulating the industry, is being regulated by it?" One reply, which had the ring of another industry citation for FDA's brass, came from Dr. Theodore G. Klumpp, head of Winthrop Laboratories and once the agency's top physician: "The agency, throughout its illustrious history, starting in 1906, has achieved a reputation of independence, of complete freedom from forces and pressures, and [has been] unswayed by the effects of those forces and pressures in a very real sense."

✓ ✓ ✓

Dr. Klumpp has said that "the regulated industries had felt that their relationship with FDA was beginning to approach what it should be in a free society and in accord with the best traditions of our Republic." He insists that an arm's length relationship, the kind that disturbs him, began in 1960. That was the year in which Senator Kefauver was zeroing in on Henry Welch, a Ph.D. in bacteriology who had become director of FDA's Division of Antibiotics in 1945.

During an eight-year period Welch collected "honorariums" totaling $224,000 from *Antibiotics & Chemotherapy* and *Antibiotics and Clinical Therapy*, two journals that owed their primary financial support to makers of antibiotics. (Of the gross of $1,065,112 derived from 15 firms through sale of advertising and reprints and charges for extra pages, by far the largest single share — $256,711 — came from Chas. Pfizer & Co., Inc.)[2] Welch also received an additional $63,000 from another extramural interest, Medical Encyclopedia, Inc.

In that way, Senator Kefauver said on August 23, 1962, "Welch received $287,000 from the industry he was supposed to be regulating." This exchange on the Senate floor, with Senator Paul H. Douglas, followed:

MR. DOUGLAS. Should not the Food and Drug Administration have known about that?

MR. KEFAUVER. The Food and Drug Administration had the matter called to its attention several years ago by Mr. John Connor, then chairman of the predecessor to the Pharmaceutical Manufacturers Association. They did this to their great credit. They asked his superior about the so-called honorariums Dr. Welch was receiving. They were apprehensive about the propriety of these "honorariums." In not going into that matter, his superiors were derelict in the performance of their duty; I say that very frankly. Instead, they whitewashed it. At our hearings we brought out that matter fully; and at about

---

[2] The afterword to this chapter gives further details about Welch and Pfizer's advertising campaign for Sigmamycin.

that time Dr. Welch was allowed to resign. We believe that the FDA officials should have gone into the matter thoroughly several years earlier. He was not even asked by them how much his "honorariums," as he called them, amounted to. That was an outrageous conflict of interest; and the matter is now before a grand jury.

MR. DOUGLAS. Does not the Senator from Tennessee think that in permitting Dr. Welch to resign, rather than dismissing him from the public service, the then Secretary of the Department of Health, Education, and Welfare [Arthur S. Flemming] was derelict in the performance of his duty?

MR. KEFAUVER. Yes, I think so.

MR. DOUGLAS. Does the Senator from Tennessee believe that situation has really been cleared up?

MR. KEFAUVER. I think there needs to be a great deal of vigor injected into the Food and Drug Administration.

In an interview reported in *Science* for December 6, 1963, Commissioner Larrick disclosed what he terms "my philosophy." It is "that people in industry are by and large just about as honest as people in Government." Coming as it did after the Welch affair, which ended in 1963 with the dismissal of a federal grand jury that failed to indict, Larrick's philosophy seemed to be distinguished by a singularly elastic ambiguity. But it may help to explain why a self-seeker need fear to knock on the doors of the Food and Drug Administration only if he pinned on a badge proclaiming "I Am a Self-Seeker."

No such badges are worn. However, industry's nonmedical "contact men" have had almost unrestricted access to FDA medical officers, who, one might naïvely hope, would be making their difficult, sensitive decisions involving our lives in a detached scientific atmosphere. One would be naïvely wrong.

Dr. Barbara Moulton, an FDA medical officer for five years, resigned in a deliberate protest against the agency's policies. Here is a description she gave the Kefauver Senate Subcommittee on Antitrust and Monopoly in 1960 of the pressures to which medical officers have been exposed:

When a drug firm submits a new drug application for an important new drug, it is common practice for their representative to call the Chief of the New Drug Branch a few days later and inquire which medical officer is handling the application. The name is promptly supplied.

The medical officer then receives a call to the effect that the firm wishes to send representatives in to discuss the application, and he is expected to make such an appointment promptly. If he does not do so, perhaps for the very valid reason that he has not as yet studied the application, he is reprimanded by his Chief as uncooperative, and the appointment is made anyway by a clerk.

A day rarely passes without several such conferences in the New Drug Branch. If the firm anticipates no difficulties, they send a single representative. If the medical officer has suggested over the phone that the new drug application may not be completely satisfactory, four or five men may appear in his office to argue the case. He may also be invited to attend a medical meeting sponsored by the firm at which the drug in question will be discussed by the clinical investigators.

Frequently, at such meetings, the investigators who have been lukewarm or cold about the merits of the drug are not invited to participate.

If the medical officer handling the new drug application is still not satisfied with the evidence of safety, the company will frequently make an appointment with the Medical Director, who has not seen the data on the new drug application, to present their side of the story to him. I have known such conferences to be followed by an order to the medical officer to make the new drug application effective, with the statement that the company in question has been evaluating new drugs much longer than the medical officer and should, therefore, be in a much better position to judge their safety.

No one in the Bureau of Medicine would deny the value of occasional conferences with industry, particularly about technical details in the new drug applications. However, when a drug company representative spends 3 or 4 days a week in the New Drug Branch offices, arguing each point step by step, wanting to know and being told exactly where the application is at all times and which chemists and which pharmacologists are assisting in its review, I submit that the medical officer responsible for making a wise decision in the interest of the public is suffering under an almost insurmountable handicap.

In April 1964 Commissioner Larrick acknowledged to the *Christian Science Monitor* that "there is a lot of pressure on me, yes. It came from both industry and Congress. But it was not crooked pressure. It is part of my job to withstand it. Pressure is not something to be critical of."

✓ ✓ ✓

It will be recalled that Robert Fischelis, in testimony given in 1953, had deplored the dominant anticrook, or police, emphasis in the Food and Drug Administration, and had called the downgrading of the role of scientific personnel the real cause of their failure to make their careers in FDA. The agency went on alienating scientists for years after Fischelis spoke.

No result worth mentioning was visible after the first Citizens Advisory Committee on FDA recommended, in 1955, that consideration be given to the creation of an expert council to advise FDA on complex problems in the field of new drugs, and that the "stature, prestige, and salaries of the professional personnel who must bear the burden of passing on new drugs . . . be increased." The appointment of "a Scientific Advisory Board of distinguished scientists from universities, foundations, industry, and other government laboratories" was urged in July 1959 by Paul L. Day, the noted biochemist who had become FDA's first scientific director nine months earlier. This and other recommendations made by Day which sought to, raise the standard of science in FDA were brushed aside.

In 1960 there were several outspoken criticisms and warnings. In October of that year, Day was a guest speaker before the Animal Nutrition Research Council in Washington. As printed in the official program, the title of his speech was "Long-Range Program of the Food and Drug Administration." When he spoke, however, Day changed the title to "Long-Range Program *for* the Food and Drug Administration," and pointedly called the attention of his audience to this significant modification. Despite sharp increases in FDA appropriations and manpower since 1957, Day said in the speech, and despite the presence of many more scientists in FDA laboratories than ever before, "there is good evidence that imaginative scientific work is at a low ebb." He added that the agency's research productiveness in recent years had been "at an alltime low." Day went on to quote from an article he had written in January 1960 in which he had said: "I am confident that the Congress could be convinced of the need for adequate research support if the Food and Drug Administration had sufficient vision of its proper role in the protection of the health of the American people, and if the FDA had the courage to present, adequately, a bold program."

The significance of the change in the title of the speech from "of" to "for" was, plainly, that Day had not found such vision or such courage in FDA. "I have been telling you what I believe to be the proper destiny of the Food and Drug Administration," he said in his peroration. "Only history will record whether mine is a voice crying in the wilderness." History will record that thereafter Day found life at FDA intolerable, and he resigned. In February 1962 he joined the National Institutes of Health. He has declined to discuss what happened, which gives an unintended bite to the finding made in 1960, the year of his speech, by a firm of personnel specialists employed by FDA. The agency's general atmosphere, the firm found, was "perceived by employees as one which discourages and stultifies communication."

Also in 1960, a committee of the National Academy of Sciences and the National Research Council urged FDA's layman Commissioner to establish an expert advisory council similar to that which had been advocated by the Citizens Advisory group in 1955 and by Day in 1959. In addition the NAS-NRC group found that new-drug applications "are not always of sufficient quality and quantity to permit a sound decision." The then Secretary of Health, Education, and Welfare, Arthur S. Flemming, added his voice to the chorus. "The complexity of . . . new drugs and the constant flow of progress and new developments in the drug field," he said, "makes it essential that the Food and Drug Administration have for its guidance the most competent scientific resources available in the United States."

Before the Kefauver subcommittee at about the same time, Dr. Moulton acknowledged that FDA's budget was woefully inadequate. But, she testified, "I cannot stress too much [that] no amount of increased budget will compensate for the gaps in the law, nor will any conceivable appropriation of millions of dollars do the job unless it is administered by individuals capable of understanding the full public health significance of the problems with which they must deal, willing to look at scientific facts and able to understand and evaluate them, and interested more in the public welfare than in the financial gain of the industries which they regulate."

Dr. Moulton, who had resigned "to retain [her] own self-respect" and to be able to speak with the freedom of a private citizen, read to the subcommittee the text of a letter to Commissioner Larrick that she had drafted a few days after she left

FDA. She had not sent the letter, but she submitted it to the subcommittee. The letter said in part:

I believe also that hundreds of people, not merely in this country, suffer daily, and many die because the Food and Drug Administration has failed utterly in its solemn task of enforcing those sections of the law dealing with the safety and misbranding of drugs, particularly prescription drugs.

The pharmaceutical industry, the medical profession, the legal profession, and the public all share in the guilt, but the responsibility and the authority rest primarily with the Food and Drug Administration, which has neither made full use of the powers it has nor asked Congress for the further power it needs to insure the marketing of none but safe and useful drugs with honest labeling . . .

I have watched with deep regret as more authority has been removed from the one group within the [FDA] with the training, experience, and wisdom to advise you on medical problems. I have watched with even deeper regret as promotions have been given almost exclusively to those officials within the [FDA] who have, in my opinion, allowed considerations of private gain to becloud their intellectual honesty and pervert their sense of duty to the public, or to incompetent individuals who, nevertheless, can and do protect you temporarily from knowledge of uncomfortable or disturbing facts.

✓ ✓ ✓

A frightening confirmation of the inadequacy of new-drug applications as seen by the National Academy of Sciences–National Research Council committee was given in 1961 in a talk to the FDA staff by William Weiss, who had been a statistician with the agency for thirteen years:

. . . I contend that the low quality of research data in New Drug Applications is general and not isolated; that the degree to which our doctors are inhibited in the proper performance of their duties due to deficiencies in NDA data is serious and merits the prompt attention of the Administration . . .

I believe, too, that the physicians of the Food and Drug Administration are in something of an untenable position, from which they can be extricated only with well-planned help. In my opinion, it has become clear that FDA's physicians cannot rely heavily on the drug industry to determine the proper efficacy/safety relationship that should move a drug to the market, to discard, or to additional research. Unfortunately for the medical officers, they must within short periods of time make decisions one way or another, and their decisions affect the health and safety of many citizens.

Yet, from the point of view of the evaluation of mass data — and most of their decisions of a medical nature rest on the evaluation of mass data — they are forced to gamble; the information which they need to reduce almost to zero the risks of an incorrect decision too often is unavailable to them, because of weaknesses in research methods.

I say that the medical officer is in an untenable position because if he were to adopt the view that an application were incomplete unless the research supporting it was properly conducted, he would pass few applications. But this would result in a major shift in FDA policy, and have a far-reaching effect on a major industry.

Senator Humphrey's subcommittee, which acquired a copy of this statement, asked Commissioner Larrick for comment. He said all he cared to in these two sentences: "The paper presents a statistician's view of the operations of our Bureau of Medicine. Representatives of other disciplines did not agree with all of the conclusions reached by the statistician, and stated so at that time."

Angered, the Senator said:

The agency neither concedes nor implies that anything is wrong with testing. It states that there is simply a disagreement.

The agency could have responded otherwise; it could well have used the opportunity afforded by my letter to present a frank statement as to the problems of testing confronting the pharmaceutical industry and the scientific community. Instead, as on so many other occasions, it failed to be forthright with the Congress. It replied in a manner which would open up the least possible avenues for further congressional inquiry. The reader has a right to ask, "Why?" "Why the lack of candor?" "Why the failure on FDA's part to present a fuller story to the Congress — an illuminating account of the situation as it really existed?"

In 1962, the year after FDA statistician Weiss had expressed his concern, Senator Humphrey told the Senate that it was "incredible [that] FDA has made little systematic use of outside consultants." Also in 1962, even the industry-oriented second Citizens Advisory Committee expressed concern about the agency's structure. The committee went so far as to recommend that FDA's top posts "no longer . . . be held primarily by persons whose backgrounds have been as inspectors, but should include scientists with broad experience as well." When reporters asked the committee chairman if that applied to nonscientist Larrick, he said it certainly did not — the recommendation was directed to the future. The chairman was George Y. Harvey, a University of Missouri political scientist, who has said he is an old friend of Larrick. He became a consultant to the Department of Health, Education, and Welfare on FDA matters. "I have no intention of getting rid of Mr. Larrick," his boss, HEW Secretary Anthony J. Celebrezze told the New York *Times* in July 1963. "He has 40 years of experience which we need."

Yet, in October 1962, the Kennedy White House had let Senator Humphrey know that Larrick was expendable. Larrick was approaching retirement age — he was then sixty-one — and was under fire. Mr. Humphrey is a kindly man, and he said no.

✓   ✓   ✓

The alienation of scientists by the Food and Drug Administration was but one manifestation of the erosion of its zeal to protect the public.

Not until 1956 — eighteen years after enactment of the Food, Drug, and Cosmetic Act — did FDA start to require inclusion in the packages going to pharmacists of brochures listing the authorized dosages, side effects, and contraindicated uses. Even this step had a highly limited effect, because physicians generally do not see the packages: the pharmacist dispenses what he is told to dispense, as he must, no matter what the brochure says, and the brochure usually ends up in the wastebasket, where it may be seen by the trash collector but not by the doctor.

A bitter protest against this arrangement was made by Dr. Martin A. Seidell, who appeared before the Senate Antitrust subcommittee after resigning as medical director of the J. B. Roerig & Company division of Chas. Pfizer & Co., Inc. Writing in connection with Chloromycetin, the Parke, Davis antibiotic that continues to be prescribed needlessly for millions of people despite a death rate estimated at 1 in 60,000 by California State Department of Public Health authorities, Dr. Seidell asked in the Orange County, California, *Medical Bulletin* for March 1963: "Where was the official brochure all these years? It failed to reach the prescriber because it was discarded by the pharmacist. There was no requirement for 'full disclosure' to the prescriber in the promotional materials being received from any company on any type of agent."

Finally manifesting more interest in helping physicians to have access to the facts they need in order to prescribe intelligently, FDA took a second small step in 1960 by directing that the brochures (which, unfortunately, often are inconvenient to read and file) be enclosed with the drug samples distributed to physicians. For the time being, Commissioner Larrick was unwilling to support a change in the law. Ever optimistic and trusting, he believed, Stephens Rippey wrote in the December 12, 1960, *Drug Trade News*, in "the willingness of the principal pharmaceutical manufacturers to provide complete information . . ."

The Kefauver-Harris drug reforms of 1962 brought some order and sense to the situation. The amendment that requires drug advertising to state side effects and contraindicated uses imposes the identical requirement on brochures, folders, and other descriptive printed matter about drugs seen by physicians. This is the "full disclosure" amendment that, it will be recalled, was opposed by the industry and the American Medical Association.

*   *   *

As would be expected in an agency dominated by former inspectors rather than scientists, the Food and Drug Administration is oriented toward secrecy. The Humphrey subcommittee's physician member, Senator Ernest Gruening of Alaska, pointed out in 1963 that "no information is more crucial in drug therapy than detailed knowledge of prior animal and clinical experiments." Yet for a quarter-century FDA has "veiled in almost complete secrecy" the 13,000 new-drug applications in its files. This has been done, FDA's counsel William W. Goodrich has acknowledged, as "a matter of policy." Not law, but "policy." A number of years ago, *Drug News Weekly* reported on December 19, 1962, FDA tried to make new-drug information public, but "was overruled by industry protests."

Consider what happened in 1962. As the law stood, FDA was forbidden to disclose information that could endanger trade and manufacturing secrets. Quietly FDA sought a change that would have prohibited disclosure of additional information on hazards found in new drugs, and of a great deal of other officially obtained data on drugs, foods, food additives, and pesticides. FDA's effort to accomplish this far-ranging suppression was itself concealed, hidden in the legal language of the bill that passed the House.

By a close reading of the text Dr. Barbara Moulton spotted what was happening. FDA's effort was revealed in the press, the Department of Health, Education, and Welfare disassociated itself from the maneuver, and, when the bills that became the Kefauver-Harris amendments went to a conference committee, Kefauver knocked out FDA's attempt to be legislated into mandatory secrecy.

FDA is so oriented toward secrecy, toward not taking the scientific community and the public into its confidence, that if a manufacturer investigates a new chemical agent, finds it dangerous and so reports to FDA, the agency does not tell another manufacturer who, by sheer coincidence, may be interested in the same drug. He will be allowed to proceed, left unaware of the hazard, not knowing that what he is about to do has already been done. FDA's policy is justifiable "only so long as the company does not suffer too badly," it was suggested by William C. Spring, Jr., former secretary of the Council on Drugs of the American Medical Association, and Frank Honicker, Jr., a former drug firm staff member. But, they asked, "must one company duplicate iatrogenic deaths or serious illnesses when another has demonstrated that these occur? Must they even remain unaware of suspected causal relationships before confirmation?"

In a memorandum prepared in June 1964 for inclusion in Part 5 of his subcommittee hearing volumes, Senator Humphrey dealt at length with the secrecy problem. One of the first things he took up was the attempt by FDA, discussed in Chapter 3 of this book, to deny information on Flexin and MER/29 to Representative Fountain. For this the Senator found "not the slightest justification." The agency's policy of enveloping its drug files in total secrecy, he continued, is contrary to expressions of national policy — for example, that of the President's Science Advisory Committee in regard to pesticide data in FDA's possession. Senator Humphrey also reported that at least twice the National Institutes of Health, FDA's sister agency in the Department of Health, Education, and Welfare, had sought information from FDA files and had been rebuffed.

> This situation [he said in the memorandum] represents quite a paradox — NIH, the "right hand," so to speak . . . (which spends $70 million of taxpayers' funds for drug research), asks the "left hand" of the Government, FDA, for a look at either investigational drug files and/or approved drug files, but is turned down flat.
>
> Thus, millions of victims of heart disease will be interested to learn that one Institute, the National Heart Institute (spending $160 million for overall research, including, over the years, several millions in collaboration with the drug industry), has had the door slammed shut in its face by FDA as regards access to files on new heart drugs.
>
> [The National Heart Institute] was specifically interested in drugs to lower serum cholesterol. But FDA took the issue up to the office of the Special Assistant to the Secretary of HEW for Health and Medical Affairs [Boisfeuillet Jones]. That office apparently sustained FDA in keeping the "iron curtain" intact against [the National Institutes of Health].
>
> And on what basis? FDA apparently contended that since 1938 (when FDA was in the U.S. Department of Agriculture) secrecy had been uniformly followed. This amounts to the same ridiculous excuse . . . heard from other Federal agencies whenever the agencies have tried to block freedom of the

press: "We observe secrecy, because, in the past, secrecy has been our policy, and no one has changed our policy."

The policy can change if things become hot enough, as the Senator demonstrated when he caught FDA in a striking inconsistency involving Parnate, a psychotherapeutic drug examined in Chapter 9. When it appeared that there would be a public hearing at which FDA would be challenged, the agency proposed to enter as an exhibit the total file on the new-drug application for Parnate — trade secrets, the names of patients on whom the drug had been tested, everything. The hearing was not held, and the file was never made public.

Since August 1963, through the Commissioner's office, FDA has been making public a list of new-drug applications it has approved. This fuller disclosure may have been made possible by the aggressive stand taken on the matter by Hubert Humphrey. However, at this writing FDA still does not go along with the chief medical director of the Veterans Administration, Dr. Joseph H. McNinch, who wrote to the Senator, "Once a new-drug application is made effective . . . all information about the drug and its effects should be made available to practitioners."

HERE, reprinted from the Appendixes to *The Therapeutic Nightmare*, are the "further details" mentioned in footnote 2 in Chapter 6 on the promotional campaign for Sigmamycin, the Chas. Pfizer & Co., Inc., antibiotic, and on the role of Henry Welch, former director of the Division of Antibiotics of the Food and Drug Administration. This material is followed by discussions of FDA's personnel and information policies.

✦ ✦ ✦

In 1956, Pfizer's Sigmamycin, a combination of antibiotics, was the only product of this type being widely promoted with the claim of synergistic effect — that the components were more effective when taken in combination than when taken separately.

A witness before the Kefauver subcommittee, Dr. Gideon Nachumi, testified that during 1956, while he was working at Pfizer as a medical copywriter, someone in the executive echelons had come up with a dramatic promotional phrase for a campaign for Sigmamycin. The phrase was "a third era in antibiotic therapy." Later, in editing papers to be given at the 1956 International Antibiotics Symposium (an annual event organized by Welch and sponsored by FDA and the Medical Encyclopedia, Inc.) Nachumi, who later became a physician, came across Welch's welcoming address, which the official had written and submitted to Pfizer for approval.

He and his colleagues, Nachumi said, added the sentence "It

is quite possible that we are now in the third era of antibiotic therapy." This "amounted to the endorsement [of Pfizer's campaign for Sigmamycin] by the head of the Antibiotics Division [and] was exceedingly valuable," the subcommittee was told by Warren Kiefer, who at the time was a Pfizer public relations man.

Authorities on antibiotics were dismayed at what they believed to be a surprising and unwarranted boost to fixed combinations of antibiotics, no matter who produced them. Dr. Maxwell Finland, of the Harvard Medical School, for instance, testified as to his doubts that such combinations "can be justified." He said that claimed advantages for combinations had not been proved, that their use discouraged proper diagnosis while encouraging "shotgun therapy," and that some were actually harmful.

The degeneration of the Food and Drug Administration into a scientific backwater, which was accelerated by the regime of Commissioner George P. Larrick, was halted and reversed with the appointment of Dr. James L. Goddard as his successor. Now, as Robert P. Fischelis said in 1953 when he was secretary of the American Pharmaceutical Association, it would be possible for "professional personnel to look upon this activity as a career." Dr. Goddard was not only a physician replacing an amiable policeman, but he was also a career officer in the commissioned corps of the Public Health Service with no soft gloves for the drug industry. There began a great exodus of higher- and middle-level officials (including Deputy Commissioner John L. Harvey even before Larrick officially left on December 27, 1965; Allen E. Rayfield, director of the Bureau of Regulatory Compliance, whose incompetent handling of a mixup at Abbott Laboratories involving labeling of bottles of sugar solution as salt solution, and vice versa, was exposed in October 1965 by the House Intergovernmental Relations Subcommittee, and Morris L. Yakowitz, director of the Division of Case Supervision, another departure that would, if it were deemed a loss to the public interest, be mislabeled). There followed an impressive but by no means unflawed influx. Dr. Goddard was able to make an arrangement under which a substantial number of newly commissioned Public Health Service physicians would do a tour of duty at the FDA — a good and helpful idea. The new image he gave the agency brought an unprecedented flow of job applications from scientific and technical personnel, many of whom would not have seriously considered applying in the old days. To succeed Dr. Joseph F. Sadusk, Jr., as director of the Bureau of Medicine (Dr. Goddard abolished the additional title of Medical Director that Dr. Sadusk had obtained for himself), the Commissioner named Dr. Herbert L. Ley, Jr., an old friend who came to the agency in September 1966 from the Harvard School of Public Health. Dr. Ley, who was then 43, already had built an outstanding record in research and administration (from 1961 to 1963, for example, he was chief of the Biological and Medical Sciences Branch of the Army Research Office) and in teaching (including three years as professor and chairman of microbiology and community health at George Washington University School of Medicine followed by the three years preceding his FDA appointment as associate professor of epidemiology and microbiology at Harvard). Dr. Ley lacked the background in clinical and investigational medicine one would expect in an appointee to the agency post, but after several months the impression he gave was of an able and intelligent scientist who was anxious to learn and who was determined to do a good job. If he made some mistakes they were not in the same ballpark as those of Dr. Sadusk, whose big-league status had been validated by *Medical World News*. In announcing its selection of "medical newsmakers" for 1965, this publication listed Dr. Sadusk before Dr. Albert Schweitzer, the late physician-missionary, but after Dr. James Z. Appel, who had become president of the American Medical Association.

Certain other of Dr. Goddard's personnel moves were at least on the surface not inspiring and somewhat inscrutable. An example was the transfusing of several friends from the Federal Aviation Agency, which had not been known as a cadet training school for the FDA. As suggested in the Preface to this edition, one of these friends, Dr. Arthur E. Wentz, had demonstrated an inability to get a wasteful research project off the ground for FAA when the Commissioner arranged for him to become the pilot of extramural research for FDA. There was also the puzzling selection of Earl L. Myers, who is not a physician and whose academic credentials are less than overwhelming, to head a medical unit of what in a reorganization came to be called the Office of New Drugs.

The apparent warmth of Dr. Goddard's consideration for his old friends, which may be shown someday by their dedication to the public interest to have been fully justified, was not extended to those brave persons who had spoken out, taken risks, and made sacrifices, all of which helped to bring about the shakeup that finally resulted in Dr. Goddard's accession to office. Surely these "lonely soldiers of the common good" were owed a measure of appreciation and respect that might have been, but was not, given genuinely and generously by the new commanding general.

✦ ✦ ✦

The secrecy that characterized the Food and Drug Administration in the era of Commissioner George P. Larrick has been attacked with vigor by his successor, Dr. James L. Goddard. He has a natural flair for public relations, and certainly it acquired a synergistic, or $1 + 1 = 3$, effect when it was combined with the natural flair for the same thing possessed by the aide who became Assistant Commissioner for Education and Information. That very able and formidable person is Theodore O. Cron, who had been in the Office of Education until he joined FDA at the start of the Goddard era. Together, the Commissioner and

Cron tried, all at once, to cut away needless secrecy (while eliminating leaks to reporters), to make the Commissioner and other agency personnel accessible to newsmen, to build efficient and well-manned public information and speech-writing units — in sum, to do those things that would enable the agency at last to make an imprint upon public awareness reasonably commensurate with its importance. This importance was neither diminishing nor remaining static — it was growing rapidly because of new responsibilities such as those for controlling drugs with a potential for abuse and for administering the Fair Packaging and Labeling Act. Virginia might still ask if there is a Santa Claus, but she no longer had to ask if there is a Food and Drug Administration. There were some slips and doubtful judgments. For instance, there are, I think, valid reservations about the wisdom of Dr. Goddard's decision to break completely with custom and meet with groups of financial counselors who play key roles in the investment of large sums in the securities of the industries he regulates. Meetings with analysts and investors that would be open to the public would be one thing; Dr. Goddard's closed meetings with the financial specialists designated by the particular host company, even with the strict ground rules set by Theodore Cron and the undisputed good intentions and respect for the proprieties which arm the Commissioner, may carry certain risks. One such risk is of *inadvertent* disclosure of information that could be of financial benefit to those investors who happen to be represented at a session where the slip occurs. The general position of the Securities and Exchange Commission is, of course, that any information which may be of substantial impact ought better to be disclosed publicly, rather than to limited groups.

Cavils such as the foregoing aside, there is, I believe a more important point to be made. The "opening up" of the agency has been insufficiently appreciated. In August 1966 the FDA Advisory Committee on Obstetrics and Gynecology submitted an extremely important report on the oral contraceptives. Assistant Commissioner Cron saw to it that the full text was made available well in advance to newsmen. A briefing was held four days before the designated publication date; and there was some very searching and tough-minded questioning. All of this was as it ought to be — but was *not* under the predecessor regime.

Indeed, it should be recognized that criticism is owed news media which have repeatedly given insufficient attention to news of consequence — even life-and-death consequence — available to it on FDA's big new platter. The examples are almost numberless. Here is one. An April 4, 1967, in Atlanta, Dr. Goddard told the American Association of Planned Parenthood Physicians that side effects of the oral contraceptives (and other drugs) are "grossly under-reported," that the lack of information on the pills is a "grave issue," that a "mild side effect may preface a more serious one" and be recognized as a signal with which the alert physician could save a patient's life, and that their use in girls whose bone growth is incomplete is "inadvisable." Texts of the speech were made available in Atlanta and Washington. Little attention was paid. It was not surprising, then, that the hazard to bone-joint closure almost escaped notice when Baltimore authorities announced a plan to give birth control pills to teen-age girls in welfare programs who were expected to be promiscuous. Was this not information of the kind that, as Walter Lippmann put it, "the public will in the longer run need to know"?

On October 3, 1966, Assistant Commissioner Cron dealt with some of these points with acidity and wit in a speech to the annual meeting of public relations directors of the Pharmaceutical Manufacturers Association. He took note of "the peculiar relationship that exists between Washington and the Second City, New York, as far as press coverage of the government is concerned" and continued:

I'm afraid I must give the term "Second City" to New York . . . since I have been in Washington in government information dealing with the Washington press corps, I have become uncomfortably aware of the pretense and foolishness that exist in New York editorial offices. . . . One thing that New Yorkers really believe is that Manhattan is *omphalos,* what Stephen Daedalus called the "belly-button of the world." If New York doesn't know about it or if a New Yorker didn't do it, then it can't be too important. . . . The result is such an imbalance of information to the public that it is a wonder we make the kind of progress we do.

Last spring, I can confess to you this morning, I informed the Science Editor of the New York *Times* [Walter Sullivan] that I thought the FDA was skimpily covered in Washington and that the Washington bureau, as everyone in town knows, couldn't make a decision to do better until New York decided. Until that conversation I had made it a point to have one of my staff — or myself personally — call stories into the *Times*.

But then I got fed up. I told the Editor that from then on he would get his FDA stories from the AP ticker until he realized he needed a man to cover us as a public agency with our kind of responsibilities ought to be covered. . . .

7

DRUG TESTING

WHAT SENATOR KEFAUVER learned about the Food and Drug Administration during two and one-half years of hearings by his Subcommittee on Antitrust and Monopoly disturbed him profoundly. This was particularly evident in August 1962, when the drug-safety legislation for which he had fought against hopeless odds was on the verge of passage by the Senate. In these triumphant moments he and a few other senators engaged in a despairing colloquy about the need for an infusion of "new blood" into the agency that was to enforce the reforms.

One of these senators was Hubert Humphrey, the versatile and dynamic Assistant Majority Leader. During 1962 his Subcommittee on Reorganization and International Organizations was well launched on its inquiry into FDA's regulation of an industry that was currently spending $251 million a year on research and development, a share of which was for drug testing and evaluation; an industry that was using 8.5 million animals in experiments; that was testing 168,000 substances pharmacologically, and that was trying 1295 agents in humans which included 157 psychotherapeutic drugs, 111 pain-killers and anesthetics, and 104 antibiotics.

All of this later was assessed by Senator Humphrey: "On the one hand, superb testing . . . often was conducted by drug companies of unimpeachable reputation on many outstanding drugs. On the other hand, mediocre and substandard testing was often conducted on good, bad, or indifferent drugs. Both types of testing seemed to be approved by FDA." Well before this time Mr. Humphrey had been expressing horror at what he was finding. In an agency in which one slip can cause injury and death, he found practices, he said in October 1962, "so lax that there was, in effect, no real regulation at all."

✓   ✓   ✓

Since 1938 the Food and Drug Administration had had the power to define "an expert qualified by scientific training and experience to investigate the safety" of a new drug limited to investigational use in interstate commerce. For twenty-four years FDA failed to decide what an "expert" is, its principal justification being a reluctance to interfere in the practice of medicine.

As a result it was not uncommon for manufacturers to have experimental drugs tried out on patients by private physicians who often were far removed from their scientific training, unable to collaborate closely with scientists of other disciplines (scientists whose help may well be essential), or were hard pressed by the demands of their practice and unable to assess the full significance of what they were doing. There were even occasions when experimental drugs were tried out by persons completely untrained in medicine. On the other hand, some manufacturers were scrupulous to arrange testing by qualified and utterly impartial scientists, in the universities and elsewhere.

We know that out of the milieu of inadequate testing came drugs like Altafur, the anti-infection agent released despite lack of evidence of safety and efficacy. What we don't know is how many *good* drugs were, as the result of superficial examination, lost.[1] During the same quarter-century FDA also had the au-

[1] An example of this was cited to the Kefauver subcommittee by Dr. Allan M. Butler, professor of pediatrics emeritus at the Harvard Medical School. He told of Atabrine, which was:

thority to set standards for experiments in humans and to re-quire manufacturers to keep it informed about clinical tests, but FDA let these powers lie fallow.

One indication of what was going on during the casual years was provided by Dr. Louis Lasagna, the distinguished Johns Hopkins clinical pharmacologist. "I have been approached to start human testing of a drug," he has said, "with the only information available" being the dose required to kill half of the test mice receiving it in a single injection. While some pharmaceutical houses were performing extensive animal tests before giving drugs to man, others were performing "almost none," Dr. Lasagna told a Kefauver hearing. He termed it "reprehensible" that man should have been "the first experimental animal" on which tests were run, "simply because bypassing toxicity tests in laboratory animals saves time and money." [2]

In 1956–1957 thalidomide, which was later found to be baby-

---

discarded as a drug too toxic to use in malaria, because the way practicing physicians were using it in their clinical medicine was resulting in serious toxicity. When quinine became unavailable in the past world war, the Office of Scientific Research and Development set up a committee to study anti-malarial therapy and I was on that committee.

Within a few months by careful clinical testing under controlled conditions it found that Atabrine had been misused by the practicing physician and is a very valuable drug discarded.

And it was just through a few months of carefully controlled clinical testing that the usefulness of Atabrine was reestablished and that Chloraquin and the very effective antimalarials available today were developed.

[2] What Dr. Lasagna described was in clear violation of the ethics of the American Medical Association. In 1946 the AMA's Judicial Council said that before human experiments can begin three requirements must be satisfied: (1) the voluntary consent of the person on whom the experiment is to be performed, (2) the danger of each experiment must be previously investigated by animal experimentation, and (3) the experiment must be performed under proper medical protection and management.

In 1949 "Ten Commandments of Medical Research Involving Human Subjects" were developed for the Nuremberg War Trials. The "Commandments" included obtaining the informed, voluntary consent of the patient. Experiments must be "such as to yield fruitful results for the good of society . . . and not . . . unnecessary . . . designed and based on the results of animal experimentation," and with a risk factor that "should never exceed that determined by the humanitarian importance of the problem to be solved . . ."

deforming, was tested in 875 persons by Smith Kline & French. No deformities were reported to FDA. Because the firm lost interest in the drug and did not file a new-drug application, and because FDA did not require reports in such circumstances, the agency knew nothing of all this until March 1962, when it was told about it by the firm.

The William S. Merrell Company's "experimental" trials of Kevadon, as it called thalidomide, followed. In an interoffice memorandum dated October 10, 1960, which is one of numerous company documents published by the Humphrey subcommittee, a vice president, R. H. Woodward, said, ". . . we have sufficient raw material for 15 million tablets." On October 25 and 26, personnel connected with what was termed the "Kevadon Hospital Clinical Program" were convened for a meeting in Cincinnati at which an instruction manual was distributed. The manual contained highly detailed instructions to the firm's detailmen on precisely how to get "experiments" under way at hospitals around the country. The following section appeared under the headline "A WORD OF CAUTION"; the italics are in the original:

Bear in mind that these are not *basic* clinical research studies. We have firmly established the safety, dosage and usefulness of Kevadon by both foreign and U.S. laboratory and clinical studies. This program is designed to gain widespread *confirmation* of its usefulness in a variety of hospitalized patients. If your work yields case reports, personal communications or published work, all well and good. But the main purpose is to establish local studies whose results will be spread among hospital staff members. You can assure your doctors that they need not report results if they don't want to but that we, naturally, would like to know of their results. Be sure to tell them that we may send them report forms or reminder letters but these are strictly reminders and they need not reply [of those ultimately enlisted, less than 25 per cent actually did reply in writing]. Their reports or names would not be used without getting their express permission in advance.

At the beginning of your interview, don't be secretive — lay your cards on the table. Tell the doctor that present plans call for Kevadon to be marketed early in 1961 [these were the plans with which the FDA's Dr. Frances Kelsey interfered]. Let them know the basic clinical research on Kevadon has been done. Don't get involved in selling a basis [sic] clinical research program instead of Kevadon. *Appeal to the doctor's ego — we think he is important enough to be selected as one of the first to use Kevadon in that section of the country.*

The goal set at the meeting was the establishment of 750 Kevadon "studies" involving 15,000 patients during the month of November 1960. The goal was exceeded in two weeks. On November 17, Kevadon representatives were sent air mail, special-delivery directives saying, "Cease Fire — You Made It." On November 29, a company news sheet, "Kevadon Clippings," reported that 762 studies involving 29,413 patients had been set up. ". . . you have exceeded the 'quota' for the number of studies and doubled the 'quota' for the number of patients," the bulletin continued. "Congratulations."

Merrell representatives, who with their colleagues in affiliated Richardson-Merrell firms ultimately raised the number of physician-investigators to more than 1200, had been feeding back to headquarters information on the reactions they had been encountering among physicians. "The main area of interest," a company summary said, "has been the drug's safety." One representative, however, had been asked by Dr. E. B. Linton, of the Acuff Clinic in Knoxville, Tennessee, about the possible effect of Kevadon on the fetus. The question was forwarded to an associate director of clinical research at Merrell, Dr. Thomas

L. Jones. On December 5, 1960, he wrote Dr. Linton: "Unfortunately, I am unable to assess this question since it has not been established whether or not there is any transfer of Kevadon across the placental barrier. However, we feel that, even if transfer does occur, it would be completely safe . . ."

"Certainly, the most casual observer would reject the desultory returns from over 1,200 physicians, to whom was entrusted the clinical trial of thalidomide," the then chief medical director of the Veterans Administration, Dr. William S. Middleton, wrote to Senator Humphrey in September 1962. "Their results could have no scientific significance or validity. Yet, this formula for deriving new drug introduction and acceptance has obtained for many years." [3]

Although Commissioner Larrick has denied — "firmly" — that new drugs have been allowed to go on the market "on the basis of inadequate laboratory and clinical investigation work," others had been expressing thoughts like Dr. Middleton's, and for a long time. In 1951 Dr. O. B. Ross, Jr., wrote in the January 13 *Journal* of the American Medical Association that the majority of reports of therapeutic studies failed to include adequate controls. Six years later, Dr. Harry F. Dowling of the University of Illinois wrote in the October 12, 1957, *Journal* that the "tre-

---

[3] In this regard, Dr. Walter Modell told the American Association for the Advancement of Science in 1962 this little-known story about Sigmund Freud:

The story of the origin of the cocaine habit in Europe is well authenticated. Sigmund Freud was largely responsible for its development in Europe. Freud was, by his own account, the first European to take cocaine after it had been isolated. He liked the effect it had on him, and he continued to take it from time to time thereafter, and even boasted to his fiancée about its effects on him. He assumed that he had performed a valid experiment with his own trials on himself, although he had not applied the safeguard of setting up rigorous controls. Without further ado he proclaimed cocaine to be a treatment for a large number of ailments and attested to its harmlessness. The habit quickly spread in Europe and hooked, of all people, Sherlock Holmes (with, of course, the blessing of Dr. Conan Doyle). Eventually Freud was publicly condemned for his role in bringing about what was then called the third scourge of mankind.

mendous multiplication of new drugs exhausts the existing facilities for clinical investigation and inexperienced investigators are cajoled into assessing drugs in patients."

In 1960 Dr. Mindel C. Sheps, an associate professor of biostatistics and preventive medicine at the University of Pittsburgh, told the American Public Health Association of her review of 394 investigations in all medical specialties. All of the evidence she gathered "suggests that," she reported, "a great part of the so-called clinical evaluations of new drugs is unscientific, lacks adequate provisions to eliminate bias, and cannot be objectively judged." The New York Academy of Medicine agreed with Dr. Sheps in a report issued in 1962. The report advised that the possibility of drug testing by "untrained, inexperienced, or otherwise incompetent investigators" not be rejected out-of-hand as "impossible, fantastic, and incredible . . ." Difficult as it may be for Commissioner Larrick to admit and for the reader to believe, such testing was going on.

George Larrick's own Assistant Commissioner for Planning, Winton B. Rankin, was very blunt about the situation in the fall of 1963, when he participated in the University of Pennsylvania symposium on medical research and communications. He said it is quite true that the new regulations and the Kefauver-Harris drug amendments "may interfere with some types of research conducted in years past. They were intended to do so, because there was some lousy investigation being performed under the guise of science."

The Food and Drug Administration had failed, as we have seen, to define an "expert" qualified to test drugs and to create standards for testing. "An unparalleled example of bureaucratic inertia," said the Senate Minority Leader, Senator Everett M. Dirksen.

The inertia ended, after twenty-four years, on August 10, 1962 — more than two months before enactment of the Kefauver-Harris amendments but during what elements of the drug indus-

try are disposed to call the thalidomide "hysteria." Acting under the 1938 Food, Drug, and Cosmetic Act, FDA proposed
regulations — which became effective in February 1963 — requiring that FDA be notified of *all* human trials of a new drug, and
that it be kept fully informed of what happens during clinical
testing. In addition, human testing must be preceded by adequate animal studies. These experiments must be properly
planned, and must be carried out by qualified investigators.
The precise meaning of "qualified" was not stated. However,
manufacturers now are required to submit to FDA "the scientific
training and experience considered appropriate by the sponsor to
qualify the investigators as suitable experts to investigate the
safety of the drug, bearing in mind what is known about the
pharmacological action of the drug and the phase of the investigational program that is to be undertaken."

Many defenses can be made of the record of the Food and
Drug Administration. Suppose, for example, that the Commissioner were a very tough-minded George Larrick bearing a modest resemblance to his early predecessor, Dr. Harvey Wiley.
Who are the allies to whom he might turn? Merely to ask the
question is to see the man in a more sympathetic light than may
have appeared up to now to bathe this essay.

First, there are the Secretaries of Health, Education, and
Welfare who have been Larrick's bosses. As their very titles
make clear, they have vast, unrelated responsibilities. They are
at the mercy of powerful figures on Capitol Hill who control
HEW's appropriations. None has been a scientist. None has
been eager to grapple with the politically powerful drug industry.
Besides, all of them come and go. Oveta Culp Hobby, who was
in office during the blitz campaign that helped to assure Larrick's
promotion as Commissioner, has returned to Houston. Marion
B. Folsom is back with Eastman Kodak in Rochester. Arthur S.
Flemming praised FDA as "one of the finest examples we can
have of what a career civil service can mean," but that was

several years ago, and he is running the University of Oregon in Eugene. Abraham A. Ribicoff is in the Senate. The present Secretary, Anthony J. Celebrezze, may someday go back to Cleveland, where he was Mayor. Until September 1964 he, like his predecessors, had on his personal staff no scientifically trained adviser to whom he could turn for counsel.

Now to the rest of the list, to the powers that never go back to Texas, Oregon, New York, or Ohio. As he calls the roll — the American Medical Association, Congress (apart from a very few men, that is, and between disasters), the press (ditto), the fickle, uninformed public — as the Commissioner reads the roster he surely could be forgiven if he were to paraphrase the late A. J. Liebling and tick off one and all as weak slats under the sickbed of democracy.

One who has been highly sympathetic to Commissioner Larrick and Deputy Commissioner John L. Harvey is Representative John D. Dingell of Michigan. His is a voice that deserves to be heard. The public is deeply indebted to John Dingell and a fellow liberal Democrat, Representative John A. Blatnik of Minnesota. Using blowups of advertisements for Norlutin, Diabinese, and other drugs with frightening side effects, they led the brilliant and totally effective fight on the House floor which restored to the Kennedy Administration drug bill the provisions for full disclosure of side effects in advertising and promotional materials.

In a letter dated March 21, 1963, to the *Reporter*, Dingell put primary responsibility upon Congress and a number of Administrations for treating FDA "as a stepchild" for at least twenty years. He considered it "remarkable . . . that it has done as well as it had with limited staff, reduced appropriations, antiquated facilities and fearful work load. Indeed, it is to the Food and Drug Administration's great credit that it has stood up to heavy industry pressure in the remarkable way in which it has over the years." Dingell has for years worked to strengthen

FDA. He has known Larrick and Harvey well and come to praise them. "I have found them," he wrote to the magazine, "to be honorable, dedicated and remarkably courageous men who would stand up against heavy pressure . . ."

Although Mr. Humphrey has been given to outbursts of kindness in which he has praised the Commissioner's personal qualities, he has felt impelled time after time to renew his criticism of the way George Larrick has run FDA. One of his sharpest attacks was made in February 1964 in a long memorandum distributed to his subcommittee colleagues and then printed in a subcommittee publication. This issue was the quality of drug testing and evaluation. FDA has known of the weaknesses in this life-and-death area for more than two decades, he said, but it "does not appear to have been forthright." He continued:

> FDA did not present the necessary facts to Congress. It did not use any opportunity afforded by the Congress to broach the subject. It did not urge with all the strength at its command that changes in the law be made. And it did not use its own power to make changes via administrative regulations.
>
> The net effect of FDA's silence and inaction was a "cover up." This condition ran utterly contrary to FDA's own best traditions, dating back to the days of the crusading Dr. Harvey Wiley . . .
>
> . . . as late as June 1960, even when the tide of public opinion had begun to run strongly for drug reforms, FDA expressed to the Senate Antitrust subcommittee nothing but "firm denials," as to weaknesses in FDA's evaluation of drugs. The agency, at the time, could well have pointed out that it could hardly properly evaluate drugs if the evidence in the New Drug Application was weak to begin with; the agency chose not to do so; it chose to try to assure the Congress that all was reasonably well. Thus, the "dust" which had been

"swept under the rug" remained under the rug. This was not innocent, or meaningless "dust"; it involved suppressed data, affecting human lives.

FDA's silence over the situation is not without explanation. As Dr. May [Dr. Charles D. May, in testimony before the Humphrey subcommittee] implied, the "atmosphere of the times" seemed to be against strong regulation. But why do we have Federal regulatory agencies? Are they supposed to remain silent while the public interest is harmed? Are they supposed to sit passively until some great tragedy like thalidomide comes along, so that the "atmosphere" can change?

All too often an agency has acted and Congress has legislated only after tragedy has struck. But that is no excuse for any agency not to use its fullest resources to inform the Congress and the people of the approaching danger.

Not that FDA was alone in trying to soothe Congress. Spokesmen for the industry and the medical profession were trying to do the same thing. Even in August 1962 — two months before the reforms bearing his name were enacted — Representative Oren Harris, chairman of the House Committee on Interstate and Foreign Commerce, was being told by a leading physician who is on the board of Merck & Co., Inc., that drug companies use "extraordinary care in selecting highly trained clinical investigators." He was Dr. Chester S. Keefer, who is on the faculty of the Boston University School of Medicine and on the staff of the Massachusetts Memorial Hospitals.

FDA finally brought itself to admit that testing had not been adequate, but it did so as if it hoped that no one would notice. Deep and almost buried in its budget justification for 1964 there was this paragraph:

. . . recent evidence indicates that some of the clinical investigations have been improperly planned, executed by unqualified investigators, and the results improperly reported to the Food and Drug Administration in New Drug Applications. There is evidence indicating that in many cases recipients of experimental drugs have failed entirely to report their experience with the drugs. Another problem has been that some drug manufacturers, in sending investigational drugs to practitioners, have not provided sufficient information about the drug to guide the physicians in testing the drugs on patients.

FDA used an old bureaucratic face-saving technique here. The evidence was *not* "recent" — and FDA knew it. "The adjective is inappropriate," said Senator Humphrey in a piece of understatement. "The evidence has existed since 1938 (not to mention before then)."

In other fundamental areas FDA behaved like a sleepwalker in a town full of agencies that struggle ceaselessly for more money and more power. This was brought out by the Senate Antitrust subcommittee when it undertook to find out why it was that drug companies had been so successful in persuading physicians to prescribe drugs under their trade names. This practice is immensely more expensive to the consumer — and immensely more profitable to the manufacturer — than prescribing by generic name. But brand-name prescribing was predominant despite FDA's inspection and enforcement powers, which are intended to assure acceptable quality of all drug products. The subcommittee majority commented in its report of June 1961:

To overcome whatever natural inclination the physician might have to prescribe generically . . . the drug companies have sought to create the impression that FDA has regrettably been derelict in its duty. The agency, it is stressed, simply cannot get around to policing all of the companies which make up the industry, and therefore, it is held, the wise physician should rely on those companies whose products he can be sure of. It is a considerable understatement to say that this campaign has in no way been hindered by the Food and Drug Administration.

It is not unusual for an agency to accept and indeed join in the criticisms of its own shortcomings. What is unusual is for it to do so without having grounds to transfer the responsibility elsewhere. It is in precisely this situation that the Food and Drug Administration now finds itself.

It can avail itself of neither of the two defenses traditionally employed by Government agencies to excuse their own derelictions — inadequate authority and inadequate funds. In 1952 the agency felt that it needed stronger inspection and enforcement powers to police the drug industry. It sought those powers and was rebuffed by Congress. During the ensuing 8 years it did not renew its request.

The shoring up of an agency's enforcement powers is usually accomplished only after the need for the enlarged authority has been clearly demonstrated; this usually and properly takes a period of time . . .

When an agency fails to renew a request for broader authority, the Congress has reasonable grounds for assuming that the conditions which originally prompted it have disappeared or at least are no longer as pressing.

Nor can the Food and Drug Administration have recourse to the inadequate funds defense. During the period 1952-60 appropriations for the agency were increased by 60 percent. What is more relevant here, the Congress has usually appropriated substantially the amount requested, or more.

In every year since 1952, with the exception of 1954, the amount appropriated has been 95 percent or more of the amount requested for the agency.

In 3 of the last 5 years Congress has appropriated the full amount requested, while in the other 2 years it has given the agency more than was requested.

Moreover, the manner in which the agency apportioned its appropriation on work involving ethical drugs as contrasted to other and perhaps less important types of activities is open to question.

This would particularly be the case if the problem of inferior quality of products offered by small firms is as serious as the large companies profess it to be.

In 1964 Representative L. H. Fountain refused to accept uncritically Commissioner Larrick's pleas that he had had insufficient staff to handle certain new-drug applications properly. At a hearing of his House Intergovernmental Relations Subcommittee, Fountain reminded the Commissioner of his appearance in January 1956 before the House Committee on Appropriations. He was asked what he needed in the Division of Medicine. Representative Fountain told Larrick, "And you responded by saying, 'I think we may need one additional [medical] officer and in the succeeding years we would plan to request more.' "

THE QUALITY OF DRUG TESTING is an issue inseparably related to that of obtaining, in accord with medical ethics such as those summarized in the footnote on page 149, the voluntary and *informed* consent of patients to participate in clinical trials. Clearly, for example, an investigator about to undertake an experiment of low quality — if he has the wit to recognize what he is doing — is less likely to win a patient's *informed* consent if the patient is told the facts. Since November 1965, when *The Therapeutic Nightmare* was published, new evidence has emerged that drug testing is too often of low quality (fraud is taken up in Chapter 16 and its Afterword); at the same time, the ethical issues of medical experimentation on human beings have aroused a productive professional and lay concern. I now will illustrate this point and counterpoint and then take up the illuminating case of Indocin, a drug that on the basis of highly doubtful testing quickly became used more than anything but aspirin by victims of rheumatoid arthritis, of whom there are 3½ million in the United States, and by many among the additional 10 million Americans afflicted with other arthritic disorders.

In December 1965 Dr. Jean K. Weston, then director of the Department of Drugs of the American Medical Association, told a meeting of The Proprietary Association that clinical drug studies scientifically well-designed and executed to produce

reliable and useful data are "not yet in the majority," although
the "almost universal occurrence of bias . . . should be taken for
granted. . . ." In April 1966, shortly after becoming Commissioner of the Food and Drug Administration, Dr. James L.
Goddard told the Pharmaceutical Manufacturers Association
that the "hand of the amateur is evident too often for my comfort" in data submitted to justify going from animal to human
testing. "I have been shocked at the quality of many submissions," he said. On March 14, 1967, in a roundup story on
"Sloppy Research," William M. Carley of the *Wall Street
Journal* quoted Dr. John L. Decker, chief of research on arthritis
and rheumatism at the National Institute of Arthritis and Metabolic Diseases, as saying that "perhaps half the studies proposed
on the two diseases won't answer the questions posed because of
inadequate design of the investigations." Stanley Schor, a professor of medical statistics at the Temple University School of
Medicine, critically evaluated 149 research reports in ten leading
medical journals. He found, reporter Carley said, that in three
cases out of four (73 per cent) "conclusions were drawn when
the justification for these conclusions was invalid."

Concern about clinical experimentation — including new surgical procedures — was manifested in many places and ways.
Surgeon General William H. Stewart of the Public Health Service promulgated new rules to protect patients in studies receiving
PHS funds; in a cooperative project, the PHS and the American
Academy of Arts and Sciences made plans for a conference on
the problem to be held in 1968. Much interest was aroused by
Dr. Henry K. Beecher, of Harvard Medical School, with an
article in the *New England Journal of Medicine* that chronicled
shocking abuses; by editorials in that distinguished publication,
and by a broad and provocative treatment of the subject in
Saturday Review. An especially challenging idea was suggested
by Irving Ladimer, a National Better Business Bureau counsel
who is a consultant to the National Institutes of Health. The

idea was for compensation insurance for volunteers who suffer unexpected injuries that require loss of time from work or hospitalization. But there was no more important action than that taken — initially in August 1966 — by the Food and Drug Administration under the patient-consent provisions of the Kefauver-Harris Amendments of 1962. The agency proposed guidelines which, as modified in March 1967, would require physicians using investigational drugs to obtain the consent of the patient (or his representative). This would be in writing when clinical testing is in the early phases (to determine effectiveness against a specific disease or to determine toxicity or dosage ranges), and when the primary purpose of an experiment is not to advance the welfare of the volunteer, but to accumulate scientific knowledge. Written or oral consent would be required "in all but exceptional cases" when an investigational drug is used for treatment. In the final phase of a clinical trial, in which a number of investigators administer an experimental drug essentially as they would if the product had been approved for general medical use, it would be "the responsibility of investigators, taking into consideration the physical and mental state of the patient, to decide when it is necessary or preferable to obtain consent in other than written form." If such consent is not obtained in writing, "the investigator must obtain oral consent and record that fact in the medical record of the person receiving the drug." In *all* phases of clinical trials the investigator would be required to give "pertinent information" to the patient on the test drug and disclose to him ". . . the nature, expected duration, and purpose of the administration of said investigational drug; the method and means by which it is to be administered; the hazards involved; the existence of alternative forms of therapy, if any; and the beneficial effects upon his health or person that may possibly come from the administration of the investigational drug." Surely these regulations, which were expected to be promulgated in basically unchanged and final form in mid-1967, were a major achievement in behalf of medical ethics and against careless, mindless, and reckless experimentation with human beings. Commissioner Goddard had a right to be proud.

I turn now to the disclosures about Indocin, some of which were the basis for the story in the *Wall Street Journal* on "Sloppy Research":

INDOCIN

In January 1966 an informal poll was taken among the 100,000 practicing physicians who receive *Medical Research Digest*. An "overwhelming percentage of responses," a sister publication, *Drug Research Reports*, recalled on March 22, 1967, "named Indocin in answer to the question: 'What was the most significant advance in medical therapy (during 1965)?'" Let that be our benchmark.

The Food and Drug Administration of Commissioner George P. Larrick and Medical Director Joseph F. Sadusk, Jr., gave marketing approval on June 10, 1965, to Indocin, a drug intended for the management of certain arthritic disorders. The manufacturer, the Merck Sharp & Dohme division of Merck & Co., Inc., said that the drug produced "improvement" in 50 to 80 per cent of patients among the 10,000 on whom it was tried by more than 300 clinical investigators, William M. Carley recalled in the *Wall Street Journal*. By the end of 1965 an estimated six million dollars' worth had been sold. For as long as two years earlier the drug, which has the generic name indomethacin, had been sold in other countries. This largely unaudited experience produced at least one published alert several months before the FDA let Indocin go on sale here. An "imposing list of side effects" was detailed in the *Medical Journal of Australia*, but this had no more impact on the Bureau of Medicine of Dr. Sadusk than had the strict requirement of the law that a manufacturer must demonstrate efficacy with "substantial evidence" — defined as "adequate and well-controlled investigations, including clinical investigations, by experts, qualified by scientific training and experience to evaluate the effectiveness of the drug involved. . . ." What *had* been demonstrated, as Dr. John L. Decker of the National Institute of Arthritis and Metabolic Diseases would tell *Medical Tribune* later, was that instead of a few pre-marketing trials carried out with "exquisite exactitude," we had a great many studies that were "less than adequate" and that would require "several years of re-evaluation." Far less time is needed to wage a promotional campaign that may be executed with exquisite inexactitude — but that may be more than adequate to assure a happy annual meeting of the stockholders and, simultaneously, to facilitate the gearing up needed to bring out a successor compound which will be greeted as yet another miracle by large numbers of supposed men of medical science. In the first paragraph of its article on "Sloppy Research," the *Wall Street Journal* noted that Indocin had "produced a large jump in Merck's sales and profits. . . ."

Promotion of indomethacin was not restricted to physicians. *Pageant*, the same magazine that in December 1966 and January 1967 would give cover-story treatment to the so-called Rand vaccine and set off an appalling pilgrimage of terminal cancer victims to Cleveland, carried a piece in July 1966 headlined "INDOCIN," the brand name of the drug. The article, written by freelancers Phyllis and Robert P. Goldman, was distinguished by comparable subtlety. Using testimonials supplied by Merck, these writers proclaimed indomethacin's usefulness in conditions which the maker was not allowed to promote to physicians — "bursitis," "trick knee," "tennis elbow." "The only support for these claims," FDA counsel William W. Goodrich has said, "was user testimonials which, according to the article, were made available to the writers by the sponsor of the drug." The company said that the initiative for the article had come from the Goldmans, that the writers had originated a request for "feature material" which Merck met by turning over letters from grateful Indocin patients, and that the company acted out of a "responsibility to assist the press."

Another responsibility was imposed when reports of adverse reactions to indomethacin began coming in. Merck met that one in October 1966 by mailing the nation's practicing physicians a revised prescribing brochure. This was accompanied by a letter that mentioned "new cautionary information" and "important changes" in the FDA-approved prescribing brochure. The letter, signed by Dr. Frederick K. Heath, vice president for professional communications of Merck Sharp & Dohme, had, overall, a clear promotional tone. It was a performance reminiscent of the one put on by E. R. Squibb & Sons 19 months earlier, when that firm tried to turn what should have been a warning letter about Naturetin c̄ K, a thiazide-potassium diuretic, into a promotion that would handicap competitors—including Merck. One thing that gave Dr. Heath's communication a promotional rather than a professional tone was a statement that "144,000,000 patient days of therapy in 99 countries" had been accumulated with Indocin, which "has become, next to aspirin, the most frequently prescribed antirheumatic drug." A spokesman for the FDA has said that the agency never should have allowed indomethacin to be characterized as "antirheumatic." Shortly Merck was required to delete the claim — but not until after it had contributed to Indocin's immense popularity and to Merck's immense profits.

On October 20, 1966, William Goodrich made the speech to the Pharmaceutical Advertising Club which was mentioned in the Afterword to Chapter 4. That speech, it may be recalled, cited the deception found by FDA to infect advertisements for the "big eight" drugs introduced in 1965, including Upjohn's Lincocin and Indocin. "Like most new drugs offered to replace established products," the agency counsel said, Indocin "was offered as safer and more effective."

(One of Merck's own predecessors to Indocin was the anti-inflammatory hormone it called Decadron and which entered the United States market in November 1958. Then and after, and, to some extent, even before, Merck flooded the medical profession with ads and broadcast and print lay news media with "news" releases and interview scripts, all to make claims such as that Decadron had wondrously fewer and less serious side effects than the corticosteroids that had preceded *it.* When the late Senator Estes Kefauver asked about a Decadron ad that went all the way and claimed "NO STEROID SIDE EFFECTS," John T. Connor, then president of Merck and later President Johnson's Secretary of Commerce, replied, "This particular ad is used by our international division. . . ." The claim of no side effects was acknowledged by Dr. Augustus Gibson, director of medical research at Merck, to be "not true." Even in 1958, "at the very time Merck's advertising claims were being intensified," Kefauver's Senate Subcommittee on Antitrust and Monopoly reported, "the volume of clinical reports by unbiased observers was confirming earlier evidence to the contrary." But ten months after Decadron entered the American market it had captured 26.9 per cent of the prescription business in corticosteroids.)

Goodrich went on to say about Indocin that as new experience with it was gained — as with Decadron and *its* predecessors before that — "more side effects have been noted and more warning information has been required." Only a few days earlier, he continued, Merck had mailed the revised prescribing brochure "with new cautionary information in heavy print." Yet, the FDA attorney said, the current ad for Indocin, which had been carried in the *Journal* of the American Medical Association, "continues the headline 'extends the margin of safety in long-term management of arthritic disorders.'" He added:

There is not yet enough experience to support the claim for greater long-term safety. To the contrary, the longer the drug is used the more side-effect information appears.

This ad quotes authoritative sources, without the full impact of the actual articles. And it uses one reference which is from a two-inch abstract, apparently of a 1964 speech. This latter reference is used to support a claim for "ankylosing spondylitis" [arthritis of the spine], but the ad does not inform the reader that this same abstract also states "Excellent results have also been obtained in some cases of rheumatoid arthritis . . . there have been striking failures as well."

The claim for gout is not supported by the package insert [prescribing brochure] or by the scientific data.

And, finally, the "Brief Summary" omits some very important warning information that is required in the package insert — and thus in the ad.

Goodrich then related how Indocin had been "featured" in *Pageant*. This article appeared *after* the Merck product was marketed. Perhaps progress was being made: Decadron, referred to as an un-named "new steroid," had been plugged in the *Reader's Digest* for August 1958 — three months before the drug was released for sale. The article, by Paul de Kruif, was called the Merck Sharp & Dohme "shoehorn" in a June 1958 memo prepared by the Medical & Pharmaceutical Information Bureau, a public relations firm whose clients have included Merck, many other drug firms, and the New York Academy of Sciences, which has sponsored symposia on new drugs in co-operation with some of those firms. The MPIB was shown in the Kefauver hearings to have had extraordinary success in getting lay news media that do not carry ads for prescription drugs to carry stories that provide free advertising. The title of the *Reader's Digest* piece was "Taming the Wild Hormones."

Following the Goodrich speech several developments occurred. Merck appeared at a closed FDA hearing in Philadelphia to show cause why it should not be prosecuted for the Indocin ad; at the time in January 1967 when I wrote a story about this for the Washington *Post* no inkling of the outcome could be ascertained, and that situation prevails as of this writing in May 1967. In November, the Food and Drug Directorate in Ottawa itself sent a letter to Canadian physicians which told of several indomethacin deaths in children and of a number of unexpected adverse reactions, including "not uncommon" and sometimes severe effects on the central nervous system, serious blood diseases that are sometimes fatal, and blurred vision. The Canadian Government letter said that "INDOMETHACIN SHOULD NOT BE USED IN CHILDREN. . . ." In addition, doctors north of the border were warned that the drug "can mask the signs and symptoms of an infectious process or activate a latent infection." When Sandy Koufax retired from baseball he had taken indomethacin after being on cortisone. In a story about the great pitcher in the New York *Times* of November 19, Science Editor Walter Sullivan pointed out that cortisone may have adverse effects; his story said nothing about the adverse effects of indomethacin. "Indocin has the dual ability to reduce pain as well as inflammation," was deemed a sufficient comment. By December, the FDA in Washington knew of 329 adverse reactions, including seven deaths in children (only one of which was said to have had a clearcut relation to Indocin) and nine in elderly persons (of which three were said by the agency to have had a "possibly clearcut" relation with the drug). The presumption must be that the usual gross incompleteness of reported cases of adverse drug reactions existed in this situation. And, it should be noted, until persons with rheumatoid arthritis began receiving corticosteroids and then Indocin, that disease, as was said by the late Dr. Michael Kelly, director of Australia's Institute of Rheumatology, was one "which once had no mortality."

In December, the month following the Canadian Government letter, FDA decided against sending a letter of its own in favor of one negotiated with Merck. The company letter, signed by Dr. Frederick Heath, carried the words "DRUG SAFETY IN-FORMATION," in deep blue, above the "Dear Doctor" salutation. Promotional plugs for Indocin were absent. The Merck official emphasized that Indocin "should not be prescribed for children because safe conditions for use have not been established." That same warning appeared three times, in boldface type, in the new prescribing circular enclosed with the letter. The same typographical emphasis was given to a statement that severe and even fatal reactions have occurred in a few cases of severe juvenile rheumatoid arthritis in children who received indomethacin along with other drugs.

Early 1967 brought reports on rheumatoid arthritis studies done on indomethacin with that "exquisite exactitude" valued by Dr. John Decker of the National Institute of Arthritis and Metabolic Diseases. In the *British Medical Journal* for January 14 was a report by three physicians in Wales — Drs. Phelim Donnelly, Kenneth Lloyd, and Hubert Campbell — on a 10-week double-blind study of highly sophisticated design; with neither patients nor physicians knowing it, some among the 28 patients had been "crossed over" from drug to fake pill, or from fake pill to indomethacin. The study indicated that the drug was no more effective than the placebo pill. Side effects were found more frequently with indomethacin, but the report inferred that "suggestion played a large part in determining both the incidence and the variety. . . ." In the *New England Journal of Medicine* for March 2, Drs. Robert S. Pinals and Sumner Frank, both of Boston, reported on another double-blind crossover study done on 24 patients. Of these, two on Indocin, including one who also was taking aspirin, dropped out with "intolerable side effects." Another quit for an unrelated reason. Among those who remained in the month-long trial seven preferred aspirin, seven preferred indomethacin, and seven were unable to detect a difference in the effects of the two. As for the physicians themselves, they rated Indocin superior in five patients — and aspirin in six; in ten patients they discovered no difference in the symptomatic relief provided. The blockbuster was a study that was in the planning and analysis stage for about 18 months, that was intended to overcome the deficiencies of earlier trials, that was aided by a grant from Dr. Decker's National Institute, that was sponsored by the American Rheumatism Association, and that was published in the January-February issue of *Clinical Pharmacology and Therapeutics*. The article, prepared by Donald Mainland, professor of medical statistics at New York University, gave the results of a three-month blindfold trial conducted in 11 research institutions co-operating with the Rheumatism Association. All told, there were 71 patients treated with Indocin and 65 with placebo — but both groups were permitted to take aspirin, because they needed it to control their pain. "Without questioning the possibility that indomethacin benefits some patients," Professor Mainland said, the drug and placebo groups were "indistinguishable in frequency, extent and rate of symptoms, evaluated either singly or in combination. Undesirable symptoms, especially headache, dizziness, and light-headedness, were more frequent in the D[drug] group than in the P [placebo] group. In the week after trial medication had ceased, and before therapy assignments were revealed, physicians' and patients' impressions reported more deterioration in the D [Indocin] group than in the P group. . . ." In addition, the literature on indomethacin back to its introduction in 1963 was reviewed by Dr. William M. O'Brien, then of the Yale University Cooperating Clinic and now professor of preventive medicine at the University of Virginia. He found, in general, that the degree of enthusiasm for indomethacin varied inversely with the quality of the investigation — the lower the quality, the higher the enthusiasm.

In a statement on the Rheumatism Association's blindfold trial in the 11 clinics, Merck said the study did not demonstrate "the clinical effectiveness of Indomethacin used alone or the relative effectiveness of Indomethacin and aspirin used separately." In addition, the company said, its drug has worked in rheumatoid arthritis patients in whom aspirin has failed, and in other arthritic conditions for which its use is approved by the FDA. Merck also said that the whole situation illustrates the extreme difficulty of doing double-blind studies, because patients consume aspirin to relieve active rheumatoid arthritis "without regard to their MD's directions."

Doubtless indomethacin has some uses. But it had been heralded as a great breakthrough — as a super-drug, as — the reader may recall — the nomination of practicing physicians for "the most significant advance in medical therapy" during 1965. For this unscientific exuberance some patients paid with their health if not their lives — and their money cost in every case was vastly greater than for aspirin. The blame falls widely — on an FDA that failed to demand the "substantial evidence" of efficacy specified in the law, on the gullability of so many physicians, on the distorted advertising campaign carried on by Merck — but also, certainly, on what the *Wall Street Journal* called "Sloppy Research." On March 18, 1967, FDA said it was re-evaluating Indocin and the prescribing instructions for it.

8

THE DRUG INDUSTRY ASCENDANT

IF THE Food and Drug Administration, the American Medical Association, the press, the journals, the public — if all of these have come to play vastly different roles than in earlier years, the mainspring of change has been the pharmaceutical industry. And the mainspring of drastic change in the industry has been a technology that pours out new compounds and variants by the tens of thousands. F. Ellis Kelsey, a special assistant to the Surgeon General of the Public Health Service, and a pharmacologist whose wife is Dr. Frances Kelsey, has reported, for instance, that a computer can search a file of 50,000 chemical compounds and within a few minutes report on those that share certain biological properties and structural configurations.

Unlike drugs of an earlier time, the powerful agents produced by the new technology often have personalities that may not be fully unveiled until they have been used for years, and in great numbers of people. This means that testing of these products must be extraordinarily cautious, thorough, and imaginative before marketing begins. The decisions to be made — how much testing is enough? how long should trials in humans continue? — are, under the best of circumstances, delicate and difficult. Just as it is intolerable to have a drug released too quickly, so would it be intolerable — although this has not been shown to be a problem — to hold back a valuable new drug out of fear, or out of unwillingness to take a knowledgeable and intelligently calculated risk.

✓ ✓ ✓

New drugs require large investments — for development, for testing, for meeting the costs of other agents that are found wanting and abandoned, for meeting the requirements of the Food and Drug Administration's procedures, and, finally, for advertising and promoting them to physicians. Modern corporations, whether they make automobiles, detergents, or drugs, do not make large investments casually. They make them after extensive planning that seeks to control not only costs and prices but also, Professor John Kenneth Galbraith points out, demand. Planning to control demand for the product is impelled by a need to assure a corporation's stability, growth, and even its survival.

Advertising and promotion are basic tools in planning to control demand. Ford, Chevrolet, and Plymouth all are cars in the same price range, and all will carry you from one place to another with reasonably equal efficiency, reliability, and comfort. Insofar as possible, the corporation making each car tries to assure an adequate and steady demand. It does so, in part, by seeking through advertising to distinguish its car from its rivals' — its style, safety, dimensions, power, durability, trade-in-value, and the like. Nonetheless, each make remains an automobile; each make fulfills the same basic needs.

The demand for prescription drugs, however, arises from a market of an extraordinary character. It is a market in which *caveat emptor* has little, if any, real application. You may be quite capable of deciding whether your car is good or bad, and directing your patronage accordingly; but you cannot reliably ascertain whether your medicine is good or bad. The better it is, indeed, the *less* likely you may be to buy it again. A crucial, closely related difference is that although you a buy a prescription drug you do not order it. The decision as to what you buy is made by the prescribing physician. He orders but does not pay the bill. In many cases, in fact, he does not even know the cost of the medicines he tells you to buy. In this context, therefore, your importance as a consumer is secondary. It lies, that is, principally in the extent to which you can be induced, by publicity and other devices, to demand of your physician that he prescribe a certain drug.

There is no difference between various brands of the same chemical compound — aspirin is aspirin no matter what the trade name. But there is little glamour, little feeling of movement toward some vague new frontier, little corporate growth, little chance at really big profits — little chance for any of these things in merely sitting back and turning out the usual.[1]

The challenge, consequently, is to develop a new product, patent it, promote it, advertise it, make a big profit, and then repeat the cycle. If the patented drug catches on, if physicians believe it is *the* product to be used, what is a competitor to do? The answer, so greatly facilitated by the new technology, is to pour out imitations in which the molecular structure is modified sufficiently to avoid infringement on the patent of the original drug. These imitations are variously called pharmacologic shadows, congeners, analogs, and me-too drugs.

Although cars and other consumer products retain their basic generic characters no matter what trade names are given them, or what changes may be made in them, the story is not the same with drugs. A molecular modification may avoid a court fight,

[1] In a speech before a group of security analysts several years ago John McKeen, president of Chas. Pfizer & Co., Inc., said that antibiotics marketed under their generic names, such as penicillin and streptomycin, fail to furnish ". . . any real indication of the outlook for the antibiotic industry. From a profit point of view . . . the only realistic solution . . . lies in the development of new and exclusive antibiotic specialities. This . . . is an exceedingly costly and vigorous alternative; nonetheless it is the avenue of approach being most extensively explored by certain antibiotic houses today. This is the approach being followed by Pfizer." McKeen's speech was recalled during the Kefauver hearings.

and be very profitable, but its impact on the human body may be very different. The side effects can be more numerous and more serious than those of the original drug, while conferring no advantage over it.

Dr. A. Dale Console, former medical director of a drug manufacturer, testified before the Kefauver Senate Subcommittee on Antitrust and Monopoly:

> The problem arises out of the fact that they [the drug companies] market so many of their failures. Between these failures which are presented as new drugs and the useless modifications of old drugs . . . most of the research results in a treadmill which moves at a rapid pace but goes nowhere. Since so much depends on novelty, drugs change like women's hemlines and rapid obsolescence is simply a sign of motion, not progress as the apologists would have us believe . . .
>
> I doubt that there are many other industries in which research is so free of risks. Most must depend on selling only their successes. If an automobile does not have a motor, no amount of advertising can make it appear to have one. On the other hand, with a little luck, proper timing, and a good promotion program a bag of asafetida with a unique chemical side chain can be made to look like a wonder drug. The illusion may not last, but it frequently lasts long enough. By the time the doctor learns what the company knew at the beginning, it has two new products to take the place of the old one.

The marketing of failures, Pierre R. Garai suggested in *Drugs in Our Society*,[2] may be economically unavoidable. "No manufacturer of drugs can afford to restrict his production to genu-

---

[2] Edited by Paul Talalay (Baltimore: Johns Hopkins Press, 1964). This volume is a collection of twenty-one formal papers presented at a conference sponsored in 1963 by the Johns Hopkins University to discuss problems associated with the discovery, development, manufacture, testing, pricing, and use of drugs. Mr. Garai's paper was entitled "Advertising and Promotion of Drugs."

inely significant pharmaceutical innovations," the late senior writer for the advertising agency of Lennen and Newell, Inc., said. "There simply aren't enough of these around in any given fiscal year or, for that matter, in any dozen fiscal years."

The physician who is informed about drugs and their uses, and whose judgments in prescribing are models of scientific detachment, is the mortal enemy of the inferior, ineffective, or unsafe product. His interest is synonymous with yours — but it is not necessarily identical with that of a drug manufacturer.

The manufacturer has made a large investment in a drug, he seeks to profit from that investment, and he therefore makes plans to control demand — which, in a real sense, means to control the physician. It is the physician who prescribes, and it is the physician who must be sold. If he is to prescribe a drug that rationally should not be prescribed, his rationality must be overcome. The doctor may have to be misinformed, confused, denied easy access to information about adverse reactions, bewildered by a multiplicity of brand names for similar products, and subjected to the blandishments of advertising and salesmen.[3]

Can physicians be induced to join the ranks of those who "praise what is outlandish before they know whether it is good, rather than the customary which they already know to be good;

[3] There is a serious question whether a great many physicians do not *prefer* being misinformed to being rationally informed. For $12.50 a year a physician can subscribe to the nonprofit biweekly, the *Medical Letter*. In *Drugs in Our Society* Pierre R. Garai said of this independent publication: "By drawing on an advisory board and on consultants of unquestioned integrity and distinction, by bringing together in a single, easily available source the best-founded, most objective findings about new drugs, and by publishing these evaluations at the very time the drugs are being intensively promoted, *The Medical Letter* is making a unique contribution whose value simply cannot be overstated."

Although the *Letter* costs less per year than a daily newspaper and provides a tough shield against "confusion, ignorance, and error," the profession as a whole has not flocked to buy it. In late 1963, after four and one-half years of publication, the *Letter* — "this indispensable adjunct to conscientious practice," Garai called it — had a circulation of 25,000. About seven out of every eight physicians did not receive it. For Dr. Louis Lasagna's comments on opposition encountered to the *Medical Letter*, see the afterword to this chapter.

the bizarre rather than the obvious?" In May 1960 *Fortune* recognized that they could: "Drug companies have learned that doctors are influenced by the same advertising techniques that are used for mass consumer advertising. They accept new drugs with amazing rapidity . . . in part because it would appear that a physician's own market position is strongly influenced by his reputation for using the latest drug."

"As an advertising man," Pierre Garai told the 1963 conference on drugs sponsored by the Johns Hopkins University, "I can assure you that advertising which does not work does not continue to run. If experience did not show beyond doubt that the great majority of doctors are splendidly responsive to current ethical [prescription-drug] advertising, new techniques would be devised in short order. And if, indeed, candor, accuracy, scientific completeness, and a permanent ban on cartoons came to be essential for the successful promotion of ethical drugs, advertising would have no choice but to comply."

This is the way Senator Kefauver had described the situation a year before:

> For the entire industry, promotion expenses run around $750 million a year . . . For the 22 largest drug companies, approximately 24 cents of every sales dollar is expended for promotion, or roughly four times the amount spent on research.

> That promotional expenditures have reached such proportions in this industry is particularly surprising in view of the fact that the most expensive media normally used for advertising — television, newspapers, and magazines — are not employed in the regular course of prescription-drug advertising. In this industry there is a separation of the buyer from the orderer. The former, namely the patient, pays the bill but the latter, the physician, places the order. And it is therefore to the physician that this vast expenditure of advertising re-

sources is directed . . . So important [are visits by salesmen] that from 1 out of 5 to 1 out of 8 of all employees of major drug companies is a detail man. So much money is spent in sending advertising literature to the physician's office that he is literally inundated . . .

But above and beyond the quantity of this advertising and promotional material, there is the further and more serious question of its quality. It is indeed a serious question because if the physician is misled, the public health is endangered. It was therefore most dismaying to learn from medical authorities that this advertising is often misleading and sometimes downright false. For 3 years one medical college has included in its course work for second-year medical students an evaluation of drug advertising. According to Dr. Solomon Garb, who conducted the course [at Albany Medical College]: "in all 3 years it was found that the majority of the mailed ads were unreliable, to the extent that a physician trusting them could be seriously misled."

Dr. Walter Modell warned of the dangers of the misled physician in an editorial for January–February 1961 in *Clinical Pharamacology and Therapeutics:*

> It makes little difference if, under the impression that it is the best, a housewife buys the next best detergent. *But you may not fool any of the people any of the time about drugs!* For even the slightest deviation from fact may be vital; if, under the misapprehension that it is the best, a doctor prescribes something less than the best, it may be the difference between life and death. Unlike the housewife and her detergent, it is clearly immoral if the physician is even *slightly misled* by claims made for the drugs he is importuned to use on the sick. It matters to him, it certainly matters to the patient, and it should matter to the pharmaceutical industry.

There is the very real ethical question of whether the pharmaceutical industry has the right to sell all the drugs it creates
and whether it does not have the moral obligation to select
only the elite of its creations for use in man.

ⵏ   ⵏ   ⵏ

Also operating in all of this is Gresham's Law — bad money
drives out the good. The situation is more complicated, however, than that bald statement indicates.

In any large corporation the *timing* of a decision may be more
important than its correctness. That is, Professor Galbraith has
explained, the corporate planning process is such that at certain
critical points it may be better to make a wrong decision that
can later be overcome (as was the Edsel fiasco in motordom)
than it is to disrupt and demoralize the organization by making
no decision. An application of this to the drug industry can
help to explain why certain drugs have been marketed before
their potentials for harm were established by thorough testing.

"When a drug of unquestioned merit is put on the market,"
Dr. Louis Lasagna of Johns Hopkins testified before the Senate
Antitrust subcommittee, "the company whose imagination and
know-how has been responsible for the breakthrough is faced
with the possibility that within a short period of time a half-
dozen or more pharmacologic shadows will be introduced by
competing firms, almost all of them representing minor advances
or no advances at all, but one or more of which may purloin a
good share of the market away from the first drug. The result
is a fantastic pressure on drug houses to assemble data in a
hurry and to market at the earliest possible date."

Dr. William Bean of the University of Iowa testified:

I am not concerned with the many pharmaceutical companies
which exercise scrupulous caution in releasing new drugs. The
problem is with companies whose sole concern is business.

The stockholders' appropriate interest is in income. The richest earnings occur when a new variety or variation of a drug is marketed before competing drugs can be discovered, improvised, named, and released. This bonanza time may last only a few months. Unless there are large earnings, the quick kill with the quick pill, the investment does not pay off. Commercial secrets must be kept dark, lest a competitor get the jump. Under this system it is impracticable to do tests extending over a long period of months or years to establish the range of usefulness and potential dangers from toxicity. Such tests usually have to be done in hospitals and often in medical schools, where secrecy in science cannot be tolerated. Thus, after extensive laboratory tests on toxicity and pharmacologic properties, but sometime[s] with a minimum of clinical trial, a drug may be marketed.

Dr. Dale Console had this exchange with Senator Kefauver about what happens when a "crash program" is begun to get a product out before a competitor does:

DR. CONSOLE. . . . it is not unusual for a worthwhile research program to be postponed so that the people can be taken off it to be put on the "crash program." Very frequently some of these programs are never picked up again. So that I think that good research is actually hampered by this type of thing.

SENATOR KEFAUVER. Is there much of this type of research that you are talking about that really produces nothing worthwhile and is not intended to?

DR. CONSOLE. I think the majority of it is in that category. I think more than half is in that category, and I should point out that with many of these products, it is clear while they are on the drawing board that they promise no utility; they promise sales. It is not a question of pursuing them because something may come of it. It is quite clear that there is no point in pursuing this; that you won't end up with a product that has any real value; but it is pursued simply because there is profit in it.

Dr. Maxwell Finland of Harvard believes that "even some of the older and respected members of the industry have relaxed some of their standards . . . all of them protest that the objectionable practices have been forced upon them by the actions of their competitors."

A similar view was expressed by the economist Seymour Harris in *The Economics of American Medicine,* which was published in 1964. He said that "competition forces even the highly moral firms to become less ethical in their behavior."

Although no one has been more forceful and eloquent in denouncing "this kind of rat race" than Dr. Modell, he took encouragement, in his American Association for the Advancement of Science address, from the fact that probably the most successful company "from the point of view of gross profits introduces the smallest number of new drugs for a company of its magnitude and indulges in virtually no molecule manipulation as the means of encroaching on markets established through the original research of other manufacturers."

To cut down on the flow of "manipulated molecules," and of useless combination drugs as well, Senator Kefauver proposed that such products not be patentable unless the Secretary of Health, Education, and Welfare has determined that the therapeutic effect is significantly increased. The proposal got nowhere.

The multiplicity of brand names has caused confusion that has been responsible for dangerous misprescribing. ". . . it is becoming exceedingly difficult for physicians to keep things clear," Dr. Solomon Garb, the Albany Medical College Pharmacologist, told the Senate Antitrust subcommittee. Consider what would happen, he suggested, "if drug manufacturers took over the manufacture of baked beans. They would all stop using the word 'beans' and each would give the product a new, coined name." He continued: "Some might use anagrams of beans, like Sneabs, or Nabes, and others might call them Lo Cals, or Hi Pros. Picture the confusion in the grocery store if beans were no longer named beans, but if each maker gave a completely new name to his product. Further, try to imagine what would happen if there were 300 to 500 additional new names of this type in the grocery store every year.

"This is approximately what is happening in medicine . . ."

The Kefauver-Harris amendments eased the problem. They directed the Secretary of Health, Education, and Welfare to designate an official (generic) name for a drug where necessary for usefulness and simplicity. This name must be printed prominently on every drug label and on advertising materials legally considered labeling.

Demand for a product cannot be controlled solely through the exertion of direct influences on physicians, since the impact of advertising and promotion on the physician can be offset or nullified by other factors, like professional journals and organizations that could aggressively circulate information on shoddy testing, adverse reactions, and irrational combinations of drugs. Automatically, therefore, all such potential threats to corporate planning for demand tend to generate efforts in the industry to neutralize or frustrate them.

Consider the labeling of a drug. The more emphatic the warning it gives the greater the threat to sales. Some firms, therefore, carry on prolonged resistance to FDA's efforts to make the labels reflect actual dangers. To give an illustration — in a staff memorandum published by the Humphrey subcommittee, Dr. Irving Cooperstein, an FDA medical officer, said in February 1963:

> The immediate problem is to cease the laxity the FDA and industry have maintained about the scientific caliber of label-

ing . . . It is impossible for one or several physicians to operate in the hit-or-miss fashion this Division has done in the
past . . . A firm will ignore your requests, and the only
response may occur when an inspection is made. The long,
tedious negotiations over changes begin, as the firm is reluctant to have mediocre claims for a mediocre product.

It is common practice for firms to send nonmedical and
even nonscientific, personnel to discuss medical matters. Little
is accomplished, since they are the equivalent of the detail
men some of us encountered in practice. Some firms merely
ignore requests we initiate, because they do not want to submit
anything like a supplement. Promises have been made over
the telephone with no attempt to fulfill them.[4]

Congress, of course, is a unique and potentially enormous
check. That Congress was not disposed to enact strong legislation was evidenced by a comment in *Fortune* for March 1963.
"Conservative Congressmen," it reported, *"responding to industry opposition,* had practically emasculated the Kefauver bill by
the time the thalidomide story broke . . ." (My italics.)

The story of a second example of the industry's power in Congress began in 1961. Two liberal Democrats, Senators Stephen
H. Young of Ohio and Quentin N. Burdick of North Dakota,
sought appointments to vacancies in the Committee on the
Judiciary, the parent of Senator Kefauver's Antitrust subcommittee. They had more seniority than their rivals, Senator Edward V. Long of Missouri and former Senator William A.
Blakley of Texas, an arch-conservative. The assignments were
to be made by the Democratic Steering Committee. According
to two members, Senator Humphrey and Senator Joseph Clark
of Pennsylvania, Robert G. (Bobby) Baker, then Secretary to
the Senate Majority, appeared at a meeting of the Steering

---

[4] For details published by the Humphrey subcommittee on relabeling difficulties
with regard to Sigmamycin, see the afterword to this chapter.

Committee and said that Burdick and Young "weren't interested" in the Judiciary vacancies. During the Bobby Baker scandal in 1963 it came out that Burdick and Young, whose rivals were given the Judiciary seats, hadn't lost interest at all. "I know Bobby Baker threw the harpoon into me," Young told Bernard Nossiter of the Washington *Post*. "I thought it was a damn outrage to have this cold fish millionaire put in my place." The reference was to Blakley.

In 1963, when Senator Kefauver was trying to get an investigation under way into the fixing of drug prices in South America by United States firms, Long joined Republicans on the Antitrust subcommittee to stymie the proposal. Senator Philip A. Hart of Michigan succeeded Kefauver after the Tennesseean's death. The challenge was to issue subpoenas to compel the testimony of drug manufacturers. Long opposed it. In December 1963, because they were still outnumbered, Hart and his allies failed again in their effort to launch the inquiry. In the New York *Herald Tribune* William Haddad said that observers viewed this "as a major victory for the drug industry and Washington lobbyist Thomas G. Corcoran ('Tommy the Cork' of Roosevelt days)." The effort was to be renewed in the spring of 1965.[5]

✓　✓　✓

Dr. Dale Console, the Kefauver witness who was once with E. R. Squibb & Sons, has termed the pharmaceutical industry "unique in that it can make exploitation appear a noble purpose." Shows of righteousness do, in fact, come from unexpected quarters. This was learned by John Lear, who in 1959 broke the story in the *Saturday Review* about the outside activities carried

---

[5] In the spring of 1965 the Hart group, unable to break the deadlock, let it become moot after the Department of Justice, conducting its own inquiry into the same area, began receiving relevant documents obtained through the service of civil investigative demands by its Antitrust Division.

on by Henry Welch while he was head of the Division of Antibiotics in the Food and Drug Administration.

Lear came across a brochure for Chas. Pfizer's Sigmamycin. It proclaimed that "every day, everywhere, more and more physicians find Sigmamycin the antibiotic therapy of choice." Under this headline were what seemed to be reproductions of the professional cards of eight physicians in various cities. The cards listed addresses, which Lear established were nonexistent, and telephone numbers, which he also found did not exist. Pfizer's president, John McKeen, indignant about Lear's exposures of goings-on like these, fired off a letter to Commissioner Larrick that recited the medical accomplishments in which the Commissioner, Welch, the industry, the medical profession, and scientific institutions could take pride. "Instead of being criticized," McKeen said, "the American health team should be used to much greater advantage . . . in fostering better international understanding and, frankly, in counteracting Communism."

Dr. Louis Lasagna said in one of the New York Academy of Medicine's "Lectures to the Laity," Series XXVIII, *Horizons in Medicine, Science and Health* (1963):

> . . . I do not wish to minimize the contributions of the drug houses to medical progress. The American public owes them a great deal . . . But I resent exaggerated claims that pretend that every life saved in the last 20 years, and every decrease in death rates from *any* disease, is the gift of the drug industry. There are many factors responsible for our better health today, and the pharmaceutical industry is only one of them.
>
> Granting the contributions of drug company scientists the contributions of nonindustry scientists and physicians also are enormous. Looking back to the drugs I have discussed . . . it is striking the number of them that owe their genesis or development to academic figures: Fleming (of St. Mary's Hospital)

and penicillin, Waksman (of Rutgers) and streptomycin; Farber (of Harvard) and the antileukemic drugs; Astwood (of Tufts) and antithyroid chemicals; and Hench and Kendall (of the Mayo Clinic) and cortisone.

Even when both the drug *and* the basic theory originated completely at the drug house lab bench, it is only on the rarest of occasions that physicians outside the firm have not provided the ultimate testing of the drug in practice. There is here, it seems to me, more than enough credit to go around — Why gild the lily?

There are a variety of occasions on which pharmaceutical firms approach information about drugs in ways colored by their natural desire to turn out successful compounds. Like most parents, they want their chemical progeny to perform well in public, and resent it when told that their pharmacologic offspring are not handsome, or are threats to the general welfare . . .

Despite many years at the game, I confess that I am still amazed and angered whenever a scientist is attacked personally, or his integrity or ability impugned, simply because the results of an experiment fail to support drug house claims — or hopes — for a new compound.

✓ ✓ ✓

The "subtle and potentially most dangerous aspect of the FDA setup," Dr. Lasagna said in his book *The Doctors' Dilemmas,* published in 1962, is "the well-traveled, two-way street between industry and Washington." The Johns Hopkins pharmacologist added, "Men from the drug industry have gone on to FDA jobs and — more important — FDA specialists have gone on to lucrative executive jobs in industry. While there has been no clear-cut evidence of collusion or corner cutting by FDA executives dealing with drug companies applying for new drug approval, it does not seem desirable to have in decision-making positions scientists who are consciously or unconsciously always contemplating the possibility that their futures may be determined by their rapport with industry."

With different emphasis, the question was raised early in 1964 by Representative Melvin R. Laird, the Wisconsin Republican who headed the platform committee at the Republican National Convention later in the year. At a hearing held by a House Subcommittee on Departments of Labor and Health, Education, and Welfare and Related Agencies Appropriations, he put into the record a letter to Commissioner Larrick in which he commented on reports that two FDA employees had gone to work for two companies that had been in their regulatory purview. The Congressman said in the letter that the reports

> reawaken a concern I have had for several years . . . that individuals in Government who exercise regulatory authority over major segments of American industry may so position themselves as to (1) obtain lucrative positions with the regulated enterprises and (2) open themselves and their agencies to perhaps valid accusations of conflicts of interest.
>
> . . . .
>
> . . . I do believe . . . that it is poor public policy to allow such individuals who are vested with broad discretionary authority to arm themselves with extensive information on the activities of a group of sharply competing businesses, then suddenly bob up working for one of them. It also stands to reason that while still employed by FDA and while still passing judgments on the problems of competing companies, they were in the process of agreeing to this outside employment.

We in Congress faced up to this issue long ago in respect to Defense Department personnel. A statute was passed prohibiting career military personnel from working on defense matters for private industry until at least two years had passed following their retirement. I strongly incline toward a requirement of this same kind in respect to FDA personnel, forbidding their employment, for a period of 2 years after their leaving FDA, by any company whose business is under FDA jurisdiction.

In response to a request from Laird, the Commissioner supplied information on where former FDA employees had gone after leaving the agency. Between January 1, 1959, and December 31, 1963, he said, 813 scientific, medical, and technical employees had left FDA: 632 — including an unstated number who retired — were found definitely not to have taken direct or indirect employment with regulated industries. However, 83 appeared from available records to have taken positions with companies FDA regulates. Information about the status of the remaining 98 was being sought.[6]

Although no name was mentioned, a specific case had been described to the Kefauver subcommittee by Dr. Barbara Moulton, once an FDA medical officer. The case involved Marsilid, the "happiness pill" that the agency said had been associated with 53 fatal and 193 nonfatal cases of liver damage. In a statement to the subcommittee she said:

Eventually, after many conferences with representatives of the company, it was decided that they should issue a special

[6] But FDA's low salaries must be taken into account. Dr. Theodore G. Klumpp, head of Winthrop Laboratories, is one of those in industry who has worked to correct this situation. He told the Humphrey subcommittee in June 1963:

. . . there is a severe shortage of scientists and physicians with the skills and aptitudes required by the FDA. Because of this, and the fact that many will not accept a position with a law enforcement agency under any circumstances, the FDA will never succeed in filling its vacancies with men of high caliber unless the salaries paid are reasonably competitive . . .

A recent survey showed that whereas the top medical post in FDA (i.e. the Medical Director) draws a salary of $20,000 a year, a number of universities pay their medical school deans as much as $30,000. The same survey showed that, while the average FDA medical officer in FDA receives a salary of $15,200, the average medical school professor receives $20,700, and the medical specialist in private practice earns $24,800.

warning letter to physicians, advising caution in the use of the drug because of new evidence of danger . . . I happened to have an appointment on official business with a professor of psychiatry at a well-known medical school on the day on which he received this letter from Hoffmann-La Roche. He had put aside the letter to ask me its meaning. Only after I had pointed out the few sentences in one of the last paragraphs in a rather lengthy epistle did he realize the alleged purpose of the communication. In this instance the important facts were obscured by so much irrelevant material that the letter failed to serve as an effective warning . . . The "relabeling" of Marsilid and the warning letter were handled by a physician who shortly thereafter left the [Food and Drug] Administration to accept a position on the staff of Hoffmann-La Roche. His salary at [FDA] must have been approximately $12,500. His salary at Hoffmann-La Roche was to be, so I was told, approximately twice that figure.

There has also been a rather more complicated series of movements among the three power centers, the Food and Drug Administration, the Pharmaceutical Manufacturers Association and its member firms, and the American Medical Association — the three components of the FDA-PMA-AMA molecule.

The following are cases in point. Before becoming head of Winthrop Laboratories, Dr. Theodore G. Klumpp had in the late 1930's been chief medical officer of the Drug Division at FDA, subsequently leaving to take a post in the AMA. C. Joseph Stetler, who had been counsel of the AMA and head of its Socioeconomic Division, found it possible to improve his socioeconomic position by becoming executive vice president of the PMA. Dr. Jean K. Weston was with Parke, Davis from 1951 to 1962, when he left his position as head of the firm's Department of Clinical Investigation to join Burroughs Wellcome & Co. In June 1964, Dr. Weston became director of the

AMA's Department of Drugs and secretary of its Council on Drugs.

Easily the most interesting study is provided by Dr. Austin Smith, who was editor of the *Journal* of the AMA for almost ten years and head of its Council on Pharmacy and Chemistry (now the Council on Drugs) for seven years before that. In 1944 Dr. Smith was a co-author of a report by the Council that found — even so long ago — "too many instances of disastrous results that have followed incomplete or inadequate investigations on new drugs." The authors, in a supplemental statement, also said that it is "extremely risky" to assume that a chemical modification of a well-known drug will have a similar impact in the body.

Five years later, Dr. Smith participated in another report by the Council entitled "Too Many Drugs?" The answer, in a word, was yes. But it is worth quoting excerpts published in the AMA *Journal* for February 5, 1949.

A fundamental requirement to successful treatment is that the physician have the clearest possible understanding of the remedial agents that he prescribes. This is difficult at best, and is rendered increasingly difficult with multiplication of agents that are nearly but not quite equivalent. Each may show minor differences, which may or may not be practically important, but which are difficult to learn if he spreads his experience too widely and therefore too thinly, as he is urged to do when pharmaceutical firms introduce and promote many actual or near duplicates, with the chief purpose of profiting in a presumably lucrative field, rather than with any real consideration for the welfare of the public or of the interest of medical science and practice . . . but the catalogs of drug houses continue to be overcrowded. The processes of natural selection and the operation of economics tend toward the final survival of the fittest and the eventual elimination of the less fit, but they operate slowly. In the meantime, as new fields open, there is the gold rush to stake out claims and make a killing while the going is still good. But it is particularly in these new and relatively unexplored fields where the harm of unnecessary duplication is greatest, where it interferes most seriously with the acquisition of the precise information that is essential to the proper evaluation of the scope and of the dangers of new medications. Two examples that come to mind are the estrogenic preparations and the "anti-histaminic" drugs. In both cases, synthetic chemistry is able to produce practically numberless agents. Both fields are already crowded and overcrowded, but new agents are still being introduced at an alarming rate which makes it practically impossible to acquire the experience that is necessary to determine what advantages, if any, they possess over the older similar agents.

However, Dr. Smith's postgraduate education continued, and he was transfused into the presidency of the PMA, where denunciation of irrational therapy is not one of the qualifications for employment. In his new post he wrote an article for *New Medical Materia* for October 1962. The title was "Too Much Medicine?" a slight molecular modification of "Too Many Drugs?" Dr. Smith's answer to the question "Too Much Medicine?" was, in a word, no. "Competition forces each drug company, as a matter of economic survival, to dedicate itself to obsoleting its own products," he said. "Any slackening of competitive research carries with it the prospect of grave decline in future progress."

On December 22, 1958, the Pink Sheet, the drug-industry weekly newsletter, was speculating about a vacancy in the post of FDA medical director. Dr. Smith had just resigned as Editor of the AMA *Journal*. If he "could afford to take the job at FDA's $19,000-a-year salary," the Pink Sheet confided, "his appointment would be welcomed by the drug industry as being solely on the basis of outstanding qualifications."

Of course. Solely on the basis of outstanding qualifications. It was an almost-great play — Tinker to Evers but, by chance, not quite to FDA.

Although the FDA-PMA-AMA molecule had been synthesized in laboratories specializing in the social rather than the medical sciences, it had not been generally known that it could be materialized at a banquet table. It happened on the night of December 9, 1958, in New York City (I am indebted to Senator Humphrey's subcommittee for making excerpts from the Pink Sheet available to a reader of ten-cent newspapers). Dr. Smith, who had been the AMA's major contact with the drug industry for more than sixteen years but was serving here in his capacity as a member of the PMA Award Committee, at a gala dinner arranged before his resignation from the AMA had been announced, presented the 1958 PMA Award to George Larrick of the FDA.

During the Kefauver hearings Dr. Smith submitted a statement claiming that "for the most part, our advertisements are more like scientific treatises . . . that tell not merely the good things . . . but deal exhaustively with the bad ones as well. Toxicity, side effects — all must be exposed in full detail."

That Dr. Smith could make this fantastic claim may illuminate one of those outstanding qualifications solely on the basis of which the industry reportedly was prepared to welcome him into the medical directorship of the FDA. "Dr. Smith," *Drug Trade News* said admiringly on July 25, 1960, "has well shown his ability to speak for the PMA . . . By common consent Dr. Smith is properly regarded as the man of the hour, the right man, in the right place, at the right time." But which hour, which place, which time, and which Austin Smith?

"The extent of the problem which faces the physician is difficult to envision," Dr. Walter Modell testified in 1961. A statement about the enormity of the number of medicaments available, Dr. Modell continued, "is difficult to evaluate because, on the one hand, it was published by Dr. Austin Smith in the

Journal of the American Medical Association when he was its editor, while, on the other hand, it was challenged by Dr. Austin Smith as president of the Pharmaceutical Manufacturers Association and called a libel on the industry."

✓ ✓ ✓

Although it occurred in a modification of the FDA-PMA-AMA molecule, a later play for the post of FDA medical director went like this: NYU to HEW but, by chance, not quite to FDA. It was 1962. Dr. Austin Smith's outstanding qualifications had been recognized by the PMA rather than the FDA, and the new candidate was Dr. Charles D. May, professor of pediatrics at the New York University School of Medicine. He is also a former member of the AMA's Council on Drugs and a former editor of *Pediatrics,* the official journal of the American Academy of Pediatrics. His sponsor was Commissioner Larrick, who surely could claim that he had nominated a man with outstanding qualifications, including Dr. May's willingness — arising from "a sense of public duty" — to take the post at a financial sacrifice.

The need for a medical director had been seemingly urgent. In 1959 Larrick had canvassed the country for a qualified candidate, but finally promoted Dr. William D. Kessenich to the post from within the Bureau of Medicine. Dr. Kessenich declared his intention to resign in September 1961, and did resign in August 1962.

In January 1963, nine months after Dr. May was nominated, he withdrew his name from consideration. During all that time the decision had been in the hands of Boisfeuillet Jones, who until his resignation in June 1964 had been special assistant for health and medical affairs to Secretary of Health, Education, and Welfare Abraham A. Ribicoff, now a Democratic Senator from Connecticut, and his successor, Anthony J. Celebrezze.

It turned out that Dr. May's qualifications were offset by grave disqualifications. Not only had he sinned by testifying before the Kefauver subcommittee, but also he had written an article — "Selling Drugs by 'Educating' Physicians," published in the January 1961 issue of the *Journal of Medical Education* — in which he had pointed out that drug companies selling their products through doctor's prescriptions had been spending an estimated $750 million in 1959 on promotional activities, or more than three and one-half times the $200 million available to all medical schools in the United States in 1957 for their educational programs. It is within the bounds of possibility that leaders of the pharmaceutical industry were not captivated by passages like this one:

> . . . the pharmaceutical companies go to great extremes to sell an appealing "House Image" to the physician to soften his resistance. Lowest on the scale are overt gestures like ordinary entertainment and personal favors. One "ethical" drug company (Eli Lilly) gives medical students new diagnostic instruments each school year to foster "the close association of our two professions," with the proud boast of having enlisted "the co-operation of the dean of your college"! A particularly regrettable maneuver is the exploitation of the natural sympathy between doctors and students by hiring the needy and unsuspecting student as a detail man (Pfizer, Schering).
>
> More subtle wooing takes the form of conspicuously sponsored conferences and television clinics and give-away lavish medical magazines and newspapers sometimes made more fetching with pseudo-culture and racy human interest. Grants are made in partial support of independent research, but these usually cover only part of the cost and tend to favor utilitarian studies; and the investigator may unwittingly find his results subject to exploitation.
>
> Medical organizations are given monies to support a large part of their activities, and then are in a poor position to

criticize practices that infringe on the prerogatives of the medical educator and imperil the knowledge of the physician.

The question might well be raised: How does all this courting differ from payola?

Although HEW's Boisfeuillet Jones denied to the Washington *Evening Star* that Dr. May's writings or testimony had aborted his nomination — which had been gestating in Jones's desk drawer for nine months — *Drug Research Reports*, the blue-tinted sister publication of the Pink Sheet, said in June 1964, that "Jones had won the confidence of the pharmaceutical industry by blocking the appointment of Dr. Charles May . . ." The physician, of course, suspected before he withdrew his application that those who had opposed his appointment considered anyone who advocated legislation to reform drug practices automatically "hostile to industry."

Terming Dr. May "a subject of controversy," Jones told the Washington *Evening Star*'s Miriam Ottenberg that he was looking for somebody "acceptable to the industry, the consumers and the academic world, but [HEW was] not trying to satisfy the industry per se." The batting order was industry, *then* consumers.

The search ended in April 1964 with the selection of Dr. Joseph F. Sadusk, Jr., who was chairman of the Department of Preventive Medicine at George Washington University and director of clinics for the District of Columbia institution. A 1935 graduate of the Johns Hopkins University, he had been at George Washington for two years and before that at Stanford since 1949. He has been chairman of the American Medical Association's committee on medical-legal problems and a consultant to the Committee on Medical Sciences of the Defense Department's Research and Development Board.

THE SEQUENCE HERE will be: first, the further discussion mentioned in the footnote on page 165 of opposition to the *Medical Letter*; second, the report mentioned in the footnote on page 172 of the Signemycin relabeling difficulties; third, an updating of material on page 173 about price-fixing in Latin America; fourth, additional comment on pharmaceutical advertising, accompanied by summaries of actions concerning the coronary vasodilators, Orinase, Eutonyl, Ortho-Novum SQ, Indoklon and Renese and Renese-R, and fifth, more on our own counterpart of the military-industrial complex, the FDA-PMA-AMA molecule.

THE MEDICAL LETTER

In a lecture of 1963 sponsored by the New York Academy of Medicine and published in *Horizons in Medicine, Science and Health* as Series XXVIII in the Academy's "Lectures to the Laity," Dr. Louis Lasagna said that a common reaction to the *Letter* in the drug and advertising industries has been: "Who gave these guys the right to tell everyone how good or bad drugs are?" Dr. Lasagna commented:

This comes with bad grace, and an amazing intellectual myopia, from people who try to do just that for products in which they have strong vested interests.

Noteworthy also is the strong opposition of others who have, quite rightly, pointed out occasional defects in the *Medical Letter's* reports on drugs; while these men do not deny, a priori, the right for such a service to exist, they seem totally unwilling to aid in its improvement. Instead, they give the impression that they wish it would shrivel up and die — something which, fortunately, will not happen.

SIGNEMYCIN

The Humphrey subcommittee has published an example contained in a memorandum by an FDA medical officer, Dr. David S. Davis, concerning relabeling of an antibiotic combination with the jawbreaking name of triacetyloleandomycin, which Chas. Pfizer sells as Signemycin. A partial text follows:

> On January 4, 1962, Mr. A. C. Von Oehsen phoned me and assured me that the firm [Chas. Pfizer] had incorporated all of our recommendations in their latest revision of the labeling, which, at our meeting of January 2, 1962, we had been assured we would receive no later than January 8, 1962. Mr. Von Oehsen called me again January 8th and told me the revised labeling had been mailed January 5th. I received this material January 9th in an envelope postmarked January 8, 1962. My review of this latest labeling reveals that our basic recommendations — the first three [of 11] have been completely disregarded:
> 1. The firm continues to make recommendations for the management of acne and chronic pyodermas;
> 2. Prophylactic uses continue to be recommended;
> 3. Whereas we have recommended beginning of monitoring no later than the 10th day of continuous therapy, the firm continues to recommend monitoring of the liver profile on the 14th day.
> It is readily apparent that this latest "relabeling" is a con-

tinued illustration of the Pfizer firm's bad faith in their negotiations with us on this matter. It is my conclusion that further attempts at negotiation by the Bureau of Medicine in this regard would be unwarranted, fruitless and degrading. I recommended that this matter be transmitted to the Commissioner for further action at once.

More than 3 months ago, Wyeth Laboratories furnished us with proposed revised labeling which contained all of the basic recommendations which we agree to be appropriate. At all times, during this period, and most recently, in a communication dated December 29, 1961, Wyeth has demonstrated their complete willingness to relabel triacetyloleandomycin products which they market in accordance with our recommendations. Accordingly, I recommend favorable action in the Wyeth proposals at once.

PRICE-FIXING

The documents obtained by the Antitrust Division of the Department of Justice concerning price-fixing in Latin America by American firms — specifically including Chas. Pfizer & Co., Inc., American Cyanamid Co. and its Lederle Laboratories division, the Bristol-Myers Co. and its Bristol division, the Olin Mathieson Chemical Corporation and its E. R. Squibb & Sons division, and the Upjohn Co. — were examined by a Federal grand jury in Washington, but as of May 1967 what course of action would be taken by the government was not known. Copies of the documents, or most of them, were, however, obtained by Senator Russell B. Long, the Assistant Majority Leader, from William Haddad who, in turn, had gotten hold of them while an investigative reporter for the late New York *Herald Tribune*. Long then used the papers as the foundation for a speech on February 10, 1966, in which he told the Senate that for at least twelve years the aforementioned manufacturers had engaged in a "reprehensible and shameful" conspiracy to fix the prices of tetracycline

and certain other broad-spectrum antibiotics, that one of the
aims of the conspiracy was to prop up prices in the United
States, and that the principal victims have been the aged and
the poor here and in Latin America. The documents, some of
them marked "personal and confidential" and "please destroy,"
consist of communications among officials of the five accused
companies. What the Senator termed "the most startling price-
fixing document I have ever seen" was a letter written in part
in a code that, Long said, was intended "to disguise price-fixing
and 'pay-off' communications." The letter was dated November
7, 1958, was written in Caracas, was signed "Pluto" — the code
name for Rafael N. Silva, Pfizer's manager in Venezuela — and
was addressed to Frank P. Wilson, Pfizer-International's pricing
manager in New York City. In explaining the letter to the Senate, Long had to use a glossary. He said, for example, that
"Special G-13" denoted "Pfizer-Venezuela's 'pay-off' fund to
'facilitate' sales to governmental purchasers in Venezuela." A
"sinner" denoted a violator of a price-fixing agreement. A "powwow" was a price-fixing meeting. A "disturbed family" meant
that someone had cut prices. An unpronounceable "brstlhstchldrllpttpfzr" denoted five companies — Bristol; Hoechst, the
German firm it licensed to make tetracycline; Lederle; Lepetit,
the Italian firm licensed by Pfizer to make tetracycline; and
Pfizer. The letter told of an antibiotics "powwow" recently "con-
voked in our office with brstlhstchdrllpttpfzr in attendance."
"Pluto" noted that "our friend sqbb [Squibb] could not attend
but was no party to any offense [competitive price variation] and
was fully desirous of others re-establishing the previous atmosphere of confidence . . . it became evident that brstl [Bristol]
was engaged in a nationwide pricecutting scheme . . . ldrl [Led-
erle] had followed suit without consulting the remaining
partners. . . ." The letter recounts that the "powwow" succeeded in restoring "the previous confidence" in a spirit of "let's
try again!" — but only a day later there came a report, "Pluto"

said, that "ldrl was at it again." Another "powwow" was scheduled "to thrash out this [new] violation." The "meetings, agreements and understandings to fix the price in Venezuela," Long told the Senate, "were part of the same conspiracy which 'fixed' the price in the United States" (see Chapter 17 and its Afterword). With evidence in hand of the kind illustrated by the "Pluto" letter, one can only say that a failure to indict would be as hard for the Justice Department to explain as it would be for me to pronounce "brstlhstchldrllpttpfzr."

PHARMACEUTICAL ADVERTISING

I return to this subject because of its pervasive importance. I do not mean exclusively that importance indicated by Commissioner James L. Goddard of the Food and Drug Administration when he said that "it is through advertising that most busy physicians get their messages about drugs";[1] nor do I mean exclusively that importance indicated by Dr. Goddard when he estimated that drug manufacturers spend between $600 million and $800 million a year — or at least $3000 per physician — to advertise and promote prescription products to doctors (that expenditure is between a quarter and a third of the $2.4 billion grossed from these products in 1965).[2] The mainspring of all of this is the fantastic profit made possible by a patent system that does (but should not) grant unlimited monopolies equally to drugs and can openers, by the Corporate Conscience, by the able counsel of Washington lawyers whose service in the New Deal or the cause of civil rights has given them the right liberal credentials, by sleeping watchdogs, by bought legislators, and by a profession — the noblest profession — whose uneasy blends of ignorance and dedication, innocence and sophistication, and arrogance and

[1] In a speech on April 4, 1967, in the Lowell Lecture Series on "The Medicated Society." The Series was sponsored by the Lowell Institute in cooperation with Tufts-Northeast Medical Center.

[2] These were the figures used by the Commissioner in testimony on May 25, 1966, before the House Intergovernmental Relations Subcommittee.

gullibility have made it an easy mark for betrayal by leaders who are indistinguishable from the drug makers. I do not know what can be done about doctors, politicians, and doctor-politicians, who get exercised about the alleged virtue of brand-name prescribing and the evil of counterfeit drugs — an evil that would be negligible if brand-name prices were less often near-extortionate — but *not* about the profits which, inexorably, incite the drug makers to lie in ads for the products that rake in those profits. I do not know what can be done about the banal evil of advertising men whose idea of a good day's work is the contrivance of an ad which is considered successful in the degree to which it is deceptive without actually being illegal — but who go home at night to be good husbands, good fathers, and generous contributors to the United Givers Fund. What I do know is that until such time as the profits in drugs should be miraculously moderated so as to eliminate incentives to abuse pharmaceutical advertising — until such a time comes, if it ever does, we must look to that government agency and those few men who are charged with *regulating* that advertising. We are blessed today that the head of the Medical Advertising Branch of the FDA is Robert S. McCleery, a physician who sees the medical advertising process, *Business Week* said on February 4, 1967, as "a real frontier for private industry," who asks if "the private competitive spirit [can] be harnessed for a public purpose?" and who hopes very much that the answer is yes. We are blessed also that Dr. McCleery, who followed a distinguished career in surgery with a study at the Institute for Advanced Study in Princeton of the relation of nuclear warfare to Christian ethics, and who himself has been the medical director of an ad agency, has won the resolute backing of Dr. Goddard.

The Commissioner signaled that support only eleven weeks after he took office. In his speech to the Pharmaceutical Manufacturers Association on April 10, 1966, he said that Dr. McCleery — then aided by only one other physician — had in 1964 originated a number of complaints "involving nearly one-third of the membership of the PMA"[3] and continued:

> Some advertising cases have been quite abusive of regulations. They have trumpeted results of favorable research and have not mentioned unfavorable research; they have puffed up what was insignificant clinical evidence; they have substituted emotional appeals for scientific ones. . . . I think some of you have been led astray — astray of the law and astray of what physicians need and want to know. Facts *do* sell drugs, facts presented in a professional way for professional men to read with care and respect.
>
> Maybe I am talking about tone, *professional* tone. For example, no drug categorically "relaxes both physical and emotional tension" all by itself. . . . But a drug can *help* relax these conditions or can *often* relax these conditions.

The corrective or remedial letter, in which a manufacturer quickly corrects a misleading ad with a communication mailed individually to each prescribing physician, was the inspiration of Dr. McCleery. In 1964 he got the approval of the FDA for the first such letter — only to see it mysteriously withdrawn by the top echelon of the regime of George P. Larrick. Two years later, Dr. McCleery broached the idea to Dr. Goddard, who vigorously endorsed it. The benefit to the public health was clearcut and undeniable: Within a couple of weeks after a seriously deficient ad appears, a physician can be warned against claims that could lead him to administer a drug which could be harmful or at least wasteful and which could delay proper treatment. In contrast, ordinary regulatory procedures are not only slow, but have no built-in mechanism for alerting physicians. When Dr. McCleery

[3] The accuracy of this figure was effectively challenged with a fanfare of speeches and press releases by C. Joseph Stetler, president of the PMA, and co-author of what in this book is called the Hussey-Stetler Test of Time. He thought it highly significant that the complaints of violation had been shown to involve one out of five rather than one out of three members of the PMA.

and his small staff determine that there is a serious problem with an ad requiring a corrective letter, they consult as necessary with others in the Bureau of Medicine and then seek the approval of its Director, Dr. Herbert L. Ley, Jr. When this approval is granted the matter goes at once to the Commissioner. If Dr. Goddard concurs that "a major untruth is involved," and not a minor or technical violation, *Drug Trade News* for March 27, 1967, reported:

> he personally telephones the president of the company involved, explains what has been placed before him, and asks the officer to come to Washington within a day or two for a conference . . . [with] whomever he wishes to participate. . . .
>
> Dr. Goddard presides at the conference, detailing what FDA believes is wrong and listening to company objections. Sometimes additional time is given for submission of further data. . . . If Dr. Goddard still believes action should be taken, he notifies the company and gives it the alternative of issuing a correcting letter . . . or of having its product seized with an announcement by FDA. The agency does not publicize issuance of a letter by the company.
>
> If the company agrees to send a letter, its wording is worked out in subsequent conferences. . . . Usually the initial draft submitted by the company reads like a promotion . . . but FDA will not accept this. . . .
>
> FDA insists that the letter be mailed first class and that the envelope carry in the lower left-hand corner the statement "Important: Correction of Drug Information."

CORONARY VASODILATORS

In February 1966 the Food and Drug Administration began a seizure action based on false advertising for Peritrate, one of the drugs produced by about 180 manufacturers that contain nitrates or nitrites and that are prescribed for millions of persons with heart conditions. The Peritrate action led to the punch against other so-called coronary vasodilators that came on April 19, 1966. FDA undertook its largest direct mailing — 286,000 letters to physicians and medical institutions — to say that claims of carefully limited usefulness in angina pectoris would be allowed — but that claims of efficacy in any other heart condition would be prohibited. The reason was that substantial evidence of efficacy in those other conditions had not been provided.

ORINASE

On August 22, 1966, in District Court in Grand Rapids, Michigan, the Justice Department started criminal proceedings against the Upjohn Co. in connection with Orinase, the oral antidiabetic that is its biggest-selling prescription drug. Marketed in 1957, it was said to have been used by more than 750,000 patients. The 1-count information charged that the entry for Orinase in the 1965 edition of *Physicians' Desk Reference*, the most widely used prescribing guide, omitted information that under law was required and that was included in the prescribing brochure which had been approved by the Food and Drug Administration — and which usually ends up in the pharmacist's wastebasket. The omitted information, which may be of especial interest to those who may tend to exaggerate the relevance of *caveat emptor*, included a statement that "[t]he *safety* and the usefulness of Orinase during pregnancy have not been established at this time, either from the standpoint of the mother or the fetus." In animal studies, the omitted statement — which was added to the 1966 and 1967 *PDR* Orinase entries — went on, Orinase in massive doses has been shown to kill or deform the fetus. "It is not known," the missing statement said, "whether or not this finding is applicable to human subjects. Clinical studies thus far are quite limited and experimental. Therefore, the use of Orinase is not recommended for the management of diabetes when complicated by pregnancy." The fore-word to the *PDR*, all entries in which are paid for by the manufacturer, says, "Each product description has been prepared by the manufacturer, and edited and approved by the manufacturer's *medical department, medical director, or medical consultant.*" (My italics.) In other words, by a flesh-and-blood human being. The criminal information filed without announcement by the Justice Department, however, and originated by FDA, named only the company. When the charges were filed a spokesman for the company said that it had considered the entry to be advertising under the law, and as such, not required to include as full an account of warning information as the legally distinct category of labeling. The spokesman said there had been a difference of opinion on this point with FDA, which had a long-standing rule that, under the law, *PDR* entries are labeling. Upjohn has pleaded innocent and as of late May 1967 was awaiting trial. If convicted it faces a maximum penalty of a $1,000 fine. In the year of the alleged offense its net income after taxes was $37 million.

EUTONYL

On September 19, 1966, in District Court in Chicago, the Justice Department filed a criminal information against Abbott Laboratories for omitting several warnings about Eutonyl, a potent drug introduced in 1963 and widely used in severe cases of high blood pressure that failed to respond to milder therapy. This action, unlike that for Orinase, was announced by the Justice Department. As in that case, the omission was from the 1965 edition of the *Physicians' Desk Reference*, and no individuals were named. The company failed to incorporate in the *PDR* entry information from the prescribing brochure approved by the Food and Drug Administration that patients on Eutonyl should be told not to take certain nonprescription antihistamines and cold preparations, because the consequence could be a sudden spurt of high blood pressure followed by a stroke. Another omission concerned the ineffectiveness of Eutonyl in patients with malignant hypertension, an extreme form of high blood pressure. In addition, an adverse reaction can be triggered in patients in whom Eutonyl sets off a sharp rise in blood sugar levels — this, too, was not noted. In a statement, Abbott said, "This misdemeanor action is probably a test case. It involves highly technical matters and does not relate to safety or efficacy . . . leading drug firms commonly distribute various pieces of literature that provide for the medical profession even more exhaustive information about a drug than the official literature. This is true with Eutonyl." As of late May 1967 Abbott Laboratories was awaiting trial on its plea of innocent. It faced a maximum penalty of a $1,000 fine. Its 1965 after-tax earnings were $24.7 million.

(Apart from cases involving the *Journal* of the American Medical Association that were cited in the Afterword to Chapter 4, there were two major developments soon after the Orinase and Eutonyl cases. One involved reform of the *PDR* and the other the speech of October 20, 1966, by FDA counsel William W. Goodrich before the Pharmaceutical Advertising Club.

(In testimony before the House Intergovernmental Relations Subcommittee, FDA Commissioner James L. Goddard recognized that when an immediate change in drug labeling is required the quarterly supplements of the *PDR* are "really not adequate" to inform physicians. "We have asked *PDR* to provide gummed labels to be inserted to correct some of the deficiencies," he testified on May 25, 1966. But what the Subcommittee understood to be a commitment was regrettably abandoned. Fortunately, *PDR*, published by Medical Economics, Inc., announced in September 1966 that it was instituting sweeping changes to give an effective, rapid alert to physicians about new information on safety, uses, and effectiveness of drugs. The overhaul, which won agency approval for a one-year trial, was effected in the

450,000 copies of the 1967 *PDR* distributed to doctors, osteopaths, hospitals, and others in the medical community. The new system was ingenious and workable and need not be detailed here. One of its great virtues is that it provides a strong incentive to manufacturers to provide a proper entry to begin with. This is precisely what many of them have done, by publishing verbatim the FDA-approved prescribing instructions.

(The Goodrich speech, it may be recalled from the Afterwords to Chapters 4 and 7, identified the "big eight" drugs which in 1965, the year of their introduction, joined the list of the 200 most often prescribed. Two of these, Lincocin and Indocin, already have been dealt with. The others, their makers and a summary of what Goodrich said about the then current advertisements for them in the *Journal* of the AMA and elsewhere, follow.

(Aventyl, Eli Lilly and Co.: The ad features "a new psychiatric disorder ['behavioral drift'], discovered right here on Madison Avenue . . . a new catch phrase to cover a host of 'target' symptoms, so that the drug is indicated and prescribed for the ordinary frustrations of daily living to reach a much larger patient population than the scientific data will support."

(Lilly's C-Quens and Mead Johnson Laboratories' Oracon, both oral contraceptives of the so-called sequential type, in which estrogen-only pills are taken during the menstrual cycle for 15 days and combination estrogen-progestin pills for 5 days: "The central theme of the ad for Oracon is that it is safer than and superior to other oral contraceptives because it is so close to nature — that it is . . . natural, and normal. These claims are unsupported by scientific facts. . . . This ad also makes a point that Oracon was 'the first sequential oral contraceptive.' It fails to inform the physician that it was approved only thirteen days before C-Quens. The theme of the ad for C-Quens is directed to a single side effect of the oral contraceptives — weight gain. The claim that women using sequential oral contraceptives experience less significant weight gain is ungrounded in scientific fact, and the ad is thus misleading in its major implication. . . . This ad . . . [claims that C-Quens] contains 'the smallest amount of hormone substance.' The . . . claim is literally false, and [another] claim of lower incidence of side effects has no scientific support."

(Pediamycin, a Ross Laboratories antibiotic, "was featured as being especially safe for infants, but no substantial evidence existed to support the claim. And the range of its usefulness was exaggerated."

(Tegopen, a Bristol Laboratories antibiotic, was advertised under a headline saying, "This is a new, every-day penicillin for common bacterial respiratory infections." "Plainly [Goodrich said] this was to encourage indiscriminate and routine use of a drug that was approved for use primarily against penicillin-resistant staph infections. The brief summary failed to communicate the real message that it is important to identify the infectious organism and to shift to regular penicillin when the organism is later found to be sensitive to penicillin G or V.

(Pre-Sate, a Warner-Chilcott Laboratories product "for the treatment of an impossible condition — overeating and overweight. It is, we believe, the consensus of medical opinion that there are no true anorexiants, and that dieting is the only answer to obesity . . . the claims of superiority [over competitive products] and that it acts on the human satiety center of the hypothalmus are not scientifically established.")

ORTHO-NOVUM SQ

The historically first corrective letter to prescribing physicians was sent on February 1, 1967, by the Ortho Pharmaceutical Corporation. It concerned a claim in ads — carried in January issues of *Medical Economics* and *Medical Tribune* — introducing Ortho-Novum SQ. The claim was that this oral contraceptive was "the most effective" of the three so-called sequentials then on the market. The remedial letter said the claim was based on a comparison of manufacturers' inserts approved by the Food and Drug Administration for enclosure in every package. FDA, the letter told physicians "has pointed out that such a comparison is invalid because there has been neither a comparative study of the efficacy of the three sequential oral contraceptives nor individual studies of the three products in population groups shown to be comparable." Ortho ended its "Dear Doctor" letter by saying it was therefore discontinuing the promotional theme in question.

INDOKLON

On April 26, 1967, the Food and Drug Administration filed papers in District Court in Chicago for the seizure of quantities of Indoklon, which was approved early in 1964 to replace electro-shock in the treatment of certain cases of acute depression. The action was begun because of advertisements published by the maker, the Ohio Chemical and Surgical Equipment Co., a division of the Air Reduction Co., Inc., in the February 1967 *Diseases of the Nervous System* and the February and April issues of the *American Journal of Psychiatry*. The ads promoted Indoklon for use "when convulsive therapy is indicated . . ." — but omitted the required summary of side effects and of conditions in which the drug should not be used. These conditions included pregnancy, the presence of even very mild upper respiratory infections, abnormal body temperature, and severe heart, kidney, or liver disease.

RENESE AND RENESE-R

On May 22, 1967, the Pfizer Laboratories division of Chas. A. Pfizer Co., Inc., sent a corrective letter to physicians saying that promotional messages for three of its medicines were regarded by the Food and Drug Administration "as potentially misleading." One of these medicines was Rondomycin, which had been advertised in the *Journal* of the American Medical Association; that story was told in the Afterword to Chapter 4. The other products were diuretics, which have a huge market especially among the elderly and which presumably yield such high profits when sold under brand names that they tempt manufacturers into an extraordinary amount of questionable advertising. The Pfizer products in question, Renese and its chemical brother Renese-R, which combines reserpine with polythiazide, are used in congestive heart failure and conditions involving the control of high blood pressure and fluid retention. The promotional messages protested by FDA were in the 1967 edition of the *Physicians' Desk Reference* and, for Renese-R alone, in an issue of *Medical World News*. Dr. John L. Watters, medical director of the company, said in the letter that the *PDR* entry for the diuretics "is considered inadequate in presenting information for their safe and effective use"; also "inadequate" were the warnings provided in the summary of information included in the *Medical World News* ad. Enclosed with the letter was a revised *PDR* monograph — which could readily be inserted and flagged for attention with the devices newly adopted by the publisher — incorporating additional warnings and precautions concerned with, among other things, the possibility of coma in patients with cirrhosis. In the case of Renese-R the possibility of confusion and tremors was cited.

(On the same day that the Pfizer letter was mailed, FDA proposed new regulations to regulate advertising of prescription drugs. Since 1963, Commissioner James L. Goddard said, the pharmaceutical industry has asked "for clarification" of the regulations adopted under the Kefauver-Harris Amendments of 1962. The complaint had been that the regulations were "vague." That complaint could hardly be made about the new guidelines — they listed 34 specific practices which if violated would oblige the agency to brand an ad "false, lacking in fair balance, or otherwise misleading." An imaginative and persevering reader could figure out what many of the 34 "do's" and "don'ts" are by assembling the abuses in the Afterwords to Chapters 4, 7, 8, 9, and 14. But in doing so he might not get the feel of precision that characterizes the actual regulations. For example, if a drug is claimed broadly to be an antibacterial agent the ad "shall name the types of infections and micro-organisms for which the drug is effective clinically," consistent with the FDA-approved labeling. An ad will be deemed misleading if it goes beyond the approved labeling to suggest that a drug is better or safer — even if such a representation is made "through use of published or unpublished literature, quotations, or other references." An ad will be deemed misleading if it "[c]ontains information from published or unpublished reports or opinions erroneously represented or suggested to be authentic or authoritative," or if it gives information or conclusions "from a study that lacks significance because it was uncontrolled or for other reasons," or uses a quote or paraphrase "out of context to convey a false or misleading idea." In specified ways, summaries of adverse effects and contraindications must be proportionate — in placement, emphasis, and length — to the ad, e.g., the summary for a one page ad would be unacceptable for a four-page ad. In the most profound sense, these regulations are _preventive medicine_. Their adoption, observance, and enforcement will help avert more needless death and injury than can be calculated. Is this not better than trying to build more hospitals and train more doctors to treat drug-induced diseases that truth in drug advertising would help prevent? Is not the public health advanced by the Medical Advertising Branch of the FDA which, with a small staff including three physicians, continues to detect one deceitful ad after another — including many in the _Journal_ of the American Medical Association which somehow slipped by the AMA's "scientifically trained individuals" who can tap "approximately 400 consultants"?

THE FDA-PMA-AMA MOLECULE

Oscillations among the component parts of the FDA-PMA-AMA (Food and Drug Administration, Pharmaceutical Manufacturers Association, American Medical Association) molecule have continued. Dr. Austin Smith, who headed the PMA after leaving the AMA and almost becoming the top medicine man at FDA, became president of Parke, Davis, where he acquired as vice president for medical affairs Dr. Joseph F. Sadusk, Jr., who had been Medical Director of FDA. Dr. Sadusk's deputy at FDA, Dr. Joseph M. Pisani, went to The Proprietary Association. Dr. Robert J. Robinson, who on Dr. Sadusk's departure became acting (and then acting deputy) director of the Bureau of Medicine, moved northward to a high post at Hoffmann-La Roche, Inc., where he was joined by a former subordinate, Dr. Grace Pierce. Dr. Harold Anderson, director of the Division of Anti-Infective Drugs in the Bureau, went to Winthrop Laboratories. Dr. Howard Cohn, chief of the Medical Evaluation Branch, joined Dr. Robinson in New Jersey, but at CIBA Pharmaceutical Co. Morris Yakowitz, Director of the Division of Case Supervision, was nearby in Philadelphia — with Smith, Kline & French. Allen Rayfield, who headed the Bureau of Regulatory Compliance, went to the aid of Richardson-Merrell, Inc. Dr. Jean K. Weston resigned as director of the AMA's Department of Drugs to become vice president for medical affairs of the National Pharmaceutical Council, an outfit that several drug companies finance in behalf of brand-name prescribing — doubtless the switch from the AMA was an easy one. Dr. Weston was succeeded by Dr. Thomas H. Hayes, who from 1956 to 1963 was a clinical investigator for G. D. Searle & Co., Inc.; from 1963 to 1965 he was director of clinical investigation at Cutter Laboratories.

9

THE "MIND" DRUGS

THE PSYCHOTHERAPEUTIC DRUGS exploded into the market starting about in 1954. Less than a decade later, in 1963, about 95 million prescriptions for them were filled for some 30 million Americans trying to cope with anxiety, depression, tension, and other psychic disturbances. Just one group of these products, the tranquilizers, were being regularly consumed by one adult American out of every dozen. In recent years the tranquilizers alone have been accounting for 10 per cent or more of all new and refill prescriptions.

Proper use of psychotherapeutic drugs has facilitated marvels of therapy, particularly among chronically hospitalized schizophrenics. At the same time, a large share of the claims that have been made for many of the "mind" drugs, especially the tranquilizers, have been grotesque exaggeration. What is striking is the degree to which such claims, even when completely unsubstantiated, have been accepted, if not passionately advocated, not only by laymen but by physicians who supposedly are trained as scientists. This point was discussed in the *American Journal of Psychiatry* for April 1964. "Psychiatry is the only medical speciality in which generalizations about methods of treatment substitute for actual clinical experience," a practicing New York psychiatrist, Dr. Lothar B. Kalinowsky, wrote. He went on:

It is also the only speciality about which laymen have strong opinions for or against procedures in which they have either infinite faith or which they totally condemn. The prejudices of representatives of our own speciality contribute to this state of affairs. Many psychiatrists condemn treatments which, admittedly, have no rationale and adhere to others whose rationale is based on a theory that might be right but could also be wrong.

The replacement of old drugs with new ones that might be better, but are not necessarily so, is a common occurrence in psychotherapy. A summary of a study[1] that three British doctors reported in the *British Medical Journal* for March 28, 1964, points to their astonishment about one phase of this phenomenon:

> It is surprising that no trial has been previously reported in which the efficacy of a modern "antidepressant" has been compared with that of amphetamine-barbiturate combinations which were so widely employed in treatment of depressive illness before the modern drugs were introduced. The present authors conducted a controlled study of Tofranil (imipramine hydrochloride) and Drinamyl (amphetamine-barbiturate preparation) in 78 patients suffering from depressive illness. The effect of Tofranil on the clinical manifestation of depression was no different than that of Drinamyl.

Dr. A. Dale Console, it will be recalled, said that if a car does not have an engine no amount of advertising could make it appear to have one. Nor would it take the buyer a decade to find

[1] This summary of the article "Imipramine and 'Drinamyl' in Depressive Illness: A Comparative Trial," by Dr. E. H. Hare, Dr. C. McCance, and Dr. W. O. McCormick, was published in Part 5 of the *Hearings* before the Senate Subcommittee on Reorganization and International Organizations, 88th Cong., 1st Sess., June 19, 1963, p. 2845.

out if he had an ad man instead of a motor under the hood. Yet years after the antidepressants went on the market there was uncertainty among distinguished scientists as to what was really under the bottle top. An exhaustive review of these products was made by Dr. Jonathan O. Cole, chief of the Psychopharmacology Service Center of the National Institute of Mental Health. He said in the November 2, 1964, issue of the *Journal* of the American Medical Association:

> Their place in the physician's armamentarium is still far from clear, although many clinicians feel that the drugs are useful and effective. However, controlled clinical trials of these agents have not always led to unequivocally positive findings. Even when such findings have been favorable to the drug under study, the differences between the efficacy of the drug and a placebo have not been as great as one might wish, or as one might have anticipated after reading published reports of uncontrolled studies.

In reaching these mildly phrased but devastating conclusions Dr. Cole examined 72 studies in the medical literature of six nations. He grouped the antidepressants into two principal pharmacological groups, the imipramine-like compounds and the monoamine oxidase inhibitors. ". . . if one is to choose a drug for use in severe depression," he said, "imipramine, or perhaps amitriptyline [Elavil], have the best credentials in terms of available published data." These credentials are not overwhelming. In 15 controlled clinical studies among depressed inpatients, Dr. Cole said, Tofranil was shown to be significantly superior to a placebo in 9, whereas in 6 it was not.

From his careful examination of the record of the monoamine oxidase inhibitors, which inhibit a brain enzyme, Dr. Cole said the issue with those remaining on the market as well as with those that have been taken off is whether their therapeutic efficacy is sufficient to offset the potential risk of their causing severe reactions. Even those . . . that have no apparent tendency to cause liver or brain damage have, nevertheless, the innate ability to potentiate the effects of a wide variety of other pharmacological and toxic agents, including sedatives, stimulants, ephedrine, histamine, epinephrine, and bee venom, so that the possibility of unusually severe effects from the administration of some other drugs, knowingly or unknowingly, in patients receiving an effective dose of an MAO inhibitor must always be kept in mind.

Dr. Cole also dealt with a third, catch-all category — what he called "other allegedly antidepressant drugs." In the case of one, dextroamphetamine, sold in the United States as Dexedrine, he cited a controlled study reported in January 1964 in the British publication *Practitioner*. For the treatment of depression in outpatients the drug was revealed "to be significantly *less* effective than a placebo." (My italic.)

✓ ✓ ✓

The more than 200 psychotherapeutic drug products of all kinds were discussed in March 1963 before the Senate Subcommittee on Reorganization and International Organizations by Dr. Fritz A. Freyhan of the Clinical Neuropharmacology Research Center of the National Institute of Mental Health. He said that "relatively few" of them had been "demonstrated to be potent and effective." Indeed, he testified, many patients on tranquilizers "become more anxious than before." A more precise indication of how seldom efficacy had been established came a year later from Dr. Cole. In a letter dated March 25, 1964, to the staff director of the Humphrey subcommittee, Julius N. Cahn, the head of the Psychopharmacology Service Center said that as of 1958 only 2 per cent, or 1 out of 50, of the published English-language studies had been "controlled" — that is, scientifically designed to compare one drug with another form of treatment or with no treatment. By 1962 the figure had risen to 18 per cent — still less than 1 out of 5. Almost all published studies on psychiatric drugs, then, have been uncontrolled, impressionistic, subject to the wishful thinking of the patient, the physician, or both. If a doctor tells patients or indicates to them that a pill will make them feel better, a significant number *will* feel better — the "placebo effect" — even if the pill is compressed bread crumbs.

At the New York Hospital's Westchester Division, psychologist Armand Loranger and his colleagues investigated two new "drugs" that were given to patients in a typical uncontrolled "study." Between 53 and 80 per cent were said to have been benefited for between two and one-half and five weeks of the six-week trial. Both of these "drugs" were placebos.

Dr. Leon Eisenberg, a Johns Hopkins Hospital child psychiatrist, has reported on three mood drugs that have proved to be "no more effective than placebos" in treating behavior disorders in ambulatory patients. "Many tranquilizer advertisements are just short of open deception," he said. "To the extent that the physician is influenced . . . he will be exposing children needlessly to risk of undesirable effects without counterbalancing benefit."

Librium, a Roche Laboratories product, is reportedly the most widely prescribed drug for the relief of anxiety. The caption on an advertisement for it was: "When anxiety and tension create major discord in parent-child relationships . . ." There was a picture of a small boy and his distraught mother. At one side was a solid panel of 188 references. An analysis of these unearthed 11 that could not be traced, only 3 or 4 that clearly had anything to do with young children and their parents, and about 10 more in which the "children" proved to be adults whose parents were still living.[2]

---

[2] In *Drugs in Our Society* (edited by Paul Talalay and published in 1964 by the Johns Hopkins Press), the late Pierre R. Garai asserted: "Cases of willful

The *Medical Letter,* the authoritative, nonprofit drug advisory letter for physicians, made the analysis just cited. In 1960 the *Letter* found that *none* of the many reports on Librium bore any resemblance to a well-designed clinical trial. On November 22, 1963, the editors said:

> Librium is promoted . . . for use as the sole treatment in anxiety and tensions states [and also] for the relief of acute and chronic alcoholism and some physical symptoms arising from emotional disturbances. Advertisements for Librium state unequivocally that it is superior to "tranquilizers" and distinctly different in its effects from such central-nervous-system depressants as the barbiturates, chloral hydrate and meprobamate. And many physicians assume that Librium calms without drowsiness or clouding of sensorium [the ability to perceive physical sensations] and without impairing intellectual, or motor skills; it is also considered non-addicting and not capable of being used for suicide. None of these beliefs is backed by convincing evidence.

✓   ✓   ✓

In 1956, when 34 million prescriptions were written for tranquilizers, the Subcommittee on Tranquilizing Drugs of the New York Academy of Medicine had found it necessary, in a special report, to warn against the "extravagant and distorted" promotion that "may recommend a product in such a way as to lead to, if not encourage its indiscriminate use." The report cited, for instance, a pamphlet [for Roerig's Atarax] that included among indicated uses "homesickness in children . . . differing opinions . . . weddings . . . anxiety in interviews." This and

---

misrepresentation are a rarity in medical advertising. For every advertisement in which nonexistent doctors are called on to testify or deliberately irrelevant references are bunched up in agate type, you will find a hundred or more whose greatest offenses are unquestioning enthusiasm and the skill to communicate it."

other early warnings did not appear to disturb the tranquility of high officials of the Food and Drug Administration and the American Medical Association. In February 1957, a few months after the Academy report was issued, Deputy FDA Commissioner John L. Harvey was testifying at a hearing of a House Subcommittee on Departments of Labor and Health, Education, and Welfare and Related Agencies Appropriations. Do the tranquilizers, asked Representative John Fogarty, "all do what the manufacturers claim they will do?" "Well," Harvey replied, "it is a little difficult to answer that . . . In general, I have no reason to believe that they are being extravagantly labeled."

The extravagance of the promotion for these products was, however, so gross and so obvious that another House subcommittee found it necessary to schedule hearings on the subject. Months in advance, the staff, as part of its preparations, sought an appointment with Dr. Leo Bartemeier, chairman of the AMA's Council on Mental Health and a past president of the American Psychiatric Association. In a report issued subsequently, this Subcommittee on Legal and Monetary Affairs, of the House Committee on Government Operations, said that he "expressed disinterest." Despite this response, the subcommittee chairman, Representative John A. Blatnik, proceeded with plans for the hearings, and held them in February 1958.

Dr. Bartemeier came to the hearings as the AMA's principal representative. He was accompanied by Dr. Lauren A. Woods associate professor of pharmacology at the University of Michigan, representing the AMA's Council on Drugs, and Dr. Malcolm Phelps, a member of the AMA's House of Delegates and president of the Academy of General Practice. Dr. Bartemeier said he was there to "assist the committee in any way" he could, although he had no prepared statement and, to many questions, no answers. His colleagues also had no prepared statements, and said nothing. The nature of the contribution made by the AMA's authorized spokesmen is brought out by the following exchanges from which, for the sake of simplicity, I have deleted the names of the congressmen-interrogators. All the answers are Dr. Bartemeier's.

Q. . . . are you familiar with some of the writings and activity on the subject of the evils of advertising of tranquilizer drugs?

A. I do not think I am, sir.

.   .   .   .

Q. Are you familiar with the advertising?

A. I am quite familiar with it; yes.

.   .   .   .

Q. You are a member of the council of the American Psychiatric Association; do they have a journal?

A. . . . yes.

Q. Are there any advertising standards set by the association?

A. Well, I suppose that there are. I am not familiar with them.

Q. Are you familiar, by any chance, with an article that appeared in the Academy of Medicine of New York . . . on the evils of, or misleading statements in, medical literature? [This was an apparent reference to the Academy report cited above.]

A. No; I am not; I do not recall the subject.

Q. Do you have any opinions on the type of advertising that has been addressed to physicians in connection with tranquilizers?

A. Well, I know there has been a great deal of advertising, of course. I have not been impressed with excessive advertising. It would be difficult for me, sir, to know what is excessive and what is not excessive.

Q. Are you familiar with the activities of the Food and Drug Administration in connection with some of the advertising of tranquilizer drugs?

A. No, I do not think I am . . .

. . . .

Q. Have you had any reason to doubt the accuracy of the representations made in this [advertising and promotional] material that you receive [from pharmaceutical houses]?

A. I have not, so far; no.

. . . .

Q. It is fair then to assume that your knowledge and familiarity with this subject is representative of the official position of the American Medical Association; is it not?

A. Well, I think so; yes.

The ignorance-is-tranquility syndrome, pervasive as it was in the AMA and the FDA, could account only in part for the fantastic and irrational popularity the pills came to enjoy. There were many other factors. One was illustrated by the case of Sparine (promazine hydrochloride), a potent tranquilizer. Wyeth Laboratories sought to release it to the market several months *before* studies of its chronic toxicity in animals were scheduled to be completed. At that time, studies of chronic use in humans had been made on a total of 33 mental-hospital patients, one of whom had developed a blood disease with a 50 per cent mortality rate. For these and other reasons involving the safety of promazine, the FDA physician in charge of the application, Dr. Barbara Moulton, was holding up its release. What occurred in this case played a role in her decision to resign as a medical officer and to conclude that in consequence of FDA's failures "hundreds of people, not merely in this country, suffer daily, and many die . . ."

In unchallenged testimony about the Sparine episode before the Senate Subcommittee on Antitrust and Monopoly she said: "Soon an interview was requested, and four representatives of the company appeared. The Chief of the New Drug Branch [Dr. Ralph G. Smith] joined the conference, unexpectedly as far as I was concerned, and informed the firm that Food and Drug . . . would release the drug . . . I am reasonably sure that my Chief had not at that time reviewed the data . . . but was acting solely on instructions from above."

In 1956 Dr. Moulton's responsibilities included meprobamate (Miltown, Equanil, and numerous other brands). It had been introduced a year earlier as an entirely safe, mild, nonhabit-forming sedative and was, as one psychiatrist is said to have put it, being prescribed for "everything from falling arches to falling dandruff."

In the April 21, 1956, issue of the *Journal* of the American Medical Association, an early investigator of meprobamate retracted a preliminary statement that it was not habit-forming, and cited cases indicating that it could be actually addicting. Dr. Moulton's suggestion that his finding be reflected in the labeling "was vetoed."

In July 1957, physicians at the federal narcotics hospital in Lexington, Kentucky, reported withdrawal symptoms, including convulsions, in patients who had been taking large doses of meprobamate. This time, Dr. Moulton told the Kefauver subcommittee, she went directly to Dr. Albert H. Holland, Jr., then FDA's medical director, suggesting "that we should insist on a strong warning statement about this effect. I was ordered to do nothing about it because 'I will not have my policy of friendliness with industry interfered with.'"

Dr. Holland had said he believed that FDA had a "clue" that meprobamate could be addicting but that it might take two or three years to find out. That was in 1956. In 1959 he resigned from his high post with FDA and, after a spell with a medical advertising agency, went to work for American Home Products Corp. Its Wyeth Laboratories division sells meprobamate under the name Equanil.

Well before Dr. Holland joined American Home, there had been more than a mere clue that the efficacy of meprobamate was open to doubt. In June 1958, in the *Journal of Chronic Diseases*, Dr. Bernard Weiss and Dr. Victor G. Laties reported on 88 studies of the efficacy of meprobamate in the treatment of anxiety. Only 13, they said, were well controlled; 14 were poorly controlled; the majority, 61, had been completely uncontrolled. Only when meprobamate was administered in huge doses under hospital conditions had its efficacy been persuasively shown. Four years later, a thoroughgoing review of the dearth of controlled studies on the efficacy of meprobamate and other tranquilizers was published in the *British Medical Journal* for May 5, 1962. The author, Dr. M. Weatherall, of the Department of Pharmacology, London Hospital Medical College, reached this conclusion: "In spite of much enthusiasm and propaganda tranquilizing drugs have very limited effects. Perhaps their greatest value has been in just that enthusiasm which they aroused."

Brian Inglis, British author and medical writer, has stated it another way. "What doctors and patients have believed they owe to the march of science," he said, "has been faith healing." In similar vein, Dr. Fritz Freyhan has said, "No doubt, vast numbers of patients have been, and are today, the psychologically benefitting victims of their physicians' faith in worthless drugs." Both Inglis and Dr. Weatherall referred to a double-blind clinical trial conducted in 1957 in London. The products involved were meprobamate, four other drugs reputed to be effective in reducing tension, and a placebo. "When the results were compared," Inglis further wrote in his article, "The Aspirin Jungle," in the *Nation* for August 24, 1963, "the only pill which could be claimed as having a significantly tranquilizing effect was a barbiturate . . . The so-called 'tranquilizers,' including Miltown [meprobamate], gave no better results than the placebo . . . effect — or, at least, they cannot improve on it." [3]

"The simplest conclusion from all the evidence," Dr. Weatherall said, "is that barbiturates are better than any other drugs for the treatment of anxious patients, and as they have been used for much longer their possible dangers are happily much more likely to be fully known." Happily also, barbiturates cost only a small fraction as much as meprobamate.

✓ ✓ ✓

Commissioner Larrick himself has risen to the defense of the Food and Drug Administration's handling of Marsilid, going so far as to say he is "proud" of the agency's role. It is not easy to see why.

Marsilid (iproniazid) was initially released for use, with certain limitations, in critical cases of tuberculosis. This use declined when isoniamid was found to be safer and more effective. Later, Marsilid was found to act as a psychic energizer, or "happiness pill," and the manufacturer, Roche Laboratories, submitted a supplemental application to permit its use against mental depression. At least 400,000 persons received it.

---

[3] In April 1965 the semiofficial U.S. Pharmacopeia confirmed that it was dropping meprobamate tranquilizers — on which millions of Americans have spent hundreds of millions of dollars — from its list of "drugs of choice." The USP is a nonprofit "official compendium" specifically recognized in the Food, Drug, and Cosmetic Act. It is revised at five-year intervals. Revision spokesmen expressed doubt about the value of meprobamate over older, and far cheaper, barbiturates and sedatives.

Generally, their position was in agreement with the one that the *Medical Letter* had taken for years. This was not that meprobamate was worthless, but that — as the *Letter* said in its issue for April 23, 1965 — its consultants found "no acceptable support for the claim that meprobamate had unique tranquilizing properties."

Various news accounts quoted the USP's revision editor, Lloyd C. Miller, as agreeing with another consistently expressed position of the *Letter* — that meprobamate could be hazardous. As the April 23 issue put it: "The range of its side effects, from drowsiness and urticaria [a skin disease] to death from overdosage, makes meprobamate a drug no more to be prescribed casually . . . than barbiturates or other sedative drugs." FDA had no immediate comment.

The first reports of deaths and injuries were received by the company in September 1957 — but not reported to FDA until February 1958. By the end of that year the company was willing to list new warnings with respect to the use of Marsilid, but not prominently, in the brochure accompanying containers of the drug to pharmacies. FDA asked for a strong warning on the label but did not get it until September 1960. During the year and a half of negotiations about this, sales continued unabated. Finally, in January 1961, Marsilid was taken off the market because, according to FDA, "drugs with similar therapeutic usefulness but with greater safety were available." But those drugs had been on sale since 1959. Commissioner Larrick's explanation of why FDA allowed Marsilid to remain on sale until 1961 is that it was regarded as valuable in "near deathbed cases." This was true only at first, when the drug was used against tuberculosis, not mental depression.

Dr. Moulton has testified that the hazards of Marsilid were "well known in the Bureau of Medicine long before the newspapers began to carry reports on the subject. When this occurred there was prompt if not entirely effective action by FDA to revise the labeling. Prior to the newspaper publicity, however, we raised our voices in vain."

Marsilid was associated with 53 fatalities among 246 recorded cases of hepatitis.

✓ ✓ ✓

Senator Humphrey was distressed to find that most of the psychotherapeutic drugs were released by the Food and Drug Administration "without the careful evaluation of a psychiatrist or of a specialist in mental disorders, acting as a consultant on the side effects or the efficacy or the safety . . ." He was appalled at the consequences of the failure to seek that "careful evaluation."

Putting aside a long catalogue of other adverse effects, consider the problem of addiction. It is characteristic of addictive drugs that users — particularly victims of neurosis, character disorders, and alcoholism — keep trying to increase the dose. In some cases abrupt withdrawal has been followed by death.

One of the leading researchers in tranquilizer addiction, Dr. Carl Essig of the Addiction Research Center of the National Institute of Mental Health, has said the following must be considered "drugs of addiction": meprobamate, glutethimide (Doriden), ethinamate (Valmid), ethchlorvynol (Placidyl), methyprylon (Noludar), and chlordiazepoxide hydrochloride (Librium). Abuse of the listed drugs, Dr. Essig told the American Association for the Advancement of Science in 1963, can lead to violent behavior. Among 68 users of Librium, in a ninety-day study in 1962 cited by Dr. Essig, there were 6 major and 10 minor auto accidents. This accident rate was 10 times the normal incidence as projected from statistics of the Texas Department of Public Safety.

Earlier in 1963, President Kennedy's Advisory Commission on Narcotic and Drug Abuse urged that all drugs "having a potential for psychotoxic and antisocial behavior" — specifically including tranquilizers — be deemed by law dangerous drugs subject to strict federal controls. Senator Thomas J. Dodd's Psychotoxic Drug Control bill, which in 1964 was passed by the Senate but died in the House, was in accord with this recommendation. The bill would automatically deem dangerous and subject to strict federal controls amphetamines and barbiturates and products containing them — the products involved in the illicit "pep pill" and "goof ball" traffic. In regard to other drugs the bill at least takes a significant step. It would authorize the Secretary of Health, Education, and Welfare to impose the controls by administrative regulation on any substance which, after investigation, he has found to be "habit forming because of its *medically* stimulant effect on the central nervous system; or . . . any drug which contains any quantity of a substance which the

Secretary, after investigation . . . designates as affecting or altering, to a substantive extent, consciousness, the ability to think, critical judgment, motivation, psychomotor coordination, or sensory perception, and having a potential for abuse when used without medical supervision." [4]

✦ ✦ ✦

Strict controls were not, the record suggests, what the Food and Drug Administration applied to its handling of many psychotherapeutic (and other) drugs. When it did move vigorously against an antidepressant about which it had very good reason to be concerned, almost the entire medical press jumped on it — the same publications that never, or almost never, criticize the agency for releasing drugs of doubtful efficacy and safety and allowing them to be prescribed for millions of people. Virtually no one supported FDA for applying the law vigorously in this case. The mail Senator Humphrey received from physicians was almost wholly critical.

The antidepressant was Parnate (tranylcypromine), which was introduced by Smith Kline & French in March 1961. By the spring of 1964 the drug had been discussed in about 190 articles in the world medical literature. These articles disclosed only four controlled clinical studies. None was indicated to have been completed *before* FDA let Parnate go on the market.

In only two of the studies was a placebo used, and in only two was another drug (Tofranil) used for comparison. The number of seriously depressed inpatients who in all four studies

---

[4] As noted in the last footnote of Chapter 4, a bill similar to Dodd's — and tougher in some respects — was passed 402 to 0 by the House on March 10, 1965. It had been introduced on the opening day of the new session of Congress by Representative Oren Harris, chairman of the House Committee on Interstate and Foreign Commerce. The AMA had without success urged that the Secretary not be given authority to control psychotoxic drugs other than barbiturates and amphetamines. During 1965 the Senate was expected to re-enact Dodd's bill, or one like it, and a measure resulting from a reconciliation of the Senate and House bills seemed certain of enactment.

received Parnate was small — well under 100. This was made clear by Dr. Cole of the Psychopharmacology Service Center in his letter of March 25, 1964, to Julius Cahn of the Humphrey subcommittee staff.

The first study involved 64 outpatients in Australia. Half were on Parnate and only one third of these were said to be seriously depressed. The second study involved 102 seriously depressed inpatients at a state hospital. Of the 51 on Parnate about 17 apparently also had associated schizophrenia — a mental condition which is not to be confused with the moderate to severe depression at issue in the Parnate episode. In the third study were 29 depressed inpatients at another state hospital, of whom 15 were given Parnate. The fourth study concerned 70 "depressed British outpatients and inpatients." Dr. Cole's summary did not indicate how many of the 34 who received Parnate were seriously depressed. It could not very well be argued that studies on so small a scale, scattered in space among three continents and in time over three years, could clearly justify FDA's decision to release Parnate to an enormous market — even if the studies had yielded clear-cut evidence of efficacy (which they didn't) and even if the agency had had them in hand.

According to the manufacturer, Parnate was used by about 2 million persons in the United States and by another 1.5 million abroad. These figures are of special interest.

The labeling stated that the drug was "for the symptomatic treatment of moderate to severe depression," and that its "use is not recommended in mild depression reactions where more conservative therapy is indicated." Available statistics, Senator Humphrey said, do not suggest "that there are anywhere near 2 million" Americans suffering from moderate to severe depres· sion, as that phrase has been defined by the American Psychiatric Association.

Obviously, the drug was used in mild cases of depression, despite the restrictive nature of the labeling, and joined other antidepressants widely prescribed in general medical practice. "Since many of these drugs are, if not potentially dangerous, at least quite potent pharmacological agents, there is justifiable concern about their overuse for the treatment of mild depressions," Dr. Cole warned in his article in the AMA *Journal* for November 2, 1964. "There is also some concern lest physicians, lulled into a false sense of security by the existence of compounds called 'antidepressant drugs,' rely on them unduly and fail to refer patients to psychiatrists or psychiatric hospitals when this is indicated."

Parnate was prescribed for many persons with suicidal tendencies, although in his letter to Cahn Dr. Cole said that none of the four controlled studies "specifically mention[s] the inclusion of suicidal patients." The labeling approved by FDA, noting that the possibility of suicide should always be considered in depressed patients, and adequate precautions taken, warned, however: "Exclusive reliance on drug therapy to prevent suicidal attempts is unwarranted, as there may be a delay in the onset of therapeutic effect or an increase in anxiety and agitation."

Also, of course, some patients fail to respond to drug therapy. Indeed, cases have been reported in which ingestion of Parnate was the means of suicide. But there had come to be an excessive reliance on drugs generally in the treatment of seriously depressed patients. One of those who deplored this persuasively was Dr. Lothar B. Kalinowsky, in his April 1964 article in the *American Journal of Psychiatry*. He avoided an extreme view. "The original overenthusiasm for the new drugs 10 years ago was unjustified," he said. "It would be equally unjustified if some present disappointments should lead to their discreditation; but there is no reason to neglect any of the presently available methods." The method of treatment with which Dr. Kalinowsky was primarily concerned in his article was electric convulsive therapy (ECT), which is commonly, not quite accurately, and unfortunately known as "shock treatment."

The New York psychiatrist pointed out that ECT had had results "so predictable and spectacular that they had few parallels in general medicine." With the advent of powerful new antidepressant drugs, ECT fell into decreasing use; but after a decade or so the glamour of the drugs began to fade and the value of ECT again came to be increasingly recognized. This was especially significant, because ECT succeeded for patients in whom drugs had failed. This is how Dr. Kalinowsky dealt with the problem of treating suicidal patients — an issue in the Parnate matter:

> The outstanding reason to choose ECT rather than pharmacotherapy in severe depressions is the danger of suicide. Long before any treatments were available, experienced psychiatrists knew that the severely retarded patient is not the principal risk but that the patient going into a depression who still has the drive and initiative to plan suicide is in the greater danger. It was also known and amply confirmed by recent experience that the patient coming out of a depression who still had depressive thought content, but who regained some initiative, is again a suicidal risk, and this is exactly what occurs in patients who are only partly improved by antidepressant medication. Contrary to this, the patient who responds to ECT mostly loses his depression not gradually but rather abruptly somewhere between the second and fourth treatment. Experience has shown that suicide, after initiation of ECT, hardly ever occurs. After having been fortunate in our own material of pure depressions not to have had a single suicide after ECT was started, it was all the more disheartening that during the last year we had two, and know of a third suicide in patients under antidepressant medication who in previous episodes had promptly recovered under ECT.

Dr. Kalinowsky then compared the response to ECT and antidepressants as shown by several studies. In one, in a group of "pure depressions," the favorable results with ECT ran as high as 95 per cent, compared to 54.5 per cent under treatment with imipramine. In another study, ECT was found to be more effective than any of six antidepressants. In a third study, ECT's superiority over three antidepressant drugs "was clearly demonstrated," and in a large proportion of the patients the medication had to be stopped "because of the emergence of other psychopathology or because of the worsening of the depression." In yet another survey, practicing psychiatrists found that in depressions treated with drugs the failure rate was 50 per cent, but that practically all of these cases "later had a successful outcome under ECT." Dr. Kalinowsky went on to say:

> The antidepressant drugs are losing much of their popularity with the increasing recognition of their dangers. Marsilid, in our experience the most effective of the antidepressants, was withdrawn because of severe complications; so were Catron and Monase. The recent reports about Parnate (tranylcypromine) are even more frightening . . . This must be mentioned because it is often recommended to start the treatment of a depression with antidepressant drugs as the less drastic procedure. Complications with ECT are extremely rare. If one adds the subjective side effects of the drugs and the frequently resulting difficulty to reach an effective dosage, it is not surprising that ECT again becomes more and more the treatment of choice in depressions.

✓ ✓ ✓

In its monograph on Parnate for the 1962 edition of *New and Nonofficial Drugs* the Council on Drugs of the American Medical Association said that its use "should be considered investigative [a word suggestive of something less than 3.5 million users] until additional information is available concerning its effectiveness and the seriousness of its side effects." The Council also termed the available evidence "inadequate to establish . . . effectiveness of this agent inasmuch as the early [favorable] reports are based on subjective impressions in uncontrolled studies."

Parnate was used in 122 Veterans Administration hospitals and clinics on 4400 inpatients and 1600 outpatients, in general for depressive and withdrawn schizophrenic states. The VA's chief medical director, Dr. Joseph H. McNinch, told the Humphrey subcommittee that moderate to good results with Parnate were reported by half of the facilities when it was "used in combination with other psychotherapeutic agents." Forty-nine "stations" found Parnate "as effective or slightly more effective than other drugs," 5 rated it "very good," and 22 reported it "ineffective or less effective than other drugs."

In the medical profession generally, it may be briefly said, there were physicians who found Parnate invaluable, irreplaceable, and swiftly effective, although some clearly had in mind certain schizophrenic rather than severely depressed patients. Others considered one or more of the several other antidepressants equally or more effective.

Mention of side effects has been deliberately avoided up to this point. Those involved here occurred in a startling sequence that, among other things, illustrates why the products of the drug revolution require testing of a hitherto unattained quality and range. Following are excerpts from letters of physicians to the *Lancet*, published on August 24 and September 14 and 21, 1963, by that British medical publication:

> . . . I received a personal communication from a pharmacist who observed that his wife, who was taking [tranylcypromine], developed typical symptoms shortly after eating cheese. Despite the unlikely nature of this observation, dietary histories have been taken from all my patients. Of the 10 in whom recent and reliable information could be gathered,

8 had eaten cheese within two hours of the onset of the headache.

[A doctor told of having] seen approximately twenty-five
patients [on Parnate] who have all eaten a cheese meal of a
reasonably substantial kind and who then had headache about
two hours later.

She returned after four weeks complaining of frequent
attacks of disabling severe occipital headaches, with choking
feelings in the neck and pounding sensations of the heart . . .
It was discovered she relished cheese and ate large quantities
of it at any time of the day.

[From a letter quoting a patient:] "I thought I had better
tell you all my life I have always eaten cheese. Now I find if
I do so . . . I get an attack similar to what I call 'Migraine'
— heart thumping, head racked with pain, and sickness within
half an hour. Other patients having [tranylcypromine] experienced this as well after cheese but the doctors laughed at the
idea."

It was an extremely unfunny matter. By June 1963 British
physicians were theorizing along these lines: Cheddar and other
strong cheeses contain substantial amounts of pressor amines,
which produce a rise in blood pressure. Normally, an enzyme
released by the brain renders the pressor amines nontoxic. Parnate inhibits or knocks out the enzyme. This allows the amines
in the cheese to cause a sudden surge in blood pressure.

Any powerful monoamine oxidase inhibitor, of which Parnate
was one, could be expected to have had this effect, and some
others — including Nardil (phenelzine) and Eutonyl (pargyline hydrochloride) did. It was not clear why Parnate had
the effect so frequently. In England, psychiatrists, responding to

a questionnaire reported in the *British Medical Journal* for March 7, 1964, said that out of 21,582 patients treated with M.A.O. [monoamine oxidase] inhibitors, 2.08 per cent developed headaches, and 0.27 "the complete hypertensive [high-blood pressure] syndrome."

"As the majority of depressed patients are not able to co-operate fully," an article in the May 16, 1964, issue of the *Lancet* said, "the various warnings [to avoid certain substances, including cheese *and alcohol*] may go unheeded . . . In such circumstances these drugs, which represent a therapeutic advance in many respects, become potentially lethal. We are thus increasingly concerned about the ethical implications of their continued general use." [5] In the same issue of the British publication, three New Zealand researchers reported on another monoamine oxidase inhibitor, Eutonyl. Adding a new dimension, they told of patients on that drug who had experienced sudden alarming increases in blood pressure after eating whole, cooked broad beans, which are also known as fava, horse, and Windsor beans.

The chilling reports continued. One told of a physician on Eutonyl who ate four pieces of Cheddar. Twenty minutes later he developed a severe, generalized, throbbing headache, blurred vision, profuse sweating, vomiting, and generalized muscular contractions. His acute symptoms subsided within four hours after treatment of them was begun, but during the ensuing three weeks he suffered recurring headaches, neck pain, dizziness, and muscular twitching. Of seven patients on Actomol (mebana-

---

[5] In his syndicated newspaper column a few months later, Dr. P. J. Steincrohn noted that the aggravating substance is, in smaller amounts, also found in wines and beer. While recognizing that recommendations as to dietary precautions and the avoidance of certain drugs by some patients should be borne in mind, he said, "Nevertheless, I don't think it makes good sense for hundreds of thousands of people to swear off cheese, wine and beer simply because they take tranquilizers." What might make good sense would be for physicians to swear a great many of these people off tranquilizers so that they can enjoy cheese, wine, and beer.

zine), another report disclosed, three developed a severe *lowering* of blood pressure that persisted 10 to 19 days after administration of the drug had been halted. Other substances reported to be dangerous to patients taking monoamine oxidase inhibitors included certain drugs and a meat concentrate commonly used as the basis for soups served in British hospitals.

Following reports of six Parnate fatalities in England and four in Canada, as well as of numerous severe but nonfatal reactions, Smith Kline & French issued a warning letter to physicians on October 10, 1963. A change in labeling was agreed upon with FDA, and the agency said it would "keep watch." At about this time the *Medical Letter* asserted that Parnate "has no special value in comparison with less hazardous antidepressant drugs to justify the risk of its use."

Reports of deaths and injuries continued to accumulate. By February 24, 1964, the toll known to FDA was 400 cases of elevated blood pressure, of which about 50 had culminated in strokes and 15 in death. Six of the fatalities were in the United States. On this February date Smith Kline & French notified doctors that FDA believed Parnate should be removed from the market, and that the firm was complying "under protest."

Some psychiatrists complained that news of the withdrawal reached their patients before it reached them, as the result of FDA's issuance of a news release which was picked up by lay news media. Actually, Smith Kline & French had issued its own news release on February 24, the same date as the one on its letter to physicians. FDA news release was dated a day later. The *Medical Tribune* quoted an unnamed agency official as saying that the company had "very cleverly" publicized the withdrawal so as to elicit "sympathy from practicing physicians." The Pink Sheet said that the agency saw in the invitation for comment extended by the manufacturer to practitioners "an effort to develop pressure and a testimonial claque in a situation that requires calm scientific evaluation."

World medical literature contained almost 90 statements on adverse reactions to Parnate. More than half were in foreign publications — 33 of them in the *Lancet* and 14 more in the *British Medical Journal*. These publications are seen by only a minute proportion of American physicians. The number of American doctors aware of the paucity of solid evidence — *controlled* studies — about Parnate's efficacy may also be presumed to have been small.

Not surprisingly, then, FDA received negligible support from the profession. Almost all of the mail — and the volume was said to have been very heavy — was critical of its action. Smith Kline & French requested a hearing. It was the first challenge of this kind since the enactment of the Kefauver-Harris amendments in 1962. The hearing promised to be of tremendous significance. It would permit, in an unprecedented public form, a genuine confrontation on the benefits versus risk ratio. At a prehearing conference, the lawyer designated to represent FDA, William R. Pendergast, said the issue

is whether or not the drug called Parnate has been shown to be safe, under the conditions under which it *has been used* in the U.S.

This issue involves the safety of the product under the final labeling approved for it in the NDA [new-drug application] . . .

A co-issue, inherent in the issue of safety, is the problem of how effective is Parnate. A greater degree of danger can be tolerated for a drug which is highly effective than can be tolerated for a drug with only marginal or no efficacies.

Therefore, one of the co-issues will be whether or not Parnate has any appreciable efficacies in the disease condition for which it is intended . . .

Our evidence in that regard will be directed as to its safety in *its actual use* in the last three years, to the efficacies of the product for those conditions.

The phrases *"has been used"* and *"its actual use"* served to distinguish between the restricted prescribing that had been advised in the labeling and actual practice, which had been so loose that by Smith Kline & French's estimate Parnate had gone to about 2 million persons in the United States.

According to the Pink Sheet, which provided extremely thorough coverage of the matter, FDA's plan was to argue that under the labeling as it existed at the time Parnate was removed from sale, its risks did in fact outweigh its potential benefits, particularly in view of the availability of other antidepressants.

In addition to eleven physician-witnesses of its own, FDA lined up a dozen outside experts to testify in its support. Smith Kline & French, meanwhile, was preparing to try to demonstrate, as the Pink Sheet for June 15, 1964, put it, that "Parnate is an essential drug in the psychopharmaceutical armamentarium — one that has proven useful in cases for which no other therapy exists, and therefore should remain available under labeling that clearly spells out the risks, side effects, contraindications, and other information for proper use." Besides its own personnel, the company also had lined up outside witnesses, some of them men with lustrous reputations in psychiatry. In further preparation for the hearing, the firm and the agency had marked for identification approximately 150 articles on Parnate from the medical literature.

ᕯ ᕯ ᕯ

The place chosen for the hearing was the Natural History Building of the Smithsonian Institution in Washington. The time set was 10 A.M. on June 16, 1964. On the eve of the hearing, while top FDA officials were, according to the Pink Sheet, having a final session, they received a telegram from the American Psychiatric Association. Its executive committee, the telegram said, had "determined that it would not be feasible for the Association to testify," because "we do not feel we yet have sufficient evidence on which to base an expert opinion or a firm conclusion." The Association went on to say, through its president, Dr. Daniel Blain, that the executive committee thought the lack of evidence made the withdrawal of the drug "premature." Not having the evidence, the leaders of American psychiatry had made up their minds that FDA had acted impetuously, if I psychoanalyze the situation correctly. That Parnate — and a great many other psychotherapeutic drugs, as well — had been allowed to go *on* the market prematurely, without controlled studies, had apparently not troubled the Association. Proceeding further with the evidence it did not have, the Association added:

> It is our hope that the expert testimony which you will hear . . . will be sufficient for you to adopt a prudent course which will incorporate safety measures governing the use of this drug which it appears very many physicians have found clinically valuable. We are impressed that a great many of our own members have sent comments reflecting their concern about the sudden withdrawal of Parnate from the market.

Surely the decision-makers in the Association knew that by their action they were shrinking the chances that expert testimony would be heard at all. There was not one word in the telegram to suggest that in addition to the psychiatrists who had informed the Association of their pro-Parnate leanings — some of them after being prompted by external stimuli to do so — there were psychiatrists who felt that the risks of Parnate and other monoamine oxidase inhibitors outweighed their benefits. The opponents might well have included physicians who had read Dr. Kalinowsky's article in the Association's own *Journal*, the memory of which may have been sublimated by the executive committee.

The Association had telegraphed not a punch but a torpedo at FDA. It was hit, but it did not *have to* sink. It did. It did not *have to* call off the hearing, but it did. The agency could have treated a case of schizophrenia within the psychiatric profession to the electric shock of a public hearing, in order that the truth — whatever it may be — could be developed. Instead, with the help of the Association, the truth was repressed; and it will take more than psychotherapy ever to bring it out. Defeat of the public interest did not *have to* be snatched from the jaws of victory, but when the truth was repressed it was.

A matter of sixteen or so hours before the hearing was to begin, FDA issued a press release announcing its cancellation. The agency said it had accepted "a drastic revision of the labeling . . . which will allow this drug to re-enter the market for use only in severe cases of mental depression." The release went on to say that the hazards of Parnate "can be minimized and substantially avoided by careful use," and that the restrictions to be imposed included one on other than hospitalized cases of severe depression. But just as the restrictions in the old labeling were not heeded, there was no guarantee that the new ones would be, either. The drug will be stocked in drugstores, and anyone with a medical degree can write a prescription for it.

Under an agreement between FDA and Smith Kline & French the full text of the revised labeling, in the form of a thirteen-page brochure, was mailed by the company to all physicians. Among those who had been pro-Parnate or anti-FDA there may have been some who on reading the pamphlet closely felt a sense of disillusionment.

With complete candor the manufacturer said that there have been "only a small number of controlled studies" — the four mentioned earlier in this chapter — "embracing comparatively few subjects." It would be an understatement to say that the claims for efficacy for a drug that had been acclaimed as "essential" were minimal. "These and other studies," the brochure said, "disclose a remarkably high incidence, about 50 per cent, of favorable placebo effect and a statistically significant but small superiority of Parnate . . . and other antidepressant drugs over placebo." This striking admission was followed by another: "No statistically significant superiority of Parnate . . . over other antidepressant drugs, including other MAO inhibitors, has been regularly demonstrated." Then comes a deterrent to the possibly heretical notion that there may be no reason to prescribe Parnate, in view of the foregoing: "However, clinical experience also indicates that some patients who fail to respond satisfactorily to one therapy may respond to another. Because of the serious and sometimes fatal hypertensive effects that occasionally occur with Parnate . . . it is indicated only in those depressions that have failed to respond satisfactorily to other therapy." In other words, the manufacturer himself seemed to be looking on it as a last resort.

Below a red-ink "WARNING TO PHYSICIANS" Smith Kline & French said that tranylcypromine is potent, can produce serious side effects, and is not recommended in those severe depressions in which ECT is the treatment of choice or in those depressive reactions "where other antidepressive drugs may be effective."

Doctors also are told that Parnate should not be administered together or in rapid succession with Tofranil or Elavil. "In addition to the possibility of a hypertensive crisis, severe convulsive seizures have occurred in patients receiving such combinations," the pamphlet says. "Likewise, Parnate . . . should not be used with other MAO inhibitors," those used in the United States being named as Eutonyl, Niamid (nialamide), Marplan (isocarboxazid) and Nardil. Nor should Parnate be administered in combination with "amphetamines, and over-the-counter drugs such as cold, hay fever or reducing preparations that contain vasoconstrictors. Also patients should be instructed not to eat cheese while on Parnate . . . The ingestion of cheese, particularly strong or aged varieties, may also contribute to a hypertensive crisis." Other warnings include one against using Parnate in combination "with some central nervous system depressants such as narcotics and alcohol . . ."

✓ ✓ ✓

In the Natural History Building the morning of June 16, the hearing examiner, William F. Brennan, found himself writing the last chapter of the unnatural history of the Parnate episode. "Last evening at approximately 5:35," he announced, "Deputy Commissioner [John] Harvey called me into his office, and there was present Mr. Edward Brown Williams, counsel for SKF, Mr. William Pendergast, counsel for the FDA, as well as other FDA representatives." Brennan concluded his three-minute session by saying:

> Mr. Harvey informed me that FDA had been able to accept new restrictive methods of distributing the drug Parnate, as well as new labeling . . .
>
> As a consequence of this the questions which were to be determined at the hearing which was scheduled to take place this morning have become moot; and by agreement between the Food and Drug Administration and SKF, the hearing has been cancelled.
>
> Consequently, there will be no hearing, and I will not formally convene a hearing for this matter, and this statement terminates the proceedings.

On July 15, 1965, the Drug Abuse Control Amendments to the Food, Drug, and Cosmetic Act became effective. Here I will deal with the implementation of those amendments as they pertain to prescription drugs, and with a corrective letter for Librium, one of the drugs proposed for inclusion under the amendments; there will follow a new "last chapter of the unnatural history of the Parnate episode."

THE DRUG ABUSE AMENDMENTS

Early in 1966, Commissioner James L. Goddard of the Food and Drug Administration adopted criteria under which depressant and stimulant drugs not specifically designated in the Drug Abuse Control Amendments would be judged as to their "potential for abuse," as defined in the law. These criteria included evidence: of consumption in amounts sufficient to create a hazard to the user, to other individuals, or to the community; of significant diversion from legitimate drug channels; and of use on individuals' own initiative, rather than on the basis of medical advice.

Dr. Goddard then applied the criteria to specific products.[1]

[1] Those which are legally available in drugstores and which were said to have a potential abuse because of their depressant effect on the central nervous system: chloral hydrate (Chloral); chlordiazepoxide and its salts(Librium), diazepam (Valium), ethchlorvynol (Placidyl), ethinamate (Valmid), glutethimide (Doriden), meprobamate (Apascil, Atraxin, Biobamat, Calmiren, Cirpon, Cyrpon,

The intent and the effect were not to prevent physicians from prescribing these products, but merely to try to restrict them to legitimate prescription channels and approved therapeutic usages. The restrictions were essentially record-keeping requirements intended, for example, to limit the frequency with which a prescription can be refilled. Naturally, a manufacturer would prefer not to have a product officially designated as a drug with a potential for abuse, one reason being that some physicians might switch to a product not so designated. Nonetheless, all of the makers but two accepted the Commissioner's action without availing themselves of their right to a hearing. The exceptions were Carter-Wallace, Inc., producer of meprobamate, which is most widely sold as Miltown and Equanil, and Hoffmann-La Roche, Inc., producer of Librium (chlordiazepoxide) and Valium (diazepam), its near chemical twin. The extent of use of these drugs was staggering, thanks in good part to massive, sustained advertising campaigns that provided a major revenue source for publications such as the *Journal* of the American Medical Association, *Medical Tribune*, and *Medical World News*. Meprobamate, which was introduced in 1955, was prescribed for "approximately 100 million patients over the last ten years," FDA said in April 1967. At about the same time Edgar A. Buttle, the independent hearing examiner in the Hoffmann-La Roche case, "conservatively estimated" that more than 15 million patients had received Librium, which was introduced in 1960, and more than 5 million Valium, which followed in 1963.

After extensive hearings — that for Librium-Valium lasted 45

Ecuanil, Equanil, Equanil LA, Harmonin, Mepantin, Mepavlon, Meproleaf, Meprosin, Meprospan, Meprotabs, Miltown, Nervonus, Neuramate, Oasil, Pamaco, Panediol, Perequil, Perquietil, Pertranquil, Placidon, Probamyl, Quanil, Quilate, Sedabamate, Sedasil, Urbil, Viobamate), methyprylon (Noludar), paraldehyde; drugs said to have a potential for abuse and habit formation because of their stimulant effect on the central nervous system: *d-*, *dl-*Methamphetamine and their salts, and *d*, *dl-*Desoxyephedrine and their salts.

days — the hearing examiners (William F. Brennan in the meprobamate case) separately recommended that the drugs be listed as having a potential for abuse. Brennan found that chronic use of meprobamate in high dosages produces coma and stupor, mood depression and apathy, and can cause intoxication and changes in personality. The drug also has been used to commit suicide. Examiner Buttle found in the record reason to be milder about Librium and Valium but said that the evidence presented by the Government of a legal potential for abuse was "preponderant, even if not conclusive . . ." On April 12, 1967, the FDA issued a tentative order to list meprobamate. Carter-Wallace said the case had not been proved and filed formal objections. Ultimately, the case could be carried to the Supreme Court; meanwhile, meprobamate does not have to be labeled as a drug with a potential for abuse. As of late May 1967 the agency had not acted on the recommendation to list Librium and Valium.

THE LIBRIUM LETTER

In February 1967 Roche Laboratories published in *Medical Tribune* an 8-page ad for Librium. Under threat of a seizure action, the company mailed on March 10 a corrective letter signed by Dr. Robert E. Dixon, director of professional services. Like Serax, a member of the same chemical family (see Afterword to Chapter 4), Librium ran into trouble because of an impermissible overreaching for the populous market among the elderly. Thus Dr. Dixon's letter to prescribing physicians pointed to a statement in the ad that most adverse reactions in geriatric patients are mild and readily reversed by reduction of dosage. But thereafter, Dr. Dixon said, Librium ads also will say that "drowsiness, ataxia [muscular incoordination] and confusion have been reported in some patients, particularly the elderly and debilitated, and that in a few instances syncope [swooning or fainting] has been reported." The Food and Drug Administration found the ad's brief summary of warning information insufficient. Future ads, the remedial letter said, will reflect the FDA-approved prescribing instructions by reciting these points among others: Operation of machinery and driving motor vehicles are examples of activities to be cited to physicians who must caution Librium users against engaging in "hazardous occupations that require complete mental alertness"; Librium is "not recommended in children under six"; to preclude muscular incoordination and oversedation, the smallest effective dose — 10 or fewer milligrams per day — should be the initial limit in children over six and in the elderly and debilitated; because blood and liver disorders occasionally "have been reported" in Librium users, blood and liver tests are advisable when therapy is protracted.

PARNATE

Much of the truth about Parnate — repressed by the abrupt cancellation of an administrative hearing — was flushed out a year later when, on June 24 and 25, 1965, an inquiry was held by the House Intergovernmental Relations Subcommittee. The inquiry was therapeutic for the citizenry but another shocker about Dr. Joseph F. Sadusk, Jr., then the top physician of the Food and Drug Administration. It turned out that the decision to allow Parnate to be remarketed was not, as he contended, a product of let-the-chips-fall deliberation, but a result that he had foreordained; it also turned out that behind a façade of consensus which Dr. Sadusk put up in front of his Bureau of Medicine, remarketing was opposed — in the basis of solid evidence — by Dr. Matthew J. Ellenhorn, chief of the New Drug Surveillance Branch; by Dr. Arthur Ruskin, Deputy Director of the Division of New Drugs; and by Dr. Arthur Egelman, the Bureau's only psychiatrist and the medical officer responsible for the antidepressant drug. Subcommittee Chairman L. H. Fountain put into the record a memorandum to Dr. Ellenhorn dated May 21, 1964 — a few weeks before the formal announcement of remarketing — in which Dr. Egelman dissented to allowing Smith Kline & French to remarket Parnate:

> Testimonials to the contrary, from whatever source, no matter how highly placed, do not constitute scientific evidence. The well-controlled studies that we do have indicated that Parnate is in fact less effective than ECT [electro-convulsive therapy] as well as other drugs presently marketed.
>
> There is no question that this is a dangerous drug. Attempts to surround its use with a thicket of contraindications, warnings, and precautions are unwieldy and impossible to apply. In addition, this does not tell the physician that even if he should avoid all these pitfalls his patient may die from the drug anyway.
>
> If the drug were the only one available to treat a particular disease entity there might be some reason to weigh its dangers against the need for it. This is not the case with Parnate. Its other selling points have not been proven. Its supposed rapid action in the treatment of depression is felt to be due to its amphetamine-like effect. It should be underscored that this is NOT an antidepressant action. If it were we should use the amphetamines as antidepressants.
>
> I deeply regret the prolongation of human suffering and the sacrifice in human life which will follow the resumption of marketing of this relatively ineffective drug.

Subsequently Dr. Egelman resigned.

The Subcommittee inquiry repeatedly exposed Dr. Sadusk as something less than candid. He had, for example, asked Dr. Jonathan O. Cole, chief of the Psychopharmacology Service Center of the National Institute of Mental Health, for an evaluation of Parnate data. Inquiry by Congressman Fountain developed, however, that Dr. Sadusk had couched the request not in terms of *severe* depression, the specific condition in which Parnate was supposedly useful, but as to depression generally. Dr. Sadusk testified that some experts who had agreed to testify for FDA at the proposed administrative hearing changed their minds and declined. An aide identified one of these witnesses as Dr. David W. Harris, a psychiatrist at St. Elizabeths Hospital in Washington. But W. Donald Gray of the Subcommittee staff said that two days earlier he had been told by Dr. Harris that at no time had he indicated an unwillingness to testify. In announcing the cancellation of the administrative hearing of June 1964, an FDA press release initialed by Dr. Sadusk referred anonymously to experts who had been "consulted by FDA and concurred in the action taken." One of these experts was Dr. Fritz A. Freyhan, director of clinical research at the National Institute of Mental Health. It happened that Dr. Freyhan *did* favor remarketing of Parnate — but he told Donald Gray that the efficacy studies on the drug "were not very well done" and would not, at a hearing, have given Dr. Sadusk "a leg to stand on." The studies numbered 11; Dr. Cole, who also had been cited anonymously in the press release, testified that he found in them *no* substantial evidence of efficacy in severe depression. Dr. Sadusk had to be reminded by Chairman Fountain that the burden of establishing efficacy — with "substantial evidence" — was on Smith Kline & French, not FDA. At one point Dr. Sadusk, his face flushed, protested that the Subcommittee staff — Delphis C. Goldberg and Gray — were challenging "my integrity and veracity." Fountain said his aides had done no more than seek documentation. I doubt that anyone who reads the full hearings would feel that Gray and Goldberg treated the witness unfairly.

In *Clinical Pharmacology and Therapeutics* for September–October 1965 was a comprehensive assessment of 54 of the 56 published trials done on Parnate through June 1964. The conclusion was that although the toxic rise in blood pressure caused by Parnate "occurs infrequently, it is a serious risk because it is partially unpredictable and can be lethal. Moreover, the efficacy of the drug is not established. For a few patients, it may be the drug treatment of choice and for the condition for which it is used, depression, it may be lifesaving. But for most, it would seem to be inferior to or no better than several other available treatments." The authors of this study, which was aided by a Public Health Service grant, were Dr. Roland M. Atkinson, of the psychiatric service of the PHS Hospital in Staten Island, New York, and Dr. Keith S. Ditman, of The Neuropsychiatric Institute, University of California Center for the Health Sciences, Los Angeles. Their conclusion was essentially the same one that had been reached by some people in FDA's Bureau of Medicine — only to be rejected by Dr. Sadusk. In February 1966 in the *American Journal of Psychiatry* three members of the staff of the Institute of Living in Hartford, Connecticut, reported another of those bizarre things that have happened to Parnate patients. This time, ten of them ate chicken livers for lunch; six had serious episodes of high blood pressure and four had " moderately severe side reactions." On August 2, 1966, FDA Commissioner James L. Goddard, responding to a query from the Fountain Subcommittee, said that in the two years since Parnate was allowed back on the market FDA had learned of a total of 63 hypertensive reactions. Of these 31 in the United States and 9 in other countries were said not to have had a serious aftermath; nonfatal strokes totaled nine, seven of them in the United States; deaths numbered 14, 3 of them in this country. In April 1967 in *FDA Reports*, the agency's Dr. Ruskin said that the hypertensive crises from Parnate "originally suspected in less than 0.01 per cent of users of this drug were found in prospective studies to occur in 1 to 27 per cent." That is, the incidence uncovered by careful, scientific trials was at least 100 to 2700 times greater than had been thought earlier.

10

SAFETY/EFFICACY: A TRIAL
RUN WITH ANTIBIOTICS

THE LAST WORDS spoken in the Senate about the Kefauver drug bill in the moments after it was adopted on August 23, 1962, were those of Senator Paul H. Douglas of Illinois:

MR. DOUGLAS. Mr. President, the vote by which the Kefauver drug bill was passed just now — 78 to 0 — is quite a commentary on how time and history frequently bear out the views of some unpopular people and how what may seem to be a majority opinion at one moment in time is later proved not to be the case.

The Senator from Tennessee [Mr. Kefauver] has waged a long and lonely fight for an adequate drug bill. He has been attacked by the powerful drug industry, and in the press he has been derided as one of the despised band of liberals. He has not received a great deal of cooperation from some of his colleagues, although I think to their dying day, the Senator from Michigan [Mr. Hart], the Senator from Connecticut [Mr. Dodd], the Senator from Colorado [Mr. Carroll], and the Senator from Missouri [Mr. Long], can take pride in the aid they gave the Senator from Tennessee at a time when, with his back to the wall, he waged his apparently hopeless battle against these powerful interests.

But now, Mr. President, because of the many terrible tragedies which have occurred in European countries from the use of the drug thalidomide and the cases which have occurred in this country, it has been proved that the Senator from Tennessee was right all the time, and that the scoffers, scorners, and bitter opponents were wrong.

Now, by its unanimous vote, the Senate has placed its generous seal of approval on what the Senator from Tennessee and his colleagues have long fought for. Men who had openly and secretly fought him now flock to get on the bandwagon, and pretend that they were always his supporters.

As a humble American citizen, I wish to commend the Senator from Tennessee, and all those who helped him, for fighting for all these months and years for this great reform. Certainly the American people will eternally be grateful to him.

Mr. President, can we learn from this lesson; or can mankind educate itself only by disaster and tragedy?

Only four months later, the American Association for the Advancement of Science was told, "A sharp reduction in the usefulness of penicillin is . . . a real possibility; it could be a major catastrophe, costing more lives than I care to count. It would dwarf the thalidomide catastrophe." The speaker was Dr. Walter Modell, the editor of *Drugs of Choice*. The possibility or severity of the catastrophe he warned against would be reduced by the proposal the Food and Drug Administration made in August 1963 to halt the sale of about 50 oral cold compounds — lozenges or troches, principally — in which penicillin or some other antibiotic is combined with symptom-treating drugs — pain-killers, antihistaminics, nasal decongestants, caffeine.

FDA's case could scarcely be more compelling. But what it did in this episode — a trial run for enforcement of its new drug-efficacy powers — was to make a compelling case against itself.

The generally accepted estimate is that in the course of a life time 10 per cent of our population (currently, this would mean about 19 million persons) may become sensitive, or allergic, to penicillin through use of drugs, foods,[1] and cosmetics.[2] To become sensitive means that a cumulative level has been reached at which one cannot safely receive penicillin. Once this has happened, a dose very much smaller than would normally be safe may, because of previous exposure, cause a serious or even fatal reaction. In a highly sensitized person, such a reaction can be triggered by an extremely small dose. Thus, when one really needs this antibiotic for a disease against which it is invaluable — say, meningitis — the body cannot take it without a reaction ranging from a skin eruption or aching joints to an asthmatic attack or shock.

To be sure, it is argued that the risks are very small and well worth taking. How widely this argument is accepted is indicated by the figures for one year alone, 1962, when about 4 million prescriptions were filled (and 1 million refilled) for antibiotic-containing preparations intended to treat cold symptoms and prevent complications. Ninety-five per cent of the infections of the respiratory tract for which these preparations had been prescribed were caused by viruses against which no therapy, including antibiotic therapy, is effective.

Sensitivity is but one of the dangers. In the body are germ colonies that are rendered innocuous by other bacteria. When these bacteria are attacked by antibiotics and other antimicrobial agents, the germ colonies previously held in check thrive. And strains resistant to antibiotics multiply.

One result of promiscuous use of penicillin and other antibiotics has been a sharp increase in the incidence of a serious disease that in the pre-antibiotic era had been rare — staphylococcus infection of the intestine. Between 1954 and 1958, there

---

[1] For FDA's stand on antibiotics in food see the afterword to this chapter.

[2] The afterword provides some facts about use of drugs in cosmetics.

were about 500 staphylococcal epidemics in American hospitals.[3]

Another point is that what may seem to be a simple sore throat may actually be the manifestation of a disease that requires drastic and immediate treatment. Antibiotic lozenges can mask that manifestation. To take an antibiotic needlessly, then — in lozenge or any other form — is to risk serious illnesses needlessly.

As long as twenty years ago there were warnings against needless use of antibiotics. One came from Dr. Hobart A. Reimann, in the *Archives of Internal Medicine* for August 1945: "In addition to the great benefits derived therefrom, there is reason to fear that the release of penicillin [for general use] will be followed by the same abuse, waste and commercialization that followed the release of sulfonamide compounds . . . Regulation by some official body may be needed to prevent absurd combinations of penicillin with chewing gum, mouth wash, cough drops, skin lotion, and so forth."

"These predictions have been fulfilled," Dr. Reimann testified in March 1963 before Senator Humphrey's Subcommittee on Reorganization and International Organizations. The physician, who since 1960 has been professor of medicine and pre-

---

[3] Brian Inglis, British editor and medical writer, is one who despairs "that new drugs will solve the problems presented by the failure of the old. Temporarily, they may — it takes staphylococci some little time to acquire resistance to any new antibiotic." In the *Nation* for August 24, 1963, Inglis also saw a close parallel between Rachel Carson's explanation of the calamitous results of indiscriminate use of pesticides and the dangers of powerful drugs:

Microbes, like insects, are part of the evolutionary pattern. When subjected to some catastrophic inundation with chemicals, they may be wiped out; but, as a rule, a few survive, to breed resistant strains. "The drug-resistant staphylococcus," as Dr. Robert Moser put it in his *Diseases of Medical Progress*, "has risen on a grotesque spectre to haunt physicians throughout the world. It is indeed a modern plague, largely of our own creation." What is really required in these circumstances is a different kind of treatment, biological rather than chemical, taking the evolutionary aspect into account and realizing that germs and viruses, like most insects, are not necessarily harmful; they can be persuaded to lead innocuous lives if ways are found to keep them contented — but under control. Attempts to poison them off merely make them more vicious.

ventive medicine at Hahnemann Medical College and Hospital in Philadelphia, went on to say:

> Although exact figures are unavailable, it has been estimated that 90 percent of antimicrobics is prescribed unnecessarily . . . Popular magazine articles, television and radio programs, and commercial advertising have glamorized and exaggerated the value of these "wonder drugs." Because of this, lay persons often insist on the treatment or prevention of many ailments for which antimicrobics have no value. Very few diseases require antimicrobic therapy.
>
> Physicians tend to prescribe the drugs indiscriminately for any febrile disease [characterized by fever]. Many physicians and dentists, in the press of other matters, have a scanty idea of the proper use, the limitations, and the dangers of antimicrobics . . .
>
> Antimicrobic therapy saves thousands of lives and relieves much suffering, yet, as with other medicaments, untoward effects, harm, and death may occur after logical, but especially after indiscriminate prescription.

. . . .

> Owing to the almost universal use of antimicrobics, a large proportion of the population now is hypersensitive to them, *particularly to penicillin.* [My italics.]

In 1949 the American Medical Association's *New and Non-official Drugs* omitted lozenges containing penicillin because of numerous sensitivity reactions of relative severity. By 1951 the concern with the useless use of antibiotics had become worldwide and was summarized in a *British Medical Journal* report that the AMA used as the basis for a warning to the public in its magazine for laymen.

With good reason, FDA had not permitted combinations of

antibiotics with symptom-treating substances to be sold. In 1952, during the reign of Commissioner Charles W. Crawford, the agency gave in to industry pressure and permitted the combinations "for the relief of cold symptoms and the prevention of the common cold and other acute respiratory infections." In an effort to justify that decision FDA has said: "Since then well qualified medical experts have raised questions about the efficacy of such drugs for these purposes." Not only "Since then" but for years previously. There was no proof of effectiveness before 1952, just as there was not in 1964.

Inevitably, makers of over-the-counter (OTC) products, who include several "ethical" drug manufacturers, wanted to be cut in on the vast market that was about to be drummed up. The problem was the law's requirement that pharmaceutical products had to be truthfully labeled.

Dr. Barbara Moulton has said that "no truthful over-the-counter labeling could be devised" for antibiotic-containing preparations claiming to be effective against sore throats. "Rather than reaching the logical conclusion that such products should therefore not be marketed," she told the Senate Subcommittee on Antitrust and Monopoly, FDA "apparently suggested or at least condoned the addition of topical anesthetic agents which would numb the painful throat, thereby affording 'temporary relief' from the 'symptoms' of 'minor throat irritations' . . . Quite apart from the misleading nature of the labeling there is the additional problem that topical anesthetic agents . . . are known to be sensitizing." That is, an allergy can be built up — just as with the antibiotics many of these products contain (*not* including penicillin, which is allowed only in prescription compounds). Later, when the allergic person receives a comparatively large amount of the same anesthetic by, say, injection, he can be injured or even killed.

In 1958 a twenty-four-year-old soldier with a sore throat was given a lozenge containing just such an anesthetic and fell dead less than ten minutes after leaving the dispensary. This had been reported in the AMA *Journal* for January 2, 1960. Fortunately, such occurrences are infrequent, even though consumers have spent between $11 million and $25 million a year on from 300 to 500 cold remedies sold without prescription.

Although FDA actually had condoned inclusion of anesthetic agents in opposition to the tenets of preventive medicine, there was no abatement of the attacks by medical authorities on products to which antibiotics had needlessly been added, including lozenges, nose sprays, skin lotions, mouthwashes and children's "candy."

In a 1953 study of persons using antibiotic lozenges more than half — 185 out of 343 — experienced "untoward reactions," including between 20 and 30 severe inflammations of the mouth and throat. But among the 175 controls who received placebos seemingly identical with the antibiotic lozenges there were no adverse reactions.

In 1954, among 3192 Syracuse University students with acute upper respiratory infections, physicians found no difference in the effectiveness of randomly given preparations containing aspirin alone, aspirin plus an antihistamine, and aspirin plus an antihistamine plus penicillin — no difference except "a suggestion of prolongation of illness in the patients treated with penicillin."

In 1956, in a paper presented at a staff meeting at Suburban Hospital in Montgomery County, Maryland, Dr. Moulton said: ". . . for every one article that he reads advising restraint in the use of antibiotics the physician receives literally hundreds of enticing communications from pharmaceutical houses recommending their use under every conceivable circumstance. Only those of us who have actually worked in the field are fully aware of how misleading these advertisements can be; how carefully the reported studies are chosen to present only one side of the picture; and how seldom the work quoted presents an adequately controlled study."

In the following year, at an AMA section meeting in New York City, Dr. Harry F. Dowling of the University of Illinois College of Medicine reported, "As of November, 1956, there were on the market 29 preparations containing two antibiotics, 20 containing three, eight containing four, and four preparations that contained five antibiotics apiece . . . there is no good reason for the use of any of these 61 mixtures." Also in 1957, Dr. Ernest Jawetz, professor of microbiology at the University of California Medical Center, suggested that a "visitor from another planet, when informed of the proper use of antibiotics in human medicine . . . might be astonished to learn that of the 763 residents in Igloo, North Dakota, only 60, or 7.9 per cent, failed to receive antibiotics in a five-year period and that even by the most lenient criteria antibiotic administration was warranted for less than half the 2396 separate illnesses or complaints treated with these drugs." [Of the 763, 174, or 22.8 per cent, had received Chloromycetin.]

In this same year, 1957, the Asian flu epidemic began. The Public Health Service warned the public that antibiotics are ineffective against it, and said physicians should not be asked to prescribe them. The AMA told its members that in Asian flu antibiotics would be useless and might do harm. An official spokesman for FDA, however, said in October 1957 at an antibiotics symposium that doctors would continue to prescribe antibiotics for flu and would be right in so doing. The spokesman, Dr. Moulton told the Kefauver subcommittee, was Dr. Howard I. Weinstein, who had recently been transferred to Henry Welch's Division of Antibiotics.

On March 14, 1959, the AMA *Journal* printed a letter from Dr. Mervin C. Myerson of Beverly Hills, California, who said that he alone had encountered "several hundred cases" in which antibiotic lozenges — prescription and proprietary — had permitted a serious infection "to gain a foothold" and cause severely painful sore throats. "There have been cases of prolonged illness and even death from this cause," he wrote. "For some time I have questioned the moral and legal right of the manufacturer to market a product so injurious to health and at times to life itself." Pointing out that many doctors are "not aware of the danger," he said that his purpose in writing was "to ask what can be done toward a discontinuance of the sale of all antibiotic lozenges."

The nonprescription versions were the subject of an internal FDA memorandum in which the then medical director, Dr. William Kessenich, complained that the problem of whether to revise FDA's policy "has been shuttled about for some months now." He asked his superiors for a prompt decision.

✓ ✓ ✓

It was much easier for the Food and Drug Administration to let the genie out of the antibiotic lozenge bottle than it was to try to squeeze it back in after it had grown into a large and profitable business.

In March 1962 — nine months after Dr. Kessenich had sought a start on a policy decision — Commissioner Larrick put the problem before a panel appointed at his request by the National Academy of Sciences and headed by the eminent Dr. Harry Dowling.

Six months later, the panel reported that it had found "no acceptable evidence that any antimicrobial agent is of any value in the treatment of the common cold or of any other upper respiratory viral infection . . . or in preventing bacterial complications in patients with common colds who are otherwise healthy." For over-the-counter oral preparations containing antibiotics the panel said, ". . . we cannot conceive an acceptable . . . labeling." Plainly, for an entire decade FDA had been conceiving the inconceivable. Thus it deluded the trusting and helpless public it is supposed to serve. The public paid the bill in wasted health and wasted money.

Under the original law covering antibiotics, FDA was required to certify for potency — which implies efficacy, as Dr. Moulton points out — penicillin, bacitracin, and products containing them. A proposal made in 1949 by then Commissioner Paul B. Dunbar would have extended the requirement of potency to all antibiotics. In the face of industry resistance, however, Congress increased the number to a mere five and their derivatives. At any time during Commissioner Larrick's regime he could have acted against lozenges containing any of the five antibiotics. Of course this would have given the advantage to the increasing number of antibiotics that were escaping the efficacy requirement. In this situation, one might expect that Larrick at least would have pressed for extension of the efficacy requirement to *all* antibiotics. The fact is that he did not even revive the effort until the Kefauver inquiry exposed the situation in 1960. The 1958 industry award to Larrick, it may be recalled, credited the Commissioner not only with devotion to the public welfare but also with an "understanding of mutual problems." The Dowling panel had thrust a broad sword into the Commissioner's hand. He was swift to do nothing, not even to make the report public.

In March 1963 the problem of the antibiotic-containing proprietaries was shuttled to an FDA medical officer, Dr. R. E. Barzilai. He could find no excuse for the OTC labeling FDA had for a decade allowed on preparations containing antibiotics. The conditions for which they are marketed, he said, "usually clear spontaneously within a few days or could be symptomatically relieved through the use of any locally 'soothing' agent," of which honey could be one.

On July 5, 1963, the then acting medical director, Dr. Ralph G. Smith, expressed the belief in a letter to Commissioner Larrick that FDA lacked authority to remove the antibiotic proprietary preparations from the market. However, he did recommend that FDA implement the findings and recommendations of the Dowling panel on the prescription lozenges by publishing notice of intent to stop their manufacture. It could not be said that the tone was one of a crusader. In the letter Dr. Smith wrote that the proposal to have the lozenges swallowed by oblivion instead of the public "is likely to be met by substantial industry opposition," a nonmedical area of experience in which Dr. Smith is knowledgeable.

Eighteen days later, however, the Commissioner struck at last. He announced his intention to remove from the market antibiotic-containing products sold over the counter unless their makers could prove them effective. Three weeks later, FDA proposed banning the prescription versions and — eleven months after the report of the Dowling panel was received in final form — it made portions of the report public.

In defending the delays in proposing the bans, Larrick wrote to Senator Humphrey of the danger of premature action, which, if successfully challenged in court, could wipe out advances that were achieved slowly and with difficulty. On what actual FDA experience he was basing this obviously sound theory is not clear. According to Senator Humphrey, the agency has for a quarter-century neither brought nor fought a major legal battle in the courts against a leading drug manufacturer. Larrick also spoke of the unrealistic perspective of hindsight. More to the point, he suggested that there would be an advantage in delaying until enactment of the Kefauver-Harris amendments "gave us the opportunity to deal with all antibiotics across the board, rather than a case-by-case method."

✦ ✦ ✦

Although FDA's proposals did not put the genie back into the bottle, they did set off an industry sensitivity reaction comparable in fury to that which had dispatched the soldier who had swallowed an antibiotic lozenge five years earlier.

In a preliminary rash, American Cyanamid's Lederle Laboratories sent copies of FDA's proposed ban to 7500 physicians along with a suggestion that they file their opinions with FDA.

Among the first 100 responses were a number that happened to mention Lederle's Achrocidin, and one (*one*) backing FDA.

No circularization of the victims of uselessly prescribed antibiotics was attempted, which left the official record characteristically unbalanced.[4] Commissioner Larrick did receive a bit of encouragement in the form of a letter in *Medical World News* from Dr. A. Dale Console, the former medical director of E. R. Squibb & Sons. The physician said that if the industry succeeds "in urging medical leaders to lodge a formal protest . . . the caduceus should be at half-mast. If 'thousands of physicians' have found these mixtures useful," he continued, "it should be easy" for industry to collect and submit conclusive data demonstrating that utility. He urged industry to do this rather than blow up "an emotional storm over 'interference' with physicians' privileges."

It was a vain hope. The industry statement submitted to FDA by C. Joseph Stetler, of the Pharmaceutical Manufacturers Association, directed FDA's attention to the undisputed fact that antibiotic cold preparations have been "used extensively over the past 10 years." Indeed they had — in good part because the PMA's members had been pushing them. But, of course, what the industry was really saying was that the antibiotic cold "remedies" had passed the Hussey-Stetler Test of Time.

Not unexpectedly, the PMA complained that the Dowling

---

[4] "We are told," Senator Humphrey had said, that

> . . . whenever FDA has finally decided to close some loophole, antiregulatory forces have filled the "near vacuum" which tends to exist around FDA. The antiregulatory groups have often, we are told, devised elaborate campaigns to bring a flood of criticisms down on FDA's head. As a result, mail to FDA may run 10, 50, or as much as 100 to 1 against regulatory improvements. That unfortunate imbalance is one of the reasons why I, personally, spoke in the Senate in 1961, to commend FDA at the time it proposed the so-called "full disclosure regulation." As usual, its effort to protect the public health drew overwhelming rebuke from other quarters, instead of praise. Fortunately, the regulation was adopted nonetheless.

panel was composed entirely of academicians. This may seem an odd complaint, because the academicians are not only scholars of medicine but also practitioners in university hospitals, frequently with private practices as well. However, complaints of this kind have passed the test of time. They are effective. They have a kind of yahoo appeal to physicians who rely on detailmen rather than medical schools for their postgraduate medical education.

The PMA did not call attention to the balance of the Commission on Drug Safety it had set up after the thalidomide catastrophe. Of 14 members, none had advocated legislative drug-safety reforms before thalidomide, 5 were on the payroll of the drug industry, and 2 others were on the boards of directors of pharmaceutical firms. At a hearing of the Senate Reorganization subcommittee, Senator Ernest Gruening asked the Commission chairman, Dr. Lowell T. Coggeshall, a medical scientist and vice president of the University of Chicago, "Do you favor the 1962 Kefauver-Harris Law?" "I am not sure I am familiar with all the details of that law, Sir," Coggeshall replied. This was in June 1963, about eight months after the reforms had been signed into law.[5]

[5] There were other revealing exchanges:

SENATOR GRUENING: I would like to ask you, sir, whether in the years prior to 1962 . . . you had personally questioned whether or not adequate precautions were taken. The reason I ask this is because in 1960, making a speech on drug issues at the time you received an award from the Pharmaceutical Manufacturers Association, you stated: "There is no need for new drug legislation."

Do you feel that way now?

DR. COGGESHALL: Yes, sir; I do. I will be quite candid. I would qualify that statement by saying that public opinion probably required an expression of intense interest on the part of the Congress and the Food and Drug Administration.

I would remind you, sir . . . the United States came out of this terrible [thalidomide] experience looking better than any other country in the world. I think the new legislation was unnecessary from a scientific point of view, but I believe that in light of the current climate, some evidence of greater control was necessary. I am not backing away from the original answer.

For further significant quotations see the afterword to this chapter.

The principal objection in the PMA statement about FDA's proposed ban was that it "represents an unwise and unauthorized interference with the practice of medicine." Unwise for whom? For manufacturers of worthless cold "remedies"? For the AMA, which gets a huge chunk of its fight-Medicare income from pharmaceutical advertising? For the honest but busy physicians who have not the time to study the facts? Or is it unwise for the 19 million Americans who are building up a penicillin sensitivity that Dr. Modell fears could cause "a major catastrophe"?

✶ ✶ ✶

In the high administrative echelons of the American Medical Association the problem was that the July 27, 1963, AMA *Journal* in a forthright editorial had described the antibiotic cold "remedies" as "clearly violating the principles of rational therapy," had said that they "appear to sensitize as often as they relieve," and had acknowledged that "unquestionably some physicians have been guilty of misusing these agents." The hierarchy credited the editorial with "a sound scientific basis." But, undeterred, the AMA went on to urge its approximately 200,000 members to oppose the Food and Drug Administration's bans — "paradoxical as it may seem" — because of its "belief" that the bans would exceed the agency's statutory authority. The AMA statement was striking not only because of the mimeographed blush. Consider two "if" clauses that followed. "If some physicians are prescribing such mixtures . . ." If? They so prescribed 4 million times in one year. "If the rationality of the mixtures for some purpose is questionable . . ." If? The irrationality had been acknowledged four paragraphs earlier.

In any case, said the AMA, reaching reassuringly for its political prescription pad, the solution lies not in "governmental dictation of medical practice" but in "education of physicians." Certainly the solution does not lie in "governmental dictation," but the *issue* doesn't lie there, either. The issue is how the FDA exercises the statutory authority Congress gave it to protect the American people, *including physicians*, from drugs for which the scientific evidence of worth and safety is inadequate.

That education of physicians is needed cannot be doubted. Those educated by the industry to write protests to the FDA denounced the members of the Dowling panel in such enlightened phrases as "ivory-tower recluses," "cloistered educators," "pedagogues," and the like. One wonders if such physician-correspondents knew, or would care if they did know, that the panel chairman was also chairman of the AMA's Council on Drugs. The AMA position seems even more peculiar when one recalls how it is always ready to cheer FDA when it, say, bans seawater as a "tonic."

After touring the battlefield on which the bodies of logic and reason were left dead or dying, John Troan, a science writer, began a story in the Scripps-Howard newspapers on the AMA's posture about antibiotic lozenges by saying that it "is acting as though it needs to have its head examined."

While the leaders of the AMA and of the Pharmaceutical Manufacturers Association have been quick to warn FDA against denying physicians the right to prescribe drugs that can save lives and alleviate suffering, they have not been quite so ready to urge FDA to deny physicians drugs that needlessly take lives and cause suffering. What the AMA and PMA giveth the physician the AMA and PMA taketh not away from the physician.

In the summer of 1964, FDA moved to end, at last, a trial run on the safety/efficacy relationship that had come to seem almost interminable. On June 17, the agency proposed to force off the market — by demanding proof of effectiveness — 19 types of antibiotic-containing lozenges. "The Commissioner's medical advisers," the notice in the *Federal Register* said, have found "that there is a lack of substantial evidence that the drugs are efficacious for the purposes claimed in the labeling."

The proposal applied only to those 25 to 30 brands of troches containing the 5 antibiotics and their derivatives that were certified before the Kefauver-Harris amendments took effect. Included were products containing bacitracin, gramicidin, neomycin, polymyxin, tyrothricin, tetracycline, chlortetracyline, and penicillin. Following publication of the official notice, manufacturers were given 90 days to submit evidence of usefulness. What resistance would develop from the industry, and what effect it might have on actually ending sale of the affected antibiotic lozenges, was not immediately clear. The indication was that no final action would be taken until a decision be made on the larger group of lozenges containing antibiotics that were not certifiable before enactment of the Kefauver-Harris reforms. Like other uncertified drugs, they could be forced off the market by FDA starting on October 10, 1964, unless proof of effectiveness was offered. At year's end they were still on the market.

AFTERWORD TO CHAPTER 10

A death blow was struck at antibiotic lozenges and troches on March 8, 1966, when Dr. James L. Goddard, then Commissioner of the Food and Drug Administration for only a few weeks, announced that the agency would no longer certify antibiotics for such use.

From the Appendixes of *The Therapeutic Nightmare* there is reprinted here additional material on antibiotics in food which is cited from footnote one on page 216 and which is updated here with parenthetical material; on the use of antibiotics in cosmetics which is cited from footnote two on the same page; and further quotations from Dr. Lowell Coggeshall which are cited from footnote five on page 226.

ANTIBIOTICS IN FOOD

"There was a day," Senator Humphrey has said, when FDA had a

rigid prohibition against the use of antibiotics in food items. Then, said a trade publication, when commercial sources saw a "bonanza" in prospect [in 1955–1956] — ". . . a combination of pioneering research and smart legal counsel . . . made use of a gap created by the interrelationship of the Economic Poisons and the FDA Laws to overcome FDA's resistance toward use of antibiotics as food preservatives."

FDA was troubled about two questions on use of antibiotics as a food preservative:

"(1) Will their use result in sufficient antibiotic residues on food — as consumed —.to sensitize certain individuals to the antibiotic and prevent its use as a lifesaving drug in serious illnesses?

"(2) Will their use enable food packers and processors to cover up unsanitary practices, foist partially spoiled food on the U.S. public, or make inferior food appear better than it really is?"

FDA's doubts were resolved in favor of this use of antibiotics, despite numerous medical warnings. But the U.S. Department of Agriculture has had some different ideas — at least about one area in its jurisdiction — the questionable use of antibiotics as preservatives in red meats. USDA informed me:

"The Meat Inspection Division, USDA, has developed a policy of disapproval for such use."

(There was very doubtful benefit to the public in breaking the previously rigid ban on the use of antibiotics as food preservatives; rather, there was certain benefit to the Lederle Laboratories division of American Cyanamid Co. as the maker of chlortetracycline, and to Chas. A. Pfizer & Co., Inc., as the producer of oxytetracycline. Tolerances were set for residues of chlortetracycline [Aureomycin] to permit it to be used in the tanks of chilled water in which dressed poultry are dipped before marketing, for use of the same product on fish, scallops, and shrimp, and for Pfizer's product, trade-named Terramycin, also for use in "poultry dip." The assumptions accepted by then Commissioner George P. Larrick — but not by leading scientists or the Department of Agriculture — was that the tolerances had been "demonstrated" to be "safe." It was *assumed* that cooking would destroy *all* food-spoiling disease organisms before they entered the human body; it was assumed that fish products are always cooked before being eaten. Such assumptions were in error; but because they were made food processors sometimes were enabled to do precisely the kind of thing feared by Senator Humphrey, e.g., to mask decay odors that otherwise would alert the housewife to the true condition of the poultry or fish before her. Was this in the interest of the housewife or of Lederle and Pfizer? Is it the purpose of a regulatory agency to imprint the Great Seal of the United States on such practices?

(Even before Larrick started approving antibiotics as food preservatives they were added to the medicines, feeds, and water supplies of livestock and poultry, and to crop sprays. Despite tolerances intended to prevent human intake antibiotics were found in or on foods, including milk and fruits and vegetables. Then penicillin was found by the Agriculture Department in red meat, having gotten there through such routes as feeds. With this, Larrick appointed a special committee, headed by Dr. Mark H. Lepper of the University of Illinois College of Medicine, to see whether the obviously unwise action of 1955 remained obviously unwise in 1965. By the time the committee was ready to report, in August 1966, various researchers had confirmed something frightening — in animals that ingested antibiotics, bacterial strains previously sensitive to treatment were becoming resistant, the resistant strains were being transmitted into humans, and once-treatable human infections were being found to be resistant to multiple antibiotics and drugs. "It appears that unless drastic measures are taken very soon, physicians may find themselves back in the pre-antibiotic Middle Ages in the treatment of infectious diseases," the *New England Journal of Medicine* warned in an editorial. On receiving the committee report, FDA Commissioner James L. Goddard rescinded the Aureomycin and Terramycin food-preservative residue tolerances — those that eleven years earlier had been proclaimed "safe" — and set in motion an interagency examination of the whole problem of the use of antibiotics in food production. Dr. Goddard made it clear that starting at once his agency was going to be resistant to insubstantially justified claims for so-called veterinary antibiotic uses.)

ANTIBIOTICS IN COSMETICS

Senator Humphrey gave this report in 1964:

> In May, 1959, in an address prepared for delivery, an expert [the late Dr. Stephen Rothman of Chicago] of the Committee on Cosmetics of the American Medical Association presented 8 reasons against
>
> The incorporation of chemically and pharmacologically active drugs into cosmetics . . .
>
> For example, the first reason was that:
>
> There is no drug which sooner or later would not cause any harm if given without any restriction of the dosage; if it can be given without limitation, it is not a drug. It cannot be denied that in the case of cosmetics which are applied once or several times daily and often on relatively large surfaces the amount absorbed and permitted to have systemic effects is entirely uncontrolled.
>
> Twenty-nine months later, the trade press reported that this paper had not been cleared for publication until 4 months prior to that time.
>
> Four and a half years after the expert AMA paper, I asked FDA how many cosmetics contained drugs. FDA replied: 59. (But this number includes, it should be noted, many items, commended by scientific authorities, which are not "cosmetics," as such.)

DR. COGGESHALL

Subsequently in the Humphrey subcommittee hearing there was the following exchange:

SENATOR GRUENING: Now, among the abuses that were taking place at the time you felt there was no legislation needed, one was that the manufacturers were concealing reports of fatalities, and other adverse reactions. What is your comment on that?

DR. COGGESHALL: Well, if that occurred, although I know of no instance personally in which it occurred, I would be opposed to that, certainly.

Later, in a letter to the Humphrey subcommittee, Dr. Coggeshall said that in his 1960 speech he had said:

> that more scientific information rather than new legislation was needed to improve the research on new drugs and foster their development for human usage with maximum attention to safety. This is the position I still hold. However, during the public reaction stimulated by the thalidomide incident I can understand a climate was created in which legislative action occurred. It was a constructive move.
>
> On the whole, I think the Kefauver-Harris law is sound and if the Food and Drug Administration follows the intention of the Congress there will be a more orderly introduction of new compounds from industry accompanied by improved experimental data.

11

MER/29: "A SHARP INDICTMENT
OF THE FDA ITSELF . . ."

DURING THE 1950's the belief was widely promoted, and became widely and even avidly held, that a high cholesterol level was causatively related to fatty degeneration of the arteries (atherosclerosis) and related heart and circulatory diseases. In 1958 the National Academy of Sciences cautioned, however, that "the data are so incomplete and conflicting that it is impossible to draw conclusions which are universally acceptable to nutritionists and medical authorities."

The Food and Drug Administration also was concerned. Commercial interests — including producers of margarine and cooking oils — were promoting their products with anticholesterol advertising that advocated changes in diet. In *The Health Hucksters* Ralph Lee Smith wrote: "Some doctors found it increasingly difficult to get heart patients to accept and follow a proper course of treatment. Many patients insisted on stringent 'no cholesterol' diets and refused to cooperate with doctors who believed that other approaches were proper for the individual's condition."

In December 1959, FDA disclosed its official view: "A causal relationship between cholesterol levels and [heart and artery] diseases has not been proved." FDA reaffirmed this view in May 1964.

If there were such a causal relationship (and there may indeed be one), or if doctors and the public *believed* that there were, a drug that would safely lower cholesterol levels would be certain to attract a good deal of interest. Into this situation stepped the William S. Merrell Company of Cincinnati[1] with its MER/29 (triparanol). It held a dazzling promise: without changes in diet, merely by swallowing a 35-cent anticholesterol capsule before breakfast, a vast army of people — a hoped for $25 million-a-year market — could reverse or inhibit atherosclerosis and its related diseases. In a "very preliminary confidential brochure" issued in mid-1958, the Merrell firm invited physicians to try MER/29 on their private patients. At this time, Barbara Yuncker disclosed in the New York *Post* for August 8, 1962, Merrell's *own* clinical data "had not yet been collected." The animals used to demonstrate triparanol's effectiveness totaled 27 rats and 3 monkeys. Sixteen "control" animals were not given the drug. "The evidence of safety," the reporter wrote, "was derived from unstated numbers of mice and rats. The brochure said mice could not be given doses large enough to kill half of them. Three monkeys were also studied."

At the National Heart Institute Dr. Daniel Steinberg thought that the drug merited thorough study. His correspondence with Merrell, which is a vital part of the MER/29 materials assembled by the Humphrey Subcommittee on Reorganization and International Organizations, shows conclusively that he believed the utmost caution was required. Not until a year after physicians began testing MER/29 in the quite uncontrolled conditions of private practice did the Institute, where conditions for testing are unsurpassed, feel ready to try triparanol in even one patient.

The new-drug application for MER/29, filed in July 1959,

---

[1] A division of Richardson-Merrell, Inc., of New York. The name had been changed from Vick Chemical Company to Richardson-Merrell in 1960. According to Professor David F. Cavers, an authority on the history of the 1938 Food, Drug, and Cosmetic Act, Vick Chemical of North Carolina "was especially prominent" in efforts of the Proprietary Association to restrict the power of the Food and Drug Administration to make multiple seizures of products it considered a danger to health or a gross fraud on consumers. Seizures made over a wide area discouraged dealing in such products.

soon reached Dr. Frank J. Talbot, an FDA medical officer, who as "Dr. X" was interviewed in the Washington *Evening Star* for August 26, 1962. Miriam Ottenberg reported:

> As soon as the application appeared on his desk, the company started contacting him about the drug. His most frequent contacts were with F. Joseph Murray, director of scientific relations of the Merrell Co. . . .
>
> "There were many telephone calls and several meetings," [he] recalled. "It was obvious the company was extremely anxious to get the drug on the market. Some companies brought very little pressure but this company liked to keep the pressure on.
>
> "The American Medical Association convention was coming up and they were anxious to promote the drug at the convention. I was getting daily telephone calls . . ."

A few months later, at the Heart Institute Dr. Steinberg and a close collaborator, Joel Avigan, discovered that in aborting production of cholesterol MER/29 allows another sterol to accumulate in the blood. This fatty substance, desmosterol, is not normally present in the body, because in the last stage of a metabolic process it is converted into cholesterol.

Dr. Steinberg wrote Merrell's Dr. Robert H. McMaster: "I know that you are . . . anxious to obtain FDA approval . . . but I do not feel that this would be wise in view of the new data . . ."

✓ ✓ ✓

The Heart Institute discovery piled new questions on top of a structure of at least three uncertainties: the wide changes that occur unpredictably in a patient's cholesterol level; the inability of all but a few laboratories to take a "true" reading even when one can be ascertained; and, of course, the fundamental uncertainty — whether a high cholesterol level actually is causally related to heart and artery diseases.

Desmosterol is a close chemical relative of cholesterol. Is it also disease-causing in the arteries? Will an accumulation of desmosterol defeat the purpose of reducing cholesterol? Will it cause harm outside the circulatory system?

At the Food and Drug Administration, Dr. Talbot was aware of questions of this kind. The whole problem, he said in a memorandum on a telephone conversation with Dr. Steinberg, "revolves around whether desmosterol is equally as atherogenic as cholesterol or not."

Similar questions were discussed in December 1959, when about 37 scientists concerned with MER/29 held a two-day meeting on the drug in the congenial atmosphere of the Princeton Inn in Princeton, New Jersey. Merrell paid all expenses and provided generous consultation fees, although none of these pleasant benefits were accepted by the government researchers, Dr. Steinberg and Joel Avigan.

Dr. Irvine H. Page, of the Cleveland Clinic Foundation, found it "startling" that no evidence of serious toxicity in animals had been forthcoming, but the primary fount of knowledge on this had been William M. King, then head of toxicology and pathology at Merrell, of whom more will be said later.

The conference chairman, Dr. Irving S. Wright, professor of clinical medicine at the Cornell University Medical College, closed the symposium with these words: "If more drugs had been subjected to this kind of review early in their life histories, many mistakes and millions of dollars would have been spared physicians, patients and pharmaceutical companies . . ."

✓ ✓ ✓

In January 1960 the Food and Drug Administration and the American Medical Association consulted Dr. Laurance W. Kinsell, an Oakland, California, specialist in metabolism, about

MER/29. "I stated, in totally unequivocal terms," he recalled later in a letter to President Kennedy, "that the drug should not be released."

A month afterward, one of FDA's own pharmacologists, E. I. Goldenthal, submitted to the medical officer, Dr. Talbot, a devastating critique of Merrell animal data. "There is little margin of safety," he wrote. "This compound is producing toxic effects [these included eye damage, liver changes, inhibition of sexual function, even deaths] . . . at relatively low dosages . . . To use a compound that is potentially toxic [to reduce blood cholesterol] is highly questionable . . . perhaps desmosterol is itself atherogenic . . . Before we release this drug for general use . . . the company should submit results of . . . studies in which the individuals have received the drug for periods of several years." [2]

Dr. Talbot told Miss Ottenberg of the *Evening Star* that he "considered himself solely responsible for the decision" to be made on the release of MER/29. That a drug could be released for use in hundreds of thousands, or even millions of people, by a one-man decision may seem astonishing. Nevertheless, it was routine in FDA until after enactment of the Kefauver-Harris amendments.

"A medical officer in the New Drug Branch," Dr. Barbara Moulton told the Kefauver Subcommittee on Antitrust and Monopoly at about this time, "has power to release any new

[2] Later examples — in 1963 and 1964 — of unfortunate consequences that can result when insufficient attention is paid to the warnings of FDA pharmacologists were developed in hearings held in 1965 by the Intergovernmental Relations Subcommittee of the House Committee on Government Operations. The examples, involving five experimental drugs, are outlined in the afterword to this chapter.

In *Drugs in Our Society* (edited by Paul Talalay and published in 1964 by the Johns Hopkins Press) Dr. John T. Litchfield, Jr., says that the "degree of correspondence between the human and laboratory animal response will vary depending on the nature of the test." Dr. Litchfield, who is director of research at Lederle Laboratories, said: "It would seem, however, that the relation between the two must be such that a selected compound has at least a 50 per cent chance of being active in man or there would be no point to testing in animals."

drug on his own initiative, without review by any of his colleagues.

"To refuse to release a new drug, however," the former medical officer testified, "he must have the unanimous support of the Chief of the New Drug Branch, the Director of the Bureau of Medicine, the Commissioner, and usually also the Director of the Bureau of Enforcement and the General Counsel's office."

In his interview with the *Evening Star* Dr. Talbot said: "I recall talking with my supervisor, but he didn't advise on whether to pass or not to pass it. He wasn't prone to do that.

"My thinking was that here was a drug purporting to lower cholesterol. We were dealing with a highly lethal disease state . . . This drug might be helpful in dealing with the No. 1 killer of men."

To resume Miss Ottenberg's story again:

Dr. X [Talbot] in recalling what happened in the spring of 1960, said that in his last letter rejecting the drug application as incomplete, he told the company that he wanted longer trials to eliminate further potential areas of toxicity. He does not recall how long it was after he wrote that letter that he cleared the drug. [Senator Humphrey said that it was three weeks later — and before the requested data were received.]

"I was in a state of indecision where little things would have influenced me a great deal," he said.

It was then, he recalled, that he attended a meeting of the American College of Physicians in San Francisco where he heard discussions comparing various methods of lowering cholesterol.

"One paper impressed me," he said, "because the author reviewed various drugs and MER/29 came out in the No. 1 position. It was one of the things that swayed me toward passing the drug. I heard recently that the paper was never published and the author subsequently reviewed his data and questioned whether what he had said was completely valid . . .

"I released the drug," he said, "with the knowledge that things might appear later which were not obvious at the time."

In April 1960, having waited not the "several years" urged by FDA's pharmacologist but nine weeks, Dr. Talbot cleared the drug — "Solely on the evidence" of safety. His letter to Merrell actually disclaimed that efficacy had been reviewed. Yet, a few weeks later Commissioner Larrick would be dispensing assurances like these to the Kefauver subcommittee: "If the good in saving lives or alleviating suffering clearly outweighs the hazards, he [the medical officer] will permit the NDA [new-drug application] to become effective . . ." "Our decisions to permit new drugs on the market are reached only after . . . thorough appraisal of the safety and usefulness of the drugs." "I categorically deny that review of NDA's . . . may in some instances have been superficial." [3] In spite of these assurances, MER/29 was but one of 24 drugs released, only to be recalled as dangerous, during Dr. Ralph Smith's fourteen-year reign as supervisor of new drugs.

[3] Even a year later the Commissioner was being very firm about this. He had this exchange with two staff members of the Senate Antitrust subcommittee, Peter N. Chumbris of the minority and Bernard Fensterwald, Jr., of the majority:

MR. CHUMBRIS. . . . in your examination and in your tests for safety, do you also take into consideration efficacy before you grant a new drug?
MR. LARRICK. Yes.
MR. CHUMBRIS. Even though you are not required to by law?
MR. LARRICK. Yes.
MR. CHUMBRIS. In how many cases would you say was that, as to percentage of new drugs that come on the market?
MR. LARRICK. I would say we take that into account in all cases, but if we do not agree with the manufacturer on efficacy, the law does not give us clear authority to turn it down on that basis.
MR. FENSTERWALD. Mr. Larrick, you sum it up by saying you cannot separate safety from efficacy when you are testing prescription drugs?
MR. LARRICK. Exactly.

Having sold FDA on MER/29, Merrell now had to sell physicians. It unleashed a $1-million advertising and promotional campaign.[4] The Princeton conference was heavily exploited. A quite new journal, *Progress in Cardiovascular Diseases*, published the conference transcript as a supplement. But just before the date set for marketing to begin, June 1, 1960, and just when the price of Richardson-Merrell stock was about to soar — at this unpropitious time a most ominous report was made to FDA by an independent investigator, Lauretta E. Fox of the University of Florida. In the eyes of rats on MER/29, she said, she had observed diffuse cataracts.

Dr. Talbot did not ask Merrell for comment until the end of June. To the Florida researcher the company made an extraordinary, and extraordinarily insistent, "request" that she retract her report, on the ground that her animals, in which she found no evidence of infection, must be infected.

In the MER/29 advertisements, meanwhile, there were such lullabies as "remarkably free from side effects." Among those not lulled were the *Medical Letter* — which insisted that MER/29 should be used only experimentally — and Dr. Herbert Pollack, chairman of the Committee on Food and Nutrition of the American Diabetes Association. Dr. Pollack personally visited FDA to ask a review of its decision to allow marketing, which had begun six weeks earlier. The unsigned FDA memorandum on the interview consists of handwritten, disjointed notes like these: "scared to death," "Evidence that MER/29 oral contraceptive," "Sterile — male animals sterile — rats."

The interviewer has been identified as Dr. Ralph G. Smith, the longtime head of the New Drug Branch on whom the De-

[4] Medicated, however, with footnote references running from 1 to 41, or higher; and in at least one instance filling one and one-third pages of a brochure with blinding, unparagraphed small-sized type. Embedded in it were: "20. King, W. M." and "21. Van Maanen, E. F." In a later eight-page advertisement in the AMA *Journal* the careful reader would detect a shift in the batting order: "3. Van Maanen" and "11. King."

partment of Health, Education, and Welfare has conferred its Distinguished Service Award. The episode is ignored in the official FDA chronology on MER/29. Also missing from this document is any reference to FDA's official position that a causal relation between cholesterol levels and heart disease has not been established. Most notably, the chronology fails to mention the stern warning of the agency's own pharmacologist, the alert E. I. Goldenthal. This chronology is the one that was prepared by FDA for Representative L. H. Fountain's Intergovernmental Relations Subcommittee and was transmitted to Senator Humphrey's Reorganization subcommittee. Both subcommittees are charged with reviewing the activities of government agencies. One wonders how Congress can exercise appropriate supervision when an agency provides an official report as lacking in official information from its own files as was this chronology.

Meanwhile, another development was occurring at Merck & Co., Inc., where chemists had independently succeeded in synthesizing triparanol. Documents published by the Humphrey subcommittee disclose that at about the time FDA released Merrell's triparanol — MER/29 — Merck began making comparisons of the drug with a different anticholesterol drug of its own which has never been marketed. In prolonged chronic toxicity tests of triparanol, a disquieting proportion of dogs and rats developed cataracts, and several rats went blind. Merck decided it had an obligation to inform Merrell. "In the first week of January, 1961," Merck has reported to FDA, "Dr. Karl H. Beyer, Administrative Vice President, Life Sciences, of the Merck Sharp & Dohme Research Laboratories telephoned Dr. Harold Werner, Vice President and Director of Research of the Wm. S. Merrell Company, and set forth these findings for the first time."

About two weeks later, as a result of the telephone conversation, Werner and two other Merrell scientists, William King, the head of the toxicology and pathology laboratory who had startled the Princeton conference with his report that no evidence of serious toxicity in animals had been found, and Evert F. Van Maanen, King's superior, went to West Point, Pennsylvania, to confer with Dr. Beyer and his colleagues who had studied triparanol. At that time, Merck told FDA, its studies and results were described to the Merrell representatives.

About five months after that, in May 1961, the *Bulletin* of the AMA's Council on Drugs concluded that MER/29 "must be regarded as experimental," and not yet safe for general use; that claims made for it had been neither verified nor denied by adequate experiments; that its by-product, desmosterol, might be harmful, and that triparanol should not be prescribed for pregnant women. What was reported in any *Bulletin* other than this one, a copy of which was obtained by the Humphrey subcommittee, could not be learned, because the AMA designates them as confidential.

At the renowned Mayo Clinic a patient under experimental MER/29 treatment developed cataracts in August 1961. A second case was observed in October. Both victims also had experienced hair and skin changes months earlier. Mayo physicians urged Merrell to issue a warning letter, and at least two of them were said to be prepared to back any FDA moves to take MER/29 off the market.

Dr. Talbot left FDA in September 1961. Triparanol then became the responsibility of Dr. John O. Nestor, the vigorous medical officer who, along with Dr. Irwin Siegel, then deputy medical director, has been singled out for praise by Mr. Humphrey. Dr. Nestor and Dr. Siegel, who since has joined the National Institutes of Health, conferred with Dr. Steinberg at the Heart Institute. What they learned was alarming. Desmosterol *routinely* accumulated with use of MER/29. Rats heavily dosed with it had stillborn litters. The deposits left by desmosterol and cholesterol were similar — meaning that a reduction of cholesterol levels effected by triparanol could signify little or nothing.

Dr. Nestor urged FDA's laymen decision-makers to halt marketing of MER/29, at least until they could determine whether it was causing slowly developing cataracts. At the time, his investigation showed, the nationwide total was known to be four cases, but he feared this was only the beginning. Pleading that physicians be alerted "immediately," he stated his case forcefully: that MER/29 produces severe reactions is shown by "overwhelming" evidence; that it confers any material benefit has not been "conclusively demonstrated." It has produced defective offspring in laboratory animals. Merrell had made "unsubstantiated claims" for the effectiveness of triparanol in reducing cholesterol levels, and "has withheld from us some of this evidence of serious toxicity in animals and humans . . . for months."

In the AMA *Journal* for November 4, 1961, an advertisement for MER/29 claimed "few toxic or serious side effects . . ." In the *Journal* of the very next week, nevertheless, a digest of the Council on Drug's findings and a warning against the possibility of "multifarious and serious alterations . . . on prolonged therapy with MER/29" did find their way into public print.

This was *six months* after the confidential Council on Drugs *Bulletin* cited above had been given highly limited distribution. During that period, presumably, tens of thousands of persons were introduced to triparanol by physicians who had been kept in the dark about the Council findings by the hierarchy of the AMA, and hundreds of thousands continued to receive it.

Under the law as it stood at the time, the laymen administrators of the FDA felt they lacked sufficient clinical experience to prove MER/29's lack of safety and force it from the market. And so they overruled the scientists like Dr. Nestor and Dr. Siegel, who had not let MER/29 go on the market in the first place and who now wanted marketing stopped.

Getting Merrell into a cooperative posture was doubtless a tough proposition. Two months were required merely to get the consent of the Cincinnati firm to having MER/29 labeling reflect advice against use in pregnancy. In a later skirmish, which lasted five weeks, only a threat to halt the sale of triparanol won Merrell's agreement to a clear-cut statement of adverse effects.

The FDA "did all that could be done," Commissioner Larrick said later. By that he meant that the agency had required stricter labeling and a warning letter to physicians, which was issued on December 1, 1961 — two weeks after FDA had decided to demand it. The letter slowed but did not halt prescribing and use of triparanol, of which Merrell had a $2-million inventory. Merrell's vice president for marketing and sales wrote druggists two weeks after the warning letter: ". . . physicians throughout the country are prescribing MER/29 and we urge you to make sure that your stocks of this high-volume speciality are adequate."

✓   ✓   ✓

Early in 1962 a Food and Drug Administration statistician, Jerome Deutschberger, reported that an analysis of recent Merrell data indicated that in patients on MER/29 the incidence of cataracts was at least three times as great as in comparable patients not receiving triparanol.

If that was a predictable side effect, another was not. This one cropped up in February 1962, in a Cincinnati car pool. An FDA supervisory inspector, Thomas M. Rice, was riding with a man named Carson Jordan who had heard about the MER/29 warning letter issued the previous December. He told Rice that his wife Beulah had been involved with MER/29 during the approximately two years she had worked as a laboratory technician in Merrell's toxicology-pathology department, that she could not abide certain conditions there, and that she had left the firm.

This accidentally received information troubled Rice, and, alert to its implications, he arranged to interview Mrs. Jordan. His written report on the interview, which had alarming implications, was forwarded to FDA headquarters in Washington on February 27, 1962. Not until six weeks later, however, did the agency decide to dispatch Dr. John Nestor and E. I. Goldenthal to Cincinnati. Their two-day investigation determined that the MER/29 monkey data had been, as FDA put it later in its official chronology, "falsified." On April 10, two days after they had left Cincinnati, Merrell offered to take MER/29 off the market, although it engaged FDA in negotiations for an additional two days before agreeing to an announcement letter for the signature of president Frank N. Getman.

✓ ✓ ✓

"In retrospect," Deputy FDA Commissioner John Harvey told the American Bar Association a few months later, "it is apparent that the drug should not have gone on the market in the first place." [5] Senator Humphrey saw FDA's handling of the MER/29 case more harshly. It was, he told the Senate, "a sharp indictment of the FDA itself — its laxity, its tardiness in seeking to remove the drug from the market, its failure to protect the public interest."

As was the case with Altafur — the withdrawn antibacterial drug which a hearing examiner said FDA had released with inadequate evidence of safety and efficacy — MER/29 failed to incite a searching self-examination within the agency. "There has never been an appraisal," Dr. Nestor told the Humphrey subcommittee in March 1963, "to determine what . . . permitted such an application to be approved."

[5] In the twelve months ending June 30, 1961 — the first full fiscal year during which MER/29 was sold — the drug accounted for about 6 per cent of the $151.5 million in sales by Richardson-Merrell, as well as for about 13 per cent of its pharmaceutical sales, and for $1 million of its consolidated net profit after taxes. Triparanol was Richardson-Merrell's largest-selling prescription product.

There was, however, an appraisal by a federal grand jury in Washington which, in December 1963, returned an unprecedented indictment against the 135-year-old Merrell firm and its affiliate, Richardson-Merrell, Inc., and also against two Merrell scientists (who by then had left the firm), toxicologist William King and researcher Evert Van Maanen, and Harold Werner (who was retained by the firm as its vice president for research). The three scientists and the two corporations were charged with falsifying and withholding MER/29 test data.

In March 1964, no-contest pleas were entered by the William S. Merrell firm to six of the nine counts in which it was named. Richardson-Merrell, named in the three remaining counts of the twelve-count indictment, pleaded nolo contendere to two. The same plea was entered by each of the scientists. Van Maanen had been named in nine counts, King in seven, and Werner in five. The pleas were consented to by the Department of Justice.

The count that Werner and Van Maanen did not contest, the fourth, was also one of the six to which the William Merrell firm pleaded no contest. The charges in this count related to a letter of February 4, 1960, which the company sent along with a brochure to FDA. The three defendants, the count said,

. . . falsely and fraudulently represented that a caution statement reading, "Since cholesterol plays an important role in the development of the fetus, the drug should not be administered during pregnancy," had been inserted in the brochure "purely on theoretical grounds," when in truth and in fact, as said defendants well knew, investigations had been conducted by the said William S. Merrell Company, and by an independent laboratory pursuant to its request, the results of which disclosed that the administration of the drug to animals had resulted in adverse and deleterious effects upon the ovarian cycle, the rate of conception, the size of litters and the ability of the offspring to survive.

Count two in the indictment was not contested by the third scientist, King, nor, again, by the William S. Merrell Company. The charges here were that the defendants "knowingly and wilfully concealed and covered up, and caused to be concealed and covered up, by trick and scheme, material facts" in what purported to be "full reports of all investigations which were made by The William S. Merrell Company to show whether" MER/29 was safe. The true bill went on to specify that between mid-February and the end of March 1960 Werner and the Merrell firm withheld from FDA reports that certain investigations had been made, reports of results in some cases, and reports of adverse effects. Six investigations were described. In the first, all three of the female monkeys receiving daily 10 milligrams per kilogram of body weight (10 mg/kg) developed blood disorders, and one experienced ovarian changes. In the second, no evidence of recent ovulation was found in four female monkeys on 5 mg/kg per day. In the third, eight out of ten rats were dead seventeen days after being put on a dosage of 50 mg/kg per day, and the remaining two, whose dosage was cut in half, were dead a week later. In the fourth, female rats developed blood disorders. In the fifth, male and female rats that received 15 mg/kg of triparanol before and during cohabitation over a four-month period produced fewer offspring. In the sixth, pregnant rats dosed with 25 mg/kg per day had smaller litters; and among the newborn there was an increase in the death rate in the first twenty-four hours after birth.

Three months later, on June 4, the defendants appeared in United States District Court in Washington for sentencing. In behalf of Richardson-Merrell, Lawrence E. Walsh told the court:

> All I can say is there certainly was no intention by this Company or any of its employees to put on the market a dangerous drug. Whatever errors of judgment there were, this was not the intent.

I would say one further thing: That whatever these individuals did, they did what they thought they were doing on behalf of the Company and, if there must be punishment, we ask that it fall on the Company and not on them.

Chief Judge Matthew F. McGuire agreed with Walsh, who is, incidentally, himself a former federal judge and Deputy Attorney General from 1957 to 1960. "That is the view I have taken," McGuire said. Speaking only of failure to comply with the law's requirements for full reporting on drug testing, he imposed the maximum fines allowed on the corporate defendants — $60,000 on William Merrell, and $20,000 on Richardson-Merrell, which in the fiscal year that ended a few weeks later had consolidated net income of $17,790,000 on sales of $180 million, compared to $17,514,000 on sales of $170 million in the year ended June 30, 1963.

"I have taken the view," Judge McGuire said from the bench, "that responsibility in the background of this case is a failure, for want of a better term, of proper executive, managerial and supervisional control and that the responsibility of what happened falls on the Company and its executive management . . ." As vice president for research, Werner was presumably part of management. The Judge said, however, "I do not think, in this particular defendant's case, there was any willful violation of the statute." He placed Werner and his colleagues King and Van Maanen on probation for six months. Each had faced a maximum sentence of $10,000 and five years in prison.

Judge McGuire did not characterize the acts of withholding and falsifying data about a drug that was prescribed for hundreds of thousands of persons. Those who had expected him to express a sense of shock were disappointed. The sentences imposed on the scientists were unquestionably compassionate. What deterrent and educational impact they may have on others remains to be seen.

The pleas of nolo contendere, which the Judge said were

"tantamount to a plea of guilty," not only averted the publicity that would have accompanied a trial, but also precluded use of a trial record to civil litigants, who generally could not use the indictment or the pleas as evidence.

MER/29 was prescribed to an estimated 418,000 persons. According to Richardson-Merrell, "substantially less than 1 per cent" — fewer than 4180, that is — were injured. The "classical triad" of injuries was usually operable cataracts in both eyes, loss or thinning of hair, and severe skin reactions. Among those who have claimed these and other injuries were between 400 and 500 persons whose approximately 175 lawyers pooled their resources, in a "MER/29 Group," to an extent believed without precedent in a product-liability case. The "Group," whose trustee is Paul D. Rheingold of New York, one of the lawyers who took Mrs. Jordan's deposition, has filed damage suits in 36 states and the District of Columbia.[6]

In the address made by Dr. Walter Modell in 1962 at the convention of the American Association for the Advancement of Science, he described "the pattern for disaster with new drugs: a short-sighted view of all effects; faulty experiments; premature publication; too-vigorous promotion; exaggerated claims; and careless use — in brief, a break in the scientific approach some-

---

[6] In a letter to Senator Humphrey, Rheingold said that in addition to the "classical triad" of injuries there has been "a large number" of other reactions attributed to MER/29, even if less often involved. "These include," he wrote, "liver damage, spleen damage, personality change, diminished libido, impotence, damage to fingernails, sweat glands affected, vomiting and nausea, kidney damage, headaches, loss of normal circulation, pains in various parts of the body, anemia, gastrointestinal upset, ulcerative colitis, diminished adrenocortical function, and fatigue. Some of these, of course, may have only coincidentally occurred with the true reactions to MER/29."
Through April 1965 the outcome of civil damage suits brought by persons claiming to have been injured by MER/29 has been varied. Some have been won, some lost, and some settled. On April 27 in San Francisco, a man who had suffered cataracts was awarded, after a seven-week jury trial, $175,000 in actual and $500,000 in punitive damages. The judgment, which was expected to be appealed, was reportedly the largest in a product-liability case in California history.

where along the line." Perhaps this pattern was not cut to fit the MER/29 case precisely, but it comes close enough for a drug that physicians, in polls reported by the *Medical Research Digest,* had rated the most significant medical advance in medical therapy of 1960 and 1961.

AFTERWORD TO CHAPTER 11

SUBSEQUENT TO the manuscript deadline for *The Therapeutic Nightmare*, the deposition given by Mrs. Beulah Jordan was filed in federal court in New York City during the trial of an MER/29 civil damage suit. It may be recalled that Mrs. Jordan was the animal-laboratory technician whose resignation set off the chain of events which culminated in the criminal proceeding against Richardson-Merrell, Inc., the William S. Merrell Co., and William M. King, Evert F. Van Maanen, and Harold Werner — the three scientists whose crime, perhaps because it was in the laboratory rather than in the streets, brought them a sentence of six months on probation. I will now take up the deposition; other aspects of the MER/29 episode; the release of Atromid-S, which is another cholesterol-blocking drug, and the additional examples referred to in footnote two on page 234 of unfortunate consequences that have flowed from a failure to heed warnings of pharmacologists in the Food and Drug Administration.

MER/29

Mrs. Beulah Jordan gave the deposition about her employment by the William S. Merrell Co., of Cincinnati, on October 9, 1964, to William F. X. Geoghan, counsel for Sidney Roginski,[1] plaintiff in a MER/29 damage suit against Richardson-Merrell,

---

[1] Roginski was awarded $17,000 actual and $100,000 punitive damages. On appeal by the manufacturer, the Second Circuit Court of Appeals reversed the award for punitive damages. Roginski's petition for a rehearing was denied by the appellate court.

Inc. She swore that in the spring of 1959 William King, head of toxicology and pathology, sent her to Evert Van Maanen, his superior, that Van Maanen repeatedly directed her to falsify animal charts and data which were to be submitted to the Food and Drug Administration in order to get MER/29 released to the market, that she complied, that she protested to King who told her to "keep quiet," that she reported the situation to the firm's employment supervisor, and that a couple of weeks later, in June 1959, she resigned. "I wouldn't work with anyone that wanted records changed," she said in the deposition.

Elizabeth Ostopowitz and her husand, Edward, are care-takers for the Westchester County (New York) Society for the Prevention of Cruelty to Animals. After taking MER/29, Mrs. Ostopowitz suffered cataracts, which were removed in two operations; with eyeglasses her vision was corrected to 20/20. For a time her eyebrows and eyelashes were white. At times her skin became so painfully dry that she could not bear to have clothing touch her back. On November 7, 1966, a jury in Supreme Court for Westchester County awarded Mrs. Ostopowitz, a victim of the "classical triad" of MER/29 injuries, a judgment of $1.2 million. No jury in the United States had ever made such a large award in a personal injury case. Its size could be explained neither by the extent of the injuries, because actual damages were set by the jury of six men and six women at $350,000, nor by Mrs. Ostopowitz's station in life — for the loss of her services a separate award of $5000 was made to her husband. To find out why a record of $850,000 in punitive damages had been awarded,[2] I interviewed, for a story in the Washington *Post*, two of the jurors. "After we got down in the jury room," I was told by Mrs. Mary Rydgren of South Salem, New York, "we . . . all came

---

[2] The trial judge later reduced the punitive award to $100,000, for a total judgment of $450,000. The company was seeking in the courts to have larger reductions made — and, of course, counsel for Mrs. Ostopowitz — William F. X. Geoghan, of Speiser, Shumate, Geoghan and Krause in Manhattan — was pressing in the opposite direction.

out with the same remarks, that this company must be punished. Those may not have been the exact words, but this was our whole feeling." As Mrs. Rydgren, who is the wife of an insurance man, saw it, the judgment was to serve "as a warning to all drug companies, that they could not do things like this. Each one of us felt that there but for the grace of God could have been myself or any member of our family, you know." Juror Henry S. Treulieb, a maintenance man for the New York Telephone Company, said in discussing the punitive damages that the manufacturer "had a major responsibility to the public which they failed to fulfill. . . . Any criminal is certainly punished for his crimes, and this we felt was a crime so far as the company was concerned." Yet, Treulieb said, the punitive award was not made because the jury was "mad at anybody." Through most of the 5-week trial, which was held in White Plains in the court of Justice John J. Dillon, the jury sat waiting "for the defense to come out," Treulieb said. "But it never came . . ." What did come before the jury was a massive outpouring of material that counsel for Mrs. Ostopowitz had obtained from the company's files. To a large degree, the explanation for the punitive damages lay in these documents. Their damaging nature can be illustrated with a series in which the first paper was an interdepartmental memo to Dr. Robert H. McMaster, associate director of medical research in the William Merrell firm in Cincinnati. The memo, which was written in 1961, the year after marketing of MER/29 began, informed him that Dr. Garfield Duncan, of Pennsylvania Hospital in Philadelphia, "has 3 women on MER/29 who have had loss of hair." Dr. McMaster got off a letter to Dr. Duncan saying, "At the moment, we are not sure of the possible association between . . . triparanol and this phenomenon." But on March 23, 1961, a mere three days after telling Dr. Duncan he was "not sure," the Merrell executive was expressing "the feeling of the Department of Medical Research that there can be *no doubt* of the association." (My italics.) This time, however, Dr. McMaster was not writing a letter to a physician in Philadelphia, but a memo marked "CONFIDENTIAL" to Harold Werner, vice president for research of the Cincinnati firm. Attached to the memo was a tabulation of the reports of 31 physicians on 51 MER/29 patients "who have experienced hair loss, including five who also experienced changes in hair color, and six whose hair changed in texture, usually becoming dry or even brittle." A pressing problem raised about all of this was the absence of hair changes among the side effects listed in the prescribing brochure authorized by the Food and Drug Administration. Dr. McMaster recommended a listing of "changes in color, texture, or amount." The very next day, the matter went all the way to the top, in the form of a memo from Robert H. Woodward, a vice president, to H. Smith Richardson, Jr., chairman of the board of Richardson-Merrell. Woodward enclosed a letter from F. Joseph Murray, the company's liaison with FDA, which suggested that thinning of the hair — but not changes in color or texture — be listed among the side effects. Woodward also said that he and Frank N. Getman, president of William Merrell, "both feel that to protect ourselves against possible damage suits we should make the approach [to the agency] promptly." In handwritten notes on the memo, chairman Richardson said that because disclosure of one of the hair effects, thinning, could be expected in medical publications, it was "Important to get brochure change before this happens." His notation also said, ". . . desirable to play ball with Talbot who got #29 through over protest. Talbot has authority to OK." "Talbot" was Dr. Frank J. Talbot, the FDA officer who had cleared MER/29 for sale over the protest of, among others, agency pharmacologist E. I. Goldenthal.

ATROMID-S

For years, the American Heart Association, among others, has cited increasing evidence that in most persons, the level of choles-terol in the blood can be lowered, and maintained at a lower level, by determined and long-term adherence to a diet designed to decrease the intake of saturated fats and to increase the intake of polyunsaturated fats. Whether a causal relation exists be-tween cholesterol levels and arteriosclerosis remains controver-sial. But arteriosclerosis — which includes coronary artery dis-ease — afflicts millions of Americans and, each year, causes hun-dreds of thousands of them to die. Surely, then, the Association and its allies were acting reasonably when they tried to persuade the Food and Drug Administration that a food represented to be of special dietary use in the intake of fatty acids be accurately labeled as to its content of saturated and unsaturated fats. Soon after becoming Commissioner of the FDA, early in 1966,. Dr. James L. Goddard rejected the Association proposal. Scientists, he ruled, have not "conclusively accepted" manipulation of blood cholesterol levels by changes in diet "as the best way to prevent, treat, or control heart or artery disease." This was con-sistent with rulings in 1959 and 1964 that a causal relation between high cholesterol levels and arteriosclerotic disease "has not been proved," and that a misdemeanor is created by a food label which implies that consumption of polyunsaturated fats could prevent or treat heart or artery disease. The logic of this, how-ever, precluded approving for sale new drugs to lower cholesterol. But there were restraints in addition to logic which presumably were operating. One was that the requested food labeling not only did not create risks to health but held out hope of signifi-cantly reducing those risks. A second was that there is much greater scientific acceptance of the proposition that manipula-tion of blood cholesterol levels by diet is a good way, or the best way, to cope with coronary artery disease than there is acceptance of the idea that drugs are a good or even acceptable way; in fact, the need for cholesterol-lowering drugs is a *hypothesis* being tested by the Coronary Drug Project of the National Heart Institute — FDA's own sister agency in the Department of Health, Education, and Welfare. And there was, or one thought there was, the memory of MER/29.

But in an action that stands out as one of the more perplexing of the early Goddard era FDA actually did it — it approved for marketing Atromid-S (clofibrate). Developed in England, it was to be marketed in the spring of 1967 by Ayerst Laboratories, a division of American Home Products Corporation. Its biochemical mechanism to reduce cholesterol goes to work sooner than MER/29's. And it buoyed FDA to be told that more than 3000 patients had received Atromid-S — some for up to four years — without evident serious problems. The drug was said by Dr. Robert M. Hodges, director of the Office of New Drugs, to lower blood cholesterol levels by 7 to 35 per cent. But the labeling acknowledged that "only after long-term clinical trials have been completed can definite conclusions be drawn." A definite conclusion of a different sort can be drawn here and now: FDA cannot persuasively reconcile its unyielding position on factual food labeling with the release of anticholesterol drugs even before the Coronary Drug Project has established whether such drugs are necessary.

PHARMACOLOGISTS' WARNINGS

The hearings conducted by Representative Fountain, on March 23 and 24 and May 4, 1965, dealt at length with the FDA's Investigational Drug Branch, headed by Dr. Frances O. Kelsey, and its handling of four experimental drugs. A fifth experimental drug within FDA's purview was also examined.

Under the Kefauver-Harris amendments, a manufacturer who deems his testing of an experimental drug in animals sufficiently advanced to warrant the initiation of testing in humans is required to file an application for investigational exemption. However, FDA regulations — the implementation of which gave Fountain cause for concern — do not require the manufacturer to get permission from the Branch before starting clinical trials. Once he has filed the application he is free to begin these trials. The responsibility of the Branch (which, as Fountain said, has been beset by staff and other limitations) is to decide whether, and in what manner, human trials can proceed, and to require such additional animal testing as it believes necessary.

Fountain's Intergovernmental Relations Subcommittee found a pattern in the experience with the four experimental drugs. Summed up here but detailed below, it was that despite serious misgivings among FDA pharmacologists the Branch allowed human experimentation to proceed; serious side effects developed, and the manufacturers halted human testing and withdrew their applications.

The first case involved a Burroughs Wellcome and Company pain-killing and fever-reducing drug being tested for possible antidepressant properties. An FDA pharmacologist reported to Dr. Kelsey that the animal data were insufficient to evaluate its safety, that there were toxic responses, including blood, kidney, and liver disorders, and that "the data . . . do not warrant proceeding with the clinical trials."

Three months afterward, in May 1964, Burroughs Wellcome reported first that hepatitis had been found in a human patient, and then that the investigator believed the drug to have been the cause. Not until June 5 — almost six months after the application was filed — did a medical officer review the *original* data; and, disagreeing with the pharmacologist, he recommended that the human trials already under way "be permitted to continue . . . as originally planned."

Later in June, he reached the company's report of liver damage. His recommendation was merely that receipt of the report be acknowledged. On August 19, the company told FDA that it wished to end human testing, citing as its reasons the case of liver damage and long-term animal toxicity tests that revealed bladder damage at high dosages.

The second drug was an experimental cholesterol-lowering product of G. D. Searle and Co. The preclinical animal testing was found insufficient in a report to Dr. Kelsey by an FDA pharmacologist. He also suggested that there was a possibility of liver damage. His recommendation was that Searle conduct further animal experiments, and that pending submission of the resulting data "any proposed clinical investigations be terminated."

In January 1964 — almost six months afterward — Searle reported a case of myotonia (muscle spasms) in one of 50 human patients and followed up, a few weeks later, with a notification that additional cases of myotonia had been encountered in these patients. The company said it was discontinuing its clinical trials.

Searle's application had been submitted in June 1963, but not until March 1964 was it reviewed by an FDA medical officer. This was a month after the Branch had been notified that trials had been stopped. In April FDA wrote Searle to inquire about the fate of the initial myotonia case. The manufacturer failed to provide the requested information. In August the reviewing medical officer called Dr. Kelsey's attention to this and also asked if a full accounting on all 50 patients should be required. The subcommittee staff was unable to find in Branch files any response to his inquiry.

[Various drug manufacturers sent task forces to the offices of certain news media or resorted to other techniques of pressure to inhibit reviews or mention of _The Therapeutic Nightmare_. G. D. Searle & Co., Inc., distinguished itself by cranking out a multipage mimeographed attack and mailing it under assorted headings to book review editors, book reviewers, medical writers, science writers, and such others as might — and, it turned out, frequently did — have a kind word to say about the book. The candor and quality of the Searle effort is suggested by its failure to note what was clearly noted in _Nightmare_ — that the foregoing material on Searle's experimental cholesterol-lowering drug was not reporting done by me, but a straightforward summary of findings made by the House Intergovernmental Relations Subcommittee. The Subcommittee has confirmed, in writing, that its version of the episode is accurate, and that my summary of its version also is accurate.]

The third drug, a product of Geigy Research Laboratories, was phenothiazene hydrochloride, which was being considered for psychotherapeutic use. In a detailed, three-page paper, an FDA pharmacologist told Dr. Kelsey that additional animal studies were needed to establish safety. He advised that discontinuance of clinical trials be considered. The reviewing medical officer, however, saw nothing alarming in the animal data and approved the design of the clinical trial. His view prevailed.

On February 20, 1964 — ten months after Geigy had submitted its application — E. I. Goldenthal, the MER/29 case pharmacologist who is now chief of the Drug Review Branch, reminded Dr. Kelsey in a memorandum of the initial, adverse pharmacological report. He said nothing had occurred to change it.

While allowing the clinical trials to proceed, Dr. Kelsey asked Geigy on May 7 for the additional animal data that the first pharmacological report, dated July 9, 1963, had said should be obtained. Her request was followed seven weeks later by a notification from Geigy that it was halting human trials. The company enclosed a report from an investigator who said that among 20 patients 2 had developed leukopenia, a blood disease. Different side effects were noted among 6 other patients. In response to an inquiry from Dr. Kelsey, Geigy said it had terminated the experiment because of the drug's lack of efficacy "plus some questionable evidence of side reactions."

The fourth application was for an Upjohn Company antiviral eye ointment. In a one-paragraph report, the reviewing medical officer told Dr. Kelsey that he found no objection to the product, to the method of investigation, or to the investigators. But a detailed report submitted by an FDA pharmacologist pointed to a blood disease, bone-marrow depression, in test animals. He urged that human testing await a series of additional, specified animal tests.

This did not deter the medical officer from reiterating his original, favorable report. Following this, a second pharmacologist backed up the first and, a few days after that, a third adverse pharmacological report was submitted. Only eight days after the third report, Upjohn notified FDA that among 10 volunteers treated with the eye ointment 6 had developed irritations. The company said that it was suspending human testing. When FDA asked for additional information eight months later, Upjohn disclosed that in 11 normal volunteers in a previous experiment the ointment had caused severe conjunctivitis and corneal opacities, both temporary.

A fifth experimental drug was administered to 1000 enfeebled test patients. Eighty of them died within varying periods of time and with varying degrees of possibility of eliminating causal relationship to administration of the drug. Despite the requirements of the Kefauver-Harris Amendments, these deaths were not reported to the Investigational Drug Branch. The disclosure awaited the subsequent filing of a new-drug application for marketing by the manufacturer, Smith Kline & French Laboratories. The application was rejected. The drug was a combination of two diuretics, triamterene and hydrochlorothiazide. By June 6, 1963, when the application was received by the Branch, human testing on a substantial scale was already under way. In this case, the reviewing medical officer found some of the animal data inadequate and some of the results in human volunteers abnormal, but he concluded that with certain precautions the human trials should be permitted to continue. The FDA pharmacologist assigned to the drug found the animal studies insufficient to permit evaluation of its safety. In addition, he was troubled by reports of adverse blood effects in patients receiving triamterene.

In a subsequent evaluation based upon additional animal data submitted by the company, the pharmacologist found indications that the combination drug induces kidney and possibly liver damage. He urged that further human trials be ended unless certain clinical data be made available to the Branch at once. The manufacturer, he said, "has not demonstrated an adequate margin of safety between the toxic levels of the combination of drugs in animals and the human dosages indicated in the IND [investigational new-drug application]."

On April 15, 1964, Dr. Merle Gibson, assistant chief of the Branch, wrote Smith Kline & French that test patients were not being adequately monitored. He requested that frequent studies be done to measure liver, kidney, and bone-marrow function. Replying six days later, the company said it had a considerable amount of additional data of the kind requested and would include it in the new-drug application for marketing that was expected to be filed within a few days (and was filed on April 23). The new-drug application disclosed the 80 deaths. They occurred during or shortly after treatment with the diuretic combination or with the triamterene component alone. In 16 cases, the company reported, death occurred two weeks to nine months after administration of the combination or its components had been stopped, and analysis had revealed no causal relationship.

In the remaining 64 cases, the company said, there had been complications, which were set out in a table. On September 17, 1964, the reviewing medical officer, recommending that marketing not be permitted, said: "This application does not support the safety and efficacy of this drug combination. 80 deaths have been reported in a total of less than 1000 case reports with varying dosages. Although the population involved had a significantly poor prognosis . . . the possible role of this drug in the fatal outcome cannot be eliminated . . ."

[Subsequently, the FDA gave approval to the diuretic combination, which Smith Kline & French marketed under the trade name Dyazide.]

12

THALIDOMIDE AND
"EXALTED STANDARDS"

THE STORY OF THALIDOMIDE everyone knows is that the stubbornness, skepticism, and devotion to duty of a Food and Drug Administration medical officer averted a horrible tragedy, and that President Kennedy conferred upon her the nation's highest award for distinguished federal civilian service. But there is another thalidomide story, developed largely by the Humphrey Subcommittee on Reorganization and International Organizations, which puts in grave doubt any assignment of credit to FDA's top echelon for the achievement of Dr. Frances Oldham Kelsey.

The William S. Merrell Company filed a new-drug application for Kevadon, as it called thalidomide, in September 1960. By this time, Merrell's F. Joseph Murray had got MER/29 onto the market and was free to concentrate on Dr. Kelsey. She saw Kevadon merely as one more sleeping pill, insisted on proof of safety, and would not be hurried. Her pharmacologist husband, F. Ellis Kelsey, was one who saw no reason for haste. In a memorandum he commented acidly on data Merrell submitted in December 1960, about six weeks after the firm had assured its salesmen that Kevadon's safety had been "firmly established," and that they should "appeal to the doctor's ego." The memorandum, which has been published by the Humphrey subcommittee, described one section of the data as "an interesting collection of meaningless pseudoscientific jargon apparently intended to impress chemically unsophisticated readers." Of other data that he said violated an elementary concept of pharmacology, Ellis Kelsey wrote, "I cannot believe this to be honest incompetence."

The whole thing must have been maddening to the company. Other licensees were selling the stuff over the counter, like aspirin, in twenty countries. Thalidomide had passed the Hussey-Stetler Test of Time. And here — as Merrell saw it — was a bureaucratic nitpicker sitting in her drab little office not really caring a hoot about its plans to market Kevadon early in 1961.

Merrell representatives "were in day after day, trying to hurry her up to approve this," reporter Clark R. Mollenhoff of the Washington Bureau of Cowles Publications reminded Commissioner George P. Larrick on a National Educational Television program in October 1963. "Do you feel this was proper conduct?" "I don't worry about pressure," Larrick replied. "I feel that Government people, people in responsible places in Government, are going to be put under pressure. Of course there are people who respond to pressure, but I don't believe that pressure in this situation was particularly bothersome."

Not bothersome?

At one point Dr. Kelsey complained to Merrell that it had learned, but had "not forthrightly disclosed" to her, that the sedative had been associated with peripheral neuritis. This was a crucial finding, she has said. It hardened her resolve not to let the sedative go on sale. In response, the company wrote to one of Dr. Kelsey's superiors that it considered her complaint, to cite the ominous phrase, "somewhat libelous," and she was bothered enough to consult a lawyer.

After seven months of getting nowhere Murray told Dr. Kelsey's chief, Dr. Ralph G. Smith, that Merrell management "thought that he had failed to get the application through by the

usual methods and that there should be some pressure exerted"
— meaning, Dr. Smith said in a memorandum on the conversation, that R. H. Woodward, a Merrell vice president, intended
to knock on the door of the Commissioner himself "if nothing
was going to be done."

In the voluminous record compiled by the Humphrey subcommittee there is nothing to show that the FDA decision-
makers shielded Dr. Kelsey, who was handling the very first new-
drug application of her FDA career, from more than fifty Merrell "contacts," most of which were made by the persistent
Murray, who was himself under pressure from the home office.
All of this was more than "bothersome." If Dr. Kelsey had given
in, say, in February 1961, an estimated 10,000 American babies
might have been born armless and legless by the time the deforming effects of thalidomide had become known and marketing halted. Having claimed that the pressure he allowed to be
exerted was not very important, Commissioner Larrick has taken
the logical next step of asserting that "the system, the laws" provided the indispensable milieu for Dr. Kelsey's stand. He made
this assertion in October 1963, on National Educational Television, and it was challenged on the same program.

"Well, it surely wasn't a triumph of the system, because the
system was not geared to catch this sort of development," Senator Humphrey said. A Republican member of his subcommittee, Senator Karl E. Mundt of South Dakota, agreed. "I don't
think the system was successful at that time because the system
was permitting the use of thalidomide . . . the system had
some loopholes which were plugged by her [Dr. Kelsey's] feminine curiosity, I say, and her diligence and her talents . . ."

In an earlier round of the same argument, Dr. Helen B. Taussig, the Johns Hopkins pediatrician who made a firsthand,
thorough investigation of the thalidomide disaster in Europe,
told the House Antitrust subcommittee in May 1962, "Most
opinions were that the drug [thalidomide] could have passed the

Food and Drug Administration here." Dr. Taussig held to this view months later in an article she wrote for *Scientific American* of August 1962. Kevadon did not reach the American market, she said, "because of a lucky combination of circumstances" and the alertness of Dr. Kelsey, "not because of the existence of any legal requirement that the drug might have failed to meet."

> If thalidomide had been developed in this country [it was developed in West Germany], I am convinced that it would easily have found wide distribution before its terrible power to cause deformity had become apparent. The marketing techniques of the pharmaceutical industry, which can saturate the country with a new drug almost as soon as it leaves the laboratory, would have enabled thalidomide to produce thousands of deformed infants in the U.S.

✓ ✓ ✓

At the end of November 1961, word came from West Germany that thalidomide had been associated with birth deformities. A person of ordinary sensitivities might have envisioned the possibility of limbless babies being born here, found it of utmost urgency to sound a public warning, and at once ordered FDA's inspectors to retrieve every last thalidomide pill. Perhaps our scientific attaché in Bonn, Dr. Hermann I. Chinn, is an ordinary man. In a prompt, accurate, and complete dispatch to the Department of State he reported that the German pediatrician Dr. Widukind Lenz "knows of some 80 cases and has been told of 70 additional cases." Dr. Chinn suggested that the American public be warned. The copy he designated for delivery to the FDA was received by Commissioner Larrick's office on January 11, 1962.

"The conviction is universally held," *Drug Trade News* said late in 1962, "that Commissioner Larrick has conformed to exalted standards." Perhaps it was to these standards that he

was conforming when he failed to tell the medical officer responsible for the thalidomide application, Dr. Kelsey, of Dr. Chinn's
dispatch and issued no warning. The Commissioner did not
require Merrell to retrieve all the pills that could be retrieved.
He let Merrell decide what should be done. What Merrell did
was to have its medical director, Dr. John N. Premi, send out a
drug-warning letter dated December 5, 1961:

DEAR DOCTOR: We have received information from abroad
on the occurrence of congenital malformations in the offspring of a few mothers who had taken thalidomide (marketed in Canada as Kevadon) early in their pregnancies. It is
impossible at this time to determine whether, in fact, there
is any causal relationship.

However, until definitive information is available to us, as
a precaution we are adding the following contraindication to
the use of Kevadon:

Kevadon should not be administered to pregnant
women nor to premenopausal women who may become pregnant.

We are actively following this matter and you will be
advised when it is finally determined whether or not this precautionary step was necessary.

It came out later that Dr. Premi's letter was sent to only about
10 per cent of the investigators to whom Merrell had distributed
thalidomide — those the firm considered "active" because they
had received the drug in the preceding year. This distinction
managed to put into the inactive category the several hundred
physicians who had been enlisted in November 1960, when Merrell's great campaign, the "Kevadon Hospital Clinical Program,"
had been conducted. For fifteen more weeks, until Merrell sent
out letters in March 1962 to *all* of its investigators requesting

that thalidomide pills be destroyed or returned, 90 per cent had no inkling that it was dangerous to give thalidomide to women of childbearing age. Thus did Merrell proceed with what Commissioner Larrick would later, when he knew the facts, describe as "reasonable diligence."

On May 31, 1962, Dr. Kelsey sounded to Dr. Ralph Smith, head of the Division of New Drugs, what most would interpret as an alarm. In a memorandum published by the Senate Reorganization subcommittee she said:

> On February 23, 1961, we requested a complete list of investigators to whom the drug had been furnished so that we could ascertain whether adverse neurological effects had been recorded with the use of the drug.
>
> On February 28, 1961, the company supplied a list of investigators who had used the drug for periods of 4 months or longer. There were 56 physicians on this list. This was followed up by the results of a canvass among physicians for signs of neuropathy. Thirty-five physicians replied . . . Note that this did not really answer our request for a complete list of investigators to whom the drug had been furnished.

The company documents mentioned here in Chapter 7 show that the number of studies set up numbered 168 at the end of the first week in November 1960, 418 at the end of two weeks, and 762 after four weeks. Of course, few of the investigators involved had used Kevadon "four months or longer" when Dr. Kelsey's request for a complete list was received.

Dr. Kelsey's memorandum of May also reported to Dr. Smith that on April 11, 1962, she had asked Merrell to supply "a complete and up-to-date list of all physicians supplied with the drug," and for information on what the company had done to inform them of the dangers at the time the risk of deformities had first become known. Two weeks later the company had sent

her a copy of the December letter signed by Dr. Premi and sent
to an estimated 137 investigators. In response to her request for
a complete list, Merrell had forwarded a total she found staggering — 1070 physicians, including 241 obstetricians and gynecologists, in 39 states and the District of Columbia. Subsequent lists
supplied by other affiliates of Richardson-Merrell, along with
additions and corrections, increased the grand total to 1267.

Also enclosed with Merrell's letter of April 25 to Dr. Kelsey
were copies of the two destroy-or-return letters. One or the other
of these had been sent on March 20 to all physicians who had
received thalidomide. One letter, Dr. Kelsey told Dr. Smith,
was intended for physicians who had been sent Dr. Premi's
December mailing, as evidenced by the fact that it referred to
the earlier letter. The second, however, "makes no reference to
any previous communication regarding malformed babies . . ."
In a further comment Dr. Kelsey said:

> Merrell in [both March 20 letters] . . . states that from
> their investigations and surveys to date, no causal relationship
> between thalidomide and teratogenic [deforming] effects had
> been established. The National Drug Co. [a Richardson-
> Merrell subsidiary] in a letter to all investigators dated Janu-
> ary 11, 1962, stated that Dr. Lenz (who had first drawn atten-
> tion to the teratogenic effect) emphasized that an etiologic
> [causative] relationship . . . had in no way been established.
> Yet, in the "Letters to the Editor" section of *Lancet*, January
> 6, 1962, February 3, 1962, Dr. Lenz presents overwhelming
> evidence to support his belief that thalidomide is teratogenic
> in man.

In summary, the FDA hierarchy had been warned, in the most
emphatic terms, that thalidomide was indicated to be baby-
deforming, that the pills had gone to more than 1000 physicians,
and that the manufacturer's enterprise in retrieving the pills had

fallen far short of its enterprise in sowing them. Content to leave it to Merrell, the FDA top echelon did nothing.

Meanwhile, Dr. Helen Taussig had returned to Baltimore from Europe. Her investigation had convinced her that a direct relationship existed between the incidence of deformities and the introduction and sales volume of the drug — a correlation that later events established beyond question.

Although the American Medical Association rejected her proposal to print an early warning letter in its *Journal*, apparently because of pique that *Time* had published a story first, Dr. Taussig did everything in her power to communicate a warning to physicians. She wrote articles, including the one the that AMA *Journal* published much later — at the end of June 1962 — made speeches, and testified in Congress. She felt the greatest urgency about all of this, particularly because each day a new group of women entered the critical period in early pregnancy when the pill could have its horrible effects. One of her former students is Dr. John O. Nestor, the FDA medical officer. In April 1962 he arranged a meeting between her and Dr. Kelsey, which he also attended. Dr. Taussig was "most eager to give any support she could" to FDA, Dr. Kelsey wrote in a memorandum published by the Humphrey subcommittee. Her offer was not accepted.

In May, FDA's Bureau of Medicine confidentially rated no data from any Richardson-Merrell affiliate "reliable without thorough verification." In June, Dr. Taussig told Dr. Kelsey and Dr. Nestor that many physicians had an initial "reluctance" to believe that thalidomide caused deformities. FDA did nothing to dispel the reluctance.

On July 15 the Washington *Post* broke the story about how Dr. Kelsey had prevented the birth of thousands of deformed children in the United States. This set off a flareup of worldwide concern, which was fueled in no small degree by publicity about Mrs. Sherri Finkbine, an Arizona woman who had taken thalidomide during early pregnancy (and who later obtained an abortion in Sweden; the fetus was deformed).

With this Commissioner Larrick finally unleashed his inspectors in a crash program to retrieve thalidomide.

✓ ✓ ✓

"There are, perhaps, few men who can for any great length of time enjoy office and power without being more or less under the influence of feelings unfavorable to the faithful discharge of their public duties," President Jackson said at his first inaugural in 1832. The quotation, which is recalled in *Conflict of Interest in Federal Service*,[1] continued: "Their integrity may be proof against improper considerations immediately addressed to themselves, but they are apt to acquire a habit of looking with indifference upon the public interests and of tolerating conduct from which an unpracticed man would revolt."

More than a century later, Senator Paul H. Douglas wrote in *Ethics in Government* that a "disease which afflicts bureaucracy is the tendency to dehumanize decisions . . . While greater detachment is obtained, the human factor is almost always left out of consideration. The bureaucracy is defective in imagination and somewhat wanting in sympathy."

On August 1, 1962, Senator Jacob K. Javits of New York had this exchange with Commissioner Larrick at a hearing of the Humphrey subcommittee:

> SENATOR JAVITS. You have the power to order a withdrawal?
> COMMISSIONER LARRICK. I think we do, yes.
> SENATOR JAVITS. And in this case did you actually order it?
> COMMISSIONER LARRICK. No.

[1] A book by a Special Committee on the Federal Conflict of Interest Laws of the Association of the Bar of the City of New York and published in 1960 by the Harvard University Press.

SENATOR JAVITS. Was it withdrawn as quickly as you would have ordered it withdrawn, considering the data available?

COMMISSIONER LARRICK. I think the firm proceeded with reasonable diligence to get the drug off the market. I do not think any drug firm, to date, can do as good a job of getting a drug completely off the market as we can. And in spite of the fact that they tried very hard, we have, within the last few days, still found some of the drug on the market.

SENATOR JAVITS. When you say "as we can," would you have issued an order that everybody was to turn this drug in — could the FDA have done that?

COMMISSIONER LARRICK. I think we could have brought about a situation where, if we had gone to all the distributors ourselves, it would have been. But I am not quarreling with what the firm did.

SENATOR JAVITS. But we would like to know why you did not do it. Why did you not do it — you first got the first intelligence in February 1961. [This refers to Dr. Kelsey's chance discovery in the *British Medical Journal* that thalidomide had been associated with peripheral neuritis.] Apparently the case was conclusively proved to the satisfaction of the very wonderful doctor in charge, Dr. Kelsey, by November, 1961. Then what happened?

Then did you just talk to the company in general?

COMMISSIONER LARRICK. It was not conclusively proved at that stage.

SENATOR JAVITS. When was it?

COMMISSIONER LARRICK. There was strong circumstantial — there would be people who would give you an argument about it now. There is no question in our minds. But there are people whose opinions have a right to some weight, who would say that the problem here has been exaggerated. Nevertheless, the drug is off the market.

SENATOR JAVITS. When was the Department, in your opinion, in a position to make a finding that this drug should be withdrawn?

COMMISSIONER LARRICK. It never was necessary, when they issued instructions to all their doctors . . .

SENATOR JAVITS. But it was necessary, Mr. Larrick, if you had this information in your hands, let us say, in November of 1961 and it is now [August] 1962, and you say that this has been withdrawn from the doctors only really a few days ago, completely.

COMMISSIONER LARRICK. I did not say that.

SENATOR JAVITS. You did not say that?

COMMISSIONER LARRICK. I think with rare exceptions the doctors obeyed the injunctions that they got from the company.

Conclusive proof is a standard commonly invoked by drug-makers, by industries that pollute the air and the streams, and by manufacturers of pesticides that poison the land and fish and wildlife. It is, however, a standard too exalted to be workable in protecting the public health. "In law, the suspect is innocent until his guilt has been proved beyond doubt," Dr. Leroy E. Burney, Surgeon General of the Public Health Service during the Eisenhower Administration, said in 1958. In a speech before the National Conference on Air Pollution, the head of FDA's sister agency in the Department of Health, Education, and Welfare warned against applying the standard of the criminal law for determining innocence or guilt to the protection of human health, because

absolute proof often comes late. To wait for it is to invite disaster, or at least to suffer unnecessarily through long periods of time.

Many years ago, long before anyone had seen a germ or positively identified a single causative agent of epidemic diseases, farsighted leaders observed the association between epidemics and filth. Wherever they had sufficient foresight to act on this circumstantial evidence, they made striking progress. Cleaning up the city filth resulted in better health. Years later they found out why.

It was not conclusive proof that had to be in hand, but evidence of an imminent danger to the public health. Commissioner Larrick had that. Nothing prevented him from sounding a public warning. Nothing prevented him from sending out his highly capable inspectors to retrieve Kevadon pills. Nothing compelled him to leave it to Merrell.

The Commissioner said there was a doubt — some, probably in Merrell, "would say that the problem here has been exaggerated." Unfortunately, the benefit of the doubt in George Larrick's FDA went not to the children who could be spared a life without limbs, but to a drug company with which he was not quarreling. The benefit of the doubt continued to go to the company even after the FDA knew that it had delayed issuing a warning to most of its thalidomide investigators for three and one-half months, even after FDA had declared data submitted by the company on MER/29 fraudulent, and even after all Merrell data had become suspect and put into a temporary quarantine for verification. Of these things the Commissioner gave the subcommittee not the slightest hint.

✓ ✓ ✓

Six days after Commissioner Larrick testified, a plea was made — by President Kennedy — that all unidentified pills be cleared out of medicine cabinets and destroyed. The plea was made necessary by the initial tally on the crash program of thalidomide retrieval begun during the worldwide furor. It showed that substantial quantities of thalidomide pills were still at large.

Two weeks later, on August 23, 1962, the Food and Drug Administration reported a final count. Since 1959 a total of

2,528,412 "experimental" thalidomide tablets, and "lesser quantities of liquids and powders containing the drug," had been distributed. Inspectors recovered 25,076 *unlabeled* tablets from the 79 physicians who still had supplies on hand. The pills came in a variety of sizes and colors.

The FDA statement also reported that of the 1267 physicians who had received thalidomide, 1168 had been interviewed, and of these:

More than 50 percent had no record of the quantities returned or destroyed pursuant to the manufacturer's instructions. There is no way of knowing the amounts actually returned or destroyed . . .

Most of the doctor-investigators said that they had received the manufacturer's advice in March 1962 to stop using the drug, but 85 said they were not warned of adverse reactions and 42 said they did not get any message from the manufacturer. The notice to discontinue was given by letters, with followup phone calls and visits by detail men beginning in March and continuing through July 1962.

Doctors interviewed reported that 19,822 patients had received thalidomide [perhaps 2000 more had obtained it from foreign sources]. Of these, 3,760 were women of childbearing age, of whom 624 were reported as pregnant. According to the doctors, most of the pregnant patients got the drug in the last trimester of pregnancy or just prior to delivery . . .

When asked if they had signed a statement on their qualifications, required by FDA regulations to be obtained by the manufacturers, 640 doctors stated they had signed such statements but 247 said they had not. Others said they could not remember or did not answer the question.

Written reports were made to the manufacturer by 276 doctors, and 102 doctors said they gave verbal reports. Many of the verbal reports were given to company detail men. Others made no reports or did not answer the question.

According to FDA's "final figure," 10 deformed babies were born to American women who had obtained thalidomide from domestic sources and taken it in the critical first trimester of pregnancy. In 7 more cases, thalidomide from foreign sources was reportedly taken during the first trimester. In addition to these 17 cases, the agency said, there were 9 cases of deformities in which thalidomide either was taken late in pregnancy or might have been taken, since proof was lacking that it actually had been taken.

In West Germany alone the total of thalidomide babies reached 5900, according to an estimate made in 1963 by Dr. Lenz, the great pediatrician who had established thalidomide as the causal agent. In Hamburg the rate had reached one or two per thousand births. Among the first 5000 babies born in Hamburg nine months *after* the drug was withdrawn from sale were two that were deformed. Both were born to mothers who had missed the highly publicized warning issued by the West German Government. Although Commissioner Larrick and spokesmen for the American drug industry were saying even at that time that our drug laws were the strictest in the world, and that thalidomide was being freely sold abroad rather than being merely "tested" as in the United States, the fact is that the Bonn government, like the Australian and British, did not wait for conclusive proof before recalling thalidomide.

In Japan the drug was not taken off the market until May 1962, when 700 cases of phocomelia had been reported. In Italy sales were not halted completely until September 1962, despite an outbreak of birth deformities in Turin two months earlier.

In these and other countries, Dr. Taussig reported in the *New England Journal of Medicine* for July 11, 1963, part of the problem was the "evils of camouflage" — the profusion of trade names for thalidomide.

✦ ✦ ✦

On March 30, 1963, an editorial in the *Lancet* said: "With our present knowledge, it would be hard to refute the hypothesis that all drugs of therapeutic value are potentially toxic to the embryo of some animal if the right conditions of timing and dosage can be achieved. Indeed some teratologists [specialists in deformities] would not entirely oppose the view that a drug is either a teratogen or a placebo."

The fear of these teratologists was intensified by at least two reports made in the following year. In the *British Medical Journal* for April 25, 1964, Dr. Cecilia Lutwak-Mann, of the Agricultural Research Council Unit of Reproductive Physiology and Biochemistry, the University of Cambridge, said she had produced birth defects in rabbits by giving large doses of thalidomide *to the males exclusively*. The progeny of 27 out of 40 litters suffered some deleterious effect ascribable to treatment of the fathers with the drug. "It is fully recognized," the researcher wrote, "that the results of experiments limited to one species of laboratory animals must not be taken as necessarily carrying a great weight and validity for humans; nevertheless, they serve as a useful monitoring device . . ."

In December 1964 a report on two antihistamines to the annual meeting of the American Association for the Advancement of Science increased awareness that thalidomide is but one of many drugs that can cross the placental barrier and can harm a human embryo in what once had been thought to be a perfectly insulated environment. One of the antihistamines reported on by C. T. G. King, an endocrinologist at the National Institute of Dental Research, is meclizine (sold as meclizine hydrochloride). In the United States it is prescribed and also sold without prescription for use against motion sickness and against morning sickness in pregnant women; in Sweden it was withdrawn from the market in 1962 because of its suspected potential to deform the fetus. The other drug is chlorcyclizine (sold as chlorcyclizine hydrochloride), which is commonly prescribed to asthmatics.

Unlike other antihistamines tested at the Institute, King said, meclizine, chlorcyclizine, and several chemically related substances are partially converted in experimental animals to nor-chlorcyclizine, a so-called metabolic breakdown product. When the drugs in question were administered to test animals during specific days of pregnancy the unborn young were commonly found to have an array of deformities of the face and mouth, including cleft palate, fusion of the tongue to the palate, under-developed jaw, and small mouth. Skeletal deformities also occurred. In the young with malformations the metabolic breakdown product was present; in the normal young it was not. "I want to emphasize," King said in his AAAS paper, "that although at the present time we cannot translate animal experimental congenital malformations to terms of human experience we still cannot and should not ignore the results obtained." [2]

✶   ✶   ✶

"To possess the end and yet not be responsible for the means, to grasp the fruit while disavowing the tree, to escape being told the cost until someone has paid it irrevocably" — this, said the late moral philosopher Professor Edmond Cahn, of the New York University School of Law, "is the most pervasive of moral syndromes, the one most characteristic of so-called respectable

[2] A special FDA committee — none of whose findings has been made public — was said by the trade press to have recommended unanimously early in 1964 that the antihistamines reported on by King be dispensed only by prescription, with a warning in the labeling that the safety of their use in pregnant women had not been established. If implemented, this would have provided insurance against deformities — at the expense, of course, of substantial over-the-counter sales, some of which are based on manufacturers' advice to pregnant women that the products are effective against nausea.

FDA accepted neither recommendation. Instead, almost a year later, it reconvened the committee, which then proposed, the Pink Sheet reported on May 3, 1965, a substitute recommendation. This was that nonprescription sales be allowed to continue, the only suggested precaution being that the labeling advise pregnant women not to take the pills except on the advice of a physician.

Clearly, this would afford protection to the pillmakers — but not to a woman in early pregnancy who was not yet aware of her condition and who could, if she did not innocently buy the pills over the counter, get them from an airline stewardess to relieve nausea experienced in the air. Additional information dealing with birth deformities will be found in the afterword to this chapter.

man in a civilized society." In an essay in *Drugs in Our Society*[3] he went on to say:

> In the days of the outcry against thalidomide, how much of popular indignation might be attributed to this same syndrome; how many were furious because their own lack of scruple had been exposed! So many did not really care, did not even want to know what the new drugs might cost in terms of human injuries and fatalities. The dispensers of thalidomide had outraged the public by breaking an unwritten law — the law against interrupting the public's enjoyment of fruits with disagreeable revelations about the tree and the soil where the fruits have grown . . .
>
> . . . As we in our day can smile condescendingly at the primitives and ancients who practiced human sacrifice for what they considered to be the general good of the tribe or nation, future generations may ask how we could make human sacrifices more acceptable in our day by calling it "social cost" [of progress]. At least the ancients were honest; they called a spade a spade . . .

[3] Edited by Paul Talalay and published in 1964 by the Johns Hopkins Press.

The case of the antihistamines suspected to have a capability of causing birth defects was one which lent itself to a paraphrase of the pervasive moral syndrome described by the late Professor Edmond Cahn: The manufacturers would possess the end and yet not be responsible for the means, thanks to the Food and Drug Administration of Commissioner George P. Larrick and Medical Director Joseph F. Sadusk, Jr.; thus would the makers "grasp the fruit while disavowing the tree, to escape being told the cost until someone has paid it irrevocably." I will tell that story and follow it with the additional information dealing with birth deformities referred to in footnote two on page 263; this, in turn, will be followed by parenthetical material which has become available since publication of *The Therapeutic Nightmare*.

THE SUSPECTED ANTIHISTAMINES

The situation concerning antihistamines with a suspected birth-deforming potential was largely hidden until an inquiry was held on June 8 and 9, 1965, by the House Intergovernmental Relations Subcommittee. On April 5, 1963, C. T. G. King of the National Institute of Dental Research had sent a memorandum to Commissioner George P. Larrick of the Food and Drug Administration. King told of studies showing that meclizine caused congenital abnormalities in rats; soon, however, the same kind of evidence also implicated cyclizine and chlorcyclizine. For years, meclizine had been sold by Chas. A. Pfizer & Co., Inc., and its J. B. Roerig & Company division by prescription as Bonine (changed from Bonamine), without prescription as chewable tables called Bonadettes, and in a prescription combination product called Bonadoxin. Cyclizine was sold by Burroughs Wellcome & Co. as a prescription and nonprescription drug trade-named Marezine. Chlorcyclizine was sold by the same company as Perazile, and as a prescription and over-the-counter item. The meclizine and cyclizine products were available for treatment of nausea (and were *promoted* for the nausea of pregnancy), for dizziness and for motion sickness; and chlorcyclizine for allergies, colds, hay fever, and insect bites. The drugs had been taken by millions of women. At least in FDA's Bureau of Medicine there were indications that something had been learned from thalidomide. Six days after the King memo was received — that is, on April 11, 1963 — the Bureau launched a plan to consult outside experts and take other essential steps. On May 7 Dr. Ralph G. Smith, acting head of the Bureau, recommended that over-the-counter sales be ended and that consideration be given to sending a warning letter to physicians. (At the time, the Bureau knew of forty cases of birth defects throughout the world which had been reported "in association" with meclizine-containing products alone.) In addition, Dr. Smith advised that the statement "safe use in pregnancy has not been established" be added to the prescription labeling. The companies were resistant, although Burroughs Wellcome was agreeable to saying on nonprescription labeling that use in pregnancy should be only on the advice of a physician. The firm had already done this in Britain. The offer was considered inadequate and was rejected.

The thalidomide episode had produced no great sense of urgency in Commissioner Larrick and his administrative entourage. He testified at the Subcommittee hearing that he did not implement the advice of FDA's physicians because the fifteen experts on whom the Bureau of Medicine had relied did not want to be identified and would not be available as witnesses in a court action expected to be produced by the resistance of Pfizer and Burroughs Wellcome and would therefore leave the FDA with a weak case. This superficially plausible statement was demolished when the Subcommittee, which does its homework, produced a memorandum from FDA's own files in which Dr. Arthur Ruskin, then acting Director of the Division of New Drugs, said, "Experts will come to our aid if we get into court." The view of the Commissioner and Assistant Commissioner Winton B. Rankin was that an ad hoc committee should be formed from which a formal recommendation could be obtained. This group met on April 20, 1964 — nineteen days after Dr. Sadusk joined FDA as Medical Director — and agreed unanimously with the agency medical staff that nonprescription sales of the suspect drugs should be halted, and that a warning should be added to the prescription labeling. But the Commissioner's office stalled. When an inquiry was made by Dr. Matthew Ellenhorn, then Chief of the Drug Surveillance Branch, on June 11, seven weeks after the ad hoc committee met, he was told that the summary of the committee's meeting was not "official" and that an official recommendation had to be obtained. Another burden, Dr. Sadusk testified before the House Subcommittee, was preparing an acceptable set of minutes. Thus was inaction extended from April 1963 into 1965.

On January 18, 1965, the official report, which by then had been obtained, was transmitted to the Commissioner by Dr. Sadusk, who noted in writing that the Bureau of Medicine "endorses the conclusions reached by this committee." He advised that the manufacturers be asked to issue a warning letter to the medical profession; if they refuse, he said, "we would advise issuance of a notice of hearing to show cause why approval of the applications [new-drug applications under which marketing was permitted] should not be withdrawn."

But Dr. Sadusk did not really mean it, or at least did not mean it for long. He withdrew the recommendation 48 to 72 hours after it was made because, he told the House Subcommittee, more data and review were necessary. The mental attitude was indistinguishable from that in the thalidomide case: when there is, or is claimed to be, a doubt, give the benefit of it not to the pregnant woman and her embryo, but to the manufacturer. This attitude prevailed although other drugs serving the same purposes as meclizine, cyclizine, and chlorcyclizine were available and were not suspect, just as sedatives other than thalidomide had been available and were not suspect.

The ad hoc committee, now called the Advisory Committee on the Teratogenic Effect of Certain Drugs, but headed as before by Dr. Howard C. Taylor, Jr., chairman and professor of obstetrics and gynecology at the College of Physicians and Surgeons in New York City, was reconvened on April 22, 1965, two years after the alert came in from the National Institute of Dental Research. The expectation of, among others, Dr. Josef Warkany, a research professor in pediatrics at the University of Cincinnati College of Medicine who was consultant to the ad hoc group, was that essentially the same conclusions would be reached as had been reached in April 1964; in fact, he thought very little would be gained from a second meeting. However, four members of the Advisory Committee were unable to attend the second meeting and were replaced. The altered group then voted 8 to 1, with one abstention, to reverse its previous recommendation about nonprescription sales and advised that such sales be permitted to continue. The Advisory Group did suggest that a warning to pregnant women to consult a physician be added to the over-the-counter labeling, but this was not accompanied by an explanation of what use this would be to a woman who was unaware of her condition.

The Advisory Committee had, Dr. Sadusk assured the House Subcommittee, "convincing" controlled studies indicating no

risk to women who took normal doses of the suspect antihistamines. But Delphis C. Goldberg and W. Donald Gray of the
Subcommittee staff had, as always, done their homework. They
produced a letter from the National Institutes of Health, where
one of the studies referred to by Dr. Sadusk was still under way,
which said that the data he relied upon permitted no conclusions as to safety, one way or another. Dr. Sadusk also placed
great emphasis on certain incomplete studies at the University
of California at Berkeley. On July 26, 1966, Dr. James L.
Goddard, the new Commissioner of FDA, informed Subcommittee Chairman L. H. Fountain that a review of the records
of the Advisory Committee meeting had unearthed "no indication" that the statistical significance of the data in either study
had been discussed.

Another factor in the situation was the *laissez faire* attitude
of Dr. Sadusk who testified that, as a physician, he "never was
truly convinced of the desirability of putting these items on
prescription" and who failed to transmit to the Commissioner
the contrary views of his subordinates in the Bureau of Medicine, including Dr. Frances O. Kelsey. He admitted that it
was the "rank and file of physicians" — not the "scientific obstetrician" — who believed meclizine and cyclizine to be effective
against nausea in pregnancy, although the notions of the "rank
and file" had no standing under the law, which requires efficacy
to be demonstrated by substantial evidence obtained in well-
controlled clinical investigations.

At the start of the Fountain hearing Dr. Sadusk had indicated
that a final decision on prescription sales was a few weeks off.
Congressman Fountain then read aloud a letter from Commissioner Larrick saying, 5½ weeks *before* the hearing, that a decision to continue nonprescription sales was all but final. Presumably because of the heat created by the hearing, and not because
of prior intent, a decision was delayed until October 1965 when
Dr. Sadusk addressed the American Academy of Pediatrics in

Chicago. He announced that FDA intended to require in the over-the-counter labeling a warning against use not only by women who are pregnant, but by women "who may possibly become pregnant, unless directed by a physician, since this drug may have the potentiality of injuring the unborn child." This language went far beyond that which the Advisory Committee had approved, which raised the question — also suggested in the long-acting sulfonamides case (see Afterword to Chapter 2) — as to just what usefulness such bodies have. Dr. Sadusk also disclosed new warning language proposed for the labeling of the prescription antihistamines in question. But he said that for two years modified claims of efficacy in the nausea of pregnancy would be allowed "because some physicians believe these drugs exert a beneficial effect in this condition." After two years the claim could be made only if substantial evidence was provided. This was, again, contrary to the spirit of the law, which said nothing about two-year grace periods. Nonetheless, Pfizer and Burroughs Wellcome did not comply. On March 30, 1966, the FDA said it had told Pfizer that unless it adopted the required strong warning for its prescription meclizine products (now named "Bonadoxine Tablets and Drops," and "Antivert Tablets and Syrup") further distribution would be ruled illegal. The company also was told that it acted illegally when it added new claims for its nonprescription Bonine Chewable Tablets and relabeled the product for prescription use only. Commissioner Goddard notified Burroughs Wellcome that the prescription labeling for its Marezine Injection and Suppositories and Perazil must be brought into line.

During the thalidomide episode in 1962 President Kennedy made a plea to the public to take all unidentified pills out of the medicine cabinet and destroy them. But in May 1966 no public announcement was made by FDA when it requested several manufacturers to notify physicians (Do they *always* receive and read their mail?) about two more antihistamines with a suspected birth-deforming potential. The letters were sent by Pfizer for Vis-taril (capsules and oral suspension), Parenteral, and Ataraxoid, all containing hydroxyzine which is used to gain symptomatic re-lief from nasal allergy; by Pfizer's J. B. Roerig division for Atarax (tablets, syrup, and parenteral), Cartax, Marax (tablets and syrup), Enarax and Amplus, all also containing hydroxyzine; and by the Stuart Co., a division of Atlas Chemical Industries, Inc., for Bucladin and Softran, which contains buclizine, a substance used to suppress nausea in pregnancy and in other conditions. The letters said that in higher-than-normal dosages hydroxyzine and buclizine had caused fetal abnormalities in experimental animals, and that the makers had no evidence of harm to any human mother or fetus, but that data on pregnant women are insufficient to establish safety and that the products should not be administered in early pregnancy.

ADDITIONAL INFORMATION ON BIRTH DEFECTS

At a symposium in London on March 30, 1965, the FDA's Dr. Frances Kelsey said that there is "no satisfactory experi-mental animal test to determine whether a drug may safely be used during human pregnancy . . ."

Ten days before she spoke, the *British Medical Journal* cau-tioned that "tetracyclines administered during pregnancy pass through the placenta, are concentrated in the foetal skeleton, and may diminish skeletal growth. Though in view of their widespread use serious effects are probably few, there seems little doubt . . . that they should not be used to treat pregnant women unless they are specifically indicated for severe infection resistant to other less toxic drugs." FDA, however, has said it had no evidence that tetracycline may cause deformities in the unborn.

In the *Health Bulletin* for March 27, 1965, Dr. J. P. Marilac of the FDA was said to have reported that four compounds in the organic phosphate group of pesticides caused thalidomide-type malformations when injected into chick embryos.

In May 1967 at a conference on the biological effects of pesticides held at the New York Academy of Science, Drs. Marvin Legator and M. Jacqueline Verrett of the Food and Drug Administration reported that two widely used fungicides had been shown in laboratory experiments to produce genetic damage and birth defects. The fungicides were identified as captan and folpet, which the New York *Times* for May 3 said "are widely used . . . in spraying or dusting to prevent fungal growth on farm crops, garden plants and a number of consumer products." The products "had been considered relatively safe for man," the *Times* said.

13

THE ORAL CONTRACEPTIVES

In 1930, the average life expectancy in the United States was 59.7 years. In 1959, it was 69.7 years. During the three intervening decades, the death rate among babies under 12 months fell from 69 to 29.5 per thousand. Since 1944, the death rate from influenza has dropped 90 per cent, from tuberculosis 83 per cent, from syphilis 79 per cent. In such spectacular changes, not only in the United States but in other countries as well, drugs and vaccines have played an important role, along with refined surgical techniques, and improved hygiene, nutrition, and public-health measures. But if drugs have given and prolonged life, so have they contributed to the crowding of this planet.

Partly because of the successes of the drug revolution, the population is not only exploding but it is exploding at an increasing rate. The population of the world increased by an estimated 46 million persons in 1961. Only three years later, according to the United Nations Statistical Office, the annual rate of increase had reached 63 million. Another product of the drug revolution was the birth-control pills. These, along with variants being developed in the laboratories, are looked to at every hand as the most hopeful answer to the exceedingly grave problem of too many people.

To an extraordinary extent, the uses of oral contraceptives are intertwined with considerations of a socioeconomic, political, religious, and moral nature. The birth-control pills have become available in — perhaps hastened the advent of — an era in which the Roman Catholic Church is subjecting its position on birth control to profound examination. It is also an era in which the open concern of many young Americans is not with whether to engage in premarital intercourse, but with what technique of contraception is to be preferred. *Newsweek* reported on July 6, 1964:

> "Some young girls call it 'the Magic Pill,'" says Dr. Freda Kehm of Chicago's Association for Family Living . . . Not only might it foster promiscuity, Dr. Kehm notes, but it is being used on college campuses in a kind of psychological warfare: "The girl tells the boy she is using the pill when she really is not — then she traps him."

For the purposes of this book, the significant thing about quotations such as that from *Newsweek* is the implication — or confirmation — that a great many girls and women simply presume the pill to be safe. This was spelled out by a coed who wrote to the *Cornell Daily Sun* that she did not question the safety of the oral contraceptives because they had been allowed on the market by the Food and Drug Administration, which had kept thalidomide off the market, hadn't it? Her naïveté surely was no greater than that of the worldly-wise Helen Gurley Brown, who deals with contraception in a chapter of *Sex and the Office* on how to have an affair at lunch time. "If you use pills, so much the easier," says she.

✦ ✦ ✦

The safety-efficacy relationship is unusual. There is no question about the effectiveness of birth-control pills in preventing conception, for that is reportedly complete. The safety factor cannot be dealt with so readily. The question must first be asked, safe for whom?

There are poor, uneducated women who will not reliably use a diaphragm. As a practical matter, the choice for them has been an oral contraceptive or no contraceptive at all. To many of these women one more pregnancy would be fatal. More of them, in fact, face death from pregnancy than would die with use of an oral contraceptive even, says the Planned Parenthood Federation, if the pills were to be blamed for every tabulated death which someone merely *suspects* them to have caused. And in many countries millions of children are born not to live but to starve.

Surely, however, the safety factor is another matter among women who decide to forsake use of mechanical contraceptive methods for, say, convenience, or in a quest for foolproof protection against conception. "The oral preparations are the most effective contraceptives known," the *Medical Letter* affirmed on July 17, 1964. But, it said, "there are still uncertainties about their safety . . . they should not be prescribed when other methods are acceptable to the patient and can be used successfully." For the moment, mention of but one of the uncertainties will suffice.

Consider two women in their fertile period. One who normally relies on a diaphragm and jelly neglects to use them and becomes pregnant. The other woman neglects to take a contraceptive pill, and she too conceives. Not knowing that she is pregnant, she returns to regular use of the pill. What she has done, according to Dr. Allan C. Barnes, chief gynecologist and obstetrician at the Johns Hopkins Hospital, is to expose the fetus, if it is female, to a "maximal" hazard. The hazard is that the fetus will be masculinized. The reason for the hazard is that the pills contain norethindrone (Norlutin) — whose masculinizing effects on the female fetus were mentioned in Chapter 4 — or another progestogen, norethynodrel.

That the birth-control pills involve this particular hazard may come as a shock, particularly to readers of *This Week*. In the

July 12, 1964, issue of this Sunday supplement, the "Good
Health" column was by Dr. Edwin J. DeCosta, attending obstetrician and gynecologist at Passavant Memorial Hospital in Chicago. He wrote: "I have heard oral contraceptives accused of
masculinizing female babies if taken inadvertently during early
pregnancy, of interfering with future fertility, of causing uterine
fibroids or even cancer. Most of these charges are palpable non-
sense — there is no evidence to support *any* of them." (My
italic.)

Dr. DeCosta, whose column bore in the lower left-hand corner
a seal assuring *This Week*'s readers that it had been "AMA authorized," could have found the evidence to support the charge
of masculinization in many places, had he looked. For example,
in the *Journal* of the American Medical Association, the organization which thus was stated to have "authorized" him to say
"no evidence," the Council on Drugs of the AMA had published, more than five months earlier, a monograph on Ortho-
Novum. This is an oral contraceptive that, like others, combines
norethindrone with mestranol, an estrogen. The Council said
that norethindrone is "inherently" capable of masculinizing, and
that "instances of masculinization of the female fetus have been
associated with its use in pregnancy." A mere six days before
Dr. DeCosta's incredible assurance was seen by millions of laymen, the *Journal* was again carrying a warning to physicians. In
the issue dated July 6, 1964, the question was not *whether* oral
contraceptives could cause masculinization, but the *extent* to
which they cause it. The following appeared in the "Questions
and Answers" section:

Q   When patients use progestogen-estrogen mixtures such
as Enovid and Ortho-Novum for contraception during the
early weeks of an unsuspected pregnancy, or take these drugs
during pregnancy when abortion [miscarriage] threatens, what

is the incidence of masculinization of female infants? Is masculinization so induced a temporary condition?

R. Ned White, MD
Springfield, Mo.

The answer, provided for the *Journal* by Dr. Kathryn Huss of Chicago, did not question the potential of oral contraceptives to masculinize girl babies. It said that some mature as normal females, some require "plastic repair," and still others may need to undergo amputation of a clitoris so enlarged as to be "conspicuous and a source of embarrassment." Dr. Huss concluded:

The degree of masculinization appears to be determined by the dose, potency, duration of treatment, and time of exposure during gestation.

It is not possible from existing data to determine the incidence of masculinization. In view of the extensive use of progestogens during pregnancy, it occurs only occasionally, although probably cases of minor degree are overlooked. The highest incidence which we have seen published is 18% masculinization of female infants born to mothers treated with norethindrone during pregnancy.

That Enovid involves the particular hazard of masculinization of the fetus may also come as a shock to the "counselors, medical and para-medical groups, educators, clergy and other professionals concerned with marital counseling" for whom the manufacturer, G. D. Searle & Co. of Chicago, specifically prepared a 62-page handbook, *A Prescription for Family Planning: The Story of Enovid.* Unlike Dr. DeCosta's column in *This Week,* a publication of general circulation, the handbook was said in a cover letter dated November 1964 to be "not available to the general public." The handbook exudes authority and completeness. The inside cover gives a Library of Congress catalogue card number. The title page says the publication was prepared to assist professional persons "in their guidance, counselling, educational or other professional responsibilities and activities." There is a roster of the "Advisory Council / G. D. Searle & Co. Reference and Resource Program." Among the ten members are Dr. John Rock, the famed director of the Rock Reproductive Clinic and clinical professor emeritus of the Harvard Medical School. There are a table of contents and an index. With all of this, the Searle firm did not find it necessary to discuss, clearly and forthrightly, the possibility of masculinization of the fetus. Instead, this "reference for professional use" offers sets of cleverly worded questions and answers, of which these are the relevant ones:

> 4. *What is the effect on future children of Enovid users?*
> There is no known adverse effect on the child if the mother has taken Enovid before conceiving — or after . . .

This is not disputed. But the question of what may happen if a woman *neglects* to take the pill during her fertile period, becomes pregnant, and resumes its use, is ignored. The second question and answer follow:

> 6. *Is there any possibility that women who take Enovid will develop male characteristics?*
> Enovid . . . has produced no male characteristics in women and is not expected to do so . . .

This also is not disputed. But why wasn't the more pertinent question put: *Is there any possibility that women who take Enovid will have female babies with male sexual characteristics?*

✓ ✓ ✓

Enovid, the first oral contraceptive, was marketed in August 1957, chiefly for menstrual disorders. Its contraceptive potential was well known, but clinical testing of this characteristic was required. Tests undertaken in relatively small groups of women in various places, including Los Angeles and San Antonio, but most extensively among 1500 women in Puerto Rico, proved Enovid's reliability in preventing pregnancy.

In February 1960 the Food and Drug Administration sent a letter of inquiry to 61 professors and associate professors of gynecology and obstetrics. Although Enovid is a steroid that affects the endocrine system, the questionnaire was not sent to endocrinologists. All 61 of the professors replied. Twenty-six — fewer than half — said Enovid should be released to the market as a contraceptive. Fourteen "felt that they did not have sufficient data to reach a conclusion." Release was opposed by 21, who did not give specific reasons, although at least two were concerned with religious considerations.

On May 11, 1960, Commissioner Larrick was told, "The New Drug Branch has concluded that the evidence establishes the safety of Enovid tablets for oral use in conception control . . ." This assurance was provided by Dr. William D. Kessenich, FDA's medical director at the time, in a report that the Humphrey Subcommittee on Reorganization and International Organizations obtained and published. In "the entire series of cases," Dr. Kessenich said, the number of women who had used Enovid for 12 to 21 *consecutive* menstrual cycles was 66. Sixty-six additional women "have taken Enovid for 24 [*consecutive*] cycles or more to 38 . . ." Thus, the number of women in whom Enovid had been *continuously* tested for a year or more was a mere 132. On this basis, FDA released Enovid for a recommended limit of two years' use in thousands of times 132 women.

The boldness of FDA in letting a drug go *on* the market, as distinguished from its performance in taking a drug *off* the market, had once again been demonstrated. Although FDA concluded that Enovid's safety had been established, others were less certain.

"Since the average period of use has been relatively short,"

The *Medical Letter* said on June 10, 1960, "no physician can feel completely confident that long-term use will prove safe for all patients." And three years later, within FDA itself, views more cautious than those of the New Drug Branch were being expressed. In an internal memorandum on Enovid, Dr. Robert J. Robinson, an FDA medical officer, said, "In the light of our present [1963] knowledge of this drug, continued observation should be maintained in order to assure that there are not adverse effects on the pituitary, adrenal, and thyroid glands.

In December 1962, two reporters, who were unaware that Enovid had been released after it had been tested continuously for a year or longer in only 132 women, put a question to the then acting medical director, Dr. Ralph G. Smith: Were tests on 1500 women in Puerto Rico an adequate foundation for releasing a drug that would be used by millions? Dr. Smith, who was head of the New Drug Branch in 1960 when it said the evidence establishes the safety of Enovid, replied ambiguously that FDA "concluded that it was."

In assuming that FDA did in fact have sufficient justification for releasing Enovid, Dr. Smith expressed a view advocated by many of the nation's outstanding researchers and physicians. Some of them, however, may tend to think in terms of the population explosion rather than in the framework of the quality of FDA's decision-making processes. About these they may know little or nothing.

✁ ✁ ✁

Although overshadowed by the thalidomide furor, news came from Britain in the summer of 1962 linking use of Enovid to four cases of thrombophlebitis, a painful inflammation of a clotted vein. Usually it is temporarily disabling. But if the clot breaks loose the result can be fatal — the clot can lodge in a vital bloodway. The Food and Drug Administration considered the report promptly and conferred with the manufacturer,

G. D. Searle, which at once sent a warning letter to all physicians in the United States and Canada, and to all hospitals, drug wholesalers, and pharmacies. The American Medical Association said its own careful review established no causal relation between Enovid and thrombophlebitis.

About a month later, in September 1962, Searle sponsored at AMA headquarters in Chicago a conference of specialists on the possibility of a causal relation. The scientists overwhelmingly, but not unanimously, adopted a resolution saying the evidence established none.

Meanwhile, however, reports associating thrombophlebitis with use of Enovid were coming to FDA, Searle being a prime source. Although the statistics were susceptible to challenge, by December FDA knew of 272 cases, 30 of them fatal. Commissioner Larrick did not report these figures to the public, but he did verify them in response to an inquiry from the Washington *Post*. By mid-January 1963, 297 cases, of which 35 were fatal, were known.

The FDA medical officer assigned to the Enovid matter, Dr. Heino Trees, had been growing ever more concerned. Finally, he told medical colleagues at FDA he was convinced "that there is a relationship between this drug and thrombophlebitis," particularly in the first three months of use. He termed appointment of a consultant panel "critical and urgent."

Three days later, on December 18, 1962, Commissioner Larrick agreed to appoint an advisory committee. The nine-member committee, headed by Dr. Irving S. Wright, professor of clinical medicine at the Cornell University Medical College, considered the data for several months. The committee deemed the available statistics on the possible *overall* relationship between Enovid and blood clots too meager to permit a conclusion, and asked that its findings be accepted with caution. However, in the report issued in August 1963, the committee did note a statistically significant hazard of *fatal* thromboembolism in women over thirty-five. The Food and Drug Administration followed up the report by extending the period of recommended use from two to four years, asking Searle to advise physicians of the hazard in women over thirty-five, and suggesting a need for further studies.

Meanwhile, the AMA's Council on Drugs said, "On the basis of all available information and statistics . . . there does not appear to be any evidence that the use of Enovid caused the reported cases of thrombophlebitis."

✓ ✓ ✓

The Food and Drug Administration had hoped that the Wright committee report would eliminate persistent pockets of uneasiness, but this hope was disappointed to a significant extent. There were several reasons for this. To begin with, the number of cases of thromboembolism associated with Enovid continued to increase. In July 1963 FDA put the recorded total at 400, with 40 deaths.

Here and there around the country, physicians were having difficulty squaring some of the committee's findings with what they were encountering in their practices. For the first time in their experience, some doctors were finding thromboembolisms in very young women, and these very young women had been using an oral contraceptive. One such case was reported in the *New England Journal of Medicine* for May 9, 1963. The woman was twenty-one, and she had no history of inflammatory disease. She took, for contraceptive purposes, Enovid as prescribed by her psysician — 5 milligrams daily for 20 out of 30 days. Six weeks after starting on this regimen, she developed marked fatigue and, finally, a massive pulmonary embolism. Fortunately, she was successfully treated, but had to spend twenty-five days in a hospital. She was free of symptoms a month and a half later.

Within a mere fourteen months at a single institution, the Henry Ford Hospital in Detroit, six cases of thromboembolism were encountered. All of the women had been taking Enovid.

Three may have been predisposed to the disease — one, a thirty-nine-year-old woman, had no history of thrombophlebitis but had developed diabetes during pregnancy fourteen months earlier. She suffered a sudden arterial blockage in her left leg two months after starting regular use of Enovid. A below-the-knee amputation was performed. In the other three cases, however, "no predisposing cause . . . was detected."

A highly balanced and cautious report on the six cases was published in the May 11, 1964, issue of the AMA *Journal*. The authors — Dr. Irwin J. Schatz, Dr. Roger F. Smith, Dr. Gerald M. Breneman, and Dr. George C. Bower — emphasized that there exists no "acceptable experimental or statistical evidence" that the progestogen in Enovid "precipitates or enhances thromboembolism." Nevertheless, the appearance of six cases "in a short period" in one hospital compelled them to suggest that Enovid "may rarely cause thromoboembolism in susceptible individuals," and that the possibility of a cause-and-effect relation "must be considered until disproved."

In suburban Cook County, the chairman of the Committee on Maternal and Infant Welfare expressed a cautious attitude toward birth-control pills in a letter to members of the Illinois Public Aid Commission. "The tablet is *not* as innocuous as aspirin," Dr. Matthew J. Bulfin said in the letter, which was quoted by Eric Hutton in the Canadian magazine *Maclean's* for August 22, 1964:

"Every chairman of the obstetrics and gynecology departments at each of our eighteen suburban Cook County hospitals wants to voice his word of caution about the indiscriminate prescription of this drug. Every one of us who has prescribed this drug to private patients has learned of the diversity of reactions to it. Many physicians who formerly prescribed it with relative frequency now are reluctant to use it because of the unpredictability of its results.

"The tablet can be prescribed with maximum safety only

when the patient who takes it is rigidly and carefully controlled. The patient over whom the physician has little or no control should not be using the tablet."

Another focus of criticism involved the data that were made available to the Wright committee. These data did not include three deaths among Enovid users in the Puerto Rican testing. For this omission Elinor Langer, writing in *Science* for September 6, 1963, blamed the methods of record-keeping used by the manufacturer of Enovid during the experimental period. Accurate keeping of medical records is of necessity more beset by unreliability in Puerto Rico, though, than in many or most places in the continental United States. In the Commonwealth the dead are buried within twenty-four hours. Usually, a physician comes by later to ask a survivor what he assumed the cause of death to have been.

Most controversial, however, was the statistical method used by the committee to compare the rates of fatal thromboembolism among the women-users of Enovid and among comparable nonusers. No doubt confidence in the committee's statistical capabilities was shaken when, seven weeks after its report was issued, it reversed its finding of a hazard in women over thirty-five, saying that this risk had been ascertained to be statistically insignificant. In any event, the method used by the committee to determine the fatality rate indicated an incidence in 1962 of 12.1 per million among women-users. The rate among nonusers was 8.4 million. The difference, 3.7 cases per million, was regarded as, overall, too small to have statistical significance.

A critic of the committee report, Dr. Edmond Kassouf, pointed out that this method ignored the *extent* of use. That is, it did not, for example, differentiate between a woman who had taken Enovid for 20 days from another who had taken it for 240 days, or 12 times as long. More realistic, said Dr. Kassouf, is the woman-year method, which, although not used by the

Wright committee, was employed at the Searle-sponsored conference in 1962 and has been accepted by FDA. In the woman-year method, a dozen women, each taking Enovid for one month, are combined statistically to make a woman-year of use. This — not a woman using Enovid for, say, 20 days — then becomes the statistical offset to a year of nonuse. Aided by his mathematician-cousin, Sheen Kassouf, the physician calculated that the woman-year method indicates a death rate of 22.3 per million. This calculation was made from the same basic data which the committee had used to figure a fatal thromboembolism incidence of 12.1. Dr. Kassouf asked how it is possible for both methods to be correct. Dr. Wright responded that the committee relied upon competent statisticians.

At the same time, the committee was criticized by some on the ground that it had given insufficient weight to the avoidance of dangerous pregnancies and miscarriages in Enovid users. Criticism of this kind, although useful in calling attention to the great value of the oral contraceptives in other contexts, really had nothing to do with the narrow but important medical-statistical question about the incidence of fatal thromboembolisms.

At the request of Senator Humphrey, the National Institutes of Health assigned a top biometricist, William Haenszel, to review the report of the committee, which made no recommendations other than one for further study. After a close analysis of the report and the statistics on which it was based, Haenszel concluded, "There is little to be gained from prolonged debate about what the present data mean. It would be better to inquire into plans for future monitoring and collection of data designed to answer the questions which have arisen concerning the effect of Enovid." In the collection of data that can truly reveal the incidence of adverse reactions, and thus the ratio of benefit to risk, there are problems of great magnitude. It is important to understand what these problems are before turning, as I shall later in this chapter, to the way that the Searle firm overcame some of them insofar as thromboembolism was concerned and was able to issue a reassuring report.

For any drug, the incidence of each type of adverse reaction — 1 in 1000, 1 in 10,000, 1 in 50,000, or whatever it be — is the product of a fraction. The numerator is the number of adverse reactions. The denominator is the population exposed, or at risk, through use of the drug. For many reasons, as shown in Chapter 1 — reasons including failure to recognize drug-induced reactions for what they are, inadequate reporting, and deliberate suppression — the total of adverse reactions, the numerator, frequently is understated. Similarly, for reasons that will be given below, the denominator is commonly overstated. In either case — a numerator too small or a denominator too large — or if both conditions prevail, the product of the fraction will indicate a rate of adverse reactions that is artificially low. In this context, *Science* for August 16, 1963, said in a comment on the Wright committee report: ". . . if only 10 percent fewer patients took Enovid than the committee calculated, it is reported, the death rate from the drug would come very close to statistical significance for all ages; and if 50 percent fewer people took it, the rates would be very significantly greater. If 50 percent more people are presumed to have taken the drug, the danger declines for the 35–39 year group but remains significant in the 40–44 year range."

Assumptions aside, it can quickly be seen that a correct denominator — the number of users — is often as difficult to obtain as a correct numerator. I shall use examples that have nothing to do with Enovid. On September 13, 1960, Harry J. Loynd, president of Parke, Davis, testified before the Senate Subcommittte on Antitrust and Monopoly about Chloromycetin, the antibiotic with the generic name chloramphenicol. "In the 11 years since it became available," he said, "it is estimated that it has been prescribed for more than 40 million patients."

But according to *Drug Trade News*, Kenneth D. McGregor, a vice president of Parke, Davis who accompanied Loynd when he made the quoted statement before Senator Kefauver, told a California state senate fact-finding committee in October 1961, " 'more than 25 million people have had Chloromycetin administered to them since it was created in 1949' . . ." Had the cumulative total of users declined by 15 million 13 months *after* Loynd's testimony?

Another case tends to make one wonder if all that may be common about most denominators is their unreliability. The case concerns Parnate, the antidepressant discussed in Chapter 9. When Smith Kline & French issued a warning letter in October 1963, it said the drug had been taken by about 3.5 million persons, including about 2 million in the United States. In June 1964, in remarks at the convention of the American Medical Association, the FDA's new medical director, Dr. Joseph F. Sadusk, said that Parnate had been used by 1.5 million Americans, or a half-million fewer than had been reported four months earlier.

The difficulty of determining the true incidence of adverse reactions has been increased by the lumping together of estimates of foreign and domestic distribution — which was done by some publications in reporting the Parnate episode. The reporting of adverse reactions abroad is, as Senator Humphrey has described it, "pitifully weak," and this means that although the denominator is bloated the numerator is shrunken — unless it includes adverse reactions from, say, Africa, Asia, Europe, and Latin America. Again, the product of such a fraction understates the rate at which adverse reactions occur.

✓ ✓ ✓

Turning back to the question of the true incidence of side effects in women using oral contraceptives: that there is confusion about the extent of their use — the denominator — may be readily shown. On July 3, 1964, *Life* said that the pills were being used by "some 3 million American women." Two weeks later *Newsweek* said, "Searle executives claim Enovid has 2.5 million users," and that a second and more recently marketed brand, Ortho-Novum, manufactured by the Ortho Pharmaceutical affiliate of Johnson & Johnson, "is now used by almost a million women." The difference between *Life* and *Newsweek* is numerically large and statistically very large. One may be sure that both publications had made diligent, conscientious efforts to obtain and publish accurate figures. If *Newsweek* was taking foreign users into account, this was not made clear.

Whatever the figure may be, which at times seems to depend upon which newspaper or magazine one reads, the denominator used in the birth-control-pill fraction at the very least invites questions of the kind raised by Dr. Kassouf. How many of the women included in the denominator are consistent, longtime users? How many are steady users? How many are occasional users? How many women pass the pills out among their friends? No one knows the answers to questions like these, but that does not mean that they are mere statistical playthings.[1]

The importance of the duration and nature of use may be seen in a report cited by Dr. Barbara Moulton in a statement filed with the Senate Subcommittee on Antitrust and Monopoly. The report, made at a symposium which she attended in 1959

---

[1] In a statement filed with the Department of Health, Education, and Welfare, the Pharmaceutical Manufacturers Association said in March 1964, "A manufacturer has no way of knowing the quantity of the drug 'used.'" Senator Humphrey found this, however, no justification for the opposition of the PMA to reporting how much of a drug has been *distributed*. Despite this opposition, FDA has, through regulation, begun to require drug manufacturers to supply volume figures. Even so, questions about the duration and nature of drug use will not be fully dealt with by the agency. Most of the figures reported to FDA will involve sales to wholesalers. Accurate figures on sales to and by the vastly greater number of retail pharmacies have been, and will remain, much more difficult to obtain. They have no legal obligation to report to FDA. Except in extraordinary circumstances, retailers can deny FDA inspectors access to sales data, although such information is sometimes made available to detailmen and private survey firms.

in her capacity as an FDA medical officer, concerned niacin, which is part of the vitamin B complex. Among 30 regular takers of niacin in high dosages no problems were found. Not in the first year. Not in the second. But in the third year of sustained high-dose use, 22 of the 30 persons displayed blood-chemical effects — harbingers of potent, serious, future liver damage. A woman may begin regular use of an oral contraceptive when she is, say, eighteen. She may continue to rely on it for birth control during the 30 or more years when she could bear a child. Can anyone say in conscience that he *knows* what all of the long-term effects may be?

Earlier I alluded to a reassuring report issued by the Searle firm on the incidence of thrombophlebitis among users of Enovid. The company made an impressive effort to obtain a valid numerator (the number of cases of thrombophlebitis) and denominator (the number of women taking the pill). The experiment was discussed on November 20, 1964, in Washington at a meeting of Alpha Chi Sigma, the professional chemists' society, by Dr. Irwin C. Winter, Searle's vice president–medical affairs. At the time, more than 10,000 women were participating. All had been selected by Planned Parenthood Federation clinics around the country, all had been kept under continuing medical supervision at the clinics, all had been taking the pill for at least 24 months, and on joining the experiment each woman had given her medical history and undergone a thorough medical examination. The plan called for each participant to be reinterviewed and re-examined every six months.

At the time that Dr. Winter spoke, Searle's clinical research department had received and processed records on 5000 women who had been reinterviewed and re-examined once. Of the 5000, 49 had reported thrombophlebitis in their past medical history, before they began using Enovid. Among the 49, Dr. Winter said, were 5 who continued to use Enovid while having chronic thrombophlebitis.

Of the 44 remaining, who had had thrombophlebitis before taking Enovid, none has reported any new incidence . . . and 41 are continuing on the program. Of those remaining, one has been using Enovid for four years, two for nearly four years, and the remaining 38 have an average Enovid use of nearly three years.

Out of the 5,000 patients, there were only eight new cases of thrombophlebitis only . . . Furthermore, out of this carefully observed long-term study, approximately 93 percent of the women who had a pre-Enovid history of thrombophlebitis have continued on Enovid for well over two years without any recurrence of the disease.

The company calculated the incidence of new cases — 8 per 5000 over a 34-month period — at less than six tenths of a case per 1000 per year, "which is the lowest figure we have ever found for incidence of thrombophlebitis in women of a similar age group . . ."

Without question, this is reassuring. One must hesitate to say, nevertheless, that the experiment establishes absence of association between use of Enovid and thromboembolism. The most obvious reason for hesitation grows out of the fact that the incidence of the disease among the 5000 women in the study is much more precisely known than is the incidence among the general female population that do not take the pills. To put it another way: the experiment seems to show a low incidence among 5000 women who take the pill, but it does not show that the incidence may not be still lower among 5000 women who have not taken the pill. In his talk, Dr. Winter acknowledged that "the plan of the experiment could not provide an adequate control group since such was not available (the pill was too popular) . . ." He also said, "One of the most difficult . . . studies has been that of thrombophlebitis since adequate statistics of its normal incidence were not available." There would be reason for hesitation even if the company were to come up with "an adequate control group" of 5000 women not taking the pill. That is because the control group of necessity would have to be made up of women as similar as possible to those taking the pill. Thus, all 10,000 in the pill-taking and control groups would come from the lower socioeconomic groups — those who go to Planned Parenthood clinics. It may be that the incidence of thromboembolism is unrelated to socioeconomic status — but merely to assume blandly that it is would be rash.

✓ ✓ ✓

Enovid, Ortho-Novum, Norinyl (Syntex), Norlestrin (Parke, Davis) — all of these oral contraceptives contain forms of estrogen, the female sex hormone, in tiny amounts. One type of estrogen, diethylstilbestrol, which is used as an additive in food for poultry, was discussed in a letter written to the Food and Drug Administration in January 1960 by Dr. Roy Hertz, chief of the Endocrinology Branch of the National Cancer Institute. Dr. Hertz made it clear that the warnings he was conveying embraced generally all forms of estrogen, which, he said, "plays an important part in the development and progression of cancer of the breast." One death in 16 among American women is attributed to that disease.

Since 1896, Dr. Hertz wrote FDA, "it has been accepted clinical practice . . . to remove the ovaries of young women with breast cancer in order to suppress the growth of their tumors. The ingestion of estrogens has been shown to have a harmful effect in young women with breast cancer, although paradoxically the use of massive doses of estrogen in aged women with breast cancer has a favorable effect upon their disease . . ." However, he said, the use of estrogen as therapy in breast cancer should be restricted to women who are at least three years beyond menopause. Similar considerations apply, he continued, to the course of cancer's development in the uterus. Dr. Hertz said that the precautions to be taken against cancer of the breast and uterus are as follows:

> (a) to restrict the clinical use of estrogen to only those patients who present a clear indication for its use, (b) to take all available steps to eliminate the possible preexistence of cancer in the breasts or pelvis of any patient to be given estrogens, (c) to follow carefully all estrogenized patients by frequent physical examination and cytological examination of the vaginal smear, and (d) *to avoid unduly prolonged and continuous administration of the hormone.* [Italics mine.]

Dr. Hertz gave a detailed explanation for urging against continuous ingestion of estrogen. One reason is that chemically induced cancer of the breast and uterus has a very long latent period — so long that, in the case of cancer of the breast, it is well along by the time its presence is known — when a lump is felt. He said that "cases of breast and uterine cancer found in patients who have been on estrogen therapy have almost invariably arisen after *long* periods of medication." [Italic mine.] There exists, he declared, "strong circumstantial but by no means conclusive evidence of the carcinogenicity [cancer-producing potential] of estrogens . . ." He went on to say:

> . . . it is spurious to argue that since the body as well as natural food substances contain estrogen, the addition of trace amounts should therefore be tolerated [trace amounts were at issue in the case of the food additive he was discussing. Substantially more than "trace amounts" of estrogen are present in oral contraceptives]. This assumes that the threshold for potential harmful effects of added estrogen is necessarily quite high. On the contrary, I would maintain that such preexisting levels of estrogen in the body and in foodstuffs make it all the more imperative that no further continuous

estrogenic load be placed upon the individual . . . we must consider that existing levels of estrogen in the diet may very well be at the threshold of long-term toxicity and, for all that is presently known, may already play a role in the pathogenesis [course of development] of cancer in women.

. . . .

. . . we do not know the threshold for *carcinogenic* action of [estrogen] substances . . . nor do we have available scientific methods for the determination of such thresholds.

Under these circumstances it would seem the better part of reason to exclude this known potent carcinogen [diethylstilbestrol] from our diet . . .

A few days later the Surgeon General of the Public Health Service, Dr. Leroy Burney, expressed views almost identical with those of Dr. Hertz in a memorandum to the then Secretary of the Department of Health, Education, and Welfare, Arthur Flemming.

More than three years later, in October 1963, Dr. Hertz addressed a meeting in New York attended by three hundred cancer specialists. The New York *Herald Tribune* reported that, in response to a question, he said "there was no doubt in his mind that pills containing estrogen should be used only to cure disease," and that "the reduction in estrogen output obtained by cutting out a breast cancer victim's ovaries is very small . . . of the same order as the added estrogen contained in" the oral contraceptives. In short, this drastic procedure decreases estrogen output by an amount no greater than that added by ingestion of the pills.

Once again he pointed out that by the time a lump can be felt in the breast cancer "is well along," and that with a long latent period, ten to twenty years, the risk of cancer induced by estrogen "doesn't necessarily stop when the exposure to the cancer promoter stops." The taking of birth-control pills, he said, "should be carried out in a much more controlled fashion."

Dr. Hertz's views have been vigorously disputed. In the AMA *Journal* for October 27, 1962, Dr. Robert A. Wilson, a gynecologist at Methodist Hospital in Brooklyn, reported on a study of 304 women who had been treated with estrogens for as long as 27 years and for an average of 7.8 years. Among them, he said, 18 cases of breast or genital cancer were statistically indicated — but none occurred. "Estrogen does not induce cancer," he said. While his study might well have indicated that conclusion, he went beyond it, to suggest that to an unknown degree estrogen *prevents* breast and uterine cancer, and that it "would seem advisable to keep women endocrine rich and, consequently, cancer poor *throughout their lives*." (Italics mine.)

Dr. Robert Greenblatt, of the Medical College at the University of Georgia, who conducted clinical trials with estrogen for a decade, said that "there is no evidence at all of a causal relationship between the hormone estrogen and cancer in humans." Another denial that cancer in humans could be caused by oral contraceptives came from Dr. Robert W. Kistner, a Harvard gynecologist and co-worker of Dr. John Rock. However, he acknowledged that oral contraceptives could aggravate *existing* breast cancer.

After Dr. Hertz spoke, Searle, the manufacturer of Enovid, said there has "never been the slightest evidence" that Enovid caused cancer, and that "the possibility of cancer was one of the first aspects of oral contraceptives to be checked." Vice President K. D. Bowes told the *Wall Street Journal*, which carried the quotation on October 24, 1963, "Everyone who marketed such a product or considered it has carefully watched this point . . . we satisfied ourselves and obviously the [FDA] on the point before the product was ever marketed."

The issue was revived again in June 1964, by a report from the University of Oregon Medical School that in rats with preexisting cancer Enovid accelerated the growth and development of the cancer. But rats are not humans. Commenting on the report, Searle said Enovid neither causes nor promotes the growth of pre-existing cancer in humans. Again, there were suggestions from Searle and various researchers that the evidence indicates less cancer in Enovid users than in nonusers. It was not always pointed out that careful physicians examine women before prescribing the pills and, if they find cancer and certain other conditions, do not prescribe them.

Not long after Dr. Hertz spoke in New York, FDA released so-called small-dose versions of the birth-control pills. These contain less norethynodrel or norethindrone substances, which can masculinize a female fetus, but more synthetic estrogen (mestranol or ethinyl estradiol). They include Enovid-E and Ortho-Novum-2. In August 1964, Upjohn introduced Provest, which it said is a new formulation that greatly minimizes the risk of masculinization.

✓ ✓ ✓

I think it in order now to present a dispassionate summary in this most sensitive area. Such a summary can be derived from the evaluation of Ortho-Novum by the Council on Drugs of the American Medical Association. The evaluation, which appeared in the AMA *Journal* on February 29, 1964, "is based on the laboratory and clinical evidence available to the Council."

Effectiveness: ". . . virtually 100% . . . in preventing conception when taken from the 5th through the 24th day of the cycle."

Adverse reactions: ". . . reported to occur in 15% to 35% of the women, although few . . . in the large experimental trials discontinued treatment because of these reactions . . ."

The most frequently encountered reaction is irregular bleeding (breakthrough spotting, breakthrough bleeding, or failure of withdrawal bleeding to occur). Breakthrough spotting or bleeding occurs in approximately one of three patients using the 10 mg dose and in approximately one of five patients using the 2 mg dose. It usually occurs during the first five or six months of treatment . . . Failure of withdrawal bleeding to occur in one or more cycle[s] has been reported in 15% of users. An early pregnancy should be ruled out before the medication is resumed . . .

Weight gains not affected by diuretics [drugs that increase the volume of urine] are common. A recorded increase or an impression of gain has been reported by more than one half of the users. The weight gain in two thirds of these patients is less than ten pounds. A combination of increased appetite and an anabolic effect [an effect on metabolism] is believed to cause the increase in weight.

Gastrointestinal symptoms, of which nausea is most prominent, occur less frequently with the tablet containing 10 mg of norethindrone and 0.06 mg of mestranol than with the [small-dose] mixture containing 2 mg of norethindrone and 0.10 mg of mestranol, but irregular bleeding, weight gain, and acne are experienced more frequently with the former . . . Symptoms of pregnancy such as breast fullness and discomfort, chloasma [skin discolorations], headache, dizziness, and edema [excessive accumulation of fluid in the tissue spaces] have all been reported. Urticaria [hives or nettle rashes] has been noted. In most cases, these symptoms tend to diminish with continued treatment.

Depression associated with a sense of fatigue and apathy is a distressing symptom to some users. The depression tends to increase rather than diminish with continued use . . .

A diminution in the quantity or duration of lactation has been noted in about 30% of lactating women . . .

No indications of cancer or precancerous changes of the cervix or endometrium [the mucous membrane lining the uterus] have been noted after initiation of treatment. However, controversy still exists concerning the carcinogenic effect of exogenous estrogen [the additional intake of estrogen].

Preexisting fibroids may increase in size . . .

. . . an estrogenic effect on thyroid and adrenal function is to be expected . . .

. . . The effect of prolonged administration on liver function is unknown.

. . . instances of masculinization of the female fetus have been associated with its [norethindrone's] use during pregnancy. Therefore, precautions should be taken to exclude the possibility of pregnancy before a patient starts this contraceptive regimen, and also before continuing the regimen if any tablets are omitted during a cycle or if withdrawal bleeding fails to occur after any cycle of treatment.

The effects of prolonged administration . . . on the reproductive, endocrine, and vascular systems are not known. There have been no serious adverse effects reported in five years of clinical use . . . Fertility is not diminished after this method of contraception is terminated. The continued fertility of these patients indicates that the pituitary suppression presumed to occur is temporary. No effect on fetal development has been reported.

Precautions: "Indications for the use of an oral contraceptive should be carefully considered in prescribing this mixture for patients with mammary or genital carcinoma [a malignant new growth], hepatic [liver] disease or dysfunction, a history of thromboembolic disease, metabolic endocrine disorders, and any medical condition which might be affected adversely by fluid retention, such as cardiovascular disease, epilepsy, migraine, and asthma. Patients with a history of psychic depression should be carefully observed and the medication discontinued if the depression recurs."

The *Medical Letter* has mentioned an additional precaution, against giving the pills to girls who have not reached full growth. The reason offered is that estrogens are known to accelerate the process that halts the growth of the bone structure.

✓ ✓ ✓

Here are some additional evaluations of the oral contraceptives:

The *Medical Letter* for July 17, 1964: "Whether serious long-term effects — over a lifetime — can occur will not be known for many years."

From Eric Hutton's article in *Maclean's* for August 22, 1964: "One Toronto doctor told me he considered the pills so safe that he gave them to his wife and to women employees. But at a conference of the International Planned Parenthood Federation held in Warsaw, George Cadbury, of Toronto, an official of the organization, reported that he had polled doctors at the World Health Organization headquarters on the question. 'No single doctor I asked would advise his daughter to use the pill,' he said."

From *Lancet*, as reported in the same article in *Maclean's*: "Twenty years may go by before we can be sure about the safety of the present oral contraceptive. In a fortunate and well-fed country where other methods of contraception are available and effective, it seems sensible to restrict their use. Elsewhere, in overcrowded lands where starvation for many is a more serious and immediate threat than future ill-health in a few, the advantages of oral contraception might well be judged to outweigh the risks." [2]

---

[2] The safety of oral contraceptives was touched on by Dr. James A. Shannon, Director of the National Institutes of Health, at a hearing held on February 17, 1965, by a House Appropriations subcommittee. There was this exchange with Representative John E. Fogarty, the subcommittee chairman:

MR. FOGARTY. So people are really taking a chance.

DR. SHANNON. I believe so. There are a great many studies on experimental animals that indicate that they probably can be taken without hazard, but there has not been adequate human exploration to be certain.

Dr. Joseph F. Sadusk, medical director of the Food and Drug Administration, quoted in *Life* for July 3, 1964: "We are not taking a dogmatic attitude that oral contraceptives are absolutely safe — and we do intend to review the evidence immediately. But the indications so far are that they are safe, when given under the supervision of a doctor . . . We are not worried. But we're going to watch it."

There is, it may be suggested, a more adequate response that could be made. It is that FDA sponsor a conference, preferably international rather than national in scope, at which the safety of the oral contraceptives would be examined. Let the world's foremost obstetricians and gynecologists meet together. Let the endocrinologists do the same, and biostatisticians, and other specialists, too. Within each meeting of specialists let there be confrontations between men of different views. Let there then be a plenary session for interdisciplinary discussion and adoption of recommendations. The problem is too important to be left entirely to FDA or even to FDA-sponsored committees. Millions of women are using birth-control pills. Is an intention "to review the evidence," being "not worried," and planning "to watch it" enough?

THE LATE Supreme Court Justice Robert H. Jackson once said, "Where experiment or research is necessary to determine the presence or the degree of danger, the product must not be tried out on the public, nor must the public be expected to possess the facilities or the technical knowledge to learn for itself of inherent but latent dangers. The claim that a hazard was not foreseen is not available to one who did not use foresight appropriate to his enterprise." As of April 1967 there were, by the estimate of the Food and Drug Administration, 6 million women in the United States, and 5 million elsewhere, who were using oral contraceptives. For an enterprise so massive the foresight could hardly have been more inappropriate. We know now that the evidence of safety which the agency had in hand for — bear in mind, a drug to be used not by sick people, but by healthy women — was more shockingly inadequate than was known when I wrote about the pills in The Therapeutic Nightmare. For example, it has been brought out that the data FDA had — "properly documented with laboratory studies" — as to a possible relation between the pills and cancer consisted of a four-year experience in 400 women. But "all known human carcinogens," the FDA's Advisory Committee on Obstetrics and Gynecology pointed out in August 1966, "require a latent period of approximately one decade." Proper studies to determine what relation may exist between the pills and breast, cervix, and endometrial cancer would take a decade (plus four-year-follow-ups); if the objective were to be able to detect, with an acceptable allowance for possible error, a two-fold increase in risk, at least 20,000 to 30,000 women, plus a minimum of 20,000 untreated controls, would be needed. Studies of such magnitude have never been done; plans for them were being made — in 1967 — by the National Institute for Child Health and Human Development.

Having set a standard for the marketing of the pioneer pill, Enovid, that was appropriate not to its enterprise but to its dismal, sloppy habits with other drugs, the FDA of Commissioner George P. Larrick and Medical Director Joseph F. Sadusk, Jr., could not very well set significantly higher standards for manufacturers who wanted to share a lucrative market with G. D. Searle & Co., Enovid's maker. Thus in the spring of 1965 FDA released two so-called sequentials, which involved a new form of action — estrogen-only pills to be taken for 15 days in the menstrual cycle, and combination estrogen-progestogen pills to be taken in the remaining 5 days. In addition to being a new form of action, the sequentials are slightly less efficacious than the combination products, according to the FDA Advisory Committee. Despite all of this, at the time of marketing approval the number of women who had taken Oracon, the Mead Johnson Laboratories sequential, for 18 *consecutive* menstrual cycles was 274, for 24 cycles it was 148 and for 36 cycles it was 16. For Eli Lilly's C-Quens the total for 18 cycles was 445, for 24 cycles it was 180 and for 30 cycles it was 4.

Probably nothing could better reveal the quality of science prevailing than the inconsistencies in labeling arrived at by the usual bargaining process between FDA medical officers and manufacturers' representatives. One oral contraceptive formulation is norethindrone plus mestranol. But when the brand name was Norinyl the prescribing instructions were not the same as when the brand name was Ortho-Novum. If a physician had a patient with a history of psychic depression he would be told not to prescribe Brand X; so he would prescribe Brand Y, whose labeling carried no warning. Yet Brand X and Brand Y were the same thing. Order was imposed on this chaos — of which a great many physicians were unaware — in November 1966 when the FDA, implementing a recommendation of its Advisory Committee, ordered uniform labeling for all brands. Now, for example, all brands warn against use in breast-feeding mothers because, "Detectable amounts of the active ingredients in oral contraceptives have been identified in the milk of mothers receiving these drugs. The significance of this dose to the infant has not been determined." Previously, only one labeling listed this as a contraindication. Until the spring of 1965 the possibility of premature closure of bone joints in young women whose skeletal growth was incomplete was a precaution listed in none of the labels; then it was put in one, and now it is in all.

". . . nor must the public be expected to possess the facilities or the technical knowledge to learn for itself of inherent but latent dangers," Justice Jackson said. In 1963 a group of experts known as the Wright Committee was convened by the FDA to look into clotting diseases in women on the pills. But even they lacked the facilities and the technical knowledge to assess whether the pills did or did not cause nonfatal — but sometimes permanently disabling — clots, the problem being that the essential data were unavailable or, to the extent available, defied analysis. As to fatal lung clots, the Wright Committee concluded only that the available data showed a risk in Enovid users that was not significantly higher than in nonusers. But again the data were shaky — a point emphasized by the Committee when it said that "any firm reliance on the risks as calculated is tempered by the assumptions made." The Committee made one — and only one — recommendation: that there be begun carefully planned, prospective trials in which randomly selected groups of women would be started on oral contraception and conventional contraception. Certainly FDA had the facilities and technical knowledge to seek to have such controlled studies undertaken; but not until 1966 did it begin to do so. Preparations also were being made by the National Institute of Child Health and Human Development. And so we have today what the Institute's Dr. Roy Hertz, a member of the FDA Advisory Committee, has called "a statistically inadequate mass of scattered observations" about the pills and clotting — when what we could have had was the answers.

Proper studies not having been undertaken, professional proponents of the pills easily could — and did — fend off extraordinary reports of, say, strokes in young women who had taken the drugs. Their answer became almost a litany: The pills have not been *proved unsafe*. Rarely, if ever, did they provide the scientifically mandatory counterbalance, that the pills also have not been *proved safe*; rarely did they say what weight of evidence would, in their eyes, constitute "proof"; rarely did they say that if they were talking in black-and-white terms "proof" is *never* attainable, and that in matters affecting the public health decisions must be based on relative evidence — on evidence, that is, which can permit a cautious conclusion that there is between drug and adverse effect a causal relation of statistically high or low probability. The paucity of data on a causal relation between the oral contraceptives and serious adverse reactions, the FDA's Advisory Committee recognized in its report of August 1966, "makes unreliable *any assumptions*. . . ." (My italics.) If "any assumptions" were unreliable in 1966, how could the FDA have concluded that "the evidence establishes the safety" of the pills in 1960? In its conclusion, the Committee said that it found "no adequate scientific data, at this time, proving these compounds unsafe for human use." But this turned things upside down, because since 1938 the burden had been on manufacturers to provide substantial evidence that a drug proposed for marketing was safe. Nowhere in the report did the Committee say there was substantial evidence that the pills were safe. The mistaken notion that it had so declared took hold in good part because of bad journalism that told people what they were generally predisposed to want to hear. The headline provided for the medical profession by the *AMA News*, the American Medical Association's "Newspaper of American Medicine," was "Oral Contraceptives Safe,/FDA Committee Reports." *Time* magazine's headline was "The Safe and Effective Pills." *Newsweek's* was "Popular, Effective, Safe." Commissioner James L. Goddard misguidedly went on television and made matters worse. The thrust of his message — which has since become much more cautious — was that a woman need not worry about the pills, provided she went to a physician who checked to see if she had anything adverse in her medical history and who examined her at regular intervals. But was the physician relying on the labeling for Brand X or Brand Y of the same compound? If the woman had never had a clot how would the doctor know if she was, or was not, going to get one? If she had a breast cancer which in its early stages was undetectable, and whose growth might be accelerated by the pills, how would he protect her?

"We are not worried," Dr. Joseph F. Sadusk, Jr., FDA's Medical Director, told *Life* for an article published on July 3, 1964, which was shortly after he joined the agency. "But we're going to watch it," he said. Two years later, the FDA Advisory Committee, which was headed by Dr. Louis M. Hellman of the State University of New York in Brooklyn, took a look at what the agency had learned. "The results were startling," Don Oberdorfer of the Washington Bureau of Knight Newspapers wrote in January 1967:

— FDA files reportedly contained only a single case of breast cancer in a woman taking oral contraceptives.

That is "silly," says Dr. Hellman. . . .

According to the National Cancer Institute, 317 cases of breast cancer a year would normally be expected among each 1,000,000 women in the pill-taking age group. On this purely statistical basis, the 3,800,000 women known to be taking oral contraceptives would have developed at least 1,200 cases of breast cancer last year. Yet the FDA had only heard of one.

— When the Hellman Committee asked FDA how many pill-takers had died of certain rare thromboembolic disorders (clots), the agency said that a computer would make a sweeping survey of its records to find out.

FDA's answer was "a little more than 30 cases," recalls Dr. Schuyler G. Kohl of New York City, who handled this phase of the Committee's research. The pill manufacturers immediately told Kohl the FDA was wrong — since they could remember reporting at least 70 such deaths. . . .

Even this was considered to be such gross underreporting as to "preclude drawing any conclusions. . . ."

In April 1965 Dr. Sadusk spoke from his watchtower about strokes and the pills. He saw "no evidence of a cause-and-effect relationship." In fact, he said, the "information at hand is to the contrary." This was untrue. Starting in 1962 the *British Medical Journal* had carried reports on strokes in women on the pills. Such reports did not establish a causal relation — but they were not "information . . . to the contrary." A month before Dr. Sadusk's pronouncement, two Johns Hopkins University School of Medicine physicians were disclosed to have collected data on about 20 young women who suffered strokes — some of them fatal — after taking the pills. Within days of Dr. Sadusk's statement a preliminary report — which in October 1965 was presented in full form to the American Heart Association — was made on six additional cases by Dr. Sherif S. Shafey, who heads the Cerebral Vascular Disease Research Center at the University of Miami School of Medicine in Florida, and Dr. Peritz Scheinberg, chairman of neurology at the school. They urged "awareness of the possible existence of a causal relationship." About a year after Dr. Sadusk left FDA two British neurologists reported that in the years 1964, 1965, and 1966 — years of sharply increased use of the pills — they had expected to treat a total of six to eight previously healthy women of child-bearing age who had suffered strokes of unexplained origin; this expectation was based on the fact that in the decade ended in 1963 they had treated 25 such women, or an average of two or three a year. But instead of the expected six or eight such patients, 25 were referred — and 18 had used one or the other of the oral contraceptives. This report, by Drs. Edwin R. Bickerstaff and J. MacDonald Holmes, was published in the *British Medical Journal* of March 25, 1967. Ten days later Kennedy Robinson, the British Minister of Health, reported that an investigation had shown that a woman on the pill runs "a slightly increased risk" of developing blood-clotting disorders. Almost simultaneously, in a cover story on the oral contraceptives headlined "Freedom from Fear," *Time* for April 7 said, ". . . there is *no evidence* that the pills cause blood clots that might travel to the lungs or develop in the brain." (My italics.) The statement was false: Either *Time* wrote on insufficient information, or the distinction between evidence (which there was) and proof (which there was not) was not clear to it. In the course of the story, *Time* told about the mother who "announced that she story, *Time* told about the mother who "announced that she was already slipping the pill into her daughter's breakfast milk." The anonymous mother's dangerous gamesmanship with a potent prescription drug was then escalated into a banner headline across the top of a full-page promotional ad for *Time* in the New York *Times*.

At the end of April, in San Francisco, three Western Reserve University School of Medicine neurologists — Drs. John H. Gardner, Stanley van den Noort, and Simon Horenstein — reported on nine women who suffered strokes associated with sustained use of oral contraceptives. Four were permanently disabled. In an abstract submitted in advance, and printed in the program for the annual meeting of the American Academy of Neurology, the Cleveland, Ohio, specialists referred to the six cases dealt with therein as "drug-induced catastrophes." Some 200 physicians heard Dr. Gardner present a paper on all nine cases. When he asked if they had seen women with migraine who suffered strokes while taking the pills, about two-thirds raised their hands. All nine women had migraine head-aches before their strokes — and those headaches were strongly suspected by the Western Reserve neurologists to be a signal to stop taking the pills, especially if the headaches are accompanied by visual difficulties. Apart from Dr. Sadusk and *Time*, prob-ably on one had done more to downgrade the possibility of a causal relation between the pills and clotting diseases than Dr. Alan F. Guttmacher, president of Planned Parenthood-World Population. But the San Francisco report moved him to say, according to the New York *Times* of May 23, 1967, "I'm sure there is some possible connection, and I don't think we can whitewash it."

One can only speculate about the results of the kind of watching done by Dr. Sadusk, who in March 1967 became an official of Parke, Davis, a maker of oral contraceptives, or of the kind of reporting and promoting done by *Time*. Neither is it known how few or how many women on the pills have suffered, or may suffer, fatal or lifelong disabling clots in their legs or strokes in their brains, or cancer, or psychic depression, or diabetes, or other diseases. There may be no significant chance of adverse effects on those children born to women who had taken the pills. But an "adequate analysis" of this question, Dr. Roy Hertz said in a special report published by the FDA Advisory Committee, would require "a population of 100,000 children . . . followed for 6 to 9 years in order to completely appraise any possible effects upon them." All of these imprecise risks may be well worth the taking by, say, a woman who has had nine children and will die if she has a tenth — for her, complete efficacy is indistinguishable from safety. For a woman who can, and will, reliably use vaginal foam or a diaphragm with cream or jelly, however, the same risks are another matter — she hazards no disease thereby, and over a year the efficacy of these methods is up around 97.5 per cent.

When a new drug is proposed for the sick, the public expects the Food and Drug Administration to make determined, scientific efforts to ascertain the consequences of such use, through the application of recognized standards of scientific experimentation. "The claim that a hazard was not foreseen is not available to one who did not use foresight appropriate to his enterprise," Justice Jackson said. The FDA of Commissioner George P. Larrick and Dr. Joseph F. Sadusk, Jr., did not apply recognized standards of scientific experimentation when the oral contraceptives were released — and the claim that a hazard was not foreseen is not available to them. I hope very much that there is no hazard — but we are now, in 1967, when 11 million women are using the pills, about to *start* the studies which will give us some answers and which were not undertaken in advance of this massive, uncontrolled experiment in which no one has been counting.

14

PAYMENT FOR DRUG TESTING:
THE "UNEASY MUDDLE"

THE PROFESSIONAL LITERATURE of medicine has been almost devoid of discussion about the ethics of compensation for drug testing — fees, expense accounts, travel allowances, gifts, grants for research. *Fortune* has said that the practices involved create an "uneasy muddle."

The Food and Drug Administration had given this area little attention when Senator Humphrey started to explore it late in 1963. Among the cases he found, each involving a different drug company, were the following, in which the fees proposed and/or paid were:

$12,000 for a physician to try out a drug in 150 women
$3000 for trial of a drug in 30 patients with angina pectoris
$3000 for investigating a drug in 50 patients with gastric ulcers
$5000 for trial of an anti-nausea product in 50 patients
$12,000 plus options to buy 4000 shares of stock at $3 per share, which was $4 below the market price, for experimenting with a device to be used during menstruation.

One case for which details were provided involved Deprol, a best-selling mild tranquilizer combination sold by Wallace Laboratories, a subsidiary of Carter Products. This is how Deprol was described before the Kefauver Subcommittee on Antitrust and Monopoly by Dr. Heinz E. Lehmann of Montreal, clinical director of Verdun Protestant Hospital, and assistant professor of psychiatry at McGill University:

> It is a combination of Miltown [meprobamate] again, which is one of the components, and the other component is Benactyzine, which is another one of the minor, or less potent, tranquilizers which hasn't found much of a market because it produces not much freedom from anxiety but sometimes causes more anxiety.
>
> In other words, it produces very unpleasant side effects in many cases. So what has been done is to combine these two, one effective and one not so effective, minor tranquilizers, and ascribe to them a new effect; namely, one of being effective in depressions. And that was done on the basis of one article which was published, and when the promotion campaign was started, the article had not even appeared in print yet although the work had been done. There is not much to substantiate the first early claims of its efficacy in depressions.

Another witness, Dr. Fritz A. Freyhan, who was then clinical director and director of research at the Delaware State Hospital in Farmhurst, told the subcommittee of a Deprol "Dear Doctor" letter that

> raises the impression that this is a most effective drug to be used in the treatments of depressions.
>
> It says: "Also, it is good in emotional fatigue and nervous exhaustion."
>
> Then: "It acts fast to relieve tiredness, lethargy, apathy, listlessness associated with emotional fatigue. It doesn't overstimulate your patient. Thus, Deprol restores normal interest and vitality before the condition deepens."
>
> Then it goes on. Now, the trouble with this is that neither

of the two component parts which Dr. Lehmann already identified and commented on can have any conceivable effect on the conditions here stated.

Miltown certainly isn't relieving tiredness or lethargy since it is well known to have an effect which is in the nature of a sedative. As far as the other component is concerned . . . again that is a compound which induces such symptoms as dry mouth and sometimes blurred vision.

. . . .

The very intensive Deprol promotion campaign which reaches my desk at least two or three times a week really makes me feel quite concerned about what may happen to depressed patients who are treated by the general practitioner.

Even before Dr. Freyhan and Dr. Lehmann testified, an extraordinary study was being carried out, with the support of a grant from the National Institute of Mental Health, at the New York Hospital–Westchester Division. The researchers were Armand Loranger, head of the Division's Department of Psychology, and Dr. Curtis T. Prout, its clinical director. "A unique feature of the experiment was the deception employed, to promote objectivity in those who were evaluating the patients," they said. "All the participating psychiatrists were informed that one new antidepressant drug, ST50, was being evaluated in the treatment of 60 depressed patients. Actually, 20 patients received deanol [sold by Riker Laboratories as Deaner], 20 benactyzine-meprobamate [Deprol], and 20 a placebo."

The patients — 39 men and 21 women, ranging in age from 12 to 72 — were assigned at random to the three treatment groups. Each group was closely matched on the basis of age, sex, diagnosis (18 patients were diagnosed as schizophrenics, 18 as involutional psychotics, 11 as manic-depressives, 11 as psychoneurotics, and 2 as paranoiacs), length of hospital stay, and severity of illness. Each patient was studied for 10 weeks. Each patient's psychiatrist filled out a questionnaire at the end of each week. Once a week for six weeks questionnaires were completed by the patients. A behavioral-rating scale was developed and revised with the assistance of the nurses. Separate ratings were devised for cooperation, mood, restlessness, irritability, tension or nervousness, energy or drive, preoccupation with health, sociability, and interest. Sleep records were charted daily. Blood pressure was measured three times weekly. Various laboratory evaluations were made.

All of this, and more, had been deemed necessary because, the researchers said, numerous reports had appeared since 1958 about the successful treatment of depressed patients with the two drugs — but almost none of the studies of them had been controlled, "and the few investigations attempting to use controls have been either inadequately reported or poorly designed."

When it was all over, the psychologist and the physician found a dramatic illustration of "the tendency of patients, psychiatrists and nurses to attribute improvement to a placebo because they had been informed that it was a real drug." Their investigation provided "no evidence that either deanol or benactyzine-meprobamate is of any value in the treatment of depressed patients," and that "there appears to be no scientific basis for the use of either drug in the treatment of depressed patients." In brief, the patients who received the drugs, on which vast sums have been spent, improved no more than did the patients who received the placebo.

✓ ✓ ✓

In June 1963, which was thirteen months after the Loranger-Prout report was published, a Washington blood specialist, Dr. Edward Adelson, received a form letter from Dr. J. Corboy Ryan, associate medical director of Wallace Laboratories. Dr. Adelson wrote to Senator Humphrey: "I am sure that this letter was sent to many doctors throughout the country. It stated, to the best of my recollections, that exciting new studies showed how effective their drug Deprol was. It was obvious to me from the letter that these studies were not very impressive, and I felt that the letter was an attempt to mislead me."

Dr. Adelson, an assistant professor of clinical medicine at the George Washington University School of Medicine, wrote to Dr. Ryan: "I feel that the enclosed advertisement is an insult to my intelligence. Poorly controlled studies by a general practitioner and a psychiatrist published in nonscientific medical journals are no evidence at all.

"Judging by your title, I assume that you must know this as well or better than I do. I can conclude only that this advertisement is a conscious and cynical attempt to mislead the unwary physician — and I resent it."

Not knowing of Dr. Adelson's letter to Dr. Ryan, a Wallace representative telephoned the hematologist's office in October 1963 and talked to his secretary. She left this memorandum for Dr. Adelson:

From: Joe Darby, Wallace Laboratories
Re clinical research — Deprol
Clinical Study — Grant will be $4,000 over 1 year on 100 selected patients and to supply all medications.
If interested please call.

Dr. Adelson wrote Humphrey that he

returned Mr. Darby's call and learned that Wallace Laboratories would pay me $4,000 to use Deprol on 100 patients. I cannot understand how the $4,000 figure was arrived at since such a study would cost me nothing. Mr. Darby told me that my name had been selected at random from the Directory of Medical Specialists.

If we accept Mr. Darby's statement that my name was selected at random, it strikes me as a sad commentary on the drug-testing policies of Wallace Laboratories and of the regulations of the Food and Drug Administration. The Directory of Medical Specialists lists me as an internist, with special training in blood disease. It shows no competence in the field of psychopharmaceutical drugs, and says nothing about my skill as an investigator, my understanding of the technique of placebo controls, or my scientific impartiality.

In my research in hematology I know that I must be wary of the unconscious bias not only for myself but also for my technicians. Often I arrange things so that my technicians will not know what sort of results I am expecting in order to be certain of obtaining unbiased data.

It is clear to me that a drug manufacturer who is anxious to obtain data to support the value of one of his drugs will be tempted to choose investigators who are more likely to give him the data he wants. Therefore, an investigator who depends on drug funds for his income knows that if he hopes to get further grants it would be better to obtain results proving the drug he is testing is a good one. While most physicians would not consciously falsify their data the unconscious bias would still be present and could be nearly as misleading.

This awareness of the need to avoid such bias is well known to most scientists and to much of the pharmaceutical industry. Indeed, it is because my contact with some of the manufacturers in the field on antileukemia agents has been so strikingly different from my contact with Wallace Laboratories that I have decided to write you.

I feel that the guardians of the standards of clinical testing should be the various professional organizations in the field. However, the FDA, which is charged with protecting the interests of the public, might have urged these organizations to establish such rules. Furthermore, when a report is submitted to FDA by the investigator, the Food and Drug Administration should know whether or not the investigator has been paid and, if so, how much.

The medical director of Wallace Laboratories, Dr. Martin C. Sampson, disputed Dr. Adelson's argument on several points. In a letter to Senator Humphrey, Dr. Sampson insisted that the June letter had not claimed "exciting new studies," but, rather, had quoted certain papers on Deprol. The spokesman also said that Darby had merely requested an appointment and that Dr. Adelson's name had been selected not "at random" but

because the Directory of Medical Specialists indicated he was Board qualified in internal medicine, associated with a medical school and hospital and trained and experienced in medical research. The preliminary approach to Dr. Adelson was made because we were interested in clinical studies of reactive depression associated with physical diseases, such as Leukemia . . .

What Mr. Darby did was ask Dr. Adelson if he were interested in conducting a grant-supported series of double-blind, placebo-controlled tests on Deprol over a period of 1 year, making his observations on 100 selected patients . . .

When Dr. Adelson asked about the nature of the grant, he was told that similar studies had been done on a budget of approximately $3,500. When he asked what the money was for, he was told that it was to pay for his services, for technicians or others who might assist him, laboratory fees, secretarial services in making out reports and keeping records, and other necessary expenses. At 10 visits per patient during a year, each visit requiring the clinician to make and record numerous special observations on an evaluation form, the grant per patient visit would have been $3.50 — scarcely an unreasonable figure for the extra work involved . . .

Dr. Adelson commented to Senator Humphrey: "As you know, I wrote my original letter to you out of a feeling of public responsibility. I do not feel that any useful purpose would be served by my entering into a debate with Wallace Laboratories. I would like, however, to reiterate that everything which I have stated in my letter to you was the truth and the exact truth."

Wallace Laboratories has continued to repeat what it would have physicians believe to be the truth about Deprol. "Distinguished by a record of more than six years of effectiveness and safety in the treatment of depressions with anxiety," said a headline on a two-page advertisement in the May 22, 1964, issue of *Medical World News*. ". . . the 'Deprol' record of effectiveness and safety in office, clinic and hospital practice is well documented.[1-7,9-17] This experience has shown that many depressions can be relieved by 'Deprol' without recourse to more hazardous drugs.[5,10,16]" The numbers in the foregoing passage from the advertisement text refer the physician to a bank of seventeen references. They include studies on Deprol that the Loranger-Prout study found inadequate. Not surprisingly, the references in the Deprol advertisement do not include the Loranger-Prouty study, which was described by the authors in the *New England Journal of Medicine* for May 24, 1962. The article was republished by the Humphrey subcommittee in 1964.

On November 23, 1964, the Food and Drug Administration announced plans for the enforcement of the Kefauver-Harris requirement that advertising to physicians of prescription drugs include a brief, true, and nonmisleading summary of information about adverse side effects, contraindications, and effectiveness. The announcement said:

. . . FDA will seek to determine whether a fair balance exists between the information on effectiveness and that on side effects and contraindications.

The Bureau of Medicine will monitor professional journal advertising for prescription drugs. It will forward violative advertisements with appropriate recommendations to the Bureau of Regulatory Compliance.

Kinds of copy which may violate the law include the following:

1. Extension or distortion of the claims for usefulness beyond that approved in the product's final printed labeling.

2. Featuring of a quote from an article in a way which misleads by improperly implying that the particular study is representative of much larger and general experience with the drug.

3. The selection of poor quality research papers making statements favorable to the product while ignoring contrary evidence from much better research.

4. Quotation out of context of a seemingly favorable statement by an authoritative figure but omission of unpleasing data from the same article.

5. Quoting from an obviously authoritative source while failing to quote from other differing experts in the same field with the result that a properly balanced view is not given.

6. Featuring data from papers that report no side effects, but failing to quote from others that do.

7. Continuing to run ads which are constructed from data previously valid but rendered obsolete or false by more recent research.

✓　✓　✓

"I have come to the conclusion," Dr. M. Harold Book, of the University of Pennsylvania Graduate School of Medicine and Norristown State Hospital, wrote to Senator Humphrey, "that any system in which the pharmaceutical houses delegate the testing of drugs to physicians of their own choosing will not work."

Where so much potential profit is involved any honest doubts as to the value of a new drug preparation are likely to be resolved in favor of the acceptance of the new drug by non-medical officials of the firm.

On the other hand, a scientifically oriented researcher, not in the employ directly or indirectly of the manufacturer, will invariably resolve any doubt against its acceptance, since he will have the interests of the patients pre-eminent in his mind, rather than that of the stockholders.

"The question of conflict of interest of a scientific investigator receiving support of any nature from a drug firm is a very difficult one," another physician wrote Senator Humphrey in response to a questionnaire distributed by his subcommittee. The correspondent continued:

> There is actually little difference whether this support takes the form of an outright fee for service, a consultation retainer, or the acceptance of support for technicians, fellows, equipment, etc., etc. Any and all of these forms of support benefit the investigator personally, and support his work. There are other ways of course, such as dinners, conferences, railway fares, travel to distant lands, etc., etc.
>
> The danger in all this . . . is to engender the feeling, one mustn't strike the hand that feeds one; a subconscious and increasing dependency on the numerous forms drug industry support takes: this of course very much involves our medical journals through advertising.

Dr. A. Dale Console, whose experience included the medical directorship of a large pharmaceutical house, has warned, however, against any assumption that elimination of monetary rewards would assure objectivity in drug testing. He wrote to Senator Humphrey:

> . . . for every spurious report which is the result of excessive payment of fees for testing, there are 10 in which money

was a minor consideration and for each of these there are in turn 10 in which the adverse effect on objectivity was not determined by money at all. In brief, we are attacking approximately 1 to 10 percent of the problem.

Having spent some 6 years in the business of influencing clinical investigators, I can assure you that objectivity can be destroyed more frequently and more effectively by the soft sell than by a bribe. Even the fraud maintains a semblance of pride, and anyone who seeks to exploit it would be a fool to interfere with the process of self-deception which makes it possible.

Of the 946 "investigators" who are proudly reported to have "studied" a new drug, only a handful were influenced by large grants. As suggested by previous respondents, a luncheon, an honorarium, a trip to Europe are also nice and will suffice.

The vast majority, however, had other motivations. A paternalistic attitude toward the detail man who is a "nice fellow" and who requests the "study"; the positive response to the medical director "who traveled all the way from New York" to "consult" the "investigator"; the wish to be an "investigator" and perhaps to be invited to give a paper at a "symposium"; the fantasy of prestige and of the respect of the medical community; the certain knowledge that no one ever won a Nobel Prize by publishing a negative paper about an obscure drug; the fantasy of the "pioneer" who blazes the trail to the discovery of a new drug — these are only a few examples of the really potent influences which determine objectivity in drug studies.

Any employee of a drug firm who is worth his salt has an expert's appreciation of their power, a gourmet's taste for their subtleties, and the deft, delicate touch which leads the "investigator" to hang himself.[1]

[1] It might be noted here than even a double-blind trial may sometimes take place under conditions leaving some room for bias. An example of this dismaying

One with a gourmet's taste for irony might contemplate the cartoon which appeared in the *New Yorker* for February 8, 1964, with an exultant scientist in a white coat holding a test tube aloft and saying ". . . I'll phone a broker." Suppose he had been testing, say, MER/29, the anticholesterol drug. Suppose further that, three weeks before it was to be released to the market, well in advance of the predictable boom in the price of Richardson-Merrell stock (which occurred), he were to get a gracious letter (as many actually did) from the manufacturer that began this way:

Dear Dr. ——:

Events of interest concerning drugs in development should, we feel, be made known first to the investigators whose combined efforts have created the existing basic and clinical information about them. It becomes my pleasure, therefore, to announce to you that MER/29 will become available for prescription use in the United States and Canada on June 1, 1960 . . .

One of the least enlightening responses to Senator Humphrey's queries came from the president of the American Society for

---

fact was provided in the November–December 1963 issue of the *Journal of New Drugs* by Dr. Daniel M. Green, vice president for research and development of the Grove Laboratories, a division of Bristol-Myers Company. He wrote: "We have had occasion to send one investigator two drugs, each identified only by its own code number, and impressing him with the importance of expediting the trial. One drug was sent immediately and the other was forwarded after a delay of about two weeks. When the trial was concluded, the results with the first drug were significantly better than those with the second."

Apparently, the investigator thought the drug that was rushed to him was, merely by virtue of the fact, a promising new experimental product, and that the second, about which no urgency was being shown, was inferior or obsolete. Assumptions of this kind are strengthened by Dr. Green's account of what happened when there was no indication to the investigator that the first drug was better than the second: "After a lapse of several months, a new trial was established with the same investigator and the same two drugs, but completely randomized samples. This time the results failed to demonstrate any difference between medications."

Pharmacology and Experimental Therapeutics, Inc., Dr. F. E. Shideman of the University of Minnesota College of Medical Sciences. "It is imperative for industry to pick well-qualified and reliable investigators," he said. It has *always* been imperative. "The drug industry cannot financially or morally afford to market a product which does not meet the standards of the medical profession as to safety, effectiveness and quality." This assertion, blandly and blindly made, is followed by an expression of the Society's view that problems of compensation for drug testing are "delicate and must be treated with careful consideration." Presumably inspired by FDA's past record, the Society urged through its spokesman that the Humphrey subcommittee "discontinue its activities in connection with this problem," at least until FDA has had an opportunity to demonstrate how well it uses its "new and as yet untried powers to screen drug investigators." As of this writing the powers are no longer new, they are still untried, and will be allowed by FDA to remain in their pristine state.

In stark contrast to this soporific approach, the president of the American Society of Clinical Investigation, Dr. Irving M. London of the Albert Einstein College of Medicine, said: "To eliminate any influence, overt or subtle, of drug companies upon the investigator, there should be no direct payment of a fee by the drug company to the investigator." And Dr. L. Clagett Beck, president of the American Therapeutic Society, wrote Senator Humphrey that his five-hundred-member group was "very much opposed to any one individual receiving any sum for the reporting of this study [on drugs used in a Society training program for physicians] from any drug company."

THE STORY OF DEPROL seems to go on and on, with the kind of inevitability usually associated with death and taxes. The drug is made, it may be recalled, by Wallace Pharmaceuticals [formerly Wallace Laboratories], the division of Carter-Wallace, Inc., which in the Pree MT episode in the Afterword to Chapter 4 was described by the American Medical Association as "a highly reputable pharmaceutical concern." It may also be recalled that Armand Loranger and Dr. Curtis T. Prout did a carefully controlled study which produced "no evidence" that Deprol "is of any value in the treatment of depressed patients," and that this study was published in 1962 by the *New England Journal of Medicine*, in 1964 by the Senate Subcommittee on Reorganization and International Organizations, and in 1965 — in summary form — in *The Therapeutic Nightmare*. Apparently these publications have been inaccessible to the company, to its advertising agency, and to the AMA, which maintains, as Glenn R. Knotts, Director of Advertising Evaluation said in a speech in April 1965, advertising screening boards that limit claims of usefulness "to those which can be documented by scientific fact." In late 1966 and in early 1967 ads for Deprol in the *Journal* of the AMA, and in other medical publications, included a footnote saying, "A review through July 1966 of *all available* published clinical studies on 'Deprol' shows an overall response rate of approximately 75% in non-psychotic depressions. . . ." (My italics.) This was followed by 21 citations to reports published in the years 1958 to 1965. The Loranger-Prout study, which found Deprol to be no more effective than a placebo, was not among them. Not only did the company omit any reference to the Loranger-Prout study which was first published in 1962, but it also cited an article by Loranger alone which was published in the Netherlands in 1961 — and which briefly describes a Deprol study but gives *no data on results.*

In its issue of February 24, 1967, the *Medical Letter* used the Deprol ads to illustrate, among other things, the "misleading use of citations in drug advertisements. . . . Rarely," the publication said, "do physicians have time to check the references cited . . . in support of the claims made . . . long lists of references may include very few having any bearing on the claims. . . . When they relate to the claims there is often reason for questioning the quality of the studies, and therefore the validity of claims based on those studies."

The report by the nonprofit *Letter* about ads that had been highly profitable to the manufacturer and to the AMA produced an investigation by the Food and Drug Administration. Shortly Wallace Pharmaceuticals sent a corrective letter — under threat of an FDA seizure action accompanied by a press release — to the country's prescribing physicians. The remedial letter concerned not only Deprol, which was said in the ad to be "a logical first choice for depression," but also Miltown, the sedative/tranquilizer which is, as meprobamate, one of the two ingredients of Deprol. The company called attention to an ad that FDA considers "may have been misleading." The company went on to concede that the ad, which was captioned, "The published clinical studies indicate: 3 of 4 non-psychotic depressions respond to 'Deprol,'" failed to tell the physician of the exclusion of data under three significant circumstances — when "the diagnosis was not entirely clear," when the recommended daily dosage was exceeded, or when the treatment included other drugs or electric convulsive therapy. The "3 of 4" efficacy claim was derived from 323 patients who were selected from 10 of the 21 studies listed in the ads. But Wallace Pharmaceuticals conceded in the letter that 9 of those 10 studies were uncontrolled; in addition, most of the 323 patients "concomitantly received informal or structured psychotherapy." The results acknowledged by the company ranged from zero — "in a study with two non-psychotic depressed patients" — "through 64 per cent in a study with 53 such patients, to 90 per cent in two studies with 38 and 41 such patients respectively." Such hopes as this may have raised were damaged when the remedial letter admitted that, "to an undetermined degree," the results included the use of a placebo and improvements in patients that occurred spontaneously. Among the 21 studies cited in the ads were three that mentioned a report which purportedly demonstrated that either meprobamate or benactyzine, the other ingredient of Deprol, is an effective antidepressant. Actually, the *Medical Letter* said, the paper "does not even mention antidepressant effects."

In its "Dear Doctor" letter, Wallace Pharmaceuticals said the problems it had cited in connection with Deprol "exist in working with any literature and are present in some 'Miltown' advertisements carrying the theme 'one of a series.' In order to avoid any misunderstanding, we have discontinued the use of these. . . ." The series, which in each case struck the keynote of "Let's take a second look at 'Miltown,'" included one two-page ad in the *Journal* of the American Medical Association which, in lovely color, showed little boys and girls playing ring-around-the-rosie. The caption was, "What's to be learned about 'Miltown' from 50 studies with children?" What the FDA learned was enough to demand that such ads not reappear. More importantly, the abuses in the Deprol and Miltown ads became the underpinning for several of the specific "Thou-shalt-nots" in new prescription-drug advertising regulations.

15

DOCTORS' CONFLICTS OF INTEREST

Two days after Dr. Roy Hertz, the National Cancer Institute endocrinologist, spoke in New York the *Wall Street Journal* reported that his comments had affected drug stocks on the New York Stock Exchange: "Johnson & Johnson dropped $8.25 to $105 and Parke, Davis & Co. fell $1.875 to $33.125. Both make birth control pills. Searle stock, traded over the counter, dropped to $137.50 bid, $141.75 asked, from $141.25 bid, $145.25 asked . . . Syntex Corp., which supplies the raw materials for both the Johnson & Johnson and Parke, Davis pills, plunged $28.50 to $199 on the American Stock Exchange."

That was in October 1963. In May 1964, the Vatican weekly *L'Osservatore della Domenica* said that research on pills that control ovulation should be encouraged and might lead the Roman Catholic Church to "re-examine" its position on birth control. Immediately after this news broke, the New York *Times* for May 28 said, heavy trading began on the New York Stock Exchange:

> Parke, Davis soared to 32¾ before easing to close at 31, up 2⅝ on the day. Volume totaled 85,900 shares, enough to put it in third slot on the active list.
>
> G. D. Searle [previously traded over-the-counter and split 3 for 1 in December 1963] reached 66¼ before trading was

temporarily stopped. Shortly thereafter, the issue opened on a block of 10,000 shares at 66. Late profit taking pared the price to 65¼, for a 3¼ point gain on the day.

Johnson & Johnson traded as high as 107¼ and ended at 102½, up 2½.

Syntex, which had gyrated wildly from a 1963 low of 11 to 190½ in January 1964, went up 6½, closing at 91½. Volume totaled 213,600 shares, the highest of any traded on the American Stock Exchange.

This flurry of activity occurred even though news dispatches quoted the Vatican weekly as saying that existing oral contraceptive pills were not acceptable to Roman Catholics, and though a possibly acceptable pill, one that would regulate timing of ovulation rather than prevent conception, was regarded as a remote possibility by pharmaceutical sources.

The stock-price ups and downs recalled an advertisement published early in 1964 by a stock market advisory service: "The biggest 'side effects' produced thus far by oral contraceptives are to be found not among the ladies . . . but rather among the investors excited about . . . the Drug Industry's new 'glamor product' . . ."

An estimated seven physicians out of ten invest in the stock market. What of those who become investors — "excited" or not — in drug stocks? Are they as likely to make cautionary reports (like that of Dr. Hertz) about drugs manufactured by companies in which they have invested?

Are they influenced, even if unconsciously, to recommend and prescribe drugs made by companies in which they have invested? Is ownership of drug stocks by physicians in the best interests of patients? "For some patients," Hippocrates said, "though conscious that their condition is perilous, recover their health simply through their contentment with the goodness of the physician. And it is well to superintend the sick to make them well, to care for the healthy to keep them well, but also to care for one's own self, so as to observe what is seemly." In his Hippocratic Oath the physician swears, "With purity and with holiness I will pass my life and practice my Art . . . and will abstain from every voluntary act of mischief and corruption . . . may it be granted to me to enjoy life and the practice of the Art, respected by all men, in all times!"

"What I fear is the increasingly prevalent image of the physician as the businessman," Dr. Walter Modell, the Cornell University Medical College pharmacologist, said at the 1962 convention of the American Association for the Advancement of Science. ". . . If the public believes that *caveat emptor* has been substituted for the oath of Hippocrates, the whole physician-patient relationship changes. The businessman-doctor does not command the respect and does not have the authority that a physician should have." The Judicial Council of the American Medical Association, however, considers it seemly for physicians to invest in drug stocks. The reflective patient, the man who expects that the fee he pays his physician is buying professional services and skills in which his welfare is the exclusive consideration, might think otherwise. It makes no difference at all if a physician buys a Buick instead of a Chrysler solely because he owns stock in General Motors. It might make a considerable difference, on the other hand, if a physician's ownership of drug stocks influences — even if unconsciously — *whether* he prescribes, *what* he prescribes, or his decision to prescribe a brand name instead of a lower-priced generic product.

In response to an invitation to physicians to give him their views on this seldom discussed subject, Senator Humphrey was told by some doctors that they could see a genuine problem only if the amount of stock owned in a pharmaceutical house is substantial. But the chairman of a department of pediatrics at a university teaching hospital said, "I have never held any stock in drug companies during 40 years of practice simply because I felt this was a conflict of interest even though it was known only to me." Another physician in a similar university post wrote, "I believe that physician ownership of [drug] stock . . . should be prohibited." A New Jersey internist inquired of the AMA whether drug stocks were in its large portfolio of securities. Receiving no reply, he wrote Senator Humphrey that he would find it "reassuring to know that the AMA is not judging drugs in the capacity of a stockholder."

As a practical matter, the question of physician-ownership of stocks in companies whose products they prescribe is not as pressingly important as the question of such ownership in companies for which doctors do drug testing. While this problem apparently has not excited the AMA, it has been taken seriously in Washington. In response to a query from Senator Humphrey about ownership of drug securities by National Institutes of Health administrators and scientists who may be engaged in drug-related research, the Director of the Institutes, Dr. James A. Shannon, said:

> Potential conflict of interest in the conduct of public business is, and has been, of concern to us at NIH. Even prior to the formal Health, Education, and Welfare Departmental statement [dated July 26, 1960] our clinical investigators recognized the impropriety of owning stock in drug companies whose products they were evaluating. On several occasions the decision to refrain from purchase and/or to divest themselves of inappropriate holdings was made by investigator teams on the basis of personal moral convictions.

It remained for the American Society for Pharmacology and Experimental Therapeutics, Inc., to turn the whole question on its head. In a statement in May 1964 the Society said:

> In a democracy such as ours each individual can make his or her choice as to investment of earnings. The pharmaceuti-

cal industry has no right to invade the private domain of any investigator by inquiring as to whether his investments include the possession of stock in any particular company. Thus, any scientific investigator should not be restricted in his ownership of stock in the particular company for which he may be conducting an investigation.

The Society's statement then became distinctly more Orwellian, and distinctly less therapeutic:

> . . . even though an investigator may have a personal interest [ownership of stock] in the company for which he is carrying out investigational work, it is even more to his advantage to present an honest appraisal of his work. He will not personally profit by encouraging a pharmaceutical company to market an inferior product.

Why not? Hundreds upon hundreds of inferior, worthless, and even dangerous drug products — some of which are mentioned in this book — have been marketed, and vast fortunes have been made on them. Would the Council have us believe, in defiance of common sense, that investigators have never profited through timely buying and selling of stocks in firms about whose plans they have firsthand information?

✔ ✔ ✔

For the investing physician there was developed, in 1963, a new monthly magazine, a $24-a-year mutation called *Health Industry* which is intended to put money in the physicians' jeans. The magazine explores for the doctor popular areas of investment, analyzes health-industry companies in particular, and keeps its subscribers informed about how their medical colleagues are making out in investment clubs. *Health Industry* was a probably inevitable efflorescence, sprouting from soil enriched by such things as the attitude of the American Medical Association that being a physician does not ethically preclude investment in pharmaceutical stocks.

The magazine is said to be intended for physicians' eyes only, and this is understandable. The very name *Health Industry* might agitate less resilient patients to plead with their physicians, or investment counselors, for a tranquilizer, or perhaps for a good tip on the market. These remedies might not suffice if such patients were to explore the preview issue. There they would find an article on a "small but savvy" instrument specialist, the Birtcher Corporation, which has "gambled that doctors are actually people in running 'Playboy'-type ads in normally staid medical journals. And the gamble seems to be paying off . . ." But does one want to be cauterized by a Birtcher Hyfrecator not because the product is excellent, but because the manufacturer is "savvy" enough to run advertisements showing bosomy, unclad bunnies? "She's been hyfrecated," the advertisement says. "Not a blemish on her." Not on her, no.

One of the consultants to *Health Industry* is Harry I. Greenfield, the founder of Medical Securities Fund, Inc., a mutual fund. "There is," he has said, "nothing unethical or immoral in physicians serving on the boards of any companies and it certainly makes a lot of sense that they be able to contribute to the deliberations of a company which is in their field."

There may be more things in your philosophy, Harry Greenfield, than you may have dreamt of. One is doctor-ownership of pharmacies. Another is doctor-ownership of pharmaceutical houses that merchandise "private label" products — firms, generally small and generally regional in operation, that repackage and label and, in some cases, manufacture. While thousands of physicians, and possibly Harry Greenfield, saw nothing unethical or immoral in these forms of medical entrepreneurmanship, the Senate Subcommittee on Antitrust and Monopoly decided to look into them.

In August 1964 the subcommittee, now headed by Senator Philip A. Hart, Democrat of Michigan, conducted an inquiry. The primary concern was with whether physicians who prescribe drugs made or sold by firms in which they have a financial interest are engaged in unfair competition and are in possible restraint of trade. At the close of six days of hearings, Senator Hart announced, "I shall forward the transcripts of these hearings to the Federal Trade Commission and the Justice Department for a determination of whether the practices involved violate the existing antitrust laws. If not, we must determine whether reasonable legislation can be devised to halt these practices." His announcement was founded on disclosures summarized this way in his closing statement:

Clearly, a doctor's participation in the ownership and profits of pharmacies and drug companies in his geographic area puts a financial decision in front of him each time he picks up a pen to write a prescription.

. . . .

Apparently there are doctors — and I emphasize that they are a tiny minority — who use monopoly prescription power, which was given by law to protect the patient, in order to exploit that patient, to damage independent businessmen and to enrich their own bank balance.

. . . .

The record is clear that if a doctor decides to allow his financial interest in a drug enterprise to influence his prescribing of medication then the independent druggist in his area cannot compete . . . While this problem, as was pointed out by the minority [Senator Everett Dirksen] at the start of these hearings, is not as important as Vietnam, it is extremely important to the independent druggist or small company in the area affected whose very existence is threatened by the growth of these practices.

It is to be assumed that once the advantages of doctor-ownership of these enterprises are demonstrated, the practice will grow until those who see this problem as minor today will beg for action on what has become a "major" problem.

We are told — and I agree — that no ethical doctor will prescribe a product only because he stands to benefit financially. But — if the doctor is convinced that his company's — or pharmacy's — product is as good as a competitor's, he is very likely to prescribe the one which benefits him financially. As one witness explained, "This is only human nature."

We are told that these drug companies are not doing well financially. The question is whether they would be in business at all if it were not for prescription-writing doctor stockholders.

.   .   .   .

Certainly, it has been adequately demonstrated in testimony here that the intent of the companies was that doctor-owners should help sales by prescribing the company products.

This seems not only a restraint of trade, but it encourages those doctors to prescribe by trade name rather than the low cost generic names which often cost $\frac{1}{10}$ or less of the trade name drugs.

The purpose of the Drug Amendments was to encourage the generic name prescriptions. Certainly we are fighting a hard battle when a doctor is tempted to bypass generic drugs for one in which he has a financial interest.

. . . It seems to me that the doctor is charged with treating the whole man — not just one ailment. Ability to pay is a well established principle in the profession. It seems ability to pay should be a consideration too when writing prescriptions.

What amazes me is that a great and noble calling such as

medicine has members who apparently are willing to besmirch the public image of the great majority of dedicated doctors for the possible extra financial rewards involved.

What further amazes me is that this same overwhelming majority of dedicated physicians let their colleagues get away with it.

I turn now to some of the specific matters developed at the hearings that prompted such a forceful statement by a man widely regarded as the gentlest and kindest in the Senate.

✓   ✓   ✓

In 1954, the Code of Ethics of the American Medical Association said, "It is unethical for a physician to participate in the ownership of a drugstore in his medical practice area unless adequate drugstore facilities are otherwise unavailable." In the following year, this rigid prohibition was made flexible, if not limp, through the addition of a qualification under which ownership became permissible "as long as there is no exploitation of the patient." How the House of Delegates came to adopt this qualification was not made clear. The AMA's spokesmen at the hearings were not physicians but lawyers. One, Robert B. Throckmorton, its general counsel, said he did not know why the code was changed. Another witness was Dr. George A. Woodhouse of Greenville, Ohio, a former chairman of the AMA's Judicial Council, which has jurisdiction over all questions of medical ethics. His position aroused sympathy. In his prepared statement he felt compelled to defend the AMA, but under questioning he acknowledged that his personal feeling is that doctor ownership of pharmacies is "a bad practice." As to the change in 1955, he could only say, "Something did happen which caused the House of Delegates to change its mind, but what that something was, I could not tell you."

What that "something" may have been was suggested by Paul

A. Pumpian, secretary of the Wisconsin State Board of Pharmacy. A witness at the final session of the hearings, Pumpian said that policy-makers of the AMA, including a former president, Dr. Gunnar Gundersen from Wisconsin, had reshaped the Code of Ethics to escape a conflict with their own financial interest in pharmacies. The AMA's spokesman, lawyer Throckmorton, said angrily that he had "never heard anything as unfair and as un-American." Later, Pumpian arose, invoked "a point of personal privilege," and said he had heard no denial from Throckmorton that physician-owners of drugstores had influenced the AMA's change in position, which now has been in force for a decade. "It seems to me," Senator Hart said in his closing statement, "that what was declared unethical in 1954 becomes no less unethical today merely because of a change of wording in the AMA Code of Ethics."

Pumpian's accusation was denied by Dr. Gundersen, who was president of the AMA in 1958–1959, in a telephone interview with the Washington *Post.* "I had no influence — no more than any other individual," he said modestly, adding that the AMA is "a democratic organization." In 1955, when the House of Delegates modified the code, Dr. Gundersen became chairman of the board of trustees of that democratic organization. He had been a member of the board since 1948. With two of his brothers, Dr. Gundersen owns the stock of the Gundersen Clinic in La Crosse, Wisconsin. The clinic has long had a pharmacy, but, Dr. Gundersen said, it is a mile or a mile and a half from the nearest drugstore. He said that he considers this distance so substantial as to be encompassed by the original provision in the Code of Ethics permitting doctor-ownership if other drugstore facilities are unavailable. When the AMA witness, counsel Throckmorton, was testifying before Senator Hart, however, he cited as an example of remoteness a physician in Daggett, Michigan, who is twenty-four miles from the nearest pharmacy to the south and forty miles from the nearest drugstore to the north.

Dr. Woodhouse, who had been a member of the AMA's Judicial Council for eight years, became chairman in 1961. In that role, he pressed for and obtained a year-long study of the issue of doctor-ownership of drugstores. The result was a unanimous recommendation by the Council for a return to the pre-1955 prohibition, with no loopholes making ownership acceptable if there is "no exploitation of the patient." The recommendation was referred to a so-called reference committee of the House of Delegates that held a one-day hearing. The forthright Dr. Woodhouse recalled before the Antitrust subcommittee that "quite a number" of the witnesses had been physicians who themselves had a financial stake in drugstores, or who were spokesmen for a group that promotes the establishment of pharmacies in private medical clinic buildings. It was not with them but with Dr. Woodhouse that the reference committee had a quarrel, for he had outraged it by publicly disclosing the proposed tightening of the code. His medical colleagues on the AMA's committee "really ground me up pretty fine," Dr. Woodhouse testified before Senator Hart. "I looked like I had come out of a meat grinder."

With this, the House of Delegates reaffirmed in 1962 the eviscerated position adopted in 1955: that it is not evil *per se* for a doctor to have an interest in a pharmacy, or, as Throckmorton said, that the *opportunity* to exploit cannot be equated with actual exploitation. An argument can be made for this position, and the doctors chose an able lawyer to make it for them. It is difficult to see, notwithstanding, why the number of opportunities for exploitation should be expanded beyond the irreducible minimum. Perhaps the problem would be negligible if physicians were always to disclose their ownership to patients. Dr. Woodhouse thought this "might be a good practice." Throckmorton, however, did not discuss the idea.

Whatever the origins of the modification of the code, and whatever its weakness, it does *not* condone exploitation of the patient. In fact, even though the Council's recommendation was repudiated and Dr. Woodhouse was run through a meat grinder, the Council promulgated opinions demonstrating that the code could be interpreted so as to offer firm guidelines against exploitation, and to leave the patient with a free choice as to who shall fill his prescriptions. Throckmorton summarized the Council's guidance to doctors this way:

— The patient is entitled to a copy of his prescription for drugs or appliances;

— The patient must have a clear right to have his prescription filled wherever he chooses;

— The physician must not enter into any agreement to dispense prescriptions in code;

— The Council looks with disfavor upon use of a direct telephone line between physician and pharmacist;

— Prescription blanks should not include the name of any pharmacy.

In addition, it is the official position of the AMA that "the rental of space by a physician or group of physicians as a pharmacy should be a fixed one. Were the rental to be based on the amount of business, it might well be argued, and indeed be the case, that fee splitting existed. In addition, the temptation would be ever present for the doctor-owner to encourage patients to take their prescriptions to that pharmacy. The evils inherent in such practice are too obvious to be mentioned."

It is too obvious *not* to be mentioned that all of these guidelines are grossly violated. Grant that the Code of Ethics does not condone exploitation of the patient; it frequently occurs nonetheless. The Council may, for example, look with disfavor on the impairment of the patient's freedom of choice by the use of direct telephone lines between doctors' offices and particular pharmacies, but the lines exist. Often such telephone setups exist within a clinic building where the pharmacy to which the patient is steered is owned by the physician and his medical colleagues, or is leased out under the condemned arrangement that gives them a percentage of the gross. Before the Hart subcommittee, William S. Apple, executive director of the American Pharmaceutical Association, said, "I have to confess" that for two or three years his group had been unable to persuade medical societies to enforce the policy against such leases. The reason, he testified, is that those offering such leases may be the very officers of the county medical society.

A spokesman for the National Association of Retail Druggists, Philip F. Jehle, testified that although the number of physician-owned pharmacies is not great — about 2200 — the total is "steadily increasing." The most detailed examination was provided by Paul Pumpian, the Wisconsin official. In his state as of 1964, he testified, 24 pharmacies were owned by physicians, their wives and families, or their agents, and all but one were in communities with other pharmaceutical service. Half of the doctor-owned pharmacies had been opened *since 1960*. The nature of the competition was indicated by figures showing that physician-owned drugstores filled three to five times more prescriptions on the average than do other pharmacies. Often, the witness continued, the free samples manufacturers send to doctors were not given away but were used to fill prescriptions in the pharmacies they own, the patients being charged standard prices. Turning to another "unfair trade practice," Pumpian discussed the lease of space in a doctor-owned building to a pharmacist who pays an exorbitant rental. The official testified:

While it is true that a pharmacist is not forced into such an arrangement, pharmacists are often convinced by the physicians that even with a high rental they could do well in the physician's building.

Since the rental is invariably based on sales, the physicians "direct" their patients to the pharmacy operated by their lessee to increase their rental income.

A pharmacist who was recently in my office informed me that he was not going to continue to operate the pharmacy in which he had been practicing for the past five years. He had been leasing space in a building owned by the five physicians practicing there at a rental of 15% of his gross sales [which was to go to 20% when annual volume reached $60,000]. He had to provide, without charge, medication needed for use by the physicians and their families in addition to which he was providing medication at cost for the use of the physicians in their practice. He found that he was unable to continue in business under this arrangement . . .

In related testimony, Pumpian told of medication being dispensed in doctors' offices by assistants with little or no training in the handling of drugs but wearing the white uniforms that might lead some patients to think they were nurses. He displayed boxes and even kraft paper bags of pills that had been so dispensed and were barren of the information needed for refills or for antidote in case of emergency.

Apple, the Pharmaceutical Association official, told of a town of 5000 in which six physicians had been writing prescriptions that were being filled at whichever of the three town pharmacies the patient cared to patronize. Since 1963 that town has faced the prospect of a physician-owned pharmacy monopoly. Apple told the Antitrust subcommittee how this had come about:

Last year, the six physicians decided to establish a group practice and build a medical building which would include a pharmacy. The physicians invited each of the three pharmacists to submit bids on the lease for the pharmacy in their building. They made it quite clear that the lease would be awarded to the highest bidder. The basis of the bid would

be a percentage of the total gross receipts of the pharmacy.
Two of the pharmacists flatly rejected the offer . . . The
third, however, decided to take advantage of the opportunity . . .

   After only a few months . . . the other two pharmacists
[suffered a severe loss in prescription sales] . . . They discovered that the physicians had an arrangement with the pharmacist in the medical building whereby it was almost impossible for a patient to leave the physicians with a *written* prescription order. [Italic mine.]

✓ ✓ ✓

Although the implementation of the policy of the American
Medical Association on doctor-ownership of "private label" drug
firms requires some explanation, the policy itself is clear enough.
It is that it is unethical for a physician to own stock in a pharmaceutical firm "which he can control or does control while actively
engaged in the practice of medicine." The operative word is
"control." Ownership in a drug repackaging or "private label"
firm of the kind to be discussed here — small, regional in scope,
generally doing nothing more than promoting and merchandis-
ing products made by others — is, AMA general counsel Robert
Throckmorton testified, "flatly condemned." Despite this attitude, and despite similar expressions by local and state societies
in Texas, Utah, and elsewhere, there were, by estimate of the
staff of the Senate Antitrust subcommittee, some 5000 physicians who were owners of 128 such companies. The position of
the AMA's spokesman on what could be seen as a large-scale
defiance of medical ethics was in substance this: the problem
was a relatively new one; the policies cited here consequently had
been adopted not very long before the hearings; time has to be
allowed for the message to be circulated and understood; and
"within a reasonable time, physician ownership of drug repackaging companies will, in the main, disappear." Whether this

optimism will prove to be warranted remains to be seen. And, as a member of the subcommittee staff pointed out, although the AMA has declared it improper for an individual doctor to own stock in a firm he can or does control, the ban makes no provision for a company-ownership vested in several physicians, none of whom individually can be said to be in control.

A remarkable episode in Texas counsels against making hasty assumptions that medicine will easily succeed in policing its own ranks. After months of discussion, the Texas Medical Association concluded in 1962 not only that even limited physician-ownership of drugstores is unethical, but that ownership of small drug companies is also wrong. "We do not feel," Dr. James H. Sammons of Houston, a councilor of the Texas Medical Association, told an AMA Institute in August 1962, "that a physician who owns stock in a small company is able to divorce this fact from his treatment of patients in prescribing medications that his company either sells, repackages, or manufactures." Yet, two years later, Joe H. Arnette, secretary of the Texas State Board of Pharmacy, told Senator Hart's subcommittee that according to official records (which probably understate the reality), Texas physicians have an interest in 1 out of 25 of the state's pharmacies and in 1 out of 5 (26 out of 126) state-licensed pharmaceutical manufacturing firms.

One of these companies is the Merit Pharmaceutical Company, Inc., of Houston, which was founded in 1956 and has, its president, George L. Asbeck, told the subcommittee, 244 physicians among its 466 stockholders. Its volume is small — a mere $300,000 a year. If only its physician-owners would prescribe the products of the firm they own to the maximum possible extent, Asbeck said, sales would increase to $6 million. Not that Merit isn't entitled to a badge of sorts for trying. It set up a statewide franchise system whereby, Senator Hart said in his statement at the close of the hearings, "doctors entered into partnership with drug salesmen to promote company products . . . the company split 50-50 with the detail men. They in turn gave 25 percent to participating doctors . . . this appears to be nothing but a kick-back for prescribing the company products. And for a period of two years doctors were found who were willing to participate in such a scheme." Merit abandoned the scheme under fire from the Texas Medical Association. According to Asbeck's testimony, however, the Association's condemnation of physician-ownership of such firms caused *none* of Merit's doctor-stockholders to sell their stock.

A common justification cited to the Hart subcommittee for physician-ownership of small companies of the type under inquiry was that it assured the physician of the purity and quality of the products he prescribes. The record seemed to give this rationale scant support. Merit's Asbeck, for example, acknowledged that his firm's quality control had been criticized by the Food and Drug Administration, and that the firm had marketed an anticholesterol product without prior FDA clearance. In the phase of the hearings dealing with another company, Carrtone Laboratories, which is outside New Orleans, it was brought out that in 1963 FDA had reported "sometimes questionable" production methods. In May 1964 FDA found that in some respects "good manufacturing practices were still not being followed."

As to prices, the evidence indicated that they were often higher — and sometimes very much higher — than those charged by major manufacturers, even though, typically, all that the small firm had done was to merchandise products under its own label. Consider Palmedico, Inc., of Columbia, South Carolina, whose shareholders include 133 physicians and 65 wives and children of physicians. Appearing in its behalf before Hart's subcommittee was Representative Albert W. Watson, who said he had incorporated the small firm, was on its initial board of directors, and was its counsel. While he was active with Palmedico, he testified, the company stressed that it wanted to market drugs "at the lowest possible price to the patient." Questioning of Palmedico's chairman, William C. Plowden, Jr., brought out, however, that not all of the firm's prices were within the range of reason. The price for 250 capsules of its own brand of triple-sulpha formula was $22. In lots of 1000, the price charged by Lederle Laboratories was $16, or $4 for 250 capsules, whereas Wyeth Laboratories asked $23.50 per 1000. The price charged by a wholesaler for the generic product, an unbranded version also meeting established standards, was $9.65 per 1000.

The most noteworthy case involved Carrtone Laboratories, the small New Orleans firm that had experienced some difficulties with FDA. It had 3000 stockholders, of whom at least 1200 were physicians, and until about three weeks before the hearings its acting president was Dr. William W. Frye, dean of the Louisiana State University School of Medicine. Founded in 1958, Carrtone had been a consistent money-loser. In 1963, disgruntled stockholders swept out the old management and swept in Dr. Frye. In March 1964 he wrote to the company's physician-stockholders urging each of them to "do just a little bit more for his company," so that it would "start making a sizeable profit immediately." Letters like this drew a heartwarming response. In the subcommittee hearings record is a reply in which Dr. Joseph A. Thomas of Natchitoches, Louisiana, agreed that "it is up to us shareholders to make our company go and grow." From Shreveport, Dr. T. E. Strain wrote, "I do agree to prescribe and encourage my associates to use Carrtone products." Similar letters, some of them making it clear that the authors were glad to help if to do so was consistent with the patient's health needs, came from other southern states, including Arkansas, Kentucky, and Oklahoma. Dr. E. Wayne Gilley of Chattanooga wrote that he had "sent personal letters to all doctors in Tennessee who were known to have Carrtone stock." Dr. Boyce P. Griggs of Lincolnton, North Carolina, attempting to initiate a campaign of support for Carrtone among his fellow physician-stockholders, urged that "we . . . promote our stock interest by way of actively 'penpushing' Carrtone products . . ." He wrote them that "Carrtone's growth will reward you through your holding in Carrtone stock . . . I look upon Carrtone as a rosebud about to bloom, stockwise . . . Let's push the pen for Carrtone . . ."

Fortunately, the response to Dr. Frye's appeal never reached the level attained before he became acting president. In January 1961, according to documents entered in the subcommittee hearings record by a staff attorney, Mrs. Dorothy D. Goodwin, Dr. Griggs wrote a letter to the then president of Carrtone. With it Dr. Griggs enclosed a list of the attending physicians at the approximately fifteen state prison camps. The list was offered, he said, "to serve a particular mailing purpose as we pursue the state contract in North Carolina." Dr. Griggs explained: "A telephone call from me to Dr. Charles Flowers, Sr., the 'daddy rabbit' in this system, who heads the Central Prison [100-bed] Hospital service, found him very sympathetic and interested in our project . . ."

The project was of splendid simplicity: Carrtone would sell its stock to the prison physicians, after which they "would all prescribe Carrtone products" to enhance the value of their investment. This project collapsed but, undaunted, Dr. Griggs came up with another one, also a failure, in the following year. This time the target was the North Carolina state hospitals. Dr. Griggs set up a conference telephone call in which the participants were: a Carrtone official; Dr. John S. McKee, Jr., superintendent of the ·Broughton State Hospital at Morganton; C. K. Avery, assistant business manager at the hospital; and himself. Avery wrote Mrs. Goodwin the following about the telephone call:

I do not know who made the suggestion, but it was made again and again that the medical staff be advised to purchase substantial quantities of the common stock in Carrtone Labo-

ratories which was then selling at a low price . . . and that
the Hospital then switch its entire business to Carrtone Laboratories.

We were "guaranteed" that the stock would triple or quad-
ruple if we took such action . . . [it] was the baldest proposition that I have ever heard in 17 years of bulk purchasing.

This story was termed "appalling" by the AMA's lawyer
spokesman, Robert Throckmorton. It was a story that was unearthed and disclosed by the staff of the Antitrust subcommittee, which has comparatively meager resources but much determination and much devotion to the public interest. It and
other shocking episodes were not ferreted out, disclosed, and
acted upon by the AMA. Its huge resources were focused on the
fight against Medicare, the defeat of congressmen who favored
Medicare, and the election of congressmen who opposed Medicare. When Dr. James Sammons spoke at the AMA Institute in
Chicago in August 1962, he said:

It is difficult, if not impossible, to discuss intelligently and
convincingly the problems of the Socialization and Govern-
mentalization of Medicine with a patient who knows that the
doctor or doctors in town own the drug stores from which he
or they are buying their medications. This in the public eye
becomes unequivocally greed of the worst sort. It is bad
enough that the doctor's public image has been made to appear, by those forces within our government which would
destroy the private practice of medicine, one of financial concern primarily and human concern secondarily. It is folly to
lend credence to this vicious distortion by adding the factor
that we physicians may profit from the sale of the drugs used
to obtain the well being of our patients. We recognize that
this philosophy will not be acceptable to many of you. We
would only ask that you reconsider the position that you have

taken as to the effect on the public image of doctor owned drug stores and small pharmaceutical houses in your locale.

Although I know of no proponent of Medicare who seeks to "destroy the private practice of medicine," Dr. Sammons sounds to me like a Texas Hippocrates. Unlike Dr. Sammons, Hippocrates did not have to reckon with physicians who own pharmacies and drug companies.

"WHAT I FEAR is the increasingly prevalent image of the physician as the businessman," Dr. Walter Modell, the distinguished editor of *Clinical Pharmacology and Therapeutics* said in 1962 at the convention of the American Association for the Advancement of Science. Since then the difficulty of distinguishing some physicians from entrepreneurs has, if anything, become greater. The hearings held in August 1964 by Senator Philip A. Hart's Subcommittee on Antitrust and Monopoly on doctor ownership of pharmacies and small pharmaceutical houses were followed in August 1965 by hearings on ophthalmologists who dispense the eyeglasses they prescribe; the revelations of avarice, hypocrisy, and stunted or corrupted ethical perception were at least as horrifying as those of the previous year. In 1966 an indication of the climate came in a "Dear Doctor" letter mass-mailed by the Delco Chemical Co., Inc., of Mount Vernon, New York:

> We are the prime suppliers of obesity products which have been proven successful to the key men in your area as well as throughout the entire country from New York to Hollywood. These physicians enjoy incomes of $100,000.00 to $300,000.00 yearly.
>
> Also, we supply Obstetricians, Gynecologists, Internists and General Practitioners who have incorporated weight control

into their practices and have added $25,000.00 to $100,000.00 to their incomes yearly. . . .

If you are interested in a substantial increase of income, may we suggest that you return the self-addressed no postage required post card to us and our representative will be happy to call upon you at your convenience.

Early in 1967 the Senate Antitrust subcommittee held extensive hearings on the product of its earlier investigations, the proposed Medical Restraint of Trade Act. In preparation, the staff had done a spot check on the assurance, given 2½ years earlier by the American Medical Association, that, "within a reasonable time, physician ownership of drug repackaging companies will, in the main, disappear." The check showed that out of 22 firms named in the August 1964 hearing only one had gone out of business, 17 had as many physicians among their owners as before, and only three had fewer; one company did not respond. The survey did not, of course, encompass evidence obtained by the subcommittee that physician-owned firms had increased in number since 1964. On March 1, 1967, Senator Hart inquired of the AMA what it had done with the list of the 22 companies which it had been given 2½ years before. Edwin J. Holman, director of the Department of Medical Ethics, replied that it had been relayed to the relevant state medical societies "to investigate and to handle, as appropriate." This having produced no further complaints, Holman continued, "we consider that the states have handled it adequately." In 1966 another list — this one of 130 doctor-owned pharmaceutical firms — was given the AMA. It, too, was turned over to the state affiliates, but "we made no follow-up," Holman said. He then proceeded to volunteer testimony about how the value of stock in a drug company that numbered 1100 physicians among its owners had plunged 90 per cent since 1959. "Why have an ethic if the test is going to be are you going to lose money?" Hart asked. "That doesn't sound like an ethic to me; it sounds like a book-keeping decision." Holman suggested that the AMA's ethic was to be seen "as an ideal," rather than as a standard requiring swift enforcement. Suppose, Hart asked, his bill generally prohibiting physicians from profiting on their prescribing were to be enacted. Would such a law be "more respected than your ethic?" Perhaps only a man with expertise in a subspeciality as arcane as the ethics of the AMA could have responded as did Holman. "I could only answer that by saying I know some physicians are guilty of violating the Federal income tax laws," he said. I was less startled to hear this than I would have been had I not been compelled by events a year earlier to begin a story for the Washington *Post* this way:

> CHICAGO, March 6 — The keynoter for the First National Congress on Medical Ethics made an unusual slip of the tongue at the start of the 2-day meeting yesterday.
>
> Ethical principles, said Dr. James H. Berge, chairman of the Judicial Council of the American Medical Association, "ideally are not observed. . . ."
>
> The Seattle physician recovered in midsentence. He had intended to say, and did say on his second try, that ethics "ideally are to be observed rather than enforced."
>
> So far as the approximately 350 delegates to the AMA-sponsored meeting were concerned, the trouble was — "ideally" aside — Dr. Berge had a point both times.

A good deal of tension may have underlain Dr. Berge's slip. A lot was being repressed. In the open sessions there was no mention of the criminal and civil cases involving the advertising for which the medium — the AMA's own *Journal* — was the message. Nor was the name of Senator Hart or his legislation mentioned — although the bill surely helped to precipitate the meeting. The bill was a threat not because Hart really wanted it, not because of some fancied power grab in Washington, but because of the failures of an organization which Dr. Berge, a great many dedicated physicians — and, for that matter, myself — would prefer to admire. Not until 1966 did the AMA get around to convening what so pointedly was its "First" national conference on medical ethics. It then carried on like an animal such as Dr. Seuss might concoct to delight children at bedtime — a weird assembly of dinosaur body and ostrich brain trying to assure the survival of its bankrupt morality by burying its head in a mound of medicated gold dust.

If there is anything funny about all of this it is sick-funny. In the 1967 Hart hearings, Maven J. Myers, an assistant professor at the Philadelphia College of Pharmacy and Science, testified about a survey he had done in a large but unidentified city, which may have been Milwaukee, about pharmaceutical repackaging firms. Four such firms were owned by a total of 14 physicians and osteopaths. Among their private-label offerings were products containing penicillin, to which an estimated 20 million Americans are allergic or sensitive. Myers testified that out of every 1,000 prescriptions written by the doctor-owners, 104 were for penicillin-containing products. This was a rate 2½ times the national average; it was 8 times that found among a control group of prescribing physicians. A similar pattern among eye doctors was testified to by Dr. Marc Anthony. In his city of Spokane, Washington, he told Senator Hart, four ophthalmologists who sell eyeglasses stipulated in a court case that each prescribes 2,200 pairs a year. This is 1,000 more than were prescribed by the equally busy Dr. Anthony or each of his litigant colleagues who do not dispense. Dr. Anthony testified that most of the difference — an 83 per cent difference — was accounted for by exploitation of patients whose old glasses " are really ok."

16

FRAUD IN DRUG TESTING

DURING THE SIX YEARS starting in 1957 the American public spent at least an estimated $16 million on Regimen Tablets, a nonprescription "reducing pill" merchandised with such slogans as "I lost 25 pounds in 30 days taking Regimen Tablets without dieting."

In 1962 the Food and Drug Administration made multiple seizures of Regimen Tablets on charges of misbranding. In connection with this, the government took depositions from two physicians who had been engaged to conduct clinical tests with the drug (phenylpropanolamine hydrochloride), which is no longer on the market. Dr. Ernest C. Brown of Baltimore, whose fee was $1000, admitted in his deposition, FDA said in a letter to Senator Humphrey, that 30 of the 43 charts he had submitted on 50 patients "were fabricated." Dr. Kathleen E. Roberts of San Francisco and later Toledo, who was paid $4000, acknowledged in her deposition that her report was "untrue in its entirety." Her charts on 57 of 75 patients "were complete fabrications," the agency told Humphrey. Of the remainder, "only the patients' initials and starting weights were correct." Three days after making her deposition in September 1963, Dr. Roberts left the San Francisco hospital where she had been the principal investigator on two National Institutes of Health research grants, one for $10,292 and the other for $33,120. She reappeared as a grant applicant in a Toledo hospital, but NIH, having been notified by FDA of her deposition, had had enough.

In January 1964 a grand jury in Brooklyn returned what was reportedly the first federal indictment to name an advertising agency for preparing false copy for a drug product (Regimen) at the direction of a client. The agency, Kastor, Hilton, Chesley, Clifford & Atherton, Inc., said it has always "fulfilled the highest obligation of integrity and responsibility, both to its clients and to the American public." It accused the office of the United States Attorney of trying to impose "a new concept of an insurer's responsibility on an advertising agency for a client's product and business."

At least $10 million had been spent on advertising Regimen Tablets, of which the agency presumably received the customary 15 per cent. The indictment alleged mail fraud, violation of the food and drug law, and placement of fraudulent newspaper, magazine, and television advertisements. The pills were heavily advertised: on "Keep Talking," CBS television; on the Dave Garroway "Today" show, NBC television; and on Dick Clark's "American Bandstand," ABC television.[1] An unnamed physician was said in the indictment to have been induced to "change the conclusion of a clinical test he had performed with the tablets." Endorsers of the pills, the indictment asserted, were shown being weighed each week, the scales registering weight losses each time. Actually, the before-and-after models were on strict diets and, said the indictment, had been taking prescription drugs under supervision of a physician.

In addition to the agency the defendants were: the marketer, Drug Research Corporation, and its sole stockholder, John

[1] The vice president of the National Better Business Bureau, Irving Ladimer, has said that certain broadcasters and publications either never accepted or quickly discontinued Regimen advertising. But he wrote Senator Humphrey, "All of the major media had the benefit of the Bureau's views and our correspondence files show that we provided specific explanations to a large number of them." His letter, dated February 24, 1964, has been published by the Senate Subcommittee on Reorganization and International Organizations.

Andreadis, usually known as John Andre, and its chief chemist, Saul Miklean; the New Drug Institute, Inc., and its president, Arthur Herrick, a lawyer who said his firm had acted innocently, merely as consultants. The case was awaiting trial.[2]

⁍ ⁍ ⁍

"It is extremely improbable," Commissioner George P. Larrick assured the Kefauver Subcommittee on Antitrust and Monopoly in 1960, "that falsified or synthetic reports . . . would pass for long the security and review of competent [Food and Drug Administration] scientists without arousing suspicion."

Whatever euphoria a firm assurance by the Commissioner is capable of creating should have been dispelled by a five-count federal indictment returned three years later, in October 1963, against Dr. Bennett A. Robin of the Washington suburb of Silver Spring, Maryland. The charges were that he had caused pharmaceutical firms to submit erroneous reports on new drugs by supplying them with fraudulent clinical results. Actually, the government said, he had never examined patients on whom he purportedly was testing the five products mentioned in the indictment for which new-drug applications were submitted to FDA.

Dr. Robin praised the products he had "tested" in articles in

---

[2] On May 6, 1965, a verdict of guilty was returned by a jury against the advertising agency, which said it would appeal, the Drug Research Corporation, and Andre. The New Drug Institute had entered a plea of guilty. The case of Miklean was severed, leaving him subject to the possibility of a separate trial. Because of failing health, the charges against Herrick were dismissed. He died on April 26.

Assistant United States Attorney Martin R. Pollner, in his summation, said that the story of the advertising agency's promotion of Regimen was "one of fraud, deceit, and lies."

The New York *Times* for April 21 reported the testimony of a seamstress during the twelve-week trial: after seeing a Regimen television commercial, she bought some of the tablets and "got very sick." Another woman said, "Instead of losing weight, I gained it." A janitor told the court that the pills "bloated me up." A secretary testified, "I gained five pounds and got hungrier."

United States District Judge John R. Bartels set June 25 for sentencing.

medical journals, and the articles were frequently incorporated in new-drug applications that won FDA clearance. One of the three drugs mentioned in the indictment that FDA released to the market was Tigan (trimethobenzamide), a product of Roche Laboratories. In the December 1960 issue of the *Maryland State Medical Journal*, Dr. Robin reported on a "comparative study" he said he had made with Tigan and a placebo in the relief of symptoms of nausea and vomiting. "Tigan® effectively relieved the symptoms . . . within an average of 80 minutes in 94 of 96 patients," he said.

The other drugs that the indictment said FDA had released to the market were Naquival, a Schering Corporation diuretic, and Entoquel with Neomycin syrup, an antidiarrhea product of White Laboratories, Inc., a Schering Corporation subsidiary. The drugs that FDA did *not* release were identified as Rynadyne, an Irwin, Neisler and Company product for the treatment of cold symptoms, and Winthrop Laboratories' Linodil, for use in circulatory diseases.

Dr. Robin pleaded no contest to all five counts. Federal Judge Matthew F. McGuire, who had presided in the MER/29 case, said from the bench that this was an admission of guilt. On June 19, 1964, when the physician was before him for sentencing, the Judge said that he had "not only brought obloquy upon himself but obloquy upon his profession." The Judge went on to point out that

. . . drugs can have great beneficial effects and, at the same time, very detrimental and serious and in some instances fatal side effects. And yet he . . . falsely reported that his tests showed no or insignificant side effects and that the therapeutic results he observed were good and excellent and, as a consequence of that, the Government agency presumed to act.

.   .   .   .

By Prescription Only

He received his first payment of money in November of 1958 . . . The following year he undertook studies on at least four drugs. In the spring of 1960, he wrote letters to at least 16 pharmaceutical companies and offered to carry out clinical studies for them . . .

After Dr. Robin said he had no comment to make, Judge McGuire told him, "I do not think there is any justification for what you have done at all. I think it is a very, very serious thing." He imposed a sentence of two to six months, but put the defendant on probation for two years. Dr. Robin also was fined $5000. All of this was on one count. Similar penalties on the other four counts were imposed but suspended. Dr. Robin had faced a maximum possible punishment of a $50,000 fine and 25 years in prison.

According to a tally made by FDA at the request of Senator Humphrey, Dr. Robin had "tested" about 45 products for 22 firms which had paid him a total of $32,110. About 6400 patients purportedly were involved in his investigations. FDA told the Senator that a twenty-third firm, Wallace Laboratories, whose skirmish with a Washington blood specialist over Deprol was recounted in Chapter 14, had refused to tell the agency how much it had paid Dr. Robin for testing two different Wallace products, Capla and Soma.

The exposure of Dr. Robin's unorthodox activities can be traced to the decision of Dr. John O. Nestor to volunteer his services to FDA. In doing this he hoped to be able to do something about a problem he had encountered in his private pediatric practice — the illogical but frequent adoption of drug dosages for infants that were mere mathematical scale-downs of those for adults and were, he believed, responsible for making babies ill, or for intensifying their illnesses.

At about the time FDA hired him it released Entoquel, the White Laboratories product for symptomatic treatment of diarrhea in infants. A few months later, in April 1961, White Laboratories reported that a pediatrician had prescribed Entoquel — in dosages recommended in the labeling — to two infants, who had had reactions that, FDA said, "may result in death or serious injury." Dr. Nestor examined the new-drug application and found it "completely at variance" with his more than twenty years' experience. He made a trip to Newark, New Jersey, to discuss the case of the two infants with their pediatrician. He also investigated Dr. Robin, concluding that he could not have assembled the number of cases in the brief period asserted by the Entoquel application.

White Laboratories bitterly resisted FDA's efforts to delete from the labeling a recommendation for use in children under six. Not until August 1961, after FDA made multiple seizure of Entoquel stocks, did the makers agree to remove the drug from the market. In an internal FDA communication of that same month, Dr. Nestor said that a statistical analysis of Dr. Robin's papers "indicates that, in general, his results are impossible," and that he "is a fraud."

The questions this raised were obvious, and Senator Humphrey asked them: Why didn't the drug companies find the results "impossible"? And why didn't FDA so find them — *before* it released Entoquel? As Dr. Nestor saw it, Dr. Robin's work on Entoquel was an example of a "large proportion of the clinical evidence submitted . . . in support of new-drug applications" which consists of "medical testimonials from practitioners."

Dr. Robin's operations impressed the Senator as being "unfortunately, part and parcel of a larger pattern which has prevailed in recent years." In a wholly opposite way, Dr. Nestor's work in the Entoquel, MER/29, and other episodes — and his courage in giving forthright testimony in response to an official request — also impressed Humphrey. But not FDA. He was taboo on its totem pole, a low man to be passed over and humiliated while promotions were given to others with lesser qualifications, lesser seniority, lesser training, and lesser records of protecting the public interest. There were crude and obvious efforts to drive him out. One day in 1962 he returned from a session with the grand jury that returned the MER/29 indictments to find that without notice his desk and records had been moved out of his office, and that he had been transferred from the drug-evaluation unit (which decides whether a new drug goes on the market) to the surveillance unit (which deals with problems connected with new drugs already on the market). Late in 1964 it became known in FDA that the medical director, Dr. Joseph F. Sadusk, was arranging yet another transfer and that it was imminent.[3]

⁌ ⁌ ⁌

In his memorandum of August 1961, Dr. Nestor suggested that a biographical file be started on clinical investigators. He had thought of it as inclusive, with occupancy open to those who had shown themselves to be deserving of at least a suspicion that they were overly enthusiastic, poor reporters, or substandard. The Food and Drug Administration, however, made the list exclusive. To qualify, an investigator had to be suspected of "untruthfulness, psychosis, or dangerous incompetence and irresponsibility." Even so, nineteen physicians suspected of research fakery had made the grade by February 1964. The FDA began an investigation of the nineteen, focusing its effort on two of them. Commissioner Larrick wrote to Senator Humphrey:

> . . . we visited about 30 drug companies to which these doctors had submitted clinical data. These firms were asked for details of payment for this work, and more than half of them declined to furnish us with any such information.

---

[3] Early in 1965 Dr. Nestor was transferred to the Case Review Branch of the Division of Medical Review. The Branch collects evidence for prosecutions. The transfer removed Dr. Nestor from actions involving the approval or disapproval of new drugs for marketing and the surveillance of new drugs already on the market.

We believe that drug companies are under no legal compulsion to furnish FDA details on testing fees, and we contemplate no specific steps other than to make requests for the voluntary providing of this information when we feel that it is pertinent to an investigation.

Complying with a request from Senator Humphrey for the names of the manufacturers who had refused to supply the requested data, Commissioner Larrick came up with thirteen names — Eaton Laboratories (a division of Norwich Pharmacal), Smith Kline & French, the Upjohn Company, Warner-Lambert, Lederle Laboratories (a division of American Cyanamid), Ciba Pharmaceutical Company, Wyeth Laboratories (a division of American Home Products), McNeil Laboratories (a subsidiary of Johnson & Johnson), American Home Products, E. R. Squibb & Sons (a division of Olin Mathieson), Chas. Pfizer, Armour Pharmaceutical Co., and Geigy Chemical Corporation.

In early April 1964, the Senator also sent an inquiry about the matter to Dr. Austin Smith, president of the Pharmaceutical Manufacturers Association. Mr. Humphrey asked the spokesman for the trade organization of the ethical-drug industry, "Has PMA offered counsel to member companies as to cooperating with FDA in this respect? If so, what is the counsel?" No reply had been received as of this writing several months later.

The nonresponse of Dr. Smith was, however, less unexpected than the reaction in a similar situation of the American Medical Association, which is, after all, a professional organization. On March 17, 1964, Senator Humphrey wrote the AMA's executive vice president, Dr. F. J. L. Blasingame, a courteous and respectful letter of inquiry. The Senator invited the AMA to submit its written views on three matters "within the fundamental jurisdiction of the profession." The first was "possible falsification of evidence in clinical testing of drugs." The second was "possible impropriety in acceptance of exorbitant 'fees' for testing by private clinicians." The third was "the possible impropriety of some 'ethical' drug companies in subsidizing the 'planting' of (allegedly extravagant) medical claims about 'ethical' drugs in *lay* media." Senator Humphrey enclosed various materials illustrating why he, and physicians who had written to him, had cause for concern in all three areas. He asked the AMA if it believed that the materials "merit active study and follow-up" by the profession, what was the AMA's official position on the ethical issues involved, what it had done about the problems referred to, what it proposed to do about them, and what, if anything, it proposed that federal agencies do. The voice of American medicine simply did not answer — did not answer, be it understood, an inquiry from the chairman of a duly constituted subcommittee of the Senate of the United States. Perhaps an answer will come someday, but I am writing these words eight and a half months later, at the end of November 1964.[4]

As for the nineteen physicians in the special biographical file, to whom Humphrey referred in his letter to the AMA, most of them were not, he said in a memorandum published by his subcommittee, unknown to FDA. To illustrate his point, he cited a two-year-old paper in FDA files which, with names deleted by the Senator pending a Department of Justice inquiry, follows:

> For many years Dr. —— "collaborated" with Doctors —— and —— in "clinical studies" which we strongly suspect were conducted by the "graphite" method [that is, by invention with a pencil, rather than by actual testing].
>
> With Dr. ——'s death a year or so ago, we had hopes that the combination had been disrupted for good.
>
> We have learned recently, however, that —— has gained

---

[4] As of May 10, 1965, neither the AMA nor the PMA had responded to Mr. Humphrey's letters.

new allies, and the combination is back in the "clinical study" business.

These allies are:

——, M.D.

New York City, N.Y., and

——, M.D.

Brooklyn, N.Y.

Inquiries, studies, data, etc. from these men should receive *extremely* careful consideration and scrutiny.

R. C. BRANDENBURG

On January 29, 1964, Senator Humphrey had sent to FDA a voluminous confidential file on a twentieth physician, who, judging by the Senator's memorandum on the case that the subcommittee has published, might also be eligible for membership in the exclusive club. The physician, who is not named in the published materials, operated several medical organizations and services for which he arranged drug-testing deals. Several drugs now on the market, most of them sold without prescription, and made by several different manufacturers, were tested under the arrangements made by the physician-entrepreneur.

For arranging to test a laxative in fewer than 150 women in two groups — one with complaints "of constipation associated with premenstrual tension and dysmenorrhea" and a second who were pregnant — he received $12,000. A few days after the arrangements were completed, the prediction was made in an internal memorandum of the laxative manufacturer that a preliminary report would be ready a month later and "can be expected to state that . . . early observations show that (name of drug) is an effective, mild laxative for use during pregnancy . . . and also in constipation associated with premenstrual tension." Testing of a second drug, also a laxative, in 100 patients, for a fee of $3000, was undertaken after arrangements were made through an advertising agency. Both pharmaceutical manufac-

turers involved were small firms. In one of these cases — the
Humphrey memorandum does not make it clear which — the
physician wrote to the manufacturer:

> I had a talk with Dr. (name of clinical investigator), and
> while he gave me the impression that he had already done
> enough work on the new subject to indicate that the study
> would be favorable, the publication of the results bothers him.
> He can't seem to figure out how he can write such a paper
> without appearing ridiculous. Do you have ideas on it? If so,
> why don't you write a paper that would fit the concept and
> let me go on from there. I am not asking you to do my work.
> I just want to be sure that the manuscript will come as close
> to what you want as possible.

Among major manufacturers involved with the physician-
entrepreneur the situation was mixed. At least one terminated
discussions with him at a preliminary stage because, "We do
not like to use data from individuals with whom we have no
contact or where our discussion of experimental design, results
and conclusions must be made through a third party." Certain
other large manufacturers were indicated by the file, however,
to have had no hesitation about dealing only through a third
party (the physician) or refraining from direct contact with the
clinical investigators he had engaged. One large firm arranged
through the physician to pay $3000 to have a prescription tran-
quilizer tested in 39 patients.

After reviewing the file, Commissioner Larrick wrote Senator
Humphrey in February 1964 that, although it was uncertain'
whether federal law had been violated, the material was such as
to require an investigation, which FDA was undertaking.

In a "progress report" on April 8, Larrick told the Senator
that FDA had been informed by the physician that since 1960
he had arranged for testing by others of eight drugs, all of which

were previously commercially available. In the case of the non-prescription laxative whose testing brought a $12,000 fee, Larrick said the physician had farmed out the work to two colleagues who together had received only a one-eighth share, $1500.

On April 10, two months after the Senator had sent the confidential file to FDA, he protested to Assistant Commissioner Winton B. Rankin that the interim reply of two days earlier had been based "on so few interviews and other inquiries" as not to meet his original request for a "meaningful summary." [5] With that, Humphrey sent a copy of the file to the Department of Justice.

✓ ✓ ✓

As Senator Humphrey saw it, the question raised by the physician-entrepreneur and the file about him and his activities was, "How widespread are the type of substandard practices which appear to be reflected . . . ?" In October 1963, after the indictment of Dr. Robin was returned, Mr. Humphrey had voiced his confidence that "the overwhelming majority of drug testing in the United States is absolutely honest." In May

[5] The contrast between the lethargy FDA has shown in acting on abuses involving major drugmakers and those involving smalltime operators was most recently developed in three days of hearings in April 1965 by the Senate Subcommittee on Administrative Practice and Procedure of the Committee on the Judiciary. The hearings concerned what the chairman, Senator Edward V. Long of Missouri, called "police state tactics," including the use of electronic snooping in FDA investigations of smalltime operations.

Bernard Fensterwald, Jr., chief subcommittee counsel, brought out, however, that tape recorders had never been hidden in physicians' offices "to catch the spiel of detail men." He asked Allen E. Rayfield, director of FDA's Bureau of Regulatory Compliance, whether "the detail men in their sales pitches to the doctors are absolutely factual . . . ?" The response, which Long told the Senate later was "inconceivable," was: ". . . we have not run across a single . . . detail man that has made representations . . . that were exorbitant or exaggerated."

Referring to revelations at the hearings, Long closed them with a statement in which he said, "If the FDA would spend a little less time and effort on . . . small manufacturers of vitamins and milk substitute, and a little more on the large manufacturers of such dangerous drugs as Chloromycetin, MER-29 and Thalidomide, the public would be better served."

1964, in a memorandum dealing with the physician-entrepreneur, he seemed to be less certain. He noted that some may be quick to say that this case was an absolute rarity. He commented:

> I, for one, do not know the answer and reserve judgment.
> I do know that recently, after every distressing drug case has been exposed (a) the MER/29 criminal indictment, (b) the Maryland doctor's test fraud . . . (c) the two Regimen falsification cases, etc., we have heard what sounds like glib comment from some private sources: "Each case is a fluke; it is probably just one of its kind."
> Yet, FDA has told us, it *still* suspects — not one, or 2, or 10, but as many as 19 other doctors. And here is still another . . .
> So, the question is, "How many *more* such cases are there — which no one knows about, but which may come to light if investigated by FDA, the Justice Department and other Agencies?
> We do know that the pharmaceutical industry and the medical profession would be and are the first to condemn unethical practices. We deeply respect the integrity of industry and the profession.
> But Congress and the public have a right to ask: "What will actually be *done* by organized, private groups to 'clean house' —
> "(a) to cooperate actively in bringing to light any *more* such cases which may exist (if there are such) and
> "(b) to take *firm steps* to help avoid this type of case from ever recurring?"

Frauds are evil. Fraud in drug testing is an atrocity. But if all of it were to be eradicated tomorrow we would still have to cope with the problem of seriously substandard — but legal — testing which, the Senator once said, is "infinitely" more prevalent.

First, the case of Dr. Leo J. Cass, director of the Harvard Law School Health Service, and the involvement of his Cass Research Associates with questionable research; second a note on the outcome of the Regimen Tablets case; and third, a note on the Food and Drug Administration's Dr. John O. Nestor.

Once an article is submitted to a scientific publication, months — and sometimes as much as a year — usually go by before publication. This is not the case with *Current Therapeutic Research*. "Ordinarily, papers received by the first day of one calendar month, if accepted for publication, will appear in the issue released on the first day of the succeeding month," *CTR* — if I may refer to it that way — said in its November 1965 issue. In addition to being designed for "prompt publication," *CTR* requested that editorial *and business* inquiries be addressed to the Managing Editor, named as James T. Culbertson, Ph.D., at Post Office Box No. 514 in Tenafly, New Jersey. Each month, *CTR* "is distributed to the libraries of all medical schools in the world and to selected hospitals and medical societies in the United States." This being done without charge (although one can buy a subscription), and there being no advertising, the assumption is general among those who occupy themselves with such matters that *CTR* is subsidized, principally by the sale to drug manufacturers of reprints of articles which are favorable to their products. This pattern, it may be recalled from Chapter 6, was followed by Henry Welch while he was simultaneously head of the Antibiotics Division of the Food and Drug Administration and editor in chief of *Antibiotics & Chemotherapy* and *Antibiotics and Clinical Therapy*. CTR has an Editorial Advisory Board. As of late 1965 its members included, among others, Dr. William M. M. Kirby of the University of Washington, a member of the FDA's Medical Advisory Board, and Dr. Leo J. Cass, director of the Harvard Law School Health Service, head of Cass Research Associates, Inc., and Visiting Physician at Long Island Hospital in Boston. Dr. Cass and a colleague, Dr. Willem S. Frederik, identified as "Biostatistician, University Health Services, Harvard University," were frequent contributors to *CTR*. In the November 1965 issue, in fact, they had two articles. Both listed an identical set of four references, of which three were to reports by "Cass, Leo J., and Frederik, Willem S."; of the three, two had been published in *CTR* (in March and July 1965), and the third was "in press" for the *Journal of New Drugs* (the "in press" problem might have been overcome had it not been for the extraordinary speed with which the November articles, each received on September 15, had gotten into print. Each of the November offerings involved highly sophisticated double-blind comparisons of aspirin products which were said to have been conducted among arthritic and other patients at the Long Island Hospital. The first article compared ordinary aspirin and Measurin, a sustained-release aspirin which was claimed to provide immediate release of the painkiller in an amount equal to a single ordinary tablet of equivalent potency and then to continue to release the chemical at a rate sufficient to maintain the analgesic effect throughout an 8-hour period. Drs. Cass and Frederik concluded that a single Measurin tablet "provided pain relief as effective, over an 8-hour period, as did two doses of immediate-release aspirin at 4-hour intervals at the same total dosage level." The second article involved another sustained-release aspirin called Relay, which received a somewhat less glowing endorsement than Measurin. Early in 1966, a huge advertising and promotional campaign for Measurin, a non-prescription product, was begun by the manufacturer, Chese-brough-Pond's, Inc. For the medical profession, a principal effort was an advertisement that occupied four pages in the March 21 *Journal* of the American Medical Association. The ad listed two references. One was to the laudatory report by Drs. Cass and Frederik in *Current Therapeutic Research;* the second was to "Clinical reports on file" with the manufacturer.

A few months before this campaign got under way, it was later disclosed by Dr. James L. Goddard, Commissioner of FDA, the suspicions of agency personnel were aroused by "the extraor-dinarily large number of investigations" that Cass Research Associates had made "in a short period of time." On December 15, 1965, FDA notified the companies which had named Cass Research as an investigator of experimental drugs that it had failed to comply with the conditions set for the use of such drugs, and that Dr. Cass and other investigators associated with his firm were thereafter ineligible to receive investigational drugs. The companies included most of the major ones. All told, they had named Cass Research as an investigator in 84 applications to test investigational drugs in humans, and in 25 product-mar-keting applications. In three cases in which marketing approval was granted by FDA, Dr. Goddard said in a letter of June 16, 1966, to Chairman L. H. Fountain of the House Intergovern-mental Relations Subcommittee, Cass Research clinical data were "significant . . . in that other clinical evidence submitted was not sufficient of itself for us to reach a favorable conclusion on the drug's safety and/or efficacy." The three products were Norgesic, a prescription analgesic and muscle relaxant produced by Riker Laboratories, Inc., and two nonprescription sustained-

or timed-release aspirin products, Abbott Laboratories' Stendin and Chesebrough-Pond's Measurin.

On May 6, 1966, the FDA initiated action to halt the sale of Norgesic. In Cambridge, Cass Research acknowledged "certain deficiencies" in record-keeping, blamed them on "the observers [the company] retained," and said it was now out of the drug-testing business. The "certain deficiencies" were spelled out later by FDA in the Federal Register when it acted to take [the company] retained," and said it was now out of the drug-Measurin and Stendin off the market. It turned out that Cass Research had been quick with the dead: A number of patients reported to have been treated in its studies, the agency said, "in fact were not so treated . . . these persons were deceased or not hospitalized at the institution [Long Island Hospital in Boston] where the investigations were allegedly conducted." FDA said Cass Research also had supplied it with other "untrue statements," including claims that treated patients had certain medical conditions which investigation showed they did not have. Although the blame for all of this was put by the company on un-named "observers," it should be recalled that authorship of the Measurin report in *Current Therapeutic Research* had been claimed exclusively by Dr. Cass, whose perhaps fitting home address in Winchester, Massachusetts, is 4 Myopia Hill Road, and who is a consultant to the Council on Drugs for its annually revised book *New Drugs*, and by Dr. Frederik.

An inquiry into FDA's performance was held by Representative Fountain on May 25 and 26, 1966. At that time — five months after FDA had sent the notice of ineligibility to the 27 companies that had used Cass Research — no action had been taken toward removing any product but Norgesic from the market. Fountain pointed out that in the AMA *Journal* ad mentioned earlier the only published reference was to the study in *Current Therapeutic Research*. There was this exchange about Measurin:

Mr. Fountain: . . . has the work by Cass & Associates, . . . also been found to contain false data?

Dr. Goddard: Yes.

Mr. Fountain: Was the Cass data essential to prove the claims for effectiveness . . . including the claim for 8-hour relief?

Dr. Goddard: Yes.

Mr. Fountain: Has a notice of hearing been issued for withdrawing [marketing] approval . . . ?

Dr. Goddard: No.

Mr. Fountain: Was such action recommended by the Bureau of Medicine?

Dr. Goddard: Yes; it was.

The day following the Bureau's recommendation it was overruled in the office of the Commissioner. Dr. Goddard took responsibility for this, saying that a principal consideration was that Measurin was aspirin and therefore a product whose characteristics were well known. He also testified that "my decision may have been wrong, but I felt that firms should not be punished when they are entrapped by false research data. . . ." His decision was to leave Measurin on the market until Chesebrough-Pond's could submit new research data and until FDA could evaluate it. The decision was, in other words, to let Measurin remain on sale although the substantial evidence of efficacy required by the law was not present. In his testimony, Dr. Goddard said the new data had been supplied and would be evaluated "within the next few days" — but it was not until August 18, or almost three *months* later, that FDA acted to stop sales of Measurin. Two days after Dr. Goddard made his decision in March, Dr. Robert S. McCleery, head of FDA's Medical Advertising Branch, proposed that the law be observed by requiring the company, in the interim period, to remove all claims based upon the work of Cass Research from its promotional labeling — including the claim of eight-hour relief, the chief selling point. Instead of doing that, the agency told the company simply to delete the name of Dr. Cass from all promotional materials. The bizarre result of this, W. Donald Gray of the Subcommittee staff, pointed out to Dr. Goddard, was to allow the company to make claims based on fraudulent research "without citing any substantiation. . . ." This result was compounded when FDA notified the Federal Trade Commission of its action. The FTC, which is responsible for regulating the advertising (as distinguished from labeling) of over-the-counter drugs, then took matching "appropriate action" — permitting, that is, claims based on phony research to be made in ads.

When FDA finally moved in August to rescind the approval it had given to the marketing of Measurin, Congressman Fountain issued a statement interpreting this to mean that Chesebrough-Pond's additional data were "inadequate to substantiate the claims made for the product and that FDA has changed its opinion that the chemical data in the file are sufficient to support the 8-hour claim. In addition," he said, "the FDA announcement suggests that there is question as to whether the drug is safe under present labeling." The Chairman said he "cannot believe" that Congress had intended, when it enacted the Kefauver-Harris Amendments of 1962, to have the efficacy provisions "applied in such delayed fashion." Fountain went on to say:

In the five months since FDA concluded there was inadequate proof of the claims made for this drug, perhaps hundreds of thousands, or even millions, of consumers have spent their hard-earned money for a drug which may offer no more, if as much, therapeutic benefit as ordinary aspirin.

However, I think there is a lesson in this matter which I hope will not be lost on the responsible officials of the Food and Drug Administration and the Federal Trade Commission.

A regulatory agency operating in the scientific area cannot function effectively on the basis of promises. It must operate on the basis of the scientific evidence in its possession and must apply the provisions of the law uniformly and equitably. If the agency does otherwise it is the consumer who invariably will suffer.

On October 17, 1966, the FDA moved to bar sales of Abbott Laboratories' Stendin and on December 14 of Relay, the Richardson-Merrell, Inc., timed-release aspirin to which Drs. Cass and Frederik had given less than a perfect score in *Current Therapeutic Research* (this action by FDA was not based on the *CTR* data; instead, said Commissioner Goddard, it was founded on a re-evaluation of clinical data for all timed-release aspirin which had been energized by the Cass affair). Terming FDA's action "unjustified" and "incredible," the makers of the aspirin products moved for hearings. FDA put the matter before its Medical Advisory Board (whose Dr. Kirby was still a member of the Editorial Advisory Board of CTR; Dr. Cass's name no longer appeared). The agency's consultants decided that present claims for the timed-release aspirins were misleading. On April 26, 1967, FDA sent a letter to the manufacturers (including a fourth one, Grove Laboratories, for Entericin) proposing that the claims for the products be limited to those which, as FDA saw it, were warranted by the evidence — that in equivalent doses the products are characterized "by delayed absorption" compared with regular aspirin, that regular aspirin gives "more rapid onset of pain relief," that the "duration of clinical effect" of the products exceeds that of ordinary aspirin, that in chronic use the clinical effects of the two forms are the same, and that compared with two regular 10-grain tablets a 20-grain delayed absorption aspirin produces "a prolongation of effect of uncertain duration and clinical significance." As of late May it was not definitely known if the manufacturers would make their labeling conform with FDA's structures or would exercise their right to a hearing. In the separate case involving Norgesic, it also was not known whether the manufacturer would seek a hearing.

REGIMEN TABLETS

Kastor, Hilton, Chesley, Clifford & Atherton, the agency which handled the advertising campaign for Regimen Tablets, was, in June 1965, fined $50,000 and did not appeal. This was said by Kenneth B. Willson, president of the National Better Business Bureau, to ground in law the principle that an ad agency is held to the standard of reasonable care which an average prudent person would use in evaluating a claim. John Andre, sole stockholder in the Drug Research Corporation, marketer of Regimen, was fined $50,000 and sentenced to eighteen months in prison; Drug Research was fined $53,000. On September 1, 1966, the United States Court of Appeals in New York City affirmed the convictions. Subsequently, a petition for review was denied by the Supreme Court.

DR. JOHN O. NESTOR

Dr. John O. Nestor is the pediatric cardiologist whose work in the Food and Drug Administration has provided an admirable example of dedication to the public health in the face of appalling discouragements. Readers of this book will recall his work in connection with MER/29, Altafur, Elipten, the discovery of fraud in drug testing done by Dr. Bennett A. Robin, his bringing together of Dr. Frances O. Kelsey and Dr. Helen B. Taussig in the thalidomide case and his courage in testifying — while an employe of FDA — before Senator Hubert Humphrey. Readers also will recall the crude and obvious efforts made in the regime of Dr. Joseph F. Sadusk, Jr., to drive him out. Dr. Sadusk has gone to work for one of the drug companies he used to regulate; Dr. Nestor remains a public servant. Several months after Dr. James L. Goddard became Commissioner Dr. Nestor was accorded a modest recognition. He was brought back from the agency's boondocks and once again made a medical officer with a responsibility in the area of drug marketing — a responsibility he had had when he first joined FDA five years earlier. His new assignment is in the Division of Cardiopulmonary and Renal Drugs in the Office of New Drugs.

17

PRICES AND PROFITS

WHEN THERE IS price competition in drugs the price is reasonable; when price competition is absent, principally because of patent monopolies, the price is staggering. The manufacture of drugs that cannot be patented is, generally, profitable within an ordinary range; the manufacture of patented drugs is, overall, extremely profitable. These things being so, drug manufacturers seek by every conceivable means to manipulate the market into one for high-profit patented drugs. They have succeeded so well that, in spite of large-scale sales to institutional buyers at often relatively low prices, their profits remain, year after year, sensationally high.

These generalizations, which will be developed in this chapter, have an importance that transcends economics. The excessive and irrational use of patented prescription drugs has caused not mere economic waste but injury and death as well. The greater the use, the greater the profit. The prospect, or near certainty, of immense profits from the sale of drugs has depended too little upon whether they were beneficial and too much upon whether they were successfully promoted. Consequently, inferior, worthless, and needlessly dangerous drugs have been poured into the market. They have been sold through deceptive and extravagant techniques that have induced physicians to prescribe them. Then, lest the bonanza end, information on adverse effects has been suppressed. Meanwhile, more patients have been harmed.

We have seen how far pharmaceutical manufacturers will go to induce physicians to use patented drugs. Why is it that the vast majority of doctors have been so reluctant to prescribe those available, much cheaper generic versions? Here is the explanation given by Senator Kefauver to the House Antitrust subcommittee headed by Representative Emanuel Celler of New York:

> . . . it is frequently difficult for the physician to use generic names even if he wishes to do so, because the drug companies have coined long, complex unpronounceable names which it is difficult, if not impossible, for physicians to remember and spell.[1] Moreover, on occasion the drug companies have come up with several generic names for the same product or alternatively have designated no generic name whatever . . .

> The second reason for the lack of use of generic names in prescribing has been the widespread apprehension among physicians that their patients might receive drugs of inferior quality. Although there is no evidence that drugs of smaller manufacturers are generally inferior to those of large companies, at least to the degree that might constitute any danger to health, the hard fact remains that a great many physicians believe this to be the case. And as long as they hold to this point of view, their patients will never secure the savings which are possible through generic-name prescribing.

[1] Ideally, the generic name is a common, nonproprietary name that serves as an abbreviation of a much longer chemical name. Thus, Miltown is the trade name for meprobamate, which is the generic or common name for 2-methyl-2-n-propyl-1, 3-propane-diol dicarbamate.

Before the Kefauver Subcommittee on Antitrust and Monopoly, however, Dean Charles O. Wilson, of the School of Pharmacy of Oregon State College, cited instance after instance in which a multiplicity of hopelessly confusing generic names had been assigned. For example, he told of a popular pain-killer with the generic name of acetaminophen, but for which all of the following chemical names also were used as generic names: N-acetyl-p-aminophenol, p-acetylamino-phenol, acetylaminophenol, N-p-hydroxylacetamide, p-hydroxyacetanilid, APAP, and paracetamol.

The objections to generic-name prescribing were met by the Kefauver-Harris amendments. First, the Secretary of Health, Education, and Welfare was empowered to establish simple, usable names for drugs if none existed. Second, wherever a trade name appears in drug advertising, labeling, or brochures, the generic name must also appear, in type half as large. Third, in order to assure that all drugs are of high quality, the Food and Drug Administration was given broad new factory-inspection powers. Tighter manufacturing quality controls also were adopted. Congress has appropriated funds for enforcement.

Foreign-made drugs must meet the same standards if they are to be sold here. Thus, an antibiotic made in Italy must be certified by FDA for potency, safety, efficacy, and strength, just as it would if manufactured in the United States.

The savings that can be achieved through generic prescribing are huge, as shown by the following. In the spring of 1964 a firm in Mineola, New York, which sells to druggists and physicians was pricing reserpine, a tranquilizer, at 75 cents for 1000 ¼-milligram tablets. The standard price for CIBA's Serpasil was $39.50, or 52 times as much as the comparable generic product.

The price asked by the wholesaler Wolins for 100 soluble tablets containing 200,000 units of penicillin was $8.28 for brand names, but only 90 cents for the comparable generic product.

Under the Warner-Chilcott label, the price for 500 tablets of Peritrate (pentaerythritol tetranitrate plus a quarter-grain of phenobarbital) was $17. The price for the comparable unbranded product was $2.40.

The price for 1000 tablets of dextroamphetamine sulfate was $22.60 under the Smith Kline & French label, and 85 cents for the comparable generic product.

Yet the volume of prescriptions for generic products has remained low. In fact, trade studies show that the number of unbranded prescriptions was almost 9 per cent less in 1963 than in 1962. One reason for this is the influence detailmen for brand-name products have over physicians. This can be partly attributed to the ignorance of physicians about the advantages and protections conferred by the Kefauver-Harris amendments. Their ignorance is in large measure a reflection of the willingness of the American Medical Association and the medical press, both heavily dependent upon advertising revenues from branded products, to keep them that way. How zealous the AMA can be in this area was shown in the first issue of its *Journal* to be published after the 1964 general election. In an editorial, the Association's leaders, doing their best not to sound like shills for the industry, urged brand-name prescribing on the ground that this is what "Careful prescription writers" should do. There was no suggestion that physicians ought to be careful about the patient's financial health.[2] The editorial said, "The physician who prescribes meprobamate as such has no way of knowing that his patient will receive the drug in a form of highest quality and expected potency."

If all the physicians in the nation were careful prescription writers, much less meprobamate would be prescribed, whether it is called Equanil or anything else.[3] Before adding to the congestion on the road to Miltown, careful editorial writers would

---

[2] Concern about the financial health of the taxpayers without disregard of the patients' health was expressed in February 1965 by the Comptroller General of the United States, Joseph Campbell, in a report to Congress on 'the Veterans Administration's "hometown medical care program." This is a plan under which private physicians write about 1 million prescriptions a year that are filled in 67 VA outpatient clinics. Campbell said that at his urging VA had promised to implement promptly a program under which participating doctors will be encouraged either to prescribe generically or to authorize VA to dispense generic equivalents for the brand-name drugs they prescribe.

Campbell's report cited 17 examples of prescriptions written by brand name that VA could have filled with generic equivalents. The contrasting costs to VA were given as follows, with the brand-name cost given first in each case: $17 or $0.92; $13.50 or $1.87; $15.68 or $5.54; $7.48 or $2.14; $7.26 or $3.20; $4.50 or $0.62; $2.53 or $0.09; $3.57 or $1.25; $2.96 or $1.45; $1.62 or $0.11; $2.03 or $0.62; $1.65 or $0.68; $2.56 or $1.70; $0.85 or $0.08; $3.55 or $3.12; $0.85 or $0.45; $0.40 or $0.10. None of the drugs was identified.

[3] As noted in Chapter 9, the prestigious U.S. Pharmacopeia disclosed in April 1965 that it would no longer list meprobamate tranquilizers among its "drugs of choice."

have found out that in the entire United States there is but one original source of purchase for meprobamate — Carter Products, which has the American patent. Whatever the brand, or whatever the no-brand, it is meprobamate that was sold by or purchased from Carter; and it was meprobamate that met Carter's uniform quality standards. So what was there to be so careful about? Observant editorial writers would have noted that in the issue of the *Journal* in which they wrote there were: 1⅓ pages of advertising for Miltown; 1 page for Meprospan, a brand of meprobamate in sustained-release capsules; 2 pages for Deprol, the brand name for a combination of meprobamate and benactyzine hydrochloride, and 1 page for Pree MT, a combination of meprobamate and hydrochlorothiazide. All of these products are put out by Wallace Laboratories, a Carter subsidiary. In the issue of the *Journal* in question, especially observant editorial writers would have noted, no other brand of meprobamate or of products containing it were advertised.

Some pharmacists, whose profit often can be much higher on the patented products than on the cheaper generic versions, simply fill prescriptions for generic products with patented versions; and druggists who will suggest, if questioned, that the unbranded products are inferior are not unknown. Early in 1962, reporters of the Washington *Post* made a drug-buying survey showing, Nate Haseltine wrote, "that, left to his own decision, the druggist almost invariably filled generic-designated prescriptions with the more expensive brand name drugs. This is both legal and ethical." Another principal finding was "that the druggist may have as much influence as the doctor and the manufacturer in the ultimate cost of drugs when they are prescribed under their generic names." None of the pharmacists in this survey tried to sell the buyer on the worth of a more expensive brand name; but in filling generic prescriptions with brand-name drugs for buyers who said nothing about cost, "None offered the buyers a choice," Haseltine reported.

✓ ✓ ✓

Industries spend varying portions of their sales receipts to produce the goods they sell. None spend as small a proportion as the drug industry. The smaller the proportion of production costs, the larger the gross margins. Out of the gross margins come selling costs — and profits.

The staff of the Kefauver Subcommittee on Antitrust and Monopoly compiled the factory production costs in 1959 for 15 major drug firms. The range was 21.6 to 41.4 per cent, and the average was 32.3 per cent. To state it another way, the price at which the average drug manufacturer sold his product at wholesale was about three times what it cost him to make it.

The Legislative Reference Service of the Library of Congress prepared for the subcommittee the same compilations for 50 nondrug manufacturers in the same year. Each was a leading company in a different industry, and each was on *Fortune*'s list of the 500 largest manufacturers in the United States. Not one of these companies had production costs as low as the highest production costs among the 15 pharmaceutical companies. In fact, two thirds of the nondrug companies had production costs more than twice as large as those of the drug manufacturer with the highest production costs. Among the nondrug companies, production costs ranged from 42.64 per cent of sales (Coca-Cola) to 95.40 per cent (Douglas Aircraft). The average was 73.8 per cent, or about three fourths of the sales price, as compared to less than one third for the 15 drug firms.

To get a fresh perspective on the magnitude of drug prices, I calculated what would happen to the prices of other necessities if they were to be established on the same basis. That is, I applied the average for the 15 drug manufacturers — a price three times the cost of production — to the products of some of the 50 nondrug manufacturers. The results may make you want to take a tight grip on your pocketbook. The products that Colgate-Palmolive sold for $1 would bring $1.60. Similarly using a $1 base for other firms the following results were obtained:

General Foods, $2.10; International Shoe, $2.16; Cluett, Peabody (Arrow shirts) and National Dairy Products, $2.22; Socony Mobil Oil, $2.23; United States Steel, $2.25; Goodyear Tire & Rubber, $2.30; General Motors and RCA, $2.43; General Electric, $2.64; and Swift & Co., $2.73.

Suppose that these calculations could be applied to individual products. A 50-cent box of a General Foods cereal would cost $1.05. A dollar's worth of Socony Mobil gasoline would cost $2.23. A Chevrolet that GM sells for $2000 would cost $4860, and a $10,000 Cadillac $24,300. A $100 RCA stereo set would bring $243. A $200 GE refrigerator would sell for $528. The hamburgers, hot dogs, bacon, or steak that Swift sells for $1 would be priced at $2.73.

These figures are, if anything, conservative. That is because the 3 to 1 ratio of product cost to sales price in the drug industry takes into account relatively low-profit bulk sales and sales to institutional buyers. If this factor could be eliminated, the ratio would be higher than 3 to 1. A dollar's worth of hamburger would cost not $2.73, but more.

✓ ✓ ✓

The Senate Antitrust subcommittee obtained detailed financial statements on the drug operations of 22 companies in 1958. Analysis showed that promotion and profits before taxes exceeded the combined costs of production, research, administration, and all other expenses.

The incidence of illness that creates the basic demand for drugs cannot be significantly increased by expenditures for advertising and sales. Yet, the 22 firms spent an average of 24.8 cents out of every sales dollar for these purposes, ranging from 18.1 per cent, for Merck and Eli Lilly, to 40.5 per cent, for Norwich Pharmacal.

The principal justification given for high drug prices is research, and impressive sums are cited. However, what counts is the percentage, which is small: the average expenditure for research among the 22 firms was 6.3 per cent, or one fourth of that spent on advertising and promotion. Moreover, a substantial share of the research expenditure was not for the benefit of mankind, but for such medically dubious moneymakers as "me too" drugs, the molecular modifications that infringe on the sales, and not the patents, of rival manufacturers.

Of the 22 drug companies, the subcommittee majority said in its report, only 3

spent as much as 10 per cent of sales on research, while 7 firms (including such industry leaders as Pfizer and Parke, Davis) spent less than 5 per cent of sales for this purpose. Only 1 of the 22 companies in 1958, Searle, devoted as much as half the amount to research that it reported for selling expense, while 11 of them spent from 5 to 11 times as much in advertising, promotional and selling expense as they did for research.

The circularity here is obvious. The heavy expenditures on sales promotion furnishes one of the principal means by which the major drug companies are able to maintain their high prices. The high prices produce the huge gross margins in this industry which are used to finance the heavy sales promotion expenditure.

More than three years later, such conditions remained as to bring a sharp attack from three scientists participating in a symposium at the annual meeting of the American Institute of Biological Sciences. In a report of August 26, 1964, in the New York *Times,* John A. Osmundsen said that Dr. Seymour H. Hunter and Dr. Sheldon Aaronson, both of Haskins Laboratories in New York, and Dr. Robert W. Hull, of the Florida State University, "attacked the American drug industry for turning away from research and toward the 'fast buck.'" Said Osmundsen:

They charged that the big pharmaceutical companies were no longer developing new drugs against disease and were even "defecting" by licensing a growing number of foreign drug products.

Instead of taking the gamble that is associated with research to develop or discover new compounds against bacteria, viruses, cancer and other diseases, it was charged, the American pharmaceutical industry is devoting its major energies to the marketing of sure-return consumer products, such as soaps and cosmetics.

.   .   .   .

The scientists asserted that the industry's negative attitude toward research had effects that reached far beyond matters associated with protecting the nation's health.

For example, Dr. Hull said, he had stopped advising his research students to enter industry. The reason, he said, is that their talents would not be used for research but would be wasted on projects aimed strictly at producing products for immediate profit.

With a few exceptions — which included Merck Sharp & Dohme, Eli Lilly & Co. and American Cyanamid — members of the drug industry no longer share common interests with the university, which ultimately must supply the industry's talent.

I think that, in fairness, at least one thing ought to be said on the other side. Some companies have researched, produced, and stocked drugs from which they cannot possibly profit at all, because the potential number of users is very small. In the same month in which the *Times* article appeared, *Chemical & Engineering News* for August 10, in "Prognosis for the Drug Houses," gave the story of Cuprimine (penicillamine), which Merck introduced in 1963 "to remove copper in treating Wilson's disease. Wilson's disease, which had been usually fatal, afflicts about 1000 persons in the U.S. Merck figures it spent $250,000 on the research leading to Cuprimine." In *Harper's* for May 1960 Alek A. Rozental said, "It would be cynical . . . to dismiss as mere public relations Mead Johnson's drug which cures a rare mental disorder occurring in perhaps four hundred infants in this country; Wyeth's Antivenin against snake bite; Lilly's mustard gas kit; or Abbott's radioactive isotopes. These are certainly not profitable."

✓ ✓ ✓

It might be assumed, the Senate Antitrust subcommittee majority suggested, that the unique importance of drugs to the public health would induce the managers of the industry to be content with reasonable profits overall. The record indicates that little such restraint was felt. As compiled by the subcommittee, here are the after-taxes net profits on the drug operations of the 22 firms in 1958:

Company	Profit as per cent of sales	Company	Profit as per cent of sales
Abbott	11.0	Parke, Davis	16.0
American Cyanamid		Pfizer	10.5
(Lederle)	15.6	Schering	15.9
American Home		Searle	21.3
(Wyeth, Ayerst)	14.7	Smith Kline &	
Bristol Laboratories	9.9	French	17.2
Carter Products	20.4	Sterling	10.1
CIBA	12.7	U.S. Vitamin	12.2
Eli Lilly	13.3	Upjohn	13.7
Hoffmann-La Roche	8.7	Vick [now Richardson-	
Mead Johnson	11.3	Merrell]	10.4
Merck	12.9	Warner-Lambert	13.4
Norwich	11.6	Average for 22 firms	13.0
Olin Mathieson			
(Squibb)	6.8		

Six years later, in 1964, prosperity was still in the drug industry's corner. In the first half of the year — to give a few illustrations — Merck earned $22.7 million on sales of $140.4 million, or 16.2 per cent; Smith Kline & French's profits in the same period were $17.7 million, or 17.4 per cent on sales of $101.1 million; G. D. Searle's net income was $12.1 million, or 28.2 per cent on sales of $42.9 million.

Although a profit margin on sales has a degree of pertinence, a more significant figure is a rate of return on net worth, or investment. This is the standard economic measure, the one that enables investors to compare the premiums their risk dollars can earn. Figured on the basis of net worth, profits in the substantially recession-proof drug industry are again incredibly high — about double the average for other manufacturing. According to *Profit Rates of Manufacturing Corporations*, which is published by the Federal Trade Commission, the return after taxes fell below 15 per cent in only 1 of the 32 quarters starting on April 1, 1956, and ending on March 31, 1964. The low point, if that is what it may be called, was 14.7 per cent, for the second quarter of 1962. The peak was 20.9 per cent, for the third quarter of 1957. In the third quarter of 1959 the return was only 0.1 per cent below the peak. Industry executives sometimes say, "Yes, but" — and then speak disarmingly about being engaged in what they like to call a "risk enterprise." What risk?

Some of the specific cases are breathtaking. Consider Smith Kline & French. On January 1, 1949, its net worth was $10.8 million. Its after-taxes net income for 1949 and 1950, the Kefauver subcommittee found, totaled $10.3 million — or $500,000 less. In other words, SKF's net profits for two years almost equaled its net worth. SKF's cumulative net profits amounted to $134.2 million through 1959, or 12 times its net worth 11 years earlier. In 1958, SKF was ranked by *Fortune* second among 500 American industrial corporations in net profit after taxes on invested capital. Its rate of return was 33.1 per cent. The only firm that exceeded it, which also has a large drug operation, was

American Home Products, with 33.5 per cent. In 1963, although ranking fourth on the *Fortune* list, SKF's return was 30.9 per cent, and American Home, while dropping to sixth, earned 26.5 per cent.

There are other firms in the same league. One is the Schering Corporation, which originally was German-owned. For a decade after its seizure in World War II by the Alien Property Custodian, Schering was operated under government control. In March 1952 the government sold the corporation to a syndicate headed by Merrill Lynch, Pierce, Fenner & Beane. The price was $29,152,000. Within five and a half years, net profits totaled $31,959,000, or $2.8 million more than what the firm had been sold for. If owners of pharmaceutical stocks have not always found their dividends reflecting profitability on this scale, the explanation is simply that the market had bid up the price of the stocks so that the real profit was taken by the sellers.

✶ ✶ ✶

On March 15, 1964, the three television networks carried an hour-long interview with President Johnson. Toward the end he said: "I am so happy to be a part of a system . . . of private enterprise — free enterprise, where the employer, hoping to make a little profit, the laborer hoping to justify his wages, can get together and make a better mousetrap." What Mr. Johnson said, in an election year, had little relevance to the industrial economy of the United States, and almost none at all to the multibillion-dollar drug industry, in which employers hope to, and do, make enormous profits, in which the laborer's wages need no justification, and the product is too often a worse mousetrap. Surely Mr. Johnson knew of the truths about the drug industry that were developed, while he was in the Senate, in regard to the industry's place in our economy.

The subcommittee's focus was on administered prices. Set by administrative action, they are insensitive to changes in the market, are identical among producers, and are high. But, as the majority report pointed out, the prescription-drug industry has a number of features that make it unique:

> For one thing there is its critical bearing on public health and welfare . . .
>
> A second unique characteristic is the difference between buyer and orderer; in the words of Chairman Kefauver, "He who orders does not buy; and he who buys does not order." Or, as one witness observed before the subcommittee, the physician acts as "purchasing agent" for the consumer. Regardless of how well intentioned the physician may be, another party can never be expected to be as interested in price as the individual who has to spend his own money. Once the physician has written his prescription (usually in terms of a brand name), the consumer is limited to the product prescribed under that brand name; he cannot "shop around" for the same product under a different (or no) brand name at a lower price. Hence in ethical drugs the ability of the ordinary consumer to protect himself against the monopoly element inherent in trademarks by being able to choose from a number of competing brands is nonexistent. The consumer is "captive" to a degree not present in any other industry.
>
> The drug industry is also unusual in the extent to which the demand for its products is inelastic, i.e., unresponsive to changes in price. While there are undoubtedly some consumers who simply cannot pay the prices charged and must of necessity go without needed medication, they appear to constitute a small minority. Lower prices of drugs would enable consumers to expand their purchases of other products, but insofar as the drug industry alone is concerned, it appears to be relatively unresponsive to price reductions. This was emphasized by industry spokesmen during the hearings; Mr. Francis C. Brown, president of Schering Corp., testified:

Unlike consumer marketing, Schering cannot expand its markets by lowering prices. Cortisone proved this. After all, we cannot put two bottles of Schering medicine in every medicine chest where only one is needed, or two people in every hospital bed where only one is sick. Marketing medicine is a far cry from marketing soft-drinks or automobiles.

The fact that demand is inelastic means that one of the checks which might serve as a possible constraint upon corporate price policies is absent in ethical drugs. When demand is elastic, prices may become so high as to result in a significant reduction in sales volume.

✓ ✓ ✓

In both human and dollars-and-cents terms, prednisone provides a stark illustration of the contrast between administered and competitive drug prices. Prednisone is one of the corticosteroids used to relieve the pain of arthritis, a prevalent affliction of the elderly. It costs little to produce. The Kefauver subcommittee was told by Herman C. Nolen of McKesson & Robbins that all of the costs incurred by his firm in producing a bottle of 1000 5-milligram tablets came to $8.99. The price to the druggist was $20.95. A common dosage is 100 pills a month. A consumer buying this number of McKesson's generic pills would pay about $3.50.

He would, that is, if his physician had prescribed by the generic name, prednisone. If, as was most often the case, he had prescribed by trade name (Schering's Meticorten, or the same product under such brands as Upjohn's, Merck's, or Parke, Davis's) he would have fallen into quite a different situation. The price that the Kefauver subcommittee said was charged the druggist for 1000 of the brand-name versions would have been not $20.95 but $170. For his 100 pills the consumer would be paying about $27 per month.

The aged often have small, fixed incomes. "Their ability to purchase the needed drugs," the House Committee on Interstate and Foreign Commerce was told by Ernest Giddings, of the National Retired Teachers Association and the American Association of Retired Persons, "often makes the difference between sickness and health and sometimes between life and death." He said:

> When physicians, as is the general practice in writing prescriptions, identify the drug by its trade name instead of by its official name they leave our aged sick little or no opportunity for reducing costs. The patient must buy the prescribed brand and is left no opportunity of shopping around to buy at a price he can afford.
>
> Those who exist on a bare subsistence level must often sacrifice on food or some other necessity in order to afford the prescribed drug or else deny themselves or ask for charity.
>
> The opportunity to buy drugs they need at a cost they can afford, will keep them physically fit, able to work part or full time to supplement their retirement incomes and thus continue to do their part in the productivity of the Nation, and at the same time maintain their self-respect.
>
> When elderly people living on a subsistence income can be saved on drug purchases as much as $100 to $300 in 1 year, this saving alone may preserve their sense of self-sufficiency, their feeling of dignity, and keep them from being placed on the relief rolls of their local communities or State.

For victims of arthritis fortunate enough to have physicians who will prescribe prednisone generically, the situation has become even better than it had been. In the spring of 1964, for example, the wholesaler in Mineola, New York — Wolins — was listing 1000 tablets for $6.90. This was $2.09 below the cost of production estimated by McKesson & Robbins in 1959. Schering's price for Meticorten was still $170, or more than 24 times that of the comparable generic product.

It does no good for a physician to prescribe by its generic name a product monopolized by a patent, because the prescription can legally be filled only by the patented product. Prednisone, however, had remained available generically, from McKesson & Robbins and other suppliers, while the pending patent was being disputed before the Patent Office. In May 1962, in testimony before Representative Celler's House Antitrust subcommittee, Senator Kefauver warned:

> Already four of the larger companies have entered into cross-license agreements with Schering on the theory that probably Schering will get the patent. When that happens, of course, McKesson & Robbins can no longer sell the drug generically, and you can expect the price all the way around to be what Merck and the others are charging.
> [And:]
> The moment the patent is issued, under the provisions of contracts now in effect, it can be expected that the drug will be available to the druggist only at a price of 17 cents and to the consumer at 28 cents. Since a patient suffering from arthritis has to take about three of the tablets a day, this means a cost of around $27 a month, which for retired persons represents over a third of their total monthly pension.

The moment the patent was issued came in May 1964. Schering promptly notified other manufacturers of its victory. The firm said that it would adopt a liberal licensing policy — and it did. For this Schering deserves praise. Senator Kefauver was wrong in predicting that prednisone would be available to the consumer only at a price of 28 cents a pill. But one cannot assume that this would have been so had he not focused the attention of the public and the Congress on the situation.[4]

✦ ✦ ✦

The biggest seller among the drugs that relieve certain types

[4] Schering licensed some 60 firms to market prednisone. In the spring of 1965, when it was being retailed as Meticorten at a typical price of $26.70 for 100 2.5-milligram tablets, it was available generically for as little as $2.40 in the same amount.

of diabetics from the necessity of daily injections of insulin was developed in Europe. It is tolbutamide, produced and marketed here by Upjohn of Kalamazoo, under the trade name Orinase. The production cost was computed for 0.5-gram tablets at $13.11 per 1000. This price included a $6.25 royalty paid to Farbwerke Hoechst, A. G., of West Germany. Upjohn's price to wholesalers, and to retailers buying $100 or more worth of goods a year, was $83.40. Consumers buying in 50-tablet lots paid $139 for the 1000 tablets.

"After all," Dr. E. Gifford Upjohn told the subcommittee, "it is a reasonable price. It is just a matter of pennies a day." The subcommittee report recalled that Senator Kefauver pointed out:

> even pennies a day are important to people on limited incomes, especially since Orinase . . . must be taken by the patient every day of his life. According to Upjohn spokesmen, more than half a million diabetic patients are on daily maintenance dosages of Orinase, with an average dosage of three tablets (1.5 grams) per day. At 90 tablets a month, therefore, the typical patient must pay, month after month, about $12.50 for medication which costs Upjohn no more than $1.18 to produce, including the company's substantial royalty to Hoechst. On an annual basis, "pennies a day" comes to $150 a year for an amount of the drug which is manufactured at a total cost of about $14.

One more example is provided by tetracycline, an antibiotic prescribed for millions for a broad spectrum of diseases. Tetracycline has been involved in a long and almost incredibly complex series of moves and countermoves by several drug companies, each seeking issuance of a patent for itself or, failing that, a favorable licensing arrangement.

> Then suddenly the controversy was stilled [the Kefauver subcommittee said in its 1961 report]. In March, 1956, the

six lawsuits then pending were privately settled in a series of agreements among the companies. Squibb and Upjohn were licensed by Pfizer merely to sell, but not to manufacture, tetracycline. In addition to paying a lump sum for infringement, Bristol received a license from Pfizer for the manufacture and sale of tetracycline with the payment of royalties. In turn Pfizer was granted access to any Bristol patents in this field; if it exercised this option, Pfizer was obligated to pay royalties to Bristol.

With the consummation of these arrangements, the orderly and controlled marketing of tetracycline was an inevitable and expected result.

The marketing of tetracycline was certainly orderly, either because it was controlled or because coincidence moved to new frontiers. Each of the three manufacturers — Cyanamid, Pfizer, and Bristol — accounted for roughly a third of the total production. Their costs were very different from those of Squibb and Upjohn, which bought from them in bulk — but all five sold consistently at identical prices.

In the three years starting in November 1956, the Military Medical Supply Agency received sealed bids for tetracycline. The patent-holder, Pfizer, won 46.6 per cent of the business. Apart from 0.5 per cent that went to Upjohn, the rest of the sales were shared with notable equality by Pfizer's licensees. The Lederle Laboratories Division of American Cyanamid received 17.8 per cent, Bristol 17.6 per cent, and Squibb 17.5 per cent.

A federal grand jury in New York apparently thought that the marketing of tetracycline may have been characterized by violations of the law rather than by coincidence. In August 1961 the jury returned an antitrust indictment against Pfizer, American Cyanamid, and Bristol. All pleaded not guilty. Named as co-conspirators, but not as defendants, were Olin Mathieson and

Upjohn. As of late 1964, a judge had not been named to try the case.

Senator Kefauver died in the Naval Medical Center in Bethesda on August 10, 1963, a Saturday. By a genuine coincidence, the Federal Trade Commission had announced for the Sunday newspapers, which happened to be carrying his obituary, its issuance of an order to the five firms to cease and desist fixing antibiotics prices, exchanging information about those prices, and rigging bids.

The Commission said that "unclean hands and bad faith played a major role" in the private settlements of the six lawsuits in 1956. It accused Pfizer of having secured its patent on tetracycline in 1955 through "false and misleading statements of fact before the Patent Office," and through suppression of test results that, had they been known to the Patent Office, might have caused it to reverse its award of rights to Pfizer. In January 1964 the Commission, which had held prolonged hearings, issued a final order that the five firms have carried to the United States Court of Appeals. In that decree, the Commission ordered Pfizer to grant production licenses to all domestic applicants. It and the other four companies were directed not only to stop conspiring to fix prices and to rig bids, but to establish lower prices within sixty days.

There followed an outbreak of private litigation. Pfizer sued to prevent the City of New York from buying tetracycline manufactured in Italy and sold by Premo Pharmaceutical Laboratories, a small New Jersey firm, at $2.75 a bottle. Pfizer's bid had been $10.47 and Upjohn's $8.75. Pfizer complained that Premo was infringing its patent — the one the Commission said had been obtained through false statements — and that the Italian company had stolen the formula. The City filed a counterclaim, and at its request a court order was signed making all five firms defendants. In yet another action, Premo sued Pfizer, Bristol, and American Cyanamid.

Another lush growth of legal actions followed the announcement in August 1964 by McKesson & Robbins, the country's largest wholesale drug distributor, that it would offer tetracycline to druggists at a low $6.75 per hundred 250-milligram capsules — and at still lower prices to quantity buyers. This was American-made tetracycline, produced at Long Beach, California, by Rachel Laboratories, a subsidiary of International Rectifier. "We came to our decision after assurance by eminent legal and scientific opinions that McKesson does not infringe on any valid American patent," Herman Nolen, the chairman of McKesson, said. At once Pfizer said it would sue for patent infringement, and it did so. In turn, Pfizer was sued by McKesson, which asked that Pfizer's controversial 1955 patent be declared invalid. And Lederle Laboratories, which had been selling millions of dollars' worth of its products to McKesson, canceled its contract in a retaliatory action. Thereupon, McKesson filed an antitrust suit against American Cyanamid, of which Lederle is a division, and Pfizer. In November 1964, in the Philadelphia Federal Court, Judge John Morgan issued a temporary injunction against American Cyanamid, the effect of which was to compel it to resume immediately the sale of its products to McKesson.

Whatever the outcome of this profusion of lawsuits might be, the important thing, and it is refreshingly simple, is that competition and strong action by the Federal Trade Commission have brought sharp price cuts. For years, one hundred 250-milligram capsules of tetracycline that cost Bristol $1.67 to produce were sold to the druggist for $30.60 and to the consumer for $51. Price cuts were effected in August 1960 and again in the spring of 1964. The latter cuts first reduced the price to druggists for Lederle's brand of tetracycline, Achromycin, to $23.50 — $7.10 less than in 1959. Then Lederle, Pfizer, and Bristol reduced their prices still further, to $17.60 to direct-buying retailers. And in August 1964, McKesson's tetracycline became available for $10.85 less than that.

✓ ✓ ✓

Some of the most astonishing data assembled by the Kefauver subcommittee compared the prices of prescription drugs in the United States with those in other countries. A French firm, Roussel, sold estradiol progynon, a drug used in menopausal disorders, to Schering in bulk form. Schering did no research on the drug — merely put it up in tablets and marketed the pills under its own label. In a bottle of 60 tablets there was 11.7 cents worth of the drug. Schering sold the bottle for $8.40. That is a markup of 7079 per cent.

During the 1950's, the drug that largely accounted for the spectacular profits of Smith Kline & French was a potent tranquilizer, Thorazine (chlorpromazine hydrochloride). It was developed by the French chemical and drug manufacturer Rhône-Poulenc, which, through a subsidiary, sold it in France for 51 cents a bottle of 50 tablets. The exclusive American licensee, SKF, charged $3.03. The British licensee charged 77 cents, the German licensee 94 cents.

Rhône-Poulenc also developed another potent tranquilizer, promazine hydrochloride. The exclusive American licensee is American Home Products, whose Wyeth Laboratories marketed it, as Sparine, at $3 for 50 pills. Several foreign subsidiaries of American Home also are licensed to market promazine. One, in Australia, sold 50 tablets for 94 cents. Neither in Australia nor in any of four other countries did a druggist pay an American Home subsidiary half, or much more than half, of what a druggist in the United States paid to American Home itself.

Carter Products, which in 1958 reaped a fantastic net profit on invested capital of 38.2 per cent after taxes, or about 75 per cent before taxes, holds the American patent on meprobamate, the tranquilizer it sells as Miltown. Licensed by Carter as the foreign distributor is American Cyanamid's Lederle Laboratories. Carter's price to druggists in the United States was $3.25 for 50 tablets. In four well-developed nations with relatively high costs and strong demand — Germany, England, Austria, and Italy — the price for Miltown ranged from $1.38 to $1.77, or approximately half the price in this country. But in the relatively underdeveloped nations of Iran, India, and Venezuela, Cyanamid's price for Miltown ranged from $4.68 to $5.44, or about half again as much as in the United States.

The price charged by Upjohn in the United States for tolbutamide, the oral antidiabetic it calls Orinase, was $4.17 for 50 tablets when purchased by direct-dealing druggists. In none of eleven other countries checked was the price as high for this drug, which Upjohn sold under license from the West German firm of Farbwerke Hoechst, A. G. The lowest price — in Austria — was $1.66.

Pfizer's rival product, chlorpropamide (Diabinese), is marketed in most countries exclusively by Pfizer. The price to druggists in the United States was $5.40. In nine other countries Pfizer's price ranged from $3.32 in England to $6.72 in Mexico. In Italy, however, chlorpropamide was sold by Farmitalia for $1.41. In testimony before the Senate Antitrust subcommittee, Pfizer president John E. McKeen said that Diabinese was sold in Italy. He presumed that his firm would meet Farmitalia's price, which was about a quarter of what Pfizer charged the American druggist. The reader may make two presumptions. One is that Pfizer would not bother selling in Italy if it had to do so at a loss. The second is that price competition, when there is any, is remarkably effective in reducing drug prices.

Eli Lilly marketed a patented variant of penicillin, the therapeutic value of which was independently established by an Austrian firm. As V-Cillin, it was sold by Lilly to American pharmacies for $18 per 100 tablets. In Canada Lilly charged $18.75. However, in six other countries Lilly charged less than in the United States, even though the product sold in four of those nations was manufactured by Lilly in Indianapolis. The Senate subcommittee majority commented: "Thus the company ships the product from Indianapolis to Australia, where it is sold to the Australian druggist for $10.75 — 40 per cent less than what a druggist has to pay in the city where the drug is made."

Lilly has a plant in England, and the product — called Penicillin V there — sold for $6.50, or slightly more than one-third the price in the United States. Lilly's president, Eugene Beesley, was asked by Senator Kefauver if Lilly made a profit on its sales in England. "I think we do," Beesley replied. Similarly, Parke, Davis charged druggists in Detroit two and one-third times as much for Chloromycetin as it charged druggists in Iran, even though the product was manufactured and packaged in Detroit.

During debate on the drug bill in August 1962, it was suggested to the Senate that lower drug prices abroad were the result of price-control laws which, obviously, can be advocated during peacetime in this country only by those in public life bent on political suicide. The suggestion was made by Senator Roman L. Hruska, whose manifestations of sympathy for the drug industry had prompted this comment by Senator Kefauver, quoted by Richard Harris in *The Real Voice*: "In all my years in Congress, I've never encountered such harassment, obstructionism, and vilification." This time, the Nebraska Republican, who was to win re-election in 1964 by a larger margin than in 1958, aroused Senator John O. Pastore of Rhode Island. Hruska's suggestion ignored the fact that drug prices lower than those in the United States prevailed in several nations where there are no price-control statutes. And, of course, the suggestion could be interpreted — if one were bold enough to do so — as an argument *for* price control. In any event, Pastore, who would become the keynoter at the 1964 Democratic National Convention, told the Senate: "I think it is little justification to argue that because there are price-control laws in other countries, an article which is developed in the United States, on the basis of research work done in the United States, should be sold to American consumers at higher prices than those charged to the people of other countries. Regardless of the laws which may apply in other countries, I say it is immoral to gouge the American public."

Senator Kefauver then said that "if American companies do not feel they can make a profit in countries that fix prices, they do not have to do business there. They do not have to sell there at a lower price."

"I say it is immoral," Pastore declared. "It is immoral; there is no doubt about it," Kefauver agreed.

✓ ✓ ✓

Pharmaceutical manufacturers and their advocates sometimes try to explain away vast differences in prices between their products and the identical products of foreign manufacturers on the ground that wages in the United States are higher than elsewhere. This argument is hard to accept.

In the first place, we have seen that all production costs together constitute a smaller percentage of the price in the drug industry than in other industries. Labor is but one of these costs, and in the drug industry, as Professor Seymour Harris says in *The Economics of American Medicine,* its proportionate share "is minimal." One is tempted to say, negligible. A few years ago, the Military Medical Supply Agency was buying meprobamate, the tranquilizer, from a manufacturer in Denmark. From the supplier the agency obtained data on how much labor, direct and indirect, went into 1000 pills — the work needed to produce the raw material, and to tablet it, package it, and pack it for shipping. The total labor required was 46 man-minutes. The Antitrust subcommittee then multiplied 46 man-minutes by the rate of earnings in the drug industry in the United States and got an American labor cost of $1.86 for 1000 pills. This was only 25.4 per cent of the factory cost, and a mere 3.6 per cent of the $52 price at which Wallace Laboratories sold 1000 tablets of meprobamate, as Miltown, to wholesalers. That price, it may be noted, was $44.68 greater than the cost of production, as computed by the staff of the Kefauver subcommittee and confirmed by Henry H. Hoyt, president of Carter Products.

In the second place, the logic of the industry position requires some consistent relation between wages and prices. But there does not seem to be very much. For illustration, American Cyanamid's Lederle Laboratories sold tetracycline, under its trade name of Achromycin, for more in some low-wage countries than in some high-wage countries. While American druggists were charged $5.10 for 16 capsules, druggists in India were paying $6.52. This was 90 cents more than in Australia (high-wage), and $5.53 more than in Argentina (low-wage).

In the third place, American labor costs cannot very well be a decisive factor when manufacturers sell the products they make in the United States, with that high-wage American labor, for less in distant lands than at home.

Finally, consider the Bristol cost figure cited earlier — $1.67 for producing 100 tablets of tetracycline with American labor. The cost of labor is a small fraction of that $1.67, and thus could not account for prices several dollars higher than foreign firms have asked for tetracycline.

The seemingly irrational international price patterns are not to be explained by such simplistic notions as varying wage costs. The explanation lies in monopolistic practices, in licensing agreements, in price-fixing conspiracies, in cartels, and in concentration.

✓ ✓ ✓

Almost since their enactment in 1962, the Kefauver-Harris amendments have been under attack by the two parts of the FDA-PMA-AMA molecule which, at least in this respect, seem to be almost interchangeable. One need not read the publications of the Pharmaceutical Manufacturers Association and the American Medical Association to keep informed in this area. The *AMA News* alone often suffices. Hardly a week passes without the *News* reverently publishing some PMA publicity handout, just as if it were to be taken seriously. One searches in vain for the other side of the story. Well, not quite in vain. In the *News* for June 22, 1964, it must be conceded, there was a story about the disposition of the MER/29 case. The item appeared on page 12 under a one-line headline. It rated 12 lines of type, or 4 more than an item on page 11 about a $200 gift by a local medical society to a county library. Here is the item in full:

DRUG FIRM FINED

A federal district judge fined Richardson-Merrill Drug Company and a subsidiary $80,000 for alleged failure to spell out possible adverse effects from use of the drug MER-29. Three scientists with the firm were given suspended sentences by Judge Matthew M. McGuire in Washington, D.C. MER-29, used to lower cholesterol levels, was withdrawn in 1962 after reports of serious adverse reactions.

One hardly knows where to begin to cope with a piece of reporting like this. The name of the firm was given erroneously. The "subsidiary," the William S. Merrell Company division, was not identified at all. The scientists were employed by the division, not the firm named by the *News*. The middle initial of the Judge is "F" and not "M." No mention was made of the fact that pleas of no contest had been entered to charges of falsifying and withholding animal test data. The pleas, which the Judge equated to admissions of guilt, added up to something more than "alleged failure" to specify "possible" harmful effects.

I have permitted myself this digression because it may help the reader to understand why I approached a ten-paragraph piece in the March 2, 1964, issue of the *News* under the two-column headline "Drug Rules Draw Criticism" with something less than uncritical enthusiasm. However, since the article was based on statements made by high officials of the PMA I felt confident that the quotations had been carefully checked for accuracy. What interested me most were the views of Dr. E. Gifford

Upjohn, chairman-elect of the PMA, whose company, I remembered, had been one of those ordered only two months earlier by the Federal Trade Commission to stop conspiring to fix prices and rigging bids. The *News* reported:

Dr. Upjohn said the pharmaceutical industry has the right to expect assistance from the U.S. State Dept. and other government branches in its effort to retain its position in world markets.

"The protection of private property and the defense of free enterprise should be a matter of concern not only to the enterprises directly involved," he said, "but to all government agencies.

"The importance of American investments abroad and the importance of patents and trademarks in a free economy to encourage initiative are fundamental concepts of the American way of life," he added.

Because Dr. Upjohn felt the pharmaceutical industry has the right to expect the assistance of the United States Government, I thought it would be appropriate to look at the record of the assistance the industry has rendered the government.

Penicillin was discovered in 1928, by Sir Alexander Fleming in Britain. There the early investigative work was undertaken, and there the remarkable healing properties of the antibiotic were discovered. The Senate Antitrust subcommittee recalled that in 1941 a small group of British physicians came to the United States to see what might be done to manufacture penicillin in quantities adequate to the war effort. The drug companies enlisted in the effort by Dr. Vannevar Bush, director of the Office of Scientific Research and Development, did not make much progress, even with government financial aid. Nor did universities or government research groups.

In April 1943 Dr. Bush reported that the companies had cooperated "after a fashion." In a letter to an Army Air Corps consultant, Dr. Bush further said, "They have not made their experimental results and their development of manufacturing processes generally available, however . . . This is the problem." The problem, as Richard Harris described it in *The Real Voice*, "was that the firms were too busy trying to corner patents on various processes in the production of penicillin to produce much of it, and the government began pressing them to work together. It was slow going."

The coordinator of the War Production Board's special penicillin program, Albert L. Elder, became discouraged by the unwillingness of the drug firms to exchange information needed to achieve quantity production. In January 1944, more than two years after the United States was attacked at Pearl Harbor, he wrote in a memorandum to a superior: "The value of penicillin in saving the lives of wounded soldiers has been so thoroughly demonstrated that I cannot with a clear conscience assume the responsibility for coordinating this program any longer while at the same time being handicapped by being unable to make available information which would result in the output of more penicillin and thereby save the lives of our soldiers."

Fortunately, however, scientists of the Department of Agriculture's Northern Regional Research Laboratory at Peoria, Illinois, had been moving swiftly toward solving the problems of mass production. Soon afterward, the Department filed its own patent application. "In conformity with the patent policy of that agency," the Kefauver subcommittee said in its 1961 report, "patents on these developments were dedicated to the public and thus made available [free of charge] to the 20-odd companies which had been financially aided by the U. S. Government to enter into production." By the end of World War II the production of penicillin had risen to a level high enough to have saved the lives of thousands of servicemen.

One need not linger in the World War II era to determine

what kind of assistance drug manufacturers have been rendering the government. In May 1957 Bristol Laboratories bid $1.828 per bottle on a solicitation by the Military Medical Supply Agency for 454,390 bottles of tetracycline for oral suspension. The Senate Antitrust subcommittee obtained a memorandum in which the firm's treasurer defined precisely what the bid would mean in dollars and cents. Total costs and expenses were put at $268,286, or 32.3 per cent of the total sales price of $830,625. Of this the actual production cost of the goods sold was $154,493, or 18.6 per cent of the sales price. This left a net profit before taxes of $562,339, or 67.7 per cent. Net profit after taxes was shown to be $239,135, or 28.8 per cent of the bid price to the government. ". . . it is safe to say," the subcommittee majority report commented, "that a profit rate on sales of an important product of around 20 per cent, after taxes, has few parallels."

When the Supply Agency first purchased tetracycline tablets, in December 1956, the price was $11 per 100. The price was the same in May 1957. But the Supply Agency's executive director, Rear Admiral William L. Knickerbocker, USN, testified:

On the third procurement, 9 months later, the price rose, inexplicably, to $17.24 — a 57 per cent increase over the previous $11 price. As a matter of fact, in this latter procurement the low offeror refused to take more than one-half the quantity required by the Government, and the remainder had to go to the second low offeror at a price of $19.19 per bottle — or an increase of 74 per cent over the initial low price.

Aside from the foregoing peculiar pattern of cost to the Government, there are other characteristics in the procurement history of tetracycline hydrochloride tablets which should be noted. On a number of procurements, more than one supplier initially offered the identical low price. Furthermore even when only one supplier was low, others came in at higher but identical prices (i.e., either the specific prices offered were the same, or they became identical when the prompt payment discount was applied).

The record shows clearly that the Supply Agency had little success in securing price concessions on any broad-spectrum antibiotics, including Parke, Davis's Chloromycetin and American Cyanamid's Aureomycin, or on any drugs with sales controlled by one manufacturer or a few.

Because pharmaceutical manufacturers would be content with nothing less than fantastic profits, the government had to tax and tax and spend and spend in order to provide the best possible medical treatment for patients who may range, as the subcommittee pointed out, "from the newest Army recruit to Members of Congress and the President." But this was not so when there was price competition — when prices were not maintained at artificially high levels, when the product could be purchased by its generic name, when there were many bidders rather than just the monopolists, duopolists, and oligopolists.

In January 1960 Schering was selling prednisone, under its trade name of Meticorten, to the druggist at $170 per 1000 tablets. At this time Schering had not yet been awarded a patent. Faced with competition on a government solicitation, it offered the identical product at $17.97, or about one-tenth as much as it charged druggists. Even this was not low enough. The small Premo Pharmaceutical Laboratories bid $11.79, or $6.18 less, and received the contract. To the great distress of the lords of the industry, the government remains free to buy patented products generically, if they are offered and if they meet its high standards.

ダ   ダ   ダ

In the disastrous Bay of Pigs invasion in April 1961, 1200 brave men were captured and imprisoned. The Kennedy Administration felt a deep moral obligation to do everything in its power to obtain their release. Terribly delicate and difficult negotiations were carried to a successful conclusion by James B. Donovan, the brilliant New York lawyer. At the end of November 1962, when Cuban Prime Minister Fidel Castro's ransom demand had shaken down to $53 million worth of drugs, principally, and chemicals, medical and surgical equipment, and baby food, it was suggested in Washington that the manufacturers involved might be willing to make direct contributions in goods — provided that their donations could be considered as tax-deductible gifts. In *The Bay of Pigs*,[5] Haynes Johnson, in an authoritative account, said that Louis E. Oberdorfer, the Assistant Attorney General in charge of the Tax Division of the Department of Justice

. . . informally approached Lloyd Cutler, a Washington lawyer and counsel to the Pharmaceutical Manufacturers Association, about the possibility of contributions by the drug companies. Cutler, who had been contacted earlier when Donovan's negotiations were progressing, said he thought there was still a chance. But he made it clear that in order to do the job the companies would have to be able to work together without fear of subsequent antitrust or other action. And, he pointed out, because of the unfavorable public and political image of the drug manufacturers stemming from Senator Estes Kefauver's investigating subcommittee in 1960 and 1961, the companies would need some assurance from the administration that they would not be attacked because of their participation in the prisoner exchange. *They also would have to be assured that they would not be required to disclose their cost and markup data in order to secure tax deductions.* [My italics.]

The reasons for the companies' reluctance to disclose their costs and markups are so apparent as to require no elaboration,

---

[5] New York: Norton, 1964.

but some backgrounding of the situation is necessary. Under a tax ruling by the Internal Revenue Service, a manufacturer who made a contribution to charity was entitled to claim as a deduction his selling price in the lowest usual market. Applied to most industries, the ruling is a reasonable one. That is because a proximate relation exists between the cost of production and the sales price. In the drug industry, however, the sales price tc drugstores, if that be deemed the lowest usual market, vastly exceeds the cost of production — a fact that was not developed by the Kefauver subcommittee until after the ruling was adopted in 1958. Indeed, the gap between production costs and sales price to pharmacies was so great that if the ruling were to be applied here it would be possible for a drug manufacturer actually to make money on charitable contributions. This may be a startling statement, and it requires explanation.

Let us take a hypothetical example. You donate $100 to a group of medical missionaries working among an Indian tribe in South Dakota. When you claim this as a charitable deduction you will reduce your tax liability by, say, $20. You have nonetheless given a net of $80 to charity. Now suppose that a drug company donates to the missionaries a quantity of a drug that cost it $10 to produce but which it sells to the pharmacist for $100. Allowed to claim the selling price of $100 as the value of its gift, the company would, unlike you, be ahead. The $100 would be deducted from the company's income. This would reduce the corporate income tax otherwise payable by the company by about $50, and this, minus the cost of $10, would result in the company's actually being better off by $40 than it would be without the donation.

Such were the stakes while the prisoners, emaciated and suffering, lingered in prison. Continuing his account, Haynes Johnson told of a crucial meeting on December 7, 1962, between Robert F. Kennedy and top officials of the Pharmaceutical Manufacturers Association. The Attorney General, responding to an expression of concern that the industry might be criticized if it participated in the prisoner exchange, said "that the sight of the prisoners arriving in the United States on Christmas Eve would silence any critics. He also made it clear that all contributions would be voluntary — no company could expect, or would receive, special considerations from the government. Neither would there be adverse consequences if contributions were withheld."

There remained the problem of fitting the 1958 Internal Revenue ruling to the situation, not only as to what worth should be ascribed to donations for tax purposes, but also so as to permit deductions for donations made to a foreign government. The necessary tax and antitrust rulings were made. On December 11, the Internal Revenue ruled that contributions would be deductible at a value measured by the lowest wholesale catalogue prices at which the manufacturers customarily sold their products. This meant that the pharmaceutical houses would be able to claim their charitable deductions at the prices at which they sold to pharmacies.

Although a statement that the consequent tax loss to the government totaled $20 million has been attributed to the Internal Revenue Service, the IRS says the figure resulted from a misunderstanding and is an exaggeration, of unknown proportions. There are two reasons: the first is that the law limits how much can be claimed for charity — a corporate donor can claim as charitable expense no more than 5 per cent of its taxable income; the second, that there were many instances in which the donations to the prisoner exchange merely substituted for contributions that normally would have gone to other beneficiaries.

Within a matter of days after the tax and antitrust rulings — the government and the industry working together as quietly as possible — forty pharmaceutical manufacturers had put together a shipment of drugs with an ascribed value of $12 million. Haynes Johnson wrote:

There was in this industry solidarity a certain mordant satisfaction, for big business, and particularly the drug industry, felt no love for the Kennedy administration. It was good public relations to assist in the prisoner exchange, and at the same time some executives felt they were mitigating former grievances in their role of extricating the Kennedys from the Bay of Pigs debacle. Then, too, because of the high markup for drugs, it was possible for some manufacturers to realize a "windfall" . . . the government suggested that such profits be contributed to charity. The decision, of course, was left to the individual companies.

What the companies did with their profits comes close to being beside the point, which is that they were making money on charity. Merck gave its net to the Merck Foundation. Inevitably, this improved the public image of the firm.

According to Johnson:

Despite these advantages to the drug manufacturers, their motives concerning the ransom operation were humanitarian as well as personal, and the reaction of one drug industry spokesman to criticism of the tax writeoffs was understandable. "It's a little like helping a traffic victim into the ambulance," he said, "and then meeting a guy rushing around the corner to accuse you of picking the victim's pockets."

The spokesman was entitled to see it that way, but I do not think he should expect all of us to salute the PMA flag. The overriding consideration was, and should have been, the humanitarian one of getting 1200 courageous and suffering men out of prison. It was of secondary importance that Merck, according to an article by Ben Weberman in the New York *Herald Tribune* in January 1963, netted an estimated $300,000 after taxes on its wholesale-value donation of $2.5 million, or that Pfizer, according to the same source, netted $120,000 on its contribution, which had an ascribed worth of $1.5 million.

On January 19, 1963 — only a few weeks after the prisoners were released — Merck's president, John T. Connor, addressed the Texas Medical Association. Connor, who had participated in the project almost from the start, called it an "incredible success," and "a dramatic example of what free men can do in cooperation with officials of their own government to bring about results beneficial to the public interest and the interests of the participants." He described how the operation had "made possible the release of the prisoners and joyful family reunions for Christmas that we all saw on T.V." Then he got down to the "tax rulings which made the whole transaction possible." Finally, Connor spoke these brutally frank words to his audience in Austin: "Without the tax rulings, absolutely nothing would have happened. The men would still be in prison."

✓ ✓ ✓

At the Kefauver hearings, Dr. E. Gifford Upjohn, whose career had not yet brought him the chairmanship-elect of the Pharmaceutical Manufacturers Association, himself pointed up the relationship between the number of suppliers and price. When the Upjohn Company, of which he is president, was but one of several competitors on a Military Medical Supply Agency procurement of hydrocortisone tablets, it bid $4.63 per 100. This was less than one-fourth the price at which Upjohn sold the tablets to retailers who bought direct. In contrast, when the government had to buy tolbutamide it was confronted by a monopoly bid, Upjohn being the sole licensee for it. Under these circumstances, the government had to pay 90 per cent as much for the oral antidiabetic drug as Upjohn charged its direct-buying retailers.

On items like hydrocortisone, "You had competition?" Paul Rand Dixon, then of the subcommittee staff, asked Dr. Upjohn. This followed:

DR. UPJOHN. I expect you are right.

MR. DIXON. You did not have any competition on Orinase because you were the exclusive manufacturer?

DR. UPJOHN. That is right. If they specify our product then it would be filled with our product; that's right.

But why was the price for Orinase what it was, and not something else? It was revealed that the industry observed a custom of charging for a new drug the price charged for an existing drug used to treat the same general type of ailment. Production costs tend to become irrelevant under this means of eliminating price rivalry. Thus, Dr. Upjohn freely acknowledged that the price for Orinase was determined not by the cost of making it — which is very low — but by the price of a daily dosage of insulin, which Orinase would replace for many diabetics.

✓   ✓   ✓

The Sherman Antitrust Act lays down certain legal limitations on how far the holder of a patent may go in using his patent to control the market. Between these limitations and ordinary legitimate patent uses, the Senate Antitrust subcommittee said in its report, "there is a 'grey' area in which patents are used to eliminate competition in ways undoubtedly not contemplated by our Founding Fathers but which have not been specifically held to be illegal by the courts.[6] The drug industry would appear to be unexcelled in its ability to devise new and ingenious methods of using patents (or even applications therefor) which fall within this 'grey' area."

[6] Benjamin Franklin was one of the nation's early inventors who refused to take out patents. He declined to take out a patent on one of his early inventions of the stove because, he wrote, of "a principle which has ever weighed with me on such occasions, viz., That, as we enjoy great advantages from the inventions of others, we should be glad of an opportunity to serve others by any inventions of ours; and this we should do freely and generously." The quotation is from *The Writings of Benjamin Franklin*, Albert H. Smith, ed. (New York: Macmillan, 1907). 10 vols.

The simplest method of keeping control of a patented product and its price is to keep the market wholly to one's self and to license no one else. While avoiding any danger of antitrust prosecution, this method compels buyers to pay whatever price is charged. In the broad-spectrum antibiotics, this was the course followed by American Cyanamid for chlortetracycline (Aureomycin), by Parke, Davis for chloramphenicol (Chloromycetin), and by Pfizer for oxytetracycline (Terramycin).

A similar control rests in the exclusive American licensees of foreign firms. This was the situation of Smith Kline & French in respect to two drugs used in the treatment of severe mental illness, chlorpromazine (Thorazine) and prochlorperazine (Compazine), and, to provide one more example, the situation of Upjohn in respect to its oral antidiabetic drug. By various ingenious devices, the same total control over prices may be achieved when there is a duopoly or an oligopoly. Further, the patent mechanism is used, the subcommittee said, "in the formation of cartels for the international control of drug prices."

For instance, Parke, Davis had a total patent monopoly in the United States on Chloromycetin, which, in spite of the misuses to which it has been put, is regarded by many as the drug of choice in typhoid fever. Parke, Davis wanted a worldwide monopoly. The problem was not only that certain countries did not permit product patents, but that choramphenicol, alone among the antibiotics, was produced wholly by chemical methods. This enabled several manufacturers in Europe to make the product, sometimes by processes they themselves developed. "The high profits enjoyed by Parke, Davis on its sales," the Senate Antitrust subcommittee report said, "invited the entrance of outsiders who found they could sell at prices lower than the American company and still make a handsome profit on sales abroad."

To rid the market of outsiders, Parke, Davis adopted a strategy that Dr. Upjohn might have used as a case example to make his point about the obligation of the government to help the drug industry abroad.

> Complaints were filed [the subcommittee recounted] with the U. S. State Department, and our embassies abroad made formal protests to foreign governments on the sale of chloramphenicol by their nationals. Moreover, upon the prodding of American companies, including particularly Parke, Davis, the State Department urged other governments to reverse their historical position and revise their patent laws to permit the issuance of patents in the field of drugs.
> Simultaneously, a number of infringement suits were brought against foreign companies in those countries which do grant patent protection. Next, Parke, Davis took steps to bring foreign marketers under its control with patent licensing agreements containing severely restrictive provisions.

And thus, Parke, Davis achieved effective control in a number of foreign countries also.

The nations of the world handle the patenting of drugs in different ways. At one extreme are the United States, Belgium, and Panama, which grant unrestricted patent protection to both processes and products. At the other extreme is Italy, which grants patents on neither. Virtually all other countries restrict, in one way or another, the patent protection accorded to drugs. West Germany, a case in point, does not grant patents on drug products, but it does grant them on drug processes. The protection extends to a product only so long as it is manufactured by the patented process. Because drug manufacture is especially susceptible to the development of alternate processes, this protection is not only limited, but of a kind that encourages progress and research. In outlining all of this to the House Antitrust subcommittee, Senator Kefauver said: "The conceptual bases of the European system are (a) the long-held moral belief that no one should have the right to withhold from the public products which relieve suffering and may spell the difference between life and death, and (b) the assumption that the granting of process patents would stimulate the discovery of alternative and cheaper methods of production, which, because of the absence of product patents per se, would result in lower price to consumers."

Putting it another way, the Kefauver subcommittee majority said in its report, "No one, it has been felt, should make a monopoly profit on the sale of such products." This view apparently is not shared by all the leaders of the present-day industry, but it was acted upon more than a century ago by Dr. E. R. Squibb, founder of E. R. Squibb & Sons. In 1854 he succeeded in distilling for the first time pure ether of uniform strength. Declining to take out patents, he published his discovery in a pharmaceutical journal, where all could read of it and, if they cared to, use it.

With the cooperation of our embassies abroad, the Senate Antitrust subcommittee ascertained the selling prices of various drugs in several countries. Two of these countries share a common border, are highly industrialized, and have roughly comparable wage rates. In Belgium, which grants unrestricted patents on processes and products, as does the United States, a quantity of chlorpromazine (Thorazine) sold for $1.37. In neighboring Germany, where only processes are patented, the price for an equal quantity was 40 cents less. Here are other comparisons, with the higher Belgian price given first: prochlorperazine (Compazine), $1.61, or 81 cents more than in Germany; meprobamate (Miltown and Equanil), $3.25, or $1.87 more; tolbutamide (Orinase), $2.45, or 60 cents more; chlorpropamide (Diabinese in Belgium, Nadisan in Germany), $4.45, or $2.23 more, and tetracycline (Achromycin), $6.87, or $2.56 more.

✓ ✓ ✓

"I am informed," Thomas Jefferson once wrote, "that England was, until we copied her, the only country on earth, which ever, by a general law, gave a legal right to the exclusive use of an idea. In some other countries it is sometimes done, in a great case, and by a special and personal act, but, generally speaking, other nations have thought that these monopolies produce more embarrassment than advantage to society; and it may be observed that the nations which refuse monopolies of invention, are as fruitful as England in new and useful devices."

Have nations that refuse pharmaceutical patents been as fruitful in new and useful drug discoveries as those that grant such patents? Yes, and more so.

The Constitution, which nowhere uses the word "patent," says that Congress shall have the power "to promote the progress of science and useful arts by securing for limited times to authors and inventors the exclusive rights to their respective writings and discoveries." Has the progress of medical science in the United States been promoted by the granting of patents on drug products? In certain cases, undoubtedly — but in far fewer cases than one might have been led to expect. Does the benefit of the granting of drug patents justify the higher prices patents have brought?

A few things might be said. The Kefauver subcommittee staff once prepared a comprehensive table, listing the origins of basic drug inventions, made since 1875, that constituted a substantial advance in the healing arts. A partial answer to this whole difficult question can be derived by looking at the evidence disclosed in such careful documentation. The table shows that ten times as many drug discoveries were made in nations without product patents as in the nations with them. To put it another way, foreign countries that do grant patent protection on drug products can claim relatively few drug discoveries. For example, while two discoveries were listed for Belgium, where patents are granted, 16 were listed for another small, industrialized country, Switzerland, where product patents are not granted. From Germany, where product patents are not granted, came more than one quarter of the foreign discoveries, including some of the world's most widely used drugs, aspirin, atabrine, phenobarbital, tolbutamide.

The subcommittee staff had prepared a preliminary compilation that was later revised to include additional important drugs listed by the Pharmaceutical Manufacturers Association. In objecting to the original staff compilation the president of the Association, Dr. Austin Smith, contended that comparison of drug discoveries in the United States and other countries should be confined to the last twenty years. He said: "More than half of all the foreign items cited date back before 1939, when the U. S. drug industry was just pioneering modern chemotherapy. A comparison of American drug progress which has been great only in the last 20 years, when stacked up against all the rest of the world for a period reaching back centuries before the American Revolution is regarded by some as intended for only one purpose — to discredit the very real achievements that have transferred leadership in medical research from Europe to this country in the past generation."

"But this merely begs the question," the subcommittee said in its report. "If patents are in fact the key to the unlocking of new drug discoveries, why has it functioned effectively in this country only for the last 20 years? For over a century foreign countries which do not grant patent protection have been making important new drug discoveries. The fact that they were doing so prior to the last 20 years, while the United States, which has granted full patent protection since 1790, was failing to develop any important drug industry of its own, only serves to cast further doubt on the essentiality of patent grants to scientific progress in this industry."

The conclusion of a University of California professor of pharmacology, Dr. Frederick H. Meyers, was that while the American drug industry has made important contributions, it "has usually followed and often after a clear lag." This is his independent evaluation, given before the Antitrust subcommittee:

The drug business makes many references to the patients benefitted by the revolution in therapy of the past 25 years. The progress is real, but how should we distribute our gratitude?

Without going back too many years and penalizing our relatively young industry, let me provide some examples. Nonindustrial American investigators provided the anticoagulants, anterior pituitary hormones and, with help from the British, the antithyroid drugs.

Most of the progress has come from European and British researchers both industrial and independent. The antihistamines, synthetic morphine substitutes, the only recently introduced local anesthetic that has any real advantage, new antimalarials (in spite of our own screening program), synthetic estrogens, insecticides and others. The most potent treatment for hypertension, the ganglion blocking agents, is British in origin.

Reserpine, the most common treatment for hypertension, was brought to the attention of the British and Swiss by two Indian cardiologists. The first phenothiazine tranquilizers were synthesized in France and their significance, that is the idea of the tranquilizing drug effect, was developed by a French Army surgeon and by French psychiatrists.

Oral insulin substitutes were French in origin really, although best exploited by the German drug trade. Penicillin is acknowledged to be a British discovery but it is not so freely acknowledged that in the wartime developmental phase, the significant technological advance was made in a Department of Agriculture Laboratory and that American industry ventured no capital.

The War Production Board ventured the capital. What has the American industry to its credit? Following the idea of Dubos and Waksman, it screened a tremendous number of soil samples and has contributed many antibiotics beyond streptomycin.

That is, once the basic work was done, the assets of the industry are such that they could throw a tremendous effort into this, and one must acknowledge that they have contrib- uted antibiotics more useful or newer than streptomycin.

The hydrazides that are so important in the treatment of tuberculosis are American. You have already heard opinions as to how credit for the corticosteroids should be apportioned. I hesitate to reopen that discussion. [This referred to the con- flicting claims for the invention of the drugs for the relief of arthritic pain by Syntex of Mexico and Schering of the United States. Schering won the American patent.]

I personally would have felt that the Diuril type of diuretic [which offsets excessive retention of water in the tissues by increasing the flow of urine], in effect an orally active replace- ment for the mercury diuretics that had to be injected, is a great credit to the industry . . .

There was no credit at all for the American drug industry in the disclosure in the New York *Times* of November 6, 1964, that a British drug house had produced Ceporin, a new antibiotic said to have an exceptionally wide range of bacteria-destroying prop- erties. The drug, derived from a minute mold called a cephalo- sporium,[7] was reported to have been highly efficacious in treating mixed infections, particularly those of the lungs, kidney, and bladder, in treating infections resistant to penicillin, and for use in patients sensitive to penicillin. The determination of the chemical structure of the mold was a crucial preliminary. This was accomplished by Professor Dorothy Crowfoot Hodgkin, who won the Nobel Prize for Chemistry in 1964, and her collaborators at Cambridge University. That British scientists had accom- plished this was, of course, not at all surprising. But I daresay

[7] In September 1964, Eli Lilly began marketing Keflin in the United States; it is a derivative of the cephalosporium mold. Initial distribution was limited to hospitals.

many an eyebrow must have been raised by the following paragraph which appeared in the *Times* account:

> The therapeutic properties of the Cephalosporium mold were discovered *in Sardinia* in 1945 by Prof. Giuseppe Brotzu, an Italian. [My italics.]

✦ ✦ ✦

Between 1946 and 1961, according to a report presented in 1964 by the American Medical Association's Commission on the Cost of Medical Care, the use of drugs increased by 56 per cent. By July 1963 the Department of Commerce was estimating that, exclusive of medical sundries, Americans were spending more than 20 cents out of every medical-care dollar for drugs. About $2.2 billion, or $13 per person, was for prescription drugs. Clearly, this enormous and increasing burden is intimately related to patent grants that give the holder exclusive rights not merely for seventeen years, the limit set in law, but in actual practice for much longer.

The original proposal made by Senator Kefauver was to allow a drug patent to be held exclusively for three years. Then the holder would be required to license any qualified applicant, who would have to pay a royalty fee of up to 8 per cent. The powerful drug industry lobby killed this.

His final proposal, presented in the form of an amendment to his drug-safety bill, took a slightly different, but certainly generous, approach. It was confined to drugs that the Federal Trade Commission would find to be selling for more than 500 per cent of the cost of production, which was specified to include the cost of labor, materials, research, and royalties. After three years, the holders of patents on such drugs would be required to license any qualified applicant who would pay a royalty rate of up to 8 per cent. In other words, a patent monopoly could come into jeopardy only if the markup was huge — more than 500 per cent — to begin with.

This was about as far from confiscation as could be imagined, and it promised to offer the consumer a real break. The best account of what happened when the proposal came to a vote in the Senate on August 23, 1962, was given by Richard Harris in *The Real Voice*. He wrote:

> . . . to Kefauver's surprise, Mansfield [Senator Mike Mansfield of Montana, the Majority Leader] moved simply to table the patent-licensing amendment — a motion that, under the Senate's rules, is not subject to debate.
>
> Kefauver hurried over to Mansfield's desk. "Hell, Mike, if anybody's going to do that, let it be Dirksen," he said [Senator Everett M. Dirksen of Illinois, the Minority Leader]. "Why not let us vote on the merits of it?"
>
> Mansfield dismissed the suggestion, explaining that the White House had instructed him to make the motion. A buzzer rang twice, for a quorum call, and as soon as enough members had assembled, it rang three times, for a vote. Fifty-three senators voted in favor of Mansfield's motion. Twenty-eight — three times as many as Kefauver had expected — voted against it. Of the latter, all but one (Margaret Chase Smith, of Maine) were Democrats. Even Humphrey [Hubert Humphrey, the Assistant Majority Leader] voted with Kefauver. "I hate to go against the leadership," he told a colleague at the time, adding, with a nod toward the charts [charts on the prices of prednisone and other drugs that the subcommittee's chief economist, John M. Blair, had set up at the rear of the chamber], "but, my God, you can't ignore those." According to several other senators, the amendment would have got far more votes — perhaps enough to win — if the Administration had not implicitly opposed it.

Maybe another year. Maybe.

THE CONTROVERSY OVER DRUG PRICES may be in a critical stage. After suggesting why this may be so, I will take up the Olin Mathieson Chemical Corporation foreign-aid kickback case — an invaluable supplement to the record of assistance rendered to the government by the pharmaceutical industry which, it may be recalled, expects the assistance of the government in retaining its position in world markets. Finally, I will bring up to date the antibiotics litigation which, when written about in 1965 for this chapter, was in a highly unsettled state.

DRUG PRICES

As I write this in May 1967, several factors seem to be bringing the long battle over drug prices to a *possible* point of resolution of some kind. It is probably much too early to hazard any conclusions; but certainly there is a feeling that the pioneering of the late Senator Estes Kefauver in this field may yet yield a great harvest for the public. In no special order, I want to mention some of the aspects of the situation that strike me.

Some of the key drug patents, including, e.g., that of Chas. Pfizer & Co., Inc., on Terramycin (oxytetracycline) have expired, or are about to. There is increasing awareness that paying high brand-name prices for antibiotics makes no sense, because no matter where produced, or by whom, they must be certified batch-by-batch by the Food and Drug Administration for potency before they can be sold in the United States. The same kind of awareness as to drugs was given a major lift on October 15, 1966, by Deputy FDA Commissioner Winton B. Rankin. In a speech to the American College of Apothecaries in Boston, he told about a study made of 4,600 drug samples from 250 suppliers. About 2,600 were sold by their generic (or official, or public, or established) names and about 2,000 by their brand names. All told, 20 of the most important drug categories were represented. The study concerned potency, which is one of the criteria of drug quality. A drug that is above or below the accepted range of potency is a bad drug, no matter what other characteristics it may possess. Of the generics, Rankin said, 7.8 per cent were of unacceptable potency; for the brand-name products, the percentage was 8.8 — a gap too narrow to permit a valid conclusion that the generics were necessarily superior. The Pharmaceutical Manufacturers Association made a big fuss about some errors in the study, but it was clearly nitpicking. In May 1967 the *Medical Letter* reported on blindfold tests done by an independent laboratory on prednisone, the anti-inflammatory hormone. No significant quality difference — none that could be of importance to the patient — was found among the 5-milligram tablets supplied by 22 companies. But the wholesale price for 100 tablets ranged from the 59 cents charged by Wolins Pharmacal Corp. to the $17.90 — or 30 times as much — charged by the Schering Corporation for its Meticorten brand. Thanks to a recent price cut of 87 per cent (*87 per cent*) by Merck Sharp & Dohme on its Delta brand and by the Upjohn Company on its Deltasone brand, their prices were one-eighth of Schering's. This posed an awkward problem for those who argue the existence of some rational connection between price and quality. Important as it is, the *Medical Letter* is circulated among a limited number of physicians. But in May 1967 Pantheon Books published the ingenious and invaluable *The Handbook of Prescription Drugs*, which at once began enjoying a huge sale and which promised to have a major impact. The author, Dr. Richard Burack of the Harvard Medical School, tells with highly useful tables, and with intelligent guidance for physician and patient alike, how to save money on drugs by buying generically. Currently, a special task force in the Department of Health, Education, and Welfare is preparing to recommend whether prescription drugs should be made available at little or no cost to elderly patients covered by Medicare who are *not* in a hospital or institution (presently, the program provides for drug costs only during hospital or institutional care). It will be very difficult for HEW to suggest that the $17.90 prednisone should be provided. Indeed, at a press conference Dr. Philip R. Lee, the Assistant Secretary for Health and Scientific Affairs, said in response to a question that he would "tend to accept the findings of the *Medical Letter*" about the equivalency of $17.90 prednisone and brands costing as little as 59 cents.

On Capitol Hill, the big drug manufacturers are very much on the defensive. One major threat comes from a bill introduced by Senator Russell B. Long, the Assistant Majority Leader. Indirectly, this proposed legislation would generally require that drugs for several million persons in government-financed welfare programs and in hospitals or institutions under Medicare be dispensed under their established or generic names. Long, who as chairman of the Senate Finance Committee was expected to hold hearings on the bill during the summer of 1967, had introduced a relatively unsophisticated version in 1966. The industry reacted not with silence but by coming up with objections, some of which had a measure of validity.

Long then dropped his legislation for the new bill, which was carefully drafted to undercut the arguments elicited from the industry. The new measure would set up a Formulary of the United States governed by the chiefs of the FDA, the Public Health Service, the National Institutes of Health, and the Bureau of Narcotics; serving with them would be five public members. The Formulary would determine which drugs would be covered and which among the chosen medicines to be paid for — directly or indirectly — with Federal funds could be used with confidence of safety and effectiveness under their established names. For each drug listed under an established name a reasonable cost range would be specified. The drug still could be prescribed by brand name — but the government payment would have to be within the specified cost range, regardless. With certain exceptions, payments at higher trade-name prices would be permitted only when there is a ruling by the Formulary that a satisfactory generic version is unavailable. But the burden — and a heavy one it would be — would be on the manufacturer to show that its brand-name version has "distinct demonstrated therapeutic advantages that are otherwise unavailable." To provide still further assurance of high quality in established-name drugs, Senator Long would strengthen the role of the FDA, which under Commissioner James L. Goddard has already acted to set up a national drug-testing center in St. Louis. Each manufacturer, under the Long bill, would be given an official FDA registration number. No matter who *supplies* a drug to a pharmacist, that number, along with the manufacturer's name, would be on the label. If the agency found a maker not to be observing good manufacturing practices or labeling requirements, however, that number-and-name identification could *not* appear — and if it did not appear, the government would be prohibited from paying any part of the cost. It is difficult to see how the pharmaceutical industry can oppose this bill on the merits. Perhaps that is why the spring of 1967 has been marked by signs of panic — a drug-price survey undertaken by, of all organizations, the American Medical Association, and purporting to show, of course, that generics are not always cheaper than the brand-name products that yield the AMA millions of dollars in advertising revenues; an article on drug costs by Dr. F. J. L. Blasingame, the AMA's executive vice president, in *This Week*, a Sunday supplement with a marked receptivity to largely interchangeable AMA and pro-industry material; a flurry of invitations from drug makers to reporters to *please* take a tour of their manufacturing plants; a huge publicity campaign in behalf of Margaret Kreig's *Black Market Medicine*, which manages to document the unquestioned evils of counterfeiting of brand-name drugs while all but ignoring the principal incentive for such counterfeiting — the exorbitant price commanded by a pill when it is stamped with a well-known name. Low-priced generics are not counterfeited because their moderate profit margins make counterfeiting pointless. This was a point somehow missed by *Time* and other publications that gave the book laudatory reviews and perhaps by some of the newspaper editors who bought a serialized version. Strange.

But there were reasons other than those already mentioned for the drug industry to be concerned. One was the inquiry into drug prices begun in May 1967 by the Subcommittee on Monopoly of the Senate Select Committee on Small Business. It is yet another commentary on the allocation of resources in Washington that there was available for the inquiry — and for all of the Subcommittee's other David-and-Goliath undertakings as well — one staff economist, Benjamin Gordon. But the project was taken on by the Subcommittee Chairman, Senator Gaylord Nelson, a Wisconsin Democrat. The hearing opened on May 15 in the Caucus Room used by Estes Kefauver for *his* inquiry of 1959–62. The Subcommittee heard testimony about wide discrepancies in prices for drugs paid by municipal purchasing agents. William F. Haddad, appearing for the nonprofit Citizens Committee for Metropolitan Affairs, Inc., of New York City, which he heads, documented immense differences in prices paid by twelve cities and counties for ten different drugs used in public hospitals and in Federally aided welfare programs. Some of the highest prices were paid by Fulton County (Atlanta), Georgia — for example, $22.60 for a thousand tablets of the

Smith Kline & French brand of dextroamphetamine sulphate. Buying generically, New York City paid 57 cents, or one-fortieth as much. An exchange between Haddad and economist Gordon brought out the fact that in the spring of 1965 Chas. Pfizer & Co.'s subsidiary in the United Kingdom had protested to the British Minister of Health that a plan to buy drugs in Communist Poland would undermine the private companies' resources to undertake costly research. But then, it was disclosed at the hearing, the *Sunday Times* of London had reported that Pfizer had obtained oxytetracycline from Communist Hungary and sold it under its Terramycin label. In related developments, Patrick Sloyan of United Press International obtained a Department of Defense document showing that on the seven drugs it had bought abroad since 1959 it had saved $21.2 million by rejecting "unreasonable" bids proffered by American manufacturers. The foreign drugs "have been and continue to be of high quality," the document said.

Another significant development came on May 17. It concerned the prescription-drug component of the Consumer Price Index. This component had been publicly noted with approval in 1966 and 1967 by the Council of Economic Advisers and in 1966 by President Johnson who, in ordering a study of the costs of medical care, said that prescription drugs were "the only factor in medical costs that have been reduced in recent years."[1] But

---

[1] The quoted words of the President made such an impression on Dr. Howard A. Rusk that — surely inadvertently — he adopted them as his own in his Sunday medical column in the New York *Times* of October 2, 1966. The column so favorably impressed the Pharmaceutical Manufacturers Association that, ten days later, it distributed reproductions. Dr. Rusk's column of September 25 was flawed by something more serious than nonattribution. Women want to know, he said, if "the pill" is safe. The answer given by Dr. Rusk to readers of the *Times* was, "positive." That was not the answer given by the Food and Drug Administration Advisory Committee, whose report he was discussing (see Afterword to Chapter 13). Dr. Rusk said the Committee concluded there was "no evidence" that the oral contraceptives were unsafe; but what the Committee in

after hearing testimony about the component, the few drugs it embraced, and how it was arrived at, Senator Nelson felt it was unrealistic and subject to "misleading" interpretations. The statement made by the President, Nelson said in an interview, was "obviously misinformed." The evidence at the hearing showed, for example, that during the years 1954–1966 the prescription-drug component of the Price Index increased a mere 1.6 per cent. But in the same period the *average price of a prescription* — which the Index does not pretend to measure — increased 35.6 per cent, according to one industry source (the *American Druggist*) and 56.8 per cent according to another (the *Lilly Digest*). Similarly, in the years 1961–1966 the prescription-drug component in the government Index — to the delight of the industry — fell 8.7 per cent, while the average price increased 6.5 per cent (*American Druggist*) or 9.5 per cent (*Lilly Digest*).

THE OLIN MATHIESON CAPER

The Agency for International Development and its predecessor, the International Cooperation Administration, have regulations intended to prevent the use of foreign-aid funds as commissions and promotional allowances to importers for plugging brand names, and for other improper benefits including kickbacks. For falsely certifying that the regulations were complied with, the giant Olin Mathieson Chemical Corporation was indicted on March 4, 1963, by a grand jury in District Court in New York City. Although this was the first such indictment of an American manufacturer, the case received negligible attention in the general press from start to finish, despite a revelation about secret accounts in a Swiss bank and other newsworthy disclosures. Indicted with Olin Mathieson were Herbert G. Wolf, its former regional vice president in Hong Kong; the Far East

---

fact concluded was something else — that data were lacking "proving" the drugs unsafe.

International Corp., of which Wolf's wife was president and sole stockholder; the Phillip Bauer Co., Inc., of New York City, an exporter, and Kenneth B. Bauer, president of that firm. In a press release on the day of indictment, Olin said the Bauer Company "has never been an agent" for it; but subsequently, Richard A. Givens, the Assistant United States Attorney in charge of the case, filed documents in court showing that Olin had designated the exporter as its "AGENT" and frequently actually prepared Bauer's invoices. The exporter certified that the regulations had been complied with. In fact, the Government said, Bauer had concealed improper payments — including a 20 per cent agent's commission from Olin and Olin-financed promotional allowances, amounting to 10 per cent of invoice prices — that Bauer passed to foreign importers. A time even came, Givens said in an affidavit, when an arrangement was devised for Dr. Jacques Arnaud, the major stockholder in a drug importing firm in Cambodia, "to pay an additional 2 per cent royalty to Olin in order that this 2 per cent could be paid back to Arnaud through Bauer."

On March 31, 1965, Olin attempted to plead no contest. This was after District Judge Harold R. Tyler had ruled that it would not be held responsible for conduct unbeknownst to it of Wolf, its former executive in Hong Kong. But 14 days later, when Olin changed its plea to guilty to three counts — conspiracy to make false certifications and to defraud the United States, and two of 23 substantive counts — the company said in another press release that it had done so because "a jury could hold the company responsible for the conduct of a former employe in Hong Kong." At the sentencing proceeding on September 23, 1965, Judge Tyler reprimanded Bruce Bromley, of the famed law firm of Cravath, Swaine & Moore, and a former judge of the New York Court of Appeals, for overstepping "reasonable bounds of proper conduct" in approving a news release that "was at odds with the previously unequivocal ruling by the Court." Bromley acknowledged that the release was "unfortunate" and "improper" and said he had "made a mistake." When the second release was issued, Wolf had pleaded innocent and was awaiting trial. Tyler recalled that extra proceedings had to be held to determine if the release had undermined Wolf's right to a fair trial. Subsequently, Wolf pleaded guilty to the conspiracy count and was fined $7,500. Far East International was fined $21,000.

At the September sentencing proceeding, Prosecutor Givens introduced into the record 152 government exhibits and a 44-page affidavit by himself. These documents basically concerned the foreign-aid-financed shipment of $1.5 million worth of antibiotics to Cambodia and Vietnam. The shipments were made between 1958 and 1963. The antibiotics had been manufactured by Olin's E. R. Squibb & Sons division. The documents showed that deposits, which were estimated at between $30,000 and $40,000, were made in "Banque Ferrier Lullin et Ce, Geneva, Accounts No. 41-22 and 41-23." The deposits were made for the benefit of Dr. Arnaud, a French citizen, and were made by the Phillip Bauer firm (which, with its president, was convicted on all 24 counts and fined a total of $29,000; on October 28, 1966, the United States Court of Appeals in Manhattan affirmed the convictions). The Givens papers said that Olin "was well aware" that the Bauer firm was making these deposits but used Bauer "to shield itself from responsibility." One of his pieces of evidence was an Olin internal memorandum in which, on May 26, 1960, one executive told another that Bauer deducts 10 or 15 per cent "from the letter of credit receipts and transfers these funds as 'commission' to the personal account of Dr. Arnaud in Switzerland." The memo also recalled a meeting at Olin's Manhattan offices in which Dr. Arnaud disclosed that he had kept the deposit procedures from his fellow stockholders.

"There is ample evidence to show that responsible management in Olin knew what was going on and should have taken proper steps to forestall it," Judge Tyler said in the sentencing proceeding. One of Givens' exhibits was a letter of March 9, 1961, which was marked "CONFIDENTIAL" and in which Kenneth Bauer told a member of Olin's corporate legal staff that he had failed to tell a government investigator of an illegal promotional allowance. But Olin did not report this concealment to the government, Givens said. The prosecutor also said that after the grand jury investigation was begun in June 1962, Olin provided "further confirmation of the extreme willfulness of the large-scale violations involved here." The company adopted a new payments procedure, Givens said in his affidavit, under which it made illegal payments to importers directly, rather than through the Bauer enterprise — but "without disclosure" of this on the government certificates. The new method applied "only to" transactions financed by the Agency for International Development, a subpoenaed Olin document noted.

On September 23, 1965, Olin received the maximum allowable sentence on its plea of guilty — a $10,000 fine on each of three counts. It happened that there was a law which said in essence that a person who had been convicted of a felony could not transport a weapon in interstate commerce. This created a legal problem for Olin, because it had been convicted of a felony, was in the eyes of the law a person and had a division that made weapons for use by the armed forces. Congress resolved the dilemma by enacting a law that, in effect, got Olin off the hook.

THE ANTIBIOTICS LITIGATION

District Judge Marvin E. Frankel of New York City has been named to try the antitrust indictment returned in August 1961 against Chas. Pfizer & Co., Inc., the American Cyanamid Company, and Bristol Laboratories in connection with the marketing of tetracycline. The trial was expected to begin in the fall of 1967. The civil litigation involving the City of New York, Pfizer, and Premo Pharmaceutical Laboratories was settled in November 1966; Pfizer agreed to sell bulk tetracycline and to license

Premo as a producer. The McKesson & Robbins tetracycline litigation also was settled, with Pfizer and American Cyanamid agreeing to license McKesson and Rachel Laboratories.

18

"SHE WAS no fanatic trying to wish away the advantages of the 20th century," Senator Abraham Ribicoff said of Rachel Carson a few days after her death in April 1964. "She was a humanitarian insisting that man weigh carefully the consequences of his modern technology . . ."

I propose no grand solutions to the problems raised in this book. In this chapter I shall advance some ideas, very few of which are my own, that strike me as constructive, workable, and well within the boundaries of a free society and our economy as we have known it. I shall not try "to wish away the advantages of the 20th century." Quite the contrary: my hope is that the advantages brought us by medical and pharmaceutical technology will be conserved and enjoyed by ever more people.

What endangers the conservation and spread of these advantages is not criticism of the Food and Drug Administration, the pharmaceutical industry, and the political leadership of the American Medical Association. Rather, the danger is that the excesses they have generated and tolerated can bring more drug disasters, perhaps on a scale, as Dr. Walter Modell has warned, that would dwarf thalidomide.

Should that happen, we could be beset by a wave of therapeutic nihilism, an excessive revulsion against therapy with perhaps all but a few proved drugs. This, too, could be a catastrophe, and, conceivably, the worst one. It might not be recognized as such. Who would know, for instance, if important medical discoveries were delayed, not made at all, or overlooked? If this is a threat, it arises, I repeat, not because of factual, frank, and hard criticism, but because of abuse, greed, and sloth such as has been described in the preceding chapters.

✓ ✓ ✓

"Throw out opium," Oliver Wendell Holmes said in an address in 1860 to the Massachusetts Medical Society, ". . . throw out a few specifics which our art did not discover . . . throw out wine . . . and I firmly believe that if the whole materia medica, as now used, could be sunk to the bottom of the sea it would be all the better for mankind — and all the worse for the fishes."

This was an expression of therapeutic nihilism. It evidenced, Dr. Elihu M. Schimmel has said in the *Journal of Chronic Diseases* for January 1963, Holmes's "belief that the vast majority of drugs then used were either toxic or without discernible effect." Dr. Schimmel, it may be recalled, was the Yale physician who reported that 1 out of 10 inpatients on the medical service of a great hospital had suffered drug reactions, and another 1 out of 10 other iatrogenic complications. This awesome finding did not induce him to preach the therapeutic nihilism of Holmes, which he termed "impossible" in the face of the achievements of clinical medicine and modern pharmacology. Instead, he found it "appropriate . . . to take the text of iatrogenic illness for a sermon on the conservative use of the measures available to us. We may properly deplore . . . the exuberant use of drugs. We can cautiously consider the benefits of withholding premature or shotgun therapy."

Dr. Schimmel's advice was most gently stated, especially when compared with the reaction of Dr. Walter Modell of Cornell to the report that 1 out of 20 patients had been admitted in 1955 to the medical service of another great hospital ill from "sanctioned and well intentioned" use of drugs. What he found profoundly disturbing was that the hazard was not inherent in medical progress, but was in good part a result of the introduction of new drugs "to horn in on a market." Following are excerpts from his memorable editorial, "The Drug Explosion," in the January–February 1961 issue of *Clinical Pharmacology and Therapeutics*:

> . . . it is also a certainty that the incidence of reactions will increase at an even faster rate than the rate at which new drugs emerge. Even now the situation is alarming; but the future looks dismal indeed.

> . . . .

> . . . physicians are led [by extravagant, vigorous promotion] to use drugs when the indications are lacking, to use drugs that are not the best available or even those which do not apply. It is because of this that the rate of serious drug reaction is mounting. And it is because physicians are not irresponsible that they may be expected to react with some violence to this ever mounting hazard.

> . . . .

> What will happen when, as it eventually must, physicians refuse to gamble with their patients' lives and health or an enraged public demands that such gambling stop? Certainly the winning streak of the pharmaceutical industry will come to an abrupt end, but the rebound may well be excessive and may lead to unhealthy cynicism on the part of physicians and a state of therapeutic nihilism.
>
> . . . How long before the public, medicine, *and the drug industry* are the losers to this type of general reaction?

> . . . .

. . . Excessive numbers of drugs are now being introduced — excessive in view of the working capacities of those competent to test their safety and utility in man, excessive in view of the subjects available for testing their effects, dangers and uses in man, and excessive in view of the ability of those who must assimilate the essential knowledge and learn how to prescribe them effectively and safely, rationally rather than routinely. This together with drug promotion and advertising far more forceful than the comparative ignorance about them warrants, will lead just as inevitably to chaos, more insidiously perhaps than if all available new drugs were thrown on the market at one time, but the same chaos nonetheless.

In 1962, the year after Dr. Modell wrote the above, the thalidomide episode interrupted, but did not end, the drug industry's winning streak. With the Kefauver-Harris amendments, the rate of introduction of new drugs was reduced. The AMA and the PMA — but happily *not* the FDA — would have us believe that the new legislation, along with agency regulations, thus stemmed the great onward march of pharmaceutical progress. A representative complaint was made by the Commission on Drug Safety, which the industry created after the thalidomide calamity. In the *Report* issued in September 1964, the Commission's Subcommittee on State and Federal Drug Legislation and Regulations was anguished because "paper work and other controls" have "frustrated many research scientists and investigators to the point that they have forsaken these fields for others, and driven several drug companies to abandon research and development activities . . . [and] brought about a slowing down of the development and marketing of new drugs, thus depriving physicians of more effective weapons at their command with which to fight disease."

The chairman of the subcommittee was the president of the Pharmaceutical Manufacturers Association, Dr. Austin Smith, whose capacity for dispassionate observation has been shown in previous chapters. The six members of the subcommittee were the senior vice president of the PMA, the legislative counsel of the PMA, and the vice presidents of four major drug companies. A quite different approach was taken the month preceding the *Report* in an article generally laudatory of the industry in *Chemical & Engineering News* for August 10, 1964, "Prognosis for the Drug Houses." The article said that because of the new regulations "products that offer no real advantage and, therefore, are less likely to steal a sizable market seem less worth the high cost of development. The new requirements for proving safety and efficacy *have set higher standards for new drugs. Many marginal products that previously might have found their way to market never get submitted to FDA; or, if they are, fail to win approval.* (My italics.)

Statements like that of the Drug Commission tend to set up an equation in the reader's mind: new drugs = better drugs. It is a false equation. New drugs can be, and often have been, inferior drugs and worthless drugs. What *Chemical & Engineering News* — among those whose objectivity is not of the same order as Dr. Smith's — was saying was, in effect, that the law and regulations were shifting research and development away from "me too" drugs and the like into the quest for the more elusive useful product. As Dr. A. Dale Console has pointed out, in a letter of February 7, 1964, to Senator Humphrey, the research programs the industry has eliminated may be "those involving the 'dogs,' as these drugs are known in industry jargon. A 'dog' is a worthless drug or one so close to worthless that it requires obviously rigged research to prepare a new-drug application and a base for an advertising and promotion program."

I do not wish to leave the impression that the *Report* contains nothing constructive, since this is certainly not the case. It is regrettable, though, that what is frank and helpful is surrounded by such claims as the one of the Commission subcommittee quoted above; and regrettable that in releasing the *Report* the Commission chairman, Dr. Lowell T. Coggeshall, could find it possible to say, for example, "the public should know that almost without exception, drugs, if properly used, carry no risks of untoward side effects." Even apart from the very big "if" in the sentence, why at this late date should it be intimated that properly used drugs "carry no risks"? Why obscure the fact that many valuable drugs do carry risks, which sometimes must be taken? Why suggest that we can get something for nothing?

✓ ✓ ✓

Senator Kefauver proposed that patents be denied to a molecular or other modification of an existing drug, or combination of two or more existing drugs, unless the Secretary of Health, Education, and Welfare determines that the therapeutic effect of the modified drug is significantly greater. It is important to note that, contrary to claims made by industry sources, the proposal would not have made it illegal to *market* "me too" drugs. Although the limitation was solely on patent grants, it would have stemmed the tide of inferior, injurious, useless, and wasteful manipulated molecules and combinations. The proposal was killed in the Senate Committee on the Judiciary. Senator Kefauver is known to have been supported by four other Democrats, Senators Philip A. Hart of Michigan, Thomas J. Dodd of Connecticut, John A. Carroll of Colorado, and Edward V. Long of Missouri. Had other Democrats on the committee joined them, the proposal might have carried, rather than been defeated 9 to 5. The other Democrats on the Judiciary Committee were the chairman, Senator James O. Eastland of Mississippi, and Senators Sam J. Ervin, Jr., of North Carolina; Olin D. Johnston of South Carolina, and John L. McClellan of Arkansas.

The proposal is as sound today as it was in 1962. The same is true of the compulsory licensing proposal, to which the *coup de grâce* was administered on the Senate floor by order of the

Administration. This amendment, it will be recalled, would have brought about a reduction in drug prices by requiring the holder of a patent to license production after three years by any qualified applicant paying a royalty of up to 8 per cent, provided that the drug was selling for more than five times the cost of producing it.

"The moral of the drug bill," Senator Kefauver had said, "is that even on an exceedingly complex issue the legislative branch can perform in the manner originally intended [by the Founding Fathers]. With only a small staff of competent professional personnel, the Congress can prove itself to be just as able as the vast bureaucracy of the executive branch, if not more so, to assume leadership in the legislative process."

What the Senator was too modest to say was that the Congress performed as it did on the drug bill because he, aided by a few other dedicated senators and congressmen, and by a superb staff, acted with extraordinary brilliance, courage, and tenacity. In the end, he was rescued from defeat by the thalidomide catastrophe. What the Senator was too kind to say was that some of his highly influential colleagues had actively engaged in sabotage of his efforts. "The Senator from Tennessee," Senator Paul Douglas said when the drug bill was passed, "has not received a great deal of cooperation from some of his colleagues . . . Men who had openly and secretly fought him now flock to get on the bandwagon." Even Senator Dirksen and Senator Hruska voted for the bill.

The ultimate power resides in the voters. They decide who goes to Congress, who remains, and who is retired. By their letters, telephone calls, personal visits and votes they can make their views count. "We seek to make decisions about drugs solely on the basis of scientific considerations," Commissioner George P. Larrick told the Fountain Intergovernmental Relations Subcommittee. "But over a period of time, the direction of Government's decisions will inevitably be influenced by public reaction." The reaction that is needed is not an angry or emotional one, but precisely that which will encourage decisions "solely on the basis of scientific considerations."

Expressions of support from the public were an important source of encouragement to Estes Kefauver, and have been — or could be — the same to others who have worked in the consumer interest, including Senators Philip Hart, Maurine B. Neuberger of Oregon, Edmund S. Muskie of Maine, Gaylord Nelson of Wisconsin, Abraham A. Ribicoff of Connecticut, and Paul Douglas of Illinois, and Representatives John Blatnik of Minnesota, Emanuel Celler and James J. Delaney of New York, John D. Dingell of Michigan, L. H. Fountain of North Carolina, John E. Moss of California, Henry S. Reuss of Wisconsin, Kenneth A. Roberts of Alabama, and Leonor K. Sullivan of Missouri. In the 1964 election, all of the House members except Roberts were re-elected.

But what is an acute and cautious member of Congress to make of the experience of Representative J. Arthur Younger of San Mateo, California? He was the member of the House Committee on Interstate and Foreign Commerce who sponsored the amendment to the House drug bill that would have allowed pharmaceutical manufacturers to advertise the advantages of products without telling the physicians of their adverse effects. The amendment was backed to the bitter end by the committee chairman, Representative Oren Harris of Arkansas. At the time, Younger was campaigning for re-election, and his position was being used against him by his Democratic opponent. On the House floor, his position was made unbearable for him by repeated references to "the Younger amendment." To the amazement of all, he then actually stood up to deny that the amendment was his, and to say that he had "no objection whatsoever" to Representative Blatnik's proposal to knock it out.

The 1962 congressional elections were held a few weeks later. Younger was returned to office with the largest margin he had achieved since he had been first elected a decade earlier. In

1964 he was re-elected once again. Surely the voters of San Mateo County were not saying that they wanted their physicians to prescribe for them without being told in drug advertising what the side effects might be. They merely allowed an inference to be drawn that the conduct of Younger in this matter, assuming they knew about it, counted little or not at all with them.

The case of Barry M. Goldwater of Arizona merits passing mention, not only because he was the Republican presidential candidate in 1964, but also because Mrs. Sherri Finkbine, who sought an abortion rather than have a thalidomide baby, was his world-famous constituent. During the afternoon of August 23, 1962, according to the *Congressional Record,* he responded to a quorum call during the Senate debate on the Kefauver drug bill. When the bill came up for a vote a short time later, however, he was reported "necessarily absent." Had he been present and voting, the Senate was told, he would have voted "yea," as did all the 78 senators who actually voted.

What is noteworthy is that the bill substantially expanded the federal power, and thus Senator Goldwater's hypothetical "yea" may have seemed inconsistent with his rather well known denunciations of extensions of federal authority. If there was an inconsistency it was removed by the 1964 Republican platform, which was solid Goldwater. The platform pledged an end to "the ceaseless pressing by the White House, the Food and Drug Administration, and the Federal Trade Commission to dominate consumer decisions in the market place."

One wonders whether voters who support a platform plank like that believe that drug-patent monopolies and the marketing of needlessly manipulated molecules are fundamental concepts of the American way of life, and whether they are willing to uphold their beliefs with their pocketbooks and with jeopardy to their own health and that of their families.

The plank was starkly different from that in the GOP platform four years earlier. In 1960, the platform alluded with pride to what the Eisenhower Administration had done to protect consumers against harmful food, drugs, and cosmetics, and promised continued "strong support to this consumer protection program."

Despite the prominence of Senator Humphrey in Democratic affairs in 1964, the platform adopted at Atlantic City said nothing about the drug problems which the vice-presidential candidate had exposed except to boast about the Kefauver-Harris drug amendments, as if they had forever solved all the problems. Not long after the convention ended, the formation of the National Independent Committee for Johnson and Humphrey was announced. The committee named as one of its two co-chairmen John T. Connor, the president of Merck & Co., Inc. During the campaign, so far as I could ascertain, neither the Democrats nor the Republicans discussed the FDA's performance in handling prescription drugs.

Six weeks after his election Mr. Johnson nominated John Connor to be Secretary of Commerce. "He will never discard a principle nor despair of doing what is right and what ought to be done," the President said. With his background as president of Merck, Connor may believe in all sincerity that it is "right" not to hold markups on medicines to less than 500 per cent. He may believe it is "right" for patents to be granted on new drugs that are inferior to old drugs. Voters who believe such views are wrong and wonder what ought to be done may at least write their opinions to the President and other elected officials.

FDA Commissioner George Larrick may retire in the not distant future. In considering a successor it would be natural for the President to seek the counsel of John Connor, for whom he expressed the highest regard. "He is the kind of man I am proud to have serve in the Cabinet," Mr. Johnson said. "He is smart and he is loyal and he is patriotic." But a Commissioner thought by John Connor to be best for the country might strike skeptical consumers as something less. If it is not too late, those unwilling to presume that the qualifications they deem vital for leadership of FDA would coincide with those selected by Connor might take the precaution of passing on their thoughts to the White House and their senators and representatives.

✦   ✦   ✦

Among 40 of the largest drug manufacturing firms in Canada, only 4 are Canadian-owned and Canadian-controlled. Eight are subsidiaries of European firms. Twenty-eight are subsidiaries of large American corporations, which thus are dominant. These facts were revealed in the 1964 report of a three-year study made by a Royal Commission on Health Services. As would be expected, the abuses that exist in the United States also exist in Canada — except that many are even worse. Drug prices are among the highest of any industrialized nation in the world, and in many instances higher than in the United States.

In 1960, a survey of the 40 pharmaceutical makers showed that promotion and advertising accounted for 30 per cent of total sales, or about 6 per cent more than in the United States. While about 6 per cent of the sales dollar in American companies goes for research, in 1960 the Canadian subsidiaries of the following American drug firms were among those that carried on no independent research whatever in Canada: American Cyanamid, Eli Lilly, G. D. Searle, Parke, Davis, Abbott, Pfizer, and Winthrop.

The patience of the Canadian people apparently has about been exhausted by the staggering prices they have to pay for drugs, and, being unwilling to grant the industry a patent on perpetual money, they have been doing something about it. A number of provincial legislatures conducted investigations, more were expected to do so, and some were expected to adopt measures to force down the prices of prescription drugs. Alberta already has adopted legislation to facilitate generic prescribing.

The Royal Commission said in its report:

Few aspects of health services have generated so much public interest and concern as that now directed toward drugs and the drug manufacturing and distributing industries . . . It is no accident that the public interest has increased in direct relationship to the efficacy of drug therapy and the high cost of the most effective drugs. Expenditures on all drugs are equivalent to 95 per cent of the outlay on physicians' services with prescribed drugs representing about 43 per cent of medical expenditures.

Although we accept that the manufacture and distribution of drugs in this country is a private enterprise venture, we have no hesitation in stating that the public interest is dominant. When we speak of the availability of a large number of specific drugs, we are talking in terms of lives and the health of people.

Either the industry will itself make these drugs available at the lowest possible cost, or it will be necessary for agencies and devices of government to do so. We must not confuse the distribution of essential drugs with distribution of cosmetics and sundries.

The failure of the industry in Canada to make drugs available at low cost was so manifest to the Restrictive Trade Practices Commission that it recommended the abolition of patents on drugs — a far more drastic proposal than any that Senator Kefauver had advanced.

The Royal Commission suggested to the Canadian Government that it consider delaying for five years a decision to implement the patent-elimination recommendation, in order to ascertain whether other and less severe alternatives recommended by the Royal Commission could achieve the same results. The recommendations included these:

That there be created a National Drug Formulary, that it list only those drugs approved by the Food and Drug Directorate, and that only the Formulary drugs be eligible for the prescription-drug benefits proposed for inclusion in the Health Services Programme, and for exemption from the federal sales tax.

That there be a standard price and fee schedule for all prescriptions, and that steps be taken against overprescribing.

That 15 per cent of total sales be the maximum allowed to be claimed as deductible income-tax expense for drug advertising and promotion.

That in addition to the Crown, the provincial governments buying patented drugs be permitted to pay the patent-holders only such sums for the use of their inventions as the Commissioner of Patents deems to be reasonable.

That the procedures which have made compulsory patent licensing almost meaningless be revised so as to encourage responsible applicants and speed up the proceedings by which licenses are granted; and that licensing be extended to imported products.

That the Tariff Board consider reduction or even abolition of tariffs on certain imported drugs in the National Formulary, and that in the administration of "anti-dumping" regulations the Government be given discretionary power to establish "market value" at lower levels than currently, in order to reduce drug prices.

That the Government sponsor a study of the feasibility of a voluntary drug-price restraint program that would be tried out for five years.

That provincial legislatures consider passing laws that would enable pharmacists to fill prescriptions with "a drug or drug combination that is the non-proprietary name equivalent of that named in the prescription unless the physician specifically indicates otherwise." Such legislation is already in effect in the Province of Alberta.

That the Canadian Government centralize all of its drug purchases in one agency, that provinces be encouraged to adopt bulk-purchasing of drugs for all hospitals and public agencies, and that whenever possible all bids be on specifications of the ingredients of the pharmaceuticals — that they be bid on generically, in other words.

That the Canadian Government expand grants to noncommercial institutions to encourage the development of new drugs, and the improvement of existing ones, with the rights to resulting patentable discoveries being vested in the Crown.

That the Department of National Health and Welfare undertake continuing cost-price analyses of drugs and periodically publish the results.

✓ ✓ ✓

The American citizen or consumer group who may think in terms of seeking reforms such as those proposed by the Royal Commission might need a brief primer on where the power lies. Although the drug industry's lobbyists are intimately familiar with the importance in the scheme of things of certain committees of Congress, much of the public is not. Apart from the Senate Subcommittee on Antitrust and Monopoly and the House Antitrust subcommittee, headed by Senator Hart and Representative Emanuel Celler, respectively, which have been concerned with drug matters, two committees are regularly involved with food, drug, and cosmetic legislation. These are the Senate Committee on Labor and Public Welfare, headed by Senator Lister Hill of Alabama, and the House Committee on Interstate and Foreign Commerce, whose chairman is Representative Oren Harris of Arkansas.

Important purse strings are held by the House and Senate Committees on Appropriations. Each has a subcommittee that handles the appropriations for the Food and Drug Administration and the Department of Health, Education, and Welfare, of which FDA is a part; they have been in an especially strategic position to monitor the kind of job FDA has been doing. Unfortunately, the hearings conducted by the subcommittee chairmen, Senator Hill and Representative John E. Fogarty of Rhode Island, have assayed high in exchanges of mutual admiration between them and Commissioner George Larrick. Early in 1964, there were these pleasantries between Hill and Larrick and Fogarty and Larrick:

SENATOR HILL. Is there anything else you would like to add, Mr. Larrick?

MR. LARRICK. No. I want to thank you again. I have been here many times, and every time it is a real pleasure and privilege.

SENATOR HILL. I want to tell you it is always a pleasure to have you here, and I want to commend you again on the progress you have made, the job you have done, with your extensive changes, in strengthening the enforcement of our laws and the protection of our consumers.

We thank you very much.

MR. LARRICK. Thank you very kindly, sir.

.   .   .   .

MR. FOGARTY. I would just like to say for the record, you have been coming up here, to my knowledge, for the 18 years I have been on the committee, and I think you have been doing an outstanding job. When your predecessor left we were pleased that you were selected as head of the Food and Drug Administration. And regardless of what anybody in the executive branch of the Government or in the House or the Senate, or anybody outside, might say, we think you are doing a real good job.

MR. LARRICK. Mr. Chairman, coming from you —

The man it was coming from was clearly referring primarily to criticism of FDA by the chairmen of the Senate Subcommittee on Reorganization and International Organizations and the House Intergovernmental Relations Subcommittee concerned with FDA, Senator Humphrey and Representative Fountain. Rather than be content with largely uncritical hearings, they and their able staffs have examined and inquired, and, whatever Fogarty might think, they are less confident than he that Larrick has been doing a real good job. Because they have been skeptical and searching, improvements have been made. To them the public may be grateful. From the appropriations subcommittees the public has the right to expect not a diminution of generosity toward FDA, which needs all the help it can get, but a continuing, thorough evaluation of its performance.[1]

✔ ✔ ✔

"The separation of the legislative from the Executive branch has long been criticized by proponents of the parliamentary form of government," Senator Kefauver told the Senate on October 3, 1962, after the Senate-House conference report on the drug bill had been adopted. He continued: "But I doubt whether under a parliamentary system the investigation [of administered prices in the drug industry] would ever have been made [or] new and original remedies conceived . . . This was not one of the all too frequent situations in which the role of Congress was merely that of passing upon a proposal developed by the Executive branch, nor did it involve merely taking an old bill which had been rejected, updating it, and inserting some new touches to make it current. The bill involved new thinking, new ideas. They came from a legislative committee."

During the two years following enactment of the Kefauver-

---

[1] A bill for a Senate Select Committee on Consumers was introduced in March 1965 by Senator Maurine B. Neuberger. She told the Senate that the measure would provide a forum for consumers and "would bring the heat of informed public opinion to bear on the Standing Committees, stimulating them to do a better job in protecting the consumer." The Oregon Democrat added, "For every instance of the successful passage of consumer-oriented legislation, there are a dozen instances of neglect of consumers or the dominance of pressure groups inimical to the consumer."

Harris amendments, the effort to find out what our drug problems are, and to find remedies for them, was led to an astonishing
extent not by the Executive agencies but by a single, fantastically
busy senator, Hubert Humphrey, and by the one-man professional staff of his Reorganization subcommittee, Julius Cahn.
In the House a low-keyed but persistent effort has been led by
Representative Fountain, aided by the able senior investigator
of his Intergovernmental Relations Subcommittee, W. Donald
Gray. That effort will be continued into 1965, when the subcommittee plans to hold further hearings and to prepare an
investigative report for issuance by the full House Government
Operations Committee. Under the scrutiny and prodding of
the Humphrey and Fountain subcommittees, FDA began to
show signs of at least temporary improvement — a point that
will be discussed more fully later in this chapter.

The Federal Trade Commission, the independent regulatory
agency headed by Paul Rand Dixon, has shown vigor in its protection of the public interest against, for example, false and misleading patent-medicine advertising. Among certain Executive
agencies, however, the situation has been disquietingly reminiscent of that found by Senator Kefauver at the outset of his investigation, when he and his staff "were actually discouraged by
officials of the Food and Drug Administration. Not only had
they no remedies for most of the problems with which we were
beginning to be concerned; they did not even recognize them as
problems."

Consider the discouragement and frustration Hubert Humphrey has experienced in trying to get the National Institutes
of Health to establish a computerized national clearinghouse for
drug information. This would make data on drug reactions available to medical libraries and professional organizations instantly
from a single source, almost literally at the touch of a button,
rather than being hopelessly fragmented in thousands of publications, most of which physicians never see. The importance

of this cannot be overemphasized. Dr. Frances Kelsey did not learn that thalidomide caused peripheral neuritis — a piece of information that was a crucial element in her refusal to allow the baby-deforming sedative to go on the market — through any systematic means such as Mr. Humphrey has pressed for. To the contrary, she came across the information by accident — she happened to be looking through a copy of the *British Medical Journal.*

"We are making progress," the Senator was told at a hearing in May 1964 by Boisfeuillet Jones, who was then special assistant for health and medical affairs to the Secretary of Health, Education, and Welfare. Humphrey, who said he was "hot on this one," was bitter that the Institutes, which, in spite of receiving vast sums of money from the Congress, have been "damned slow," "unresponsive, and at times almost impolite." He told Jones that NIH moved as though "it has its feet in asphalt, or better yet, concrete . . . Dr. Shannon [Dr. James A. Shannon, director of the Institutes] told me two years ago this September that they were studying it. Now, that is a slow learner — if you take two years to study this business . . . when are we going to get it done? . . . You have the authority. You have some money."

Later in the hearings, Senator Humphrey recalled that President Kennedy, in a speech to the United Nations two months before his death, had adopted as a proposal of the United States an idea for a World Center for Health Communications. The idea, which the Senator had urged upon Mr. Kennedy, involves an international drug-warning network, which might have helped to prevent the birth of thalidomide babies in many countries had it been in effect in 1961, and such other steps as worldwide coordination of communicable-disease information. Although there is now a reporting network for influenza, there was none in 1957, when the Asian flu epidemic broke out. Senator Humphrey commented that it had taken the World Health Organization several weeks to ascertain where it had started and how it moved. But, he said, "had we gotten the information ahead of time, we could have saved thousands of lives . . ." What happened to the proposal for a World Center, Humphrey told the hearings, was that the State Department and other agencies of the government "didn't back it up." He recalled that Mr. Kennedy had been "excited and very much enthusiastic about it. He did ask that our Government do something about it. And it got lost between the cracks . . ." [2]

In one way or another, agencies and officials such as the following do play, or can play, important roles in drug reforms and improvements: the President, because he is the man in charge; his Special Assistant for Consumer Affairs, who is directly charged with representing consumer interests; the President's Office of Science and Technology, which could coordinate and press for such objectives as the World Center for Health Communications; the office of the Secretary of Health, Education, and Welfare, which has been complacent about its responsibilities for FDA; the National Institutes of Health, the research institutions of the Public Health Service, which, among other things, could seek to end the dependence of university departments of clinical pharmacology on grants from the drug industry by replacing them with massive injections of unrestricted funds for research and training; the Antitrust Division of the Department of Justice, which is responsible for the investigation and prosecution of price-fixing violations, and the Criminal Division of the Justice Department, which is responsible for prosecuting those who make false reports on drug testing or violate laws concerning the manufacture, distribution, and promotion of drugs.

[2] A plan to develop a worldwide warning system to report adverse drug reactions was approved on April 21, 1965, by President Johnson. He said the plan, which was recommended by the Department of Health, Education, and Welfare, calls for creation of a drug-reaction center by the World Health Organization. The plan was to be offered by the United States delegation to the World Health Assembly on May 4 in Geneva.

It is, I think, clear from the experiences of such men as Senator Humphrey and Senator Kefauver and Representative Fountain that it is foolhardy merely to assume government agencies and officials are doing all that they can in regard to federal drug issues. I think it is also a reasonable assumption that the greater the interest expressed by the public, the better the surveillance and performance will be. If the only voices heard, particularly by FDA, are those of the industry, the American Medical Association, and other special interests, the people of the United States might well be fearful of the consequences.

✓ ✓ ✓

If the public is to have and to express an intelligent interest in drug issues, it must be adequately, consistently, and fairly informed about them. This is a job not merely for the lay press, television, and radio, but also for consumer groups and publications, labor and women's organizations, the group-health associations, and the voluntary health organizations. In this regard, the American Heart Association has acted as if the MER/29 fiasco had never happened, even though the anticholesterol drug was prescribed to hundreds of thousands of people menaced by the diseases with which that Association is concerned. Similarly, the National Association for Mental Health (and the American Psychiatric Association) has failed to speak out on the abuses of psychiatric drugs, abuses affecting millions. Surely they could join with the consumer and other groups in meeting one of the greatest, and simplest, needs — for a newsletter, run by competent and respected physicians, to report objectively in laymen's language on all significant developments concerning drugs. As it is now, the kind of news that I am referring to — about FDA and the activities of congressional committees, for example — is largely confined to the trade press, which is almost never seen by the public, and to publications put out for physicians. Unlike ordinary media, these derive all, or nearly all, of their income from the advertising of a single industry, and this is glaringly obvious.

The journals published by professional medical organizations are too technical for the laymen, and generally they also depend inordinately upon pharmaceutical advertising, particularly upon that of a relatively small number of companies. Basically, this problem is susceptible of correction only by the profession. The excellent *Medical Letter* accepts no advertising, but it does not fill the need, because the last to which it sticks is a narrow one — the evaluation of drug products. Further, the *Letter* steers clear of broader issues and, in any event, is addressed to physicians.

✓ ✓ ✓

At the 1963 conference on drugs sponsored by the Johns Hopkins University, the late Pierre R. Garai, the senior writer for a New York advertising agency quoted in earlier chapters, spoke with great clarity and perceptiveness about the responsibility of physicians for drug abuses. In his paper, published in *Drugs in Our Society*, edited by Paul Talalay, he said:

In our society, the market place may be unresponsive to idealism. It is never unresponsive to sales curves. Let the sales of any product decline sharply and remain down and that product will die. Let the doctors but withhold their approval of new drugs until conclusive evidence has been presented in support of claims, and it will cease being economically feasible to market new drugs without this evidence.

Whatever waste and cynicism may be charged to the profit system, it has no equal in creativity, in productivity, and, above all, in responsiveness to the mandates of the market. Detroit didn't abandon its mastodons for compacts because it wanted to but because the public gave it no choice. The

Edsel didn't die because it was poorly promoted but because the public just wouldn't buy it.

How much easier it would be for doctors to have their way, when theirs is the sole and absolute power to determine drug sales. Without their agreement, not a single milligram of any ethical drug can reach the public. Not a cent of profit can be earned. Not a single drug company can stay in business. There is no parallel to this situation in any other industry. If doctors will express their wishes audibly — that is, on prescription pads as well as at conferences and hearings — their wishes will be heeded. And quickly. Ask any drug manufacturer.

The drug business is today, and will be tomorrow, what the doctors cause it to be. Drug advertising, too.

We know what the doctors are today. What will they be tomorrow?

Perhaps doctors in Canada will be more formidable tomorrow than they are today. One of the recommendations of the Royal Commission on Health Services was that Canada's counterpart of our Food and Drug Administration, the medical and pharmaceutical professions, and the provincial health agencies conduct educational programs concerning the cost of drugs and their prescription by generic name. Another recommendation was that the colleges of medicine and pharmacy instruct students, and physicians back for refresher courses, in the economics of prescribing and in the comparative prices of drugs with similar therapeutic quality and efficacy.

In the United States, as a practical matter, what the medical profession does about drug problems is up to its own members, leaders, organizations, and specialty groups. One of the great impediments to progress is that so many fine physicians simply are attending faithfully to their patients and time does not allow for concern with medical politics. One can do little more than hope that sufficient numbers of them will come to recognize the vital importance — to the public, to their profession, to their own image — of taking a more active role.

In their hands, more than in anyone else's, is the opportunity to do something about the astonishing postures of the American Medical Association, such as its campaign to repeal the law's requirement that drugs be shown to be effective, and its approval of the conflict of interest inherent in physician-ownership of drug stocks. In their hands is the opportunity for leadership in setting up a national prescription formulary, without which, Harvard's Dr. Dale G. Friend has said, it is impossible for the practicing physician to have the information he needs to make the best choice of medicines for his patients.

In the hands of the nation's physicians and their societies is the opportunity to make their journals fearless and free — not beholden to anyone — prepared to do such unheard-of things as to criticize specific drug companies and specific drug advertisements, willing to recognize that there are targets other than the United States Government that at least occasionally deserve editorial attack, daring enough to corral such sacred cows as payment for drug testing for frank, open discussion. A free medical press such as I dream of here probably could do wonders in bringing fundamental, lasting improvement in the whole complex of prescription-drug problems. Such a press is not impossible of realization — provided that doctors want it badly enough to reduce the addictive dependence of their publications on drug advertising, and to select, and stand behind, editors of professional excellence and proven courage, independence, and integrity.

In the hands of the nation's physicians rests the opportunity to turn from the detailmen to the medical schools for their postgraduate education, to create within each of their specialty groups committees on drug effectiveness and safety, and to persuade disinterested private foundations to underwrite conferences on important drug problems (such as efficacy, safety, evaluations of categories of drugs — potent tranquilizers, for one — fees for testing, the secrecy of FDA's files, the planting of drug stories in the lay press). So long as drug companies and certain front organizations remain primary sponsors and sources of funds, so long will the situation remain unhealthy.

✓ ✓ ✓

I do not for a moment suggest that the individual layman is without resources in all of this. If he wants such things as generic prescribing of drugs, or if he wants to prohibit such things as physician-ownership of drugstores, drug stocks, or drug-packaging plants, say, he can work for these goals, as he does for others. He can make his views known to his physician, to news media, to legislatures, and to local and state medical societies, either as an individual or through his organizations. That the legislatures of a few states have forbidden physician-ownership of pharmacies is but one indication that action can be achieved.

Many states, cities, and hospitals have greatly reduced their drug costs in recent years by switching to buying by generic names. Thousands of individuals have reduced their drug costs by joining nonprofit groups that fill prescriptions for their members at discount prices, such as the National Retired Teachers Association and American Association of Retired Persons.[8]

[8] In March 1965 James G. Patton, president of the National Farmers Union, announced the establishment of the Senior Citizen Direct Drug Service. In co-operation with the Greenbelt Consumers Cooperative of Greenbelt, Maryland, it sells by direct mail all normal items of prescription and nonprescription medicines, vitamins and health accessories.

A major innovation is that the plan issues price lists. These give the usual brand-name price, the discount Direct Drug Service price, and the still lower price for the comparable generic product. In addition the Direct Drug Service actually encourages purchasers to ask their physicians to prescribe generically. Patton estimated that the plan will save its users 20 to 50 per cent on their drug bills.

The Service is open to members in good standing of the new Farmers Union Senior Member Council and the National Council of Senior Citizens, Inc., which has about 2 million persons on its rolls. Patton said that orders will be filled within 24 hours after receipt and that 7 to 10 days should be allowed for delivery.

I would offer a word of caution. A good doctor-patient relationship is a precious thing, and a wise patient would not, it
seems to me, casually jeopardize it. A patient should not endanger the relationship by demanding of the physician that he
prescribe this or that drug he may have heard about. Nor should
he deny himself the services of a fine physician because of a
relatively unimportant disagreement about generic prescribing.
In certain critical conditions, or when life itself may be at stake,
the physician may grant that a generic product must measure
up to the same standards as a brand-name version, and may in
fact be exactly the same thing, and yet be honestly reluctant
not to prescribe the branded product which has, because of his
experience with it, won his confidence. Apart from such special
situations, there is no good reason for a physician to deny his
patients the savings of generic prescribing, particularly because
the mere fact that a drug is made by a well-known manufacturer
does not certify that it will always live up to standards. When
one does have a generic prescription, there is no reason why one
should not make certain that the pharmacist will fill it with the
nonproprietary product, and not with a more expensive brand
name. His responsibility is to carry out, not overrule, the doctor's orders. One is as free to choose drugstores as foodstores.

A final point. As a safety precaution, one can ask the physician
to direct the druggist to label the bottle as to contents and,
briefly, as to the drug's purpose, as well as to dosage. If bottles of
thalidomide pills had been labeled with that generic name,
President Kennedy would not have had to ask the public to
clean out its medicine cabinets and flush all unidentified pills
down the toilet.

✓ ✓ ✓

The help of all of those in the healing arts is needed if the
essential objective facts about the efficacy and safety of drugs
are to be assembled. For example, a nurse who assumes that a

pill she gives the patient will be effective (an assumption the physician may have had in the first place, and imparted to her) probably will tend to find that it is effective — even though the pill may actually be no more useful than a placebo. The most detached and impartial attitudes and methods are needed to promote alertness to side effects, as well as for determining drug effectiveness. If a physician, nurse, osteopath, or dentist simply assumes that a drug is safe, he may attribute to other causes reactions that are actually adverse effects of the drug.

Hospitals are among the very best places for drug reactions to be observed and recorded. The job they do in this area would automatically be improved enormously if an adequate adverse-reaction reporting system were to be made a condition for accreditation.

✓ ✓ ✓

In May 1960, *Harper's* published an excellent article entitled "The Strange Ethics of the Ethical Drug Industry," by Alek A. Rozental, an economist. "The problem is to reform an industry which is indispensable even when intolerable," he wrote. The ethics of the drug industry do not seem especially inscrutable when one examines the imperatives that undermine ethical standards. Generally, there was little use in telling a manufacturer, or preaching at him, that it was wrong to advertise a drug's purported advantages while concealing its disadvantages; his competitors were operating that way, and unless he did he would lose business, have to lay off employees, and deny himself and his stockholders high profits. Gresham's Law has a long arm. But the Kefauver-Harris full-disclosure amendment, requiring listing of side effects in advertising, shortened it somewhat. *All* manufacturers had to give a brief summary of adverse reactions, and so none could get an advantage over others in this respect. Through new legislation all manufacturers could be required to note on the labels of such drug products as may be exempted from the efficacy provisions of the Drug Amendments that they are exempt; and FDA could be required to publish and distribute, in convenient looseleaf form, bulletins on drugs found to have the potential for serious adverse effects. These would be mailed to doctors, hospitals, and medical institutions at such times as the public health is deemed to make it necessary. A requirement for such bulletins was in the Kefauver drug bill approved by the Senate, but in the House it was killed — with FDA's help. New laws could forbid manufacturers to patent a molecular modification unless it is found by the Secretary of Health, Education, and Welfare to be a significant improvement over available products. With enactment of proposals of this kind manufacturers would compete at a higher level. The reach of Gresham's Law would be shortened still further. Ethics would become less strange.

It is of crucial importance to raise the standards of drug testing. There are certain things the federal government could do. For one, Congress could give renewed consideration to a proposal in the original Kefauver bill authorizing the Secretary to require drug investigators to register with him, and to supply him with simultaneous copies of their reports to the manufacturer on their investigations of experimental drugs. However, salutary improvement would be achieved merely if medical journals were to require that articles on drugs carry a note saying whether the authors had received financial support from the manufacturer. Currently it is common practice to acknowledge that the supply of drugs used in the experiments described in an article was donated by the manufacturer. This may influence the reader to believe that the supply of drugs was the sole compensation, which often is not the case. Yet it would be perilous to overemphasize the value of reforms of this kind. They should not be allowed to obscure the fact that the best-qualified investigators doing the very best and most conscientious work may also be the most generously compensated. The greater problem that must concern us is how to take every possible trace of bias out of drug testing, and this involves more than compensation.

The record compiled by Senator Humphrey's Reorganization subcommittee contains numerous letters and articles about this. Although there is disagreement on precisely how it should be done, the principal consensus is that individual clinicians should not accept drug-company grants to test individual drugs. Instead, the feeling is, drugs should be tested in groups, or categories; and the testing should be done in nonprofit institutions. The investigator would not know, nor have reason to care, which manufacturer had developed which compound. Neither he nor his institution would benefit financially from a favorable report.

In his *Harper's* article Alek Rozental suggested a new medical specialty:

> Its governing board would be a distinguished body of physicians, chemists, pharmacologists, and statisticians. They would promulgate rules for control, methods of reporting, and techniques for comparison. The board would not conduct tests but would, subject to examinations and continued vigilance, license investigators, giving those qualified some designation such as Certified Clinical Investigator. It may be hoped that the designation would carry enough prestige to attract able men and that in due course doctors would be skeptical of all reports not signed by a CCI, just as a certified public accountant is the only accountant a respectable company would hire to conduct its annual audit.
>
> A function of the clinical tests made by these CCIs would be to pronounce not only on the effectiveness of a new drug, but also on how it compares with an existing one, in therapeutic effect and price. Perhaps a digest of these findings could

be indexed periodically and distributed, in loose-leaf form, to every practicing physician in the country.

The CCIs could be given a powerful lease on life if the FDA were to decide that an application for a new drug would not become effective unless the clinical evidence presented by the manufacturer is prepared by Certified Clinical Investigators.

If successful, this scheme would soon make much of the promotional effort, direct mail advertising, and visits from detailmen obsolete. It may lead to a substantial reduction in the number of new preparations marketed every year and divert the drug industry's research facilities to the development of really new therapeutic agents. It should also lead to lower prices for drugs. And finally, it should be a long step toward restoring the standards of morality and responsibility that entitle an industry to call itself "ethical."

Two years after Rozental offered this challenging proposal, a nine-chapter report was issued by the FDA Citizens Advisory Committee — the one whose drugs subcommittee was headed by James Bradshaw Mintener while he was representing Richardson-Merrell, Inc., before FDA in the MER/29 episode. There was no indication in the report that Rozental's proposal had even been considered, or even of any awareness of the question whether it is sound public policy to allow a drug manufacturer to do or supervise the testing of his own products in humans. Consumers Union commented in the March 1963 *Consumer Reports* that it has found over the years "that, with the best intentions in the world, the manufacturer of a product may be unable to take a view of his own handiwork that is objective enough to reveal the product's weaknesses. The results of this almost inescapable maker's myopia can be distressing enough in such goods as automobiles, typewriters, luggage, electric dryers, and so on . . . With the potent drugs now coming on the market the penalties for inadequate testing are *nearly always* threatening to the patient's health or his life." Rather than continuing to have FDA evaluate testing reports procured by the manufacturers, CU suggested that what may be needed is an objective testing agency, a public corporation responsible to both industry and the government.

Another possibility, raised by James Q. Wilson, a Harvard professor of government familiar with the cycles and syndromes of bureaucracies, is the creation by Congress of a publicly financed but privately operated organization to which not testing but the evaluation of testing would be contracted out by the government. Either organization would be a kind of RAND Corporation. By reason of its very structure, it would be capable of attracting the brilliant scientists who too often have been repelled by the inspector-dominated FDA bureaucracy. It could hold them by providing opportunities for research, by paying salaries competitive with those in industry (which FDA cannot do), and by employment and personnel policies emphasizing ability and competence rather than seniority. In building a floor under the quality of drug testing, its officers and staff members, like those of the RAND Corporation, could act and speak out with a decisiveness and freedom unknown to FDA.

In Part 5 of his subcommittee's hearing volumes, Senator Humphrey urged drug information evaluation centers that

> could be organized around specialized drugs, per se, and/or around a disease problem, e.g., diabetes, per se, which require specialized drugs.
>
> Otherwise, where can one turn for specialized information on tens of thousands of articles on specialized drugs, e.g., 40,000 articles which have appeared on cardiovascular drugs alone between 1951 and 1957?

. . . .

It is absurd that the U.S. Government should support specialized centers on metals like Titanium, but not on drugs to save lives.

Only 3 of NIH's [National Institutes of Health] 9 categorical institutes have shown any initiative toward establishing such centers — Mental Health, Cancer and Neurology (the last-named only recently and only with respect to Parkinson's disease).

Particularly outstanding progress has been made in drug evaluation by the Psychopharmacology Service Center. The stimulus for this progress came from 2 able sources: (a) in psychiatry — from leaders in drug research, (b) in Congress — from Senator Lister Hill and Congressman John Fogarty . . .

. . . .

All over the Federal Government, e.g., in Atomic Energy, Space, Military Science, specialized centers have long since proven their worth; yet, in biomedicine, agencies still stall and ask for further "study." Or they sit back and wait for "someone, somewhere, somehow" to submit a proposal . . .

Here are some other ideas. Dr. George E. Schreiner, a former president of the American Federation for Clinical Research, has proposed that drug manufacturers pool funds for testing that would be distributed to investigators by the National Institutes of Health, on the basis of formal applications made by clinicians. A similar pool was suggested by Dr. Irving London, president of the American Society for Clinical Investigation. However, he favored having the fund administered by a board made up of impartial and qualified medical scientists, representatives of the public, and representatives of the industry.

Dr. Charles D. May of New York University proposed the establishment of New-Treatment Centers, usually as part of an established medical school or institution, at which drugs would be tested in humans for safety and efficacy, and at which investigators would be trained. The financial support would be principally from public funds. Dr. M. Harold Book of the University of Pennsylvania, whose "one overriding recommendation" to Senator Humphrey was that testing in humans "be taken out of the hands of any people who might have a financial interest in favorable results," suggested an independent agency. It "might be a greatly expanded branch of the Food and Drug Administration: it might be a panel of experts chosen from the universities and research institutions; it might be [in] the United Nations or possibly a new agency of some sort."

Plainly, there is no shortage of ideas on how to take the bias out of drug testing. I suspect it would be premature to choose among them until they and others have been discussed and subjected to critical review. At this time there is little awareness even that the problem of bias in drug testing exists. Awareness, interest, debate — these are the immediate needs that must be met before sound reforms can be achieved.

From the industry there has come little but complaints, about how the Kefauver-Harris amendments and FDA's implementing regulations are impeding research — with never an admission that the research being impeded may be to develop "dogs" and with never an allusion to the small percentage of costs devoted to meaningful research.

From the industry, some elements of the press, and medical professional organizations, little in the way of proposals has been heard, except for talk of setting up some sort of nonofficial body with the power to review every FDA decision to take a drug off the market. There is never an admission that such a body might be loaded against the public interest. If the industry wants to head off proposals such as I have cited, it could at least propose to pool funds for drug testing. Some years ago, in 1957, Dr. Harry F. Dowling of the University of Illinois said in a memorable paper before a section meeting of the American Medical

Association in New York City: "Regulation there must be for those who will not work from higher motives; regulation by industry to the extent that it can be done; regulation by organizations of physicians where they can help, and regulation by government where the others fail to do the work. Let those who object to the third alternative strengthen the first two."

Despite numerous warnings over a long period, Chloromycetin, the antibiotic generically named chloramphenicol, is still promiscuously prescribed. Numerous deaths from aplastic anemia attest to this. Dr. Barbara Moulton, the physician who resigned from FDA in protest against its policies, has suggested a means of coping with the relatively few drugs which, like Chloromycetin, are believed useful for certain purposes but are so excessively prescribed — their hazards notwithstanding — that some are in favor of taking them off the market. Her thought is that such drugs should be placed in a special category of medicines that could be prescribed only with the written approval of a consultant, except in emergencies or special circumstances. In most cases this should not increase the patient's fees. Her approach is essentially similar to sound practices in many hospitals with reference to unusual surgery, Caesarean section, and sterilization operations, and also to the sound doctrine that testing of an experimental drug shall neither be initiated nor conducted by a single physician acting alone. Legislation, federal or state, would be necessary to put Dr. Moulton's proposal into effect.

✦   ✦   ✦

In *Ethics in Government*, the fine little book by Senator Paul H. Douglas that the Harvard University Press published in 1952, he inquired into why it is that the work of a public agency, perhaps as "a general law of life," tends to deteriorate with time.

When a basic reform is enacted into law [he wrote], a new agency is often set up, and the program is launched with devotion and enthusiasm. The men chosen to administer it have probably had deep sympathy with the movement which finally crystallized into law, but they seldom have been active participants in it. The people who did the pioneer work for a reform generally become so discredited in the process of getting the change, that although their cause triumphs, they generally find it impossible to hold public office. Their friends, however, frequently reap the rewards of their sacrifice. These new men begin their work with zest and the initial results are good. But as time passes, some of the pioneers die out and others, wanting a larger income, then transfer into private business. Those who stay on as vigorous administrators may be attacked, broken, and discredited by the private forces which are still opposed to the basic measure but which no longer dare to fight it openly. The opponents, therefore, carry on a subtle program to undermine the zealous administrators. They are frequently denied reappointment because they are labeled "trouble-makers" and thus the administrative body is gradually purged of its most active and devoted members. Others who see the realities about them gradually grow tired and relapse into dull routine.

Moreover, as time passes, the public interest which led to the original passage of the act inevitably slackens. Men believe their objective has been won, technical questions multiply which are hard to understand, and new and exciting problems distract the attention of even the early reformers. But the private interests do not slacken their pressure: they keep steadily at work to weaken the powers and the effectiveness of the public agency. As new men are added to the agency, they tend to be either routineers, "industry-minded," or "faceless men" . . . who are largely indistinguishable one from another.

Gradually, from all these causes the once virile agency loses its crusading spirit and becomes both lethargic and indifferent to the public interest. This may well be a general law of life. It is certainly the history of most governmental regulatory bodies. I call this degenerative disease "administrativitis." The only antidote is the continued injection of new and vigorous personalities, active work by the lonely soldiers of the common good, and, most important of all, the constant and informed interest of the general public.

It would be misleading to suggest that the Senator's analysis can be applied across the board to the evolution of the Food and Drug Administration, but an extended generalization such as that could not come closer. The devotion and enthusiasm that Harvey Wiley aroused after the turn of the century was such that he had a volunteer "poison squad" — young colleagues who served as guinea pigs to test the effects of food preservatives. Wiley's cause triumphed, although he found it impossible to continue for long in public office, and resigned. Private forces have carried on a program of undermining, which included such subtleties as conferring awards on those who regulate them and being, so long as it suits their purposes, the foremost fearless exponents of the career tradition.

The public interest that led to the enactment of the 1906 reforms slackened, just as has the public interest that led to the Food, Drug, and Cosmetic Act of 1938 and the Kefauver-Harris amendments of 1962. In recent years, able and vigorous FDA scientific personnel, men and women who asked only the opportunity to dedicate their devotion and skills to the public interest, have found themselves unwanted. Discouraged, harassed, unfulfilled, some have left and a few have been driven out. While this was happening, FDA's reputation as a scientific backwater became widely known, and promising young scientists who might have been recruited went elsewhere. The agency became too lethargic even to adopt drug-testing regulations it was empowered to adopt, or to tell Congress of the inadequacies of drug testing or of its need for more funds to do a better job. It became indifferent to the point that drugs like MER/29, Altafur, Oribilex, Entoquel, dihydrostreptomycin, and the antibiotic lozenges were released without substantial evidence of safety; psychotherapeutic drugs were released without controlled studies; and the decision to retrieve thalidomide was inexcusably delayed for almost nine months. Concurrently, the private interests were not slackening their pressure. Gradually, with almost no one noticing, the once virile agency had lost its crusading spirit.

There has been no "continued injection of new and vigorous personalities" into the highest echelon of FDA. The top generals and many of the colonels are the same. It is arguable whether the Commissioner should be a medical doctor, but certainly he should be someone of genuine scientific stature. According to *Life*, Commissioner Larrick asserted his claim to fame early in his career with "a truly slick piece of detective work. He tracked down eight poisonously bad fruitcakes from Virginia to Montreal, and saved their would-be-eaters." The *Life* article, which was published in July 1964, had this to say about the Secretary of Health, Education, and Welfare: ". . . the dapper, genial ex-Mayor of Cleveland, Anthony J. Celebrezze . . . patently recognizes that he is no expert on the drug problem. When he took office he told one of his aides, 'I don't want to hear about it. You handle it. I can't even understand those big words.' "

What FDA has had are what Senator Douglas called the "lonely soldiers of the common good," dedicated medical officers such as Dr. Barbara Moulton and Dr. John Nestor. And we have had a few lonely soldiers in the Congress, principally Senator Kefauver and Senator Humphrey. They have not accomplished the impossible task of creating a modern FDA imbued with a dedication to the public interest comparable to that of Harvey Wiley, but they have precipitated some improvements. If the process is to continue it must have, and FDA must have, what

Paul Douglas called "the constant and informed interest of the general public."

The foundation of the improvements was the Kefauver-Harris amendments, which are summarized here in Appendix II. The money needed to carry out the purposes of the amendments has been appropriated by Congress, and FDA has used it to greatly expand its corps of medical officers and other scientific personnel, and to acquire up-to-date equipment and improved facilities. In the Bureau of Medicine a limited automatic data system has been installed to improve the access of medical officers to the data needed in the evaluation of drugs for safety and effectiveness.

In November 1963 the Department of Health, Education, and Welfare approved a reorganization plan for FDA that Commissioner George Larrick hailed as "the most far-reaching overhaul of FDA's organizational structure ever to be accomplished." This was either hyperbole or a depressing commentary on FDA reorganizations of the past, or both. Even the industry's Commission on Drug Safety implicitly recognized this when, ten months after the plan had been announced, its *Report* said the need for FDA "to become scientifically oriented is readily apparent." Not *was*, but *is*. The plan entailed a substantial amount of playing musical chairs, with many of the old faces continuing to hold key positions while sitting behind new titles. However, the plan is at least a bow toward science. For example, there is now an Associate Commissioner for Science and an Assistant Commissioner for Science Resources.

It was reassuring that Dr. Frances Kelsey was promoted, in December 1962, to a new position as head of the Investigational Drug Branch. In this position she has the responsibility for deciding whether preclinical experimental tests of experimental drugs have been such as to warrant the start of testing in humans. Unfortunately, her appointment included her on the takeoffs but not on the landings. That is, her assignment does not call for her participation in the process of *releasing* new drugs — a responsibility she had even as a new medical officer years earlier. Her previous mission involved acting to prevent marketing of drugs whose safety she believed had not been established. The assignment to which she was promoted does not include responsibility for this. What happened to Dr. Kelsey is indicative of a broader malaise intensified by the reorganization — the fragmentation of responsibility for the handling of a new drug, so that one or more FDA physicians do not stay with it from start to finish. Dismay with the reorganization is felt not only within FDA's own ranks and elsewhere in government, but in the industry as well. One who expressed this was Dr. Kenneth G. Kohlstaedt, executive director of research for Eli Lilly. He told the Fountain Intergovernmental Relations Subcommittee that improved liaison was needed between Dr. Kelsey's Investigational Drug Branch and those responsible for new-drug applications. He testified, "If staff members from both groups were kept informed of the progress of a new drug project and if they would agree on the same set of standards and criteria, the approval of new drugs could be accelerated."

Without acknowledging that the approval of new drugs ought to be accelerated, I nonetheless point out that Dr. Kohlstaedt was suggesting FDA's procedures to be somewhat chaotic under the reorganization about which Commissioner Larrick spoke so proudly. He also said: "During the course of development of clinical trial, we are making progress reports to Dr. Kelsey. What might happen is that at the end of the investigation the data would be presented to another medical officer who, if he had not been informed of the course of development and if there had not been any liaison between these two branches, might have an entirely different opinion, you see, and disagree with all that had been going on before." [4]

[4] ". . . I do not believe that FDA's performance to date has been sufficiently in keeping with the spirit as well as the letter of the law and regulations," Representative L. H. Fountain said at the conclusion of hearings on the implementation of aspects of the Kefauver-Harris amendments involving the Investigational Drug Branch. He further said: "While I appreciate the staff and other limita-

FDA's new medical director, Dr. Joseph F. Sadusk, was not one of those people who, as Senator Douglas described them, "did the pioneer work for a reform [and who] generally become so discredited in the process of getting the change, that although their cause triumphs, they generally find it impossible to hold public office." He is not known to have spoken out against the practices and policies of the drugmakers or the AMA, or against the inadequacies of the administration of FDA. He had claimed little or no experience in testing drugs and little or no knowledge of or special interest in the workings and mission of FDA. Congressional aides have expressed incredulity at his lack of familiarity with the published records of the Kefauver and Humphrey subcommittees. It is an ironic commentary that one so innocent of concern with the great drug problems of our era should have been chosen to be FDA's medical director.

That Dr. Sadusk's appointment contained elements of irony did not prove that it was unwise. He did not seek the post; he accepted it, after others had declined it. Often, those best equipped to take a hard line and make others toe it are the ones who were previously not involved in controversy. Dr. Sadusk was fortunate in having a certain immunity from charges that any tough actions he may find necessary to take are wrongly motivated. In his first several months in office, however, there were no indications that he was disposed to take actions that the drug industry would consider tough.

---

tions under which the Investigational Drug Branch has been laboring, these hearings and our study have disclosed a number of important areas in which better administration was possible despite such limitations.

"We are aware of the recent actions taken to remedy some of these administrative shortcomings, and I hope the Food and Drug Administration will act vigorously to strengthen management in other areas as well."

The hearings were held by the Intergovernmental Relations Subcommittee of the House Committee on Government Operations. Fountain, who is chairman of the subcommittee, made the comments on May 4, 1965. An outline of findings on which his criticisms were based will be found in the afterword to Chapter 11.

What Dr. Sadusk did or did not do before he became the principal medical guardian the American people have against ineffective and unsafe drugs is much less significant than what he will do. That he lacks the intense pharmacological and other special training one might hope to find in a scientist holding such a post as his is less important than that he know how to recruit, use, and retain others who do have such training. The most revealing test he faces as a public servant may be what he will do to halt the sale of ineffective drugs now on the market, and what he will do to prevent ineffective drugs from going on the market. At the end of 1964, the reports from inside FDA were disturbing. Morale in the Bureau of Medicine was widely said to be low. Nor was Dr. Sadusk showing any enthusiasum for acting against ineffective medicines. No prescription drug had been removed from the market on grounds of lack of efficacy, and there was no indication in sight that any was about to be.[5]

Immediately after taking office, Dr. Sadusk put a high priority on obtaining better quarters for the Bureau of Medicine, which was housed in what he aptly called "this firetrap." Is it symbolic of the attitude of the FDA hierarchy toward medical science that the Bureau always has been relegated to inferior buildings,

[5] The nature of the FDA-AMA-PMA molecule that Dr. Sadusk was formulating was indicated by a generally adulatory article about him in the April 16, 1965, issue of *Medical World News:*

"He has repudiated the so-called Young Turks in the FDA who have demanded arms-length dealings with the industry and the AMA and excessively harsh enforcement of all drug controls. [Who wouldn't repudiate "excessively harsh enforcement"?]

"Instead, Dr. Sadusk has deliberately developed a close working alliance with the AMA on reporting adverse reactions and keeping doctors posted on all developments affecting drug use. And he has promoted a spirit of cooperation with the industry in an effort to solve drug regulation problems."

". . . the AMA should be the principal source of drug education for the doctor."

"Dr. Sadusk is just as interested in developing closer relations with the drug industry. As he puts it . . . 'We try to solve problems through fact-finding and then by voluntary compliance and cooperation rather than by enforcement . . . In most instances, we have been able to convince the industry of the wisdom of our approach.' "

while nonmedical parts of the agency have had priority claims on superior quarters? *Life* said on July 3, 1964, that the Bureau of Medicine, ". . . with its invaluable records of the drug industry, is still crammed into one of the grubbiest of the capital's remaining 'temporary' wartime buildings, sheathed in tumbledown cement board. The medical officers in it are still crammed together, three or four to a tiny office, distracted by the clank of ancient window-sill air conditioners and forced to go to another building three blocks away if they require the use of a conference room."

In March 1963 the problem had been perceptively dealt with by Dr. Theodore G. Klumpp, president of Winthrop Laboratories. In testimony before Representative John Fogarty's House Subcommittee on Labor, Health, Education and Welfare, Dr. Klumpp expressed concern that a move then contemplated would take the Bureau of Medicine "a mile or more away from the rest of the FDA organization. That means a mile from the pharmacologists with whom medical officers have to consult, from the HEW library, and from FDA's master computer."

With Dr. Sadusk's blessing a move to new quarters was approved late in 1964. The new home of the Bureau of Medicine was, however, to be across the Potomac River in Arlington, Virginia. The distance from the rest of FDA, including even the Division of Antibiotics, was about three times that which had troubled Dr. Klumpp.

Some signs of progress could be found. Under the stimulus of Senator Humphrey, FDA expanded its hitherto dormant and all but useless adverse-reaction reporting system in hospitals, as well as its use of expert outside consultants on drug problems. In a successful attack on the severe handicap imposed by standard government salaries on the recruitment and retention of scientific personnel, FDA won authority to pay a few dozen scientists and medical officers so-called supergrade salaries — $18,935 to $24,500 annually. The agency will have a Medical

Advisory Board to advise the medical director on general policies. He also will have the aid of a drug-research policy board — established by the National Academy of Sciences–National Research Council and financed by the National Institutes of Health — in which drug-research policies will be discussed by scientific representatives of FDA and other government agencies, academic medicine, the medical profession, and the industry. Although nine years elapsed before the original recommendation was acted on, the Department of Health, Education, and Welfare has at last set up a National Advisory Food and Drug Council.

✓ ✓ ✓

On May 28, 1964, Senator Humphrey conducted his subcommittee's last scheduled hearing on the Food and Drug Administration and related matters.

Humphrey was terribly pressed that morning. He was the floor manager for the Civil Rights Bill, and there were the usual demands made upon him as the Assistant Majority Leader. He was unable to take all the testimony he would have liked to take, or to say all that he felt had to be said. But he did manage to speak, even if in a fragmented way, on a few things that weighed most heavily on his mind. He wanted FDA to become a highly respected scientific agency, as befits a government body with vast responsibilities for safeguarding the nation's health. The atmosphere he wanted to see in the agency was one that encouraged its officials to do what is right, whether that happens to agree or disagree with the viewpoint of industry, physicians, consumer groups, or anyone else. "You have gone through a very difficult period," he told the Commissioner. "And I haven't made it any easier at times for you, but I did it because I thought it was important to be done." The Senator knew that he would have to be leaving to hear an address by the President of Ireland, and he wanted to be sure that his motives were understood. "It is never pleasant to investigate an agency," he said. "What we seek to do is not to punish, but to improve."

In November 1964, Hubert Horatio Humphrey was elected Vice President of the United States. In January 1965 his Subcommittee on Reorganization and International Organizations was to be broken up and absorbed into other subcommittees of the Senate Committee on Government Operations. With this development there would be no subcommittee of the Senate with an announced, continuing, and paramount dedication to overseeing the Food and Drug Administration. "What we seek to do is not to punish, but to improve," Humphrey said. But now he is himself of the Executive Branch; no longer can he be its brilliant and vocal critic in the Senate.

THERE ARE in the last chapter of this book a few things that in retrospect I wish I had not said. One was the suggestion that President Johnson might turn to his Secretary of Commerce for advice in choosing a new Commissioner of the Food and Drug Administration. If such advice was offered or requested, which is open to doubt, the appointment of Dr. James L. Goddard argues that it was not followed. I tried to restrain my pessimism about Dr. Joseph F. Sadusk, Jr.; the record argues that I was misguided. I am uncertain whether I expressed a balanced or an overstated concern about the possibility of a wave of therapeutic nihilism. And there were certain elements that were relevant only to a brief transitional period or that were otherwise overtaken by events — for example, the death of Representative John Fogarty and the appointment of Representative Oren Harris to the Federal bench.

But the note on which the chapter — and the book — ended was chosen with care and thought. With the election of Hubert Humphrey as Vice President, I wrote, "there would be no subcommittee of the Senate with an announced, continuing, and paramount dedication to overseeing the Food and Drug Administration." Overseeing, monitoring, review — this, it seems to me, is indispensable. The odds are very great that we will not (nor should we) either abandon regulation or go to government ownership. The constant problem is to make regulation work.

We skate on thin ice indeed when an agency as important as the FDA is practically exempt from Senate oversight, and will be practically exempt from House oversight when W. Donald Gray, of the Intergovernmental Relations Subcommittee, takes a six-month leave to work on his doctoral thesis at the Woodrow Wilson School at Princeton.

The one-man theme is pervasive. It would be foolhardy to assume that the backing John W. Gardner has given to Dr. Goddard will be given by a successor Secretary of Health, Education, and Welfare whose identity cannot even be conjectured, or that the support Dr. Goddard has given Dr. Robert S. McCleery, head of the FDA's Medical Advertising Branch, will be matched by a future Commissioner, or that Dr. McCleery's successor might not be much less of a man. Arrayed against this thin line is the pharmaceutical industry with — *always* with — its platoons and regiments of lawyers and public relations men.

There is, as Bernard Nossiter said in *The Mythmakers*, "nothing in the logic or practice of concentrated corporate industries that guides or compels socially responsible decision making." The evidence of that is abundant in this book. But there is also a troubling international dimension. At the very time, for example, that Parke, Davis was — because it had to, under the law — enumerating a long and frightful list of warnings, precautions, contraindications and side effects for Chloromycetin in an advertisement in the *Journal* of the American Medical Association, it was — because of a nonlaw — saying nothing at all about these risks in the *British Medical Journal*; indeed, in the British ad the company claimed what it was prohibited from claiming here — usefulness "in a wide variety of infections."

I dealt in the preface with the responsibility of the press, which in exercising its role of overseer must also be overseen. An anonymous English verse tells us, "The law locks up both man and woman / Who steals the goose from off the common, / But lets the greater felon loose / Who steals the common from the goose." Much of the time much of the press spends much of its effort on the man and woman who steal the goose, but spends very little effort watching the corporate and other therapeutic misadventurers who steal the common health. If some of the disclosures in this book are unfamiliar it is because large and influential sectors of the press reported them inadequately if at all. It must be said that among those who might not have been aware of these disclosures are readers of the New York Times. For example, it did not (according to my check of the New York Times Index) report the no-contest plea and sentencing of Wallace Laboratories on January 17, 1966; other false advertising cases involving criminal proceedings against major pharmaceutical manufacturers have been reported belatedly, trivially, or not at all. Especially in stories by Jane Brody, the Times has downplayed questions about the safety of the oral contraceptives. It has given totally inadequate attention to the episodes involving the long-acting sulfonamide drugs and the thiazidepotassium diuretics; the same applies to the false advertising cases that culminated in seizures and in corrective letters to physicians. On October 20, 1966, there was a meeting at the Roosevelt Hotel in New York City at which William W. Goodrich, the FDA's counsel, said that advertisements for the "big eight" prescription drugs introduced in 1965 were infected by deception. At the same meeting, C. Joseph Stetler, president of the Pharmaceutical Manufacturers Association, made an attack on the truthfulness of Dr. Goddard. The next morning, the Times had an item on the Stetler talk but nothing about the Goodrich talk. Doubtless this reflects aggressive public relations efforts by the PMA in distributing copies of the Stetler speech. But — along with the examples cited here — it also raises questions about the quality of the monitoring to be expected, especially from news media with smaller resources than those of the Times. The slogan of the Times is, "All the News That's Fit to Print." Maybe it is time for the Times to consider recognizing the inherent impossibility of fulfilling such a claim. This would be an appropriate expression of gratitude that newspapers are exempt from the Fair Packaging and Labeling Act.

I believe that a common thread runs through our use of technology. We have the ingenuity to build a super-tanker — and we build a *Torrey Canyon* without adequate forethought as to what might happen if it were to break up near the Cornwall beaches. We have the capacity to build Supersonic Transports — and are proceeding to build them without adequate forethought about sonic boom. We have the capacity to concoct new chemicals — and we do so without adequate forethought as to the consequences of mixing in our bodies the compounds we ingest as food additives, as pesticide residues, and as drugs.

I commend not merely for what it says about drugs, but also for its application to other human enterprises the wisdom of Dr. Robert H. Moser, author of the revealingly titled *Diseases of Medical Progress* and a Colonel in the Medical Corps of the Army. "It has been said that drug-induced adverse effects are the price we have to pay for more effective and better medicaments," Colonel Moser said on March 14, 1967, in a lecture sponsored by the Lowell Institute in co-operation with the Tufts-New England Medical Center. "There can be no quarrel with this statement; it is the *high* price we are haggling about. The thalidomide disaster indicated how expensive it can be." He ended his talk with this:

> Now we must work to create an atmosphere of rational caution and critical evaluation, where each physician will pause before putting pen to prescription pad and ask himself, "Do I know enough about this drug to prescribe it; does the possible benefit I hope to derive from this drug outweigh its potential hazard?" I do not preach therapeutic nihilism, but rather *therapeutic rationalism*.

℞

Besides, the practitioner is subjected, year in, year out, to the steady bombardment of the unscrupulous manufacturer, persuasive to the uncritical, on the principle that "what I tell you three times is true." Against bad example and persistent asseveration, only precise scientific concepts and a critical appreciation of the nature and limits of actual demonstration can protect the young physician. The laity has in this matter more to fear from credulous doctors than from advertisements themselves: for a nostrum containing dangerous drugs is doubly dangerous if introduced into the household by the prescription of a physician who knows nothing of its composition and is misled as to its effect. Experimental physiology and pharmacology must train the student both to doubt unwarranted claims and to be open to really authoritative suggestion: for it is equally important to reject humbug and to accept truth. Fortunately, even a brief concrete experience may teach one to be wary in weighing evidence.

ABRAHAM FLEXNER

Medical Education in the United States and Canada: A Report to the Carnegie Foundation for the Advancement of Teaching. *Bulletin Number Four (1910, reprinted in 1960).* New York City: The Carnegie Foundation for the Advancement of Teaching.

℞

The Afterwords and the Epilogue are not indexed.

℞

On July 15, 1962, the Washington *Post* broke the story of how Dr. Frances O. Kelsey of the Food and Drug Administration had prevented marketing of the baby-deforming drug thalidomide. The story had immense impact. Drug-reform proposals were rescued from oblivion and enacted without a dissenting vote in either the Senate or the House. Several foreign countries tightened their drug laws. People everywhere became aware of the capacity of drugs to injure as well as heal. The *Post's* reporter, Morton Mintz, won three national memorial awards — the Heywood Broun, the George Polk, and the Raymond Clapper — and the Washington Newspaper Guild's First Prize for Public Service Reporting.

Subsequently Mr. Mintz made far-ranging inquiries, from which emerged the writing of this book. For documentation he has relied on the official records of congressional investigations led by then Senator Hubert Humphrey, the late Senator Estes Kefauver, Representative L. H. Fountain, and others, and on leading medical and scientific journals. He reveals gross carelessness, bureaucratic blundering, and even some instances of conflict of interest in FDA. The AMA is shown to have all too often opposed legislation designed to afford greater protection to the consumer. There are shocking accounts of suppression of information about adverse drug reactions. Almost everyone takes prescription drugs. Almost everyone knows that they can save life and alleviate suffering. Few know of the suffering, death, and waste caused by their misuse. *By Prescription Only* tells the whole story at last.

Morton Mintz was born on January 26, 1922, in Ann Arbor and is a graduate of the University of Michigan. While at the university he was editorial director of the *Michigan Daily* and campus correspondent for the Detroit *News*. After three years of World War II Navy service, Mr. Mintz worked on the old St. Louis *Star-Times* and the St. Louis *Globe-Democrat*. Since 1958, he has been with the Washington *Post*. He was a Nieman Fellow at Harvard in the 1963–1964 academic year.